THE DEVELOPMENT OF SEC ACCOUNTING

THE DEVELOPMENT OF SEC ACCOUNTING

Edited by
GARY JOHN PREVITS
Case Western Reserve University

ADDISON-WESLEY PUBLISHING COMPANY
Reading, Massachusetts • Menlo Park, California
London • Amsterdam • Don Mills, Ontario • Sydney

Library of Congress Cataloging in Publication Data

Main entry under title:

The Development of SEC Accounting.

1. Corporations — United States — Accounting —
Addresses, essays, lectures. 2. Financial
statements — United States — Addresses, essays,
lectures. 3. Disclosure of information (Secu-
rities law) — United States — Addresses, essays,
lectures. 4. United States. Securities and
Exchange Commission — Addresses, essays, lectures
I. Previts, Gary John.
KF1446.A75D48   346.73'06648   80-21512
ISBN 0-201-05784-0

ISBN 0-201-05784-0
ABCDEFGHIJ — MA — 89876543210

To Fran

Preface

The role of the Securities and Exchange Commission (SEC) in shaping the doctrines of modern corporate accountability and reporting has become more widely recognized during the last decade. An understanding of the role of the accounting profession, the capital market, and the SEC can be traced to the perception of the independent accountant's role, corporate financial reporting officials, and the statutory power to establish accounting measurement and disclosure rules.

The first statement of SEC policy regarding this matter is contained in Accounting Series Release No. 4 (1938). This release established the concept of "substantial authoritative support" as the underlying notion for generally accepted accounting principles. Nearly forty years later, after the formation of the Financial Accounting Standards Board, the Commission reconstituted the basis of this relationship with the issuance of ASR 150 (1974). The evolution of these and other SEC accounting pronouncements has significantly influenced the form of corporate governance and content of financial reports.

This volume provides a cross-section of timely essays by prominent practitioners, academics, and SEC officials that portray the evolution of SEC accounting postures since the start of its operation in the 1930s. The earliest writings, when contrasted to the most recent, suggest the direction of developments that have taken place over this period of years, up to the recent "integration" proposals (Reading No. 36).

These essays provide a basis from which readers can assess the relevance of contemporary SEC pronouncements and trace the relationships of past and proposed SEC positions. The arrangement of articles in a chronological sequence provides a means to read selectively and/or progressively. The text of each reading is prefaced by a synoptic abstract that should assist instructors and students. The articles have been tested in professional level courses or are selected to relate to the tested materials. They give particular attention to the:

1. History and role of regulation as a vehicle in our economy (Readings 6, 14, and 21).

2. Financial markets and research on the market impact of SEC disclosures (Readings 12, 16, 24, 27, 28, 31, and 34).

3. SEC's influence on accounting standards and policy (Readings 4, 5, 8, 10, 11, 15, 17, 19, 26, and 32).

4. Legal aspects of SEC regulations (Readings 1, 7, and 23).

5. Technical, comparative, and behavioral aspects of Commission financial disclosures (Readings 2, 9, 13, 18, 20, 22, and 30).

6. Future of financial disclosure and reporting (Readings 25, 29, 33, 35, and 36)

I wish to thank Jim Childree, Lori Groden, and George Hawk, for their assistance.

Cleveland, Ohio   G.J.P.
October 1980

Contents

ONE

The Accountant
and the Securities Act

ROBERT WEIDENHAMMER

Formerly, The University of Minnesota

This 1933 article critiques the process through which the Securities Act of 1933 was developed and discusses and criticizes that act. Despite the problems in the development of the act, the author concludes that the Securities Act of 1933, with the advice of investment bankers, lawyers, and accountants, can protect the public without unduly interfering with the activities of the business community.

The significance of the Securities Act of 1933 to the accounting profession can hardly be underestimated. The accounting officer and the independent certified public accountant see their public recognition greatly enhanced, but along with this welcome enhancement of standing comes a burden of responsibility that is truly appalling. The risk assumed by an accountant-officer or by a professional accountant, who signs the registration statement submitted to the Securities Commission of the Federal Trade Commission, is quite out of proportion to the possible material benefits that may be derived from the service rendered. It is hardly surprising to hear that accounting firms accept the offer to certify registration statements only after having found protection against their liability in indemnity bonds. Needless to say that, aside from the costliness of this subterfuge, the Securities Act hardly aims at such a development. It is the irony of fate that the accountants have to thank one of their own organizations for having thrown this predicament on their shoulders. The bill (H.R. 4314, 73rd Congress) as originally submitted to Congress made no reference whatsoever to the liability of the accounting officer. The registration statement was to be signed by "the issuer or issuers, its or their principal executive officer or officers, the principal financial officer or officers, and the directors, trustees, or managers."[1] It was left to Mr. Arthur R. Tucker, the secretary of the Comptroller's Institute of America, to propose an amendment,[2] after complaining that "there is no reference made to the principal accounting officer," and "that the principal accounting officer, the comptroller of the corporation, the corporate accountant, is the original source of the information which must go into this statement, and we think that it is only fair that he should be specially mentioned in the measure." Mr. Tucker's proposal was accepted and the registration statement is now to be signed and full responsibility for its truthfulness and the "omission of material facts," are now shared by the principal executive, financial, and accounting officers.

Reprinted from *The Accounting Review,* January 1933, pp. 272–278, with permission of the American Accounting Association.

The Federal Securities Act is without a doubt the response to demands of a wide majority of the nation. More effective protection of the investor was promised in the platform of
the Democratic party as adopted in Chicago in 1932. This pledge was redeemed on March
29, in the President's message to Congress, which urged the formation and prompt adoption
of a law "to provide for the furnishing of information and the supervision of traffic in investment securities in Interstate Commerce." The most significant passages follow:

> *There is, however, an obligation upon us to insist that every issue of new securities
> to be sold in interstate commerce shall be accompanied by full publicity and in-
> formation, and that no essentially important element attending the issue shall be
> concealed from the buying public.... This proposal adds to the ancient rule of
> caveat emptor the further doctrine "let the seller also beware." It puts the burden of
> telling the whole truth on the seller. It should give impetus to honest dealing in secu-
> rities and thereby bring back public confidence.... The purpose of the legislation I sug-
> gest is to protect the public with the least possible interference to honest business.*

The hearings which followed the receipt of this message and which led to the final formulation of the Securities Act did not compare favorably with the rather high standards established in the hearings that preceded the "Banking Act of 1933." The report entitled "A Study
of the Economic and Legal Aspects of the Proposed Federal Securities Act," as prepared by
the Department of Commerce, gave scant justice to its rather ambitious title. For the most
part the report consists of a rather incomplete bibliography, a summary of existing state
blue-sky laws, and former proposals for federal regulation of the securities business as well
as a collection of quotations from newspaper articles and speeches that bewailed the lot of
the investor "who is always holding the bag." No comprehensive study of the flow of the national savings into investments, of the practices used in raising capital funds and in distributing
securities was attempted. The so-called Macmillan Report of the Parliamentary Commission on Finance and Industry as published in 1931 provided such a survey for Great Britain,
while the first really comprehensive attempt to get at the root of the problem was published
in the same year in Germany.[3]

The dignified and scholarly tone of the British report and the most impressive array of
original research presented in the German document stand in sharp contrast to the hastily
compiled memorandum of the Department of Commerce. To refer to one example only:
instead of attempting to estimate the losses suffered by American investors in recent years,
the report states that "of the $50 billion worth of new stock and bonds issued in the 13 years
from 1919–1931, unfortunately a considerable portion was of little intrinsic value and in
some cases of no value whatever." This vague contention is not substantiated by any facts
whatever, perhaps because the following reference appeared to represent ample "source
material": The author of a recent book entitled *Financial Racketeering* writes: "A 5-foot
book-shelf could without great labor be filled with scandalous volumes if some bold writer
should essay to docket and report the cases of all the financial swindlers which occurred in
the United States in, for example, the last 5 calendar years."

Were it not for the purpose of bringing into bold relief the utter inadequacy of the criticized report, I would have to apologize for wasting the reader's time on such trivialities. But
any appraisal of the legislative achievement represented by the Securities Act of 1933 has to
begin with a recognition of its rather careless preparation. Any attempt at improvement of

the act should therefore be preceded by a comprehensive analysis of this very complex mechanism by which the national savings find their way into investments.

While the chorus led by those affected by the liability clauses clamors for the repeal of some of its harshest provisions, other groups are at work to broaden out the protection of the investor as attempted by the act. Proposals for establishing "social control" over new security issues in order to direct the flow of capital is one of the devices for economic planning and management under discussion by the Administration.[4] Such plans contemplate the creation of a federal authority to prevent the sale of securities if it should be judged that the purpose of an issue was contrary to general social or economic welfare, i.e., if for instance, the proceeds were to be used to increase the capacity of an industry already deemed to be overexpanded. Sponsors of the plan point to precedents, both remote and immediate, for a governmental attempt to control the flow of capital. During the war there was a capital-issues committee which acted for that purpose. Since 1920 the Interstate Commerce Commission has had control over railroad security issues and has forbidden construction of new lines, while both preventing and permitting the abandonment of other trackage. Certain state boards have supervised the issuance of public utility securities. Both state and federal governments have controlled the chartering of new banks. Recently the National Recovery Administration refused to allow the enlargement of textile-mill capacity.

Any such attempt at economic planning would involve frequent decisions on difficult and complex questions such as the overcapacity of industries, as to comparative cost and budgeted profits. It is needless to say that the accountant, the cost accountant, and the "budgeteer" would find ample work to match his wits and to insure the orderly and sound solution of the vexing problems involved.

The time that has elapsed since the Federal Securities Act became effective has been too short to provide a test for the validity of the contention that the new law is paralyzing the flow of the national savings into investments. From July 26 to October 3, 1933, only $243.1 million of securities filed for registration, while new flotations[5] in the years 1922 to 1929 fluctuated as follows:

Year	Amount (in millions of dollars)	Year	Amount (in millions of dollars)
1922	4,304	1926	6,243
23	4,293	27	7,520
24	5,534	28	7,081
25	6,174	29	7,052

Of these $243 millions of securities registered, $159 million were investment trusts that did not represent any new flotations, while $13.3 million were accounted for by breweries and distilleries and $19.8 million by mining companies (the new gold rush!). Defenders of the act may argue that the market for new railroad issues, which are exempt from the registration, was equally unsatisfactory, amounting to only $4,923,000 during the third quarter as compared with $94,982,000 in the first two quarters. But this argument would overlook in the first place that railroad securities are not exempt from the penalties of Section 12(2) and furthermore that the paralysis of the capital market as a whole exerted its influence also on the securities exempt from registration.

Even if we take it for granted that the violent opposition of the Investment Bankers Association has its motive in partly selfish reasons, the fact remains that such bodies as the Federal Reserve Advisory Council adopted on September 19, already, a resolution, as follows:

> *It is essential that the industries of the country (including public utilities) be enabled to finance their ordinary capital requirements either for refunding or for new capital in the investment markets, and it is apparent that amendments to the law must be made to liberalize the law so that it will not stifle the legitimate flow of capital into industry.*
>
> *Accordingly it is hereby* Resolved, *That in aid of the National Recovery Program, the Securities Act of 1933 and the Banking Act of 1933 should be amended in such respects as may be necessary to enable the industries of the country to obtain capital funds in the investment markets, retaining in such laws all such provisions as may be necessary to properly safeguard the interests of the investing public.*

RELATION TO STATE SECURITY REGULATION

The Securities Act of 1933 does not supersede state control of securities as stated in Section 18. "Nothing in this title shall affect the jurisdiction of the securities commission (or any agency or office performing like functions) of any state or territory of the United States, or the District of Columbia, over any security or any person." The states, therefore, will have the sole supervision of securities sold intrastate, while control of transactions involving interstate commerce will be shared with the federal government.

STATE CONTROL OF SECURITIES[6]

Every state except Nevada has at present legislation for the protection of the investor. These "blue-sky laws" show a pronounced lack of uniformity and their effectiveness is greatly handicapped by the lack of control over interstate traffic in securities.

Of the different laws, the following groups may be distinguished: A. *Fraud Acts:* The states of New York, New Jersey, Maryland, and Delaware, which account for the bulk of new security issues, realized the enormous difficulties that would have to be overcome were they to pass upon the merits of all new issues. Instead of licensing dealers or issues, the protection of the investor was attempted by giving the Attorney General plenary investigatory powers to prosecute financial fraud, to estop fraudulent sales through temporary or fraudulent injunction and to punish those found guilty. Under this system, the effectiveness of the protection was varied in proportion to the zeal of the men administering the act and their appropriations.

B. *Control of Dealers.* The states of Pennsylvania, Maine, New Hampshire, and Colorado have adopted a system involving control of dealers and of those corporations that sell their securities directly to the public. All securities issues have to be submitted to the commissioners and if found "unjust, unfair or unequitable" can be stopped from distribution to the public by the simple device of revoking the dealer's license in case of disobedience.

C. *Control of Dealers and Enforcement of registration and licensing of new issues.*
Thirty-one states have adopted this method of protection which has found a certain degree
of national recognition by having been embodied in the "Uniform Sale of Securities Act."
The latter was drafted by the National Conference of Commissioners on Uniform State
Laws and was adopted by the National Association of Blue Sky Commissioners in 1929.
Under this plan, not only all dealers are licensed, but also all nonexempt securities have to be
registered and qualified before the commission before sale to the public will be permitted.
The commissions are charged not only with the duty of enforcing complete and trustful
publicity for new issues but are also burdened with the great responsibility of having to pass
on the adequacy of the bargain between issuer and the public.[7]

From the summary of major classifications of state blue-sky legislation it becomes evident that the Federal Securities Act goes farther than the Fraud acts, but by no means attempts the protection now provided in most of our state securities acts. The lack of efficiency
of the more ambitious blue-sky acts lies in their impotency in interstate traffic and in the
often-found inadequacy of administrative enforcement.

SUMMARY OF THE ACT

After Section 1(1–12) the terms "security, person, sale, issuer, Commission, territory, interstate commerce, registration statement, written, prospectus, underwriter, and dealer" have
been defined. Sections 2 and 3 enumerate exempted classes of securities and transactions.
Exempted securities are:

1. All municipal securities
2. Railroad and bank securities (already supervised)
3. Short-term paper (not exceeding 9 months)
4. Eleemosynary institutions
5. Building and loan associations
6. Certificates issued by a receiver or by a trustee in bankruptcy

Exempted transactions are:

1. Transactions by any person other than an issuer, underwriter, or dealer
2. Transactions not involving any public offering
3. Transactions by a dealer after one year has elapsed since bona fide public offering, provided that no sale of unsold allotments is involved
4. Brokers' transactions
5. Exchange of securities, if no commission or other remuneration is paid or given
   directly or indirectly
6. Issuance of securities to the existing security holders or other existing creditors of
   a corporation in the process of a bona fide reorganization of such corporation
   under the supervision of the court

All nonexempt securities, if offered for sale, have to be registered with the Commission.

Thus far four different registration forms have been compiled by the Federal Trade Commission:

1. For all corporations: Form A-1 (31 pages)
2. For investment trusts: Form C-1 (21 pages)
3. For certificates of deposit: Form D-1 (18 pages)
4. For reorganization: Form D-2 (29 pages)

Section 8 introduces the so-called cooling period of 20 days. Section 11 establishes the civil liabilities discussed later, while the other sections deal with ancillary functions and methods of procedure of the Commission.

CIVIL LIABILITIES

The very severe liability provisions of the act are imposed on five groups of people:

1. The issuing corporation, i.e., the stockholders, as far as their holdings are concerned
2. The directors of the corporation, whether or not they have the registration statement
3. The chief officers of the corporation, namely the chief executive, the chief financial, and the chief accounting officer
4. The experts, such as accountants, engineers, lawyers, and appraisers, and any person whose profession gives authority to a statement made by him
5. The underwriters, i.e., the investment bankers

Though all these five groups may be liable for misstatements or omissions of material facts in the registration statement, their liability is based on different standards of conduct.

A misstatement or an omission of a material fact is any statement that may have induced a person to purchase or to abstain from purchasing a security. The ambiguity of the phrasing was chosen with care: It reflects the opinion of the legislator, namely that "half a truth is no better than a downright falsehood." This statement incidentally is a quotation from the affirmation by the British Court of Criminal Appeal which in July 1931 sentenced Lord Kylsant, the president of the Royal Mail Steamship Line, to prison for one year. The conviction was based on the issuance of a false prospectus in 1928 for the purpose of inducing subscriptions to some ten millions of dollars of debentures. The prospectus stated truthfully enough the average balance available for the previous ten years, but the prosecution claimed that Lord Kylsant deliberately concealed the fact that the first three years of the ten — the war years — were extremely prosperous, as compared with the very lean years that followed. Justice Wright, who presided at the trial, remarked in his summing up, "One cannot help wondering whether those who manage big companies do not sometimes forget that the directors of a company are the agents and trustees of shareholders, and that, subject to ordinary commercial necessities, they owe them full information."[8]

OPPRESSIVE FEATURES OF THE ACT

Opposition to the act as felt by those who are affected by its severe liability provisions centers on two points. Opposition is voiced first against the imposition of full liability for all losses suffered by all purchasers. Apprehension is caused, furthermore, to experts, such as accountants by the apparent meaning of the law that full liability for all losses suffered by all purchasers of an issue is to be borne even if the registration statement contained misleading information on an item totaling only a fraction of the whole loss.

The obvious lack of proportion reflected in these two provisions has raised the question of whether this interpretation of the act is correct. Unfortunately, for those affected, however, Dr. James M. Landis, newly elected member of the Federal Trade Commission, confirmed this version in his address before the New York State Society of Certified Public Accountants on October 30. Dr. Landis deplored the practice of conjuring what he called "bogey men" to frighten those who may wish to seek new financing through public issues. In his defense of the act he really admitted all the points that have been raised against it. He admitted that each person whose liability on the registration statement has been established is responsible in damages to any purchaser of the security, whether such person shall have purchased from him or from some other person. "Theoretically," according to Dr. Landis, "this means that each person so liable can be held to a liability equivalent to that of the total offering price of the issue." Dr. Landis then claimed that several factors would operate to keep the liability within smaller bounds, because

1. The value of carefully floated issues can hardly be assumed to be zero.
2. Every purchaser would not be likely to bring suit.
3. The fixing of liability — generally, a complicated question of fact — would be retriable in every suit and it cannot be assumed that every issue would come to the same conclusion.
4. Each person liable has a right of contribution against every other person liable, unless the one suing is guilty of fraud and the other is not.

It is obvious from this statement that Dr. Landis's interpretation of the act represents an admission of the oppressive liability imposed by the act and that the "bogey men" are only too real. The liability for the full amount of the issue is imposed on all groups of persons held responsible.

CONCLUSIONS

The Federal Trade Commission's powers of regulation and interpretation of the Federal Securities Act may with the advice of investment bankers, lawyers, and accountants shape the act in its present form into a legal instrument which achieves its admirable purpose "of protecting the investor without interference with honest business." The need of advice from accountants is reflected in the numerical composition of the Securities Division of the Federal Trade Commission, where the accountants are said to outnumber the lawyers twenty-four to ten.

A general criticism of the act would urge certain restrictions on the civil liabilities and, on the other hand, certain extensions to make the act a better instrument for the social con-

trol of new investments. Instead of merely punishing fraud or negligence, the federal government may choose to advise and warn investors in regard to the economic soundness of new
ventures.

As a recommendation of a more specific nature, it may be suggested that the present liability provisions, if kept fully intact, should apply only to the issuance and public offering
of bonds, but not of stocks. The investor in bonds wants safety, and entrepreneurial initiative
is not curtailed if accountants are forced to understate assets and overstate liabilities in order
to avoid responsibility. Such enforcement of overconservative appraisals would obviously
sharply reduce the number of bond issues and of their relative amounts. This fact would be
of benefit both to issuers as well as investors. The following table shows the fatal result of the
topheavy capital structure of certain railroads during this depression. Similar examples
could be provided for industrials and public utilities. The losses on bonds suffered by our
banks, insurance companies, savings institutions, and trust funds merely reflect the other
side of the picture. Overemphasis on conservatism can only benefit society if applied to new
bond flotations; the sale of common stocks as an invitation to become a partner in a new enterprise should not be unduly restricted by civil liabilities.

Percentage of railroad bonds to total capitalization

I.   Roads with heaviest funded debt

(All in receivership)

Railroad:	1932	'31	'30	'29	'28	'27	'26	'25	'24	'23
International Great Northern	87%	87%	87%	87%	87%	75%	85%	83%	83%	83%
Mobile and Ohio	86	86	88	86	87	86	85	85	85	84
*Soo Line	80	74	81	80	80	80	80	81	80	79
Central of Georgia	75	75	75	75	75	75	75	74	73	71
New Orleans, Texas & Mexico	75	75	75	75	75	75	73	72	68	66
Missouri Pacific	73	73	72	71	69	68	67	66	64	62
St. Louis, San Francisco	72	72	72	71	71	81	84	84	84	83
Seaboard Airline	68	68	68	76	76	75	75	73	71	71

*Not in receivership because interest was paid by Canadian Pacific.

II.   Roads with lightest funded debt

(All in good shape)

Railroad:	1932	'31	'30	'29	'28	'27	'26	'25	'24	'23
Norfolk & Western	37%	38%	41%	41%	41%	42%	42%	43%	43%	40%
Atchison, Topeka and Santa Fe	46	46	46	46	44	44	44	44	44	44
Union Pacific	52	53	53	53	56	56	56	56	56	56
Chesapeake and Ohio	54	54	55	56	61	61	62	68	75	73

NOTES

1. "Federal Securities Act" Hearings, H.R. 4314. p. 3, sec. 4.

2. Ibid., p. 69.

3. Institut fur Konjunkturforschung "Kapitalbildung und Investitionen in der Deutschen Volks-wirtschaft," 1924–1928 (Berlin, 1931). For methods of approach to this investigation, see pp. 1–38 and 174–209.

4. Report by W. H. Grimes to the *Wall Street Journal,* November 4, 1933.

5. These figures represent the amount of new financing, excluding refunding issues and invest-ment trust, trading, and holding companies. Nor do they include guaranteed mortgages and cer-tificates which, in the case of the leading title and mortgage companies in New York City alone, rose from $138 million in 1913 to $2.01 billion in 1929.

6. See Jack E. Nida: "Trends in Blue Sky Legislation," Proceedings of the 16th Annual Conven-tion of the National Association of Securities Commissioners; also John E. Dalton: "The Devel-opment and Future Trends in State Security Regulation," *Harvard Business Review,* October 1933.

7. A recent case may illustrate the point. The common stock of the "Minneapolis Brewing Com-pany" was offered in July 1933 to the public through local security dealers for $8 a share. After examination of the issue the State Security Commission published its opinion that the stock should not be sold for a price higher than $3.50. To avoid this scaling down of their profits, the dealers listed the stock for $8 on the Chicago Curb Exchange, at the same time taking brokers' orders to buy at the prices quoted.

8. "High and Low Financiers (Some Notorious Swindlers and Their Abuses of the Modern Stock Selling System)" by Watson Washburn and Edmund S. DeLong, Bobbs-Merrill Com-pany, Indianapolis, 1932 (reviewed by the author in *The Accounting Review,* December 1932, pp. 306–308).

TWO

Influence of the Securities and Exchange Commission upon Accounting Principles

T. H. SANDERS

Formerly, Harvard University

Professor Sanders asserts, in 1936, that the task of the Securities and Exchange Commission (SEC) and the objectives of establishing accounting principles are compatible. SEC effectiveness depends upon the acceptance of accounting principles. After examining the SEC's effect upon accounting principles, he concludes that SEC regulation may strengthen the position of the accounting profession in providing for broader recognition of generally accepted accounting principles in the business community.

ACCOUNTING REQUIREMENTS OF THE LAW

The substance of the power of the Securities and Exchange Commission (SEC), insofar as it concerns accounting, derives from that passage in the Securities Act which in effect enables the Commission to stop the issue of new securities "if it appears to the Commission at any time that the registration statement includes any untrue statement of a material fact or omits to state any material fact required to be stated therein or necessary to make the statements therein not misleading."[1] For the Commission the various items of a balance sheet and of an income statement are "material facts," and what in accounting parlance is often referred to as the disclosure or nondisclosure of information becomes in the law the statement or omission of material facts. The corresponding powers in the Exchange Act make it "unlawful for any member . . . to effect any transaction in any security . . . unless a registration is effective"[2] as prescribed by the Commission. It is now generally understood not only that the Commission has this power to stop the issue of new securities under the Securities Act, or to prevent the effective listing of a security upon a stock exchange under the Exchange Act, but also that any misstatements or omissions, which may escape the scrutiny of the Commission and enter into the basis of transaction in the securities of the company, expose the persons responsible for such misstatements to various and much discussed liabilities and penalties.

The principles of accounting are a body of rules under which the recording in detail, and reporting in summary, of the financial transactions of a business may be accomplished in such a manner that all the important factors contributing to the showing of the company's financial condition and earnings may be made evident. In this area, the Commission's task

---

Reprinted from *The Accounting Review,* March 1936, pp. 66–73, with permission of the American Accounting Association.

is, therefore, identical in purpose with the dictates of accounting principles; in fact it may be said that the success of the Commission as a regulatory body will in large part depend upon the development and general acceptance of a body of principles upon which it can rely in the administration of the legislation committed to its charge.

A somewhat more detailed, but still very general, statement of the accounting aspects of the Commission's work is contained in those sections of Schedule A dealing with the balance sheet and profit and loss statement:

(25) a balance sheet as of a date not more than ninety days prior to the date of the filing of the registration statement showing all of the assets of the issuer, the nature and cost thereof, whenever determinable, in such detail and in such form as the Commission shall prescribe (with intangible items segregated), including any loan in excess of $20,000 to any officer, director, stockholder or person directly or indirectly controlling or controlled by the issuer, or person under direct or indirect common control with the issuer. All the liabilities of the issuer in such detail and such form as the Commission shall prescribe, including surplus of the issuer showing how and from what sources such surplus was created, all as of a date not more than ninety days prior to the filing of the registration statement. If such statement be not certified by an independent public or certified accountant, in addition to the balance sheet required to be submitted under this schedule, a similar detailed balance sheet of the assets and liabilities of the issuer, certified by an independent public or certified accountant, of a date not more than one year prior to the filing of the registration statement, shall be submitted;

(26) a profit and loss statement of the issuer showing earnings and income, the nature and source thereof, and the expenses and fixed charges in such detail and such form as the Commission shall prescribe for the latest fiscal year for which such statement is available and for the two preceding fiscal years, year by year, or, if such issuer has been in actual business for less than three years, then for such time as the issuer has been in actual business, year by year. If the date of the filing of the registration statement is more than six months after the close of the last fiscal year, a statement from such closing date to the latest practicable date. Such statement shall show what the practice of the issuer has been during the three years or lesser period as to the character of the charges, dividends, or other distributions made against its various surplus accounts, and as to depreciation, depletion, and maintenance charges, in such detail and form as the Commission shall prescribe, and if stock dividends or avails from the sale of rights have been credited to income, they shall be shown separately with a statement of the basis upon which the credit is computed. Such statement shall also differentiate between any recurring and nonrecurring income and between any investment and operating income. Such statement shall be certified by an independent public or certified accountant;

Anybody who reads these requirements minutely, and with attention to the literal meanings, will appreciate the significance and wisdom of the clause: "except that the Commission may by rules or regulations provide that any such information or document need not be included in respect of any class of issuers of securities if it finds that the requirements of such information or document is inapplicable to such class and that disclosure fully adequate for the protection of investors is otherwise required to be included within the registration statement."[3] In other words, the Commission is vested with wide discretion as to what it may require by way of information, provided the object sought for is attained, namely, a complete disclosure of all material facts.

MAGNITUDE OF THE COMMISSIONS ACCOUNTING PROBLEM

This is a particularly necessary and fortunate provision when the breadth of the Commission's assignment is borne in mind. It is charged with supervision over companies in every line of business; it will have to be flexible in its requirements if the peculiar conditions of different industries are to be adequately represented. In this respect the SEC is in a very different position from the ICC or the FCC, or the state public utility commission. These latter have a relatively small and homogeneous class of operations to cover, and may as a business proposition prescribe for them with much more assurance than the SEC could bring to the task of specific prescription of form and method. In fact the accounting task of the other commissions is more analogous to the development of a uniform accounting system such as many industries have individually and voluntarily undertaken for themselves, the only difference being that in the governmental field most of the commissions have power to require compliance.

The Internal Revenue Department has jurisdiction even wider than that of the SEC as regards the number and variety of businesses reporting to it, but far more narrow as regards the specific object of the accounting reports it receives. The Internal Revenue Department is concerned with devising a formula for taxable income, in which its main care must be the levying of a uniform charge on people in like financial position as to income. While the statements filed with this department should be reconcilable with statements prepared for general financial purposes, it has never been claimed that these should always be identical.

It should be clearly understood that the accounting rules of the SEC apply strictly to registration statements filed with the Commission, which has no direct jurisdiction over the reports furnished by companies to their stockholders. It is likely that the latter will, in form and content, continue to be largely what they have hitherto been except that, in the case of listed companies or companies expecting to offer new issues, there can be no obvious inconsistencies of a material nature between the reports to stockholders and the statements filed with the Commission. The liabilities for misstatement as specified in the Securities Act and Exchange Act apply to the registration statements and not to reports to stockholders, but no company will wish to draw suspicion upon itself by discrepancies between the two. It is clear, furthermore, that both statements must come from the same common source, namely, the books and records of the company.

APPLICATION OF ACCOUNTING PRINCIPLES

It is to these records, therefore, that the principles of accounting must primarily apply, but it is also necessary that the same principles be carried through into the reports by which the books and records are summarized for those who may have an interest in them. There is no question but that the leading companies of the country have within the past twelve months scrutinized their own internal accounting practices with extreme care in the light of the requirements of the SEC, and wherever any material difference occurred, either in the treatment of items or in the amount of information to be given, have asked themselves whether their own practices came within the SEC requirements, in view of all the latitudes there allowed.

Without doubt the SEC constitutes a potent force for the realization of accounting principles as they have long been expressed in textbooks. Without doubt the accounting conversation of our business corporations will more than ever before be of the order of "yea, yea, and nay, nay"; the deliberate disregard of fundamental principles will be a far more perilous matter than it has ever been.

But for that great majority of corporations which have always wanted to do a good job in their accounts the principal difficulties have not lain in the acceptance of the general principles, but rather in their application to peculiar conditions. It is not necessary here to dwell upon the shortcomings in the past of records in which, for example, lump sum transactions have been consummated for the acquisition of entire business units without itemizing the asset and liability elements involved. Nearly every large corporation twenty years old or over has a good deal of this sort of thing in its early records, making it very difficult, if not impossible, to be very categorical in stating the amounts and description of its various property accounts. From now on changes will occur in two directions. In the first place efforts will be made to clear up old records, even when this involves arbitrary appraisals and apportionments. This was done, for example, in the case of American Smelting and Refining Company, which during the past year has for the first time divided its property accounts as between tangible and intangible items. In so doing the company stated that although the SEC regulations did not insist upon the separation, the evident preferences of the Commission had led them to take the step. In one way or another old confusions will gradually be eliminated from the balance sheet, and the more precise practices of recent years will place the property accounts upon a more definite basis. In the second place new transactions of considerable magnitude, such as mergers or the acquisition of general properties, will be more explicitly recorded, so as to segregate the different classes of property. From a business point of view as well as for accounting purposes it will not be at all a bad thing to require the principal actors in such transactions to inventory the deal and make up their own minds as to exactly what they are getting in the purchase. If the physical assets are reasonably priced, and it has been thought proper to pay a larger amount for the entire business as a going concern, it would not seem that the common rule of regarding the excess as something of an intangible nature in the order of goodwill is improper. One would hesitate to make an arbitrary rule to this effect, and the Commission has refrained from doing so. Where properties have been acquired at something corresponding to the capitalized value of their earnings, and changing price levels and maintenance practices have resulted in a reproduction cost which would be far above the book values, it is not in all cases entirely necessary or just to require the management to make on oath an apportionment of that total purchase price as between tangible and intangible properties. On the other hand, they are required to do this for income tax purposes, and although the amounts arrived at for that purpose may not be completely satisfactory they at least represent one basis for the apportionment. It would seem that, taking all requirements into consideration, it is generally desirable that a specific allocation of investment among the various assets be made.

FLEXIBILITY IN SEC REGULATIONS

Reference has already been made to the freedom of choice allowed by the Commission's regulations; it seems desirable to define further the character of this freedom. It probably does not mean that the Commission would condone any kind of accounting, even though clearly expressed. The general preferences of the Commission are unmistakable, and the alternatives allowed are not designed to furnish excuses for any subterfuges in accounting practice that registering companies might see fit to present. The first requirement certainly is full disclosure, but if the methods disclosed are unsatisfactory the Commission has full power to require other information, and to issue stop orders not only for insufficient information, but also if the information supplied discloses a situation which seems to them fraudulent.[4] On the other hand, it is certain that the Commission will elicit much more constructive information by the policy it has followed than would have been obtained by a policy of specific prescriptions and prohibitions with respect to the various items of accounting statements. The general sanction (if one may now use that word in its ordinary sense) expressed in the provision that "the registrant may file statements and schedules in such form, order, and using such generally accepted terminology as will best indicate their significance and character in the light of the instructions" was evidently designed to encourage the adequate presentation of the special features of any corporation which might have occasion to register with the Commission. To have followed a contrary course, to have prescribed a form with specific instructions, would undoubtedly have distorted the showing in many balance sheets, and destroyed their true significance. It is this emphasis on an affirmative and constructive practice which has justified the high esteem in which the Commission has generally come to be held.

It is interesting to list the matters on which the Commission allows alternatives, or on which the requirement is merely for disclosure of the basis adopted. The following paragraphs constitute only a partial list, including the more important matters so treated.

In consolidating accounts considerable latitude is allowed, both in respect to what may be consolidated, and also in the treatment of intercompany items. The one thing insisted upon is that the practices adopted shall be disclosed.

The treatment of foreign balances converted into dollars, and of the resulting profit, is left to the company's discretion.

The inclusion of debatable items in current assets or current liabilities may be rested upon trade practices, if the practices are cited.

The classification of inventories, when there are important subdivisions, and the basis of their valuation, are left to be treated as the conditions of the industry and of the company may suggest.

In connection with all assets it is required only that the basis of arriving at the amounts or values shown shall be stated, but in no case is a specific basis prescribed.

The problem of the separation of capital surplus from earned surplus is allowed to be determined by what the accounting practice of the company has been, although future amounts added to surplus must be sufficiently described.

With respect to contingent liabilities the regulation states only that they must have "due consideration."

Although it is required that the different main sources of revenues shall be separately stated, yet the Commission does not carry this rule into small amounts; anything under 10% of the total gross revenues may be combined. This, however, does not refer to miscellaneous other income, from sources other than the company's principal operations. These are required to be separately shown.

Schedule VIII has the appearance of a hard and fast prescription as to important items of cost, but on examination will be found to be an attempt by the Commission to elicit this information in terms conformable with whatever accounting system the company may be following. These items may be shown in the income statement proper or in Schedule VIII or divided between the two, according to the cost accounting and inventory practices of the registering company.

For both debt discount and expense, and discount and commissions on capital stock, the method or basis of amortization is left to the discretion of the company.

Reacquired bonds are expressly permitted to be shown as Other Security Investments (Item 9) or as deductions from Funded Debt (Item 26), but as a separate item in either case.

In the case of reacquired stock a preference is expressed for having it shown as a deduction from capital stock or from surplus or from the two combined; though it may also be shown as an asset under Other Security Investments, provided the reasons for so doing are given. If treated as a deduction on the liabilities side the further option is allowed of making this deduction "at either par or cost as circumstances require." Presumably any reasons of substance, whether of a legal nature or connected with managerial financial purposes, would be satisfactory to the Commission, as well as informative to investors.

No prescription is given for the basis of determining cost of securities sold, for the purpose of ascertaining profit or loss. The choice of basis is left to the company, but must be stated.

It is certain that if the Commission's staff lives up to the liberal spirit of these provisions much more helpful information will be placed at the disposal of investors than would otherwise be possible. In the case of surplus, for example, everybody recognizes the desirability of explaining its nature, in cases where it contains unlike elements in substantial amounts. But if the Commission sought to require a hard and fast legal description of the balance in surplus account as shown in the balance sheet, many companies would either be unable to comply or would be forced to efforts of compliance with showings having the appearance, but not the reality, of precision. This is not only because of the uncertain character of amounts credited to surplus in the remote past; still the difficulty is caused by the impossibility of allocating subsequent deductions from surplus, whether dividend payments or other charges, as between the earned and capital elements which might formerly have been therein. The result is that it may be easy for the company to say such things as: "In 1918 the sum of $5,000,000, a capital surplus item, was credited to surplus for the following reasons." It is not possible for the same company to say "There is *now* included in surplus an amount of $5,000,000 capital surplus" because all charges against surplus subsequent to 1918 may be apportioned in almost any degree as between that capital surplus item and earned surplus credits.

The liberal spirit reflected in regulations of this character, together with their adherence to the broad principles of accounting, have gone far to win the general acceptability with which the Commission's regulations have for the most part been received. In this respect these regulations have been unlike those of the Federal Communications Commission, which, in their requirements for the substitution of property costs to some prior owner for costs to the present owner, strike at the very roots of what has always been regarded as sound property accounting. It is difficult to imagine the confusion which would be introduced to accounting principles and practices if a rule of this sort became in any way generally accepted.

MANDATORY FEATURES OF THE REGULATIONS

With all this flexibility it is important to observe the things that are insisted upon in the regulations of the SEC.

The first of these unquestionably is full disclosure of all material facts; the Commission under the law must require this, and its whole conduct has indicated a determination to do so. Wide ranges of choice at many points have been cited; latent in these options is an implied recognition that management is responsible for the conduct of its own business, and that the primary purpose of accounting is to record what management has done in the discharge of its responsibilities, not to tell management what it may or may not do. It is safe to say that the Commission will insist upon this primary function of accounting being realized in all essential matters.

The general limits of consolidation, both as to what may and may not be consolidated, and the character of information required in a consolidation, are fairly definitely indicated. Again there is room for the handling of exceptional cases, but the spirit and intent of the requirement are reasonably clear and could not lightly be evaded. That the Commission will take a critical view of consolidated statements which to them seem to fail to disclose important facts was made abundantly clear by its statement in the case of Baldwin Locomotive Works, in which the Commission held that the effect of a balance sheet which consolidated a subsidiary only sixty per cent owned was to "portray a net quick asset position better than that of the issuing corporation."[5]

While the Commission did not prescribe a precise form or wording for the accountant's certificate, its general character and substance are set forth. The American Institute of Accountants, in cooperation with the New York Stock Exchange, has evolved a form of certificate which has found wide acceptance, yet there is a good deal of feeling among public accountants against having any one form prescribed by law. Their view is that since the accountant is liable under the law for what he says in the certificate, the law should not put words into his mouth, and the regulations indicate that the Commission accepted that view, at the same time prescribing in plain terms what the substantive contents of a good certificate should be.

FLEXIBILITY IN ADMINISTRATION

In this matter of the part played by the auditor's certificate the ideas expressed by Professor C. Aubrey Smith in the December issue of *The Accounting Review* are most interesting. He there cites a number of cases of which conflicting opinions might be held as to the treatment of certain matters by the registrant company. While the accounting practices of the company might be open to criticism, or even to condemnation, the company was not, in the several cases mentioned, required to restate its balance sheets and income statements, because the comments of the auditors had made the situation clear. It would seem that Professor Smith's position is well taken; it is tantamount to saying that the entire registration statement is a unit, comprising all the representations of the registrant company, and all the supporting testimony of experts. When there is any question as to the company's handling of an item it is reasonable to suppose that the public can learn more from seeing first the company's treatment and then the dissenting views of the accountant than they could from a cut-and-dried presentation prescribed by the Commission. This is one of the happiest and most important lines of policy adopted by the Commission; it is in the spirit of its own regulations; it will undoubtedly make the statements available to the public more informative rather than less, and will increase the prestige and power of the Commission.

SIGNIFICANCE OF HISTORICAL INFORMATION REQUIRED

Another important requirement upon which the Commission can safely insist is that marked as "Supplemental Financial Information," Question 34 of Form 10. It has been shown above how impossible it often is to require a specific analysis of the present surplus balance; it is a very different thing, so far as the assurance with which one can speak is concerned, to state certain historical facts which have from time to time affected surplus, and which serve the purposes in mind even better than could a subdivision of the present surplus balance. Nor should it be assumed that the items which will here be disclosed will in all cases be matter for criticism; on the contrary, it is safe to say that the great majority of them will reflect proper exercise of managerial powers in questions of financial policy, but matters on which any intelligent investor would wish to be informed. For example, during the last four years write-downs of property and plant would appear conspicuously in this section. There has been much discussion of the accounting and financial effects of such write-downs, as they work themselves out in the balance sheet and income statement; but the far more important considerations are those of a business and economic character. Many economists, as well as many businessmen, feel strongly that when there is a general decline in price levels it is altogether desirable that a business should reduce its fixed charges accordingly, reduce its selling prices, and thereby help to maintain or increase the volume of business, employment, and the flow of consumable goods. Whatever may be one's views on such matters they are clearly management problems of the first magnitude, which are not within the province of accounting alone to determine. After they have been determined, however, it is the peculiar province of accounting to make the consequence as clear as possible, and this the regulations require. The Commission asks that the transactions be described as they occurred; it does not ask for the more dubious and difficult information as to how these matters stand in the present account balances.

BASIS OF PROPERTY ACCOUNTING

In connection with this same question of property "values" it is interesting to note that the Commission has, by the language of its regulations, lent support to the view, pretty generally accepted by accountants, that it is not the business of the accounts to reflect the "value" of the properties and plant. For lack of a better word we have all talked somewhat freely of "values" and "valuations," understanding in our own minds that what we were thinking about was the statement of assets on a cost basis, and the subsequent periodic apportionment of those costs to income. To those not primarily trained in accounting the discussions of value and valuation have always been confusing. The Commission has at least refrained from adding to this confusion, when in Schedule II it speaks primarily of the balances in the property accounts, additions and subtractions at cost, and does not use the word "value." Thus the emphasis is laid upon changes in the amount of property resulting from expenditures and retirements during the year, which are the important matters, and not upon the "value" of the whole property, which in a going concern of some age is a highly dubious and relatively immaterial fact.

With regard to current assets and current liabilities the effect of the regulations is to require a strict definition of the totals, and of the component parts which enter into the showing of the current ratio. Borderline items frequently occur, the inclusion or exclusion of which in the current bracket may be debatable; but it is certain that the company and its accountants have more information on the subject than anybody else, and they are called upon to give their judgment on the question by the requirement that the total of current assets and of current liabilities shall be shown.

SOME PRINCIPLES OF INCOME DETERMINATION

An interesting example of the kind of pressure the Commission is able to bring to bear, without prescribing a fixed rule, occurs in the regulations pertaining to the income statement for investment trusts, as given in the Instruction Book for Form 15. First of all, for income the registrant is required to "state separately the total income from (a) cash dividends, (b) interest, and (c) other income (specify)." Then it is required that the registrant "state, as to any dividends other than cash, the basis on which they have been taken up as income and the justification alleged, if any, for such action."

This is a plain hint that ordinarily the Commission would view the treatment of a stock dividend as income with marked disapproval; it is implied that in many cases no justification can even be alleged for such a practice, but it is recognized that regularly recurring stock dividends, in amounts not greater than the current earnings of the declarant company, may reasonably be treated as income, and that other circumstances may conceivably arise which would justify such a practice. By requiring the statement of the particular circumstances which are claimed to justify, or at least explain, such accounting, the Commission not only causes the public to be apprised of those circumstances, but also emphasizes their exceptional character and the fact that they are not to be regarded as satisfactory for general practice.

After all the ordinary expenses for supervision and management, and even unusual expenses, have been deducted from the income as above defined, and after the provision for income taxes, a balance of income (Item 9) is obtained. This amount is clearly regarded as the ordinary income of an investment trust, but following it are provided items for gain or loss realized, first from security transactions and next from transactions in other investments, to which items is appended the following note:

> Persons whose policy is to engage primarily in trading and who use, in determining their income for income tax purposes, opening and closing inventories on a basis prescribed by the United States Treasury Department regulations relating to the income tax, may report under caption (1) above, under a subcaption specially designated, gains or losses called for under captions (10) and (11). In such case, a footnote to the profit and loss statement shall indicate that the policy of the person is to engage primarily in trading.

Here again the Commission shows itself conversant with the very different types of business known as investment trusts, and in particular with the fact that these differences have not hitherto been adequately called to the attention of the investing public. The very name "investment trust" implies a certain fixity of the investments, with only occasional changes such as in the management's discretion are thought likely to maintain the integrity of the capital invested in the trust. A surprising number of well-informed people do not understand that operating under the name "investment trust" are numbers of businesses which buy and sell securities like groceries, aiming to make the increase between the buying and selling price their principal source of income. When such people are first confronted with this fact they are apt to say: "Then they should not be called 'investment trusts.'" The Commission has refrained from going the length of requiring such businesses to take a different name, but in the paragraph cited above has required that they shall announce the character of their business in explicit terms and not leave innocent folk under the impression that they are putting their money into a literal investment trust, if in fact it is a security trading company.

It ought to be added that there is no necessary stigma attaching to this trading business providing all interested parties, especially the investors, know what they are about. Securities properly issued are perfectly legal commodities, and if numbers of investors are willing to entrust certain managers with their money for the purpose of buying and selling such commodities, there is no good reason why they should not be permitted to do it. From the fact that the Commission has made provision in this way for the results of such operations to be shown, a member of the public may infer that it recognizes, without protest, the existence of such business, subject only to full disclosure of its nature.

EFFECTS OF THE REGULATIONS

The general effect of these regulations will undoubtedly be to strengthen the hands of all who are concerned in good accounting. Company accountants and public accountants will be able to point to these requirements in support of what they regard as necessary for accurate statement and full disclosure. While the Commission has endeavored to make its regulations liberal, practical, and adaptable to the greatly varied conditions of business, it is reasonable to believe that accounting principles, as embodied in the published statements of corporations will look more like the accounting principles taught in colleges than ever before. And this will be true whether or not the statements are filed with the Commission; it would be absurd to suppose that in the circumstances reports to stockholders, or any other publications by business corporations, could show any material divergences from statements filed with the Commission. Company and public accountants all over the country have that idea clearly in mind.

NOTES

1. Securities Act of 1933, sec. 8(d).
2. Securities Exchange Act of 1934, sec. 12(a).
3. Securities Act, sec. 7.
4. *Ibid.,* sec. 17.
5. Release no. 167.

THREE

The Relationship of the Securities and Exchange Commission to the Accountant

CARMAN G. BLOUGH

Former Chief Accountant, Securities and Exchange Commission

Carman G. Blough, first chief accountant of the Securities and Exchange Commission (SEC), discusses, in 1937, the 1933 and 1934 Acts and their effect on the practice of the public accountant. He sounds the theme that only by working together can the public accountant and the SEC make progress toward improving accounting practices.

The Securities and Exchange Commission is, at the present time, primarily responsible for the administration of three acts of Congress. They are the Securities Act of 1933, the Securities Exchange Act of 1934, and the Public Utility Act of 1935.

Extensive provisions for the regulation of accounting matters are found in each of several acts and each provides that the Commission shall prescribe the methods to be followed in the presentation of financial statements. The Public Utility Act goes still further, authorizing the Commission to prescribe the accounts to be kept and the methods to be followed in keeping them.

With such broad powers over the accounting statements of companies coming under the jurisdiction of the Commission, its decisions with reference to accounting policies, principles, and procedures will undoubtedly have a material effect upon general accounting practice. For this reason many accountants are interested in the work of the Commission even though they do not expect to represent registrants.

Many prominent accountants have expressed the belief that the profession is looking to the Securities and Exchange Commission for material assistance in solving controversial questions; and the members of the profession have, for the most part, cooperated with the Commission.

The presentation of accounting data in reports to stockholders has been improved noticeably in the last few years, and numerous accountants have stated that they have been able to improve their statements because they were supported by our rules and regulations. Undoubtedly, the acts have contributed toward more adequate disclosure and the adoption of sounder practices in the presentation of accounting statements.

Reprinted from *The Journal of Accountancy*, January 1937, pp. 23–29, with the permission of the American Institute of Certified Public Accountants.

The Commission realizes that it has grave responsibilities in these matters. Accordingly, it has sought and, I am happy to say, has received the cooperation of the leading accounting associations and numerous individual authorities on the subject. We hope, by this cooperation, to make sure that the positions we take on accounting matters from time to time may be the result of the best thought in the profession, with particular reference to the aims of the legislation being administered.

REASONS FOR THE ACTS

The reasons for the passage of the various acts are numerous and involved, having their roots in the history of American corporate policies and practices of the last fifty years, more particularly the 1920s. The Securities Act of 1933 and the Securities Exchange Act of 1934, insofar as they relate to accounting matters, are designed for the purpose of obtaining "the truth, the whole truth, and nothing but the truth." They are intended to give investors and prospective investors information regarding a registrant's financial condition and operations adequate to make sound judgments as to the value of its securities.

In this country a great many corporate stockholders are in the investing rather than the controlling class. A controlling investor, an officer, or a director is usually in possession of sufficient information about the company's affairs to make an intelligent judgment as to the desirability of buying, holding, or selling the company's stock. This has not, in a large number of cases, been the situation of the investing stockholder. He also needs comprehensive information not only as to financial conditions and prevailing trends in the industry but as to the financial situation of the individual company. The 1933 and 1934 acts were designed to enable the investor to get this information.

The Public Utility Act of 1935 was enacted with the intent to curb many of the practices that developed during the past fifteen or twenty years as a result of the rapid expansion of public utilities and the tremendous increase in the use of holding companies to finance and control them. Such practices were anything but beneficial either to consumers of public utility service or to the general investors in public utility securities.

Large holding-company systems were built up in such a manner as to place the control of tremendous aggregations of property in the hands of persons having relatively small amounts of investments at stake.

Operating companies were subjected to excessive charges for services, construction, equipment, and materials and were required to enter into other transactions with controlling and other affiliated companies upon terms fixed with a view only to the ultimate advantage of persons in control. Securities and properties were exchanged among members of the same system at exorbitant profits to the selling company. Fictitious and unsound asset values having no relation to the sums invested in, or the actual capacity of, the underlying properties were used as a basis for the issuance of securities. Paper profits from intercompany transactions, and property values inflated by the same means or by internal appraisals, induced the public to furnish the capital. Usually the public had no knowledge of the fair value of the underlying securities or property. Assumptions that the values placed on assets were the results of arms-length dealing were encouraged.

These abuses, among other reasons, brought about the passage of the 1935 act and placed upon the Commission the responsibility of exercising extensive accounting control over the public utility holding companies and their subsidiaries.

ACCOUNTING UNDER THE 1933 AND 1934 ACTS

Rules for registration under the 1933 and 1934 acts generally require the registrant to submit balance sheets, profit-and-loss statements, and various supporting schedules, certified by independent public or independent certified public accountants. Every company having securities registered upon a national securities exchange is required to file an annual report with the Commission and with the exchange. Certified financial statements constitute the major portion of such reports.

The Commission has depended a great deal upon the ability of the independent public accountants and has not attempted to lay down hard-and-fast rules regarding the type of audit or the specific form of the financial statements required. Certain minimum requirements are specified in each form, but much is left to the judgment of the accountant.

Form 10 under the Securities Exchange Act and Form A-2 under the Securities Act are used for most of the filings under those acts. As prescribed by the Commission, both these forms provide for a balance sheet, a profit-and-loss statement, and supporting schedules. While the information required in these statements is set forth in considerable detail, the following significant sentence is incorporated in the instructions to each form: "The registrant may file statements and schedules in such form, order and using such generally accepted terminology as will best indicate their significance and character in the light of the instructions."

This sentence was inserted in the instructions because these forms were devised for the registration of innumerable types of business enterprise, extending from a one-horse gold mine in Colorado to the far-flung empire of the Standard Oil Company of New Jersey. Since the registration forms were prescribed for such a widely diversified group, it was obviously impossible to draw them to incorporate the details of procedure to be followed in preparing each statement. Accordingly, the sentence quoted was incorporated for the purpose of giving the accountant enough leeway to express adequately the information for varying types of businesses.

We have had strange reactions to the sentence. Some registrants and some firms have interpreted it to mean that a statement could be prepared in almost any manner and have used it to justify omission of most of the information called for by the form. Some have even interpreted it to mean that the registrant could judge as to which financial statements would best show its condition irrespective of specific requirements as to the necessity of filing certain statements. Others seem to have overlooked the significance of this sentence entirely and have attempted to make an obviously inapplicable situation fit into the exact form set forth in the instruction book.

The rules and regulations of the Commission provide that the financial statements required shall be accompanied by a certificate of an independent public or independent certified public accountant, that such certificate shall be dated, shall be reasonably comprehensive as to the scope of the audit made, and shall state clearly the opinion of the accountant in respect of the financial statements of, and the accounting principles and procedures followed by, the registrant.

It should be noted in connection with the certification that the rule specifically provides that nothing in the instructions should be construed to imply authority for the omission of any procedure independent public accountants would ordinarily employ in the course of a regular annual audit. This provision answers the question many accountants have raised as to whether it is necessary to make certain analyses and checks in order to certify the statements to be filed. The responsibility for certification rests upon the accountant; it is his job and it is not the desire of the Commission to restrict the scope of his work; he is the judge of the type of examination necessary to make a reasonably unqualified certification.

The qualifications of accountants under the requirements of the acts has been the subject of considerable discussion. Criticisms arise for various reasons. In the first place, the auditors are often not independent. For instance, an accountant who is a director or officer or who owns a material interest in the registrant (either material as to the capitalization of the registrant or as to his own personal fortune) is not deemed to be independent, nor is one who is a regular employee of the registrant or has a continuing pecuniary interest in it. We have also taken the position that one who was an officer or director during the period under review cannot qualify as being independent even though he held no such position at the date of the audit.

In determining the right of a person to certify an accounting statement, the question of the public nature of his activities also arises. Certainly, if one is recognized by the laws of the state as having the right to practice accounting, holds himself out as a general practitioner, and actually does a variety of accounting work, there can be little question but that he is a "public" accountant. On the other hand, if he has the right to act as a "public" accountant but his only client is the registrant, the question may be seriously raised as to whether he can qualify.

A third weakness exists when the person certifying is not properly trained as an accountant. Unhappily, it has been necessary to inquire into the training and experience of a number of such persons.

Just what the Commission will have to do, or will be able to do, in the way of determining who is qualifed to certify the financial statements submitted for registration purposes is a question it is not prepared to answer at this time. While certifications have been rejected in a number of cases because the accountant could not qualify under the general rules and regulations, no attempt has been made, as yet, to name the specific qualifications for accountants. Whether it will be expedient or even desirable to limit certifications to certified public accountants is a debatable point. Effective regulatory laws in the several states would go a long way toward solving our problem in that regard.

Another criticism arising out of the examination of financial statements is the failure of the accountant to indicate the scope of his audit. I seriously doubt whether any concept of the word "audit" is sufficiently uniform among accountants that the investor may be reasonably expected to appreciate the significance of the term when an accountant certifies that he has "audited" the books of a corporation. There are a good many accountants who take the position that such a statement, without qualification of any kind, means a complete detailed audit. From this position, opinions vary all the way to the person who maintains that the sketchiest kind of an examination is sufficient to be dignified by the term "audit." For this reason, it is quite important that the auditor incorporate in his certificate an adequate explanation of the scope of the audit.

Another of the required provisions of the certification is that it shall state the opinion of the accountant with regard to the financial statements. Possibly, you may feel that if the auditor presents a statement it should be assumed that he believes it correctly reflects the financial condition of the registrant or the results of its operations, as the case may be. If the accountant always drew up the statements himself and if he were always completely indifferent to the wishes of his client, this might be a safe asumption. Unfortunately, this is not always the case. The statements are often drawn by the client for the accountant's examination, and he is seldom completely indifferent to the client's wishes.

It is not uncommon for an accountant to present financial statements and, in his certificate, point out certain facts of inclusion and exclusion without expressing any opinion as to whether the statements properly reflect the facts or not. Thus the accountant who would certify to a financial statement in which plant-and-equipment is carried at twice its cost and three times its present sale value on the basis of a 1928 appraisal, at which time the appreciation was carried to, and is now included in, the earned-surplus account, might very well attempt to protect himself by including in his certification a statement of such facts without expressing his opinion as to the propriety of such treatment. In our opinion, the protection of investors requires that the accountant who, by a narration of facts in his certificate, attempts to protect himself, should be required to express his opinion with regard to the propriety of showing the facts in the manner in which they have been shown. If all of the facts have been treated in the statement in a manner he considers to be in accordance with accepted accounting practice, he should so state. If he is prevented from properly presenting the facts, he should qualify his statement with respect to such items and should express his disapproval of handling them in the manner in which they have been handled.

Another requirement of the certification is that it shall state the opinion of the accountant with respect to the accounting principles and procedures followed by the person whose statements he is certifying. Reason should, of course, govern the statement made in that respect. I do not believe the fact that the accountant is forced, at the time of his audit, to make routine adjustments correcting minor errors in accounting procedure, should prevent him from stating that the accounts of the client have been kept in accordance with accepted principles of accounting consistently maintained. On the other hand, if the client's customary procedure is deliberately to record important transactions in such a manner as to violate accepted accounting practice or if isolated items of major importance have been improperly handled, I think the accountant is duty-bound to indicate that his client's accounting procedure has not been all it should have been.

There is, of course, a dividing line between acceptable and unacceptable accounting practices; that line is a hairline, the location of which is a matter for the individual judgment of the accountant. The determination of how far he can go in approving the practices of his client and how far he must go in criticizing them is primarily his responsibility. Certainly from the standpoint of the investor, it is of significance to know the customary accounting policies of the registrant and its subsidiary companies. Such policies reflect the likelihood of integrity in the accounts during years prior to those under review, and they also reflect the present attitude of the corporate officials.

Occasionally an accountant seeks to protect himself by including in his certification numerous qualifications and exceptions. Sometimes these are probably due to a lack of courage on the part of the accountant to insist upon being permitted to make adequate examination of the accounts and to prepare correct statements so as to make qualifications unnecessary. In other words, they may be due to the accountant's wish to hide his own inability as an auditor by citing in his certification numerous matters he has failed to cover. Occasionally, of course, the circumstances are such as to require extensive qualifications. In my opinion, good accountants will use them sparingly.

A certification covering two or three pages (to say nothing of ten or fifteen) filled with qualifications and exceptions makes proper interpretation of the accounting statement extremely difficult and leaves the reader with a feeling that there is more wrong than has been revealed. Usually it should be possible to carry an audit to such an extent and to adjust the statements in sufficient detail to permit certification with relatively few qualifications or exceptions. Just how far the Commission eventually will go in refusing to accept statements because the certifications are so extensively qualified, I do not know. The distinction between the comments a high-grade accountant considers necessary in connection with an audit that has involved peculiar difficulties and those of a less capable accountant trying to protect himself against his own incompetence may not be hard to make at the extremes, but the dividing line is often difficult to detect. Some place between the two extremes there is a point where qualifying explanations cease to be acceptable and become a fit subject for refusal on our part.

Amendments to financial statements should be covered by new certifications from the accountant. In some instances, after deficiencies have been cited with respect to financial data, the accountants are reluctant to certify a new statement or schedule that is different from the one originally filed. Naturally, I am sympathetic with the accountant who does not wish to appear to vacillate in the things to which he certifies, but on the other hand, if the changes suggested are such as to bring the statements more nearly in accord with good accounting practice, he should have no hesitancy in certifying the amended statements.

PROBLEMS INVOLVING ACCOUNTING PRINCIPLES

In the administration of the rules of the Commission relating to accounting matters, problems of wide variety are presented for consideration. To organize and discuss them in any comprehensive manner is out of the question at this time, but it seems appropriate to comment upon a few of the accounting principles that have been involved in our discussions with accountants and to relate a few specific cases.

Up to September 15, 1936, formal findings and opinions had been issued by the Commission in twenty-seven of its stop-order hearings under the 1933 act. (A stop-order is an order issued by the Commission suspending the effectiveness of a registration of a security. Until a stop-order has been lifted, it is illegal to sell the security in question through the mails or in interstate commerce.) In nineteen of these cases, the financial data submitted or accounting practices followed, or both, were cited as being at least partly responsible for the issuance of the stop-order.

All these hearings involved registrations on Form A-1 and, therefore, concerned new companies, many of a highly speculative nature. Of the nineteen mentioned as involving accounting matters, twelve were mining ventures, three were investment companies, two were distillers, one was a manufacturer of airplanes, and one was an oil-royalty company. The accountants who certified the financial data contained in these statements were principally members of small firms. While the failure properly to disclose or reflect reprehensible accounting practices probably was not intentional, it certainly indicated a lack of recognition of the accountant's responsibility.

The Commission's principal criticisms of the financial data presented in these nineteen cases may be summarized as follows:

1. Fixed assets were stated on the balance sheet as amounts equal to the par value of stock issued therefor; whereas, the value of such assets was found to be much less.

2. Stock was issued for fixed assets and simultaneously donated back to the corporation. Although the nominal value of these shares was included in the figure at which the fixed assets were carried on the balance sheet, an equal amount was also included under treasury stock, capital surplus being created to offset the charge to treasury stock. (In instances of this kind the Commission has required the elimination of the amount of the donated stock from both the asset and the surplus accounts and has required the company to state on the face of the balance sheet whether stock issued under such circumstances is fully paid and nonassessable.)

3. Fixed assets were stated on the balance sheet at appraised values that were found to be grossly overstated.

4. Fixed assets, as carried in the balance sheet, included an amount equal to the par value of the stock issued to the seller of such assets in consideration for his agreement to reconstruct certain property included therein.

5. Fixed assets, as stated, included amounts equal to the par value of stock issued to promoters for services as such.

6. Fixed assets included lease and option agreements without disclosing their nature or the fact that the obligations assumed thereunder were subject to cancellation.

7. The amount at which promotional services were included on the balance sheet was found to be greatly in excess of the value of the services rendered.

8. The balance sheet failed to indicate that certain assets were pledged as collateral to loans.

9. Donations by stockholders were treated as income rather than as donated surplus.

10. Pro-forma balance sheets were used to reflect the receipt of proceeds from anticipated sales of securities for which no firm commitment for their sale existed.

In a number of cases the accountant was not directly subject to criticism. In some he had no access to facts that would have permitted him to give the proper treatment to the items in question. In others the scope of his duties did not include a judgment as to the propriety of the values fixed by the directors.

However, the Commission did find justification for specifically criticizing the accountants for the following reasons:

1. The nature of the deficiencies in financial data was such that it appeared that the accountant had not made a "proper examination."

2. The accountant's statement that the registrant had consistently followed sound accounting practices was found to be erroneous.

3. The accountants were found to be "not independent."

The twenty-seven cases in which formal findings and opinions were issued, however, do not constitute even a major percentage of the instances in which stop-orders have been entered, and the cases taken to stop-order constitute only a very small percentage of the registrations in which accounting problems arise. As a matter of fact, the most technical accounting questions have not arisen in stop-order cases but in registrations that were corrected and ultimately became effective.

A hasty review of a few examples will serve to illustrate the type of problem with which the Commission is regularly faced.

Case I

A chemical company created a subsidiary corporation and subscribed for its entire capital stock, paying in cash approximately $1.5 million in excess of par. The subsidiary credited this excess to paid-in surplus. In the course of several years the subsidiary returned over $1.35 million of this paid-in surplus to the parent in the form of dividends.

The financial statements of the parent company filed with the Commission revealed that the company had credited the amount of the dividends received from the subsidiary to capital surplus, leaving the investment account unchanged. The Commission advised the registrant that such dividends appeared to be in the nature of a return of consideration paid for the investment and that, unless they were credited to the investment account, such account would be overstated by the amount of the dividends. Following this criticism, the registrant reversed its entry, thereby eliminating the capital surplus and reducing the investment in its subsidiary.

Case II

A glass-sand corporation recorded depletion of its deposits by direct charges to surplus. The Commission expressed the opinion that failure to include depletion charges in the profit-and-loss statements had the effect of inflating the net profits for each year by approximately 25%.

By amendment the registrant restated its profit-and-loss accounts to reflect therein proper depletion expense and attached the following note:

> *On the registrant's books of account the amounts provided for depletion have been charged to earned-surplus-unappropriated account but have been treated in these financial statements as charges against profit-and-loss account.*

Case III

An incorporated investment trust omitted from its statement of "income, expenses, and earned surplus" the expenses representing management fees paid to its sponsor corporation. The charge for this expense, which in some periods amounted to over 65% of the gross dividend and interest income of the trust, was made to paid-in surplus.

Following the Commission's objection to this practice, the income account was amended to reflect the management fee paid.

Case IV

An airplane company engaged in the development of a new type of airplane and other mechanical devices carried on its balance sheet as an asset experimental expenses incurred in the development of projects which had been abandoned prior to the balance-sheet date. In addition, the company included a substantial item of goodwill on its balance sheet, despite the fact that the company had never marketed its product.

The Commission suspended the effectiveness of the registration statement containing that balance sheet on the grounds that, among other things (1) "Sound accounting principles require that where the results of experimentation, such as has been carried on here, are unsuccessful, the respective development costs should be written off as a loss" and (2) that "In view of the fact that in this instance we are dealing with a new concern and a new contrivance, which had not been completed or proved to be a success or source of 'differential advantage,' goodwill based on actual profits cannot be contended to exist. Neither has any reasonable demonstration of future possible or prospective 'super-profits' been made. Mere speculation as to the existence of intangible values is not sufficient."

Case V

A utility holding company having assets aggregating approximately $900 million filed financial statements supplemented by numerous lengthy explanatory notes.

Upon examination of the financial statements, the Commission was of the opinion that the data as furnished was not understandable because of the numerous qualifications appearing in the notes. The Commission felt that many of the qualifications set forth in the notes, together with other adjustments recommended by the Commission's staff, should be reflected in some manner in the body of the financial statements. The objections raised by the Commission were removed by the registrant by filing financial statements in the following form:

	(1) Per company's books	(2) Footnote adjustments	(3) Amounts if adjusted as explained in footnotes
Items			

The adjustments included in column (2) resulted in reducing the assets on the balance sheet in column (3) to approximately $173 million less than they were shown to be in column (1). Corresponding reductions were made in the surplus accounts. In the profit-and-loss statements, column (3) showed a reduction in net profits from the amounts shown in column (1) by approximately $1.7 million, $1.4 million, and $300,000 for the years 1932, 1933, and 1934, respectively.

Case VI

This heavy manufacturing company created a reserve for plant retirements by charges to paid-in surplus and shortly thereafter, in 1931 and 1932, wrote off thereagainst properties retired in the amount of $1,744,213.61.

The facts in the case indicate that depreciation charges in previous years had been insufficient to provide for the normal retirement of the properties. The charge to the reserve created from paid-in surplus thus relieved the earned surplus of the charge.

The accountant had failed to express an opinion on this matter in his certificate. The Commission took the position that the auditor had not met the requirement that he express an opinion of the accounting practices and procedures followed by the registrant. The accountant thereupon inserted the following in his certificate:

> *We are of the opinion that it would have been preferable to have made such charges against earned surplus and in such event the earned surplus and paid-in surplus of the registrant, December 31, 1934, would have been $3,311,321.20 and $7,506,986.59, respectively.*

Case VII

A company charged paid-in surplus with $211,525.91, representing inadequate depreciation provision for periods prior to July 1, 1931.

Pursuant to a letter of deficiencies, the charge was transferred to earned surplus and the following note appeared in the certificate:

> *Attention is also directed to the analysis of paid-in surplus included under instruction 22 accompanying the balance sheet wherein it will be noted that a portion of depreciation provisions for the periods prior to July 1, 1931, amounting to $211,525.91, was charged to paid-in surplus as ordered by the board of directors. On March 5, 1935, the board of directors passed a resolution to transfer this charge to earned surplus, effective as of September 30, 1934, and effect has been given to such transfer in the exhibits referred to.*

Case VIII

A public utility company, prior to 1924, dealt with its unamortized debt discount and expense by making annual charges to income to provide for amortization over the duration of the issues. Also, prior to 1924, the physical properties, intangibles, and investments were written up approximately $15 million as a result of appraisal of the property of the utility and its subsidiary by an affiliated engineering corporation. Approximately $7 million was credited to a retirement reserve and $8 million was credited to capital surplus.

In 1924 and 1925 substantially all of the then-unamortized debt discount (about $8 million) was charged against the $8 million capital surplus thus created. The effect was to relieve the income account prior to August 31, 1934, of annual charges aggregating approximately $5 million. Had this method not been followed, the earned-surplus account as of August 31, 1934, instead of showing a credit balance of over $4 million, would have shown a deficit exceeding $1 million, and the capital-surplus, unamortized-debt-discount-and-expense, and the interim income accounts would have shown correspondingly different figures.

The auditors' certificate, as finally amended, included among others the following paragraphs:.

> *Substantially all ($8,402,791) of the then-unamortized debt discount and expense of the companies was charged off during 1924 and 1925 against the capital surplus arising from the appraisal. Premium and duplicate interest on refunded issues of the company were charged to unamortized debt discount and expense on refunding mortgage gold bonds, 4½% series due 1961, and are in process of amortization over the life of the refunding issue. Prior to the making of these charges to capital surplus the companies had followed the policy of making annual charges to income which, in general, were designed to provide for the amortization of debt discount and expense over the lives of the respective issues, but on the basis of carrying forward all unexpired discount, premium and expense applicable to refunded issues to be spread over the life of the refunding issue. Upon this basis, the charges against income for amortization of debt discount and expense would have been increased by approximately $337,000 for the year 1931, $314,000 for the year 1932, $315,000 for the year 1933 and $201,000 for the eight months ended August 31, 1934, the total additional charges against income for the period prior to August 31, 1934, would have aggregated approximately $5,426,000, approximately $2,977,000 of the $8,402,791 would have remained to be amortized over future years and the consolidated surplus accounts as of August 31, 1934, would have shown a debit balance of approximately $381,000 for earned surplus and a credit balance of $8,402,791 for the capital surplus arising from the revaluation of fixed assets and investments.*
>
> *Except for the matters discussed in the foregoing comments, in our opinion, the accompanying consolidated balance sheet and statement of consolidated income and earned-surplus accounts fairly present the financial position of the companies at August 31, 1934, and the results of their operations for the three years and eight months ended that date.*

The foregoing are only a few representative cases indicating the nature of the accounting problems of the Commission. A complete recital of those occurring on the registration of securities would cover most of the accounting problems in the handbook.

UNIFORM SYSTEM OF ACCOUNTS FOR PUBLIC-UTILITY HOLDING COMPANIES

Under the 1935 act, uniform systems of accounts are to be promulgated for the use of public-utility holding companies and their subsidiaries. The Commission has, to date, issued two such systems, one to be used by service companies (required to operate on a nonprofit basis) and the other to be used by public-utility holding companies deriving practically all of their income from interest and investments in other companies. Important accounting questions naturally had to be settled in the writing of these classifications. Some of them are, undoubtedly, of sufficient general interest to mention at this time, so I have selected a few for comment.

Investments acquired subsequent to the effective date of the systems are required to be entered at cost to the accounting company and to be retained in the accounts at cost until sold or otherwise disposed of or written down or off. No write-ups of investments are permitted.

If a company emerges from receivership, bankruptcy, or reorganization proceedings as the owner of investments of undetermined value, and at the time of recording such investments on its books does not have a satisfactory valuation of some portion of the items, it may enter such investments at figures representing a reasonable estimate of their value. Each item of investment is to be recorded separately, and if the amount so recorded, plus other assets acquired, exceeds the aggregate par value of its capital stock plus its debts, an amount equal to such excess is required to be set up as "reserve for adjustment of assets acquired in reorganization." That reserve is to be available only for the adjustment of the investment figures. When values have been determined and adjusted, any excess in the reserve may be disposed of as the Commission may approve or direct.

Three special classifications of surplus are provided, as follows: (1) paid-in surplus, (2) other capital surplus, (3) earned surplus. Paid-in surplus is to include amounts paid in for capital stock over the amount credited to the capital-stock account; surplus arising from donations of the company's stock by stockholders or from a reduction of the par or stated value of the company's stock; net gains from the acquisition or resale of the company's stock; and debt of the company forgiven by stockholders. It may be charged for losses arising from the reacquisition or resale of the company's own stock to the extent that such losses do not exceed the amount of accumulated net gains previously included in the paid-in surplus account arising from reacquisition or resale of the company's own stock. Any excess of such losses must be charged to earned surplus.

If any discounts, commissions, or expenses on the issuance of capital stock attributable to shares reacquired are still carried in the accounts at the date of reacquisition, they must be written off.

Bond discount and expense attributable to reacquired long-term debt is required to be written off when the bonds have been reacquired, irrespective of whether they may be subsequently resold.

A holding company is not permitted to take up on its books the undistributed earnings of subsidiaries except to the extent that such undistributed earnings have been declared as dividends and may properly be included as dividends receivable.

A stock dividend may not be included in the accounts of the receiving company at more than the amount charged by the paying company to its income or earned-surplus account or the market value of the stock received, whichever is less. A dividend in stock of a paying company may not be included in income if the dividend is paid from sources other than income or surplus of the paying company earned subsequent to the receiving company's acquisition of the stock with respect to which the dividend was paid.

CONCLUSION

There have been inquiries as to what the Commission expects in the various financial statements required to be filed with it. There have been some criticisms of the information required, as well as some protestations of inability to obtain the necessary information without undue hardship. These questions and protests have been surprisingly few in view of the large number of statements filed. I have the feeling that those registrants and accountants who have made up their minds that they will carry out the spirit of the act have not been seriously troubled by the requirements.

We are striving to obtain the greatest amount of information that will be of real assistance to the investors with a minimum of effort on the part of the registrant. There are certain specified rules that have been laid down in the preparation of the forms. Necessity dictates that such should be the case. However, when specific situations present problems that do not fit into the requirements, an approach to the problem with an honest desire to present full disclosure of the facts involved has usually made it possible for the registrant or the accountant to comply substantially with the rules and regulations.

The Securities and Exchange Commission is anxious to develop accounting practice and procedures on a high level, to bring the investor for whose protection it was created a more dependable body of information than he has ever had before. To do so will require the support of the accounting profession. The accountants and the Commission working at cross-purposes will accomplish little, and in my opinion the cause of accountancy will suffer. On the other hand, if the accountants and the Commission cooperate, they can do much toward correcting undesirable accounting practices.

FOUR

RELEASE NO. 4

April 25, 1938

Administrative policy on financial statements

This 1938 Accounting Series Release established the concept of substantial authoritative support as the basis for acceptable accounting principles to be used in preparing financial statements filed with the Securities and Exchange Commission.

The Securities and Exchange Commission today issued the following statement of its administrative policy with respect to financial statements:

"In cases where financial statements filed with this Commission pursuant to its rules and regulations under the Securities Act of 1933 or the Securities Exchange Act of 1934 are prepared in accordance with accounting principles for which there is no substantial authoritative support, such financial statements will be presumed to be misleading or inaccurate despite disclosures contained in the certificate of the accountant or in footnotes to the statements provided the matters involved are material. In cases where there is a difference of opinion between the Commission and the registrant as to the proper principles of accounting to be followed, disclosure will be accepted in lieu of correction of the financial statements themselves only if the points involved are such that there is substantial authoritative support for the practices followed by the registrant and the position of the Commission has not previously been expressed in rules, regulations, or other official releases of the Commission, including the published opinions of its chief accountant."

FIVE

Accounting, Reports to Stockholders, and the SEC

MAURICE C. KAPLAN AND DANIEL M. REAUGH

Former Staff Attorney, Securities and Exchange Commission

In 1939 the authors make two main points that reflect their time. First, that there is a serious gap in the regulations governing accounting reports to stockholders under the SEC and, second, that there are a number of limitations inherent in the accounting material made available to investors. They assert that unless these matters are resolved, the SEC will have to impose standards to protect the investing public. They foresee as one possible solution a type of "all-purpose" disclosure system.

This article is exploratory. Two jobs — both focused upon the adequacy and reliability of corporate accounting reports to stockholders — are attempted: first, to point out the serious gap in the regulation of accounting reports to stockholders under the Securities Exchange Act, especially as it is reflected in seventy selected corporate balance sheets and income statements for 1937; second, to discuss a number of the limitations inherent in the accounting material made available to investors: limitations which may indicate the deceptiveness of such current catchwords as "truth in securities" and "full disclosure." These objectives make it necessary to discuss the categories and classifications upon which the accountant rears an apparently precise and certain structure.

A vigorous legal literature in the past two or three decades has made lawyers aware of the very general nature of many legal categories or rules and their necessarily varying nature in changing environments. A similar development has not yet taken place in the field of accounting, at least not to the same extent. Many of the accountant's most important categories — "income," "cost," "fixed assets" — and the criteria used in allocating particular items into one category or another — "extraordinary," "maintain," "current" — are as broad and permit as much discretion as legal rules. But one can find only occasional appreciation of this fact in an accounting literature largely preoccupied with existing techniques and repolishing of definitions.

This article undertakes to break additional ground in the inevitably forthcoming critical analysis of accounting categories and accounting concepts.[1] Little excuse is needed for un-

Reprinted from *The Accounting Review*, September 1939, pp. 203–236, with permission of the American Accounting Association. Another version of the article appears in the *Yale Law Journal, Vol. 48, pp. 935–980, 1939. Reprinted by permission of the Yale Law Journal Co. and Fred B. Rothman and Co.*

dertaking this task. The Transamerica, Associated Gas and Electric, and Missouri Pacific Railroad delisting proceedings, and the McKesson-Robbins auditing investigation indicate that, to a considerable extent, the fight for protection of the interests of investors and public regulation of corporate enterprise has shifted to the accounting front.[2]

Despite the Securities Act and the Securities Exchange Act, corporate reports to stockholders remain unregulated to any effective degree.[3] The Securities Act does not embrace securities already issued, or subsequent dealings in securities issued in compliance with its provisions. The original scope of the act did not contemplate periodical supplemental reports after the securities were already in the hands of the public.[4] Obviously, information supplied in a prospectus for the new issues becomes misleading and unreliable in a relatively short time.

To remedy these apparent deficiencies, among others, the Securities Exchange Act of 1934 was enacted.[5] The objectives of the act, in this respect, as later expressed by the Commission, were:

> ... to make available to the average investor honest and reliable information sufficiently complete to acquaint him with the current business condition of the company, the securities of which he may desire to buy or sell.[6]

In Congress, the publicity features of the Exchange Act were particularly emphasized, and apparently the act was regarded as providing sanctions which would result in the disclosure of corporate information to investors, existing and prospective, in securities already in the hands of the public and thus beyond the reach of the Securities Act.[7]

Unfortunately, the Exchange Act does not require that corporations follow Commission standards in their annual reports to stockholders.[8] The act applies only to corporations with securities listed on national securities exchanges and requires such corporations to file with the Commission and with the exchange annual reports which comply with the standards imposed by the Commission and the exchange.[9]

Reports filed with the Commission, except where regarded as confidential, are available in Washington to the public either by personal examination[10] or by paying the cost of duplication.[11] Except for institutional or other substantial investors, who before the Exchange Act often managed to get the information anyway,[12] such cost is likely to be prohibitive, and the effort to obtain it is so great that only the most energetic investor will bestir himself. Under a rule of the Commission, the national securities exchanges are required to keep the registration statements and periodic reports of issuers open for public inspection.[13] This rule enables investors and investment analysts in cities where the exchanges are located to secure the information by examination. These are the only *official* sources and sanctions by which corporate information is made available to the investing public. In other nonofficial ways, perhaps a fairly large quantity of general information manages to trickle down into investors' hands. In instances where the Commission summarizes the reports in a press release, the financial sections of the daily or financial newspapers may publish the summary in a digested form.[14] More important, a large percentage of investors rely upon the advice of investment services which presumably scrutinize and evaluate these reports with care. And perhaps more important still, brokers and large-scale and institutional investors do obtain the information filed, and their judgment on the value of the security, presumably reflected in its market price, affords the ordinary investor some protection.

Thus reports to stockholders, unsupervised under the present rules of the Commission, remain the stockholders' most important source of corporate information.[15] A study of balance sheets and income statements appearing in the 1930 and 1937 published reports of 70 large corporations, herein presented, indicates that, despite a marked improvement since 1930, such reports fall considerably below the accounting standards which these same corporations are required to meet in their reports to the SEC and to the exchange on which their securities are registered.[16] The results of this study are presented against a background of critical comments on accepted accounting conventions.

INCOME STATEMENTS

The balance sheet is a highly technical document, as will be seen later, of relatively small value to those who buy or sell securities. It does not purport to give an investor *present values;* it merely reports that portion of historical and current disbursements which remain, after depreciation, obsolescence, depletion, and amortization have been charged periodically to the fiscal periods in which the capital assets are assumed to have been consumed. Accountants and investment analysts today are agreed that the income statement is much more significant and informative to the investor than the balance sheet.[17] It is of cardinal importance, because the "value" of a business depends not on the historical costs incurred in the process of building it up, but upon its earning capacity.[18]

In the not-so-distant past, many corporations omitted the income statement completely, but protests in accounting and economic literature and pressures from the New York Stock Exchange and the securities acts, have forced more and more corporations to disclose information on their current operations. Of the 70 corporations studied, three did not include any income statement in their annual reports to stockholders in 1937,[19] and the income statements of at least 17 of the corporations are considered by the writers to be totally inadequate.[20] In 1930, four corporations omitted income statements and the statements of at least 34 were inadequate. Although in both years there was a striking lack of uniformity as to form and content, 1937 showed some improvement in this respect.[21]

As with all generic words, the abstraction "income," which the accountant uses with an appearance of certitude, acquires meaning only in a particular setting and in connection with a particular purpose. "Income" for the economist, "income" under income tax laws, "income" in the determination of national income, "income" to determine the relative rights of remaindermen and life-tenants in property held in trust, and "income" to the accountant for a partnership and for a corporation all vary enormously; within each field the word acquires different shadings and permutations, with changing emphases.[22] The contrast between the economist's point of view and the accountant's is particularly significant, especially since, with important social consequences, the accountant's viewpoint has dominated industrial life.[23] The economist regards "income" as the distributive rent, wages, interest, and profits accruing to each of the four factors of production — land, labor, capital, and the entrepreneur.[24] The accountant focuses his attention on "profits" alone, as reflected in the costs and revenues of a particular business enterprise, from the viewpoint of its entrepreneur. Wages, rents, and interest flowing from a business enterprise are "income" to the economist, but the accountant considers them, when actually paid, as "costs of production" and "expenses." The "efficient business" constantly strives to keep these "expenses" down — "profit" is regarded as the sole desideratum of business enterprise. Cost and income recordation are, thus, designed in the interests of the businessman.[25]

The accountant's function in a business enterprise is the rather narrow one of reflecting the interest of the owners and management.[26] In preparing the income statement, the accountant devotes himself to determining the portion of historical and current disbursements and receipts which should be allocated to the current fiscal period, when "expenses" are "incurred," and when "revenue" is to be "recognized." Judgment and discretion play a tremendous role. No accounting omniscient can with assurance say what charges should have been made for depreciation, depletion, amortization, and obsolescence during a particular year, what amounts should be provided for doubtful accounts, whether a borderline charge or disbursement is to be handled as an expense of the current fiscal period, a charge to surplus, or whether it is assignable to future income and consequently handled as an asset or deferred expense account, and what extraordinary gains or losses should be credited or charged to income, to assets, or to surplus accounts. A large degree of discretion is present in the choice of the various available and sanctioned methods of computing depreciation[27] or stating inventories.[28] Income for the year will vary sharply with the method selected.

The extent of the judgment factor in accountancy is not widely appreciated by investors — statistics and figures inevitably lend an air of mathematical certainty. It is fundamental, in the understanding of income accounts and balance sheets as well, to appreciate that the figures appearing in the annual reports of corporations "are largely the reflection of individual judgments"[29] and the judgments of other men, equally honest and competent, surveying the same economic phenomena, would have differed — perhaps sharply.[30]

Divisions of the income statement. To present a reasonably informative picture of the activities, and sources of income and character of expenses of a corporation, total figures must be broken down into categories which describe broadly the business of the corporation for the year, and which furnish an investor some basis for analyzing the business and for intelligently forecasting future developments. According to the conventions of present-day practice, such a segregation is obtained best by the rather arbitrary division of the income statement into the classical operating, nonoperating, and nonrecurring subdivisions.[31]

Most accountants agree that the first major division of the income statement, the operating section, should disclose the net sales and revenues, and the expenses resulting from and attributable thereto. Within this section, it is necessary, from the investors' viewpoint, that the major sources of operating income and the applicable expenses be itemized. The Securities and Exchange Commission has divided the operating section, roughly speaking, into income from the sale of goods, and income from the sale of services; each must be disclosed separately where the lesser amount is 10% or more of the sum of the two items. No further subdivision of the "gross sales less discount" figure is required other than a separate listing, where practicable, of sales to parents and subsidiaries.[32]

While the segregation of "goods" and "services" is of some benefit, it places sole emphasis on the distinction between them and ignores other possible breakdowns of the gross figure which may be much more significant to the stockholder. Furthermore, relatively few nonutility, nonrailroad corporations receive as high as 10% of their total income from the sale of services. Investors are not so much interested in whether income comes from the sale of goods or from the sale of services, as they are in knowing from *what goods and what services* the income is derived. For instance, in the income statement of General Motors, it would be far more important for investors to know the percentage of the gross revenue derived from the sale of each line of cars, the percentage derived from the sale of Frigidaires, and from the corporation's other major activities than to know that a certain amount was derived from the sale of "goods" and the remainder from the operation of a railroad. In large corporations, with many diversified types of activity, the disclosure of net sales and operating revenues, cost of goods and services sold, and net operating income in total figures is not particularly enlightening to the investor. In fact, the larger the corporation and the more activities it engages in, the less significant gross figures will be to an investor or investment analyst for purposes of forecasting.[33] Segregation within these items is necessary for intelligent forecasting and evaluation.[34]

The second division, nonoperating income,[35] usually includes the amounts received from interest, dividends, commissions and fees, rents, royalties, etc., which, while normally recurring, do not arise from the corporation's operations. This disclosure is significant to the investor in that it apprises him more fully of the relative importance of the operating and financial income of the enterprise. Of course, the amount of detail will and should vary somewhat with the nature of the business.

The third major breakdown in the income statement is called by the accountant "nonrecurring" income.[36] The accountant uses this term to categorize business events which are not conceived to be part of the "normal" operations of the business, e.g., profits and losses from the sale of fixed assets or portfolio securities, abandonment of property, fire and flood losses, etc. Frequently, these items are attributed directly to some surplus account and hence never appear in the income statement at all. The concern here, however, is not with the problem of credits or debits to income versus credits or debits to surplus[37] but with methods of reflecting the item involved after the decision to allocate it to income has been made. The purpose of segregating "nonrecurring" income is to reveal to the investor specific income items which "normally" may not be expected to recur in each major accounting period. Clearly the inclusion of sizable, sporadic items with "regularly recurring" income would present a misleading picture of the return to be anticipated from the enterprise. Sale of assets, a major item in this category, occur constantly in large businesses, however, and it is somewhat misleading to label them without discrimination as "nonrecurring," thus asking the investor to discount their presence in the income statement. From the investor's viewpoint, the test should be whether submerging the transaction in some other item, "sales," or "other operating income," will distort his evaluation of the company's operations and future prospects of income.

Itemization within these major categories of income is an essential minimum of income disclosure. An investor is not interested merely in learning the total earnings for the current year which an indivisible total gives him; his primary interest in earnings is based, to a large extent, on the ability it gives him to forecast the future. Total figures must be broken down to enable him to obtain some information as to the sources of past income in order that his guess as to the future, precarious at best, is something more than a wild shot in the dark.[38]

This discussion has accepted the classical segregations of the income account, and has been concerned with a criticism of its internal constructions. The classical division is not, however, inevitable or exclusive. Income statements of the future may use other starting points or a number of alternative starting points varying with the purpose at hand to describe functionally the phenomena encountered by the business enterprise.[39] Much hard work and critical thinking remain to be done on these accounting classifications.

Gross revenue from sales and services. In modern accounting practice, the generally accepted view is that revenue is realized by a valid and enforceable sale.[40] The sale may be for cash, other valuable consideration, or for a legal claim, e.g., note or account receivable.[41] The sale is not only of great theoretical importance in the determination of when revenue is realized, but its aggregate total — net sales[42] and operating revenues — especially when segregated into major operating activities, is regarded by accountants as secondary only to net profits as the most significant figure in the income statement.[43] It aids in indicating whether a corporation is growing or declining, and it provides a measure for an analysis of the competence of the management. Many of the investment analysts' most important ratios depend upon its disclosure.[44]

Under the Securities Exchange Act, and the regulations thereto, corporations coming within the Act are required to list net sales in their registration statements and periodic reports to the Commission and exchanges, unless under Section 24(b) written objection to its disclosure is filed with the Commission. The Commission then "may . . . make available to the public the information . . . only when in its judgment a disclosure of such information is in the public interest."[45] A large number of companies objected to the disclosure of these figures, and, in the early years of the administration of the Act, the Commission was very liberal in granting such petitions.[46] The usual reason given for refusing to disclose sales and cost-of-sales figures was that it created consumer resistance where the gross-profit margin was wide and that its publication invited competition or gave an advantage to existing competitors, especially where the competitors' figures remained undisclosed.[47] Investigations later revealed that in most cases competitors and customers already had obtained the "confidential" information, and that disclosure had little effect upon buying policy.[48] As a result of this finding the Commission sharply reversed its policy and now denies most of the requests.[49]

Generally speaking, these figures now reach the Commission and the stock exchange on which the security is listed and they are available, theoretically, to the public. But as we have seen, this does not assure that the information is revealed in the annual reports to the stockholders.[50] In the absence of rules to the contrary[51] by the exchange on which the security is listed, the scope of disclosure in annual reports rests purely in the management's discretion. Of the 70 corporations included in this study (which probably are representative of the best accounting practices) 37 corporations or only 53% reported net sales to their stockholders in 1930, whereas 55 corporations or 79% reported the item in 1937. The 21% which did not report gross sales included such leading corporations as National Biscuit, Quaker Oats, J. I. Case, Allied Chemical and Dye Corp., and Union Carbide and Carbon Corp.[52]

Cost of goods sold. "Cost of goods sold,"[53] assuming traditional classifications, is an equally significant figure to investors when coupled with a disclosure of "net sales."[54] If sales and cost of sales of the past are revealed, the investor is furnished with some basis for predicting the relationship of future costs with future sales, and the resulting gross-profit margin.[55] If both sales and costs of sales are given, any knowledge the investor may have as to the future in-creases or decreases in wages or other components of cost of sales and their possible effect upon gross-profit margin will be useful. In addition, a knowledge of sales and cost of sales provides the investor with a basis for accounting for variations in gross or net profit from one period to another.[56] Yet despite its required itemization under Securities and Exchange Commission regulations, only 47 of the corporations studied listed the amount of the item "cost of goods sold" in their 1937 annual reports to stockholders. In 1930, the number was 33. Very few of these corporations allocated "cost of sales" to minor operations, a segrega-tion which, if the concept is to realize its maximum value, should be made where practicable.[57]

The mere notation of the figure "cost of goods sold" on an income statement is not of much aid to an investor. Aside from the variations which might be expected to appear due to differences in the nature of businesses or industries, accountants, unfortunately, are not in accord as to what elements of expense should be included in the item "cost of goods sold." Investors are not so much interested in the exact way in which this item is finally defined as they are in having a complete description of the contents of the figure together with such uni-formity and constancy in its application as may practically be obtained.

Accounting Terminology defines "cost of goods sold" as "the cost of those goods that have been sold and delivered during the period covered by the account. This consists . . . in the case of manufacturing concerns of the total production cost of the goods sold, including raw materials, labor and manufacturing expenses."[58] "Total production cost of goods sold" and "manufacturing expenses" are themselves broad categories permitting great latitude in the inclusion or exclusion of specific items. With these loose phrases as their standard of judgment, accountants are called upon to allocate the myriad transactions encountered by modern business. Most items fall into familiar patterns which history and the traditions of the business assign to a particular category with little question; but borderline items must constantly occur, and there the discretion of the management and the quality and integrity of its judgment play important roles. These factors are, undoubtedly, not constant from business to business or from year to year within a business.

"Cost of goods sold," as used in accounting, is a rather artificial concept excluding other costs — selling, general and administrative expenses, maintenance and repairs, depreciation, taxes, etc. — which, from an economic standpoint, are as primary as those costs which "con-tribute directly" to the physical fabrication of the goods or services. But the concept has some utility, and if it is to be of service to investors as a basis of analysis and comparison, there should be some understanding as to what it includes and some consistency in its appli-cation from period to period by each business within an industry. Little uniformity is present today. Some corporations exclude wages; others include selling and administrative expenses, depreciation, and even taxes in its determination.[59] Frequently, it impossible to determine what is included from the information given in the statements. The Securities and Exchange Commission, consistent with its approach to accounting problems generally, has proceeded very cautiously in obtaining adherence to an agreed definition, and merely requires an item-ization of the amount of "cost of goods sold as regularly computed under the system of ac-counts followed."[60] Consistent treatment as to the component items in this concept within an industry seems highly desirable.[61]

Selling, general, and administrative expenses. The considerations which suggest disclosure of "cost of goods sold" apply equally well to "selling, general, and administrative expenses." Disclosure of its total is valuable for the purposes of comparison with previous years, with similar expenses of competitors, and as a basis of estimating net profit figures of the future. Despite its importance, only 13 of the 70 corporations listed it in 1930 and but 24 in 1937, even though the SEC includes the item in its four principal forms.[62]

Selling expenses are usually defined to include all expenses in selling, salaries of salesmen, commissions, advertising, etc. Administrative expenses are those expenses incurred in conducting a business as distinct from the expense of manufacturing, selling, etc. It usually includes the salaries of officers, rents of the general offices, office and general expenses. General expenses are considered to be those expenses which do not fall under the category of manufacturing, selling, or administrative.[63] Again, each of these concepts is extremely broad and loose, and unquestionably many borderline expenditures make it difficult for the accountant to determine proper allocation.

Accountants, at least in their reports to stockholders, usually follow, as does this article, the division of total costs of operations into costs of sales, selling and distribution costs, and administrative and general costs. This classification puts into "cost of goods sold" only those costs which have an "observable effect" upon plant operations — labor, material, and manufacturing overhead costs. These costs are assigned by the cost accountant to the units sold. Other costs, selling, administrative and general expenses are often not allocated to the operations or units or period which they may affect, but are thrown into the income account of the period in which they are incurred.[64] Where these costs bulk large, the inconsistency in handling the two types of costs may make the income account of a particular period misleading not only to investors but to management. Underlying this practice is not only the practical difficulty of allocating selling and other costs to the period they affect, but an inarticulate premise that the "observable costs of production" are alone the "real" productive costs.[65] From an economic point of view, all of the costs supply utility and are productive.

In recent years, accountants, for purposes of securing more adequate internal control, have set up cost or expense classifications based upon more functional lines. Under these new classifications, the cost analysis may be in terms of operating or producing departments, by various revenue divisions, by territories, by types of commodities, etc.[66] The components of each classification change with the purpose and emphasis sought. While accountants have secured to management the benefits of these functional classifications, it has been assumed without question that the orthodox segregations are sufficient for investor purposes. Few, if any, studies have been made to see whether other classifications, along lines suggested by the work of the cost accountants, specifically directed toward the needs of investors, would serve those needs more adequately.

Maintenance and repairs. It is a generally accepted principle of accounting that expenditures made for maintenance and repairs should be treated as a current operating expense, whereas expenditures for additions or betterments should be capitalized. The problem of allocating a particular expenditure to one of these two categories — perhaps the most troublesome question with which accountants and auditors are confronted[67] — brings into high relief accountancy's fundamental problem: charges to capital versus charges to current operations.[68]

Certain cases are clear. A new system of elevators is installed whose useful life will extend considerably beyond the current year's operations. Theoretically, there is little question but that its cost should be treated as an addition to the building account to be written off through depreciation allowances during its estimated life. Minor, regularly occurring adjustments are made in the plant to keep it in good working order. Accountants agree that these should be charged to current operations. But the borderline cases, coming up in everyday operations, create more difficulty.[69] A part is replaced in an old machine; new tires are bought; a roof is reshingled with new composition material rather than slate, or spruce is used rather than cedar — the cost and the utility may be greater, may be approximately the same, or may be less than the original. Increased utility may correspond with increased cost. Again, it may not; increased utility may result even though the cost of the new material is less than the old. The benefits of the expenditure may be fleeting, or may be extended beyond the current accounting period. In the past, accountants have considered the problem soluble by the application of definitions. If the expenditure merely "replaced ... wear and tear on property," and was not "an improvement or addition";[70] if it merely "maintained" and did not "increase ... the efficiency of the property repaired," it was a "maintenance" or "repair"[71] and chargeable to profit and loss; otherwise the expenditure was a "betterment" or "addition" and chargeable to assets.[72] But these definitions were, like most definitions, tautological and merely spelled out the mental pictures invoked when the word itself was suggested. All the definition could do in an actual situation was to pose the problem and present it to the expert engineer or plant manager for his judgment: a judgment which might vary in individual experts, in different businesses, with different assets and for different purposes.[73] Usually these definitions were considered from the standpoint of broad classes of property or a whole enterprise, although in recent years better-managed businesses have introduced detailed plant accounting and have reduced the size of the asset unit.[74]

Few accountants seem to appreciate that the allocation of expenditures to capital or income on the basis of the prevailing metaphysical distinction between maintenance and repairs and additions and betterments violates cherished principles of accrual accounting and historical cost.[75] The fundamental basis of accrual accounting is that expenditures should be allocated to the period whose operations they can fairly be said to benefit. Thus, that portion of an expenditure which benefits current operations should be treated as an expense, and the portion which benefits future operations should be capitalized and then amortized during the applicable periods. If an item whose benefits extend for future periods is classified as maintenance or repairs and is thus charged wholly to current operations, the result is that expenses for the current period are overstated and the income of that period correspondingly understated. Conversely, if future periods are not benefited and the item is classified as an addition or betterment and capitalized, present income is overstated and future income understated.[76] The distinction between a capital expenditure and an income expenditure should not rest on whether the property is either "bettered" or "maintained" thereby, but rather upon the relation between the anticipated useful life of the asset required and the length of the accounting period for which the income is being determined.[77]

Historical cost accounting principles are violated also by the application of the generally accepted definition of maintenance and repairs. Parts of a machine wear out and new parts are purchased at prevailing prices, not necessarily comparable with the cost of the original parts. If such replacements are charged to current operations, the asset account continues to reflect the cost of the original asset, whereas in fact after a period of years the asset consists of numerous replacements purchased at entirely different prices. Finally, by virtue of this cumulative process, the books reflect not the cost of the assets now in use but assets long since consigned to the junk heap.

Such are the theoretical criticisms of the accepted definitions and distinctions between maintenance and additions as they are currently applied in practice. The writers do not overlook the practical difficulties which may in some situations confront the accountant in applying a strict accrual system. In some businesses, or for some types of assets, a strict accrual system may involve an unreasonable amount of record detail for which more accurate results are not sufficient compensation.[78] The prevailing question-begging definitions, however, under which specific expenditures are categorized, prevent the application of accrual accounting even where bookkeeping economy is not a factor.

What other interests does the investor have in this problem? Obviously, an investor has a primary interest in the managerial-engineering problem of maintaining and advancing the plant's physical equipment to keep it abreast or, if possible, ahead of the normal progress in the industry. In the long run, the particular account charged for expenditures for this purpose is of secondary consideration. No balance sheet or income statement, unless the recorded sums are clearly inadequate, can indicate definitely whether management is doing its job in making the necessary expenditures for maintenance and betterment. Only the results of future operations may throw some light upon it. But the income statement and balance sheet reflect the judgment of the management as to the allocation of these expenditures. Since it is so often a close question of fact, especially under the current practice, as to whether a particular expenditure should be charged to current revenue or not, management is in a position to allocate those expenditures to suit its particular purpose. If a favorable showing is desired, expenditures which normally would be charged to current operations could be charged to assets, with the result that both assets and current profits are inflated.[79]

Or if an unfavorable showing is desired, the reverse process is instituted. Often, distortions in allocation may come as a result of the desire of a plant manager to keep "costs" of operation down and thus increase the apparent profits by charges to asset accounts rather than to current operations.[80] The investor or stockholder is in no position to prevent this manipulation. His first line of defense is the independent auditor who, he hopes, is able to resist the strong forces arrayed against him, and who will refuse to approve unreasonable allocations. His second defense is a disclosure of the allocation of these expenditures during a particular year to the income and the asset accounts, supported, where practicable, by more detailed and illustrative schedules.[81] Comparison with previous years and with other companies in the same industry may bring to light practices sufficiently flagrant to put him on guard. Both itemization in the income account and the schedules of changes in assets and the accounts charged with maintenance and repairs are now required by the Commission. Important as this information is, very few corporations in their annual reports to stockholders, even in 1937, presented this figure in their profit-and-loss statements, and almost as few presented schedules of the changes in the asset accounts and the maintenance-and-repairs charges during the years examined. In 1930 only two, and in 1937 only four, corporations gave a maintenance-and-repairs figure in the income statement. Six companies presented schedules of changes in assets both in 1930 and 1937 and three companies tendered mainte-nance-and-repairs schedules in both years.

Depreciation. Until fairly recently, many corporations did not make any provision for de-preciation in computing income. In an investigation conducted in 1916, the Federal Trade Commission discovered that out of 60,000 apparently successful corporations doing at least $100,000 a year of business, fully one-half did not take depreciation into account at all.[82] In the years before the federal income tax laws made depreciation allowances profitable, it was not very difficult to disregard the *fact* of daily wear and tear on physical equipment in the urge to make favorable showings and pay dividends.[83] Depreciation—the loss of physical or functional value, due primarily to ordinary wear and tear and obsolescence[84]—is as much a cost of doing business as is the cost of coal consumed in running the plant; it differs from other costs only in that it does not represent an immediate, current outlay of cash.

The annual provisions for depreciation affect both the income statement and the bal-ance sheet. The debit entry represents an expense charge to income, increasing operating expenses and thereby diminishing income. The reciprocal credit entry to the depreciation reserve results in a reduction in the net book value of the asset on the the balance sheet unless the reserve is presented on the liability side. The latter practice is objectionable in that assets then will not reflect the estimated loss due to wear and tear; unsophisticated investors may be misled by the larger aggregate balance-sheet totals.

An investor has essentially two major interests in accounting for depreciation: Is the allowance for depreciation treated as an operating expense? Are the allowances reasonable and adequate?

No respectable accountant today, despite a curious confusion as to the nature of ac-counting for depreciation,[85] would deny that the annual allowances should be treated as an operating expense and disclosed separately on the income statement. The SEC, of course, in all of its forms requires its itemization.[86] Despite this unanimity of opinion, 22 corporations of the 70 studied in 1930 did not separately note their depreciation charges for the year; of the 22, ten mentioned that depreciation charges had been deducted but did not disclose the amount; in 1937, 66 companies mentioned and disclosed a depreciation charge; four cava-lierly continued to ignore it.[87]

Depreciation allowances have always been a fertile source of manipulation of income; they may be played with either to pack or minimize current profits.[88] Unless the manage-ment is like Caesar's wife, a careful investor must be prepared to compare the depreciation charges of his company over a period of years (assuming he can obtain the figures) in order to see if a consistent depreciation policy has been followed and if one year's charges are not meager or overgenerous in relation to other years.

A further comparison of the depreciation figures and methods of similar-sized compa-nies in the same industry is desirable.[89] Accounting authorities disagree sharply as to the preferable system or theory of accounting for depreciation—retirement or depreciation systems. Among companies following the retirement system, there are no accepted methods of determining the amount of the annual provisions for retirements.[90] Many companies arbitrarily allocate an amount which they deem sufficient to cover the currently expected retirements. Others appropriate a fixed percentage of the gross revenue or sales. Many varieties of allocation are also available under the depreciation system—the straight-line method, the reducing-balance method (used in England), the sinking-fund method, the annuity method, and the working-hour or production method. As the Report of the Committee of the American Institute of Accountants on Cooperation with Stock Exchanges pointed out, each of these methods is "supported by respectable argument and by usage, and the charges against a particular year may vary a hundred percent or more according as one or the other permissible method is employed."[91] The wide area of discretion presently available to management in the choice of methods of depreciation and the important consequences of that choice upon the net income figure for the year require, in the investor's protection, that the income statement should contain some explanation of the method used. Any change in method or significant changes in the technique of applying that method should be disclosed and the effect upon the year's income noted.[92]

Depreciation figures reported to stockholders frequently differ, as do other figures on the income statement, from the depreciation deductions allowed by the Bureau of Internal Revenue under the income tax laws. As a result, net income for income tax purposes differs from net income for corporate purposes. In any given case, however, the divergence may be perfectly justifiable from the investors' viewpoint as well as the management's.[93] It is not until the termination of a business that anyone can say with some certainty what depreciation charges should have been made during any particular year. Prior to that, the "proper" depreciation charge is a rather loose estimate, varying with the judgment of men, the past experience and traditions of the particular company and the industry, the method employed, and other innumerable variables. It is not at all surprising that a judgment reached for income tax purposes—a reconciliation of the conflicting interests of a taxpayer and his government—will differ from a judgment reached for the purposes of reporting to stockholders or for internal control. Nevertheless, since the depreciation estimate has a long history of abuse and since it is always a potential source of manipulation, investors should inquire more closely into the reasons for known differences.

Extraordinary gains and losses—Income versus surplus allocations. A corporation sells a building or securities in its investment portfolio and suffers a loss. Shall this loss, in either or both cases, be reflected in the income statement, be charged against earned, capital surplus, or an anachronistic unsegregated surplus account, or be set up as an asset to be amortized out of income of future years?[94] Would the same rule apply if a gain were realized? The corporation decides to write its plant down because depreciation and obsolescence charges in past years proved to be inadequate or because the corporation wants to reduce future depreciation charges in order to increase the net income of future accounting periods. Shall this charge be reflected in the income of the year in which the decision is made or shall it be attributed to some surplus account? Similarly, how shall the writing off of goodwill, adjustment of prior years' inventories or taxes, abandonment of property, losses from flood or fire, moving expenses, recovery of items previously written off, and all other "nonrecurring gains and losses" be handled? Is the same rule applicable to all of these items or to any one of them irrespective of its history and surrounding circumstances? The problem is far from academic, for the policy followed in allocating these "extraordinary" incidents of a business will affect the reported income very materially. If the United States Steel Corporation, for example, had followed an alternative advocated by the Tentative Statement of the American Accounting Association in handling these extraordinary items,[95] its income account for 1935 would have shown a net loss of almost $269,000,000 rather than the net income actually reported of $1,146,708.[96] This incident is, of course, spectacular, but variations from 30 to 50% in the total income reported if another policy had been adopted are not uncommon.[97]

The investor's needs in the handling of these gains and losses are twofold:

1. The itemization and segregation of these "nonrecurring incidents" from the results of "normal" current operations;

2. Greater agreement among accountants both in theory and in practice as to a workable general policy to be followed in allocating these items in order to minimize the possibilities of manipulation and to provide investors with a comparable basis for determining past results of the same company and other companies in the same or other industries.

Accountants are probably agreed that substantial "nonrecurring profits and losses," whether reflected in the income statement, or elsewhere, should be itemized and segregated from the "ordinary recurring income" of the period.[98] Obviously, if these items are included in income without a specific indication of their presence and amount, the investor is misled in his estimate of the probable future earning power. Accounting practice, however, has been far from meticulous in its observance of this principle of segregation.[99]

In the writers' study of 70 corporations, over twice as many itemizations of extraordinary credits or debits, whether to income or surplus, were found in 1937 as in 1930. While some of the increase may be attributable to a greater number of transactions affecting surplus in 1937, most of it seems due to a policy of nondisclosure in the 1930s. The extent of nondisclosure persisting today is very difficult to determine, since the item may be assimilated into another disclosed item or may be debited or credited without notation to some reserve account. Undoubtedly, credits are more likely to be revealed than debits. It seems clear that accounting morality requires both full disclosure and segregation in all instances of substantial nonrecurring gains or losses.[100]

There are few accounting problems on which both theory and practice are in such confusion as in the allocation of "nonrecurring" incidents of a business. The problem raises a fundamental query as to the nature and function of an income account. One school of accounting, including most practitioners (to judge by their published reports) and many writers[101] have a mental picture of "normal" or "recurring" operations of a business, producing financial transactions "applicable to the period under review"—which are to be reported in the income statement while nonrecurring transactions are not. The business activities and their resulting financial items which do not fall within this picture of the "normal" operations of the business are categorized as "extraordinary," "nonrecurring," "not applicable to the period under review" and are dumped into some surplus account, preferably earned surplus. Vitality is supplied to this symbolism by the opposition to the capital-gains tax.[102]

Unfortunately, the lines between "normal" and "abnormal" business are in practice very difficult to draw,[103] and, once drawn, may lead to serious distortions in the presentation of income. There is the tendency of management, except for income tax purposes, to classify all doubtful gains as income and to charge all doubtful losses to surplus. Depreciation may be kept at undersized figures in order to increase the reported net income—the eventual loss being charged to surplus, not to income. Where an item is debited or credited to surplus directly, it never is reflected in income reported, and the income statement becomes only a partial view of the total gains and losses encountered by the business.

More important perhaps than any of these reasons, the dichotomy of "recurring" and "nonrecurring" items results in a diversity of accounting practices which makes comparison between corporations difficult and permits an easy manipulation of these items to either income or surplus as management may desire. As a reaction to the uncertainty and abuses of the "recurring" school, the Tentative Statement of Accounting Principles of the American Accounting Association, proposes a drastic solution. Postulate 8 states:

> *The income statement for any given period should reflect all revenues properly given accounting recognition and all costs written off during the period, regardless of whether or not they are the results of operations in that period: to the end that for any period of years in the history of the enterprise the assembled income statements will express completely all gains and losses.*[104]

The postulate contemplates an important change in the scope of the income statement; under the "recurring" view, reported income reflects only a portion of the total of the company's business activities of the year. The Tentative Statement proposes that income should include *all* changes in proprietorship from any causes during the period under review as well as any adjustments made to allow for profits and losses "which are not strictly applicable to the current period but which have been recognized in the accounts during that period."[105] In unusual situations, where the "material losses or gains recognized during the current period actually apply to earlier periods," the comment to Postulate 8 suggests either of two alternatives:

> ...*show the extraordinary charges or credits in the current income statement or ...restate the income statement of the proper number of past periods. Should the latter alternative be adopted, the revised statements of past periods should accompany the statement for the current period. It seems obvious that in any series of statements of corporate results adjustments of previously stated profits should not be excluded—adjustments which have been known to outweigh the total stated gain or loss for a considerable period of years.*[106]

Postulate 8 and its accompanying comments suggest many advantages. It makes the income statement present a total view of business activities; it is a simple rule, relatively easy to apply; it provides a more uniform basis for comparison between corporations (under Postulate 11, these "nonrecurring" items are to be segregated from the operations section in the income statement); it shuts off an important source of manipulation and abuse. On the other hand, the postulate may be too rigid and too simple a solution for a highly complex problem. It may well be that it does not serve the interests of all concerned—the corporation, stockholders, creditors, and the public—to have all of the transactions of the year reflected in the income statement. Some substantial adjustments and capital gains and losses have little relation to current operations and their inclusion in the income statement, even when segregated, may be misleading.[107] As Professor Hosmer has pointed out, application of the postulate to the United States Steel Company's $270,000,000 plant write-down charge to earned surplus in 1935 may have had disastrous consequences for the corporation and its stockholders.[108]

Hosmer has suggested that Postulate 8 should be accepted as a presumptive rule only; that presumptively all extraordinary gains and losses should be reflected in the income statement of the period in which they are recognized, unless the interests of the corporation, stockholders, creditors, or the public are affected adversely by such an allocation.[109] This formula, however, may be loose enough to enable management to rationalize under it many objectionable present practices.[110]

The Securities and Exchange Commission under the Exchange Act has, until recently, permitted management a wide range of discretion in the allocation of "extraordinary" items. The instructions to the forms merely require disclosure and segregation of the "nonrecurring" items reflected in the income statement,[111] and a complete itemization of all additions and deductions to surplus in an attached surplus schedule.[112] These additions and deductions from surplus must "be so designated as to indicate clearly whether they are of the nature of capital or earned surplus items."[113] Nothing is said as to what items may or may not be charged to income, earned surplus, capital surplus, or reserve accounts.[114]

In the administration of the Securities Act, the Commission has had sharp internal disagreements over the charging of certain items to capital surplus rather than to current operations or earned surplus. In the *Northern States Power Company* and *Chesapeake Corporation* cases,[115] the registrants had written up their assets, creating large capital surplus accounts. Against this account, both companies wrote off millions in unamortized debt discount and expense instead of amortizing by charges to profit and loss. In a third case, the Thermoid Company, among other doubtful accounting practices, charged off debt discount against an existing capital surplus account.[116] In another case, the Monongahela West Penn Public Service Company made a running "horseback appraisal" of its properties, crediting the writeup to an appraisal surplus and, in the following five years, charged abandonments of traction properties to this surplus. In all of these cases, the Commissioners unanimously disapproved the accounting, but the majority were content to force an amendment to the accountant's certificate stating the alternative treatment of charging to profit and loss and what the effect of such a procedure would have been. A minority of the Commissioners took the view that reservations in footnotes or an accountant's certificate were not enough, and that the company's earnings records and earned surpluses as stated in their registration statements were untrue and amounted to misrepresentations.[117]

In at least two subsequent instances, the Commission indicated a tendency to depart from the majority policy. In one case, a reproduction appraisal credited the resulting increase in "value" to capital surplus, and the company announced its intention of charging certain items such as organization expenses to this surplus. The Commission threatened stop-order proceedings, and the company erased the entries and recorded its property at cost.[118] In another case, the registrant wrote down the net cost value of plant and equipment to a valuation established by the officers and charged the write-down against capital surplus rather than earned surplus. This capital surplus was created specifically for this purpose by a reduction of stated capital pursuant to resolutions adopted by the directors and stockholders. The opinion of Carman Blough, then Chief Accountant of the Commission, issued as Accounting Release No. 1, pointed out that the write-down of assets was a recognition of inadequate depreciation charges against the income of prior years, and then stated:

> *It is my conviction that capital surplus should under no circumstances be used to write off losses which, if currently recognized, would have been chargeable against income. In case a deficit is thereby created, I see no objection to writing off such a deficit against capital surplus, provided appropriate stockholder approval has been obtained. In this event, subsequent statements of earned surplus should designate the point of time from which the new surplus dates.*
>
> *Accordingly, in my opinion, the charge here in question should have been made against earned surplus. In view of the stockholder action that has been taken, I see no objection to the deficit in earned surplus resulting from this write-off being eliminated by a charge to capital surplus created by the restatement of capital stock.[119]*

Following changes in the personnel of the Commission,[120] a firmer stand, approaching the minority view, was taken. The new administrative policy was announced in Accounting Release No. 4:

> *In cases where financial statements filed with this Commission pursuant to its rules and regulations under the Securities Act of 1933 or the Securities Exchange Act of 1934 are prepared in accordance with accounting principles for which there is no substantial authoritative support, such financial statements will be presumed to be misleading or inaccurate despite disclosures contained in the certificate of the accountant or in footnotes to the statements provided the matters involved are material. In cases where there is a difference of opinion between the Commission and the registrant as to the proper principles of accounting to be followed, disclosure will be accepted in lieu of correction of the financial statements themselves only if the points involved are such that there is substantial authoritative support for the practices followed by the registrant and the position of the Commission has not previously been expressed in rules, regulations, or other official releases of the Commission, including the published opinions of its chief accountant.[121]*

It marks a major step forward to require that the laggards of the profession live up to the level of accounting practice for which there is "substantial authoritative support." The release, however, contains many problems of interpretation. What constitutes "substantial authoritative support"? Is the approval of a respectable minority of accountants sufficient? What will the Commission do if there is no generally recognized practice or literature in regard to the handling of a particular transaction? Is the release applicable to "closed" transactions of past years—in other words, would the result of the *Northern States Power Company* case have been changed if this release had been in existence? If so, a large percentage of balance sheets now filed with the Commission will require substantial restatement in the light of an audit going far back into the company's history. Furthermore, many a corporate dividend, authorized in reliance on the accountant's certificate, will, by the changed entries, now appear improper; directors conceivably may thus be subjected to criminal penalties and both stockholders and directors to restitution. These practical considerations suggest that it may be inadvisable to interpret Release No. 4 retroactively. On the other hand, other techniques, despite comparable inconveniences, constantly revise old practices in the light of current knowledge. Unless the costs of restatement are prohibitive, accountancy and business should not insist upon the preservation in today's accounting statements of the errors of the past.

Segregation of the sources of surplus. To the accountant, surplus is merely the balancing figure remaining after deducting the sum of the par or stated value of capital stock and all liabilities from the total of all assets. Surplus plus the amount of the capital stock represents the stockholders' equity in the assets of the corporation. The surplus reported may be only a book arithmetical surplus not realizable in the marketplace; it usually is no more than that where a substantial percentage of the total assets are fixed and are entered on the balance sheet at historical cost figures or at conjectural and usually sanguine appraisal figures.

Surplus arises from highly diverse sources. Earned surplus, paid-in surplus arising from the sale of stock at a premium, revaluation surplus, donated surplus, surplus from the sale of treasury stock, surplus from the reduction of stated capital are among the subdivisions of generic surplus. Their categorizations reflect their origin.

Genealogy is of great significance to surplus. Earned surplus holds an honored position because of its relation to earnings and to dividends. Some of the other surpluses are offspring of illicit affairs (revaluation surplus); others of less dubious ancestry are not welcomed in the best corporate circles (surplus from restatements of capital); still others have such ambiguous origins that they dare not, and frequently cannot, be revealed (unsegregated general surplus account). And commonly, all surpluses, other than earned, veil their past in the protective anonymity of the label "capital surplus."

Because of its relation to earnings and dividends, earned surplus should be segregated and disclosed separately from all other surplus accounts. The Securities Act itself in Schedule A provides specifically for disclosure of the "surplus of the issuer showing how and from what sources such surplus was created."[122] The Exchange Act is not explicit on this point, but the Instruction Book for Form 10-K provides for the division of this item into (a) paid-in surplus and/or (b) other capital surplus; and (c) earned surplus.[123]

In practice, however, these divisions for past accounting periods are often impossible to ascertain. The surplus account may never have been segregated in the past, and no one can tell in what proportion dividends are to be taken to have been charged against its earned and nonearned components. Further, no one can tell how other past charges or credits, e.g., capital gains and losses, should be apportioned now in the general surplus account. And accounting theory, much less accounting practice, is not crystallized sufficiently to enable one to say with certainty whether certain doubtful items are to be charged against earned rather than capital surplus, or the converse.[124]

These inherent and historical difficulties have prevented the Commission from insisting upon its divisions of surplus in all cases. Surplus must be segregated, but

> ... *if in the accounts, separate balances for these are not shown at the beginning of the fiscal year, i.e., if the company has not, up to the opening of the fiscal*

year, differentiated in its accounting for surplus as above indicated in (a) and/or (b) and (c), then the surplus may be stated in one amount.[125]

In the future, however, segregation of capital and earned surplus will be required.[126]

There has been a marked improvement in the disclosure of sources of surplus from 1930 to 1937 in the 70 corporations studied. In 1930, 44 corporations of the 70 had a single general surplus figure and no other; in 1937 the number had dwindled to eight. In 1930, 26 corporations indicated an earned surplus figure. Many of these divisions are, presumably, arbitrary segregations of an old general surplus account.[127]

BALANCE-SHEET ASSET FIGURES

Fixed assets. The properties and resources of a business—the accountant's assets—are divided broadly by the accountant for reporting purposes into two major groups—fixed and current assets. Fixed assets include those assets which are held more or less permanently, are not for sale, and, excepting investments, ordinarily are consumed in the production of goods and services; their cost recovery is achieved only in the gross revenue received from the sale of such goods and services. Current assets, on the other hand, are assets which will be converted into cash or notes and accounts receivable in the forthcoming accounting period. Numerous other classifications of the resources of a business are possible, of course, but from the viewpoint of recording cost and income, and the presentation of the liquidity of the business, the almost universally employed categories of fixed and current assets are presently regarded as the most useful. As one might expect, however, there is no clean-cut distinction between them, and accountants are troubled frequently by borderline items. A variety of rules of thumb exist which are employed in distinguishing the two classes.[128]

Within the category of fixed assets, accountants crowd into a few simple subcategories—land, buildings, equipment, and one or two other groupings[129]—all of the phenomena of the physical and man-made world which pass in the marketplace. This compression of a world into three or four neat pictures is accompanied by an intellectual exploit through which the physical world is transmuted into dollar values; Michigan soil and Texas mules, by the use of a quantitative unit, are made comparable and sometimes identical. All of this is presented in precise, unequivocal terms.[130]

Since dollar symbols do not attach inherently to physical objects, some rational principle must be employed as the basis of making the transmutation.[131] "Cost," "reproduction cost," and "sound value" or similar phrases attempting to express "current value"[132] have been most widely used in accounting history. With few exceptions,[133] accountants deny that accounting should purport to set forth current values for fixed assets,[134] since it is almost impossible to attribute verifiable market or realizable values to specialized plant equipment permanently committed to a business. "Reproduction cost," at best a factor of remote interest to investors, leads to a periodic revaluation of the assets with its attendant expenses and involves accountants or appraisers in a highly speculative game of estimating what it would cost to reproduce a specific piece of property which no one is actually thinking of duplicating. The accountant finds it safest, therefore, to resort to historical cost figures, and accountancy becomes "not essentially a process of valuation, but the allocation of historical cost and revenues to the current and succeeding fiscal periods."[135] As such, the dollar values attributed to fixed assets on the balance sheet must be viewed not as an available source of funds for the business or an indication of what the corporation is "worth" as of the date of the accounting statement, but as charges to future operations whose predominating function is to insure cost recovery and a proper computation of income. Few investors appreciate that the asset figures must be interpreted so narrowly.[136]

Thus the balance sheet, especially where fixed assets bulk large, is primarily a historical document reflecting original costs (or costs less depreciation). Such costs, at best, represent the "fair value" of the assets as of the date of *acquisition*. Frequently, however, they include sums "imprudently invested" in the business as a result of engineering mistakes, insiders' profits, and other elements. Original cost, while more objectively verifiable than the estimates of the appraiser, frequently is an elusive concept also, the contents of which vary according to purpose and definition. It may refer to the cost of construction to the builder or to the cost of acquisition to the owner to whose order it was made or to the cost of acquisition incurred by the present owner.[137] Thus any specific piece of property may have a number of "costs."[138] In accountancy, "original cost," or "historical cost," usually refers to the cost to the present owner, except in the public utility field where two sets of cost figures are required by state and federal commissions—"cost of . . . property to the person first devoting it to public service" and cost to the present owner.[139] Cost to the present owner rather than being a precise, ascertainable fact to be stated dogmatically on the balance sheet is often no more than an estimate. Where corporate stock is given in exchange for property, resort must be had to the "value" of the property or the stock to determine "original cost,"[140] and "value," as Bonbright has shown,[141] is not a very clear concept. And where two properties are purchased jointly in a lump sum payment or where plant assets are constructed by the company itself, the difficulties of segregating the joint costs or allocating overhead requires resort to the techniques of appraisers or cost accountants; their resultant figures—a "fair allocation"—may be little more than shrewd guesses. Cost figures, furthermore, are usually stated minus accrued depreciation allowances, which means, of course, that the depreciated cost figures are subject to all of the judgment factors that enter into the estimate of the depreciation allowance. Struggles of public utility commissions with operating utilities and of the Interstate Commerce Commission with railroads in the determination of "original costs" indicate that more is involved here than specious fault finding. Investors cannot regard cost figures as mathematically precise quantities which do not include a complex of speculation and discretionary elements virtually inherent in the cost-recording process.

Current assets. Not all the assets of the corporation, however, are presented on the balance sheet at their historical cost. Under prevalent accounting practice, valuation enters in the representation of current assets. These assets consist of cash, realizable securities, and inventories intended to be converted into cash in the course of the year (items, unlike fixed assets, of estimable market value). The market value of these assets is of importance to creditors of the company, and, in view of their interests and the accountant's tradition of conservatism, no more than this value is frequently shown on the balance sheet. This is the well-known rule of "cost or market, whichever is lower." A balance sheet therefore presents, at the very least, two "values." Apples and horses are added together, *mirabile dictu,* but the result is neither four apples nor four horses but a very strange medley of the two. An identical pecuniary symbol attributed to each obscures the working of this magic. And no balance sheet exhibits as few as two different bases of values. Frequently, distinct categories of items in inventory will be represented at different bases on the same balance sheet.[142] Investment securities, securities of affiliates, marketable securities may not be valued by the same criterion.[143] As we have seen, "cost" itself is far from being a readily determinable unitary concept. On a single balance sheet, reflecting a long corporate history, "cost" may be used in a number of different senses. This may be and frequently is true in a single balance sheet of all the other bases used in determining the value of assets.[144] In view of these circumstances, inherent in an all-purpose balance sheet called upon to serve the divergent functions of internal control, interests of creditors, taxation, and reports to stockholders, investors must regard the "total assets" figures of a corporation with substantial skepticism.

Current assets, representing the working capital of the business, are the most significant items on the balance sheet to management, investors, and creditors. The questions arising from their disclosure, from the investors' viewpoint particularly, are: what items are to be included in this category (basis of classification), what basis of "value" should be used in computing each category of items, and the extent of the disclosure necessary to serve the investors' needs.[145]

Accounting literature indicates that many companies exclude all items from current assets which are not readily convertible during the course of a year. But this rule is by no means followed universally.[146] An investor is interested in knowing the company's particular scheme of classification (it may have one which is no more than a very rough working rule) in order to evaluate its current credit position in the light of the highly significant ratio of current assets to current liabilities, and other ratios,[147] and the current credit position of competitors. Disclosure is also of value in inducing the corporation to use the same basis for current liabilities as for current assets — a necessary step in the analysis of the current credit position. Under both securities acts, the Commission regulations provide that "items classed as current assets should be generally realized within one year," but "generally recognized trade practices with respect to individual items, such as installment receivables or inventories long in process are admissible, provided such trade practices are stated."[148] The word "generally," while probably a necessary grant of discretion, may permit items to enter which would distort an investor's estimates. But while the Securities and Exchange Commission may consider basis of classification of current assets a significant item of disclosure, not a single corporation of the 70 studied, in either 1930 or 1937, revealed its basis of classification for either current assets or current liabilities.

Marketable securities. When this item is included in current assets, it should represent only securities having a ready market, which can be liquidated without a material impairment of their values.[149] Since this item figures so largely in the analysis of current assets, it is desirable that the basis of determining the balance-sheet amount be shown. The Securities and Exchange Commission requires that if the amount is not shown on the basis of current market, such aggregate amount should be stated parenthetically.[150] Of the 70 corporations studied, only 23 indicated the basis in 1930; by 1937, the number had jumped to 48. Great diversity exists in the basis employed.[151]

Notes and accounts receivable. Since notes and accounts receivable appear as a current asset on the balance sheet, they should consist of items which, normally, will be liquidated in the regular course of business during the succeeding fiscal year. Receivables from officers, employees, and parent and subsidiary companies, if included, should be listed separately. Such receivables have a long record of abuses in corporate history and experience has shown that they often remain on the books for years. Inclusion of these items in current assets may thus result in an overstatement of the current position. Where significant differences in the light of trade practices exist, notes and accounts receivable should be listed separately. The Securities and Exchange Commission permits the consolidation of the two items under the Exchange Act, but requires detailed segregation under the Securities Act.[152]

Adequate reserves should be set up, as a deduction from listed assets, "to cover any difference between the book amount and reasonably probable realization."[153] The judgment of management and its accountants in the light of current conditions and the company's past experience will determine the margin.[154] Normally, unless warranted by increasing volume of sales on credit, or greater anticipated losses, the reserve, unlike the depreciation reserve, should not increase from period to period, since it is considered applicable to existing and presumably collectible receivables only. Such an increase may indicate that a "secret" reserve is being created. Unless a company has a background of dissimilar results in the collection of notes as distinguished from accounts receivable, there is little point in setting up a separate reserve for each. Few accountants would disagree, in principle, with these working rules.

Of the 70 corporations studied, 34, in 1930, presented a single figure for both notes and accounts receivable, and 24 of the 70 did not provide a reserve. In 1937, 23 corporations presented a single figure for both accounts and 19, despite the standard of accounting practice prescribed by the SEC, did not disclose a reserve.[155]

Inventories. In view of its importance in the analysis of the current credit position of the company and in the determination of income, full disclosure of information as to inventories is of material benefit to the investor-analyst. In addition to the desirability of segregation of major classes of inventories which is required by the Securities and Exchange Commission,[156] the investor is primarily interested in the bases used in the determination of the valuation of inventory. There are numerous possibilities: cost, replacement cost (market), cost or market whichever is lower, base stock, selling price, retail method, and others. The same corporation may, and frequently does, employ a different basis for distinct items in the inventory.[157] And the same basis because of the nature of the materials with which it is concerned, means something entirely different with varying items in the inventory.[158]

The particular inventory method chosen has an important effect in the determination of income. "Cost or market, whichever is lower," perhaps the most widely used method,[159] seems to have been adopted in this country on the advent of the Federal Income Tax law, largely as an immediate method of reducing taxable income.[160] But the accountants who adopted it for this purpose were short-sighted. While the method results in an understatement of income in the first period, it causes an overstatement in the very next.[161] Either may have serious consequences for an investor.

Andrew Barr has shown that under the first-in, first-out method of determining cost advocated by Paton, higher profits are noted in the income statement with rising price levels and lower profits with falling prices.[162] These gains and losses are "realized" gains and losses only if the fiction of first-in, first-out is not questioned. The replacement cost method (market), however, in its own way, clearly results in the inclusion of unrealized profits in the case of rising prices and losses not incurred in the case of falling prices. A growing school of accountants and economists are now advocating adoption of such methods as the base-stock method, the last-in, first-out, and the inventory reserve method as more satisfactory means of eliminating fictitious gains and losses.[163]

In view of the important differences in the statement of income resulting from the adoption of one method rather than the other, an investor cannot "give the same weight to profits of companies in the same business without knowing whether the profits to which their calculations are applied have been computed on the same basis or how great the effect of a difference in method might be."[164] Few investors, and not all accountants, seem to realize this fact. And even when the same basis is employed in estimating distinct items in the inventory of the same company or where the same basis is employed by two different concerns, results may be far from uniform.

A "cost" of an individual item in the inventory seems a simple matter to determine. But so simple a word turns out to be the most generic of concepts, and its estimation creates endless difficulties for the accountant. Investigators for the Bureau of Internal Revenue in 1919 discovered, for example, that it meant very little to note that a particular company was on a "cost" basis; the nature of the basis could only be brought out by a careful study of the theories and procedures adopted by the management in working up its estimate.[165] First is the question of how cost is to be defined. It usually includes invoice price, transportation charges, handling prices, and insurance. Sometimes buying expenses and unpacking costs are added. There is also the very difficult task of allocating costs to specific items in instances of joint products and by-products. The highest arts of the cost accountant may produce no more than an arbitrary division. The second major question which arises is what method is to be used in determining invoice costs. Many methods, each producing different results, compete for attention: first-in, first-out; last-in, last-out; average cost; weighted average cost; base stock method; actual cost of specific lots on hand; and others. Mere enumeration of these competing methods indicates some of the difficulties inherent in cost determination. Almost equal difficulties exist in the determination of the other available bases of inventories.[166]

The SEC, thus far, has adopted no rules on inventory valuation other than to require a statement of the method of valuation adopted by the company.[167] William Werntz, Chief Accountant of the SEC, reports that practically all of the generally recognized methods of inventory valuation have been used by one company or another in the statements filed, and that the Commission seldom has found occasion to object to the use of any particular system.[168] Werntz, however, has expressed serious doubts as to whether the mere designation of the system followed—"cost or market," for example—constitutes sufficient disclosure.[169] The apparent solution is to call for more detail, but the problem is not so easily disposed of. As Werntz reports:

> When a requirement was proposed calling for a clear indication of what was meant by cost or market, numerous commentators made the point that if the operations of a company were at all complex, several pages of explanation would be required by reason of the use of diverse methods. Others indicated that not

much less than a text on cost accounting would suffice to illumine "standard" costs.[170]

What does all this mean to the investor? First of all, he must learn to be extremely cautious and skeptical in his use of inventory figures both for credit ratios and for comparative purposes with corporations in the same industry. Second, he must not place too much faith in the disclosure of the basis of valuation since the nature of any one of the bases varies so greatly, depending upon the method and procedure employed and the item with which it is concerned. Inventory figures, as so many other figures in accounting, must be taken as broad, loose estimates, as (if the procedures and theories were acceptable) one of a number of alternative pecuniary valuations attributable to the unit of goods in the inventory. Accounting technique in its present stage of development cannot do more than this.

Disclosure of an accepted basis, however, assuming that the basis has been followed honestly and with an effort at consistency from year to year, does give an investor an opportunity to make his rough calculations; looseness of concept does not imply that concepts are not valuable. While 1937 shows some improvement over 1930 in disclosure of the basis of inventory figures, the record is not altogether clean.[171]

THE NEED FOR "SINGLE-PURPOSE" STATEMENTS

Reports to stockholders, whether judged by the standards set by the SEC or by one's own lights, seem very inadequate. On vital counts, investors are left conjecturing — sales, cost of sales, depreciation, inventories, and surplus generally are so inadequately described that an investor does not have a minimum of information upon which to form an intelligent opinion on buying or selling.[172] The 70 corporations included in this study represent the best in American reporting practice, yet their accounting to stockholders falls far short of the minimum requirements which these very corporations must meet in their reports to the SEC. Unless accounting morality with respect to annual reports to stockholders improves substantially within the next few years, imposition of standards of conduct by the SEC seems necessary in the interest of the shareholding public.

Accounting conventions and rules of thumb attempt to bring "a sprawling domain of unsubdued facts"[173] and an almost infinite number of individual transactions into clean-cut, neat categories, each denominated with some pecuniary value. Classification of these myriad and individualized events into categories and subcategories — the components of which bear to the observer some similarity to each other — is, of course, essential if the phenomena of modern business are to be controlled. The types of classifications and categories developed in any discipline — and accounting is not an exception — are the products of a long evolution; the reasons for their origin, usually unknown to us now, may have been to serve some temporary convenience or more persistent business need. Their survival today in accounting practice is not conclusive of their survival value for all accounting purposes.

Most of the classifications in accounting are broad and generic — very loose, abstract words and phrases into which we attempt to pack the divergent transactions of business life. Like most abstractions, they have no "real meaning" apart from concrete situations and specific purposes for which the abstraction is being employed. No single definition of "value," for example, however convenient and simplifying it might be, can describe the word's changing meanings with changing purposes. "Value" for rate-making purposes is a term meaningless to anyone unfamiliar with the struggles in American public utility law.[174] The accountant's "valuation" of inventories at "cost or market, whichever is lower," makes sense only in the light of its use by "conservative" accounting practice to report the accountant's "realized income." Another set of "values" used by the accountant, "historical costs," is meaningful only in the light of the accountant's conception of his function as a reporter of "the allocation of historical costs and revenues to the current and succeeding fiscal periods."[175]

A fuller realization by accounting practitioners and teachers of the generic nature and purposive character of accounting categories should lead to a paring off of the broader concepts, the elimination of those which are meaningless or which no longer serve specific needs adequately, an application of existing concepts and the formulation of new ones in terms of specific situations and specific functions, and to a healthy skepticism to counteract the appearance of certitude induced by mathematical symbols. More concretely, it should lead to a realization that accounting rules designed to serve the interests of management in private business may reflect, inadequately and unfairly, the interests of employees, consumers, and the public in the enterprise, and that such rules may be rather irrelevant as applied to the fiscal activities of a government.[176] It should lead, further, within the precinct of accounting for management, to a far greater development in the preparation of accounts for specific purposes—to "single-purpose" statements, varying according to the purpose for which they are prepared. A statement which attempts to account for the money presently invested in the business and to record costs during each income period—the historical balance sheet—cannot serve the purpose of determining the "present financial worth" of a business; and rules designed to insure adequate tax returns or rate control or internal control for management or to reflect liquidity for creditors—all intermingled in the present "all-purpose" balance sheet—hardly suffice to guide an investor in his trading of securities.[177] Professor Bonbright has indicated the technique for the development of the functional account:

> It is to be hoped that the accounting profession will give far more attention than it has heretofore given to the effect on the "proper" balance sheet and earnings statements of the specific purposes for which these financial documents are customarily used. A good beginning could be made by assuming, first, that no use will be made of the company's reports except by buyers and sellers of the corporate stock. In the light of this single assumed objective, all of the alternative procedures of accounting, such as the valuation of fixed assets at original cost versus replacement cost, the use of straight-line versus sinking-fund method of depreciation, the booking of current assets at cost versus the lower of cost and market, and so forth, might be subjected to a critical rating of their relative merits. This task having been accomplished, the accountant might then forget the stockholder and assume that an "ideal" set of financial reports is such a set as will best fit the needs of the credit department of a commercial bank. Still other objects... would be taken up in turn. The result of this inquiry would be the creation of standards for "single-purpose" balance sheets and earnings statements. Further research would consider the question whether a workable multiple-purpose scheme of accounts might not be so devised that, by the aid of pencil and paper, a reader could reconstruct the accounts to fit his own requirements.[178]

The SEC has accepted the all-purpose accounting categories as sufficient for investors and has confined its role to an insistence upon more adequate disclosure within the framework of those categories and upon a conformance with the standards of accounting conduct recognized by the better text writers and more careful practitioners. Almost alone of all agencies — governmental or private — the SEC has the resources, staff, and sanctions, where necessary, to undertake the work of a reclassification of business data pointed toward the needs of stockholders and investors. If the exploratory remarks in this essay are well conceived, investors and the general public will inevitably benefit if the SEC finds it possible to undertake this task.

NOTES

1. Hamilton and Till, *The Cost Formula for Price* (March 1, 1935) N.R.A. Consumers Division, Rep. No. 9, partially reprinted as "Cost as a Standard for Price" (1937) 4 *Law and Contemp. Prob.* 321, is, undoubtedly, the outstanding piece of critical writing on accounting. Bonbright, *Valuation of Property* (1937) contains many passages subjecting accounting to the functional approach. Of professional accountants, George O. May, senior partner of Price, Waterhouse, & Co., seems most aware of the purposive nature of his techniques. See his Dickinson Foundation Lectures, Harvard Graduate School of Business Administration, reprinted in (1937) 63 *J. of Accty.* 333 and "Eating Peas with Your Knife" (1937) 63 *J. of Accty.* 15.

2. *In re* Missouri Pacific Railroad Company (Feb. 15, 1938) Sec. Exch. Act Release No. 1586; Transamerica Corporation (Nov. 25, 1938) Sec. Exch. Act Release No. 1950; Associated Gas and Electric Company (Jan. 13, 1939) Sec. Exch. Act Release No. 1985; McKesson & Robbins, Inc. (Dec. 30, 1938) Sec. Exch. Act Release No. 1975.

3. Some state corporation statutes contain accounting and reporting requirements. See the study by American Institute of Accountants of several state incorporation laws, cited in Payne, "The Effect of Recent Laws on Accountancy" (1935), 10 *Accounting Review* 84, 87 *et seq.*

4. Section 15(d) of the Exchange Act, as amended in 1936, requires under certain conditions, an undertaking by the issuer of new securities under the Securities Act, to file the supplemental and periodic information required of persons with securities listed and registered upon a national securities exchange.

5. See, generally, Hanna, "The Securities Exchange Act as Supplementary of the Securities Act" (1937), 4 *Law and Contemp. Prob.* 256–68.

6. Securities and Exchange Commission, Second Annual Report (1936) 2.

7. H.R. Rep. No. 1383, 73d Cong. 2d Sess. (1934) 11–13.

8. Sections 14 and 6, governing the solicitation of proxies and registered exchanges, respectively, provide a possible statutory basis for the promulgation of rules regulating the form and content of corporate reports to stockholders.

9. See sec. 13(a) of the Securities Exchange Act of 1934.

10. Securities Exchange Act of 1934, sec. 24(b).

11. "10 cents per photostatic copy of each page, for all copies up to and including 100 in a single order; 7 cents per photostatic copy of each page, for all copies over 100 in a single order." Securities Act Regulations, Rule 121(a).

12. The Fourth Annual Report of the Securities and Exchange Commission for the fiscal year ended June 30, 1938, states that approximately 24,000 members of the public visited the Washington, New York, and Chicago Public Reference Rooms of the Commission "seeking registered public information forms, releases, and other material." The Commission filed more than 3500 orders for photocopies of material. Pp. 93–94.

13. Exchange Act Regulations, Rule X-24B-3.

14. Even this as a practical matter is of little use to the investor, since it is too summary an account—being a digest of a digest—and also, since most people discard their daily papers, it is unavailable when the investor wants it.

15. Nonvoting investors in the business—bondholders, nonvoting preferred, etc.—by a strange convention are not considered to be entitled to a yearly accounting from the custodians of their funds. See, however, secs. 313 and 314 of the Trust Indenture Act of 1939. Reports to stockholders, usually available on request without charge, or newspaper or financial-chronicle digests of and comments on those reports, are probably the nonvoting investors' principal source of information.

16. The method followed in making the study was to select items in income statements and balance sheets which accounting authorities, investment analysts, and the Commission in its forms and regulations under both the Securities Act and the Exchange Act regard as significant in reflecting the corporation's business condition and progress, and to note the number of corporations in 1930 as compared with 1937 which furnished information in regard to each item. While this method does not present a complete picture of the extent of the information supplied by any specific corporation, it does indicate in a general way what the 70 corporations chose to reveal on specific items. The aggregation of these items and the number of corporations disclosing each reflect, it is believed, in a rough measure, the extent of the financial information given to stockholders in the years selected. 1930—prior to the Securities Act—was selected rather arbitrarily as the year with which to contrast 1937. The 70 corporations, chosen because of their national scope and because their financial statements were available in the Yale University library, are believed to represent a rather fair sampling of the 500 or 600 largest nonutility, nonrailroad corporations in the United States. Presumably the larger corporations furnish more information to stockholders than smaller ones. If this assumption is true, this study is weighted toward greater disclosure.

The following is a list of the corporations studied: National Biscuit Co.; Quaker Oats Co.; American Sugar Refining Co.;Holly Sugar Corp.; Liggett & Myers Tobacco Co.; R. J. Reynolds Tobacco Co.; Firestone Tire & Rubber Co.; United States Rubber Co.; International Salt ·Co.; Armour & Co. (Illinois); J. I. Case Co.; Deere and Co.; International Harvester Co.; Allegheny Steel Co.; Bethlehem Steel Corp.; United States Steel Corp.; Federal Mining & Smelting Co.; Old Dominion Co. (liquidating); Pittsburgh Coal Co. (of Pa.); Columbia Oil and Gasoline Corp.; Standard Oil Co. of Ohio; The Barber Co., Inc.; Johns-Manville Corp.; National Lead Co.; American Window Glass Co.; Owens-Illinois Glass Co.; Air Reduction Co., Inc.; Allied Chemical & Dye Corp.; Union Carbide & Carbon Corp.; Virginia-Carolina Chemical Corp.; Atlas Powder Co.; Lehn and Fink Products Corp.; Parke, Davis & Co.; General Electric Co.; American Type Founders, Inc.; Baldwin Locomotive Works; Crane Co. of Chicago; The Fairbanks Co.; International Business Machines Corp.; Lima Locomotive Works, Inc.; Midvale Co.; National Cash Register Co.; Remington Rand, Inc.; United Shoe Machinery Corp.; Chrysler Corp.; General Motors Corp.; Packard Motor Car Co.; Reo Motor Car Co.; Studebaker Corporation; E. I. du Pont de Nemours & Co.; Hercules Powder Co.; Remington Arms Co.; American Chain and Cable Co.; Torrington Co.; Container Corp. of America; American Woolen Co.; Gotham Silk Hosiery Co., Inc.; Julius Kayser and Co.; A. G. Spalding & Bros.; Eastman Kodak Co.; Curtis Publishing Co.; Colgate-Palmolive-Peet Co.; Procter & Gamble Co.; Warner Bros. Pictures, Inc.; Kaufmann Department Stores, Inc.; S. H. Kress & Co.; May Department Stores Co.; J. C. Penney Co.; Sears, Roebuck and Co.; American Stores Co.

17. This statement will not hold for banks, finance companies, or, possibly, public utilities.

The history of the recent shift in emphasis of investment analysts from the net worth of a business to the earning capacity is discussed in Graham and Dodd, *Security Analysis* (1934) 299–313. While current literature emphasizes the importance of the income statement, most writers continue to devote a disproportionate amount of attention to balance sheets in their written treatments of the subject. See, for example, the report of the American Institute of Accountants on Cooperation with Stock Exchanges, Reports to Stockholders (1932).

18. The writers do not mean to suggest that the balance sheet can be ignored safely by investors. The results of current operations can be appraised best in light of the financial resources of the company to maintain those operations and to weather adverse business conditions. In addition, the balance sheet sheds light on the questions of claims against the corporation and the relative priorities of the different classes of securities. The use of both net worth and earnings gives an investor an additional test of attractiveness rather than a single one of earnings alone. See Graham and Dodd, *Security Analysis* (1934) 350 *et seq.*

19. Curtis Publishing Co.; Torrington Co.; and United Shoe Machinery Corp. A study of 1934 published annual reports indicated that 2½% of the corporations studied omitted income statements. Sunley, "Seen in Published Financial Statements" (1935) 15 *C.P.A.* 682.

20. Of the 70 studied the 1937 income statements of the following corporations are obviously inadequate: Allied Chemical & Dye Corp.; American Sugar Refining Co.; American Window Glass Co.; The Barber Co., Inc.; The Fairbanks Co.; J. I. Case Co.; Liggett & Myers Tobacco Co.; Lima Locomotive Works, Inc.; Midvale Co.; National Biscuit Co.; National Cash Register Co.; Old Dominion Co.; Quaker Oats Co.; R. J. Reynolds Tobacco Co.; Remington Arms Co.; Studebaker Corporation; Union Carbide and Carbon Corp.

21. See Stockwell, *How to Read a Profit and Loss Statement* (1927) 4.

22. For a discussion of variations in the purpose of the corporate income statement and the consequences of such variations see Hatfield, *Accounting* (1927) 380–2. See, also, Canning, *The Economics of Accountancy* (1929) 92–4; Kimball, "The Importance of Understanding Income and Profits" (1935) 10 *Accounting Review* 131–5; Crandall, "Income and Its Measurement" (1935) 10 *Accounting Review* 380–400; Paton, *Accountants' Handbook* (1935) 1075–8; Littleton, "Concepts of Income Underlying Accounting" (1937) 12 *Accounting Review* 13–22.

23. "The nineteenth century carried to extravagant lengths the criterion of what one can call for short 'the financial results,' as a test of the advisability of any course of action sponsored by private or by collective action. The whole conduct of life was made into a sort of parody of an accountant's nightmare. Instead of using their vastly increased material and technical resources to build a wonder city, the men of the nineteenth century built slums; and they thought it right and advisable to build slums because slums on the test of private enterprise, 'paid,' whereas the wonder city would, they thought, have been an act of foolish extravagance, which would, in the imbecile idiom of the financial fashion, have 'mortgaged the future'—though how the construction to-day of great and glorious works can impoverish the future, no man can see until his mind is beset by false analogies from an irrelevant accountancy..." Keynes, "National Self-sufficiency" (1933) 22 *Yale Rev.* 755, 763. See also Hamilton and Till, *supra* note 1; Kimball, "The Importance of Understanding Income and Profits" (1935) 10 *Accounting Review* 131–5.

24. Some economists have contended that government constitutes a fifth factor in production—with taxes as its legitimate share in distribution. See Wasserman, "Taxes as a Share in Distribution" (1938) 28 *Am. Econ. Rev.* 103.

25. See Hamilton and Till, *supra* note 1, at 26–27. The accountant excludes psychical income which the economist includes; income to the accountant must be cash or an immediate, readily obtainable claim to cash. The accountant excludes economic costs such as salaries of the owners in individual proprietorships, rent on owned property, interest on capital invested by the owners, all of which are contained in his net profit figure, since he, usually, is interested only in recording costs resulting from explicit transactions. This limited interest enables the accountant to ignore some economic costs spawned by modern industry—waste of natural and human resources, etc. Despite these significant distinctions, it does not seem to be widely appreciated that accounting values are but one phase of economic values.

26. Some accountants have urged that the accountant is not confined necessarily to this parochial niche in the economic life of a nation, and that he can widen the scope of his work to reflect

broader economic values. See Borth and Winakor, "Some Reflections on the Scope of Auditing" (1935) 10 *Accounting Review* 174.

27. See Report of Committee of American Institute of Accountants on Cooperation with Stock Exchanges, Reports to Stockholders (1932) 6. See the discussion on depreciation, *infra* p. 217 *et seq.*

28. See the discussion on inventories, *infra* p. 217 *et seq.*

29. Report, *op. cit. supra* note 27, at 6–7. Many of the leading accountants share this view. See May, "The Accountant and the Investor" in *Northwestern University, Ethical Problems of Modern Accountancy* (1933) 26; "American Institute of American Society, Joint Report to the Securities and Exchange Commission on Forms A-2 and 10" (1935) 15 *C.P.A.* 107, 111; and Sanders, "What Is Most Satisfactory Form of Reports to Stockholders?" (1935) 3 *The Controller* 162, 163.

30. See Editorial, "Three Decades of Profit" (Dec. 17, 1938) 133 *The London Economist* 584.

31. The Tentative Statement of the American Accounting Association apparently divides the income statement into operating and nonoperating sections, but its terminology would be far more descriptive if the divisions were called "recurring" and "nonrecurring" income. "American Accounting Association, A Tentative Statement of Accounting Principles Affecting Corporate Reports, Postulates 9, 10, and 11" (1936) 11 *Accounting Review* 187, 189. Professors Sanders, Hatfield, and Moore, in *A Statement of Accounting Principles* (1938) 28–44, follow a similar classification. They do suggest, however, that in the operating section further subdivision is sometimes necessary. *Id.* at 28.

32. The SEC in Form 10-K requires the segregation of sales (and operating revenues if they equal 10% of the sum of the two items), dividends, interest, profits arising from transactions in securities, and separate listing of "any substantial nonrecurring items of miscellaneous other income, and any other substantial amounts." Form 10-K, Instructions, pp. 20–21. Forms A-1, A-2, and 10 are similar.

33. The reports examined were definitely deficient in this respect:

ITEMIZATION OF OPERATING REVENUE

	Number of Companies	
Operating Revenue Section:	*1930*	*1937*
One figure	34	48
Some segregation	3	6
Minor sources segregated	3	6

34. This problem has been considered by the Securities and Exchange Commission. See Address of Harold H. Neff, Director, Forms and Regulations Division, entitled "Revision of the Rules Affecting Registration under the Securities Act and the Securities Exchange Act," delivered before the Controllers Institute of America on January 19, 1939.

35. "The distinction...between operating and nonoperating income is...always a relative one and will be determined in any given instance on the basis of major activities and supplementary or minor activities." 1 Kester, *Accounting Theory and Practice* (3d ed. 1930) 46.·

36. As remarked in note 31, *supra,* many accountants use the term "nonoperating" income to include the items here classified as nonrecurring. See Paton, *Accountants' Handbook* (1934) 1093. For a discussion and illustration of the importance of segregating nonrecurring items, see Graham and Dodd, *Security Analysis* (1934) 353 *et seq.* See also Sanders, Hatfield, and Moore, *A Statement of Accounting Principles* (1938) 27.

37. See *infra.*

38. See Graham and Dodd, *Security Analysis* (1934) 478 *et seq.* for a discussion, with illustrative case histories, of the importance of segregating sources of income.

39. It has been suggested, for example, that the income statement be reclassified on the basis of "controlled" or "uncontrolled" costs. Uncontrolled costs are fixed interest charges, depreciation, etc., which accrue, irrespective of the volume of business done. Controlled costs are costs which may be varied with the volume of the business; the most variable of these costs are raw materials, and, in the absence of labor unions, wages. The larger the uncontrolled costs, the less ability management has to adjust itself to unfavorable business conditions.

40. Logically, income is earned not by sales alone, but by each step in the process of production. No one specific event is responsible for its creation. Theoretically, each stage in production should be credited for its proportionate share of the revenue earned. Accountants, however, to avoid "counting their chickens before they are hatched," treat the sale as the crystallization of the earning process and of the amount earned. In long-term projects, however, such as shipbuilding or large construction projects, where the amount of earnings can be reasonably estimated, income is frequently attributed to the productive process rather than to await its crystallization in the sale. See Husband, "Accounting Postulates; An Analysis of the Tentative Statement of Accounting Principles" (1937) 12 *Accounting Review* 386, at 394.

41. The receipt of cash and cash alone is not an adequate basis for income determination. The accrual basis is generally used. If revenues were recognized only in terms of cash, comparison of the results of periods would be impossible, since revenues "properly allocable" to one period would not be recognized until another, and there would be no assurance that such errors would cancel each other in the long run.

42. In connection with any particular income statement it is important to note whether "gross" or "net" sales is the figure given when making comparisons. There is no uniformity of practice as to what is the beginning figure of the income statement, or what deductions are made from the gross figure to give the net sales figure. See Hatfield, *Accounting* (1927) 351, 368; Sanders, Hatfield, and Moore, *A Statement of Accounting Principles* (1938) 28; and Sunley, "Seen in Published Financial Statements" (1935) 15 *C.P.A.* 682, 683. The accounting forms of the SEC require that the net sales figure (gross sales less discounts, returns, and allowances) or gross revenue should be the first figures on the income statement.

Of the 37 companies in 1930 and 54 in 1937 giving a sales figure, the following chart indicates the nature of the beginning figures used:

Beginning Figures:	Number of Companies	
	1930	1937
Gross Sales	3*	1*
"Sales"	9	10
Net Sales	15	31
Sales and Operating Revenue	10	12
	37	54

*In 1930, two of these companies also gave net sales; and the one company in 1937 also gave net.

43. J. M. B. Hoxsey, in his address to the American Institute of Accountants, "Accounting for Investors" (1930), declared that so important is this figure regarded "that one of the great statistical companies has adopted the policy of refusing to recommend to its clients the securities of companies which do not give this information, on the ground that not enough information is disclosed to permit an adequate analysis." Dean Landis, as Chairman of the SEC, characterized sales and cost of sales as "the most important" figures for income statement analysis. *N. Y. Times*, April 14, 1937, p. 46, col. 1. See also Graham and Dodd, *Security Analysis* (1934) 34; *Twentieth Century Fund, Security Markets* (1935) 581.

44. The following ratios of the investment analyst depend upon the disclosure of the net sales figure: Ratio of operating profit to net sales; ratio of net income to net sales; ratio of net sales to average inventory; ratio of net sales to receivables; ratio of net sales to fixed and to total assets, and to net worth; and ratio of operating expenses to net sales. See Montgomery, *Financial*

Handbook (1925) 233; Wall and Dunning, *Analyzing Financial Statements* (1930) 245 *et seq.;* Foulke, "Financial Ratios Become of Age" (1937) 64 *J. of Accty.* 203, 212.

The following chart indicates the number of companies which gave sufficient information to compute the operating income–net sales ratio:

Net Sales and Net Operating Income Figures:	Number of Companies	
	1930	1937
Sufficient information to make the computation	28	48
Of these no adjustments were necessary in	15	27
Adjustments were necessary in...................................	13	21

45. Securities Exchange Act, sec. 24(b).

46. For a rather full discussion, see Comment, "Confidential Treatment of Information Required by the Securities Exchange Act" (1938) 47 *Yale L. J.* 790, 794.

47. See Hoxsey, *Accounting for Investors* (1930) 15; *Twentieth Century Fund, Security Markets* (1935) 581. Sunley, "Seen in Published Financial Statements" (1935) 15 *C.P.A.* 682, 683, reports that of the apparently hundreds of statements examined by him, exactly 50% failed to indicate their volume of business.

See note 42 *supra,* for a summary of the opening items contained in the income statements of the 70 corporations included in this study.

48. *Id.* at 795. Professor Sanders seems to have more faith in the protests against disclosure of sales figures than most commentators. See Sanders, "Accounting Aspects of the Securities Act" (1937) 4 *Law and Contemp. Prob.* 191, 212–3.

49. See Landis, *The Administrative Process* (1938) 42 *et seq.*

50. Compare the remarks of William W. Werntz, Chief Accountant of the SEC, in an address delivered before the Controllers Institute of America on September 27, 1938.

51. Apparently the listing rules of the New York Stock Exchange do not require a disclosure of net sales or gross revenue, cost of sales, and selling, general, and administrative expenses in the annual reports to stockholders.

52. Of the 70 corporations examined, the following did not disclose net sales in 1937: Allied Chemical & Dye Corp.; American Window Glass Co.; J. I. Case Co.; The Fairbanks Co.; Lehn and Fink Products Corp.; Lima Locomotive Works, Inc.; Midvale Co.; National Biscuit Co.; Old Dominion Co.; Parke, Davis & Co.; Quaker Oats Co.; Torrington Co.; Union Carbide and Carbon Corp.; United Shoe Machinery Corp.; Virginia-Carolina Chemical Corp.; Warner Bros. Pictures, Inc. In June 1938, Allied Chemical & Dye Corp. had a case pending in the Second Circuit Court of Appeals to determine the validity of the Commission's order under sec. 24(b) denying an application for confidential treatment of this and other figures. The National Biscuit Co., R. J. Reynolds Tobacco Co., and the Torrington Co. had all filed similar suits but later dismissed them. Securities and Exchange Commission, Third Annual Report (1937) 179.

53. In concerns where services are sold rather than goods, "cost of goods sold" is not a workable concept, since the allocation of the direct costs of the services rendered is too difficult because "expenses" are inextricably mixed with "costs."

The figure "cost of goods sold" is normally subtracted from net sales and the resulting figure is usually called "gross profit" and by some "margin of sales." The emphasis which has been placed on this item has been severely criticized by Professor Paton. Paton, "Shortcomings of Present-Day Financial Statements" (1934) 57 *J. of Accty.* 108, 123–5.

54. The uses which may be made of the category "cost of goods sold" by the investor are outlined comprehensively in Morrison, "The Interest of the Investor in Accounting Principles" (1937) 12 *Accounting Review* 37, 40–1. And see Stockwell, *How to Read a Profit and Loss Statement* (1927) 65.

55. A wide or narrow gross or net profit margin as compared with competitors in the industry is

inconclusive and suggests further investigation. Either may be a sign of strength or weakness. See Morrison, "The Interest of the Investor in Accounting Principles" (1937) 12 *Accounting Review* 37, 41. In some situations, where the buyer is convinced that a rise in the cost of the product is imminent, a higher cost of production than that of competitors may be an inducement to purchase speculative stocks of a low price range. See Graham and Dodd, *Security Analysis* (1934) 477–8.

56. The causes of variations in profits from one period to another in accounting terminology are outlined in 1 Finney, *Principles of Accounting — Intermediate* (1937) 477.

57. Sanders, Hatfield, and Moore, *A Statement of Accounting Principles* (1938) 30, recommends that this segregation be made. In many companies, undoubtedly, the percentage of error in attempting to segregate expenses may render the breakdown of dubious value. See Hamilton and Till, *supra* note 1, for a summary of the inherent difficulties in allocating and segregating costs.

58. American Institute of Accountants, *Accounting Terminology* (1931) 109. Accounting terminology defines "manufacturing expenses" as "the cost of manufacturing, other than material consumed and direct labor." *Id.* at 60. This definition is almost the purest tautology.

59. The lack of uniformity is illustrated in the following chart:

Contents of "Cost of Goods Sold" Figures Given:	Number of Companies	
	1930	1937
Did not include depreciation or selling, general, and administrative expenses	8	17
Included depreciation but not selling, general, and administrative expenses	0	6
Included selling, general, and administrative expenses, but not depreciation	16	19
Included both depreciation and selling, general, and administrative expenses	9	5
	33	47

While there were 37 companies in 1930 and 54 in 1937 which reported a net sales figure, 4 of them in 1930 and 6 in 1937 omitted the "cost of goods sold" item.

60. Form A-2, Instructions, p. 36; Form 10, Instructions, p. 21; and Form 10-K, Instructions, p. 20. The SEC in Exchange Act Release No. 174 permitted mercantile establishments to include occupancy, buying, and publicity costs in "costs of goods sold"; in the proposed new forms, however, publicity costs must be excluded.

61. See, as indicating another attitude, Sanders, Hatfield, and Moore, *A Statement of Accounting Principles* (1938) 31: "The division of expenses into those to be included in cost of goods sold and those to be treated as subsequent income deductions may be left to the judgment of the management. In making this division it should be borne in mind that usually, though not necessarily, it determines also the cost items to be included in the inventory valuation."

62. Form A-1, p. 24, and Form A-2, Instructions, p. 37, under the Securities Act; and Form 10, Instructions, p. 22, and Form 10-K, Instructions, p. 21, under the Exchange Act.

63. The above definitions follow those given by the American Institute's Committee on Terminology. American Institute of Accounting, *Accounting Terminology* (1931) 59–60.

64. See Paton, *Accountants' Handbook* (1934) 157–8.

65. *Id.* at 158.

66. See Cogburn, "Burden Application" (1938) 65 *J. of Accty.* 208–12; Paton, *Accountants' Handbook* (1934) 157–8, 1332–63.

67. "In the audit of a large manufacturing establishment, this is the most troublesome account which the auditor is called to pass upon." Montgomery, *Auditing Theory and Practice* (5th ed., 1934) 516.

68. "The intimate relationships of depreciation, repairs and betterments is seldom adequately treated in most books on accounting.... The student is led to believe that these items are readily classified by the accountant from an examination of invoices, although nothing could be further from the truth..." Borth and Winakor, "Some Reflections of the Scope of Auditing" (1935) 10 *Accounting Review* 174, 180.

69. See the illustrations given in Kohler and Morrison, *Principles of Accounting* (1927) 313-4.

70. This is the definition of "betterment" in American Institute of Accounting, *Accounting Terminology* (1931) 28.

71. See the definition of repairs, *id.* at 101. Not all "repairs" are allocated to profit and loss in accounting practice. "Repairs" are divided into two groups—"ordinary" and "extraordinary." The latter is charged to asset accounts.

72. Treasury regulations are partially responsible for perpetuating these definitions in accounting practice. See U. S. Treas. Reg. 94, Art. 23(a)-4.

73. *Cf.* Saliers and Holmes, *Basic Accounting Principles* (1937) 483.

74. Paton, *Accountants' Handbook* (1934) 526 *et seq.,* describes and criticizes these practices. See, also, Mason, *Principles of Public Utility Depreciation* (1937) 23.

75. But see Paton, *op. cit supra* note 74; Mason, *op. cit supra* note 74, and compare Kohler and Morrison, *Principles of Accounting* (1926) 313-5; Graham and Katz, *Accounting in Law Practice* (1932) secs. 119, 120.

76. *Cf.* Paton, *Accountants' Handbook* (1934) 526-7. Justice Brandeis, dissenting in *United Railways* v. *West,* 280 U. S. 234, 260-1 (1930), expresses this point of view as clearly as any other commentator.

77. "If the accounting period were increased from the customary year to a decade, most of which is now treated as capital expenditure would become chargeable to income; while if the period were reduced to a day, much of what is now treated as current maintenance would become capital expenditure." May, "Improvement in Financial Accounts" (1937) 63 *J. of Accty.* 333, 334.

78. For large nonrecurring types of expenditures, concededly, the general accrual method should be followed. But where the expenditures are frequent and constantly recurring, the theoretical solution may not always prove practical, due to the infinite amount of accounting detail necessary to carry it out. For instance, to follow the theoretically accurate method, where a firm has a large fleet of delivery trucks, would require a separate account for each truck. This amount of detail might be considered too expensive. Consequently, the cost accountant may devise a more practical method of arriving at a reasonably accurate figure. In the case assumed, the cost accountant of the firm, from past experience, might have found that during past years, with a given number of trucks, so much per mile must be spent for tires, so much for repairs, and so much for partial replacements in order to maintain a reasonably efficient fleet of trucks. The sum of these items would then be treated as "maintenance and repairs" and charged to current operations. This device should work reasonably well where the number of items is large and constant replacement is necessary.

79. See Montgomery, *Auditing Theory and Practice* (5th ed., 1934) 516.

80. See 1 May, *Twenty-Five Years of Accounting Responsibility* (1937) 158-9; Montgomery, *Auditing Theory and Practice* (5th ed., 1934) 517.

81. The forms of the Securities and Exchange Commission require such itemization. See Form A-2, Instructions, p. 36, and Schedules II and VIII.

82. Ripley, *Main Street and Wall Street* (1926) 174.

83. It was not until 1909 that the Supreme Court recognized that allowances for depreciation were a legitimate expense of operations of public utilities. See *Knoxville* v. *Knoxville Water Co.* 212 U. S. 1 (1909).

84. This definition follows *Accounting Terminology* (1931) 48-9.

85. See Hatfield, *Accounting* (1928) 26; Hatfield, "What They Say About Depreciation" (1936) 11 *Accounting Review* 15–26.

86. Form A-1, p. 24; Form A-2, Instructions, p. 36; Form 10, Instructions, p. 22; and Form 10-K, Instructions, p. 22 and Schedule X.

87. The following chart indicates roughly the accounting treatment of the depreciation allowances in the income statements examined:

Depreciation Item in Income Statement:	Number of Companies	
	1930	1937
Amount not disclosed separately	22	4
Item mentioned but not disclosed	10	0
Amount given	48	66
Deducted prior to operating income figure	14	36
Deducted after operating income figure..........................	43	28
Allocated — deducted in two places	1	2

88. Ripley, replying on Cole's *American Wool Manufacture,* points out that it is practically impossible to determine whether the American Woolen Co. earned its preferred dividends in the 15 years prior to the World War [1] since part of its surplus was the result of inadequate provision for depreciation. Ripley, *Main Street and Wall Street* (1926) 177. On the other hand, the National Biscuit Co., prior to 1922, resorted to highly excessive charges to depreciation in order to conceal its large profits. The policy was abandoned in that year—the company multiplied its number of shares by seven and quadrupled the amount of dividends paid. *Id* at 180.

89. Investment analysts' ratios are also helpful. Graham and Dodd, *Security Analysis* (1934) 398 *et seq.*

90. The retirement system, while still used by many utility companies, is gradually being abandoned. A substantial number of states have adopted the uniform system of accounts of the National Association of Railway and Utility Commissioners and of the Federal Power and other federal regulatory commissions which all provide for the depreciation system.

91. Report of Committee of American Institute of Accountants on Cooperation with Stock Exchanges, Reports to Stockholders (1932) 6.

92. See Sanders, Hatfield, and Moore, *A Statement of Accounting Principles* (1938) 32.

93. Such differences may arise from the fact that a different base is used for tax purposes than for corporate purposes. Companies with a long corporate existence often have undergone one or more reorganizations or mergers under which they are permitted to use the same base for income tax purposes as was used by the predecessor corporation, whereas the base for corporate purposes may be the reorganization or merger price. Similarly, the rates for depreciation prescribed by the Bureau of Internal Revenue may legitimately be considered too liberal or inadequate for corporate purposes and therefore a different rate may justifiably be used.

94. Another possibility is to carry the gain or loss as an additional item in the net worth section, leaving the existing surplus accounts untouched, and at some future time absorbing it in one or more of the surplus accounts. See Sanders, Hatfield, and Moore, *A Statement of Accounting Principles* (1938) 39. See generally Hatfield, *Accounting* (1928) 245–6.

95. "American Accounting Association, A Tentative Statement of Accounting Principles" (1936) 11 *Accounting Review* 187, 189–90. See postulates 8 and 11.

96. The corporation wrote its plant down $270 million—charging a previously appropriated earned surplus account. The "Tentative Statement," *supra* note 95, would have charged it to the income account for the year, or would have had the income figures for the past years recast.

97. Hosmer, "The Effect of Direct Charges to Surplus on the Measurement of Income" (1938) 13 *Accounting Review* 31, 43; Greer, "Uniformity in Accounting Statements," *Proceedings of the First Institute on Accounting* (1938) 133.

98. Schedule A of the Securities Act requires a disclosure of all "charges... made against its various surplus accounts" and a differentation of "recurring and nonrecurring income." Subdivision (26). The Exchange Act leaves the scope and contents of the financial statements required to the discretion of the Commission. Sec. 12(b) (J) and (K).

The instructions to Forms A-1 and A-2 under the Securities Act and Forms 10 and 10-K under the Exchange Act contain almost identical requirements as to disclosure of all substantial nonrecurring debits and credits. In addition, the required surplus schedules must specify all additions and deductions from surplus and indicate whether "they are of the nature of capital or earned surplus items." Form A-2, Instructions, Schedule VI, at 46; and Form 10-K, Instructions, Schedule IX, at 32.

The listing requirements of the New York Stock Exchange also require a disclosure of "any substantial item of an unusual or nonrecurrent nature." New York Stock Exchange, Committee on Stock List, Requirements for Listing Applications (1937) 8. See also Investment Bankers Code of Fair Competition (1934) 12; "Tentative Statement" (1936) 11 *Accounting Review* 187, 189 (postulates 8 and 11).

99. See Graham and Dodd, *Security Analysis* (1934) cc. 31, 32, for specific instances of abuses of this sort.

100. *In re* American Terminals and Transit Co., 1 SEC 701 (1936), the Commission held that the designation of a nonrecurring income item as "other income" was misleading. One of the principal deficiencies cited in the Commission's Order for Hearing in the Associated Gas and Electric Co. delisting case was the "failure to charge to registrant's income account" certain extraordinary expense items. Securities Exchange Act Release No. 1985 (January 13, 1939).

101. See Stockwell, *How to Read a Profit and Loss Statement* (1927) 367; Kester, *Advanced Accounting* (3d ed., 1933) 356-7; Rowe, "Surplus Adjustments" (1933) 56 *J. of Accty.* 291-3; Littleton, "Dividends Presuppose Profits" (1934) 9 *Accounting Review* 304; Marple, *Capital Surplus and Corporate Net Worth* (1936) 144; 1 Finney, *Principles of Accounting—Intermediate* (1937) 112; and 1 May, *Twenty-Five Years of Accounting Responsibility* (1937) 325. In England, gains and losses on the sale of capital assets are regarded as increasing or decreasing capital, and are not reflected in the income account.

102. The carryover is reflected clearly in 1 May, *Twenty-Five Years of Accounting Responsibility* (1937) 319 *et seq.;* Littleton, "Dividends Presuppose Profits" (1934) 9 *Accounting Review* 304 *et seq.*

103. See Hosmer, "The Effect of Direct Charges to Surplus on the Measurement of Income" (1938) 13 *Accounting Review* 31, 44-5.

104. (1936) 11 *Accounting Review* 187, 189.

105. *Id.* at 190.

106. *Ibid.*

107. See Sanders, Hatfield, and Moore, *A Statement of Accounting Principles* (1938) 39.

108. Hosmer, *supra* note 103, at 49-50. If U.S. Steel had charged the $270 million to income, with a resulting $269 million loss for the year, the effect upon the price of the company's stock, and, perhaps upon business confidence, might have been of serious proportions. The alternative suggested by the Tentative Statement of recasting the income accounts would be very difficult to apply in practice, since "the proper number of past periods" for which depreciation and obsolescence were computed wrongly is perhaps impossible to ascertain. Furthermore, recasting past income statements, of course, cannot undo the effects of their previous publication upon investors and the country at large. People have acted upon them already for good or evil. For future action, however, recasting may throw more light upon the corporation's past than retention of old figures known to be wrong.

109. Hosmer, "The Effect of Direct Charges to Surplus on the Measurement of Income" (1938)

13 *Accounting Review* 31, 43 *et seq.* See also Hoxsey, *Writing Down Assets and Writing Off Losses* (1933) 12.

110. A fundamental source of the difficulty lies in the attempt to allocate gains and losses realized from transactions, years in the making, to one short fiscal period. Accounting marks off arbitrarily a continuous flow of interrelated events into periods measured by the fiscal year; an attempt is then made to isolate the related events into clean-cut transactions allocable to a definite period of time. The sharp distinction drawn between income statements and surplus statements — between income of one period and the income of past periods, and the resulting premium placed on a strategic allocation of a particular item to one or the other of the statements — further heightens the difficulty. It has been suggested that the cleavage wrought by the calendar year concept can be bridged somewhat by combining the income statement and the earned-surplus statement into a single net-worth statement, thus decreasing the importance of allocating a particular item to either income or earned surplus. Such a statement might start with the net worth at the beginning of the period. To this should be added, in the first subdivision, new capital contributions. The next subdivision would be devoted to changes in net worth resulting from "normal operations." The last section would reflect the payments of dividends and credits or debits for "extraordinary gains and losses" not fairly applicable to "normal operations," finally arriving at the net worth at the end of the period. While a net-worth statement of this type does not solve the problem of allocating borderline items between income and surplus, it does tend to minimize the distinction and shifts the emphasis to a more complete disclosure of all accounting transactions recognized during the period — which, after all, is what the investor needs.

111. Form A-2, Instructions, at 37; Form 10, Instructions, at 23; and Form 10-K, at 21.

112. Form A-2, Instructions, at 35 and Schedule VII; Form 10, Instructions, at 21 and Schedule VII; and Form 10-K, Instructions, at 19 and Schedule IX.

113. Form 10-K, Schedule IX.

114. Form A-1, under the Securities Act, more than any other form, directs the registrant to allocate his extraordinary items along approved accounting channels. Instructions, at 32.

115. These cases are commented upon by Commissioner Healy in an address, "The Next Step in Accounting" (1938) 13 *Accounting Review* 1, at 2–4, delivered before the American Accounting Association in December 1937.

116. *Ibid.*

117. Healy, *supra* note 115, at 4–5. See, as supporting the minority view, "Accounting and the SEC" (1937) 12 *Accounting Review* 309, 310.

118. Healy, "The Next Step in Accounting" (1938) 13 *Accounting Review* 1, 5.

119. SEC, Accounting Series, Release No. 1 (April 1, 1937). A similar position was previously taken by a committee of the American Institute of Accountants in a report to the Committee on Stock List of the New York Stock Exchange in 1932. Postulates 17 and 19 of the Tentative Statement of Accounting Principles state the same proposition. "American Accounting Association, A Tentative Statement of Accounting Principles" (1936) 11 *Accounting Review* 187. The New York Stock Exchange has a standard clause in its listing agreement with corporations which is similar to Accounting Release No. 1.

William W. Werntz, Chief Accountant of the SEC, in an address before the Annual Meeting of the American Accounting Association, December 28, 1938, at Detroit, stated that the Commission, in a number of cases settled over the conference table, has insisted that the absorption of an operating deficit through charges to capital surplus can be made only by stockholders' consent after full disclosure of all surrounding circumstances. Such transactions are considered to be quasi-reorganizations, whereby, through stockholder consent, earned surplus is relieved of the burden of absorbing past losses, thus facilitating the future payment of dividends.

120. Chairman James M. Landis resigned September 15, 1937, and was succeeded by Mr. William O. Douglas on September 21, 1937; Commissioner J. D. Ross resigned October 31, 1937; Mr. Jerome N. Frank took office on December 27, 1937; and Mr. John W. Hanes on January 14,

1938. The release was issued on April 25, 1938. Subsequently, Mr. Hanes resigned (June 30, 1938), and was succeeded by Mr. Edward C. Eicher.

121. SEC Accounting Series Release No. 4, April 25, 1938.

122. Securities Act, Schedule A (25). See also Instruction Books for Forms A-1, at 32, and A-2 at 46, n. 1, for the schedules and detail required by the Commission under the Securities Act.

123. Schedule IX, at 32. Similar requirements are contained in the Instruction Book for Form 10, Schedule VII, at 26.

124. *Cf.* Sanders, "Accounting Aspects of the Securities Act" (1937) 4 *Law and Contemp. Prob.* 191, 200–2; Sanders, Hatfield, and Moore, *A Statement of Accounting Principles* (1938) 92–7.

125. Form 10-K, Instructions, at 19.

126. A new form, now in the process of preparation, may contain the following provisions concerning the segregation of surplus: "That companies organized since January 1, 1928, give a complete segregation of surplus as between (a) paid-in surplus, (b) surplus arising from revaluation of assets, (c) other capital surplus, and (d) earned surplus." Healy, "The Next Step in Accounting" (1938) 13 *Accounting Review* 1, at 8.

127. The following chart indicates the number of corporations disclosing the important surplus divisions:

TREATMENT OF SURPLUS AND SURPLUS RESERVES

	Number of Companies	
Names of Surplus Accounts	*1930*	*1937*
One item, usually called "surplus"	44	8
Earned surplus..	26	57
Capital surplus...	12	30
Paid-in surplus...	10	5
Revaluation	1	0

Appropriated Surplus Reserve Accounts		
Companies with one figure......................................	23	16
Companies with reserves itemized	37	44
Companies with reserves included in Capital and Surplus section.......	6	3

128. Paton, *Essentials of Accounting* (1938) 745, states that the principal tests used in distinguishing fixed and current assets are: "... degree of liquidity; (2) normal term or length of life; (3) rate of transfer to expense or loss; (4) technical character or method of use; (5) nature of business and intent of management."

129. Instruction 1 to the Form A-1 balance sheet, under the Securities Act, requires a schedule indicating the major classifications of the plant, property, and equipment account. Similar segregation is required by Schedule II of Forms 10 and 10-K under the Exchange Act. Forms 10 and 10-K require that, where practicable, depreciation reserves shall be shown to correspond to classifications of property, "separating especially depreciation, depletion and amortization."

The following chart indicates the disclosure of these accounting requisites in the 70 corporations studied:

	Number of Companies	
Fixed Assets and Related Reserves	*1930*	*1937*
Single entry	8	0
Single entry (net)..	4	2
One figure and one reserve......................................	39	41
Itemized but no reserve indicated................................	2	0
Itemized with one reserve	8	11
Itemized with allocated reserves	9	17
Reserve on liability side	14	6

130. Compare Hamilton and Till, *supra* note 1.

131. A minimum of disclosure impels, regardless of the alternative employed, an adequate description of the basis used in recording fixed assets. In the recent delisting proceedings instituted against the Associated Gas and Electric Co., one of the deficiencies cited was the "failure to explain adequately the basis of determining" the amount of fixed assets. *In re* Associated Gas and Electric Co., Securities Exchange Act Release No. 1985 (January 13, 1939). In 1937, only 43 of the 70 annual reports examined contained any indication of the basis—not an impressive record. It was, however, a decided improvement over 1930, when only 21 of the 70 indicated the basis.

132. See May, "The Influence of Accounting on the Development of an Economy" (1936) 61 *J. of Accty.* 11, 17, pointing out that in a single act of the English Parliament the word "value" is said to have been used in 27 senses.

133. See May, *supra* note 132, at 15–21. There are a few dissenters, however. See Husband, "Accounting Postulates: An Analysis of the Tentative Statement of Accounting Principles" (1937) 12 *Accounting Review* 386; Lorig "Remarks on Tentative Statement" (1937) 12 *Accounting Review* 401–3.

134. The SEC has not as yet passed upon the question of whether a balance sheet, under the Securities Act, may include write-ups, "based on a proper appraisal," of the increased value of assets over original cost. *In re* Breeze Corporations, Inc., Securities Act Release No. 1786 (1938), a stop-order proceeding, the Commission was faced with the question of whether the inclusion in the balance sheet of a substantial appreciation in the book value of registrant's intangibles was materially misleading. The Commission side-stepped the question of write-ups since it found that the appraisal methods employed were arbitrary and unsound. See also, *In re* Unity Gold Corp., 1 SEC 25 (1934); *In re* Haddam Distillers Corp., 1 SEC 37 (1934); *In re* Continental Distillers and Importers Corp., 1 SEC 54, 79 (1935); and *In re* American Terminals and Transit Co., 1 SEC 701, 720 (1936).

135. "American Accounting Association, Tentative Statement of Accounting Principles" (1936) 11 *Accounting Review* 201.

136. Financial analysts use capitalized earnings as their principal basis of judging the value of a business. Capitalized earnings, however, usually, except perhaps in the case of public utilities, bear little relation to either original costs, reproduction costs, or revaluation appraisals of the fixed assets. Accountants do not conceive it to be their function to correlate balance-sheet figures with capitalized earnings, or to note separately the latter on the balance sheet.

137. *In re* Breeze Corporations, Inc., Securities Act Release No. 1786 (1938), predecessor companies of the issuer effected substantial write-ups by arbitrary appraisals of intangibles. The registrant's acquisition of these assets at the inflated figures was not an arms-length transaction and the Commission held that the statement of the cost figures without the inclusion of an additional statement showing to what extent these figures represented write-ups by the predecessor companies was materially misleading.

138. 1 Bonbright, *Valuation of Property* (1937) 140–1.

139. Federal Power Commission, *Uniform System of Accounts Prescribed for Public Utilities and Licensees Subject to the Provisions of the Federal Power Act* (1937) 6.

140. In a number of cases under the 1933 act the Commission has issued stop-orders suspending the effectiveness of registration statements for securities of enterprises in the promotional stage on the grounds that the balance sheet did not properly record the cost or value of assets acquired through the issuance of securities. In each of these cases the Commission indicated that the basis for the asset figure should be "sound" appraisal methods competently and honestly applied or the fair market value of the stock at the time the property was acquired. See *In re* Unity Gold Corp., 1 SEC 25 (1934); *In re* Continental Distillers and Importers Corp., 1 SEC 54 (1935); *In re* Big Wedge Gold Mining Co., 1 SEC 98, 107 (1935); *In re* American Terminals and Transit Co., 1 SEC 701 (1936); *In re* Yumuri Jute Mills Co., 2 SEC 81, 85 (1937); *In re* National Boston Montana Mines Corp., 2 SEC 226, 250 (1937); *In re* Rickard Ramore Gold Mines, Ltd., 2 SEC

377, 389 (1937); *In re* Bering Straits Tin Mines, Inc., Securities Act Release No. 1498 (July 2, 1937); and *In re* Virginia City Gold Mining Co., Securities Act Release No. 1615 (Nov. 16, 1937).

141. Bonbright, *Valuation of Property* (1937).

142. As in the 1937 balance sheets of such corporations as American Sugar Refining Co.; Holly Sugar Corp.; Armour & Co.; Federal Mining and Smelting Co.; Columbia Oil and Gas Corp.; Baldwin Locomotive Works; Warner Bros. Pictures, Inc.; May Department Stores Co.

143. Paton, *Accountants' Handbook* (1934) 319, lists the following principal bases of security valuation for accounting purposes: "(1) Actual cost or amount invested; (2) market price; (3) appraised or estimated value; (4) value on issuing company's books; (5) cost modified by accumulation or amortization; (6) maturity value."

144. Doran, "The Impact of Economics on Accounting" (Jan. 1939) *Edison Inst. Bull.* 26, 28; Committee of American Institute of Accountants on Cooperation with Stock Exchanges, Reports to Stockholders (1932) 6 [reprinted in 1 May, *Twenty-Five Years of Accounting Responsibility* (1937) 115]. In addition, adjustments for price level changes are seldom made.

145. Even in regard to this very significant figure, there were six companies in 1930 and two in 1937 which did not give a total for current assets. In 1930, nine companies included obviously improper items such as treasury stocks and bonds; and in 1937, eight companies made such improper inclusions. The SEC has found similar deficiencies. Accounting Series, Release No. 7 (May 16, 1938) 3.

146. See Sanders, "Reports to Stockholders" (1934) 9 *Accounting Review* 201, 208.

147. See Graham and Katz, *Accounting in Law Practice* (1932) 168; Bowman, "Reporting upon the Corporate Investment" (1938) 65 *J. of Accty.* 396, 407–10. On investment analysis ratios generally, see authorities cited *supra* note 44.

148. Form 10-K, Instructions, at 14.

149. "Include only securities having a ready market. State in the balance sheet the basis of determining the balance sheet amount and, if not shown on the basis of current market quotations, state such aggregate amount parenthetically." Form 10-K, Instructions, 14. It is understood that the proposed new forms contain a provision requiring in addition a parenthetical statement of the original cost of the securities.

Professors Sanders, Hatfield, and Moore indicate an additional requirement: "This market should be sufficiently stable to absorb an orderly liquidation of the particular securities held by the company without materially impairing the currently quoted values, or at any rate without reducing them below the prices at which the company carries them in its balance sheet." Sanders, Hatfield, and Moore, *A Statement of Accounting Principles* (1938) 72. Thus duPont de Nemours & Co. does not list its vast holdings in General Motors as a current asset. See, also, Accounting Series, Release No. 7; and *In re* American Gyro Co., 1 SEC 83, 87 (1935).

150. Form 10-K, Instructions, at 14, quoted *supra* note 148. Forms 10 and A-2 contain similar instructions.

151. In a study of 155 balance sheets and income statements published in 1934, the valuation of marketable securities was as follows: "No basis indicated, 54; cost, 50; market, 28; 'cost or market,' 10; miscellaneous, 13; a total of 155. Among the miscellaneous bases were: book value; lower than cost; subject to a 'reserve'; lower of par or market; listed securities 'at market,' unlisted at 'cost'; par; below market; bonds 'at par,' stocks 'at par,' stocks 'at market.'" Daniels, "Corporation Financial Statements" (1934) 6 *Michigan Business Studies* 51, n. 1.

152. The instructions to Forms 10 and 10-K permit "Notes and Accounts Receivable" to be combined. Instructions, at pages 17 and 15, respectively. Form A-1, Item 54, requires segregation in considerable detail, and apparently segregation is also required in Form A-2. Form A-2, Instructions, p. 31. In the tentative drafts of the proposed new forms, trade notes and accounts receivable are to be segregated, but a consolidated reserve is permitted.

153. Sanders, Hatfield, and Moore, *A Statement of Accounting Principles* (1938) 73.

154. There are two generally accepted methods of determining the amounts of the annual allowances for losses from uncollectibles. One is by analyzing the individual accounts and the other is by basing the allowance upon the general past experience of the company. See Paton, *Essentials of Accounting* (1938) 411 *et seq.*

155. The statistics for notes and accounts receivable and related reserves of the 70 corporations are as follows:

	Number of Companies	
How Disclosed:	1930	1937
Single entry ("net" not indicated)	16	4
Single entry ("net" indicated)	8	15
One entry and one reserve	10	9
Itemized but no reserve	15	2
Itemized and one reserve	17	30
Itemized and allocated reserves	3	8
Reserves on liability side	25*	3†

*In 1930, two companies had the reserve separated, ten mentioned doubtful accounts in the name of the entry, and thirteen had reserves for contingencies with no mention of doubtful accounts.

†Three companies listed reserves for contingencies with no mention of doubtful accounts.

156. Form 10-K, Instructions, at 15.

157. Examples are found in the 1937 annual reports of American Sugar Refining Co., Holly Sugar Refining Co., Firestone Tire & Rubber Co., Bethlehem Steel Corp., Pittsburgh Coal Co., Columbia Oil and Gasoline Corp., and others.

158. See Paton, *Accountants' Handbook* (1934) 418, 420.

159. Of the 70 annual reports studied, 39 in 1930 and 45 in 1937 employed the "cost or market" method.

160. Paton, "Comments on a Statement of Accounting Principles" (1938) 65 *J. of Accty.* 196, 202.

161. See Graham and Katz, *Accounting in Law Practice* (1932) 191; Paton, "Comments on a Statement of Accounting Principles" (1938) 65 *J. of Accty.* 196, 203; and Barr, "Comments on a Statement of Accounting Principles" (1938) 65 *J. of Accty.* 319–23.

162. Barr, "Comments on a Statement of Accounting Principles" (1938) 65 *J. of Accty.* 319–23.

163. Fictitious inventory profits have serious economic consequences. See Arthur, "Inventory Profits in the Business Cycle" (1938) 28 *Am. Econ. Rev.* 27–40.

164. May, "Influence of the Depression on the Practice of Accountancy" (1932) 54 *J. of Accty.* 336 [reprinted in 1 May, *Twenty-Five Years of Accounting Responsibility* (1937) 87].

165. Paton, *Accountants' Handbook* (1934) 423–4.

166. See Paton, *loc. cit., supra* note 165. For variations in the meaning of "market" see "The Value of Inventory" in "Report of the Special Committee on Inventories to American Institute of Accountants" (1938) 65 *J. of Accty.* 29, 30.

167. The forms require: "State separately in the balance sheet, or in a schedule therein referred to, major classes of inventory such as (a) raw materials; (b) work in process; (c) finished goods; (d) supplies, and the basis of determining the amounts shown in the balance sheet. Any other classification that is reasonably informative may be used." Form A-2, Instructions, p. 31; Form 10, Instructions, p. 17; and Form 10-K, Instructions, p. 15. It is understood that the proposed revision of accounting forms requires, in addition, a description of the basis to the extent practicable.

168. Werntz, "An Approach to Accounting Problems" (An address delivered before the India-

napolis Chapter of the National Association of Cost Accountants on December 14, 1938; before the Illinois Society of Certified Public Accountants on December 16, 1938) 7.

169. *Ibid.*

170. *Ibid.* Consistency in the application of a particular method from year to year and a clear indication in the company's accounting statements of any changes of method from year to year may provide more protection to the investor than attempts at detailed description of the method employed. The Bureau of Internal Revenue's regulations, designed, of course, clearly to reflect income for income tax purposes, do not prescribe specific methods to be followed, admitting that "inventory rules cannot be uniform." The emphasis is on consistency, and "greater weight is to be given to consistency than to any particular method of inventorying or basis of valuation so long as the method or basis used is substantially in accord with these regulations." Treasury Regulations 94, Art. 22(c)–2. The Bureau, however, is interested in the income, from year to year, of individual businesses only. Consistency in the application of a particular method over a period of years will, theoretically at least, result in the ultimate absorption of *fictional* inventory profits or losses produced by a method in a particular year. Investors, however, have a broader interest. They are interested in a method of inventorying which reflects most fairly the inventory for the *particular* year since they may decide to buy or sell on the basis of the income statement for the particular year. Furthermore, they are interested in a greater uniformity of inventory methods from corporation to corporation and more detailed disclosure of the methods followed so that a basis of comparison of operating results of different corporations is available.

171. Presentation of inventory figures:

	Number of Companies	
	1930	1937
Inventory itemized with amounts indicated	16	17
Basis Employed:		
Not indicated	19	5
Cost	8	6
Cost or market	39	45
Miscellaneous	6	16

172. The Twentieth Century Fund came to a similar conclusion: "We have found that, despite some improvement during the past few years, a majority even of those companies whose issues are listed on the New York Stock Exchange do not disclose enough information to render their balance sheets and income accounts intelligible to the average, well informed investor." Twentieth Century Fund, Security Markets (1935) 601.

173. Hamilton, "Cost as a Standard for Price" (1937) 4 *Law and Contemp. Prob.* 321.

174. See 2 Bonbright, *Valuation of Property* (1937) 1168.

175. "American Accounting Association, A Tentative Statement of Accounting Principles" (1936) 11 *Accounting Review* 187.

176. See note 23 *supra.*

177. See, as expressive of another point of view, Berle, "Accounting and the Law" (1938) 13 *Accounting Review* 9.

178. 1 Bonbright, *Valuation of Property* (1937) 253–4.

SIX

Some Antecedents of the Securities and Exchange Commission

J. R. TAYLOR

Taylor examines the history of the period prior to the creation of the Securities and Exchange Commission. Beginning with the Ultra Mares case he discusses several important events prior to the Great Depression and the various events leading to the Securities Act of 1933.

Someone has said that not only does history repeat itself but also historians repeat themselves. We who are associated with accounting have materially benefited through this reiteration. Most often, we are more impressed by the current happening than with those antecedents which precede the event. However, a sound reaction and a judicious forecasting of possible developments must be predicated upon a study of those events which precede the incident at hand. Historical perspective may be said to be an essentiality to a sound judgment. Especially is this true with respect to the development of accounting techniques and legal responsibilities under regulations in general, and the Securities and Exchange Commission legislation in particular.

BACKGROUND OF SECURITIES AND EXCHANGE COMMISSION LEGISLATION

There is a current feeling among many accountants that this legislation was the outgrowth of the professed philosophy of the political party then in power — to protect the small capital-furnishers from exploitation by corporate financiers. Moreover, it was held by some that this philosophy was fostered by the security and safety attitude attendant with the depression era. A review of the facts, however, shows that these are but half truths, for there were many historical antecedents. Fundamentally, the regulations were directed toward the financial practices of a prosperity period rather than at those found most often in an economic and financial valley.[1]

Time and again the prosperity malpractices of corporate management were the subjects of erudite discussions. Moreover, the courts have always had a tendency toward setting up rules of law which they felt would protect the small absentee owner. Perhaps this depression philosophy may be said to be accountable for the desire to limit the capital-raising activities of those large corporate entities in future prosperity periods who had demonstrated themselves to be given to faulty procedures during the prosperity era of the twenties. But it must be

Reprinted from *The Accounting Review,* June 1941, pp. 188–196, with permission of the American Accounting Association.

emphasized that there was a trend toward such financial regulations even during the preceding prosperity period. Furthermore, during this period there were evidences indicating that the accountants' responsibility would likewise increase under this financial control philosophy. Perhaps the first forecast of accountants' increasing responsibility was the Ultra Mares case, which began early in 1924.

ACCOUNTANTS' RESPONSIBILITIES PRIOR TO THE ULTRA MARES DECISION

Before the Ultra Mares case, public accountants in America had not had their responsibility clearly interpreted, nor had the limits of their liability to third persons been defined under common law decision to the accountants' complete satisfaction. In England, however, the reverse was true; there the courts had rendered a sufficient number of decisions, and a responsibility concept for the accountant was fairly well outlined under the rules of law which the English courts had set up. Moreover, the greater age of auditing in England as well as the passage of certain laws (the Company Act in 1908 is an example) had enabled the English auditors to know their position more clearly. Finally, in England there had been no major shift in the sources of capital.

English businessmen have always secured the larger portion of the necessary capital from stockholders. This practice dates back to the Industrial Revolution. On the other hand, up until the World War [I] the large corporate entity in the United States was financed primarily through advances from short- and long-term creditors. After 1922, however, corporate management turned to selling securities in order to secure the captal needed.[2] This shift in the capital sources utilized by corporate management resulted in a need for a change in the auditing technique by the American public accountant, as well as a shift in the relative importance of the two principal financial statements, the balance sheet and the profit-and-loss statement.[3]

Since the auditor's client was most often no longer a trustee of capital but an agent for absentee principals, emphasis should have been shifted from the debt-paying valuations to going-concern valuations, and the profit-and-loss statement should have become the more important report rendered by the public accountant. In other words, the profit-and-loss statements of succeeding periods were connected by a balance sheet, while the reverse had been true as long as the major portion of capital funds was secured from creditors. Furthermore, a property need no longer have the ability to retire debts to be classed as an asset. All that it needed to demonstrate was the ability to be a necessary adjunct to revenues arising in subsequent fiscal periods.

Prior to the Ultra Mares case the accounting profession in the United States had presumed that the American courts would follow English precedents in most of their decisions. However, the profession was not always confident that these English precedents would be followed, for it was aware that its audit was limited, while the English profession most often performed a detailed examination. There was, no doubt, added reason for the practicing accountant in the United States to feel that the American courts would follow British precedent (that is, common law precedent), after he had shifted his emphases to one which was more closely synonymous with English audit philosophy — security holder rather than creditor audit — even though his program most often was not as detailed. Of course, the American accountant could never be certain that his courts would look behind this facial difference

—test checking as opposed to a detailed audit—to the underlying sameness in the audit philosophy. That is, how well are the assets entrusted being used (stockholders' viewpoint), rather than how valuable are the assets of debt payers (creditors' viewpoint). Because of this uncertainty, accountants in the United States were aware of their difficult position and many articles were written by them during this period concerning their perturbation.

Furthermore, in an attempt to limit their responsibility and its extension to third persons when coupled with a circumscribed audit program, many accountants wrote extended and excessively qualified certificates. The result was that the average reader, who was most often not versed in the technical and obtuse phraseology used, was more confused than enlightened by the certificate which accompanied the auditor's report. It is interesting to review the early samples of certificates and compare them with later examples. One is almost forced to the conclusion that there was support for the accusations that accountants were attempting to evade their responsibility by qualifying their certificates. Whether or not the responsibility should have been attached to the accountant is open to question. There are, however, few supporters for the thesis that the certificate should afford a screen behind which the auditor may conceal the lack of a professional attitude.

ULTRA MARES CASE

If the certificates of the period had anything in common it was the freedom with which the individual composers mixed freely statements of fact and statements of opinion. The Ultra Mares case indirectly but roundly criticized this current trend of using the certificate as an escape mechanism on two scores:

1. The confusion of statements of fact and opinion.
2. The certification of an opinion based upon an unseasoned judgment arising out of an unprofessional attitude on the part of the auditor.

The first criticism clarified the court's position for auditors in that it indicated that a fact is a statement and not a certification. Moreover, the court saw the obvious redundancy in certifying to one's own opinion. The more pertinent question was whether the opinion expressed by the certifying accountant was the result of a whimsy or grew out of a measured consideration based upon sufficient evidence, objectively verified. The second criticism, then, was the more significant issue which the court evolved, for it dwelled upon an accounting and auditing problem rather than upon a rhetorical question.

Under the common law decisions, auditors had had the feeling that their responsibility to third persons was limited to that of fraud, and that privity of contract disburdened them from any legal responsibility to third parties even though negligence was proved. Here, however, the court said the accountant must act as a professional man. Obviously, this represented an extension of responsibility from that attached to the accountant's work under the "prudent man," and "privity of contract" concepts. Furthermore, the court reiterated that "privity of contract" did not represent a satisfactory defense if fraud were proved by the plaintiff. Proof, of course, depended upon the facts in a particular case. However, it is to be noted that the editor of *Certified Public Accountant* (vol. 2, p. 35, 1931) said: "This decision would seem to narrow materially the ground which accountants heretofore believed was covered by the general term 'negligence,' and correspondingly increased the sphere of what might legally be denominated 'fraud.'"

To the practicing accountants it was apparent that a fraud could be perpetrated much easier by them after this decision than under the older concept of negligence and fraud. Most certainly it removed any and all temptation to use the standard audit certificate while varying from the standard audit program (to do less than the program required), as well as indicating that it would be prudent to determine the use to which the submitted report would be put by the client.

NEW YORK STATE PROPOSAL

In 1925, there was a movement to amend the corporation laws in the state of New York. No doubt, some accountants would contend that the proposed amendment grew out of the Ultra Mares case. Perhaps this case was the initiating force, but this writer can think of the case only as an accentuating influence rather than as a causal factor. The interim from 1924 (the year the Ultra Mares case began) to 1925 seems too short for the real importance of the case to have been appreciated by the public generally, and the New York State legislators particularly. Moreover, the appeal decision was not rendered until 1931. Rather it would seem that both the Ultra Mares case and the New York State proposal grew out of:

1. The concentration of economic capital in a limited number of corporations.
2. Faulty methods of corporate financing.
3. Evidences of insufficient managerial control.
4. The government trend toward the controlling of the large corporate entities, instead of attempting to break up these economic units.
5. The appreciation of predicating effective and fair controls upon a knowledge of the facts.
6. The desirability of independent audits for securing the needed financial and economic information.

Although the proposal was not enacted, it is interesting to the accounting profession, for an inherent feature was a compulsory yearly audit of corporations by an independent public accountant. The directors were to appoint the auditor, outline his duties, and designate the scope of the audit program.

Not only did this proposal acknowledge the need of independent audits, but at the same time it would have increased the auditors' responsibility beyond that outlined in the decision of the London and General Bank (*Accountants' Law Reports,* 1895, p. 173), and reiterated by Mr. Justices Lindley, Kay, and Lopez in the appeal of the Kingston Cotton Mill Case (*Accountants' Law Reports,* 1896, p. 77). Under this New York proposal, the auditor was not to be excused even though he brought "to bear on the work ... that skill, care, and caution which a *reasonable competent,* and *careful,* and *cautious auditor* would use." Apparently as long as it was demonstrated that there were:

1. An omission of an essential fact,
2. A misstatement of an essential fact,
3. A third person suffering a loss because of this omission or misstatement,

then the auditor was liable to this third person, regardless of whether he was "reasonably competent, careful, and cautious," or whether he even knew of this third person's existence.

Thus, a trend can be traced in audit responsibility. The language in the English cases seems not as strong as that used in the Ultra Mares case, yet they attached somewhat more responsibility to the auditor than did the earlier decisions based upon the "prudency" concept. The Ultra Mares case narrowed the field of negligence and stressed the necessity of a professional attitude on the part of the public accountant. Further, it may be inferred that the New York State proposal represented a step before the Securities and Exchange Act of 1933, for the former would not have placed the auditor under as extended responsibility as did the Securities and Exchange Commission Act of 1933.

At this point, a pertinent question represents itself: even if the American auditor had not been placed under the responsibility attendant with the Securities and Exchange legislation, would not eventually the common law developed rules and precedents, and changes in the various state corporation laws, increased accountants' responsibilities to the point comparable to that of today? There seems to have been a more or less clearly defined trend in that direction. Certainly the New York proposal was not spontaneous but must have been somewhat representative of current philosophy, namely:

1. Interested persons outside the immediate management of a corporation should be presented with certain factual information;

2. Public auditors were in a position and had the ability necessary to secure this information and present it;

3. And, to assure themselves of a complete and satisfactory report, auditors were to assume added responsibilities and legal obligations.

One cannot of course say, even if the above were the philosophy of New Yorkers, that it was representative of American philosophy as a whole. Perhaps, however, it may be held that the New York viewpoint was somewhat indicative of the feelings throughout the corporate investing public. There were evidences that indicated the feeling was current and rather widespread within the corporate investing public for additional and objectively verified information, reference of the task to public accountants, and increased auditor responsibility. Principal among these evidences were:

1. Writers of semipopular literature were indicating the current financial practices (Professor William Z. Ripley's book, *Wall Street and Main Street* (1927), exemplified such literature).

2. Courts were beginning to recognize the almost complete alienation of ownership and control in our larger corporations and the need for third-party protection (although the courts did not say so directly, apparently they were attempting to set up protections for actual and potential shareholder-owners rather than attempting to extend the auditor's responsibility to third persons as a whole).

3. Concentration of the money market and the financial agencies in New York City.

4. In the early 1930s, there was much talk of federal incorporation and compulsory audits by independent accountants.

If it were true that such a feeling was current, and if this group were large enough that its pressure became apparent, then its common law trend toward increasing auditor responsibility would have become increased proportionally. However, the American public is an impatient one and seldom permits trends to develop fully. If it discovers what it considers to be an evil practice, regardless of whether it is a common or an unusual event, it must have a law enacted which evidences its disapproval and prescribes suitable legal action.

AMERICAN INSTITUTE AND NEW YORK EXCHANGE COOPERATION

Professor Ripley's book, *Wall Street and Main Street,* indicated that the financial practices of the period were faulty and that a corrective control should be brought to bear upon these practices. Ripley also suggested that these corrective measures, to be soundly enacted and administered, must be predicated upon more informative statements. Further, he expressed the hope that the stock exchange would support public accountants in fulfilling this need.

Accountants were impressed by Ripley's suggestions. As early as 1927, accountants attempted, through the American Institute, to have the New York Stock Exchange and the Institute appoint a joint committee to study the whole reporting problem. However, the Exchange was not ready at that time to enter into such a cooperative effort, and it was not until 1930 that J. M. B. Hoxsey, in the *Journal of Accountancy,* October 1930, suggested that such cooperation would prove helpful and that the Exchange would welcome the opportunity to make a joint study of the mutually interesting problem. Since this cooperation marked another historical incident before the Securities and Exchange Commission legislation, it seems appropriate at this time to analyze why this cooperation occurred in 1930, and to give the outcome of it.

As has been indicated, the failure of the American Institute and the New York Stock Exchange to appoint a joint committee in 1927 was because the cooperation lacked support among the members of the Exchange. Not only had the Institute's spokesman suggested that such cooperation would be mutually beneficial, but accountants evidenced, by their writings and discussions in the Institute's organization meetings, that they were dissatisfied with their auditing technique and its adaptability under varying situations, as well as with the general inadequacy of the 1917 audit program. This dissatisfaction was witnessed as early as 1925 and culminated in the study of the possibilities for engagement classification. The attempt to classify the auditor's work grew out of the exposures of current financial practices and the growing legal responsibility under the rules of law being developed by the courts. Although Mr. Wildman, chairman of the committee appointed by the Institute to study audit classification, and his committee suggested that there could be several audits with the recommendation that a standard certificate for each type be adopted, the members of the Institute were unwilling to accept the report. These members must have felt that if audit engagements were classified, this would stereotype auditing practice and leave only a restricted area in which the accountant could exercise his professional judgment. It is interesting to note that although accountants realized the inherent weakness in their techniques and the growing financial and economic complexities attendant with the concentration of capital in the corporate form of business enterprise, they were unwilling to accept self-imposed restrictions. Yet, in the thirties, they had to accept restrictions imposed by external groups.

Furthermore, their reaction to Mr. Wildman's committee report indicates that even if the American Institute and New York Stock Exchange had actually cooperated in 1927, the members of the Institute would have been unwilling to accept any drastic departure from commonly accepted auditing procedures. It is doubtful whether any constructive suggestions would have been accepted by the Institute's members, for accountants like all humanity have to be moved into action by forceful and dynamic circumstances rather than by seeing and accepting inevitable developments arising from historical trends. These forceful and dynamic circumstances were the reason for the Exchange, expressing through its spokesman Mr. Hoxsey, the feeling that active cooperation with the Institute would be beneficial.

Perhaps the stock market crash in 1929 had influenced the change in the Exchange's disposition toward cooperation with the Institute, but this must not be overstressed as a causal factor. In 1930, the Exchange felt that the aftermath of the crash was but a temporary recession and that recovery was "just around the corner." This belief was based upon:

1. The 1922 price-structure break had been of short duration.

2. Since financing had shifted to the raising of needed capital by selling securities rather than borrowing from bankers, bankers had been the major source of capital before 1922, management would not be pressed for repayment of loans, and, therefore, there would be no further depressing of the market by the dumping of inventories to satisfy the banker demands. In other words, because of the absence of this forced inventory liquidation the price structure would regain lost ground more quickly than it had after the 1922 break.

3. During the prosperous 20s, it was accepted as a fact (and the philosophy remained long into the '30s) that we had mastered the art of production—highest production per capita, cheapness of production per unit output, and larger purchasing power per worker. This mastery of production and the distribution of larger purchasing power to the workers, whose marginal valuation of their income was relatively high, would make the return of prosperity inevitable.

4. Historically, before the break in 1929, wholesale prices for a number of years had been relatively stable, with a trend toward a permanently higher level. This stability of the price structure introduced the philosophy that we had overcome the economics of price; therefore the break in 1929, being counter to this trend, would soon be overcome.

Probably the strongest activating force was the Kreuger and Toll crash. Here was the dynamic incident that focused attention upon the evils possible under the holding-subsidiary form of corporate enterprise, in spite of frequent audits by competent public accountants.

Mr. Ivar Kreuger's technique was one of retaining managerial control in a way that the authority delegated to subsidiary managements was such that no person, outside of Kreuger, knew about the economic entity. Moreover, by skillful manipulation between these subsidiaries and the restriction of audits to legal entities, he was able to conceal these dexterously executed frauds.[4]

The investigation which followed the Kreuger and Toll crash made it apparent that these manipulations would not have been possible had the examination covered the economic entity rather than being restricted to the legal entities, or had the audits of the legal entities been correlated in such a manner that a complete review of the economic entity would have been possible. Finally, many of the transactions carried on among and between the subsidiaries and the parent company, as well as the verifying and reporting technique used by public accountants for this company, came under critical analysis. The transactions accepted by accountants, and the verifying and reporting techniques utilized by them, cannot be said to be representative of what were considered then to be the best practices; but they were acceptable as approved departures from auditing standards.

This departure from professional standards is a case at point where accountants based their concepts upon legal doctrine rather than upon those peculiarly adaptable to their auditing and reporting techniques. Legal limitations were never intended by the courts or legislatures to be used as auditing or accounting standards. This use of legal limitations as if they are auditing prescriptions is denied by the mere fact that a standard should never be expressed in a negative sense. A standard to be classed as such should express what is the better solution, rather than what is not acceptable. Moreover, auditing, particularly, is in essence a research technique, and research cannot be directed by legal prescriptions or concepts.

Finally, the auditor, since he is conducting a financial and economic review, should not be limited to examining only a legal entity if the development of his report is dependent in a large part upon the authentication of an investment in a subsidiary, or in those cases where a large number of intercompany transactions indicate an audit of these transfers. One cannot set up any rules regulating the extension of auditing technique; materiality should be the governing factor, as in all research. It must be noted that during this period, accountants sometimes deviated from what was then considered a standard for auditing practice and relied upon legal acquittal even though professionally they retained their ethical responsibilities. Not only were they accepting practices which afterward proved to be faulty, but one finds in the current literature of the period reasons why these practices were not only acceptable but preferable to the commonly prescribed auditing and accounting methodologies. Accountants, however, cannot be too strongly criticized; their fees were limited, the clients were overly persuasive, and even they were not impregnable to the economic and financial philosophy prevalent during the thirties.

Turning, finally, to the results of the cooperation between the American Institute and the New York Stock Exchange, there were at least three important outcomes and, since they have been currently discussed and are well appreciated, listing them seems sufficient:

1. Agreement on five broad accounting principles.

2. A new certificate in which there was a complete separation of fact and opinion.

3. The issue by the Stock Exchange of new rules for listing.

SUMMARY

Accounting has developed from an extremely simplified memorandum technique into a complex recording and reporting methodology. As the activities of the commercial world and its economic form became more complex, new and expanded services were demanded from accountants. The whole history of accounting and the evolving of its concepts, as well as the attainment of a professional status, has been one of development in response to these new and greater demands by businessmen, bankers, stockholders, and the courts. As accounting has accepted these added recording and reporting tasks, likewise its members have been forced to accept greater legal as well as moral responsibilities. If the accounting profession had been keenly aware of the ever-increasing number of accounting services which it was offering and its clients were accepting, and that there was a synonymous growth of legal and professional responsibility, as well as a historical trend, leading up to the Securities and Exchange Commission legislation, the members of the accounting profession would have been less startled by the enactment. They would have appreciated the fact that the Act of 1933 was but a culmination or the capstone to a pyramidical growth of historical antecedents.

NOTES

1. During a prosperity era the financial malpractices usually arise out of corporate creation or expansion. In a depression era, however, these financial malpractices are attendant with the consolidation or liquidation of corporate entities.

2. See page 80 for the reasons for this shift.

3. In many instances corporate management shifted from bankers to bondholders for its capital. Theoretically the relationship was still one of trustee and beneficiary, but practically the bondholder's position was closely synonymous to that of a stockholder.

4. For a more complete expose, the reader is referred to "Hearings before a subcommittee of the Committee on Banking and Currency of the United States Senate," Seventy-second Congress, Second Session, Part 4. The testimony of George O. May on pages 1259 to 1274 should be of particular interest to the accountant, especially pages 1267 and 1270.

SEVEN

Accountants' Financial Statements and Fact-Finding in the Law of Corporate Regulation

HOMER KRIPKE

School of Law, New York University

With the advent of public corporations, the accountant became involved in assessing the rights of the various classes of corporate investors and creditors. Kripke explores the conflict between legal and accounting principles as it relates to the determination of financial disclosure. The author also discusses the concepts of value and earnings as influenced by the historical cost accounting basis determination of income. He calls for a capitalization of anticipated earning power. Kripke subsequently revised his views on cost versus value in "The SEC, the Accountants, Some Myths and Some Realities." NYUL Rev. *45:1151 (1970) and in his 1979 book,* The SEC and Corporate Disclosure: Regulation in Search of a Purpose.

The accountant, traditionally portrayed as a modest clerk perched on a high stool before a ponderous ledger, has emerged in recent years as a man of professional stature with a unique importance in the business community. Three broad stages mark the accountant's evolution from scrivener to professional man. In the first stage, he appeared as the bookkeeper for a sole proprietor, recording such prosaic and incontrovertible facts as arrival and shipment of goods, receipts and disbursements of cash, and accounts receivable and payable. In the second stage, he was the servant of business management, digging out the vital statistics of the enterprise for its officers and directors and their commercial bankers. Today the accountant has reached a third stage in his development: He now deals with the financial statements of the large publicly owned corporations which have assumed major importance in our economy.

The gigantic aggregations of capital which these corporations bring together have precipitated two problems of peculiar significance in the evolution of the accountant's work. First, this capital has been invested in land, buildings, and heavy machinery, items enduring for many years — unlike the short-lived items of cash, receivables, and inventories with which the bookkeeper was once concerned. Such long-term assets require allocation of depreciation expense over their life expectancies and necessitate valuation at times when value may be far removed from cost. Second, these large aggregations of capital, collected from diverse

Reprinted by permission of the Yale Law Journal Co. and Fred B. Rothman and Co. from the *Yale Law Journal* vol. 50, pp. 1180–1205, 1941.

classes of investors, present the problem of accounting for the contributions and of defining the respective rights of each class—a problem never faced by the bookkeeper of simpler business units. Thus, the accountant has been thrust into the role of arbiter: He must demarcate the rights of the various groups interested in and affected by the corporate enterprise—common stockholders, preferred stockholders, bondholders or debenture holders, and, in the case of public utilities, consumers. Under state and federal security legislation, the accountant is, in effect, obligated to protect prospective investors against promoters, underwriters, and existing investors, and to afford existing investors security against corporate insiders. These new burdens stem primarily from the fact that the application of many legal rules governing the interrelations between these interests largely depends on business facts which are classified in terms of accounting concepts.

Many such legal rules are found in the modern law of corporate distributions to security holders. Dividends, for example, may be paid only out of "net profits" or out of an "excess of assets over liabilities plus capital stock," both accounting concepts. Likewise, the classification of stock as par or no par, the use of a low stated value with a high paid-in surplus, the use of a high par value or of a low par value combined with a high paid-in surplus—all these questions depend on legal or strategic considerations which arise out of the same accounting concepts.[1] Again, the payment of dividends on certain preferred stocks or the payment of interest on the corporate income bond is dependent on the accountant's determination of whether income has been earned. Similarly, the status of bonds as legal investments for savings banks and trust funds turns on whether the corporate income has afforded the necessary earnings coverages.[2] Finally, the "voluntary reorganization" frequently takes the form of a "quasi-reorganization," which is nothing more than a manipulation of accounts. The extent to which such an accounting manipulation may legally occur, the extent to which it may have legal consequences, and the extent to which it must be accompanied by legal safeguards are some of the most rapidly developing problems of corporation law.[3]

Accounting concepts are no less significant when they appear as devices of control in the public regulation of business. Apparently, the Interstate Commerce Commission has made the right to issue securities under Section 20 (a) of the Interstate Commerce Act dependent on rules of accounting.[4] In order to protect investors, the Securities and Exchange Commission has promoted standardization and reform of accounting practice,[5] not merely because accounting manipulation is characteristic of fraudulent stock-selling schemes,[6] but also because accounting conventions underlie many of the business facts upon whose disclosure the federal system of investor protection is based. So complete is the permeation of accounting concepts into the business fabric that prescription of uniform systems of accounts is one of the most common regulatory devices in the public control of enterprise.

It will be the purpose of this article to explore two questions which appear to be basic to the future cooperation of lawyers and accountants in corporation law generally and in the domain of public regulation in particular. The first is whether accounting principles which are used to interpret business facts have independent validity in themselves or are merely conventional techniques which should be adapted to the disclosure of legally operative facts. An important aspect of this controversy is the question of whether financial statements should adhere to a cost basis, or should attempt to disclose value, a factor more important than cost in the solution of many legal problems. The second question to be explored is whether, assuming that the financial statements do show legally significant facts with respect to an enterprise, that enterprise and the persons with whom it deals, including public agencies, are bound by the facts thus disclosed or can successfully contend that the operative facts in issue differ materially from the facts disclosed by the accounts.

A. FINANCIAL STATEMENTS AND CONFLICTS BETWEEN LEGAL AND ACCOUNTING PRINCIPLES

The literature of legal-accounting problems is replete with discussion of the extent to which accountants need recognize legal rules in the preparation of financial statements. Reasoning purely *a priori,* the solution of this question seems to depend on the answer to the somewhat philosophical question of whether accounting is a science or an art. If it is a science in the sense that its principles have external validity, these principles should not be distorted to meet the exigencies of man-made law. If, however, accounting is an art, a technique, it ought to be adapted to the structure of law which governs the enterprises for which the accountants account.

Leading accountants recognize that accounting is an art based on conventions — not immutable principles — which are justified by their utility proved in practice, not by their truth proved scientifically. Thus the committee on terminology, American Institute of Accountants, recently said:

> *Initially, accounting rules are mere postulates derived from experience and reason. Only after they have proved useful, and become generally accepted, do they become principles of accounting. . . . An accounting principle is not a principle in the sense that it admits of no variation, nor in the sense that it cannot conflict with other principles.*[7]

Most accountants acknowledge that accounting involves such substantial elements of judgment that two equally reputable and competent accountants may disagree widely as to the proper income statements and balance sheets of the same enterprise. Such matters of choice and discretion as the allocation of expenditures to capital account or to expense, the amortization or the writing off of debt discount and expense, the use of "last-in, first-out" or "last-in, last-out" as a basis for inventory valuation, and the selection of depreciation formulas allow much latitude to corporate managements and their accountants in shaping financial statements.

Nonetheless, many accountants argue that this selective process need not be controlled by applicable legal considerations.[8] Lawyers, conversely, are quite convinced that accountants must heed legal rules[9] — and some accountants side with the lawyers.[10] This conflict can best be illustrated in terms of the example which is most discussed in the literature: the accounting treatment of the acquisition of a corporation's own shares. The most prevalent accounting treatment is, or at least was, to show the cost of the shares acquired as a deduction from the capital account, on the theory that reduction of capital is the practical and economic consequence of the purchase. But most modern writers now recognize that, without formal legal steps, the stated capital of the company is not reduced by the acquisition; the legal effect of the transaction is to reduce surplus, and any form of accounting which fails to present the legal realities is misleading, and may impose liability on the officers and directors[11] — and even the accountants.[12] Accordingly, accounting practice is moving toward a presentation of treasury stock as a deduction from surplus, or from the sum of stated capital and surplus.

Such an attitude apparently assumes that a primary responsibility of accounting is to state correctly the corporate legal obligations with respect to the capital and surplus accounts, and particularly, not to state earned surplus in an amount greater than is legally available for dividends.[13] This aspect of accounting responsibility has not often been articulated because, ordinarily, this function of the accountant is automatically performed by a statement of income and surplus accounts according to established accounting conventions. But there is other evidence of its recognition in practice.[14]

While the legal situation should not, therefore, be ignored, accountants who insist that the law cannot justify departures from accounting principles in financial statements do have a plausible argument: The meaning of economic facts in a financial statement is a function of the conventions on which that statement is based. Even though these conventions have not achieved complete uniformity, a certain degree of standardization already achieved has made for the ready analysis of financial statements. Consequently, if variations in law from state to state were permitted to destroy the existing uniformity of conventions, the present utility of financial statements would be gravely impaired. Any departure from standard conventions, whether or not justified under state law, may be deceptive even with the clearest explanation and may render the financial statements useless as a basis for making comparisons with other enterprises.

Without attempting finally to decide whether accounting principles have such independent validity or utility that financial statements may be prepared in reliance upon them without regard to legal considerations which might point to different treatment, it seems probable that there is a compromise course which is preferable and practicable in almost every case. Where the law is such that financial statements prepared according to accounting principles do not reveal legally significant information, accounting techniques permit compromise by a presentation which discloses both the legal facts and the facts as they would be stated under currently recognized accounting principles. In practice, such techniques are evolving at many points. Thus, a short time after a quasi-reorganization has been legally accomplished, an enterprise may have an earned surplus legally available for dividends, although by ordinary accounting standards the results of operations over its life span may have left no surplus available. In such a case both the legal situation and the deviation from basic accounting standards may be revealed by dating the earned surplus account subsequent to the reorganization.[15] Again, where preferred stock with a very small par value is issued at a price which creates a large capital surplus — the liquidating preference approximating the entire consideration received by the corporation — the accounting convention of carrying stock at par value in the balance sheet would not disclose a possible equitable restriction on the availability for dividends of the surplus which arises out of the disparity between the par value and the liquidating preference. Hence, the better practice is to supplement the standard accounting presentation with a disclosure of the amount of the liquidating preference coupled with a legal opinion as to the availability of dividends.[16] Again, in states where revaluation surplus is legally available for dividends, such a surplus can be displayed by a technique which reveals both the accountant's traditional cost-less-depreciation basis and the appraised value reflected on the corporation's books. Where dividends may be paid out of earnings for the current and next preceding years without regard to the existence of a deficit,[17] surplus and deficit accounts may be presented so as to show clearly both the overall deficit and the earnings available for dividends for the current and preceding years. The solution in each case lies in the development of accounting techniques which disclose both the legal status of the capital and surplus accounts and their status according to accepted accounting principles. Both aspects of this disclosure are of fundamental importance to investors.[18] Accountants who insist upon presenting their own principles without regard to the legal considerations lose sight of the function of accounting as an art designed to tell people what they need to know.

B. FINANCIAL STATEMENTS BASED ON THE COST CONVENTION AND LEGAL PROBLEMS OF VALUATION

Extensive controversy has revolved around the contention that accountants are not revealing legally significant facts because they persist in adhering to their convention of carrying fixed assets on the balance sheet at cost. In view of the importance of the cost convention in the structure of the accountant's financial statements, this contention puts at issue the ultimate utility of financial statements in the solution of legal problems:

1. Nature of financial statements based on the cost convention. It is commonly assumed that the accountant's balance sheet is an instantaneous photograph of the financial condition of a business at a given point of time, and that his income (or profit-and-loss) statement is a picture of the results of business operations between two such points of time. But such generalizations are descriptive, not analytic; they distinguish the accountant's statements from each other, but indicate nothing specific about their respective contents.

For present purposes, the outstanding characteristic of the conventional balance sheet is the use — in general — of cost as a basis for recording fixed assets, with appropriate deductions for depreciation. Broadly speaking, no appreciation or decline in asset value is recorded until realized by a sale. A reserve for depreciation is shown for depreciable items; the annual accretion to this reserve has its counterpart in an annual charge for depreciation expense in the income statement to record the *pro tanto* exhaustion of the utility of the assets during the year. The sum of the annual charges during the life of the asset will theoretically equal cost less salvage value. Thus, the successive income statements distribute the entire net cost as expense over the life of the asset, and the depreciation reserve is eventually sufficient to retire the asset from the balance sheet. It follows that the balance sheet at the end of any accounting period shows the portion of cost which has not yet been charged to operations, and does not purport to show value. Consequently, the characterization of a balance sheet as a "statement of condition" is misleading if that phrase is taken to mean a representation as to value.

Because the balance sheet based on the cost convention does not in fact show value, its advocates have been perennially criticized. Although the proponents of balance sheets based on value gained ground in the twenties,[19] by the middle thirties their gains had been irretrievably lost, partly by reason of the gross errors and abuses which had occurred in write-ups and write-downs of value for income-puffing and security-selling purposes.[20] Consequently, the cost convention remains the fundamental concept of accounting.

The accountant is not necessarily wrong, however, in adhering to the cost principle, and he need not seek justification on the unconvincing grounds that cost is the best and only nonspeculative evidence of value available,[21] or that cost is "going concern value."[22] A better justification is that value is not an accounting concept[23] and the accountant's job is not one of valuation. His function is to account for the funds expended in the business. To him an asset used in production or distribution is merely a prepaid expense like insurance or rent; balance-sheet assets (other than cash and its equivalents) are merely records of costs incurred and not yet charged to operations.[24]

2. The utility in the law of balance sheets based on cost. But the question still remains as to whether the use of the cost convention rather than value in the balance sheet has not impaired the usefulness of the accountant's work for many legal purposes. Both law and accounting make use of certain important concepts — net worth, assets, capital, income, surplus, depreciation, and the like. Consequently, it is frequently assumed and asserted that the law follows accounting rules.[25] Yet the balance sheet often is not directly useful in the solution of legal problems, because the meaning of familiar terms in the balance sheet based on the cost convention is not the meaning which the law gives to them.[26]

a. *Dividends.* Weiner and Bonbright[27] have pointed out that legal rules concerning dividends have evolved in American statutes and cases in two major patterns. Under the "net profits rule," dividends may be paid only out of earned but undistributed profits. Under the "capital impairment rule," dividends may be paid out of any excess of the value of assets over liabilities plus capital stock. In other words, under the latter rule dividends may be paid only if capital will not thereby be impaired.[28] Thus, the "net profits rule" places particular emphasis on events which the accountant records in his income statements — the net results of operations over the history of an enterprise. In contrast, the "capital impairment rule" apparently emphasizes the value of an enterprise at a given point of time — the information supposed to be revealed by the accountant's balance sheet as traditionally understood. Applied literally, the "capital impairment rule" would take account of unrealized appreciation; the "net profits rule" would not.

Although recognizing that the status of the law was uncertain, Weiner and Bonbright were of the opinion that the courts have not realized that their two verbalizations embody separate rules having different consequences. These writers contended that the courts have really assimilated the two rules into one, that of net profits.[29] This has been accomplished by adopting for dividend purposes the accountant's rule of "valuing" assets — a rule which refuses to value assets on any basis other than cost[30] — with the result that the surplus account contains only those realized earnings which are recognized by the accountant. To the extent that the courts in fact follow this standard, no matter how verbalized, the accountant's income statements, summarized in the earned surplus caption of the balance sheet, guide the lawyer in respect to the legality of dividend payments.

But, in a recent New York case,[31] a statute framed in "capital impairment" terms was held to require determination of value at the time of each dividend declaration rather than acceptance of the accountant's book figures. Other cases likewise suggest that value rather than the accountant's figures may be decisive in dividend litigation, particularly before judges unfamiliar with these mixed legal and accounting concepts.[32] Under such decisions, the accountant's traditional balance sheet founded on the cost convention is of slight value in dividend law. And confusion of theories regarding the availability of dividends will persist unless lawyers and accountants are careful to recognize the differences in meaning which they respectively attribute to the same terms.

b. *Value in public utility regulation.* So long as *Smyth* v. *Ames*[33] survives,[34] public utility rate regulation will purportedly be concerned with value, not with cost. Hence, financial statements founded on systems of accounts prescribed by regulatory bodies and based on cost perforce cannot control in such litigation. As a result, a public utility executive was able to say:

> *The most unfortunate feature of regulation in this country is that the book values*
> *of operating companies are totally unrelated to the legal values under which these*
> *companies operate, sell their electricity, and do their business. In other words,*
> *you have got a value on your books that has nothing to do with the income you*
> *earn.*[35]

Cost is nonetheless one of the "elements" of value recognized in *Smyth* v. *Ames,* and state commissions tend to give it as much weight as they dare in rate base determinations.[36] But to the extent that the law is still based on value rather than cost, the accountant's financial statements will play a minor role in rate litigation.

The specific issue of the amount of depreciation, like the general problem of the rate base, is treated by the courts in terms of value rather than accounting language. For the accountant a reserve for depreciation, in harmony with his other book figures, shows the extent to which cost has been amortized by charges to earnings, not the extent to which value has diminished.[37] But it is obvious that a balance sheet in which the reserve for depreciation reflects amortization of cost will not be conclusive in matters involving depreciation in value.

It was to be expected, therefore, that in determining accrued depreciation for purposes of fixing the rate base the Supreme Court would reject formulas for amortizing cost[38] or the book accounts for depreciation reserve,[39] and would lean toward the "observational method," under which the appropriate depreciation reserve is determined by inspecting the property to compare its condition and value with that of a new plant.[40] Hence, so long as the rate base depends on value, the litigated cases will discuss depreciation in terms of value, not cost.[41] and the accountant's balance sheet will be of little assistance.

c. *Regulation of security issues under the Public Utility Holding Company Act.* In the light of the limited importance of the cost concept in the dividend and rate-fixing situations, it might be expected that balance sheets would be given scant attention in determining the soundness of security issues, where safety lies in value, not in cost. But experience has proved the contrary to be true. Recent opinions of the Securities and Exchange Commission under the Public Utility Holding Company Act of 1935 illustrate the persistence of value terminology in balance-sheet analysis, with resulting semantic difficulties, even among persons who know that balance sheets record cost, not value. The Commission has consistently found it necessary to eliminate appraisal write-ups from property accounts, in order to reduce these accounts, and the balance sheet in general, to a cost basis.[42] This policy reflects recognition of the principle that "the purpose of accounting is to account, not to present opinions of value."[43] Undoubtedly, the Commission realizes that a balance sheet stated at cost does not show the present values of properties. Nevertheless, in considering applications and declarations under sections 6, 7, and 11 of the act,[44] the Commission has used language which seems to assume that property accounts thus adjusted to cost indicate value for the purpose of determining the soundness of security issues.

A recent example is *Community Power and Light Company,*[45] a case involving not only the issuance of securities but the question of whether sufficient value existed to entitle common shareholders to participate in a reorganization. In its opinion, the Commission first pointed out that on the basis of *book* figures there was an equity for the common stock; then, by eliminating revaluation write-ups, it said that on the basis of *cost* figures, there was no equity for this stock. From this part of the Commission's opinion an uninformed reader might reasonably assume that book figures corrected to show cost were significant in determining the existence of an equity; otherwise, he might perceive no purpose in the elimination of the write-ups. But, in contrast to its own demonstration that there appeared to be no value by the test of cost, the Commission concluded that the existence of residual earnings for the common stock demonstrated that there was sufficient value. If, however, on the basis of earning power, there was an excess of value over cost, the existence of such an excess tended to support the company's revaluation—thus invalidating the Commission's assumption that these write-ups had to be eliminated for valuation purposes.

Newport Electric Corporation[46] and *Public Service Company of Colorado*[47] similarly appear to have used book values as indicia of value, with the not surprising result that the conclusion based on book value was contradicted by more apposite evidence. The Commission said in the *Newport* case:

> *The common stock equity in the net tangible property per books amounted to approximately $575,000.... On these bases the proposed price of $1,756,725 for the common stock appears high but in relation to the earnings record of the company... it appears not unreasonable.*[48]

And in the *Public Service Company* case the Commission said:

> *Declarant's record of earnings and dividends... indicates that the equity is more substantial than might appear by merely subtracting total intercompany appreciation from book figures and comparing the difference with the face value of securities to be held by the public.*[49]

It is possible that the Commission, or some of its members, actually intend to hold that public utility property should be capitalized only to the amount of its book value after squeezing out write-ups. This would accord with a position taken by some state commissions.[50] It might be said in justification of such a position that if and when *Smyth* v. *Ames* is finally overruled, historical cost or some similar test may become the measure of rate base. If so, rates will be fixed so as to earn a fair return on cost; consequently, cost will tend to approximate value.[51] Finally, it may be argued that if any value above cost resulting from excess earning capacity is shown on the balance sheet, it is preferable that it be shown under some such caption as "goodwill," rather than concealed by purported revaluation of the physical assets themselves.

Up to the present time this question seems never to have been squarely presented to the

Commission, partly because many of the revaluations recorded on utility company books in the twenties were arbitrary or based on intrasystem transactions, and consequently are not now seriously defended as estimates of value.[52] Whether insufficient asset coverage on the basis of cost figures could be obviated by proof of higher enterprise value has not become an acute question. The present writer, however, hazards the guess that when the Securities and Exchange Commission is squarely presented with such a situation, it will not fail to recognize that a balance sheet based on cost is a record, not a statement of financial condition, and as such does not in itself show the value upon which the safety of a security issue depends. It is hoped that the Commission will soon abandon the language which treats cost as direct evidence of value, and state more precisely the real reason for its discussion of original cost in opinions dealing with security issuance — namely, that the influence of original cost on the rate base may affect value.

Once it is clearly recognized that book values do not purport to be representations of present values, much of the motive for recording appraisal values on corporate books will be eliminated. Thus, it will no longer be necessary to use appraisal write-ups "to balance security issues."[53] In one sense, the write-up has never been necessary to "balance" an issue sold for cash, for the issue is balanced by its proceeds, or the property in which the proceeds are invested. Of course, the "balancing" refers to past practice of writing up the property mortgaged as security for a bond issue to the point where it appeared to be adequate security, or to the practice of writing up the total assets to the point where there appeared to be an adequate margin of equity investment to safeguard an unsecured debt or preferred stock. But only so long as balance-sheet figures are regarded as estimates of value is "balancing" necessary. When it is realized that they are based on cost, not value, the motive to distort the accounting records for valuation purposes will in large measure disappear.[54]

3. The cost convention in the ascertainment of enterprise value. What has been said thus far demonstrates that, inasmuch as the accountant's balance sheet is based on cost, it does not adequately answer legal questions concerned with value. But this does not mean that accountants are not justified in adhering to the cost convention. Paradoxically enough, financial statements are more useful in determining enterprise value when they reflect asset cost than when they reflect asset value.

It is apparent that a balance sheet in which the individual assets are stated on a cost basis rather than on a value basis affords no guide to enterprise value.[55] But this would be equally true of a balance sheet which purported to show the values of the assets separately. George O. May has well stated the reasoning:

> *Turning now to the objection that if balance sheets do not reflect values they ought to do so, because that is what the investor is interested in—a number of minor exceptions to the position thus asserted might be taken, but the answer to the objection is that ... the figures would be of no real interest to the investor if they could be ascertained. ... what the investor or speculator is interested in is the value of the business as a whole, and that is dependent mainly on what it will produce in the future and is not determinable by any purely accounting process. Not only so, but if the accountant were to assume the task of valuing the busi-*

ness as a whole, he would have met the assumed need, and it would be entirely superogatory for him to attempt to allocate that value as between the different assets of the business.[56]

May concludes that the greatest service which the accountant can render to a person desiring to know value is to shed light on earning capacity, and that this can best be done by ignoring fluctuations in the values of capital assets. This thesis has a sound economic basis: enterprise value is a summation of the present worth of future anticipated earnings.[57] As this fact gains recognition, the income statement becomes the account to which the investor attaches the greatest significance.[58] Emphasis in accounting, therefore, shifts from accuracy of balance-sheet account totals to accuracy of income recording.

Accounting procedure will reflect income most accurately if it ignores fluctuations in the value of assets. A fixed asset which is not for sale, but to be used in production, cannot produce income except as its use in production creates a flow of assets back to the enterprise. Therefore, no income results from appreciation in value of production goods, except insofar as that appreciation is reflected in the prices realized from finished goods sold.[59]

It is sometimes argued that since the effective price determinants are current rather than historical costs, current costs should be shown on the books. It may be conceded that in a competitive market current replacement costs rather than historical costs of individual producers determine supply,[60] and that supply and demand determine price. Nevertheless, it does not follow that individual producers should revalue their assets at present replacement costs so that their books may reflect the effective price determinants. On the contrary, their books are kept to measure their own income,[61] which is determined by excess of price over the costs which they have incurred, not the excess of price over costs which determine price.[62] If a particular producer's plant cannot be replaced except for a price greatly in excess of its original cost, he is a low-cost producer, and his margin of price over cost will be great. Conversely, if his costs are substantially higher than present replacement costs, he will have little or no margin of price over cost. His position as a high- or low-cost producer is reflected by his maintenance of gross-profit margins above or below average margins in the industry over a period of years. For his own purposes and those of the investors in his business, the important facts are the costs he charges to the sale of his product, not the costs of the group of producers as a whole, or the costs of the marginal producer. Until the fixed assets are sold, any rise or decline in their value is important only insofar as it is reflected in the increase or decrease of income over the periods in which the cost of such assets is amortized. If, on the other hand, a producer revalues his assets in an attempt to show the effective price determinants, amortization of the amount recorded on the books will overstate his real costs and understate his true income,[63] or conversely, understate his real costs and overstate his true income.

Therefore, from the standpoint of accurate income reporting, the most useful income statements are those which are based on cost, and which are supplemented by balance sheets showing costs not yet charged to operations. Of course, this conclusion does not mean that earnings statements based on cost provide a direct guide to the value of the enterprise once a capitalization rate is determined. Value is the present worth of *future* anticipated earnings, and past earnings are significant to the investment analyst only insofar as they help predict future earnings.[64] But the accountant is not an analyst and cannot be expected to supply all the information on which the analyst bases his conclusions as to value. Just as the analyst must adjust past results in the light of forecasts and trends in demands, prices, competitive conditions, and the nonrecurrence of certain items, so he must adjust past earnings as guides to future earnings in the light of probable changes in the costs of the particular enterprise. Among these changes may be the replacement of low-cost old plant with high-cost new plant, which will require greater charges to operations. For that reason it may be that the accountant will want to supply information as to replacement values of present plant as footnotes or collateral notations on financial statements, or the management may want to supply information in its published reports outside the financial statements. Similarly, the management for its own purposes in determining pricing policies may want to have supplementary records showing replacement costs rather than actual costs. All such considerations, however, are incidental to the fundamental point that any estimate of the value of an enterprise must begin with the record of past earnings, which can be shown only if the financial statements reveal cost.

The ultimate conclusion is that accountants who persist in retaining the cost convention are not thereby ignoring the need of the lawyer for information as to value, but are in fact supplying the basic information from which value can be determined. But, of course, value determination must remain an inexact science so long as possibilities of conflicting results exist within the limits of accepted accounting principles.

THE CONCLUSIVENESS OF THE ACCOUNTS IN THE DETERMINATION OF LEGALLY OPERATIVE FACTS

Even though the conclusion has been reached that a financial statement should be drawn to show legally operative facts, the problem of resolving conflicts which arise from the actual or potential existence of inconsistent financial statements for the same enterprise still remains.

The possibility of such inconsistency arises primarily because accountants do exercise judgment in suitable conventions and in interpreting financial transactions. Not only may accountants at large differ in these matters but, from the same facts, a particular accountant may derive different conclusions shaped by the particular interest of the person for whom he is preparing the financial statement. For example, the commercial banker will be interested in the ability of an enterprise to liquidate assets quickly, the executive in matters of internal management, the investor in long-term prospect; the accountant will wish to interpret the facts so as to direct the emphasis accordingly.[65]

Possibilities of diversity also arise out of the fact that public regulatory agencies may prescribe different conventions for their several purposes. The courts recognize that the power to regulate accounting goes beyond mere prescription of the formal titles and breakdown of the accounts, and extends to dictation of the appropriate interpretation of particular transactions. Thus, the Supreme Court has recognized the power of the Interstate Commerce Commission to require a railroad to charge to earnings the entire cost of a railroad line newly replaced and to capitalize the cost of replacement, instead of charging to capital the difference between the cost of the improvement and the cost of the line replaced.[66] Similarly, the Court has upheld an order of the Interstate Commerce Commission requiring a railroad to classify its coal mines as property not used for carrier purposes rather than as property used for carrier purposes.[67]

Income taxation creates still a third opportunity for diversity. The concept of income embodied in the revenue acts is not always identical with the economic,[68] or accounting,[69] or corporation-law concept. Thus the recent undistributed-profits tax penalized the failure to distribute income, distribution of which might have been unlawful under state law.[70] Likewise, depreciation may be taken on one basis for tax purposes and on another for general purposes. Again, tax law may not recognize deductions of certain expenses which lawyers and accountants recognize as proper charges to income.[71] As a consequence of these situations the taxpayer must frequently keep two or more sets of books or memoranda accounts reconciling the books with the tax reports.

Where financial statements potentially conflict, problems of adjustment arise. Where there is no public control of accounting, the key to the question of the conclusiveness of statements appearing in a corporation's books is the evidentiary rule concerning admissions.[72] But where a public regulatory agency has prescribed the accounts involved, the problem may become one of determining the effect of action by one agency on another agency. Much litigation seems to have settled on one point at least: Taxing authorities, operating under statutory schemes for determining taxable income, are not bound by the accounting prescribed by other agencies. Thus, the Commissioner of Internal Revenue need not base his computations of taxable net income on accounting permitted or prescribed by the Interstate Commerce Commission,[73] a state public-service commission,[74] or a national bank examiner.[75] Likewise, a state is not required to base its system of railroad taxation on income as determined by the Interstate Commerce Commission's classification of accounts.[76] And it seems reasonable to assume that this rule with respect to tax problems will apply to all other situations outside the field controlled by the particular agency which prescribes the accounting.[77]

The problems of conclusiveness of accounts prescribed by a regulatory agency with regard to matters within its own jurisdiction are more complex. On this point the Supreme Court cases appear confused. Recently, the Court seems to have indicated that the financial condition of a company as portrayed by mandatory accounts is not necessarily conclusive in the determination of regulatory questions. This attitude is best illustrated in *Norfolk & Western Railway Company* v. *United States*,[78] where the railway sought to enjoin enforcement of an Interstate Commerce Commission order requiring it to classify its coal mines as property not used for carrier purposes in its accounts. The Court said:

> *With great earnestness the appellant characterizes the order as in several aspects a denial of due process....* But this is to ignore the fact that the order is one touching accounting merely; *that before any rate base can be ascertained or any basis of recapture determined the carrier will be entitled to a full hearing as to what property shall be included; and not until the Commission excludes the assets in question from the calculation may the carrier assert the infliction of injury to its rights of property....*
>
> *We are not convinced by the assertion that the necessary effect of classifying the mines as noncarrier properties is to exclude them from consideration as capital in the issuance of securities*... the mere accounting classification can conclude neither the Commission nor the appellant upon the hearing of an application

under § 20a(2)....

Appellant also characterizes the Commission's action as a denial of the legal right of the railway to adopt fair and reasonable methods of accounting.... But there is no right to a particular form of accounting as such.[79]

In *State Corporation Commission of Kansas* v. *Wichita Gas Company,*[80] the Commission prohibited gas distributing companies from recording on their books as expenses any payments made to an affiliated pipeline company in excess of thirty cents per thousand cubic feet. A three-judge federal court enjoined enforcement of the order. The Supreme Court, reversing the lower court, held that, irrespective of the merits of the order, no injunction should have issued unless the company could prove irreparable injury. Since the findings and directions of the Commission were held to be merely legislative in character, designed only to secure information[81] and thus not binding on the companies in subsequent rate proceedings, no present injury was found and the injunction was vacated. This case indicates clearly that accounting orders are not conclusive in subsequent rate litigation.

Neither the Supreme Court nor any other courts have recognized that these two cases apparently abandoned a position which the Court had earlier assumed in one of its leading cases on accounting, *Kansas City Southern Railway Company* v. *United States.*[82] In that case the railway sued to enjoin enforcement of a regulation of the Interstate Commerce Commission which would have required it to charge to earnings the entire cost of a railroad line which had been recently replaced. The railway showed that it had been cheaper to build a new line than to improve the old line and that, if the old line had been improved, the entire cost of that improvement could have been charged to capital, with no charge to operating expenses. Since, under the accounting procedure prescribed, the railway's books showed no operating income during the year in which the replacements were made, the railway could declare no dividends for that year on its preferred stock, which was noncumulative. Moreover, this regulation prevented the railway from increasing its capital account by the full cost of the improvements to balance the bond liability incurred to finance the improvements.

But the regulation was upheld against the contention that it impaired substantive rights. The Court did not question that substantive rights were involved; on the contrary, it definitely assumed that the prescribed accounting treatment was conclusive for all purposes, and precluded the payment of dividends. It said:

> *The preferred stockholders as such are not before the court, and this is not a proper occasion for determining their rights. Supposing, however, that the enforcement of the accounting system does require them to forego their current dividends, we do not concede that this amounts to an unlawful taking of their property.*[83]

The question whether the accounting methods prescribed by the Commission were conclusive for dividend purposes was not directly in issue in the *Kansas City Southern* case. But the case embodied a considered dictum which has been cited in other cases to demonstrate that accounting controls matters of substance. Thus, it was cited by the three-judge district court in the *Norfolk & Western* case in support of the following language:

> *Accounting under the order of the Commission is not merely a matter of form, but one of substance.* It sets forth the condition of public carriers for the infor-

mation of their stock and bondholders and the investing public *as well as for that of the Commission.* It furnishes the basis for corporate financing *and many other matters affecting their very existence.*[84]

Some lower federal courts, reflecting the confusion of the Supreme Court decisions in regard to the conclusiveness of regulatory accounting orders, have differed as to the proper jurisdictional theory for the judicial review of such orders. Two district court cases have assumed that jurisdiction exists because accounting orders relate to substance.[85] The Supreme Court itself has never spoken directly on the point. But the Court's decision in the *Wichita Gas* case that an accounting order was merely legislative in nature but was buttressed by citing *United States* v. *Los Angeles & Salt Lake Railway Company,*[86] which had held that because the order was legislative in nature, an order of the Interstate Commerce Commission determining a final valuation under Section 19(a) of the Interstate Commerce Act[87] was not reviewable even under a statute authorizing review of that Commission's orders.[88] If accounting orders are in fact merely legislative, the *Los Angeles* case would appear to preclude review. But the Supreme Court *has* reviewed accounting orders.[89] It has been suggested, however, that since violation of such orders is punishable,[90] they must be reviewable for that reason.[91] If this suggestion correctly explains the basis for review, the cases dealing with review shed no light on the issue of the conclusiveness of accounting orders in litigation of substantive matters.

The rules of law that will emerge from the existing welter of decisions — which demonstrate only that the courts have not clearly analyzed the problem of conclusiveness of accounts — are, of course, not predictable with certainty. It is probable, however, that in matters relating to the interpretation of financial events, prescribed accounting will be conclusive for all purposes within the jurisdiction of the regulatory agency which prescribes it. Where the agency has direct regulatory power to deal with the particular problem involved, this result seems to be inevitable: No agency would stultify its regulatory powers by directing that financial events be interpreted on the books in a manner inconsistent with their treatment for other regulatory purposes. But in matters relating to "confiscation," prescribed accounting will not be conclusive, for the courts will make their own determinations as to value and expense.

Unlike agencies with comprehensive regulatory powers, the Securities and Exchange Commission under the two securities acts[92] has no statutory purposes to achieve with respect to the financial statements of corporations beyond requiring full and truthful disclosure.[93] It is clear, nonetheless, that Congress intended the Commission to exercise such control over accounting as would insure accurate disclosure and make the accounts of different companies comparable.[94] To make this uniformity possible, Congress deliberately refrained from requiring that the accounting prescribed by the Commission be consistent with accounting prescribed by state law.[95] This freedom of action has enabled the Commission to require adherence to accounting standards in financial statements filed with it even when state law permitted other treatment.[96] But, generally, the Commission has no control over the accounting of a registrant for purposes of internal management other than reports to the Commission.[97] Although no case has arisen on this point, it seems clear that a registrant will not be concluded by the accounts it files with the Commission, except where the evidentiary rule of admissions is applicable.

Two hypothetical cases will illustrate the problems which might otherwise arise:

For instance, should a registrant accept the Commission's view that a particular item should be charged to earned surplus rather than capital surplus in reports filed with the Commission, no earned surplus might remain available for dividends.[98] Yet, if on its own books the registrant should charge the item to capital surplus and pay dividend out of earned surplus, it seems evident that in a suit against the registrant's officers and directors for unlawful declaration of dividends, a report filed with the Commission showing no earned surplus should not be conclusive evidence of improper accounting treatment.[99]

Again, if a financial statement filed under the Securities Exchange Act of 1934 shows fixed assets at cost less depreciation, although the assets be "worth" more than cost, the registrant should not be liable under Section 18(a)[100] for failing to disclose value to a stockholder who made a computation of the value of his stock from the report and sold it at a price determined accordingly. The result should follow even in states where the increased value could have been made the foundation for a write-up which would create a revaluation surplus available for dividends.

In summary, it appears probable that, except for the use of the accounting prescribed by a regulatory agency as evidence of facts in matters arising within the purview of that agency's regulatory powers, the financial statements of an enterprise will conclude neither the enterprise nor persons nor public agencies which deal with it. Such statements will be considered to be essentially purposive — rebuttable by challenging the applicability of the conventions or assumptions upon which they were based to the problem at hand.

NOTES

1. See Berle and Means, *The Modern Corporation and Private Property* (1932) bk, II, cc. II and III; SEC Accounting Release No. 9, Dec. 23, 1938; Healy, "The Next Step in Accounting" (1938) 13 *Accounting Review* 1; Werntz, "Some Current Problems in Accounting" (1939) 14 *Accounting Review* 117.

2. On the income bond, see Hansen, "Legal and Business Aspects of Income Bonds" (1937) 11 *Temple Law Quarterly* 330; Dewing, "The Position of Income Bonds as Illustrated by Those of the Central of Georgia Railroad" (1911) 25 *Quarterly Journal of Economics* 396. For a similar problem with reference to stock, see *MacIntosh* v. *Flint & P.M. R.R.,* 34 Fed. 582 (C.C.E.D. Mich. 1888). On the earnings requirement for legal investments, see Wabash Railway Income in 1930, Senate Report No. 25, pt. 23, 76th Cong., 3d Sess. (1940)

3. See *Matter of Kinney,* 279 N.Y. 423, 18 N.E.(2d) 645 (1939); *Associated Gas & Elec. Corp.,* 6 SEC 605 (1940); *New Mexico Gas Co.,* 6 SEC 547 (1940); *The Philadelphia Co.,* 6 SEC 752 (1940); SEC Accounting Releases Nos. 15 and 16, March 16, 1940; Committee on Accounting Procedure, American Institute of Accountants, Accounting Research Bulletin No. 3 (1939); Paton and Littleton, *An Introduction to Corporate Accounting Standards* (1940) 112 *et seq.;* Note (1940) 49 *Yale Law Journal* 1319; Werntz, *supra* note 1.

4. See Locklin, *Regulation of Security Issues by the Interstate Commerce Commission* (1925), particularly cc. IV, V, and VII, and pp. 85–87.

5. For cases under the Securities Act of 1933, see, e.g., Metropolitan Personal Loan Corp., SEC Securities Act Release No. 2256, Aug. 23, 1940; *The Republic Co.,* 6 SEC 1062 (1940); *cf. Potrero Sugar Co.,* 5 SEC 982 (1939). For cases under the Securities Exchange Act of 1934, see, e.g., A. Hollander & Son, Inc. SEC Securities Exchange Act Release No. 2777, Feb. 6, 1941; *Alleghany Corp.,* 6 SEC 960 (1940); *Missouri Pac. R.R.,* 6 SEC 268 (1939). See also Frank, "The Sin of

Perfectionism," in *Experiences with Extensions of Auditing Procedures and Papers on Other Accounting Subjects* (1940); Sanders, "Accounting Aspects of the Securities Act" (1937) 4 *Law and Contemporary Problems* 191; Kaplan and Reaugh, "Accounting, Reports to Stockholders, and the SEC" (1939) 48 *Yale Law Journal* 935; Henderson, "Practice under the Securities Act of 1933 and the Securities Exchange Act of 1934: From the Viewpoint of the Attorney" (1934) 58 *Journal of Accountancy* 448; Werntz, *supra* note 1.

6. See *SEC Report on Investment Trusts and Investment Companies* (1940) pt. III, c. VI.

7. Committee on Accounting Procedure, American Institute of Accountants, Accounting Research Bulletin No. 7 (1940). See also Freeman "Accounting Principles and the Law" (1934) 57 *Journal of Accountancy* 467, 469; May, "The Influence of Accounting on the Development of an Economy" (1936) 61 *Journal of Accountancy* 11, 13; May, "Uniformity in Accounting" (1938) 17 *Harvard Business Review* 1. For an even more objective approach, see Hamilton, "Cost as a Standard for Price" (1937) 4 *Law and Contemporary Problems* 321.

8. Thornton, "Accounting Principles and Local Statutes" (1934) 57 *Journal of Accountancy* 302; Thornton, "Law and Accounting" (1933) 56 *Journal of Accountancy* 151; Paton, "Shortcomings of Present Day Financial Statements (1934) 57 *Journal of Accountancy* 108; Clader, "Principles Related to Earned Surplus," in *Papers on Accounting Principles and Procedure* (1938) 36, 37. Compare Paton and Littleton, *op. cit. supra* note 3, at 4, 106, with the doubts as to the position there taken expressed by a subcommittee of the American Institute of Accountants (1941) 71 *Journal of Accountancy* 48, 57. See also the somewhat uncertain positions taken in Bowles, "Treasury Shares on the Balance-sheet" (1934) 58 *Journal of Accountancy* 98; Wakefield, "When Lawyers and Accountants Disagree" (1934) 58 *Journal of Accountancy* 117.

9. Hills, "Stated Capital and Treasury Shares" (1934) 57 *Journal of Accountancy* 202, 472; Hills, "Accounting in Corporation Law" (1937) 12 *Wisconsin Law Review* 494, 501; Hills, "Federal Taxation vs. Corporation Law" (1937) 12 *Wisconsin Law Review* 280, 306; Katz, "Accounting (1933) 8 *Accounting Review* 1; Payne, "Accounting as Affected by the New Illinois and Pennsylvania Corporation Acts" (1933) 13 *Certified Public Accountant* 669.

10. Marple, *Capital Surplus and Corporate Net Worth* (1936) 45; Watson, "Principles Related to Treasury Stock" in *Papers on Accounting Principles and Procedure* (1938) 31, 32; Freeman, "Accounting Principles and the Law" (1934) 57 *Journal of Accountancy* 467; Herrick, "Law and Accounting" (1933) 56 *Journal of Accountancy* 148; Marple, "Treasury Stock" (1934) 57 *Journal of Accountancy* 257; Payne, "Net Worth under the Delaware and Michigan Corporation Laws" (1933) 8 *Accounting Review* 1; Payne "Accounting as Affected by the New Illinois and Pennsylvania Corporation Acts" (1933) 13 *Certified Public Accountant* 669.

11. See Freeman, Herrick, and Payne, *supra* note 10; Hills and Lewis, *supra* note 9; Marple, "Treasury Stock" (1934) 57 *Journal of Accountancy* 257.

12. Lewis, *supra* note 9, at 151–59.

13. There may be some question whether accountants should be bound to disclose restrictions on dividends arising from contractual rather than statutory limitations on surplus.

    The text is stated in terms of a duty not to *overstate* surplus; accountants would recognize no obligation not to *understate* surplus available for dividends, e.g., by failing to disclose a potential revaluation surplus.

14. The duty of accountants to disclose the legal situation concerning dividends seems to have been an underlying postulate of many of the viewpoints on accounting disclosure expressed by the Securities and Exchange Commission and its staff; e.g., their emphasis on balance-sheet disclosure of the liquidating preference and issue price of preferred stock. These amounts may be so greatly in excess of par or stated value as to raise problems as to the legal availability of surplus for dividends. The Commission requires an opinion of counsel as to the availability of dividends. SEC Accounting Release No. 9, Dec. 23, 1938. See Werntz, "Footnotes and Financial Statements" (address May 3 and 9, 1939); Lewis, *supra* note 9.

    In Foster, *The Application of Accounting Concepts to Legal Standards* (1938) 13 Ohio O.

62, 65–66, it is said, "When the members of the legal profession survey the accountant's work and make use of the financial statements he prepares, they must remember that he is embattled between at least two points of view. One of his jobs is economic; it is a business administration job. He must arrange his procedures in such a manner that his accounts and reports will be of use in the control of the agents of production under the hands of his boss, the businessman.

"His other job is more legalistic; it is a protection-of-equities job. He must arrange his procedures in such a manner that the various contributors to the enterprise, creditors and owners, will not suffer injustices through an improper statement of relationships ... the user of the accountant's end results, the financial statements, must appreciate the difficulties of putting two different tasks together in a single report."

15. See Committee on Accounting Procedure, American Institute of Accountants, Accounting Research Bulletin No. 3 (1939); SEC Accounting Release No. 15, March 16, 1940.

16. SEC Accounting Release No. 9, Dec. 23, 1938.

17. See Delaware Revised Code (1935) c. 65, § 2066.

18. This solution may not be practicable in every instance. Some writers believe that dividend law has grown so complex that it is not possible to show a balance-sheet figure for surplus which represents legally distributable surplus. Sanders, Hatfield, and Moore, *A Statement of Accounting Principles* (1938) 93; Henderson, *supra* note 5, at 448, 454; Littleton, "Dividends Presuppose Profits" (1934) 9 *Accounting Review* 304; *cf.* Paton and Littleton, *op. cit. supra* note 3, at 106.

19. See table indicating the enormous number of write-ups and write-downs between 1925 and 1934 in 272 large industrial corporations studied, prepared from a study by Solomon Fabricant, in Committee on Accounting Procedure, American Institute of Accountants, Accounting Research Bulletin No. 5 (1940). See also Graham, "Valuation for Profit Determination" (1940) 15 *Accounting Review* 145.

20. See Paton and Littleton, *op. cit supra* note 3, 122 *et seq.;* Sanders, Hatfield, and Moore, *A Statement of Accounting Principles* (1938) 58–59, 63; Daniels, "Principles of Asset Valuation" (1934) 9 *Accounting Review* 114; Paton, "Accounting Problems of the Depression" (1932) 7 *Accounting Review* 258; May, "The Influence of Accounting on the Development of an Economy" (1936) 61 *Journal of Accountancy* 11, 15–16; "A Tentative Statement of Accounting Principles Affecting Corporate Reports" (1936) 11 *Accounting Review* 187.

21. Kelley, "'Value' as an Accounting Concept" (1935) 60 *Journal of Accountancy* 50.

22. Daniels "Principles of Asset Valuation" (1934) 9 *Accounting Review* 114.

23. Paton and Littleton, *op. cit. supra* note 3, at 10–12; Littleton, "Value and Price in Accounting" (1929) 4 *Accounting Review* 147; May, "The Influence of Accounting on the Development of an Economy" (1936) 61 *Journal of Accountancy* 11, 15; Peloubet, "Is Value an Accounting Concept?" (1935) 59 *Journal of Accountancy* 201, 60 *Journal of Accountancy* 53.

24. Sanders, Hatfield, and Moore, *A Statement of Accounting Principles* (1938) 58–59; Paton, "Economic Theory in Relation to Accounting Valuations" (1931) 6 *Accounting Review* 89.

25. "The principles developed by accountants will be adopted by the law tomorrow." Fisher, "Legal Regulation of Accounting" (1933) 55 *Journal of Accountancy* 9. See Berle, "Accounting and the Law" (1938) 65 *Journal of Accountancy* 368; Berle and Fisher, "Elements of the Law of Business Accounting" (1932) 32 *Columbia Law Review* 573; Fisher, "The Integration of Legal and Accounting Concepts" in *Papers on Accounting Principles and Procedure* (1938) 49; Hills, "Accounting in Corporation Law" (1937) 12 *Wisconsin Law Review* 494.

26. An exception is in the field of income taxation. Even though some accounting concepts are modified by the income tax laws, concepts based on the cost convention are extremely important in taxation: e.g., the concepts of realization of profit, cost as the starting point of "basis," and depreciation based on amortization of cost. See 2 Bonbright, *Valuation of Property* (1937) c. XXVIII; Hills, "Federal Taxation vs. Corporation Law" (1937) 12 *Wisconsin Law Review* 280.

27. Weiner, "Theory of Anglo-American Dividend Law: The English Cases" (1928) 28 *Columbia*

Law Review 1046; Weiner, "Theory of Anglo-American Dividend Law: American Statutes and Cases" (1929) 29 *Columbia Law Review* 461; Weiner and Bonbright, "Theory of Anglo-American Dividend Law: Surplus and Profits" (1930) 30 *Columbia Law Review* 330, 954; Weiner, "The Amount Available for Dividends Where No-Par Shares Have Been Issued" (1929) 29 *Columbia Law Review* 906. These articles are summarized in 2 Bonbright, *Valuation of Property* (1937) c. XXVII.

28. Recent writers have pointed out that the use of no par and low par value stock, and the accompanying development of paid-in surplus, have impaired the usefulness of the old tests. Suggestions are made for formulation of tests based on ratios of assets to liabilities. See Littleton, "Business Profits as a Legal Basis for Dividends" (1937) 16 *Harvard Business Review* 51; Littleton, "A Substitute for Stated Capital" (1938) 17 *Harvard Business Review* 75; Hills "Model Corporation Act" (1935) 48 *Harvard Law Review* 1334; *cf.* California Civil Code (Deering, 1937) § 348(b); *N.C. Code Ann.* (Michie, 1939) § 1179.

29. They cite *Bank of Morgan* v. *Reid,* 27 Ga. App. 123, 107 S.E. 555 (1921) and *American Steel & Wire Co.* v. *Eddy,* 130 Mich. 266, 89 N.W. 952 (1902) as examples of interchangeable use of the two rules.

30. See *So. Calif. Home Bldr's* v. *Young,* 45 Cal. App. 679, 188 Pac. 586 (1920); *Kingston* v. *Home L. Ins. Co. of America,* 11 Del. Ch. 258, 101 Atl. 898 (1917); *Sexton* v. *Percival Co.* 189 Iowa 586, 177 N.W. 83 (1920); *Coleman* v. *Booth,* 268 Mo. 64, 186 S.W. 1021 (1916); *Wilson* v. *Barnett,* N.Y.L.J., Aug. 2, 1928, 1870 (Sup. Ct., 1st Dep't); *Hutchinson* v. *Curtiss,* 45 Misc. 484, 92 N.Y. Supp. 70 (1904); *Hill* v. *International Products Co.,* 129 Misc. 25, 220 N.Y. Supp. 711, 751 (1925), *aff'd without opinion,* 226 App. Div. 730, 233 N.Y. Supp. 784 (1929).

31. *Randall* v. *Bailey,* 23 N.Y.S.(2d) 173 (Sup. Ct., 1st Dep't 1940) discussed in (1940) 50 *Yale Law Journal* 306.

32. E.g., *Titus* v. *Piggly Wiggly Corp.,* 2 Tenn. App. 184 (1925) discussed in (1929) 7 *Harvard Business Review* 467, where it was held that although unrealized appreciation might not be used as a source of dividends, it might be used to absorb losses, thereby permitting dividends to be paid out of realized profit.

33. 169 U.S. 466 (1898). This is the case which held that present reproduction cost is one of the "elements" of value to be considered for rate-making purposes. In practice, at least until recently, the doctrine of *Smyth* v. *Ames* has resulted in paramount emphasis being placed on reproduction cost. For a recent article on this much discussed topic, see Kauper, "Wanted: A New Definition of the Rate Base" (1939) 37 *Michigan Law Review* 1209.

34. Some persons believe that the changed composition of the Supreme Court and the following cases foreshadow the demise of *Smyth* v. *Ames. R.R. Comm. of California* v. *Pacific Gas and Elec. Co.,* 302 U.S. 388 (1937); *McCart* v. *Indianapolis Water Co.,* 302 U.S. 419 (1938); *Driscoll* v. *The Edison Light & Power Co.,* 307 U.S. 104, *rehearing denied,* 307 U.S. 650 (1939). Presumably the rule of *Smyth* v. *Ames* would be succeeded by the principle of returns on "prudent investment." See the dissent of Mr. Justice Brandeis in Missouri *ex rel. Southwestern Bell Telephone Co.* v. *Public Serv. Comm.,* 262 U.S. 276 (1923).

35. Floyd L. Carlisle, Chairman of Niagara Hudson Power Corp., quoted in testimony of Leland Olds in "Hearings before the Joint Committee on the Investigation of the Tennessee Valley Authority," pt. 13, 75th Cong., 3d Sess. (1938) 5803.

36. Compare *R.R. Comm. of California* v. *Pacific Gas and Elec. Co.,* 302 U.S. 388 (1938) with *Los Angeles Gas Co.* v. *R.R. Comm. of California,* 289 U.S. 287 (1932). See Northwestern Power Co., Fed. Power Comm. Opinion No. 56, Dec. 6, 1940, where the utility wanted to reaccount for cost on its books because of the increased importance of cost in rate regulation.

37. See 1 Bonbright, *Valuation of Property* (1937) 185.

38. *Pacific Gas & Elec. Co.* v. *San Francisco,* 265 U.S. 403 (1924); *McCardle* v. *Indianapolis Water Co.,* 272 U.S. 400 (1926); *cf. United Railways and Elec. Co.* v. *West,* 280 U.S. 234 (1930).

See Haun, "Inconsistencies in Public Utility Depreciation; Deduction of Depreciation for Rate Base Purposes" (1940) 38 *Michigan Law Review* 479.

39. *West* v. *Chesapeake & Potomac Tel. Co.*, 295 U.S. 662 (1935). Compare *Board of Public Utility Comm'rs* v. *New York Tel. Co.*, 271 U.S. 23 (1926) with *Lindheimer* v. *Illinois Bell Tel. Co.*, 292 U.S. 151 (1934).

40. The writer does not suggest that the "observational method," as ordinarily employed, is accurate even on a "value" theory. Observational methods will not disclose loss of service life, and hence, loss of value. See 1 Bonbright, *Valuation of Property* (1937) 204–5.

41. But see Mr. Justice Brandeis dissenting in *United Railways & Elec. Co.* v. *West* 280 U.S. 234 (1930) to the effect that depreciation charges should be based on cost even when *Smyth* v. *Ames* controls the determination of value. *Cf.* Committee on Accounting Procedure, American Institute of Accountants, Accounting Research Bulletin No. 5 (1940).

42. E.g., Community Power & Light Co., 6 SEC 182, 201 (1939); Central Ill. Elec. and Gas Co., 5 SEC 115 (1939); Public Serv. Co. of Colorado, 5 SEC 788 (1939); Middle West Corp., 7 SEC 566 (1940); Appalachian Elec. Power Co., SEC Holding Company Act Release No. 2430, Dec. 14, 1940.

43. Healy, "The Next Step in Accounting" (1938) 13 *Accounting Review* 1, 6.

44. For a general discussion of the Commission's regulatory functions under these sections, see "Comment" (1940) 49 *Yale Law Journal* 492.

45. 6 SEC 182, 201 (1939).

46. 4 SEC 999 (1939).

47. 5 SEC 788 (1939).

48. 4 SEC 999, 1017 (1939).

49. 5 SEC 788, 820–21 (1939).

50. See *In re* Pittsburgh Rys., C.C.H. Bankr. Serv. § 52821 (Penn. Pub. Serv. Comm., 1940); *Re* California Water Service Co., P.U.R. 1928C 516 (Cal. Ry. Comm.); *cf.* Healy, "Financing the Utility Property Account," an appendix to Report of the Committee on Corporation Finance of the National Association of Railroad and Utilities Commissioners (1940).

51. In fact, one member of the Commission has recognized the importance of cost in security regulation from this point of view. See the concurring opinion of former Chairman, now Circuit Judge, Frank in Central Ill. Elec. and Gas Co., 5 SEC 115, 134 (1939).

52. But *cf.* Federal Water Service Corp., SEC Holding Company Act Release No. 2635, March 24, 1941.

53. See the remarks of Commissioner Healy in Central Ill. Elec. and Gas Co., 5 SEC 115, 127–29 (1939), and in Pub. Serv. Co. of Colorado, 5 SEC 788, 837, 850–51 (1939).

54. It is suggested in Fryxsell, "Should Appreciation be Brought into the Accounts?" (1930) 5 *Accounting Review* 157, that the balance sheet be stated on a cost basis, with representations as to value in the prospectus. Other accountants assume that revaluations showing present value are necessary to support security issues. 2 Kester, *Accounting Theory and Practice* (3d rev. ed. 1933) 104.

55. "...but there is nothing in the statistical procedure of the accountant that implies either that these valuations are capital valuations or that the sum of them bears any simple relation to the capitalized value of a concern's earning power." Canning, "Some Divergences of Accounting Theory from Economic Theory" (1929) 4 *Accounting Review* 1, 6.

56. May, *supra* note 7, at 18–20. See also *Consolidated Rock Products Co.* v. *Dubois*, 61 Sup. Ct. 675 (U.S. 1941).

57. *Consolidated Rock Products Co.* v. *Dubois*, 61 Sup. Ct. 675 (U.S. 1941); 1 Bonbright, *Valuation of Property* (1937) 156–60, 237 *et seq.*; Canning, *The Economics of Accountancy* (1929)

197–98, 317–18; Littleton, "Value and Price in Accounting" (1929) 4 *Accounting Review* 147.

58. May, *supra* note 7, at 20. Henderson, *supra* note 5, at 448, 455; Frank, "Accounting for Investors" (1939) 7 *The Controller* 380.

59. The Supreme Court recognized this point in *LaBelle Iron Works* v. *United States,* 256 U.S. 377, 393–94 (1921), where it said:

> *There is a logical incongruity in entering upon the books of a corporation as the capital value of property acquired for permanent employment in its business and still retained for that purpose, a sum corresponding not to its cost but to what probably might be realized by sale in the market. It is not merely that the market value has not been realized or tested by sale made, but that sale cannot be made without abandoning the very purpose for which the property is held, involving a withdrawal from business so far as that particular property is concerned...*

See also 2 Bonbright, *Valuation of Property* (1937) 954–55; May, *supra* note 7, at 18–20.

60. Daniels, *Financial Statements* (1939) 178–81; Paton, "Economic Theory in Relation to Accounting Valuations" (1931) 6 *Accounting Review* 89, 94; Littleton "Value and Price in Accounting" (1929) 4 *Accounting Review* 147; *cf.* Canning, "Cost of Production and Market Price" (1931) 6 *Accounting Review* 161.

61. "It is the purpose of accounting to record as nearly as possible actual costs for the individual enterprise..." Daniels, *Financial Statements* (1939) 179.

62. "Naturally, the actual costs of different companies operating plants made up of parts purchased at different times and different prices will differ. But is it not the very function of accounting to show these variations?" Daniels, "The Valuation of Fixed Assets" (1933) 8 *Accounting Review* 302, 310.

63. Corporations which have thus confounded their books have struggled to devise compensating errors to correct their income accounts. See Daniels, "The Valuation of Fixed Assets" (1933) 8 *Accounting Review* 302; Sanders, Hatfield, and Moore, *A Statement of Accounting Principles* (1938) 31–32, 65; Committee on Accounting Procedure, American Institute of Accountants, Accounting Research Bulletin No. 5 (1940); Graham, "Valuation for Profit Determination" (1940) 15 *Accounting Review* 145.

64. See *Consolidated Rock Products Co.* v. *Dubois,* 61 Sup. Ct. 675 (U.S. 1941); *Palmer* v. *Conn. Ry. & Lighting Co.,* 61 Sup. Ct. 379 (U.S. 1941); 1 Bonbright, *Valuation of Property* (1937) 249 *et seq.* For examples of the practical problem of estimating future earnings from past earnings, see Minnesota & Ontario Paper Co., 7 SEC 456 (1940); Flour Mills of America, Inc., 7 SEC 1 (1940); Griess-Pfleger Tanning Co., 5 SEC 72 (1939); La France Industries, 5 SEC 917 (1939).

65. Originally, accountants emphasized the interpretations which commercial bankers extending short-term credit placed on the financial condition of the enterprise, with resulting conservatism in balance sheets. Montgomery, "Accountants' Limitations" (1927) 44 *Journal of Accountancy* 245, 259; Littleton, "Value and Price in Accounting" (1929) 4 *Accounting Review* 147, 148. See Paton, "Aspects of Asset Valuation" (1934) 9 *Accounting Review* 122, 124, deploring the effect which this emphasis has had on the development of accounting principles. The present tendency is to emphasize information for the investor, with particular emphasis on accurate income reporting. Paton and Littleton, *op. cit. supra* note 3, at 1–3; Staub, "Uniformity in Accounting," in *Papers on Accounting Principles and Procedure* (1938); Frank, *Accounting for Investors* (1939) 7 *The Controller* 380; "A Statement of the Objectives of the American Accounting Association" (1936) 11 *Accounting Review* 1; May, "Improvement in Financial Accounts" (1937) 63 *Journal of Accountancy* 333, 340 *et seq.;* Paton, "Accounting Problems of the Depression" (1932) 7 *Accounting Review* 258, 266. To eliminate the possibilities of ambiguity latent in efforts to make a single set of financial statements serve all needs, it has been suggested that the "all-purpose" balance sheet be recognized as inadequate, and that different balance sheets be prepared for different purposes. 1 Bonbright, *Valuation of Property* (1937) 253; Canning, *The Economics of Accountancy* (1929) 86–88; Brink, "The Need for Single-Purpose Statements" (1940) 69 *Journal of*

Accountancy 284; Frank, "Accounting for Investors" (1939) 7 *The Controller* 380; May, "Eating Peas with Your Knife" (1937) 63 *Journal of Accountancy* 15, 17; May, "Improvement in Financial Accounts" (1937) 63 *Journal of Accountancy* 333, 337, 367; Montgomery, "Accountants' Limitations" (1927) 44 *Journal of Accountancy* 245, 255, 259; but see "Single-Purpose Statements" (1940) 69 *Journal of Accountancy* 186.

66. *Kansas City So. Ry.* v. *United States,* 231 U.S. 423 (1913).

67. *Norfolk & W. Ry.* v. *United States,* 287 U.S. 134 (1932).

68. *New Colonial Ice Co.* v. *Helvering,* 292 U.S. 435 (1934); *Weiss* v. *Wiener,* 279 U.S. 333 (1929).

69. *Surety Finance Co.* v. *Comm'r,* 77 F.(2d) 221 (C.C.A.9th, 1935); *Lucas* v. *American Code Co., Inc.,* 280 U.S. 445 (1930); *Brown* v. *Helvering,* 291 U.S. 193, 203 (1934); *Securities Allied Corp.* v. *Comm'r,* 95 F.(2d) 384 (C.C.A.2d, 1938).

70. See *Helvering* v. *Northwest Steel Rolling Mills, Inc.,* 61 Sup. Ct. 109 (1940); Paul, *Selected Studies in Federal Taxation* (2d Series 1938) 19–20.
    The subject of the divergence of the tax law of income and dividends and the corresponding field of corporation law is exhaustively explored in Hills, "Federal Taxation vs. Corporation Law" (1937) 12 *Wisconsin Law Review* 280.

71. The diversity of accounts has provoked much criticism. See Healy, "Before the Auditor Comes" (mimeographed address, May 15, 1939) 7; Paul, *Selected Studies in Federal Taxation* (2d Series 1938) 19–20; *Citizens' National Bank of Orange* v. *Comm'r,* 74 F.(2d) 604 (C.C.A.4th, 1935).

72. *Bessemer Investment Co.* v. *Comm'r,* 31 F.(2d) 248 (C.C.A.2d, 1929); see cases collected in 1 Prentice-Hall 1941 Fed. Tax Serv. § 6004; *cf. Northern Pac. Ry.* v. *Helvering,* 83 F.(2d) 508 (C.C.A.8th, 1936).

73. *Old Colony R.R.* v. *Comm'r,* 284 U.S. 552 (1932); *Kansas City So. Ry.* v. *Comm'r,* 52 F.(2d) 372 (C.C.A.8th, 1931), *cert. denied,* 284 U.S. 676 (1931); *Chesapeake and Ohio Ry.* v. *United States,* 5 F.Supp. 7 (E.D. Va. 1933); Minneapolis, St. P. & S.S.M. Ry., 34 B.T.A. 177 (1936); Union Pac. R.R., 26 B.T.A. 1126, 1142 (1932).

74. Fall River Elec. Light Co., 23 B.T.A. 168 (1931).

75. Second Nat. Bank of Philadelphia, 33 B.T.A. 750 (1935), refusing to follow *Citizens' Nat. Bank of Orange* v. *Comm'r,* 74 F.(2d) 604 (C.C.A.4th, 1935) and *Lebanon Nat. Bank* v. *Comm'r,* 76 F.(2d) 792 (C.C.A.3d, 1935).

76. *Atlantic C.L. R.R.* v. *Daughton,* 262 U.S. 413 (1923).

77. The writer, however, knows of no cases other than tax cases which involve such situations.

78. 287 U.S. 134 (1932).

79. 287 U.S. 134, 141–43 (1932). Italics supplied. See also Telephone and Railroad Depreciation Charges, 177 I.C.C. 351, 381 (1931); *In re* Classification of Accounts of Gas and Electric Companies, P.U.R. 1921D 385, 386 (Mass. D.P.U., 1921); *Re* New York & Richmond Gas Company, 23 P.U.R. (N.S.) 463 (N.Y. Pub. Serv. Comm., 1938); *Re* Uniform Classification of Accounts for Electric Utilities, 14 P.U.R. (N.S.) 57 (N.H. Pub. Serv. Comm., 1936). Note that the conclusion of the *Norfolk & Western* case was reached although carriers are forbidden by statute [41 STAT. 493 (1920), 49 U.S.C. § 20(5) (1934)] to keep any accounts other than those prescribed by the Commission.

80. 290 U.S. 561 (1934).

81. On this point, see also *I.C.C.* v. *Goodrich Transit Co.,* 224 U.S. 194 (1912).

82. 231 U.S. 423 (1913).

83. 231 U.S. 423, 453 (1913). The Court's attitude was not dependent solely on its expressed agreement with the principle of the regulation, for it went on to say:

But, did we agree with appellant that the abandonments ought to be charged to surplus or to profit and loss, rather than to operating expenses, we still should not deem this a sufficient ground to declare that the Commission had abused its power. So long as it acts fairly and reasonably within the grant of power constitutionally conferred by Congress, its orders are not open to judicial review.

Id. at 456–57.

The Court reasoned that the regulatory power of the Commission was over the corporate entity, and could not be defeated by agreements of stockholders *inter sese* as to the disposition of profits. Such reasoning could not advance the Court very far, however, for precisely the same basic questions would have been presented if the corporation had had only one class of stockholders on whose behalf it complained that the regulation deprived it of the right to declare dividends.

84. Italics supplied. *Norfolk & W. Ry.* v. *United States,* 52 F.(2d) 967, 970 (W.D. Va. 1931). As has been pointed out, the Supreme Court decision in this case held that accounting orders deal with "accounting merely." See also *Chesapeake & Ohio Ry.* v. *United States,* 5 F.Supp. 7 (E.D. Va. 1933); *New York Edison Co.* v. *Maltbie,* 244 App. Div. 685, 281 N.Y. Supp. 223 (3d Dep't 1935), *questions certified,* 245 App. Div. 897, 282 N.Y. Supp. 550 (1935), *aff'd,* 271 N.Y. 103, 2 N.E.(2d) 277 (1936); *People* ex rel. *New York Rys.* v. *Public Serv. Comm.,* 223 N.Y. 373, 119 N.E. 848 (1918); *Passaic Consolidated Water Co.* v. *Board of Pub. Util. Comm'rs,* 5 N.J. Misc. 1078, 139 Atl. 324 (Sup. Ct. 1927), *aff'd without opinion by a court divided 6 to 5,* 104 N.J. Law 666, 141 Atl. 921 (1928).

85. *Norfolk & W. Ry.* v. *United States,* 52 F.(2d) 967 (W.D. Va. 1931); *Chesapeake & Ohio Ry.* v. *United States,* 5 F.Supp. 7 (E.D. Va. 1933).

86. 273 U.S. 299 (1927).

87. 37 Stat. 701 (1913), 49 U.S.C. § 19(a) (1934).

88. Urgent Deficiencies Act, 38 Stat. 208 (1913), 28 U.S.C. § 41 (28) (1934).

89. *I.C.C.* v. *Goodrich Transit Co.,* 224 U.S. 194 (1912); *Kansas City So. Ry.* v. *United States,* 231 U.S. 423 (1913); *Norfolk & W. R.R.* v. *United States,* 287 U.S. 134 (1932); *Am. Tel. and Tel. Co.* v. *United States,* 299 U.S. 232 (1936).

90. As to penalties for disobedience of accounting orders of the Interstate Commerce Commission, see 34 Stat. 594 (1906), 35 Stat. 648 (1909), 59 U.S.C. § 20(6) and (7) (1934). As to orders of the Federal Communications Commission, see 48 Stat. 1078 (1934), 47 U.S.C. § 220(d) (1934).

91. *Atlanta, B. & C. R.R.* v. *United States,* 28 F.(2d) 885, 887 (N.D. Ga. 1928).

92. Securities Act of 1933, 48 Stat. 74 (1933), 15 U.S.C. § 77a *et seq.* (1934); Securities Exchange Act of 1934, 48 Stat. 881 (1934), 15 U.S.C. § 78 (1934).

93. The relevant provisions of the Securities Act are §§ 7 and 19(a) and schedule A, items 25 and 26. The relevant provisions of the Securities Exchange Act are §§ 3(b), 12(b), 13(b), and 23(a).

94. See "Hearings before Committee on Interstate and Foreign Commerce on H.R. 7852 and H.R. 8720," 73d Cong., 2d. Sess. (1934) 652–53; 15, 16 "Hearings on Stock Exchange Practices before Senate Committee on Banking and Currency," 73d Cong., 1st Sess. (1934) 6532–33, 6537, 6690–91, 6693, 6698–99, 7175, 7182, 7521.

95. See "Hearings on Stock Exchange Practices before Senate Committee on Banking and Currency," 73d Cong., 1st Sess. (1934) 7599–7601; 78 *Congressional Record* 8033, 8282, 8284, 8567 (1934).

96. See SEC Accounting Series Release No. 16, March 16, 1940.

97. This limitation, deducible from the language of both statutes, was expressly pointed out in the Senate Report on the Securities Exchange Act, Sen. Rep. No. 792, 73d Cong., 2d Sess. (1934) 10. See Kaplan and Reaugh, "Accounting Reports to Stockholders and the SEC." (1939)

48 *Yale Law Journal* 935, for a study of the extent to which corporate reports to stockholders adhere to the requirements imposed by the Securities and Exchange Commission for reports filed with it.

It is emphasized that the statement in the text is not applicable to the Commission's functions under the Public Utility Holding Company Act of 1935 and the Investment Company Act of 1940.

98. This assumes that capital surplus is not available for dividends under applicable state law.

99. Doubtless, however, the report filed with the Commission should show the condition of the corporation's own books, in order not to conceal facts which affect the availability of dividends.

100. Section 18(a) of the Securities Exchange Act of 1934, 48 Stat. 881 (1934), 15 U.S.C. § 78r (a) (1934) provides that any person who files a report which is misleading as to a material fact shall be liable to any person who purchased or sold a security at a price which was affected by such statement for damages caused by the reliance.

EIGHT

Current Accounting Problems

EARLE C. KING

Former Chief Accountant, Securities and Exchange Commission

King discusses the "current problems" of 1950 era accounting professionals, which he sees as arising from either new methods of doing business or areas where there have been disagreements in the past. He shows how these problems have been solved by accountants who clearly stated the change in accounting principle and its effects.

Accountants, it seems, always have "current problems." Some of us would not have much to do, but our lives would be much less interesting, if that were not the case. If all concerned had a better gift of prophecy, or perhaps if all could be convinced that economic or business disturbances, both inflationary and deflationary, are recurring, and consequently some accounting problems are also recurring, we might make more headway in reaching mutually acceptable solutions.

From its inception the Securities and Exchange Commission (SEC) has had the active cooperation of accounting teachers and practitioners, both public and private, in the development of its accounting rules and regulations. Reciprocally, the Commission has had an active interest in the work of the American Accounting Association in the preparation of its successive statements of "Accounting Principles Underlying Corporate Financial Statements" and in the work of the American Institute of Accountants' Committees on Accounting and Auditing Procedure.

All of you, of course, are familiar with your own Association's statement, the bulletins of the Institute's committees, and with the accounting requirements of the SEC as reflected in Regulation S-X, Accounting Series Releases, and in published opinions. While I realize that registrants with the SEC represent only a small fragment, in numbers, of business units in the United States, I think we can assume that sooner or later accounting students training to enter the profession of public accounting may serve such registrants. When they do, in serving commercial and industrial clients, they will deal with an agency interested in obtaining a reasonable degree of consistency in the form and content of financial statements of companies not required to comply with a uniform system of accounts, as in regulated enterprises. Although the first registration and report forms adopted by the Commission included rather specific instructions as to the content and, more especially, the form of the financial statements to be filed, the instructions now found in Regulation S-X permit a certain amount of variation in terminology, form, and content. After some disturbing experiences and dif-

---

Reprinted from *The Accounting Review*, January 1950, pp. 35–44, with permission of the American Accounting Association.

ference of opinion on the basic question, the Commission in 1938 issued a statement of its administrative policy with respect to financial statements:

> *In cases where financial statements filed with this Commission pursuant to its rules and regulations under the Securities Act of 1933 or the Securities Exchange Act of 1934 are prepared in accordance with accounting principles for which there is no substantial authoritative aupport, such financial statements will be presumed to be misleading or inaccurate despite disclosures contained in the certificate of the accountant or in footnotes to the statements provided the matters involved are material. In cases where there is a difference of opinion between the Commission and the registrant as to the proper principles of accounting to be followed, disclosure will be accepted in lieu of correction of the financial statements themselves only if the points involved are such that there is substantial authoritative support for the practices followed by the registrant and the position of the Commission has not previously been expressed in rules, regulations or other official releases of the Commission, including the published opinions of its Chief Accountant.*

This statement of policy is a declaration by the Commission consistent with recommendations made by Professor Paton at an Illinois accounting conference in 1946 that, "First, management must become more receptive to the view that accounting is not designed to paint pictures corresponding to managerial whims and prejudices. In other words, management must become more willing to let the accountants call a spade a spade — show things as they are rather than as management would like to see them. Second, accountants must become more resourceful, adaptable, less hidebound, so that management may be effectively assisted. Third, both management and accountants should remember that their primary responsibility is still to the investors — those who put up the money — the folks who have been the forgotten men for some time." I certainly have no quarrel with those sentiments. They remind me of a particularly difficult conference in which counsel for the registrant did most of the talking in support of a treatment of reserves to which we had taken exception. After the conference broke up one of the group was overheard to remark that "they seem to want us to tell the truth rather than be conservative."

Most of our "current problems" arise in the appraising of transactions reflecting new methods of doing business or matters upon which there has been a wide difference of opinion among recognized accounting authorities for many years. Thorough analysis and discussion of the new problems and reappraisal of the old controversial problems are matters of mutual interest for all of us here, as well as for the registrants and certifying accountants directly concerned. Two articles which appeared in the *Accounting Review* a year ago suggest the possibility of discussing some of these problems under the general theme of consistency in accounting.

One of the articles expresses the fear that the doctrine of consistency is being followed blindly by accountants and therefore improvement in accounting practices is being prevented. This view is somewhat in contrast with the other article dealing with examination of 150 current (1946–1947 vs. 1945–1946) reports to stockholders. This article contained the statement that "none of the opinions [of independent public accountants] included exceptions, qualifications, or explanations bearing *directly* upon the question of consistency with respect to generally accepted accounting principles." The author listed ten classes of items gleaned from the reports which *seemed* to him to be cases of inconsistency.

Dealing with this problem is a major part of our work in reviewing the financial statements filed with us and I think I can assure you that our efforts are not directed to suppressing disclosures of inconsistencies from year to year. On the contrary, we insist upon exceptions being noted if the changes are significant. And there is where the element of judgment enters. There are usually four parties involved in a conference over such matters if a registration under the 1933 Act is involved — representatives of the registrant (usually the chief accounting officer), a partner of the firm of certifying public accountants, a representative of the underwriters, and accountants of the Commission's staff. If the conference is a prefiling one, it may have been suggested by any one of the parties; if after filing, it probably resulted from a letter of deficiencies. Such a conference is an informal means of getting at the facts behind the accounting and usually leads to a conclusion as to whether an exception as to consistency or a change in method of accounting or reporting is necessary.

The rules that govern whether an exception should be taken as to consistency are found in Regulation S-X. Among other requirements, Rule 2-02 says that "The accountant's certificate shall state clearly: ... the opinion of the accountant as to any changes in accounting principles or practices, or adjustment of the accounts, required to be set forth by Rule 3-07; ..." Rule 3-07 requires that "If any significant change in accounting principle or practice, or any significant retroactive adjustment of the accounts of prior years, has been made at the beginning of or during any period covered by the profit and loss statements filed, a statement thereof shall be given in a note to the appropriate statement, and, if the change or adjustment substantially affects proper comparison with the preceding fiscal period, the necessary explanation." To complete the disclosure, Rule 2-02 goes on to require with respect to exceptions that, "any matters to which the accountant takes exception shall be clearly identified, the exception thereto specifically and clearly stated, and, to the extent practicable, the effect of each such exception on the related financial statements given."

Experience seems to indicate that most registrants and their independent public accountants prefer to have the financial statements and accountants' opinion contained in the report to stockholders in substantial agreement with the report to be filed with the SEC. Since the report to stockholders usually is published weeks or months before their report is filed with us, our requirements must be anticipated, or, if a troublesome point is known to be present, conferences are sometimes requested prior to publication of the report to stockholders. Occasionally when agreement has not been reached before such publication the report to us may be different from the report to stockholders and attention may be called to that fact.

There is no real difference in our requirements for disclosure of inconsistencies in accounting from those which prevailed in the accounting profession prior to the existence of the SEC. In the three-way correspondence relating to audits of corporate accounts between the American Institute of Accountants, the Controllers Institute of America, and the New York Stock Exchange in December 1933 and January 1934, agreement was reached as to a short form of accountant's report in which the opinion paragraph contained the phrase "in accordance with accepted principles of accounting consistently maintained by the Company during the year under review." One of the notes referring to this report contained the warning that, "This certificate is appropriate only if the accounting for the year is consistent in basis with that for the preceding year. If there has been any material change either in accounting principles or in the manner of their application, the nature of the change should be indicated." The form of report and the accompanying instructions as to its use were included in 1936 in the American Institute of Accountants' bulletin entitled "Examination of Financial Statements by Independent Public Accountants," which was in use unamended until the series of Statements on Auditing Procedure was launched in October 1939 following the disclosures in the McKesson case. The first of these statements recommended a short form report or opinion which closed with language still in general use—"in conformity with generally accepted accounting principles applied on a basis consistent with that of the preceding year."

It may be noted that Rule 3–07 speaks of "any significant change in accounting principles or practice," whereas the note to the Institute's 1934 certificate refers to "any material change either in accounting principles or in the manner of their application." Occasionally an accountant has maintained that in a particular case there was no change in accounting principles—the difference in the figures as between years being due only to the manner of applying the principles. A revision of Regulation S-X now in process will eliminate this opportunity to quibble by amending our rule to include change in manner of application as well as change in principle.

Sometimes attention is directed in the statements themselves to a change in the method of their preparation. When two years' figures are presented and the earlier year is adjusted to conform to the later year the statements are comparable and of course no exception as to consistency is necessary. A good example of this situation recently came to my attention. (My reference here, as well as the other examples I shall use, unless clearly indicated otherwise, is to the published report to stockholders.) In 1947 a substantial profit on the sale of land and buildings had been shown as a nonrecurring credit to net income. In the 1948 report, presented in comparative form, this item was shown in earned surplus for 1947, where the change in procedure was noted, and in the 1948 earned surplus there was a substantial debit for development costs abandoned. Handling the 1948 extraordinary debit as the extraordinary credit had been reported in 1947 would have resulted in net income being reported as approximately one-seventh of the preceding year whereas by the change in procedure the net income for 1948 was shown as one-eighth more than 1947. The latest revision of one of the leading accounting texts in discussing extraordinary debits and credits to income or surplus endorses the method adopted here for 1948, although the author recognizes that advocates of a "clean surplus" would show these items in the income account. The example I have cited seems to be a clear-cut case of handling the extraordinary items in the two successive years to attain the result desired. The amount of the debit was clearly large enough to come within the exception in the American Institute of Accountants' Research Bulletins Nos. 32 and 35 but to which the Commission has objected on the grounds that such exclusion of profit-and-loss items from the income account is misleading. The outline for an income account set forth in Regulation S-X includes items of "Other Income" and "Income Deductions" requiring separate disclosure of significant amounts with explanations designating clearly the nature of the transactions involved.

This matter of a "clean surplus" compels me to observe that the teaching that adjustments of prior years' profit-and-loss items must be made through earned surplus is reflected in many financial statements. Perhaps the most persistent single item given this treatment is adjustment of prior years' income taxes. Supporters of either the American Accounting Association's statement of accounting concepts or the Institute's Research Bulletin No. 23 on "Accounting for Income Taxes" would report such adjustments in the income statement for the year in which the transaction took place, except that Institute members might follow the suggestion contained in their bulletin that if the corrections were so large as to be likely to produce distorted interpretations of income the entries might be charged or credited to surplus, with an indication of the period to which they relate. A statement I saw a few days ago contained two tax adjustment credits to earned surplus and one debit for an additional assessment, none of the gross amounts being significant by any test and the net result being $19 one way or the other. Cluttering up earned surplus with such small items seems absurd even though the entries as made do have strict theoretical support in some quarters.

Accounting for the cost of vacation allowances has been the subject of comment in the 1947 and 1948 financial statements of several large corporations, with a variety of treatment. In one case, in which the company apparently disapproves of footnotes, for there are none, a short lucid paragraph in the accountants' opinion reports the change in accounting and takes a clear-cut exception as to consistency in the following language:

> Prior to 1947 it was the policy of the company and its subsidiaries to charge vacation payments to income account as and when the amounts were disbursed. Effective January 1, 1947 the companies adopted the policy of accruing the estimated cost of vacation payments in the year the vacation pay is considered to be earned, which change we approve. The profit for the year 1947 has, therefore, been charged with the cost of vacations paid as well as vacations earned in that year with the result the profit has been reduced by $1,630,000. In all other respects the principles of accounting maintained by the companies during the year were consistent with those of the preceding year.

The amount of the duplicate charge to income here was 2 percent of wages and salaries, and approximately 5 percent of net income and current liabilities.

In another company in the same industry served by the same firm of independent public accountants a similar change in policy was explained in a footnote, with the accountants' exception as to consistency expressed in their certificate as follows: ". . . in conformity with generally accepted accounting principles applied on a basis consistent in all material respects with that of the preceding year, except in the change in accounting for vacation allowances explained on page 13, which has our approval." In this case the duplicate wages were charged to surplus among other extraordinary debits and credits. The amount in this case was 3 percent of wages and salaries, 17 percent of net income and 7 percent of current liabilities. In still another company in the same industry, served by the same accountants, the change in accounting for vacation pay is referred to in a footnote which in turn refers to an explanation in the text of the report. No exception as to consistency as to this point was taken by the accountants in their certificate, although another change in accounting was mentioned. In this case the duplicate charge was to income and amounted to 2 percent of wages and salaries, 15 percent of net income and 4 percent of current liabilities. In statements filed with us the administrative problem of reconciling these varied treatments of the same situation becomes one of judgment as to significance of the accounting in each case, which is the same problem as faced the accountants. But we don't always agree!

As was to be expected, the published report of a correspondence school affords an example of exception to consistency in the application of generally accepted accounting principles. The accountants in this case expressed their exception by the insertion of a phrase in the standard certificate to read: "which, except for the change (which we consider proper) in the treatment of recoveries and the provision for losses, as explained in Note A." Note A explained that in the current year recoveries and provisions for losses were recorded in a manner which had the effect of increasing sales and provisions by approximately the same material amount but with no effect on gross or net income. The change in income tax regulations late in 1947 relating to deductions for bad debts by banks should be the cause for a somewhat similar comment in bank reports where the change has been adopted, as I have seen in one well-publicized bank report, which, however, contained no accountants' certificate.

Exceptions taken because of changes in accounting policy are not always related to transactions affecting profits. Two cases appeared in my small sampling in which the accountants noted changes (approved by them) in the manner of making provisions from surplus in connection with preferred stock retirements. The changes related only to the timing of the charges to surplus. Different accounting firms were involved.

A paragraph from the accountants' report to the board of directors and stockholders of a department store company will serve to introduce a subject which has had the attention of the Commission for a number of years but which has achieved considerable prominence in the last two years or so. The paragraph reads:

> *The accounting principles followed by the companies during the year have been consistent with those of the preceding year, except that payments under the employees' retirement plans applicable to services of prior years have been charged to earnings, whereas in the prior year such payments were charged to accumulated earnings retained in the business; this change, which has our approval, is explained in Note G to the financial statements.*

Note G spells out the effect of the change and adds a paragraph:

> *It is estimated that the aggregate amount which may ultimately be paid in future years in respect of such services for prior years, if the plans continue, will approximate $4,850,000.*

The policy to charge earnings for pensions based upon past services is in accord with the policy advocated by the Commission for some time and recommended by the Committee on Accounting Procedure of the American Institute of Accountants in Research Bulletin No. 36. The reasons for reaching this conclusion are adequately stated in the bulletin. However, an unsolved problem not even mentioned in the bulletin is suggested by the $4,850,000 in the note just quoted. Since a realistic approach to the problem leads to the conclusion that the liability must eventually be met, barring serious economic reverses, we feel that the liability actuarially determined should be reflected in the balance sheet. In the absence of a strict legal liability for the pensions based on past service, our practice has been to require a footnote representation as to the company's obligation under its pension plan.

Inventories are a recurring cause of trouble for accountants and for us, and should demand close scrutiny by the investor. Exceptions taken by certifying accountants on grounds of lack of consistency in the accounting principles applied in valuation are common. The accountants' certificate attached to the statement of an oil company refers to two footnotes dealing with changes in accounting principles. The first of these, dealing with changes in inventory valuation, sounds a bit complicated for a layman but should be interesting to a cost accountant:

> *Prior to 1948, additions to inventories from current production of natural gasoline products were valued at prices based on market, and additions to inventories of refined products at manufacturing cost computed on the by-product method, with crude oil charged at market value. For the year 1948, with minor exceptions, additions to inventories of natural gasoline and refined products were priced at manufacturing cost computed on the relative value method, refined product costs including crude oil at cost. This change in accounting procedure has resulted in reducing net income for the year 1948 by $5,245,017.*

The other note dealt with a change in accounting for dry holes and concessions with a similar effect on income for 1948. A third note refers to the company's policy of making minor revisions in accounting procedures to conform to changing conditions and experiences, the effect of which, except for the two dealt with specifically, was not deemed significant.

Some of the airplane companies have had inventory problems since the war. For example, one such company noted a change to exclude commercial selling expenses from inventories (giving the amount in work-in-process at the beginning of the year). The abandoned procedure was a wartime practice appropriate under government contracts. The certifying accountants called attention in their certificate to the change.

In a certificate addressed to the stockholders of an old company in financial difficulties, the public accountants omitted a statement as to consistency with the preceding year but called particular attention in their certificate to the notes applicable to the financial statements. While somewhat long, I think the four paragraphs are of sufficient interest to quote:

> *Members of our staff were present at the plant of the Company when the inventories were being checked physically and observed the work of the Company's employees in that connection. We reviewed the methods used in taking and compiling the inventories and made physical tests sufficient to satisfy ourselves as to the substantial accuracy of the inventory quantities. We also reviewed the pricing of the inventories and ascertained that they were stated on the basis of materials and direct labor, as customarily computed by the Company for inventory purposes, with provision for slow-moving, obsolete and irregular items. Pursuant to the Company's consistent practice, all indirect manufacturing costs were omitted from the inventory stated on the balance sheet.*
>
> *If effect were given in pricing the inventory to the Company's current costs as to materials and direct labor and to an application of estimated indirect manufacturing costs, the inventory at the close of the period valued on the basis of*

lower of cost or market would have been increased approximately $1,580,000. It is estimated further that if the opening inventory had been valued on a similar basis, the operating loss for the year 1947 would not have been materially changed.

During the year ended December 27, 1947, the Company made no provision in its financial statements for the customary contribution under its pension plan for past services. The Company also changed its basis of providing for current costs of the pension plan from the previous practice of making annual provision therefor and now meets current costs of the pension plan on a monthly basis. It is estimated that the loss for the year ended December 27, 1947, would have been approximately $170,000 greater if the Company had continued to make provision for pension plan payments on the former basis.

In our opinion, the accompanying balance sheet and the related condensed statements of profit and loss and surplus, together with notes to financial statements, and comments contained in this certificate, present fairly the position of [the]————Company at December 27, 1947, and results of operations for the year then ended.

In contrast to the above case, in the examination of the financial statements of a new registrant under the Securities Act it was observed with respect to inventories that "costs as to work in process and manufactured stock include material and labor only, without manufacturing or other overhead." Despite this comment in the note the certifying accountant expressed the opinion that the statements "with their footnotes" were in conformity with generally accepted accounting principles and practices applied on a consistent basis. The footnote dealing with inventories as it became effective was amended to show what the inventories at the several year ends would have been if manufacturing overhead had been included. The effect on income was also set forth. The accountant's certificate was amended to include a paragraph taking exception to the inventory methods of the company, in the following language:

Under the Company's practice, work in process includes material and labor only, without manufacturing or other overhead. I am of the opinion that the inventory valuation of work in process more properly should include the applicable proportion of manufacturing overhead, but the effect of such inclusion upon the Company's assets and net income would be relatively insignificant, as shown in footnote D in the accompanying financial statements.

However, the first annual report filed with the Commission reflected a change in the accounting to include manufacturing overhead in the inventory and the accountant expressed an appropriate exception as to consistency in his certificate. On this point *Montgomery's Auditing,* seventh edition, has this to say:

Overhead Methods — In practice there is great latitude in the application of overhead to inventories. On the one hand, it is generally accepted that all overhead should not be charged off as incurred (Accounting Research Bulletin No. 29), and on the other, it is very rare that all items of overhead are appropriate to apply to inventories. As a corollary to the principle that all overhead should not be charged off, there is, in the author's opinion, a presumption against the exclusion of reasonably determined overhead costs from inventory. The exclusion of such costs may sometimes be tantamount to a reserve which reduces the inventory below an accepted basis; such reserves are discussed in Accounting Research Bulletin No. 31, issued in October, 1947. There has recently been further support of the method of charging off fixed overhead as incurred and of applying to inventories only such items as vary with production; while this method is not widely in use and is not generally recommended, it may have merit under certain circumstances.

There are indications that this subject warrants further study.

The popular inventory method of "Lifo" [last in, first out] has been praised and condemned so generously in poetry and prose by such masters of the English language as Peloubet and Wilcox that I hesitate to say anything on that subject. However, the topic is too important to pass over. Even opponents of the method must concede that "Lifo" is a generally accepted method for valuing inventories. The question before us then is whether the method presents any special problems of disclosure in financial statements intended to inform investors. Certainly a change from some other method of valuation to the "Lifo" method is a significant change in principle and usually results in sufficiently material effect on balance sheet and income figures to warrant full disclosure and an exception by the certifying accountant on the matter of consistency with prior years. For some elaborate disclosures of this type it is only necessary to turn to the department store field, in which some companies had adopted the method in 1941, then abandoned the practice in the face of adverse Treasury Department rulings, and then readopted the method after the favorable U.S. Tax Court decision in 1947. Some of the notes reciting these changes have required a full page in reports to stockholders. In situations such as these, where the differences in valuation between "Lifo" and a basis reflecting more nearly "current values" are material, we have required the disclosure in financial statements filed with the Commission that such differences exist. It seems desirable, also, that where the "Lifo" method is used and no "cushion" exists, that fact should also be disclosed to avoid the possible interpretation by the investor that "Lifo" always indicates a safety factor.

A statement with respect to depreciation policy is a requirement of Regulation S-X and, as any reader of accounting literature knows, depreciation accounting is a popular subject for discussion. Certainly, the topic has not been ignored in the last few years in corporation reports to stockholders. Just what constitutes a significant change in depreciation policy has been the cause of some disagreement among accountants. Some have maintained that a mere change in rate is not a change in the policy to amortize the cost of the asset over its useful life and that such a change is a normal part of applying the policy, as it is customary to alter the rate as more accurate estimates of remaining useful life become possible. Others insist that if the change results in significantly different depreciation charges, notice should be taken in the accountants' certificate so that the statements may not be misleading. This view was expressed by the first chief accountant of the Commission in an address in 1937. As indicated earlier in this article, a literal reading of Rule 3–07 does not seem to require this strict interpretation. A reexamination of the matter with leaders of the accounting profession led to the conclusion that the rule should be clarified on this point to include change in manner of application as well as change in policy. In the application of this rule it should be understood to apply to changes effected by management decision and not to changes in amounts of items due to outside factors beyond the control of management. A change in amount of depreciation, for example, due to a change in operating rate of a plant when depreciation is measured by rate of production, would not require any comment as to consistency in the application of accounting principles. However, a change from a straight-line basis to a productivity basis would require an exception as to consistency, as in this note to which the certifying accountant called attention, with approval, in his certificate:

> It is the policy of the company to depreciate fixed assets over their estimated useful lives. Effective January 1, 1948, however, instead of the straight-line method heretofore used, it has been decided to allocate depreciation over future years based upon activity of each year as related to "normal" activity. For this purpose the average activity for the 20 years ended December 31, 1943 has been chosen as representing "normal." The depreciation charged for the year ended December 31, 1948 is $95,721 in excess of what the charge would have been if the previous policy had been continued.

A year ago depreciation based upon purchasing power recovery or to provide for excessive construction costs, depending upon the circumstances in particular cases and the interpretation of their economic condition by management, was the subject of active discussion in accounting and business circles. Today, to a large extent, accelerated depreciation has gained the center of the stage. For those who are interested in the immediate past history of this subject the 1948 annual reports to stockholders of United States Steel Corporation and E. I. du Pont de Nemours & Company furnish the most accurate statements available of the views of those exponents of these methods. Further discussion seems unnecessary here except to suggest that there is much to be said for substituting a method of depreciation based upon plant activity for straight-line depreciation. I think we should start with the assumption that a decision to build a plant, a new store, or an addition is based on the best business judgment of the management at the time as to the prospects for profitable employment of the property. It seems reasonable to me to assume also that demand in the immediate few years is easier to predict than that of the later years of a plant's potential physical life. The basis for accelerated amortization of the cost of plants during periods of anticipated peak demand seems to me to be well founded and much more realistic than the uniform application of a straight-line rate of depreciation over a plant's anticipated useful life. Also obsolescence as a factor is recognized in any theoretical discussion of depreciation and should be taken into account in the early period of a plant's life for substantially the same reasons and also in anticipation of some possible new competing gadget. While recording plant assets at cost remains the generally accepted basis of accounting, the adequate recognition of activity and obsolescence factors should serve to produce a proper matching of costs with revenues.

In conclusion I want to revert to one of the articles I mentioned in the beginning. The author said that "the inclusion of words of exception, qualification, and even explanation in the accountant's opinion tends to carry or imply some stigma of wrongdoing or deviation from the authority. How to attain adequate disclosure in the face of this reaction is a real question." I confess that in our work at the Commission we see something of the background for the view here expressed. But I think I have shown by many examples that such a feeling is not universal and should not apply at all to an exception as to consistency when the change reported reflects an improvement in accounting policy. The examples I have quoted serve to illustrate how many accounting firms solve the problem very simply by stating the change and its effect on income, or other accounts affected, in their certificate or by referring to a footnote or, in some cases, to a page in management's report, in either case followed by the simple statement that they approve of the change. If the accountants' certificate carries any weight at all, and I assume it does, this treatment should serve to reassure the investor.

NINE

Amendment of Regulation S-X

E. L. KOHLER

Former Consulting Accountant

Kohler, in a rare instance of writing on Securities and Exchange Commission matters, discusses the changes in Regulation S-X brought about by Accounting Series Release (ASR) No. 70. Two particular areas affected by ASR No. 70 are the auditor's certificate as it relates to a position on internal controls and the concept of materiality. This article provides substantial insight into several topics of continuing interest to auditors of publicly held companies.

Originally issued in February 1940, Regulation S-X of the Securities and Exchange Commission (SEC) has been amplified and amended in a number of important respects. Details of the changes appear in SEC Accounting Series Release No. 70, dated December 20, 1950, and they have been made effective for fiscal years ending on or after December 31, 1950, except for Article 6B which became effective one month later. The purpose of Regulation S-X has been and continues to be the setting of minimum standards of form and content for financial statements filed with the SEC. Though the jurisdiction of the SEC does not extend to corporate reports to stockholders, the influence of the Regulation on such reports has always been marked.

THE INCOME STATEMENT

The most publicized change has been in Rule 5.03, which now commences with the following language:

> Except as otherwise permitted by the Commission, *the profit and loss or income statements filed for persons to whom this article is applicable shall comply with the provisions of this rule.* [Italics supplied.]
>
> (a) All items of profit and loss given recognition in the accounts during the period covered by the profit and loss or income statements shall be included.
>
> (b) Only items entering into the determination of net income or loss may be included.

Aside from the italicized material, the above-quoted language is new. It reflects in some measure the Commission's previously expressed preference[1] for the "all-inclusive" income statement long advocated by the Executive Committee of the American Accounting Associ-

Reprinted from the *Illinois Certified Public Accountant,* March 1951, pp. 50–55, by permission of the Illinois CPA Society.

ation,[2] as opposed to the "current-operating-performance" income statement favored by the Committee on Accounting Procedure of the American Institute of Accountants.[3] In response to representations by the AIA Executive Committee, the Commission receded somewhat, its change of viewpoint being reflected in the presentation at the bottom of the income statement:

16. Net income or loss.

17. Special items — State separately and describe each item of profit and loss given recognition in the accounts, included herein pursuant to rule 5.03a, and not included in the determination of net income or loss (Item 16).

18. Net income or loss and special items.[4]

and in the statement of surplus (Rule 11.02), following the opening balance of surplus:

2. Net income or loss (or net income or loss and special items) from profit and loss statement.

3. Other additions to surplus — State separately any material amounts, indicating clearly the nature of the transaction out of which the items arose.

4. Deductions from surplus other than dividends — State separately any material amounts, indicating clearly the nature of the transactions out of which the items arose.

An estimate of the consequences of these changes is hazarded in the following observations:

1. The Commission will doubtless review carefully any proposal to use items 17 and 18 of the income statement; only rarely will it be likely to permit items to appear on line 17.

2. The seven words added to the introductory sentence of Rule 5.03 (see above) seem to imply an even more restrictive attitude of the Commission toward direct surplus charges and credits.

3. Many types of charges to reserves, such as reserves for contingencies now recognized as surplus reserves, although in some instances created by charges to expense in prior years, may have to be included in the income statement and may even have to be shown as expense above line 16.

4. Reserve charges permitted to remain as such (and thus not treated as expense) may be limited to those affecting reserves that are in the nature of valuation accounts or liabilities, where the debit creating the reserve was properly recognized as an expense.

5. Contingency and other reserves originally created by charges to surplus may of course be restored to the same surplus account. If what would now be designated as a surplus reserve (e.g., a "general" or even a "special" contingency reserve) was set up in an earlier year by a charge to expense, there is some chance that the Commission may require the credit eliminating the reserve to appear in line 17, unless the statement for the earlier year is recast or its rectification is otherwise noted.

6. The write-off of a large intangible such as goodwill originally created as the result of the issue of capital stock having a par or stated value in excess of tangible values acquired will probably be regarded as a permissible charge to earned surplus, since it bears a distant but nevertheless conceptual relationship to a stock dividend.

7. There may be some pressure on the Institute's Committee on Accounting Procedure to revise a number of the Committee's bulletins, particularly 28, 32, and 35. A clarification of recommended reserve and income-statement procedures would undoubtedly have the effect of eliminating a number of divergent points of view still existing between the Commission and the AIA Committee.

8. Income statements appearing in reports to stockholders accompanied by certificates of accountants will doubtless be conformed to whatever is agreed to between the Commission and registrants as "net income," "net income and special items," and surplus charges and credits, if any other than dividends and the carryover from the income statement.

9. Investment analysts are likely to quote the net-income figure on line 18 rather than that appearing on line 16, but will probably footnote the item by some such qualifying phrase as "after special charges." Some of them have long been in the habit of adjusting per-share earnings by surplus charges and credits, particularly where displaying earnings over a period of years.

10. The trend in the direction of the all-inclusive statement has probably been given a notable, if somewhat restricted, impetus.

THE BALANCE SHEET

A good deal of attention has been paid at one time or another in accounting pronouncements to the use of the words "significant" and "material." They proved to be useful, but probably unconscious, fill-ins at spots where such theories and practices as had not been fully developed were being left, in particular varying situations, to whatever formulation the common sense of the accountant would dictate. When overused, as they often were, they were little more than irksome and sententious in effect, and not infrequently cloaked the real purpose behind their employment. The Commission has taken a needed, though hesitant, step in the amended regulation by substituting "material" for most of the "significants" and by identifying more closely with the regulation the definition of "material" it had prescribed elsewhere. The definition, now appearing in Rule 1.02, indicates that the word is intended as a limiting term confining required information "to those matters as to which an average prudent investor ought reasonably to be informed before purchasing [and presumably holding or selling] the security registered"[5] (bracketed material supplied). But this definition is still far from satisfactory; it delimits too narrowly and uncertainly rather than adds substance to whatever notion the word might otherwise be made to convey; a straw man, the average, though prudent, investor who, being an average, cannot be assumed to exist, nevertheless conscionably desires information of a sort even though he doesn't, or can't, ask for it; if he does ask for it, the plain implication is that he may make little or no use of it. From so tenuous a concept, what can one gather as the kind of minimum information the investor should have? Possibly no one can answer the question at this time and it may take several years before a better definition can be found; in lieu thereof, the Commission and professional accountants alike are trying to present historical information through conventional forms: as much, as briefly, and as easily read as possible. This laudable aim of information, brevity, and readability is exemplified by the Commission in a number of ways in the revised regulation:

1. The old 5% test for materiality, and hence separate disclosure, has been changed to

10% for any item appearing in the following general categories: current assets, assets other than fixed and intangible, current liabilities, liabilities "other than funded debt, capital shares, and surplus" (Rule 5.02, items 7, 12, 21, 25, 31)[6].

2. Fixed assets are to be broken down on some class basis "such as land, buildings, machinery and equipment, leaseholds," and the basis of valuation is to be indicated for each class (Rule 5.02, item 13A). Public utilities that have been required by regulatory bodies to determine original cost are required to display such cost, plant-acquisition adjustments, and plant adjustments (Rule 5.02, item 13b).

3. Valuation and qualifying reserves are now to be deducted on the balance sheet from the current assets, fixed assets, or intangibles to which they relate (Rule 3.11). Public utilities had previously been permitted to classify replacement and similar reserves among liabilities.

4. The basis of patent and other intangible valuation must be disclosed (Rule 5.02, item 15).

5. The amortization method applicable to capitalized organization expense and commission and expense on capital shares is to be stated (Rule 5.02, items 18, 20).

6. Details displayed on each long-term-debt issue are to include: general character, interest rate, date of maturity or general indications of maturities, aggregate amount of maturities, and sinking-fund requirements for each of the five years following the balance-sheet date; if payment of principal or interest is contingent, an indication of the contingency; some indication of priority; and the basis, if any, of convertibility (Rule 5.02, item 28).

7. Defaults, under credit agreements as well as security issues, "in principal, interest, sinking-fund, or redemption provisions . . . or any breach of covenant of a related indenture or agreement, shall be stated," and noted in the balance sheet (Rule 3.19c).

8. Brief disclosure is now required of material commitments "for the acquisition of permanent investments and fixed assets, . . . for the purchase, repurchase, construction, or rental of assets [including the minimum payable] under long-term leases; . . . for rentals under such leases" and of the periods during which they are payable; also to be shown are "any important obligation assumed or guaranteed made in connection therewith" (Rule 3.18). It is the apparent intention of the Commission to have commitments and contingent liabilities noted on the balance sheet after long-term debt, perhaps in a total supported where necessary by a footnote (Rule 5.02, item 32).

9. If the reserve classification following liabilities is to be retained, each class and a clear indication of its purpose must appear (Rule 5.02, item 33).

10. The basis of conversion of convertible shares must now be disclosed on the balance sheet (Rule 5.02, item 34).

11. Pension-plan details are to be disclosed that will include: the general basis of the pension or retirement plan, the estimated annual cost, and, if the plan has not yet been funded, "the estimated amount that would be necessary to fund or otherwise provide for the past-service cost of the plan" (Rule 3.19e).

12. Surplus must, if possible, be split between paid-in surplus, revaluation surplus, other capital surplus, and earned surplus appropriated and unappropriated, with a parenthetical notation of included undistributed earnings of unconsolidated subsidiaries, if any. Earned surplus following a quasi reorganization must be dated, and for the first three years thereafter the amount of the absorbed deficit must be shown[7] (Rule 5.02, item 35, a, b, c). Restrictions limiting the availability of surplus for dividends are to be described (Rule 3.19f).

Most of these requirements have long been standard practices in many accounting firms; even where they have not been observed, they will add no onerous tasks to audit and reporting procedures. Deviations from these more detailed balance-sheet rules, where exceptional situations do not permit their observance, are specifically provided for in the opening sentence of Rule 5.02, by application to the Commission.

CONSOLIDATED FINANCIAL STATEMENTS

A number of changes were made in Article 4 of the regulation governing the preparation of consolidated statements; in most cases their effect will be minor:

1. The definition of "significant subsidiary" has been changed by increasing the 5% therein appearing to 15%: that is, to come under this classification, the subsidiary's assets "or the investments in and advances to the subsidiary by its parent and the parent's other subsidiaries" must exceed 15% of a similar consolidated figure; or the subsidiary's sales and operating revenues must exceed 15% of a similar consolidated figure; or the subsidiary is "the parent of one or more subsidiaries and together with such subsidiaries would, if considered in the aggregate, constitute a significant subsidiary" (Rule 1.02).

2. A registrant in the promotional, exploratory, or development stage, and subject to the provisions of Article 5a, may not submit consolidated statements but is required to submit the statements of itself and subsidiaries in parallel columns (Rule 4.14).

3. Where consolidation is made of a foreign subsidiary, the effects of foreign-exchange restrictions (e.g., limiting the withdrawal of profits) on the financial statements are to be disclosed (Rule 4.02c).

4. The basis and amount of affiliates' securities, both consolidated and eliminated, are to be indicated (Rule 5.02, item 9).

5. A previous rule required disclosure of "significant intercompany profits and losses (on sales or other charges by persons for which statements are filed) included in the profit-and-loss statement . . ." The rule has been modified so as to require a disclosure of "the effect on any balance-sheet item of profits or losses resulting from transactions with affiliated companies," which of course may include a parent company, subsidiaries less than 50% owned, and other companies under common control (Rule 3.19b).

THE ACCOUNTANT AND HIS CERTIFICATE

During the eighteen years of its existence the Commission has dealt with numerous cases in which the independence of the accountant has been questioned. By 1940, when the regulation was first promulgated, the Commission's position was that a *substantial* interest of an accountant in a person indicated a want of independence in his certification of the financial statements of that person; by 1950 it was ready to state that *any* interest was enough to demonstrate that lack. A review of the cases presented by Donald C. Cook, SEC vice-chairman, at the last AIA annual meeting, tends to justify the present position of the Commission. At the same time the Commission has broadened the application of the rule to *any affiliate* of a person, it being remembered that an affiliate in the language of the Commission continues to be defined as "a person that directly, or indirectly through one or more intermediaries, controls, or is controlled by, or is under common control with, the person specified," while "control" is "the possession, direct or indirect, of the power to direct or cause the direction of the management and policies of a person, whether through the ownership of voting securities, by contract, or otherwise" (Rule 2.01b). It may be noted in passing that these and other definitions previously appearing in general regulations have now been incorporated in Regulation S-X (Rule 1.02).

Rule 2.02, Accountants' Certificates, has been somewhat simplified by omitting reference to the determination by the accountant of the adequacy of the system of internal control and to the weight he may give to the work of internal auditors. There is no ground for believing that the Commission would assign any less importance to these audit factors; rather the presumption is that there are many audit factors and that the mention of two of them (justified undoubtedly in 1940 when the McKesson & Robbins case and the subsequent disclosure of auditing practices were fresh in mind) might well be subordinated to a fuller reliance and emphasis on the implications of the term "generally accepted auditing standards," and on the requirement that the certificate must recount any omission, with reasons therefor, of "any auditing procedures generally recognized as normal, or deemed necessary by the accountant under the circumstances of a particular case."

The opinion of the accountant must now be given on *"Material* changes in accounting principles or practices, *or method of applying the accounting principles or practices"* [the italics denote additions to the previous rule] (Rule 2.02c); and the effect (presumably material also) of any such change on the comparability of "financial statements with those of prior or future periods, and the effect thereof upon the net income of each period for which financial statements are filed" must be disclosed in a footnote accompanying the statements of the affected years. Like disclosure must be given to any "material retroactive adjustment" affecting prior years. In substance this represents no change in attitude by the Commission, but the intended coverage and method of disclosure are more specific. Apparently some accountants had drawn a distinction between primary and secondary accounting policies,[8] notwithstanding a very large effect on operating results by switches in such secondary policies. Differences defined as the consequence of a change in method of application are now covered (Rule 3.07).

Reliance may still be had by a principal accountant on certifications by other accountants of the accounts of branches or subsidiaries; the rule has been recast to permit any of three procedures: (a) a filing of the certificates of such other accountants; (b) no mention of the examination by other accountants in the principal accountant's certificate; or (c) mention of the examination by the other accountants and a statement in the principal accountant's certificate "that he assumes responsibility for such other accountant's examination in the same manner as if it had been made by him" (Rule 2.05).

NOTES

1. Fourteenth Annual Report (1948) of the Securities and Exchange Commission, p. 111.

2. Originally advocated in 1936; in the Committee's 1948 revision, items (9) and (10) under *Financial Statements* read as follows:

(9) The income of an accounting period should be reported in a statement providing an exhibit of all revenue and expense (including losses) given accounting recognition during that period. This practice assures that the income statements for a period of years will disclose completely the entire income history of that period.

(10) The income statement should be arranged to report consistently and in reasonable detail the particulars of revenue and expense pertaining to the operations of the current period, measured as accurately as is possible at the time the statement is prepared and also any items of revenue or expense not associated with the operations of the current period. Such arrangement of data in a single statement discloses both the earning performance and the entire income history of the enterprise during a given period.

3. Accounting Research Bulletin No. 32, page 263, lists for exclusion from the income statement five types of transactions, provided their amounts are material "in relation to the company's net income and are clearly not identifiable with or do not result from the usual or typical business operations of the period." These are: nonrecurring prior-year adjustments; sales of assets not acquired for the purpose of resale; unusual losses against which insurance would not normally be carried; the elimination of an intangible; and the write-off of bond discount or premium and expense upon an originally unscheduled retirement or refunding before maturity. Three members of the committee, favoring the "all-inclusive" type of income statement, dissented; the committee, doubtless influenced by these dissents, was careful to state that "there should be a general presumption that all items of profit and loss recognized during the period are to be used in determining the figure reported as net income." The "all-inclusive" sense of this statement is, however, negated by the exceptions noted.

4. Although the arrangement of items 16–18 meets the AAA Committee concept partway—in that all items recognized during the period as profit or loss are to be included in one statement and extraordinary items are to appear in a "bottom" section—the caption of item 18 leaves the major issue still undecided.

5. Originally appearing in Regulation C, rule 405. Rule 3.02 in the revised regulation gives the word general application to all financial-statement items, thereby making possible the merger of inconsequential amounts with others; moreover, specific tests have been provided for several subclass disclosures as noted in paragraph (1), following.

6. An item may still be material, in the judgment of the certifying accountant, even though exempted from disclosure by the application of the 10% test. A literal reading of the revised regulation would require the permission of the Commission if such a disclosure were to be made. Doubtless this was not the intent.

7. First appearing in Accounting Series Release No. 15 (1940).

8. E.g., the valuation of inventories at cost or less (a primary policy) and "actual" cost, "cost or market," FIFO [first in, first out], or even LIFO [last in, first out]—four very different subpolicies having in almost every case a material effect on income if a switch is made from one "subbasis" to another.

TEN

The Impact of Federal Legislation upon Accounting

WILLIAM W. WERNTZ

Former Chief Accountant, Securities and Exchange Commission

Werntz discusses the influence on accounting of federal regulatory agencies over the years. The author, a former chief accountant, traces the effect these agencies have had on the profession and what the result has been. He concludes that, despite some problems, the overall effect on the profession has been positive and has tended to stimulate accounting thought.

There is no need whatever to debate the questions of whether administrative agencies of the federal, state, and even local governments have exerted an influence on accounting. They have—and it has been a powerful and in some areas an almost dominant influence. The matters for consideration are: (1) what is the nature of this influence and how has it been brought to bear; and (2) on balance, is such influence helpful or hurtful, both as to its short-term and long-term effects.

A listing of those administrative agencies which have influenced accounting in one way or another would be lengthy and of little usefulness. We may, perhaps roughly, map out, with illustrations, certain types of situations, as follows:

1. Purely record keeping requirements, e.g., wage and hour requirements, or sales tax collection requirements;

2. Agencies creating problems which accounting and accountants must handle in the records and give effect to in financial statements, for example, contract termination regulations, renegotiation boards;

3. Indirect influence on accounting concepts and thinking, as, for example, price control and procurement regulations with their discussions and definitions of costs, overheads, allocation of costs, etc.;

4. Direct influence on accounting—income tax requirements, state and federal regulatory agencies, and the SEC.

Many individual agencies will of course fall into more than one, and perhaps in all, of the above categories. For example, in its administration of the income tax, the Internal Revenue Bureau (including for this purpose the courts passing on individual cases) has certainly been a powerful influence toward keeping better records; discussions of cases arising under its requirements have been persuasive and, in some areas, controlling authority for the deci-

Reprinted from *The Accounting Review*, April 1953, pp. 159–169, with permission of the American Accounting Association.

sions as to the accounting treatment to be followed in general financial statements; and the peculiarities of the income tax have certainly created problems for the accountant — witness Bulletin 23 of the Committee on Accounting Procedure of the American Institute of Accountants and Bulletin 53 issued by the SEC.

For today's purposes I plan to confine our consideration to analysis of the last two categories, i.e., the influence exerted directly or indirectly on accounting thought, and its reflection in accounting theory and practice.

There are two principal avenues by which to explore the effect which federal administrative agencies have had on the development of accounting theory and practice. It would be possible to amass a multitude of actual instances in which published administrative opinions or rulings in specific cases had forced changes in accounting methods or accounting presentation, and, conversely, to seek to catalog examples or areas in which accounting generally is at odds with the rulings of such bodies. Such a summation would today be a monumental task and, perhaps, most useful only in a historical sense.

The alternative approach of considering the purposes underlying the assignment of accounting powers to governmental agencies, and the varying ways in which such powers are implemented, and of speculating as to their influence on accounting thinking, while perhaps less objective and demonstrable, is more amenable to the requirements of brevity. It is probably also a good deal more useful in seeking to anticipate the action of such an agency in unsettled areas and undecided cases.

THE CONCEPT OF ACCOUNTING

Business accounting, for purposes of internal control of personnel, costs, and policies and for reporting to inactive owners, has largely developed within the last half century. It was impossible that this development of accounting as a control device originating in the business world would go unnoticed by legislative bodies and judicial and administrative officials. It was inevitable that, in the search for effective means of obtaining data as to social and economic phenomena, resort should quickly be had to accounting data. Thenceforth it was but a short and logical step to reliance on the accounting process, first as a means of regularly observing the activities of economic units, and then as a means of prescribing and proscribing various courses of action.

The use of accounting for governmental control purposes has generally followed a set pattern. First, there will be a mere requirement for informational returns, the filing of financial statements as prepared or published by the enterprise. Next, there may be an administrative or statutory requirement that data filed conform to some general standard, such as general trade practice or, more recently, "generally accepted" accounting principles. Next, there may be a statutory generalized grant of power to an administrative agency to prescribe rules or, perhaps, a more or less detailed group of accounting rules may be incorporated in the statute itself, the stated objective being, for example, to attain "uniformity" or to avoid "misleading statements." At this intermediate stage, prescribed rules are generally few and directed at a handful or so of specific points, either positive or negative. The ultimate stage, not always reached, is the statutory grant of broad powers and their exercise administratively through a more or less complete prescription of accounting methods, as by a uniform system of accounts, together with prohibition against the keeping of records that are inconsistent therewith.

It is not to be assumed, however, that every use of accounting or accounting data for purposes of control by the government through statutes or administrative agencies will necessarily follow the above evolutionary pattern. New controls will frequently start far along the evolutionary pathway, particularly if the area to which the control is directed is not a new one or if the particular government involved has already felt its way for some time in the use of accounting controls in other areas. It is also not to be assumed that every resort to accounting powers will necessarily evolve to the ultimate stage noted. In many instances, regulatory needs may be satisfied or considered best served by stopping at one or the other of the intermediary steps as a matter either of statutory restrictions or of administrative discretion.

In analyzing this role of administrative agencies, it is essential that some analysis first be made of what "accounting" itself is. Accountants have sought for many years and in many ways to develop and state what are now generally called "accounting principles." First overt efforts in this direction were quite naturally textbooks prepared by leading practitioners and teachers. Later there were efforts by groups such as the Federal Reserve Board, the New York Stock Exchange acting in conjunction with the American Institute of Accountants, and by the Institute itself. These were mixed approaches to accounting principles, audit procedures, and statement forms. Much more recently, there have been efforts to isolate and establish accounting principles as such. These have taken the form of statements issued by groups within a technical organization such as the American Accounting Association or by established committees of a national professional association, the American Institute of Accountants. Indeed, in certain instances, statements of particular "principles" have been adopted by the membership of this Institute, thus attaining a substantially more authoritative position than bulletins released by a committee, which carry essentially only the persuasive authority of the committee.

"Principles" thus established must, however, be sharply distinguished from what in other fields are frequently, though not necessarily accurately, called laws in such expressions as the "law of gravity." They must equally be set apart from "laws" in the sense, for example, of particular statutes such as the uniform negotiable instruments "law." In contrast to both of these they basically represent methods of dealing with economic events, expressed in dollars, which are recommended for use in order to convey information about such events in a reasonably understandable way. Departures from or nonobservance of such "principles" are generally to be condemned because the user of data so prepared is certainly or likely not to understand the information given, or to misunderstand it. To this there is often stated a corollary — that it is seldom practicable to depart from such "principles" and to cure the situation by seeking to disclose the use of a different or unusual method that has been generally condemned. "Principles" thus are a good deal like definitions of the words in a language — they are recommended and accepted meanings whereby the shorthand expression that is a financial statement can be expected to have a common meaning to its readers.

In selecting or rejecting one of these "definitions" or "principles," a major criterion is necessarily the purpose or objective which the observer has in mind. There can be enumerated at least ten different interested groups — management; stockholders or owners; creditors and credit agencies; employees; government agencies; legislators and the judiciary; lawyers;

the academic public; the press; and other accountants. Each of these is a principal user of financial data, with the rather clear resulting inference that the needs and desires of each group may differ in varying degrees. To the draftsman of financial statements, to the critic of accounting principles, or to one who seeks to draft an integrated statement of accounting principles, selection of the interests of one or the other of these groups as paramount necessarily colors his approach and conditions his judgment. This is purposive accounting.

Purposive accounting is nevertheless not to be regarded as bad or unsound or improper accounting. To the extent that a particular scheme of accounting adequately satisfies a chosen group of underlying purposes, it must be deemed good as "accounting" and approval or disapproval must then be based on agreement or disagreement with the announced or implicit underlying purposes and objectives. A very fair share of the written arguments about this or that accounting method or principle or presentation is in reality a debate over the purpose of the accounting rather than over the "accounting" as such; in a great many cases, the debates arise only because the contestants have in mind the interests of different groups.

This view of accounting necessarily defines it as basically utilitarian in nature, a conclusion or possibly a premise both of the Committee on Accounting Procedure of the American Institute of Accountants and of many, if not the large majority, of accounting writers. Three groups, at least, apparently take a different view. At one extreme are those who are inclined to ascribe to accounting the status of a basic "truth" and the efforts of accountants to formalize principles simply as attempts to discover and state these fundamentals. Even this approach tends to recognize the accounting standards of any given time as legitimate and acceptable at the time, even though subsequent developments of accounting thought and practice may discredit them. The second school seeks to ascribe so large an area of common purposes and objectives to each of the various groups listed above as to posit a body of accounting "principles" common to all areas, differences where required being merely part of a definable superstructure. A third group cuts across the strictly utilitarian approach and both of the above views. This comprises those who ascribe to accountancy a measure of artistry in the interpretation of economic events and the construction of financial statements. This group tends to recognize a basic body of accounting concepts (which may be the purposive or utilitarian concept, the fundamental truth idea, or the "common purpose" belief, or some mixture of the three) but feels that in applying such concepts or principles to the facts of a given case the "best" picture can be gotten only if the accountant exercises the widest discretion and gives full play to an intuitive judgment born of experience and familiarity with his field.

Which of these views of accounting, if any, may ultimately predominate cannot be predicted. Recognition of such basic differences in approach is, however, important and is often essential to the understanding of an accounting discussion and to the preparation of successful arguments and counterarguments. For present purposes, it may be sufficient to suggest with great temerity that most administrative agencies necessarily combine in their approach parts of two of these schools of thought. Substantially all administrative bodies operate on the basis of a fixed set of purposes, usually set out in the preamble to the enabling statute, but sometimes merely implicit in or inferable from the specific statutory powers granted the agency. Oftentimes the short title or the common name of the act gives the key to this basic set of purposes such as, for example, the "Revenue Act of 1950." In other cases, such as the principal acts administered by the Securities and Exchange Commission, there are introductory sections setting out quite specifically and in varying detail the purposes of the act and consequently the purposes of any accounting authority granted. Conscientious adherence to these announced and restricted purposes necessarily places an agency in the position of regarding accounting as essentially utilitarian — i.e., responsive to the maximum achievement of its objectives. Superimposed on this approach, however, there is likely to be the overt or implicit tendency to regard that method of accounting which is conceived to be best adapted to achievement of these fixed purposes as a basic or fundamental "truth," other possible methods being deviations which should be considered unsuitable for these particular purposes. In practice, there is seldom in the discussion of particular matters full recognition of this ellipsis in reasoning, either on the part of agency representatives or on the part of those appearing before the agency.

The daily work of most public accountants is necessarily of such a nature as to require at various times recognition of the interests, both mutual and adverse, of each of the different groups under discussion, and usually under circumstances which require consideration simultaneously of the problems and objectives of several of the groups. In consequence, it is believed that most observers in this group tend to support the idea of a relatively broad area of basic accounting concepts common to the interests of all groups mentioned with, however, equally broad leeway whereby to resolve conflicts in interest or to arrive somewhat intuitively, perhaps, at a presentation which best gives expression to a particular set of facts under consideration and also with considerable latitude in presenting supplementary data or special statements to satisfy the needs of one or more groups.

This modification of the "basic truth" philosophy perhaps ascribes to accounting an origin in pure economics so that accounting becomes a practical attempt to reflect basic economic concepts such as income, profits, costs, and capital values in terms of day-to-day transactions. As such, accounting will tend to reflect, though by no means always succeed in reflecting, whatever economic philosophy is predominant at the time. It may even reflect basic notions common to a variety of economic philosophies and in such sense be more fundamental than any one of such philosophies. It is probable, however, that in this view the basis for accounting is best limited to the economic system and philosophy then predominant in the economic society under discussion. "Accounting" would thus have for itself only a purely "utilitarian" function, but would at the same time enjoy a derivative independence stemming from the economic philosophy it seeks to reflect.

THE ADMINISTRATIVE AGENCY

In the somewhat disorderly and contradictory development of the accounting concept, administrative agencies have played an important but not always beneficial part. Perhaps the most hurtful is a tendency toward inertia, which may at times characterize the accounting required or preferred by such agencies. One of the earliest uses of accounting by an administrative agency was the prescription of a uniform classification of accounts for railroads by the Interstate Commerce Commission (ICC). At the time, the accounting embodied in the regulation doubtless reflected the best contemporary thought and may well have been then considered progressive, if not radical. However, in many respects of principle, the classification remained unchanged for so long a period as to diverge materially from the accounting mores of later times. In the effort for uniformity and consistency, the benefits of progress were lost through resistance to change. Some commentators have pointed out (with the benefit of hindsight) that accounting under the old ICC resulted in data of questionable usefulness to the average reader through adherence to ideas and treatments since discarded in other areas. Much the same sort of discouragement to progress was caused in the utilities field through adherence, specifically or by interpretation of the older classifications of accounts, to the idea of retirement accounting in lieu of depreciation accounting, which is followed in substantially all other business areas.

A second undesirable effect of administrative agencies on accounting development stems from a possible lack of breadth in coverage of different viewpoints. Even putting to one side the fact that administrative agencies by hypothesis have a specific and limited set of purposes in mind, there is also the fact that, organizationally, ultimate responsibility for technical development and for selection from among variant policies is necessarily centered in the hands of a relatively small group. It is apparent that, without such centralization, administrative accounting would fail as a control device. Nevertheless, the existence of centralized authority means that the policies adopted will reflect to a greater or lesser extent the particular philosophy embraced by the group, to the exclusion of others. It is not intended to infer in any way that decisions and choices are reached capriciously or without the most extended and thoughtful consideration of conflicting ideas and optional methods, but only that selection ultimately rests on the conclusions reached by relatively few rather than on "general acceptance." It is also important to note that once a policy has been adopted, the very size of the group tends to strengthen the natural and understandable reluctance to reconsider.

There is finally, as a possible nonbeneficial influence of administrative agencies in the development of accounting, the efficacy of the sanctions of the enabling statute in controlling conduct and thought and so modifying development. No better illustration of this can probably be found than in the field of income tax. Ever since adoption of the income tax in 1913, and more powerfully as rates have risen, the tax treatment of items has become a major consideration in accounting thought. Initially, and still in language, taxable income is supposed to be determined by generally accepted accounting methods which will clearly reflect the taxpayer's operations. On this generalized and especially sound foundation, there has been built a mass of court decisions, and statutory exceptions and prescriptions, as well as rulings, interpretations, and opinions based thereon, which have resulted in an edifice of tax accounting theory only superficially similar to general accounting and possessed of a rigidity wholly inconsistent with what is probably the present majority view of accounting. It is not intended to imply that tax accounting theory is "bad" accounting or unsound for tax purposes, but only that it has developed along its own functional lines, is not well suited for many other purposes, and at many points runs contrary to most modern thought. It can even be agreed that many or most tax rules which are subject to criticism accountingwise are necessary or desirable taxwise. But when one considers the tax accounting approach to such matters as deferred income or premiums or subscriptions received in advance or property taxes, to name a few of the simplest matters, it is readily apparent that tax and general accounting theory have become widely divergent. Yet the impact of taxes on the economy is so significant from the dollars-and-cents point of view that the tax effect of a particular treatment is often determinative of the adoption or rejection of such treatment for general purposes and, what is more significant perhaps, of the decision to complete or not to complete the transaction. The area of departure of the two fields is well illustrated by the fact that both the American Institute of Accountants, through its Committee on Accounting Procedure, and the Securities and Exchange Commission, in one of its Accounting Series Releases, have felt it necessary to develop rules of procedure and theory to apply in cases in which a material item is treated differently for tax and for financial purposes. It is also an interesting commentary to note that conformance to the principles required by one administrative agency, the Bureau of Internal Revenue, because of statutory provisions and court decisions, has resulted in a major problem for another administrative agency, the Securities and Exchange Commission, which is charged with responsibility in accounting matters in another area and which, by its very concern with the problem, has by implication rejected as unsatisfactory the accounting required or accepted under the tax statutes.

These tax "sanctions" are monetary in a direct and immediate way, since they govern the amount of dollars to be paid in taxes. Other statutes such as the Securities acts impose a quite different type of sanction. Under such acts, those who participate in the issuance of financial statements may incur liabilities to users of the statements if such statements "contained an untrue statement of a material fact or omitted to state a material fact required to be stated therein or necessary to make the statements therein not misleading." As applied to the usual financial statements, these liability provisions encompass not merely full disclosure but go much farther, according to the interpretations established by the Commission. Such rulings provide that a failure to conform to "generally accepted accounting principles" renders the balance sheet or income statement misleading. In other words, a statement of property or of a provision for depreciation or any other material item on a basis not generally recognized among accountants as acceptable and proper may be held to be a misstatement. Much the same idea permeates the common-law liability for issuance of misleading statements, although there is seldom a conscious recognition that failure to follow a "sound" accounting principle is to be considered a misstatement. Instead, most court cases merely examine the item in question — property, for example — and conclude on the facts that the "amount" shown is therefore wrong or misleading. However, scrutiny of those opinions which contain some reasoning in support of the conclusion will generally show that there is testimony or other authority to the effect that the "amount" was arrived at by means or on the basis of methods which most accountants would consider to be improper. The rules, opinions, and releases of qualified administrative agencies, particularly one such as the Securities and Exchange Commission, can be expected to be given considerable weight by most courts which have before them a question on which the agency has ruled, even though the case was not raised under the agency's enabling statute and the agency was not a party thereto. Such material would probably be accorded more weight than, for example, textbooks, and might also outweigh some types of testimony by expert witnesses.

This concept that failure to utilize accepted principles is a misstatement was adopted by the Commission in its Accounting Series Release No. 4. That release indeed went further and specified as misleading the use of any principle of accounting which was contrary to any of the Commission's rules, regulations, or formal opinions, including the opinions of its chief accountant. This statement of policy was reaffirmed at the time the recent Federal

Administrative Procedures Act became effective through republication of the release in the Federal Register at that time.

The pressure generated by statutory liability for misstatements has been increased and enlarged by the requirement of "independence" as a necessary attribute of accountants who report on statements filed with the Commission. Under the Commission's interpretation of this requirement, all relations of an accountant with his client are to be given consideration in determining his independence, not merely relationships incident to the filing of a statement with the Commission. Among other things given consideration are differences between statements filed with the Commission and those included in annual reports to stockholders or otherwise published. Lack of independence will itself make the filing deficient (misleading) and may under some circumstances also result in disciplinary action.

Still another type of "sanction" attaching to such legislation as the Securities acts is the possibility of widespread publicity of disagreements and adverse decisions which is afforded through the medium of public hearings and published opinions. Such publicity is undesired and undesirable for both corporations and practicing accountants. This may even be true where the opinion cites an accountant with approval rather than criticism, since many lay readers may not be able to distinguish the cases or may not take the trouble to do so.

Because of these sanctions and because the SEC field of activity closely parallels or overlaps a major area of corporate and public accounting activity, the conclusions and policies of the SEC have been particularly influential and formative in much of the development in accounting concepts during most of the last two decades. Evidence that this is so is easily found. Both the annual reports of the Commission and the annual reports of the major committees of the professional accounting societies are replete with references to the usefulness of a long course of collaboration in the discussion of mutual problems such as the selection or rejection of particular accounting treatments, the development of methods of handling new situations in financial reporting, and so on. Companies and their accountants are understandably reluctant to file statements with the Commission which differ in any essential way, except perhaps in the amount of detail, from those furnished to stockholders or otherwise related to the general public. This reluctance can be specifically illustrated. In a fairly recent annual report to stockholders, this note to the income statement was prominently displayed: "At the request of the staff of the Securities and Exchange Commission, these items are included in the consolidated statement of income rather than in Earned Surplus as previously reported."

An even more significant illustration is found in Bulletins 5, 6, and 12 issued by the American Institute of Accountants Committee on Auditing Procedure in 1941 and 1942. Early in 1941, the SEC had revised its rules so as to require that accountants' reports include "if with respect to significant items in the financial statements any auditing procedures generally recognized as normal have been omitted, a specific designation of such procedures and of the reasons for their omission." An earlier conclusion of the Committee on Auditing Procedure had been that no disclosure of omitted procedures was necessary unless the procedures would have been reasonable and practicable under the circumstances, but, nevertheless, had not been carried out.

Approximately a year later, the committee issued an amended statement in which it was recommended that certificates for general use conform to the SEC requirement on this point even though the company involved or the particular statements under consideration were not subject to the jurisdiction of that agency. The reason advanced was that it was undesirable to create the appearance of a "double standard" as between companies subject to SEC and those not so subject. This stand may, however, have been modified somewhat in the recently published booklet on auditing standards.

It is not possible to tell in how many cases the accounting of otherwise unregulated companies has been shaped or modified by reason of the penalties and risks that would have had to be assumed had not the rules or administrative requests of the Commission been met. That they are numerous will be readily conceded by all familiar with the field. There are certainly even more cases wherein a possible accounting treatment was dismissed from serious consideration simply because it was apparent that the use of such treatment would be inconsistent with prior opinions or rulings of a federal agency. To the extent that compliance with agency preferences in accounting matters is due to fear of sanctions, to the exclusion of a consensus of informed and honestly held contrary views, the influence exerted by the agency must be classed as undesirable.

The influence of such agencies as the Bureau of Internal Revenue and the SEC are especially pervasive and far reaching because of the great variety of businesses affected; but they are not so all-powerful in any specific area as the decisions of agencies in which regulatory accounting powers over particular industries are vested, such as the several state and federal commissions regulating utilities, insurance companies, or banks. Most of the statutes creating such commissions proscribe the keeping of basic records other than or inconsistent with those called for by the regulatory agency. Under such conditions, the subject company or its accountants may have little basic freedom of action except as to the relatively few matters for which the agency has issued no controlling rule. Even here, however, there will be found a few, a very few, instances in which a company's published accounts will be different in form or content from those prescribed, but accompanied by a very positive disclosure of the difference in treatment. These cases differ from the instance cited earlier in that the first group reflects recognition of a persuasive authority, while the latter and very rare group of cases reflects, in reality, a revolt against rigid and possibly antiquated procedures.

Up to this point the influence of administrative agencies on accounting has been dealt with in terms of the restrictions exerted on freedom of development and from that point of view has been characterized as possibly, though not always necessarily, nonbeneficial. This, however, is only one side of the problem. Like other social and economic organizations, the administrative agency would not have attained its present widespread use and general acceptance had there not been much to recommend it both in theory and as it has worked in practice. This has been as true in the direction and development of the accounting concept as it has in most other areas of social or economic activity.

Administrative agencies have played an important and commendable role in this area, and it is intended next to catalog some of the ways in which this influence on accounting development is felt to have been beneficial in the past and to offer promise for the future.

Consideration of the interests of corporate management and direct credit grantors such as banks is inherent in corporate accounting work being done by company-employed personnel. The same applies to the work of public accountants, whether acting in an advisory or special service capacity, or in the course of a regular examination. This is true because such interests are in a position either to control the accounting or to force consideration of their interests through economic pressure. In privately owned companies, much the same situation usually exists with respect to stockholders who are active in the management or who personally select the management. Other groups have not nearly so direct a means of forcing direct recognition of their interests and in practice are often not articulate as to their needs or desires. These groups ordinarily include the stockholders and bondholders of large publicly held corporations; prospective investors; consumers; employees, at least until recently; and frequently the government or certain aspects of government, usually characterized as "the public interest."

In an enlarging and increasingly complex society, events such as the depression of 1929 or widespread uneconomic competition of natural monopolies such as utilities frequently bring about reexamination of economic practices and result in new emphasis on or attention to the needs of particular groups. Such events often cause companies and accountants on their own initiative to reexamine their practices and thinking with a view to giving more attention to the needs of special groups. A particularly frequent result is new legislation and the establishment of a continuing administrative agency specially charged to represent or "look out for" the needs of important but "hitherto neglected" groups. Such agencies are endowed with varying degrees of regulatory or disclosive powers. As a result, the interests of the selected groups will thenceforth play a much more important part in the subsequent development of practices, including accounting practices and concepts. In brief, the agency practices purposive accounting and to the extent that it thereby restores or tends to restore an equitable balancing of interests, its activity is both theoretically and practically beneficial. Turning once again to the SEC, it is a simple matter to show that since its inception there has been constant improvement in the scope and nature of data furnished investors as well as in the amount of thought and effort expended to develop for investors new and better data. On the negative side, the fear of punitive action by the agency undoubtedly has deterred many from the use of questionable practices and improper statements. This influence on "thinking" and this discouragement of substandard performances are probably the most important and beneficial influence of the administrative agency. Indeed, it is beneficial even when an agency sponsors a position which is generally unpopular, since it tends to stimulate opposition, and from the conflict will often emerge an equitable solution which might not otherwise have been hit upon or developed until much later, if ever.

Another beneficial influence is the development of a more highly specialized knowledge or "expertise" in a particular field than would be possible for any single outside group. In the usual case, an agency will have to consider a far wider variety of situations than would be possible for any single company or any single accountant or even any manageable group of companies or accountants. As a result, the agency is in a prime position to compare methods and results and to collate data and test solutions. It will also serve as a forum in which to debate the merits of alternative practices and to develop treatments to meet new conditions. Wisely handled, this function can be of especial usefulness in the field of accounting both by acting as a bar or deterrent to individualistic or irrational deviations and by establishing minimum standards of conduct. It can also effectively police standards adopted by accountants through their own voluntary actions.

SUMMARY

There can be no doubt that administrative agencies have been a significant influence in the development of the accounting concept during most of the last half century. To the very considerable extent that they have enforced recognition of the interests of unorganized or inarticulate groups, and have accelerated progress in accounting thinking, their influence can only be regarded as beneficial and their continued existence desirable. To the extent that they have curtailed freedom of thought in accounting matters or have kept accounting in outdated molds or have required observance of principles well suited for limited purposes but ill suited for most uses, their influence must be regarded as hurtful. On balance, it seems probable that accounting thought and practice has progressed farther and faster under the stimulus of such agencies than it would otherwise have done.

ELEVEN

The Independent Accountant and the SEC

ANDREW BARR

Former Chief Accountant, Securities and Exchange Commission

Barr reexamines the concept of independence and how it has related to the Securities and Exchange Commission's (SEC) work. He concludes that the SEC has carefully guarded the concept of independence and, despite criticism, views the overseeing of the independence of public accountants as being one of its most important functions. In this regard Barr suggests ways which in time became accepted in the process of revising the American Institute of Certified Public Accountants' concept of accountant's independence.

In January 1900, shortly after the passage of the Pennsylvania CPA law, *The Public Accountant* of Philadelphia invited leading practicing public accountants to write a definition of a public accountant. The responses from twenty-nine accountants in eight cities are interesting reading. Most replies stressed breadth of experience and nature of the work, but one is remarkably succinct in stating what is expected of an independent public accountant today. Charles C. Reckitt, a brother, and partner for a few years, of Ernest Reckitt, one of the founders of the profession in Illinois, said:

> *A public accountant acknowledges no master but the public, and thus differs from the bookkeeper, whose acts and statements are dictated by his employers. A public accountant's certificate, though addressed to president or directors, is virtually made to the public, who are actually or prospectively stockholders. He should have ability, varied experience and undoubted integrity.*[1]

The other replies included those of leaders in the profession whose names are perpetuated in major firms today. An account of the building up of the moral obligations and independence of the public accountant would not be adequate without a reference to Robert H. Montgomery, who had expressed himself with vigor in responding to the request mentioned above and restated his views with equal vigor in the first edition of his *Auditing*[2] where he emphasized his point with a quotation from another leader of the profession.[3] Three years later, in his second edition, Montgomery noted the absence of decided cases in the United States on accountants' legal liability and observed that the British cases would serve as guides

Reprinted from *The Journal of Accountancy,* October 1959, pp. 32–37, with the permission of the American Institute of Certified Public Accountants. Copyright © 1959 by the American Institute of Certified Public Accountants, Inc.

to the American courts in the event of litigation. In this connection he said:

> *In my opinion the quickest way to weed out the incompetent men who now hold themselves out as public accountants would be to make them understand the civil responsibility of a professional accountant. Naturally, an unreliable, incompetent man cares nothing about his moral responsibility, and so long as he knows that American courts have never laid down specific rules regulating the duties or obligations of public accountants, he probably feels safe from any legal responsibility. One sure and very desirable result of the weeding out process would be the raising of the professional standard, for a few irresponsible men can offset the good work of ten times their number.*[4]

One more reference will complete this short sketch of professional development before the Securities Acts became law. The rules of professional conduct of the American Institute of Accountants declared effective May 16, 1929, include this important rule:

> *(2) The preparation and certification of exhibits, statements, schedules or other forms of accountancy work, containing an essential misstatement of fact or omission therefrom of such a fact as would amount to an essential misstatement or a failure to put prospective investors on notice in respect of an essential or material fact not specifically shown in the balance-sheet itself shall be,* ipso facto, *cause for expulsion or for such other discipline as the council may impose upon proper presentation of proof that such misstatement was either willful or the result of such gross negligence as to be inexcusable.*[5]

Note the resemblance here to Sec. 11(a) of the Securities Act of 1933 which says in part:

> *In case any part of the registration statement, when such part became effective, contained an untrue statement of a material fact or omitted to state a material fact required to be stated therein or necessary to make the statements therein not misleading, any person acquiring such security (unless it is proved that at the time of such acquisition he knew of such untruth or omission) may, either at law or in equity, in any court of competent jurisdiction, sue . . .*

This is enough to demonstrate that the concept of independence was well developed, and the value of a review by independent accountants who are in no way connected with the business was established before the passage of the Securities Act — the first of the several acts now administered by the Securities and Exchange Commission (SEC). These acts either require or give the Commission power to require that financial statements filed with it be certified by independent accountants, and, with minor exceptions, the Commission's rules require that such statements be so certified.

The passage of the Securities Act, however, is an important landmark in the development of the concept of the responsibility of the independent accountant to the investor and the public. The original draft of the Securities Act did not require certification by independent accountants. A representative of the accounting profession appeared at the hearings on the bill before the Committee on Banking and Currency of the United States Senate to suggest revisions of the bill.[6] He pointed out that the bill as drafted imposed "highly technical responsibilities upon the Commission as to accounting principles, their proper application, and their clear expression in financial statements," and suggested that the bill be revised to require that "the accounts pertaining to such balance sheet, statement of income and surplus shall have been examined by an independent accountant and his report shall present his certificate wherein he shall express his opinion as to the correctness of the assets, liabilities, reserves, capital, and surplus as of the balance sheet date and also the income statement for the period indicated."

VALUE OF AUDIT STUDIED

The committee studied at length the value to investors and to the public of an audit by accountants not connected with the company or management and whether the additional expense to industry of an audit by independent accountants was justified by the expected benefits to the public. The committee also considered the advisability and feasibility of requiring the audit to be made by accountants on the staff of the agency administering the act.

In the report on the bill the Senate committee stated that it was intended that those responsible for the administration and enforcement of the law should have full and adequate authority to procure whatever information might be necessary in carrying out the provisions of the bill, but it was deemed essential to refrain from placing upon any federal agency the duty of passing judgment upon the soundness of any security.[7] The proposal to require certification by independent public accountants was incorporated in the bill as passed.

With the passage of the act it became necessary for the Federal Trade Commission to publish rules. This it did in a pamphlet of eight pages which could be obtained from the Superintendent of Documents for five cents. Article 14 of these rules related to accountants and in two paragraphs set the pattern for our present rules. The first of these corresponds to the present Rule 2-01(a) which states who will be recognized to practice, and the second paragraph dealt with the matter of independence in these words:

> *The Commission will not recognize any such certified accountant or public accountant as independent if such accountant is not in fact independent. Unless the Commission otherwise directs, such accountant will not be considered independent with respect to any person in whom he has any interest, directly or indirectly, or with whom he is connected as an officer, agent, employee, promoter, underwriter, trustee, partner, director, or person performing similar function.*[8]

Note that in the first rule and in its republication by the Securities and Exchange Commission[9] in 1935, the independent accountant could not have *any* interest, directly or indirectly, in his client. In a 1936 edition of the rules "any interest" was qualified by the word "substantial."[10] This brought the rule into accord with the October 15, 1934 resolution of the Council of the American Institute of Accountants "that no member or associate shall certify the financial statements of any enterprise financed in whole or in part by the public distribution of securities if he is himself the actual or beneficial owner of a substantial financial interest in the enterprise or if he is committed to acquire such an interest."[11] The Commission deleted the "substantial" qualification in 1950 but the Institute's rule is essentially unchanged as it applies to public issues of securities. Further comment on the present status of the rules must wait while I explore some of the Commission's experience with accountants.

VIOLATION PERCENTAGE SMALL

Lest you get the impression that all of our experience has been discouraging, I want to inject here that it is the violation of the independence rule, or other unprofessional conduct, which gets the publicity. I am sure the profession knows that the Commission appreciates the valuable work that has been done by committees and individual accountants in assisting in the drafting of forms and regulations in the first strenuous years and the constructive comments that have been offered in the same way throughout the life of the Commission. This certainly is acceptance of social responsibility. In our daily work the breaches of the rules are a very small proportion of the total number of cases in which the professional skill of the accountant has resulted in financial statements presented fairly in accordance with generally accepted accounting principles after an audit meeting generally accepted standards. I am sorry that I cannot give you the details of the cases in which the extraordinary diligence and persistence of the independent accountant have resulted in significant disclosures for the protection of investors. This is what the public expects, so it comes as a shock to laymen to find that sometimes accountants are not infallible.

INDEPENDENCE RULES REVIEWED

I have reviewed the writing of our rules relating to independence. A few cases in which the concept was developed warrant examination. Recurring questions of surprising frequency demonstrate that we have a new generation of accountants in practice today. Many of these are not familiar with our rules and have not read the history imbedded in our reported cases and summarized or identified in more accessible form in the Accounting Series releases.

The first proceeding[12] involving independence dealt solely with independence and the failure to disclose certain matters with respect to the certifying accountants. The propriety of the financial statements was not questioned and the proceedings were dismissed when an amendment to the registration statement containing the certificate of a new and independent accountant was filed.

The Commission found in this case that a most unusual relationship existed between the registrant and the accountants who signed the certificate as independent public accountants. An employee of the accountants did the accounting and auditing work and at the same time was comptroller of the registrant and in this latter capacity signed the registration statement as the unsalaried principal financial and accounting officer of the registrant. The certifying accountants' compensation was a fixed fee plus a percentage of the gross proceeds of metal sales of the mine for one year. Furthermore, the employee owned shares in the registrant, which he had purchased before the filing was made. In their certificate the accountants said, among other things, that their relationship with the registrant was "the usual relationship of independent accountants to their client." The Commission found that this was an untrue statement and that the certification was not made by an independent accountant.

The purpose of certification by an independent accountant is so well stated in this case that it warrants quotation:

> *The insistence of the Act on a certification by an "independent" accountant signifies the real function which certification should perform. That function is the*

submission to an independent and impartial mind of the accounting practices and policies of registrants. The history of finance well illustrates the importance and need for submission to such impartial persons of the accounting practices and policies of the management to the end that present and prospective security holders will be protected against unsound accounting practices and procedure and will be afforded, as nearly as accounting conventions will permit, the truth about the financial condition of the enterprise which issues the securities. Accordingly, the certification gives a minimum of protection against untruths and half-truths which otherwise would more easily creep into financial statements. Hence a statement which serves such a high function cannot be dismissed under the Act as a mere "tag" attached to financial statements. It is a material fact, for it gives meaning and reliability to financial data and makes less likely misleading or untrue statements.

MEASURE OF INDEPENDENCE

We hear that the real measure of independence is in the accountant's integrity and attitude of mind in dealing with the problems before him.[13] These are certainly fundamental qualities which the Commission was quick to recognize. In an early case,[14] it was said that where an accountant has consciously falsified the facts an inference of actual absence of independence would seem to be justified. An accountant must approach his "task with complete objectivity—critical of the practices and procedures of registrants, and unwilling to aid and abet in making statements which the facts do not warrant."

From time to time it has been urged upon us that an accounting firm should be permitted to certify financial statements when one or more of the partners could not be considered independent because of a financial interest in the client or other complication under the rules. In these cases it is represented that other partners will supervise the audit and the disqualified partners will not participate in any way. This argument was used in an early mine promotion in which one of the partners accepted his fee in stock of the registrant and the staff applied the rule. An amended balance sheet, which was certified jointly by an individual and the original firm, was filed. The individual was said to be an employee or associate of the senior partner of the firm but was paid directly in cash by the registrant. The Commission found that the independence rule would be defeated and evaded if the senior partner was disqualified but his partner or employee was not and concluded that the amended balance sheet was not certified by an independent accountant as required.[15] In a recent case it became necessary to apply the ruling in this case and a similar ruling of the American Institute of Certified Public Accountants Committee on Professional Ethics.[16]

UNUSUAL CASE CITED

In an unusual case twenty years ago it was found that, unknown to the certifying accountants, their supervisor in charge of the audit had kept certain books of a client. The situation came to light when it was discovered that the client's financial statements for several years were false and that the accountants' employee was responsible for the false entries. The Commission in its opinion agreed with the partner of the accounting firm who testified that "an audit should be a check by an outsider of original work done by the client's employees; 'if an accountant is permitted to do original work the whole purpose of the audit is lost.'"[17]

These few cases from the first five years of the Commission's experience have been the guides in deciding cases in the last twenty years. There have been variations in circumstances, but we have in these cases examples of conflicts of interest due to financial interest, direct employment by the client, and apparent submission to the will of the client without other complicating factors. These matters are covered in our rules[18] and in part in the codes of professional ethics of the Institute and of the state societies of certified public accountants. The frequency with which my office must answer questions on matters of this kind suggests the possibility that greater emphasis could be put on the subject of professional ethics in the colleges and by the accounting societies.[19]

I am, of course, aware that much effort is directed along these lines, but it cannot be relaxed. The codes of ethics, in my opinion, could be reexamined in one major area at least. Most of the codes have a double standard on the subject of financial interest — permitting no substantial interest in a client with a public distribution of securities, but only requiring disclosure of such an interest to private lenders. Many cases coming to our attention are those of accountants who have served closely held corporations and are entering the public financing area for the first time. I was encouraged by Thomas G. Higgins's remarks at Detroit last October, at the American Institute's annual meeting (*Journal of Accountancy,* Nov. 1958, p. 34), when he discussed this dual standard and said, "It is really difficult to see why the rule should be different for statements used for public financing and those used as a basis of credit." He also remarked, "There is a growing feeling that the Institute's rule on investments in clients should be more comprehensive than it is and that it should probably parallel the Illinois rule, which is essentially the rule of the SEC." Most accountants seem to recognize that they should not be an officer or director of the client whose statements they certify, but perhaps the codes could be strengthened by covering this point too. Such strengthening might relieve accountants from pressures by well-meaning clients.

SEC INVESTIGATION NOTED

I have not dealt with the general problems of the improvement in auditing procedures and the definition of generally accepted auditing standards which have received a great deal of attention in the profession and by the SEC — particularly since the *McKesson & Robbins* investigation. This case may be cited as an example of the profession coming forward both individually and in national and state organizations to examine a serious problem among themselves, by assisting the SEC as expert witnesses, and thereafter in promoting the use of the extended auditing procedures which were found necessary as a result of the investigation. The fraud had been exposed on or about December 5, 1938. On January 6, 1939, committees of the American Institute of Accountants and the New York Society of Certified Public Accountants made a joint statement at a meeting with the attorney general of the state of New York in which they said:

> *Professional accountants, in sponsoring CPA legislation, adopting codes of ethics, and establishing standards of procedure, have assumed heavy responsibilities, and by statute and court decision additional responsibilities have been imposed upon*

them. All reputable accountants assume a responsibility to persons other than those who employ them. The greatest asset of a public accountant being his reputation for competence, care and integrity, it is essential that he guard that reputation with all diligence. The legal penalties imposed on accountants for fraud, deceit, or gross negligence are so severe that no practitioner would deliberately risk incurring them.

Strengthening the understanding of the meaning of independence by all members of the profession is a vital factor here. In this connection I want to highlight one finding in the *McKesson* report, that an audit which relies heavily on a proper appraisal of the client's system of check and control "should not . . . exclude the highest officers of the corporation from its appraisal of the manner in which the business under review is conducted."[20]

INDEPENDENCE — CLOSELY GUARDED

By this brief review of the concept of independence I believe I have demonstrated that the Securities Acts embraced what had become good professional practice. Any course of conduct by the profession which may have the effect of undermining public confidence in the independence of the accountant who certifies financial statements upon which third parties are asked to rely would destroy the usefulness of the accountant's work in the securities field. It is for this reason that the SEC has vigilantly guarded the concept of independence — so firmly in some cases as to bring criticism from the properly constituted guardians of the profession's code of ethics. These reactions have been disturbing, but, at the same time, I know that our intent has always been to promote the highest standards in one of the most important qualities of the accountant in public practice.

NOTES

1. *New York Certified Public Accountant,* December 1944, p. 707.

2. At p. 30 (1913).

3. A. Lowes Dickinson, CPA.

4. *Auditing Theory and Practice,* 2d ed., rev. and enl'd, 1919, p. 4.

5. Quoted in Montgomery, *Auditing Theory and Practice,* 5th ed., 1934, p. 12.

6. Statement of Col. A. H. Carter, President of the New York State Society of Certified Public Accountants, before the Committee on Banking and Currency, United States Senate, 73d Cong., 1st Sess., on S. 875, p. 55.

7. Senate Report No. 47, 73d Cong., 1st Sess., p. 2.

8. Rules and Regulations under the Securities Act of 1933, Federal Trade Commission, July 6, 1933.

9. Compilation of Regulations Issued by the Securities and Exchange Commission and Its Predecessor, April 29, 1935.

10. Rule 650(b), General Rules and Regulations under the Securities Act of 1933, January 21, 1936.

11. American Institute of Accountants, *Year Book,* 1935, p. 354.

12. *In re Cornucopia Gold Mines,* 1 SEC 364 (1936).

13. "Essentially it is a state of mind." John L. Carey, *Professional Ethics of Public Accounting,* American Institute of Accountants, 1946, p. 7. The short quotation was qualified by citing the need for objective standards. Ten years later Mr. Carey said, "It is most important that the CPA not only shall refuse to subordinate his judgment to that of others but that he be independent of any self-interest which might warp his judgment even subconsciously in reporting whether or not the financial position and net income are fairly presented. Independence in this context means objectivity or lack of bias in forming delicate judgments." (*Professional Ethics of Certified Public Accountants,* American Institute of Accountants, 1956).

14. *In re American Terminals and Transit Company,* 1 SEC 701, 707 (1936). See also *In re Metropolitan Personal Loan Company,* 2 SEC 803, 813 (1937) in which the Commission found that the accountants were not independent and commented, "The requirement that the certifying accountant be independent is not mere verbiage. The testimony reveals that...and...completely subordinated their judgment as accountants to the desires of their client in setting up items questioned in the balance sheets and profit-and-loss statements...testified that he wasn't sure of an accountant's function in this respect and that he generally did what his clients requested."

15. *In re Rickard Ramore Gold Mines, Ltd.,* 2 SEC 377, 389 (1937).

16. *C.P.A. Handbook,* Chapter 5, Appendix A, Rule 13, p. 7.

17. *In re Interstate Hosiery Mills, Inc.,* 4 SEC 706, 717 (1939).

18. Rule 2–01, Regulation S-X.

19. See Accounting Series Release No. 81, December 11, 1958, for a Compilation of Representative Administrative Rulings and references to published cases on independence.

20. Accounting Series Release No. 19, p. 35. (1956 ed.).

TWELVE

Public Regulation of the Securities Markets

GEORGE J. STIGLER

University of Chicago

In this classic article Professor Stigler critiques the Report of the Special Study of the Securities Market, *the Cohen Report, and concludes that it failed to consider market evidence and made little use of the data available at the time to support its recommendations. To support his view Stigler tests pre- and post-Securities and Exchange Commission (SEC) market transaction data in order to assess the benefits of disclosure and SEC market regulation.*

It is doubtful whether any other type of public regulation of economic activity has been so widely admired as the regulation of the securities markets by the Securities and Exchange Commission (SEC). The purpose of this regulation is to increase the portion of truth in the world and to prevent or punish fraud, and who can defend ignorance or fraud? The Commission has led a scandal-free life as federal regulatory bodies go. It has been essentially a "technical" body, and has enjoyed the friendship, or at least avoided the enmity, of both political parties.

The *Report of the Special Study of the Securities Markets,* which was recently released, is itself symptomatic of the privileged atmosphere within which the SEC dwells.[1] This study investigated the adequacy of the controls over the security markets now exercised by the SEC. The study was well endowed: it was directed by an experienced attorney, Milton H. Cohen; it had a professional staff of more than thirty people; and it operated on a schedule that was leisurely by Washington standards. The study was not an instrument of some self-serving group, nor was it even seriously limited by positions taken by the Administration. Such a professional, disinterested appraisal would not even be conceivable for agricultural or merchant marine or petroleum policy, or the other major areas of public regulation. Disinterest, goodwill, and money had all joined to improve the capital markets of America.

The regulation of the securities markets is therefore an appropriately antiseptic area in which to see how public policy is formed. Here we should be able to observe past policy appraised, and new policy defended, on an intellectually respectable level, if it ever is.

We begin with an examination of the *Special Study*'s policy proposals. Cohen presents a vast number of recommendations of changes in institutions and practices. Most are minor, and some are even frivolous (market letters should not predict specific price levels of stocks).

Reprinted from "Public Regulation of the Securities Market," by George J. Stigler, *Journal of Business,* April 1964, pp. 117–142, by permission of The University of Chicago Press. Copyright © 1964 by the University of Chicago.

The content of the proposals, however, is not our present concern; what is our concern is the manner in which the proposals are reached. More specifically: (1) How does the Cohen Report show that an existing practice or institution is defective? (2) How does the Cohen Report show that the changes it recommends (a) will improve the situation, and (b) are better in some sense than alternative proposals? In answering these questions I shall use the discussion of the qualifications of brokers and other personnel in the industry (chap. 2), although the numerous other areas would do quite as well.

1. THE FORMULATION OF POLICY

The Cohen Report tells us that there is cause for dissatisfaction with the personnel of the industry: "From the evidence gathered by the study, it appears that the existing controls have proven to be deficient in some important regards. The dishonest broker-dealer, that 'greatest menace to the public,' to use the words of one Commission official, continues to appear with *unjustifiable frequency*. Also, the inexperienced broker-dealer *too often* blunders into problems for himself, his customers, and the regulatory agencies."[2] So there are too many thieves and too many incompetents.

How does Cohen prove that there are enough thieves and incompetents to justify more stringent controls? After all, one can always find some dishonest and untutored men in a group of 100,000: not all the angels in heaven have good posture.

The "proof" of the need for further regulatory measures consists basically and almost exclusively of four case studies. These studies briefly describe four new firms with relatively inexperienced salesmen who were caught in falling markets and in three cases became bankrupt or withdrew from the business. No estimates of losses to customers are made. The studies were handpicked to emphasize the shortcomings of *new* firms, because this is the place where Cohen wishes to impose new controls. The studies are of course worthless as a proof of the need for new policies: nothing Cohen, the SEC, or the United States government can do will make it difficult to find four more cases at any time one looks for them.

Cohen's second, and only other, piece of evidence is a survey of disciplinary actions against members of the National Association of Security Dealers (NASD) from 1959 through 1961. To quote the report: "The results of this analysis revealed that the association's newest member firms, which are generally controlled by persons having less experience than principals of older firms, were responsible for a heavy preponderance of the offenses drawing the most severe penalties" (pt. 1, p. 66). Cohen's summary of the statistical study, of which this sentence is a fair sample, would not meet academic standards of accuracy. The study reveals that of 1014 firms founded before 1941, 223 were involved in disciplinary proceedings between 1959 and 1961; of 1072 firms founded in 1959–60, only 103 were involved in such proceedings. The data are poorly tabulated (dismissals are included, and duplicate charges against one firm are counted as several firms), but however viewed they do not make a case for the need for more regulaton, or for more severe screening of new entrants.[3] Yet Cohen believes that the basis has been laid for his main finding:

> *The large number of new investors and new broker-dealer firms and salesmen attracted to the securities industry in recent years have combined to create a problem of major dimensions....*

> *More than a generation of experience with the Federal securities laws has demonstrated, moreover, that it is impossible to regulate effectively the conduct of those in the securities industry, unless would-be members are adequately screened at the point of entry (pt. 1, p. 150).*

These alleged findings lead to a series of policy proposals, such as the following:

1. All brokers should be compelled to join "self-regulatory" agencies (such as the NASD).
2. No one who has been convicted of embezzlement, fraud, or theft should be allowed in the industry for ten years thereafter.
3. A good character should be required for entrants.
4. Examinations should be required for prospective entrants.

The *Report* approves strongly of the six-month training period now required of customers' men in firms belonging to the New York Stock Exchange (NYSE).

Cohen believes that the people dealing in securities with the public should have extensive training and screening such as his own profession requires. My lengthy experience with "account executives" of major NYSE firms has not uncovered knowledge beyond what would fit comfortably into a six-hour course. It would have been most useful if Cohen had investigated the experience of customers of a randomly chosen set of account men with diverse amounts of training and experience: Have differences in experience or training had any effect on the profits of their customers? But he never even dreamed of the possibility— or perhaps it was of the need — of pretesting his proposals.

The report takes for granted not only the effectiveness but also, what is truly remarkable, the infallibility of the regulating process:

> *There is no evidence that these practices are typical . . . but regardless of their frequency they represent problems too important to be ignored (pt. 1, p. 268).*
> *The mere fact that there have been any losses at all is sufficient reason to consider whether there are further adjustments that should be made for the protection of investors (pt. 1, p. 400).*

Observe: no matter how infrequent or trivial the damage to investors, the regulatory process must seek to eliminate it (no doubt inexpensively). Surely rhetoric has replaced reason at this point.

As for alternative methods of dealing with the problem of fraud, only one is mentioned: "A number of persons have suggested that a Federal fidelity or surety bond requirement be imposed in addition to or in lieu of a capital requirement. It would seem, however, that such a requirement would present a number of practical difficulties and that more significant protection to the public can be assured through a Federal net capital requirement. No recommendation as to bonding, therefore, will be made at this time" (pt. 1, p. 92). I must confess to being shocked by this passage. A number of "practical difficulties" exclude the sensible, direct, efficient way to deal with the problem of financial responsibility — difficulties so obvious and conclusive they do not even need to be mentioned.

When one looks at a well-built theater set from the angle at which the audience is to view it, it appears solid and convincing. When one looks from another direction, it is a set of two-dimensional pieces of cardboard and canvas, which could not possibly create an illusion of validity. So it is with the Cohen Report. Once we ask for the evidence for its policy proposals, the immense enterprise becomes a promiscuous collection of conventional beliefs and personal prejudices.

2. A TEST OF PREVIOUS REGULATION

A proposal of public policy, everyone should agree, is open to criticism if it omits a showing that the proposal will serve its announced goal. Yet the proposal may be a desirable and opportune one, and the inadequacies of a proposer are no proof of the undesirability of the proposal. And—to leave the terrain of abstract and unctuous truth—the past work of the SEC and Cohen's schemes for its future may serve fine purposes even though no statistician has measured these probable achievements. Quite so. But then again, perhaps not.

The paramount goal of the regulations in the security markets is to protect the innocent (but avaricious) investor. A partial test of the effects of the SEC on investors' fortunes will help to answer the question of whether testing a policy's effectiveness is an academic scruple or a genuine need. This partial test will serve also to illustrate the kind of study that should have occupied the *Special Study*.

The basic test is simplicity itself: How did investors fare before and after the SEC was given control over the registration of new issues? We take all the new issues of industrial stocks with a value exceeding $2.5 million in 1923–28, and exceeding $5 million in 1949–55, and measure the values of these issues (compared to their offering price) in five subsequent years. It is obviously improper to credit or blame the SEC for the absolute differences between the periods in investors' fortunes, but if we measure the stock prices relative to the market average, we shall have eliminated most of the effects of general market conditions. The price ratios (p_t/p_0) for each time span are divided by the ratio of the market average for the same period. Thus if from 1926 to 1928 a common stock rose from $20 to $30, the price ratio is 150 (percent) or an increase of 50 percent but, relative to the market, which rose by 68.5 percent over this two-year period, the new issue fell 12 percent.[4]

The prices of common and preferred stocks were first analyzed to determine whether they varied with size of issue after one, three, or five years. In each case there was no systematic or statistically significant variation of price with size of issue. The elusiveness of quotations on small issues makes it difficult to answer this question for issues smaller than the minimum size of our samples ($2.5 million in the 1920s, $5 million in the 1950s). One small sample was made of fifteen issues in 1923 of $500 thousand to $1 million for which quotations were available, and this was compared with the twenty-two larger issues of the same year. The differences were sufficient to leave open the question of the representativeness of our findings for smaller issues.[5]

The annual averages of the quotations (relative to market) are given for common stocks in Table 1. In both periods it was an unwise man who bought new issues of common stock: he lost about one-fifth of his investment in the first year relative to the market, and another fifth in the years that followed. The data reveal no risk aversion.

Table 1   New stock prices relative to market averages, common stocks
(Issue year = 100)

	Year after issue				
	1	2	3	4	5
Pre-SEC:					
1923	92.7	85.0	77.8	62.1	67.0
1924	98.0	76.3	69.1	65.9	51.0
1925	85.0	66.9	54.8	42.2	33.0
1926	90.2	81.8	77.1	62.6	66.9
1927	84.7	69.1	60.1	72.6	103.4
1928	71.6	50.4	40.8	45.0	57.0
Average	81.9	65.1	56.2	52.8	58.5
Standard deviation	43.7	46.7	43.7	48.5	65.1
No. of issues	84	87	88	85	84
Post-SEC:					
1949	93.3	88.1	86.7	86.9	64.9
1950	84.3	76.0	53.0	57.8	46.9
1951	83.6	78.7	76.3	80.4	74.5
1952	87.7	74.3	70.7	70.4	69.8
1953	88.1	79.2	75.4	70.4	93.6
1954	53.2	48.7	56.4	48.1	42.4
1955	71.8	64.9	82.3	77.8	83.4
Average	81.6	73.3	72.6	71.9	69.6
Standard deviation	23.9	27.7	31.0	30.9	38.9
No. of issues	47	47	47	47	47

The averages for the two periods reveal no difference in values after one year, and no significant difference after two years, but a significant difference in the third and fourth, but not fifth, years. The ambiguity in this pattern arises chiefly because the issues of 1928 did quite poorly, and the number of issues in this year was relatively large — one-third of all issues of the 1920s was made in 1928. It may well be that these enterprises did not have sufficient time to become well launched before the beginning of the Great Depression. With an unweighted average of the various years, there would be no significant difference between the averages in the 1920s and the 1950s.

The proper period over which to "hold" a new stock in these comparisons is difficult to specify: presumably it is equal to the average period the purchasers held the new issues. With speculative new issues one would expect the one-year period to be much the most relevant, for thereafter the information provided by this year of experience would become an important determinant of the investor's behavior.

These comparisons suggest that the investors in common stocks in the 1950s did little better than in the 1920s, indeed clearly no better if they held the securities only one or two years. This comparison is incomplete in that dividends are omitted from our reckoning, although this is probably a minor omission, and may well work in favor of the 1920s.[6]

The variance of the price ratios, however, was much larger in the 1920s than in the later period: in every year the difference between periods was significant at the 1 percent level, and in four years at the 0.1 percent level. This is a most puzzling finding: the simple-minded interpretation is that the SEC has succeeded in eliminating both unusually good and unusually bad new issues! This is difficult to believe as a matter of either intent or accident. A more plausible explanation lies in the fact that many more new companies used the market in the 1920s than in the 1950s—from one viewpoint a major effect of the SEC was to exclude new companies.[7]

The preferred stocks, which were far more numerous than the common stocks in the 1920s, pose a special problem. We use the market average as the base for measuring investor experience in order to minimize the influence of other factors, but no such market average exists for preferred stocks. The existing preferred stock indexes are actually indexes of the yields of preferred stocks, and exclude defaults or failures, so they do not measure the fortunes of investors in preferred stocks.

Table 2   New stock prices relative to issue year, preferred stocks

	Year after issue				
	1	2	3	4	5
Pre-SEC:					
1923	95.3	96.9	92.0	97.6	96.2
1924	84.6	71.2	72.9	71.9	56.3
1925	107.6	108.3	118.4	107.2	78.6
1926	101.1	96.2	94.7	85.7	60.5
1927	101.4	97.8	91.7	63.0	44.6
1928	93.7	69.7	50.0	29.9	31.9
Average	97.8	87.0	79.1	65.0	53.2
Standard deviation	20.4	33.4	45.1	53.7	50.3
No. of issues	110	115	117	111	108
Post-SEC:					
1949	112.3	101.7	101.1	97.7	105.2
1950	99.6	96.5	97.5	103.9	105.7
1951	101.1	94.3	101.8	108.8	113.1
1952	95.7	93.6	113.2	95.0	91.2
1953	148.1	117.6	119.5	104.5	n.a.
1954	112.1	102.7	88.5	77.3	88.3
1955	103.6	102.0	109.2	190.5	205.7
Average	107.1	99.0	102.0	107.7	114.3
Standard deviation	18.6	13.7	20.2	51.8	66.5
No. of issues	40	38	36	33	29

The price relatives for preferred stocks are given in Table 2, and it will be observed that the break in the market in 1929 had a decisive influence on the absolute values of these issues. We may in fact summarize the salient numbers:

Year of issue	Average price relative	
	1929	1930
1925	107.2	78.6
1926	94.7	85.7
1927	97.8	91.7
1928	93.7	69.7

As a result of this heavy impact, the price relatives are substantially lower after two years in the 1920s than in the 1950s.

Accordingly, we need a deflator, and again use the common stock index (Table 3). The common stock index seems more appropriate than the unsatisfactory preferred stock indexes, especially since most of the recent preferred issues were convertible.[8] The average experience, on this basis, was superior in the 1950s for the first two years after an issue was purchased; thereafter there was no difference.

Table 3   New stock prices relative to market averages, preferred stocks
(Issue year = 100)

	Year after issue				
	1	2	3	4	5
Pre-SEC:					
1923	91.2	72.9	60.0	50.9	37.2
1924	66.5	48.4	39.7	29.0	18.0
1925	93.1	75.1	60.8	43.6	41.6
1926	81.0	57.1	44.5	52.4	57.7
1927	75.1	57.4	70.0	75.1	104.0
1928	74.2	71.8	80.6	94.4	70.9
Average	79.2	66.6	66.9	69.7	65.3
Standard deviation	17.4	24.9	40.0	65.9	42.0
No. of issues	110	115	117	111	108
Post-SEC:					
1949	91.9	67.2	61.2	59.0	52.2
1950	80.5	71.4	62.8	63.0	45.7
1951	92.5	86.1	76.3	58.2	51.5
1952	95.5	76.7	66.2	47.3	47.4
1953	121.6	68.9	59.6	54.5	n.a.
1954	79.9	62.4	56.2	47.4	43.5
1955	88.2	90.8	93.8	131.4	146.8
Average	91.5	76.9	69.6	62.2	59.0
Standard deviation	15.2	14.0	13.6	37.2	49.3
No. of issues	40	38	36	33	29

The undeflated preferred stock experience is the same in both periods for the first two years, and the deflated experience is the same in both periods for the last three years; the opposite indexes show a superior performance in the 1950s. This combination of results suggests that our deflators are inappropriate, and we can only repeat our lament at the absence of a relevant preferred stock index.

Since convertibility is much more common in the later issues, there is an argument for comparing the earlier issues to the base year, and the later issues to the common-stock index. The average period these new issues are held may also be longer than common stocks are held. These various considerations combine to suggest that the preferred-stock performance was not significantly better in the 1950s than in the 1920s.

These studies suggest that the SEC registration requirements had no important effect on the quality of new securities sold to the public. A fuller statistical study — extending to lower sizes of issues and dividend records — should serve to confirm or qualify this conclusion, but it is improbable that the qualification will be large, simply because the issues here included account for most of the dollar volume of industrial stocks issued in these periods. Our study is not exhaustive in another sense: we could investigate the changing industrial composition of new issues and other possible sources of differences in the market performance of new issues in the two periods.

But these admissions of the possibility of closer analysis can be made after any empirical study. They do not affect our two main conclusions: (1) it is possible to study the effects of public policies, and not merely to assume that they exist and are beneficial, and (2) grave doubts exist whether if account is taken of costs of regulation,[9] the SEC has saved the purchasers of new issues one dollar.

3. THE CRITERIA OF MARKET EFFICIENCY

So far as the efficiency and growth of the American economy are concerned, efficient capital markets are even more important than the protection of investors — in fact efficient capital markets *are* the major protection of investors. The *Special Study* devotes considerable attention to the mechanism of the most important single market, the New York Stock Exchange.

One can ask whether this market is competitively organized: are the prices of brokers' services set by competitive forces? The answer is clearly in the negative, and the Cohen Report is properly critical of the structure of commissions of the NYSE, which is highly discriminatory against higher-priced stocks and larger transactions. The *Report* explicitly refrains from discussing the compulsory minimum rates set by this self-regulating cartel. The reason for silence is obscure: the present scheme of compulsory private price-fixing of brokers' services seems to me wholly objectionable. The replacement of cartel pricing by competition with review lodged in the Antitrust Division, would confer larger benefits upon investors than the SEC has yet provided.

The mechanism of response to changing conditions is a more subtle matter, dealt with especially in Chapter 6 ("Exchange Markets") of the *Special Study*. The task of providing continuity and orderliness of markets in specific stocks is now performed by the specialists, aided or observed (as the case may be) by the floor traders. How well do they presently perform their tasks?

1. The NYSE uses a "tick-test" of the effects of specialists on short-run price fluctuations. If a transaction takes place below the last different price, it is called a minus tick, and if above the last different price, it is a plus tick. Purchases on minus ticks and sales on plus ticks are considered stabilizing, and in three sample weeks, 83.9 percent of specialists' transactions were of this type. The *Special Study* rejects this test on two grounds:

1. "A tick by itself does not necessarily represent a change in the public's evaluation of the security." Thus, after a transaction at 35, the specialists will often offer 34½ and ask 35½, and a transaction at either price is a so-called stabilizing tick. This represents "only a random sequence of buy and sell orders."

2. The specialists' own profit incentive is to buy low and sell high—and presumably (but the *Special Study* does not say explicitly) no virtue attaches to profitable activity.[10]

The *Special Study* demands that the test be applied to a longer sequence of transactions; on individual pairs of transactions the test "can be expected to reveal only cases of grossly destabilizing activity."[11] Specialists engage in only a third of all transactions, but as a rule at least one-third of the ticks are negative and one-third positive in a day. Hence the specialists could foster market movements while appearing to stabilize them, or so the Report argues. Thus if the specialist sells in the underlined transactions in the following sequence:

$$3\,5 \quad \underline{3\,4} \quad 3\,4¾ \quad \underline{3\,4} \quad 3\,4½ \quad 3\,3¾ \quad \underline{3\,4,}$$

he is stabilizing by the tick test while riding with the market trend. This prescient behavior is not documented, nor is a specific tick test proposed.

2. The preferred test of the specialist's effect is how his inventory of stock varies as the market price fluctuates: "That is, a member trading pattern which tends to produce purchase balances on declining stock days and sales balances on rising stock days would indicate that members exert a stabilizing influence on the stock days in which they traded" (pt. 2, p. 55). An analysis is made of changes in specialists' stock inventories on four days. In each case inventories moved with the market—that is, they were destabilizing. But if the analysis is performed on stocks classified as rising or falling, balances moved in a stabilizing fashion in seven of the eight cases (pt. 2, p. 108). But *within* these eight groups there were a substantial number of cases in which inventories of stocks moved with the market, so specialist performance left something to be desired. Cohen's standards have not flagged: he expects every specialist to do, not his best, but perfectly.[12]

The economist will have observed that the *Report* has no theory of markets from which valid criteria can be deduced by which to judge experience. The tick test and the "offsetting balances" tests are both lacking of any logical basis: these tests assume that smoothness of price movement is the sign of an efficient market, and it is not. Let us sketch the problem of an efficient market.

The basic function of a market serves to bring buyers and sellers together. If there were a large number of people who sent their bid and ask prices to a single point (market), we should in effect observe the supply-and-demand functions of elementary economic theory. *The* price that cleared this market would be established—it would be a unique price if there were sufficient traders to produce continuity of supply-and-demand functions — and trading would stop.

This once-for-all, or at most once-per-period, market differs from most real markets in which new potential buyers and sellers are appearing more or less irregularly over time. Existing holders of a stock wish to sell it — at a price — to build a home, marry off a daughter, or buy another security which has (for them) greater promise. Existing holders of cash wish to buy the stock, at a price. Neither group is fully identified until after the event: I would become a bidder for a stock that does not fall within my present investment horizon provided that its price falls for reasons which I believe are mistaken.

So demand and supply are flows, and erratic flows with sequences and bids and asks dependent upon the random circumstances of individual traders. As a first approximation, one would expect the number of holders of a security to be proportional to the total value of the issue. Then the numbers of bids, offers, and transactions would also be proportional to the dollar size of the issue. This is roughly true: the turnover rate of a random sample of one hundred stocks in one month is classified by the total value of the issues, in Table 4, and only in very small and very large issues was there a considerable departure from proportionality.[13]

Table 4   Turnover rates of 100 stocks on the New York Stock Exchange, March 1961

Value of issue (millions of dollars)	No. of stocks	Ratio of shares traded to total outstanding
Under 5	9	0.012
5–10	12	.026
10–25	18	.037
25–50	10	.043
50–75	11	.073
75–100	12	.034
100–250	13	.027
250–500	8	.029
500 and over	7	0.008

Let us take a very primitive model of a random sequence of bids and asks, and see what this sequence implies for (1) the level of transaction prices, and (2) the time until a bid or ask is met and a transaction occurs. We start with a demand schedule (Table 5) for a given stock of which 710,000 shares are outstanding, so the equilibrium price is between 29¾ and 30. A sequence of bids and asks now appears. They are truly random: two-digit numbers from a table of random numbers are drawn, and the first digit determines whether it is a bid or ask (even or odd, respectively) and the second digit determines the level of the bid or ask (0–9, or, in market price units, 28¾–31). (This uniform distribution is replaced by a normal distribution later, but it suffices for the present.) The sequence of random numbers (here called "tenders") proceeds:

Table 5   Demand schedule for a security

Price		Aggregate demand
28¾	(0)	800,000
29	(1)	780,000
29¼	(2)	760,000
29½	(3)	740,000
29¾	(4)	720,000
30	(5)	700,000
30¼	(6)	680,000
30½	(7)	660,000
30¾	(8)	640,000
31	(9)	620,000

(1)   2 8: a bid (2 is even) of 8 (= 3 0¾) ,

(2)   3 0: an ask (3 is odd) of 0 (= 2 9¾) ,

Here a transaction occurs at 30¾ because this highest outstanding bid exceeds the seller's minimum ask. To proceed:

(3)   9 5: an ask of 5 ,

(4)   0 1: a bid of 1 ,

(5)   1 0: an ask of 0 .

This last trader sells at 1 (= 29) to the fourth tender. The process continues with the further rule that any unfulfilled bids or asks are canceled after twenty-five numbers. The transaction price and the minimum unfulfilled asking price and the maximum unfulfilled bid are shown in Figure 1.

The transaction prices fluctuate substantially, as will be seen — indeed, the mean absolute deviation from the equilibrium price (taken as the closer of 29¾ or 30) is $0.34, or 34 percent of the maximum possible absolute deviation. The average delay in fulfilling a bid or ask is 3.8 units of (tenders).[14] These particular results depend upon the special distribution of bids and asks we assume, but any reasonable distribution will generate significant fluctuations in price and significant and erratic delays in filling bids or asks.

The time unit involved in the foregoing analysis is the interval between successive bids or asks. If tenders are proportional to transactions, and the latter to dollar size of issue, this time unit will be inversely proportional to the size of issue. The time unit will be roughly 1/1000 as long for American Telephone and Telegraph as for Oklahoma Gas and Electric common. In addition the effective price unit for trading may be ¼ or ½ dollar for the less active stock where it is ⅛ for the active stock.

In addition to allowing buyers and sellers to deal with one another, an efficient market is commonly expected to display the property of resilience (to use an unfamiliar word for a property whose absence is called "thinness"). Resilience is the ability to absorb the *market* bid or ask orders (i.e., without a price limit) without an appreciable fluctuation in price. No

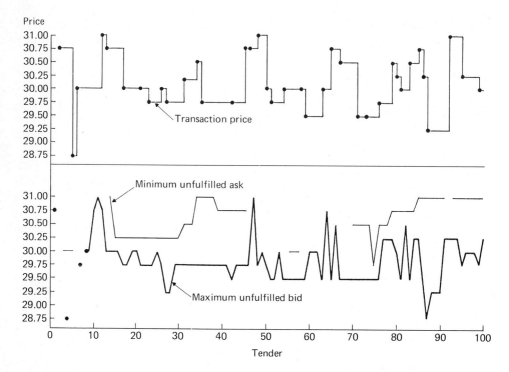

Figure 1 *Hypothetical sequence of transaction prices, generated by sequence of random numbers, and maximum unfulfilled bid and minimum unfulfilled ask prices (equilibrium price of 29¾ or 30).*

market can absorb vast orders without large price changes, so this condition must be interpreted as follows: market buy and sell orders of a magnitude consistent with random fluctuation in tenders with an unchanging equilibrium price should not change the transaction prices appreciably.

The reason for making resilience a property of efficient markets may be approached through an analogy. If in a geographical area prices of a product differ, in response to random demand changes, by more than transportation costs, we say that the allocation of the product will be inefficient: A will buy the good for $6 when B is unable to obtain it for $7 (including transportation costs). Alternatively, the owners of the good are not maximizing its value.

Similarly if random fluctuations in price—under our assumed condition of a stable equilibrium price—lead to price changes greater than inventory carrying costs (the cost of transporting a security from one date to another), the allocation of the product will be inefficient among buyers. Alternatively, the sellers are not maximizing the value of their holdings.

If access to the market is free, speculators will appear to provide resilience by carrying inventories of the stock; they are in fact primarily the specialists of the NYSE plus the floor traders. The speculators will charge the cost of carrying inventories and of their personal services by the bid-ask spread they establish, and in competitive equilibrium this spread will be just remunerative of these trading costs. The technical efficiency with which this inventory management is conducted will be measured by the spread between bid and ask prices.

In addition there are costs of the provision of the machinery of exchange, and these are also part of the cost of transactions. The performance of the main function of the exchange as a marketplace is subject to economies of scale. The greater the number of transactions in a security concentrated in one exchange, the smaller the discontinuities in trading and the smaller the necessary inventories of securities. As a result the price of a security will almost invariably be "made" in one exchange.

Specialists would then alter the price pattern of Figure 1 by setting fixed bid and ask prices (under the present assumption of fixed supply and demand conditions). They will offer to buy all shares at, say, 29¾ and sell to all buyers at 30, and the difference (the "jobber's turn") will be the compensation for the costs of acting as a specialist.[15]

To summarize: the efficient market under stationary conditions of supply and demand has the properties:

1. If a bid equals or exceeds the lowest asking price (and similarly for offers), a transaction takes place.
2. Higher bids are fulfilled before lower bids, and conversely for offers.
3. Prices will fluctuate only within the limits of speculators' costs of providing a market (under competition).

In this regime the cost of transactions (half the bid-ask spread plus commissions) will be the complete inverse measure of the efficiency of the markets. Bid and ask prices will be (almost) constant through time.[16]

Let us consider now the formidable task of real markets, in which the equilibrium price changes without precise or advance notice. We illustrate the characteristic price patterns in the absence of speculation with Figures 2 and 3. The sequences of bids, asks, and transaction prices follow the procedure of Figure 1 with four changes:

1. The random numbers are normally distributed (with $\sigma' = \$1.00$)
2. In Figure 2 the equilibrium price is dropped from \$25.00 to \$23.75 after 50 tenders
3. In Figure 3 the equilibrium price begins a linear upward trend of 5 cents per tender after 25 tenders
4. No tenders are canceled because of staleness.

In each case, after the equilibrium changes the unfulfilled tenders are alternatively (1) retained, and (2) changed by the amount of change in the equilibrium price — the two alternatives bracket the most reasonable assumptions. If the reader will compare the equilibrium prices with the observed sequences he will better appreciate the task of the specialist in detecting true changes and avoiding false changes in the equilibrium price (= population value).

If the impacts on equilibrium are sudden and unexpected — as in the examples underlying Figure 2 — the appropriate market response is an immediate and complete shift to the new price level. Under this condition the demand for "continuity" in a market is a demand for delay in responding to the change in demand conditions, and, the *Special Study* to the

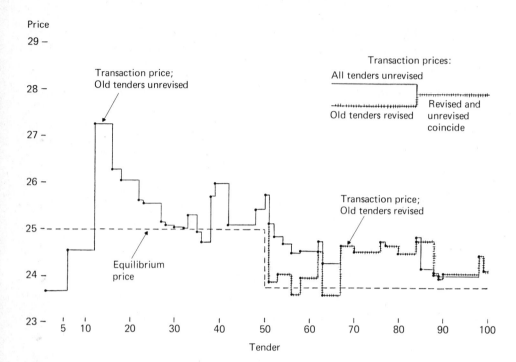

Figure 2 *Sequence of transaction prices generated by random normal deviates: Equilibrium price of $25.00 for first 50 tenders; equilibrium price of $23.75 thereafter.*

contrary, there is simply no merit in such delay.

The popular NYSE practice of suspending trading until buy and sell orders can be matched at a "reasonable" price is open to serious objection. To prevent a trade is no function of the exchange, and any defense must lie in a desire to avoid "unnecessary" price fluctuations. An unnecessary price fluctuation is surely one not called for by the conditions of supply and demand of the *week* even though the fluctuation may reflect supply and demand of the *hour*. This suspension of trading means that the exchange officials know the correct price change when there is a flood of buy or sell orders. We need not pause to inquire where they get this clairvoyance; it is enough to notice that the correct way to iron out the unnecessary wrinkles in the chart is to speculate: to buy or sell against the unnecessary movement. The omniscient officials should be deprived of the power to suspend trading but given vast sums to speculate. Since omniscience can surely earn 20 or 50 percent a year on the market, there should be no trouble in raising the capital. To disassociate random from persistent changes is sufficiently difficult, however, to make me very admiring of the courage of those who invest in Omniscience Unlimited.

The wholly unexpected shift in market conditions occurs infrequently — as the assassination of President Kennedy and the heart attack of President Eisenhower illustrate. But almost every event casts a shadow before it: the outbreak of war, the expropriation of foreign

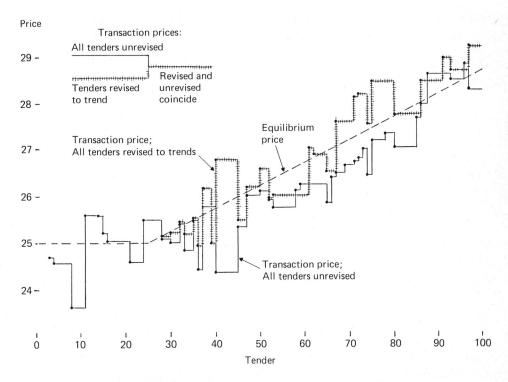

Figure 3 *Sequence of transaction prices generated by random normal deviates: Equilibrium price of $25.00 for first 25 tenders increasing by $0.05 per tender thereafter.*

subsidiaries, the growth of imports of a product, the glowing income statement—all are more or less predictable as to date and import. The speculators then act within a system in which there is partial anticipation of most events that occur (and many that do not). They will attempt to guess the future course of events, and to the extent that they succeed they will make profits and smooth the path of the price quotations.

In appraising the performance of the market under changing conditions we must abandon our criterion of efficiency in a stationary market that price should be constant over time (p. 129). We now must judge the performance of two functions by the speculator:

1. How efficiently does he perform his function of facilitating transactions by carrying inventories and making bid and ask prices?

2. How efficiently does he predict changes in equilibrium prices, or, in other words, how closely does he keep bid and ask prices to the levels which in retrospect were correct?

The first of these functions is analytically the same as that encountered in the stationary market, but it is now more difficult to discharge or appraise. It is much harder to judge the proper inventories and the proper amount of resources to devote to ascertaining the "true" market price than in the stationary market. The criterion of efficiency is still the cost of consummating a transaction. Much current work on inventory theory, queueing, and related subjects should contribute to the power of our tests of the efficiency of speculators.

The second function, the anticipation of price changes, has one measurable attribute: the trading profits of the speculators are a measure of their skill in anticipating price movements. What is more interesting is that the positive profits of the speculators also demonstrate that their activity stabilizes prices in the sense of reducing the variance of prices over time.[17]

These profits as reported by the *Special Study* have been quite attractive: on liquid capital of $76.3 million in 1960, specialists made a trading income of $21.2 million (pt. 2, pp. 371, 373), as well as making $19.6 million in commissions. No profitability data are given for floor traders.

4. CONCLUSION

I have argued at length that the Cohen Report makes poor use of either empirical evidence or economic theory, so its criticisms are founded upon prejudice and its reforms are directed by wishfulness. Full disclosure is the rule of the hour, so I must add that the academic scholars have not given the capital markets the attention they deserve because of their importance and analytical fascination. The area is replete with problems in the economics of information: What over-the-counter transactions should be required to be reported? Should floor traders' orders be delayed in execution to achieve parity with outsiders? and the like. It is an equally attractive area for the theory of decisions under uncertainty: what are the ex post criteria of efficient speculation? The prospectuses of research are glowing—should we start censoring this form of literature too?

APPENDIX

The lists of new flotations of common and preferred stocks are taken from the *Commercial and Financial Chronicle* for the earlier period, and *Investment Dealer's Digest* for the later period. Issues first offered only to stockholders and privately placed issues are excluded, as are public utilities and railroads.

The price quotations are the initial asking price and, at subsequent twelve-month intervals, the averages of the weekly high and low for the week nearest the middle of the month. Averages of monthly highs and lows are employed where weekly quotations are not available. Stock splits and dividends are eliminated, that is, the price of a share is multiplied by the number of shares the original share has become. If an issue of preferred stock is retired, its retirement value is used in the year of retirement, after which it is dropped from the sample.

The price relatives presented here are relative to issue price.

The market index is *Standard and Poor's Annual Industrial Index.* It is said to be biased upward in the early period but not in the later period; this bias would of course exaggerate the influence of the SEC in our tests. *Standard and Poor's Index* covers only common stocks. Tables 1 and 3 of the text summarize information for these price relatives deflated by the relative value of the market index for the same period.

Table A1   Price relatives of common stocks

(Issue price = 100)

Month of issue and stock name	Value of issue (thousands)	Year after issue				
		1 Year	2 Years	3 Years	4 Years	5 Years
1923						
1 — Cuy Amel Fruit Co.	$ 2,942	135.0	99.3	90.6	61.8	99.8
2 — Household Products, Inc.	9,350	97.1	105.7	132.4	142.1	195.8
4 — Inland Steel	8,006	72.2	85.8	80.8	93.7	115.9
4 — Eaton Axle & Spring Co.	4,200	51.7	50.4	91.2	87.5	116.5
5 — Munsing Wear, Inc.	3,780	81.2	75.0	84.5	87.2	137.5
11 — Wm. Wrigley Jr. & Co.	12,000	111.2	140.5	132.5	165.0	190.0
12 — National Dairy Corp.	4,125	129.2	233.7	223.9	195.3	358.2
1924						
3 — Transcontinental Oil Co.	$ 8,000	117.2	93.8	112.5	195.2	248.5
6 — Game Well Co.	3,000	n.a.	n.a.	112.5	140.1	156.0
11 — Brunswick Balke-Callender	6,435	65.4	70.3	67.9	113.5	46.2
12 — Long-Bell Lumber Co.	7,912	93.7	80.4	53.1	55.9	24.6
12 — (Frank G.) Shattuck Co.	2,750	252.2	229.5	327.3	444.3	460.9
12 — The Symington Co.	996	95.0	87.1	87.9	30.1	20.9
1925						
1 — Music Master Corp.	$ 3,000	15.6	0.0	0.0	0.0	0.0
2 — The Gould Coupler Co.	3,675	82.0	35.0	36.5	30.0	36.5
2 — The Cudahay Packing Co.	4,280	85.5	48.7	64.7	61.6	42.1
4 — Dodge Bros. Inc.[1]	20,986	110.6	79.2	86.3	75.3	31.8
4 — Gabriel Snubber Mfg. Co.	4,950	132.5	138.7	77.5	92.0	34.0
5 — Sun Oil Co.	5,767	88.4	91.1	136.5	190.2	218.7
6 — Hunt Bros. Packing Co.	2,600	n.a.	89.6	91.4	90.4	81.7
7 — Atlas Plywood Corp.	2,500	120.0	104.8	169.5	109.1	37.5
7 — Lehn & Fink Products	8,578	99.5	99.0	132.7	140.9	81.5
8 — The Maytag Co.	5,000	114.0	158.8	89.4	128.1	56.9
8 — Vick Chemical Co.	4,100	118.4	136.7	164.8	175.1	164.6
8 — Industrial Rayon Corp.	3,000	42.5	47.8	85.2	99.8	91.9
9 — Safety Insulated Wire & Cable Co.[2]	6,250	104.6	133.2	145.0	219.0	72.4
10 — Tung-Sol Lamp Works Inc.	2,940	98.0	116.9	142.8	220.5	n.a.
10 — American Brown Boveri Electric	13,000	76.5	19.6	28.6	35.2	26.5
10 — Gotham Silk Hosiery Co.	2,750	205.4	285.4	280.4	134.2	33.1
10 — Western Dairy	3,600	100.0	115.8	129.9	116.9	51.1
11 — Fox Theatre Corp.	12,500	95.7	77.2	115.0	50.3	28.0
11 — Rice-Stix Dry Goods Co.	2,650	76.9	82.1	71.2	55.7	37.3
12 — Consolidated Laundries Corp.	2,750	98.9	71.0	86.1	48.0	59.4

Month of issue and stock name	Value of issue (thousands)	Year after issue				
		1 Year	2 Years	3 Years	4 Years	5 Years
			1926			
1 — North American Car Corp.	$ 2,588	94.4	106.6	210.7	128.2	95.2
1 — Congress Cigar Co., Inc.	2,800	135.0	200.8	204.2	113.1	56.2
1 — Beacon Oil Co.[3]	5,700	105.3	84.2	122.0	78.3	52.0
2 — American Home Products Corp.	5,962	120.8	238.2	290.6	221.2	217.9
2 — Grief Bros. Cooperage Co.	2,560	105.6	106.9	100.6	56.2	50.8
2 — Amerada Corp.	3,250	141.6	112.5	123.6	74.5	74.5
3 — Lambert Co.	7,958	176.5	223.8	234.5	255.7	205.8
7 — American Solvents & Chemicals	632	n.a.	158.7	270.5	61.3	9.9
8 — Liquid Carbonic Corp.	3,220	102.9	178.6	267.3	205.3	61.5
9 — Penn-Dixie Cement Co.	12,900	59.6	34.0	21.5	15.7	4.0
11 — Pacific-Clay Products	2,800	100.9	98.7	105.4	54.9	33.9
12 — Patino Mines Enterprises Consol.	5,000	89.8	132.7	117.2	34.0	26.0
12 — Fulton Sylphon Co.[4]	3,900	118.4	115.4	64.1	32.2	22.4
			1927			
1 — National Tile Co.	$ 2,970	n.a.	105.3	82.2	21.2	8.3
3 — W. T. Grant Co.	2,688	250.0	267.6	71.3	72.6	60.6
3 — Mandel Bros. Inc.	3,638	78.4	71.1	29.8	10.4	5.2
6 — Pillsbury Flour Mills, Inc.	3,500	37.2	43.8	30.0	27.5	13.2
8 — (John W.) Watson Co.	4,900	27.6	13.5	8.6	1.6	1.3
10 — Hershey Chocolate Corp.	3,468	174.3	311.8	243.0	238.4	169.4
11 — National Radiator Corp.	2,535	45.2	9.8	3.2	0.3	0.0
11 — United Biscuit Co. of America	2,800	181.9	130.8	126.8	95.8	66.5
12 — McKeesport Tin Plate Co.	6,000	120.0	106.2	114.4	80.2	74.8
			1928			
1 — Consolidated Film Industries	$ 1,575	83.1	63.5	46.2	19.0	13.8
2 — National Trade Journal Inc.	2,529	29.8	12.3	3.0	0.0	0.0
3 — Cutler-Hammer Mfg. Co.	3,088	129.7	219.5	84.6	21.2	13.9
4 — Neve Drug Stores, Inc.[5]	4,000	56.2	23.3	14.8	n.a.	n.a.
5 — H. W. Gossard Co.	2,588	90.0	64.8	12.8	2.0	4.6
5 — Speigel, May, Stern & Co.	4,060	178.6	57.3	13.4	2.8	10.3
6 — Grasselli Chemical Co.[6]	4,700	274.0	155.3	129.2	33.7	112.8
6 — International Printing Ink Corp.	4,945	119.8	83.7	18.3	9.3	27.0
6 — National Aviation Corp.	3,525	281.7	52.7	27.5	14.6	45.0
6 — The Wayne Pump Co.	820	52.1	35.7	8.2	1.2	2.2
6 — Consolidated Automatic Merchandising	824	55.9	6.8	2.3	0.7	3.4
7 — Kimberly-Clark Corp.	7,280	99.5	102.9	60.9	19.2	41.9
9 — Anchor Cap Corp.	4,239	166.5	96.5	46.2	25.3	62.9

Month of issue and stock name	Value of issue (thou-sands)	Year after issue				
		1 Year	2 Years	3 Years	4 Years	5 Years
9 — Curtis Flying Service[7]	9,450	146.4	35.7	16.1	11.9	17.9
10 — Hershey Corp.[8]	1,338	94.2	18.5	11.4	8.0	9.8
10 — Sonora Products	3,000	15.0	0.0	0.0	0.0	0.0
10 — Allied Products Corp.	2,500	120.1	33.8	20.0	11.5	12.8
10 — Lane Drug Stores Inc.	785	60.5	4.1	1.3	n.a.	n.a.
11 — Joseph T. Ryerson & Son	3,900	84.6	66.0	37.7	19.2	31.4
11 — Associated Rayon Corp.	3,352	12.7	3.7	6.2	n.a.	n.a.
11 — Bellanca Aircraft Corp.	2,972	31.9	16.8	6.4	2.6	17.0
11 — United Aircraft & Transport	1,116	112.5	69.0	38.6	59.9	74.1
11 — Great Lakes Aircraft Corp.	4,900	32.4	9.2	10.2	2.5	2.8
11 — Ranier Pulp & Paper Co.	3,325	81.2	36.1	30.1	19.6	58.6
11 — Ritter Dental Mfg. Co.	2,580	102.3	70.4	29.2	20.9	23.3
11 — Universal Aviation	4,300	40.7	23.5	16.1	35.3	44.3
11 — Pacific Western Oil Corp.	16,080	58.3	38.5	20.8	17.7	32.3
11 — Merritt-Chapman & Scott	2,500	84.5	72.0	40.0	1.1	19.2
11 — Strauss (Nathan) Inc.	2,695	54.9	20.4	0.2	0.0	0.0
12 — Aluminum Goods Mfg. Corp.	4,000	113.1	71.6	49.7	42.2	46.2
12 — Helena Rubenstein	3,147	28.4	8.3	3.8	3.2	1.9
12 — Hahn Dept. Stores	17,252	39.0	20.7	8.6	4.0	14.1
12 — Kroger Grocery & Baking	9,194	51.5	21.8	21.4	18.9	26.4
		1949				
1 — Bethlehem Steel Corp.	$20,409	99.0	171.0	161.4	172.1	165.8
1 — Affiliated Gas Equip., Inc.	9,250	113.5	106.2	97.3	104.8	86.5
1 — Koppers Co., Inc.	12,400	94.0	122.8	152.6	128.6	102.6
3 — Sylvania Electric Products, Inc.	5,469	99.8	130.6	176.8	162.3	178.2
4 — Liggett & Myers Tobacco Co.	38,729	163.9	135.5	128.2	151.8	121.4
		1950				
4 — Dumont (A. B.) Labs, Inc.	$ 6,250	43.9	46.4	38.8	26.6	40.2
6 — Sunray Oil Corp.[9]	9,469	152.5	166.4	139.1	151.5	201.1
9 — Canadian Superior Oil of California, (Ltd.)	19,350	145.6	121.2	72.5	108.8	120.0
10 — Kaiser Steel Corp.	31,616	104.0	102.5	102.5	112.6	120.2
12 — International Min. & Chem.	10,224	75.4	77.6	58.7	77.1	60.4
		1951				
3 — Jones & Laughlin Steel Corp.	$25,250	92.6	90.4	84.9	139.8	197.0
3 — Kimberly-Clark Corp.	9,000	102.1	96.1	119.4	202.8	235.6
5 — Sylvania Electric Products, Inc.	11,650	114.8	121.3	121.9	158.0	177.9

Month of issue and stock name	Value of issue (thousands)	Year after issue				
		1 Year	2 Years	3 Years	4 Years	5 Years
6 — Squibb (E. R.) & Sons[10]	15,375	49.5	41.6	53.0	68.3	62.8
10 — Aluminium Ltd.	7,095	94.9	87.5	125.8	197.4	237.8
10 — Sharon Steel Corp.	7,314	81.9	80.7	69.0	106.9	110.0
10 — Lion Oil Co.	14,788	82.7	71.9	98.2	155.8	131.1
12 — Federated Dept. Stores	10,030	112.8	99.6	141.9	173.9	157.3
			1952			
2 — Koppers Co., Inc.	$11,250	85.3	76.4	103.9	119.4	120.6
2 — Owens-Corning Fiberglass	16,088	125.2	156.6	196.1	281.4	312.6
2 — Rheem Mfg. Co.	6,200	89.1	88.3	141.7	110.5	60.1
2 — Marathon Corp.	10,900	86.7	80.3	108.9	137.8	107.8
2 — Monsanto Chemical Co.	39,200	94.0	86.2	108.2	135.6	96.6
3 — Ga.-Pacif. Plywood & Lumber Co.[12]	5,250	81.2	53.9	127.4	217.7	292.7
3 — Can. Chem. & Cellulose Co.	7,750	81.0	53.6	67.0	64.9	48.0
5 — Lion Oil Co.[11]	16,048	86.9	100.3	122.4	156.6	133.9
5 — Food Mach. & Chemical	13,425	82.7	95.4	112.0	147.5	139.1
5 — Federated Petrol. Ltd.[13]	5,175	52.9	38.6	49.6	59.5	100.1
7 — Deere & Co.	22,121	81.4	90.1	113.7	86.1	91.2
8 — Pillsbury Mills	5,640	107.0	139.7	155.1	143.2	131.8
12 — Colorado Fuel & Iron	6,000	89.6	120.6	167.0	180.4	109.0
			1953			
2 — Sylvania Electric Products, Inc.	$20,141	92.7	135.4	135.9	122.4	108.5
4 — Clevite Corp.	5,076	82.7	86.7	84.7	81.8	65.0
4 — P. Lorillard	8,290	105.9	96.8	85.0	72.9	226.9
9 — Stauffer Chemical	7,750	148.0	221.5	299.4	262.6	343.4
			1954			
1 — Colorado Oil & Gas	$12,500	108.0	128.0	154.0	108.5	132.5
2 — Wagner Electric Corp.	5,400	87.8	95.5	136.1	107.6	143.8
4 — American Tide Lands[14]	20,000	11.8	8.8	6.5	1.7	4.2
12 — Monterey Oil Co.	10,950	91.1	88.5	58.2	96.1	64.0
			1955			
1 — United Artists Theatre Circuit	$ 6,802	50.0	34.9	25.7	56.2	50.7
2 — Allied Stores Corp.	16,425	96.7	76.6	77.3	102.6	98.1
4 — Storer Broadcasting Co.	6,469	99.2	113.7	93.2	130.0	116.3
10 — Copperweld Steel Co.	6,000	115.5	109.5	132.5	196.3	135.0

Month of issue and stock name	Value of issue (thou-sands)	Year after issue				
		1 Year	2 Years	3 Years	4 Years	5 Years
11 — Marquette Cement Mfg.	8,688	98.0	84.2	152.9	136.7	139.6
11 — Kimberly-Clark Corp.	18,552	93.4	94.1	148.2	144.2	177.2
12 — LeCuno Oil Corp.	4,060	61.6	41.0	35.7	17.9	10.7
12 — Minute Maid Corp.	6,900	59.8	29.0	100.4	118.0	207.2

[1] Acquired by Chrysler Motors on July 30, 1928.

[2] Name changed to Safety Cable Co., October 6, 1925, and changed to General Cable Co., November 14, 1927.

[3] Name changed to Colonial Beacon Oil, 1930.

[4] Acquired by Reynolds Metal Co., January 1929.

[5] Acquired by United Retail Chemists, December 1928.

[6] Acquired by DuPont Chemical Co., November 1928.

[7] Acquired by Curtiss Wright, August 1929.

[8] Name changed to Houdaille-Hershey Corp. on January 30, 1929.

[9] Name changed to Sunray Mid-Continent Oil Company, 1955.

[10] Merged with (Olin) Mathieson (Chemical) Corp., 1952.

[11] Acquired by Monsanto Chemical, September 30, 1955.

[12] Name changed to Ga.-Pacific Corp., April 1956.

[13] Merged with Home Oil, December 1955.

[14] Name changed to Marine Drilling Inc., September 1, 1957.

Table A2   Price relatives of preferred stocks

(Issue price = 100)

Month of issue and stock name	Value of issue (thou-sands)	Year after issue				
		1 Year	2 Years	3 Years	4 Years	5 Years
				1923		
1 — (Edward G.) Budd Mfg.	$ 3,000	n.a.	n.a.	n.a.	n.a.	73.7
1 — Hammermill Paper Co.	3,000	101.0	105.0	108.8	108.8	109.0
1 — Reliance Mfg. Co.	2,500	96.2	87.1	88.4	99.0	99.2

Month of issue and stock name	Value of issue (thousands)	Year after issue				
		1 Year	2 Years	3 Years	4 Years	5 Years
1 — Armour & Co.	60,000	93.6	93.2	98.4	95.2	90.0
1 — Lyon & Healy, Inc.	2,500	98.2	103.5	110.0	*	*
1 — American Rolling Mill	7,000	100.5	107.2	110.2	112.8	110.0
2 — Onyx Hosiery, Inc.[1]	3,500	89.5	80.5	97.5	114.3	122.2
2 — National Dept. Stores	5,000	95.5	99.5	95.8	91.5	91.2
2 — Rosenbaum Grain Corp.	3,625	95.1	94.1	7.8	29.4	33.3
3 — American Chain Co.	8,750	87.0	93.9	94.6	118.6	*
3 — National Cloak & Suit Co.[2]	4,000	93.5	101.0	84.5	90.8	99.9
4 — Inland Steel	10,000	98.0	100.6	105.3	108.4	111.4
5 — Sherman Clay & Co.	3,000	n.a.	n.a.	94.8	97.7	98.6
9 — Remington Arms Co. Inc.	4,000	n.a.	n.a.	100.3	94.1	101.6
11 — Palmolive Co.[3]	4,000	n.a.	n.a.	n.a.	107.9	110.0
		1924				
9 — Franklin Simon & Co.	$ 4,000	101.7	103.9	107.1	104.6	96.4
10 — R. Hoe & Co. Inc.	4,000	90.0	59.0	66.0	38.0	52.0
12 — Universal Pictures Corp.	3,000	94.9	97.8	99.1	93.5	39.5
12 — The Symington Co.	4,504	51.8	24.2	19.4	51.6	37.2
		1925				
2 — Artloom Corp.	$ 3,000	111.0	113.6	113.0	99.0	60.9
2 — First National Pictures, Inc.	2,500	103.7	97.6	107.5	106.0	115.0
2 — Spear & Co.	4,500	81.9	78.6	80.4	80.2	79.1
2 — General Outdoor Advertising	5,812	118.7	124.2	123.7	109.1	92.3
4 — Dodge Bros. Inc.[4]	64,014	108.2	99.2	96.3	152.7	*
7 — International Cement Corp.	6,750	101.8	106.8	107.3	*	*
7 — International Match Corp.	20,250	144.9	157.9	229.4	203.6	173.2
7 — The Outlet Co.	3,500	101.1	110.5	114.5	82.0	105.0
9 — (Edward G.) Budd Mfg. Co.	2,500	n.a.	n.a.	n.a.	75.6	61.9
9 — Real Silk Hosiery Co.	2,500	n.a.	88.8	93.0	97.1	89.5
10 — The Miller Rubber Co.[5]	4,000	96.6	96.6	77.8	42.5	13.1
10 — National Tea Co.	3,250	124.8	164.4	287.2	250.0	71.0
10 — Gotham Silk Hosiery Co.	4,500	114.9	121.0	111.0	82.9	68.6
11 — Firestone Tire & Rubber Co.	10,000	98.8	107.9	108.0	111.1	*
12 — St. Maurice Valley Corp.	3,806	n.a.	100.4	96.6	91.0	50.0
12 — Abraham & Strauss, Inc.	4,250	110.1	110.8	109.6	104.4	106.4
12 — New York Canners Inc.	5,100	89.4	55.0	38.9	27.9	14.5
		1926				
1 — Chandler Cleveland Motors[6]	$ 3,360	48.0	35.3	40.8	11.2	4.4
1 — Crown-Williamette Paper Co.	20,000	99.9	97.8	96.5	100.6	68.0

Month of issue and stock name	Value of issue (thou- sands)	Year after issue				
		1 Year	2 Years	3 Years	4 Years	5 Years
1 — White Sewing Machine Co.	5,000	113.5	109.1	112.8	58.5	13.8
1 — Louisiana Oil Refining Corp.	4,000	96.6	90.0	92.2	86.0	55.0
2 — Bethlehem Steel Corp.	35,000	107.7	120.6	121.8	126.4	121.4
2 — Zellerbach Corp.	5,850	99.0	141.9	98.0	82.3	41.3
3 — Collins & Aikman Co.	5,000	152.7	99.9	94.1	83.2	73.9
6 — American Seating Corp.	3,000	123.3	99.3	92.7	28.0	12.7
7 — American Solvents & Chem.	2,868	69.7	110.5	174.3	69.7	10.9
8 — The Halle Bros. Co.	2,500	102.5	102.5	102.0	97.5	90.0
9 — Sculling Steel Co.	3,850	85.7	93.8	76.0	45.4	13.0
9 — Pacific Coast Biscuit Co.[7]	2,910	99.5	88.7	101.6	359.9	352.5
9 — Penn-Dixie Cement Corp.	7,215	94.1	75.8	44.7	40.4	10.1
10 — Central Alloy Steel Corp.[8]	6,189	100.5	103.5	104.2	69.5	17.8
10 — (Edward G.) Budd Mfg. Co.	3,000	n.a.	32.8	81.1	63.9	23.7
10 — Broadway Dept. Stores	3,000	108.4	102.3	93.4	71.7	n.a.
11 — Gotham Silk Hosiery Co.	5,000	117.2	117.0	83.1	62.3	58.8
12 — Flintkote Co.	2,500	n.a.	110.0	*	*	*

		1927				
2 — General Motors Corp.	$25,000	104.2	104.6	101.6	83.1	70.2
2 — L. Bamberger & Co.	10,000	106.7	105.3	104.1	101.6	91.4
3 — American Chain Co.	11,000	100.3	82.0	94.0	35.6	17.5
3 — Richfield Oil Co. of Cal.	5,000	111.2	180.5	107.0	24.7	2.5
4 — United Cigar Stores of America	20,000	104.7	92.2	40.8	70.0	8.3
5 — Crown-Zellerbach Corp.	2,992	127.3	92.0	81.2	21.6	13.8
5 — Sun Oil Co.	4,500	109.8	102.9	104.1	95.0	73.4
6 — International Paper Co.	15,000	105.2	87.9	78.2	25.0	4.8
6 — Pillsbury Flour Mills Inc.	3,000	111.4	109.4	75.0	68.8	33.1
7 — Auto Strap Safety Razor Co.[9]	3,762	104.9	99.7	145.4	163.1	157.6
7 — Collins & Aikman Corp.	5,500	89.6	90.3	80.3	77.9	55.3
7 — Pennsylvania Sand Glass Corp.	3,000	n.a.	115.0	105.0	90.0	n.a.
7 — Foster Wheeler Corp.	3,500	n.a.	n.a.	205.0	100.0	75.0
8 — National Radiator Corp.	5,850	66.7	15.9	4.0	0.9	0.0
8 — Weber & Heilbroner, Inc.[10]	2,500	98.5	90.6	49.0	13.7	4.9
10 — Hershey Chocolate Corp. (6 percent cum. prior pref.)	15,000	104.6	107.6	108.6	*	*
10 — Hershey Chocolate Corp. (conv. pref. cum. $4/sh.)	22,432	124.4	221.3	143.5	132.6	122.3
10 — St. Regis Paper Co.	2,740	86.3	99.0	106.4	n.a.	30.9
12 — The Cuneo Press Inc.	2,500	92.4	78.7	89.0	65.4	61.7
12 — George A. Fuller Co.	4,478	104.9	96.5	82.9	30.2	9.2
12 — F. & W. Grand 5-10-25¢ Stores	2,500	72.8	38.6	21.4	2.4	0.9
12 — Loews Inc.	15,000	101.4	44.3	90.5	59.2	59.6

Month of issue and stock name	Value of issue (thou-sands)	Year after issue				
		1 Year	2 Years	3 Years	4 Years	5 Years
			1928			
1 — General Tire & Rubber Co.	$ 3,500	99.5	88.7	82.4	58.3	35.3
1 — Consolidated Film Industries	6,375	126.2	92.3	82.1	50.6	43.2
1 — Walgreen Co.	4,500	95.5	91.0	85.0	64.7	92.4
2 — Hamilton Watch Co.	4,800	100.2	103.5	102.0	64.7	19.9
2 — United Piece Dye Works	3,750	103.4	93.7	102.2	88.4	68.0
2 — Interstate Dept. Stores Inc.	3,250	128.3	70.8	58.0	46.0	17.4
2 — Keith-Albee Orpheum Co.	10,000	112.4	99.5	94.3	24.8	10.9
2 — Neisner Bros. Inc.	2,500	178.3	106.5	68.9	2.8	12.8
2 — Schulte-United 5¢-$1 Store	10,000	76.0	18.0	1.1	0.0	0.0
3 — Spang Chalfant & Co. Inc.	2,500	94.9	96.9	93.4	43.4	20.7
3 — Barker Bros. Corp.	3,000	96.0	78.5	55.0	25.0	1.1
3 — Standard Dredging Company	4,350	123.3	103.4	33.2	7.8	2.1
4 — Brown Co.	10,000	97.4	28.3	34.0	4.7	2.8
4 — Cavanagh-Dobbs, Inc.[11]	3,500	96.4	70.2	22.0	7.6	6.0
4 — Unit Corp. of America	3,135	98.2	79.0	16.7	0.9	0.0
4 — Metropolitan Chain Stores	3,500	99.1	72.6	8.7	0.0	0.0
4 — Peoples Drug Store, Inc.	2,500	107.9	100.5	95.6	81.9	60.5
4 — Consumers Co.	5,000	79.0	67.4	41.6	4.2	1.6
5 — I. Miller & Sons, Inc.	2,500	90.5	77.1	39.3	13.9	5.8
5 — Speigel, May, Stern & Co.	7,000	89.2	69.4	17.6	19.8	35.1
6 — Borg Warner	3,500	109.8	95.0	95.6	51.7	85.7
6 — Hart-Carter Co.	4,480	78.9	56.6	20.3	7.8	25.2
6 — International Printing Ink Corp.	7,000	95.7	94.0	59.1	31.7	68.1
6 — The Wayne Pump Co.	2,218	78.1	65.9	30.4	5.2	4.7
6 — California Dairies Inc.	4,312	50.4	44.9	21.4	4.1	9.8
6 — Consolidated Automatic Merchandising	10,176	38.8	6.9	1.0	0.3	1.5
6 — Crosse & Blackwell, Inc.	2,704	94.7	71.2	46.8	n.a.	n.a.
6 — Leath & Co.	2,642	78.8	65.4	17.3	13.5	8.2
7 — Miller & Hart Inc.	2,860	82.0	60.6	33.6	15.4	22.1
9 — Anchor Cap Corp.	3,060	139.3	104.9	85.3	69.2	88.0
9 — Kendall Co.	3,888	88.7	68.0	40.5	26.2	67.0
9 — McKesson & Robbins	9,889	107.4	77.4	57.4	18.1	40.0
10 — Houdaille-Hershey Corp.	1,329	97.2	44.2	40.3	19.8	26.9
10 — Mullins Mfg. Co.	3,060	83.3	40.3	22.7	15.4	10.4
10 — Chase Brass & Copper Co.	2,500	99.4	100.1	87.8	72.2	84.4
10 — Mid-Continent Laundries	3,400	65.4	6.6	3.7	n.a.	n.a.
10 — Lane Drug Stores, Inc.	1,717	79.5	3.8	2.4	n.a.	n.a.
11 — Associated Rayon Corp.	17,648	39.8	48.2	33.1	*	*
11 — United Aircraft & Trans. Corp.	4,194	112.5	116.3	103.0	118.8	131.6
11 — Kraft Phenix Cheese[12]	6,000	96.0	45.5	37.7	30.0	28.6

Month of issue and stock name	Value of issue (thousands)	Year after issue				
		1 Year	2 Years	3 Years	4 Years	5 Years
12 — Thompson & Stanet Co.	8,800	67.7	50.6	34.3	30.1	39.7
12 — Hahn Dept. Stores	22,700	76.6	54.8	30.3	12.9	24.9
12 — Koppers Gas & Coke	20,000	98.5	97.0	63.6	49.5	59.4
12 — The Newport Co.[13]	6,500	104.0	70.5	110.2	4.4	14.5
			1949			
4 — Merck & Co. Inc.	$ 7,192	130.4	n.a.	110.2	98.0	101.7
5 — United Biscuit Co. of America	8,280	104.1	103.6	101.4	98.8	102.9
6 — Caterpillar Tractor Co.	25,000	105.1	102.9	103.8	98.5	102.5
11 — Clinton Industries Inc.	5,025	109.6	98.5	89.1	95.4	113.8
			1950			
7 — Spencer Chemicals	$ 6,821	100.9	101.2	99.2	102.0	102.5
10 — Kaiser Steel Corp.	31,616	104.0	102.5	102.5	112.6	120.2
11 — Safeway Stores	6,400	94.0	85.8	90.9	97.2	94.5
			1951			
1 — City Stores Co.	$ 6,000	86.1	82.1	75.8	96.0	105.8
1 — Food Fair Stores, Inc.	8,000	94.2	97.2	93.5	100.0	101.2
6 — Minn.-Honeywell Regulator Co.	16,000	108.8	105.4	103.4	*	*
6 — Pfizer (Chas.) & Co. Inc.	15,000	110.7	93.8	103.3	113.8	98.7
6 — Rheem Mfg. Co.	7,000	92.1	89.7	100.5	118.4	90.2
6 — National Tea Co.	12,000	105.0	107.9	125.9	104.0	*
8 — U.S. Plywood Corp.	6,150	94.1	82.6	88.8	99.8	116.8
8 — National Distillers Prods.	50,000	101.5	88.8	93.8	99.8	100.6
9 — National Container	12,600	87.1	74.3	92.6	141.7	231.4
10 — Ashland Oil & Refining	5,045	100.5	97.7	99.5	101.8	97.9
10 — Shell Mar Products[14]	5,200	123.2	118.5	127.4	*	*
12 — (Olin) Mathieson Chem. Corp.	18,000	109.8	103.9	122.5	120.9	108.1
12 — Diamond Alkali Co.	12,000	108.2	100.1	114.1	116.8	103.0*
12 — Pittsburgh Coke & Chem.	6,000	94.2	78.4	84.0	92.2	90.5
			1952			
1 — Kaiser Aluminum & Chem.	$18,750	92.5	95.2	169.4	104.0	*
1 — Consolidated Grocers[15]	9,800	86.2	92.9	99.0	103.6	98.8
1 — Atlas Plywood Corp.	5,700	86.3	75.0	82.7	77.9	70.5
5 — Elliott Co.	6,000	107.5	102.1	101.8	94.5	104.2
6 — Safeway Stores	20,000	106.0	103.0	*	*	*

Month of issue and stock name	Value of issue (thou- sands)	Year after issue				
		1 Year	2 Years	3 Years	4 Years	5 Years
		1953				
3 — P. R. Mallory	$ 7,500	109.5	109.5	105.5	105.0	*
11 — General Precision Equip.	5,408	192.5	106.0	*	*	*
11 — Dixie Cup[16]	7,623	142.2	137.2	133.5	104.0	*
		1954				
2 — Gulf Sulphur Corp.	$ 7,000	111.2	125.0	70.0	31.9	55.0
4 — I.T.E. Circuit Breaker	5,000	101.8	97.0	93.0	74.4	92.1
5 — Allis-Chalmers Mfg.	35,700	121.6	110.3	113.0	93.6	108.8
9 — Spencer Chemical Co.	15,000	99.2	97.0	81.2	91.0	87.2
10 — Mead Corp.	7,800	132.9	103.8	*	*	*
11 — Tung-Sol Electric	5,000	111.5	103.5	103.6	*	*
11 — Penn Fruit Co.	5,225	106.2	82.3	70.3	95.7	98.6
		1955				
3 — General Tire & Rubber	$10,225	108.6	126.0	143.8	380.4	428.7
3 — Western Auto Supply	5,000	105.0	96.0	99.8	99.1	96.4
5 — Minn.-Honeywell Regulator Co.	16,320	102.9	*	*	*	*
9 — Kaiser Aluminum & Chem.	35,000	97.8	84.0	84.0	92.0	92.0

* Issue retired.

[1] Acquired by Gotham Silk, December 1926.

[2] Name changed to Bellas Hess Co., March 1927.

[3] Name changed to Palmolive-Peet Company, February 1927, and to Colgate-Palmolive-Peet Company, June 1928.

[4] Acquired by Chrysler Corp., July 30, 1928.

[5] Acquired by B. F. Goodrich, March 1930.

[6] Merged with Hupp Motor Car, 1930.

[7] Acquired by National Biscuits, June 1930.

[8] Merged with Republic Steel, April 1930.

[9] Acquired by Gillette Safety Razor, November 1930.

[10] Name changed to Fashion Park, 1929.

[11] Merged with Hat Corp., May 1932.

[12] Acquired by National Dairy, June 4, 1930.

13 Name changed to Newport Industries, 1931.

14 Name changed to General Package Corp., July 1953.

15 Name changed to Consolidated Foods Corp., February 1954.

16 Acquired by American Can, June 1957.

NOTES

1. *Report of the Special Study of the Securities Markets of the Securities and Exchange Commission* (88th Cong., 1st Sess., House Document 95, 1963 [Washington, D.C.: Government Printing Office, 1963]), part 1. All citations in text to part, chapter, or page refer to this work.

2. *Ibid.,* p. 51. (My italics.)

3. The Report discusses only the higher rate of use of expulsion as a penalty against younger firms. The Report does not relate sanctions to violations, so the interpretation of heavier penalties is obscure, even if the more lenient enforcement against older firms remarked upon by the Report is waived.

4. The data are more fully described in the Appendix.

5. The preferred stocks had almost identical means in the large and small samples, but the small common stock issues had much lower prices than the large issues for the first three years, after which they were essentially equal to those of the large issues. But only the first-year price relatives differed significantly at the 5 percent level with the small samples available. There were no systematic differences in the variances of the price relatives of large and small issues.

6. An estimate of the role of dividends for two years in each period were made as follows: The aggregate dividends received on stocks issued in 1923 and 1924, and in 1950 and 1951, are expressed as rates of return on the initial costs to investors of the issues:

Rate of return on initial cost

Year and type of issue	1924*	1925	1926	1927	1928
1923–24:					
Preferred	7.11	7.10	6.77	6.50	6.30
Common	7.11	6.16	6.56	6.77	7.62

Year and type of issue	1951†	1952	1953	1954	1955
1950–51:					
Preferred	6.89	4.78	4.81	4.86	4.81
Common	1.62	4.17	4.11	4.08	4.26

* 1923 issues only.
† 1950 issues only.

This sample suggests that dividends were a larger component of return in the 1920s.

7. Of twenty-six issues of common stock in 1949–54, only six were by companies less than three years old; the corresponding figure for 1923–27 was thirty-eight less than three years old of a total of fifty-three issues.

8. In the 1920s, thirty-six of 121 issues were convertible and in the 1950s twenty-eight of forty issues were convertible.

9. The costs of the program, that is, probably exceed even a reasonably optimistic estimate of benefits. Costs of flotations due to registration have apparently never been estimated even ap-

proximately; the SEC data (e.g., *Cost of Flotations,* 1945–49) exclude costs included in commissions of underwriters and costs of the delays imposed by the process, as well as costs of operating the SEC. The full costs of registration for new stock issues could be 5 percent of their value.

10. *Special Study,* pt. 2, pp. 102–3.

11. *Ibid.,* p. 104.

12. The *Special Study* shows particular concern with the specialist who "reaches across" the market, i.e., who initiates transactions by buying stock at the offer or selling at the bid, instead of waiting for someone to trade. This alarm again reflects the study's identification of the specialist's proper role with strict price stabilization. Suppose the bid is 30 and the ask 30½, and the specialist anticipates that the market will soon go to 32–32½. He buys at 30½ so the effective ask becomes (say) 30¾. He has initiated a price move, but one called for by his function of achieving equilibrium, if his anticipation is correct.

13. Of course, the frequency of transactions depends upon the size of the individual transactions, but this is not closely correlated with frequency. A short sequence of the transactions of the NYSE was tabulated for November 5, 1963:

No. of transactions	No. of stock issues	Average transaction size (shares)	No. of transactions	No. of stock issues	Average transaction size (shares)
1	264	225	7	3	200
2	97	181	8	3	196
3	51	199	9	3	144
4	30	190	12–16	9	172
5	13	192	18–67	3	236
6	12	303			

14. This delay is the average of 7.59 units for the earlier tender plus zero units for the tender that makes a transaction. If we include bids or asks cancelled after twenty-five time units, the average delay is 8.04 units—perhaps a half-hour for an active stock, a week or a month for an inactive stock.

15. Specialists affect our model in the following ways: (1) the bid of 29¾ effectively eliminates all offers by nondealers at less than 29¾, so the frequency distribution of offers now ranges from 29¾ to 31, with the lowest offer arising ½ of the time on average; (2) the offer of 30 effectively eliminates all bids by nondealers at more than 30, with similar consequences.

16. In the absence of specialists, the gains or losses of buyers measured from an expected price of 29⅞ were exactly offset by the corresponding losses or gains for sellers. (We ignore commissions, which will be the same with or without specialists, at least as a first approximation.) The parties now lose the jobber's "turn" of (say) ¼, which is the price they pay for one of two things: (1) immediate availability of a buyer or seller; (2) the elimination of short-run fluctuations in price. These two gains are analytically one: there is always an available buyer at a low enough price, and an available seller at a high enough price, so the gain of immediate marketability is at a price which contains no random elements. (Strictly speaking, we should say a price with much reduced random elements. The specialists' inventory will be exhausted from time to time when unusually long runs of bids or asks arise, since inventories will not be held in quantities sufficient to cope with the longest runs.)

With perfect foresight, the analysis would be modified in only one respect in order to be applied to changing equilibrium prices: the equilibrium price of a security could never fluctuate by more than the cost of holding it.

17. See Lester G. Telser, "A Theory of Speculation Relating Profitability and Stability," *Review of Economics and Statistics,* August 1959.

THIRTEEN

The CPA—and the
Securities Acts Amendments

CURTIS E. YOUNGDAHL

Retired Partner, Deloitte, Haskins & Sells

The 1964 amendment to the Securities Act significantly changed some of the requirements for annual and periodic filings with the Securities and Exchange Commission. This article examines the technical changes and how they affect the CPA and public companies, noting that the accountant who fully understands the 1964 amendment is in a position to provide very valuable services to an expanded client market.

INTRODUCTION

Many CPAs, whether engaged in private accounting or public practice, will discover an opportunity to render a valuable service through an effective understanding of the 1964 Securities Act Amendments which affect a substantial number of companies.

INITIAL SUMMARY

A Special Study of the Securities Markets, initiated by the Securities and Exchange Commission in 1961 and completed in August 1963, produced some 175 recommendations. As a result, legislation, which eventually led to the enactment of Public Law 88–467 signed by President Johnson on August 20, 1964, was subsequently introduced in Congress. This resulting law is called the "Securities Acts Amendments of 1964."

These amendments:

Increase substantially the number of companies required to register their securities with the Securities and Exchange Commission (SEC);

Extend the SEC's regulation of proxy statements and its rules relating to insider trading to these companies, and to similar companies having unlisted securities previously registered with the SEC at the time such securities were sold;

Change certain reporting requirements for companies registered and to be registered; and

Impose stricter controls on brokers and dealers in securities.

Financial officers and legal counsel of companies that may be affected, as well as their auditors, should familiarize themselves with these amendments and their possible impact in particular circumstances. The auditor who understands them is in a good position to render

Reprinted from *The Financial Executive*, April 1965, pp.10–16, 45, with permission of the Financial Executives Institute.

constructive service to his clients, including those clients who may not have given consideration to the possible effect of the amendments.

REGULATION PRIOR TO ENACTMENT OF THE 1964 AMENDMENTS

In order to understand the impact of the amendments, it is necessary to refer very briefly to
regulation as it existed prior to enactment of the 1964 amendments.

The Securities and Exchange Commission administers several acts which require companies to register with it. These are:

The Securities Act of 1933, commonly called the 1933 Act;

The Securities Exchange Act of 1934, commonly called the Exchange Act or the 1934
Act;

The Public Utility Holding Company Act of 1935; and

The Investment Company and Investment Advisors Acts of 1940.

The 1933 Act requires companies offering their own securities for sale to the public to
register these securities with the SEC pursuant to the provisions of that act. Certain types of
securities are exempted from its provisions. The exempted securities include those of building and loan associations, charitable corporations, governments, railroads, and banks, as
well as securities sold wholly within the bounds of a single state. In addition, a conditional
exemption is available for issues of $300,000 or less, although the offering circular relating
thereto must be submitted to the SEC in order to qualify for the exemption. Also, the exemption may be withdrawn.

The 1934 Act has for many years required registration with the SEC of securities of companies listed on national securities exchanges. The SEC has exempted foreign corporations
from certain provisions of the law. Railroads have not been exempt, but have been permitted
to file copies of reports filed with the Interstate Commerce Commission (ICC) in lieu of financial statements certified by independent public accountants. The 1934 Act also contains
rules relating to proxy solicitation, insiders' transactions, and various other matters which
applied in the past to listed companies only. The 1934 Act also contains the periodic reporting requirements which apply to companies which have registered under the 1933 or 1934
Acts.

Registration under either the 1933 Act or the 1934 Act requires the submission of specified information, including financial statements for specified periods prepared in accordance
with regulations prescribed by the Commission, and this information usually must be brought
up to date annually on prescribed forms. The SEC requires that audited financial statements
be accompanied by certificates of public accountants who are independent by its standards.

The 1934 Act contained rules relating to proxy solicitation (in Section 14 of that Act)
and, in Section 15, rules requiring reports of ownership of equity securities of a registrant by
its directors, officers, and principal stockholders (who are usually described as "insiders").
These rules related to listed companies only.

THE 1964 AMENDMENTS

The amendments change the 1933 Act in only a few respects, but the amendments to the 1934
Act are numerous and important and will have a considerable impact on accounting by com-

mercial and industrial companies, and, directly or indirectly, on reporting requirements, proxy solicitation, and insider trading activities of these companies and many others.

The SEC estimated, many months ago, that perhaps 3900 unlisted companies would be affected. However, different categories of companies are affected in different ways, as will be explained subsequently. This figure included some 1700 unlisted firms already reporting to the SEC as a result of previous "undertakings." Of the remainder of 2200, perhaps 275 represent insurance companies not reporting to the SEC. That leaves 1925, which includes perhaps 600 banks. Deducting the banks, we arrive at a remainder of 1325 of which perhaps 600 may not be required to register until 1966.

These figures are probably low, but the plain fact is that no one knows the right numbers. The SEC recently sent out thousands of questionnaires to unlisted companies in order to alert them to the new requirements and to try to get some reliable figures on the number of firms which may be required to register under the new requirements.

The amendments importantly affect unlisted companies. The amendments include Section 12(g), which extends the 1934 Act registration requirements to a large number of companies not presently listed on any exchange; after registering under 12(g), these companies become subject to the reporting, proxy, and insider-trading requirements of that act. These requirements will apply to companies having assets in excess of $1 million and 750 or more stockholders at the close of their first fiscal year ended after July 1, 1964. They will apply similarly, effective July 1, 1966, where the number of stockholders will be 500 or more.

The amendments provide that companies meeting the $1 million and 750 stockholder requirements must file a 1934 Act Section 12(g) registration statement within 120 days after the close of their first fiscal year ended after July 1, 1964. The SEC, however, has exempted foreign issuers from 12(g) until November 30, 1965, and has adopted a rule to the effect that the earliest date on which a domestic company is required to file is April 30, 1965, except for companies already reporting. A related rule states in effect that unlisted companies are not subject to the proxy solicitation rules until two months after the date their registration statement is due, or December 31, 1965, whichever is earlier. This rule, however, does not apply to solicitation of proxies from security holders of a holding company, or its subsidiaries, registered under the Public Utility Holding Company Act of 1935.

The SEC may exempt companies, or classes of companies, if it believes such exemptions to be in the public interest.

Total assets are to be determined by reference to a balance sheet prepared pursuant to Regulation S-X, which governs the form and content of financial statements prepared for filing with the SEC. The test is met if either the corporate or consolidated balance sheet shows total assets in excess of $1 million.

"Equity security" includes any security convertible into stock or similar security, and thus includes warrants and certain convertible debentures. Rules to be followed in determining the number of holders of securities of record may be found in 1934 Act Release No. 7492.

To terminate a registration of a particular class of equity securities under Section 12(g) after the number of holders of record of that class of equity security falls below 300, the company must file a certification to that effect with the Commission. The latter issues a notice and affords an opportunity for a hearing. If all goes well, registration will be terminated 90 days after filing the certification.

Because the degree of change in regulation varies, depending upon how much a particular company was regulated in the past and how much it is now regulated, we shall examine the impact of the amendments by classes of companies grouped as follows:

1. Unlisted companies not previously reporting to the SEC (other than special industries);
2. Special industries;
3. Unlisted companies already reporting to the SEC;
4. Listed companies.

IMPACT ON UNLISTED COMPANIES

First, then, let us consider the unlisted companies which have not previously reported to the SEC. The 1964 amendments have their most abrupt impact on certain categories of companies in this group. In the discussion of this group, I will mention some of the detailed requirements which will affect these companies; these details will not be repeated in the discussion relating to other categories of companies. In no cases will these details be complete.

Companies not listed on a national securities exchange include companies having unlisted trading privileges on the American and other stock exchanges and companies listed on the exempt exchanges — Honolulu, Richmond, Wheeling, and Colorado Springs. Unless they are members of special industries, companies in this category, which have 750 or more holders of record of one class of equity security at the end of their fiscal year ended after July 1, 1964 (500 or more effective July 1, 1966), and whose total assets exceed $1 million, become subject to the registration, reporting, proxy, and insider-trading provisions of the 1934 act, and will continue to be subject thereto unless the number of stockholders is reduced below 300.

DISCLOSURE REQUIREMENTS

The registration statement to be filed with the SEC will include an audited balance sheet as of the close of its first fiscal year ended after July 1, 1964 (July 1, 1966 for a company with 500 to 749 stockholders) and audited statements of income and surplus for the three years then ended, all in the form prescribed in the Commission's Regulation S-X. These statements must include notes setting forth certain specific information with regard to principles of consolidation, depreciation policies and practices, preferred stock, stock options, stock reserved, basis of valuation of inventories, pension plans, and similar matters. The financial statements will be accompanied by schedules prescribed in Regulation S-X. Schedules required, where appropriate, include schedules of investments, of amounts due from directors, officers, and principal holders of securities other than affiliates, of property, plant and equipment and related reserves, of long-term debt, of reserves, of capital shares and warrants, of supplementary profit and loss information, and of income from dividends and equity in net profit and loss of affiliates.

Other requirements, not covered by the accountant's certificate, include a description of the company's business and properties, regulation, and other matters. Copies of important contracts, the charter, pension plans, and other documents must be filed as exhibits to the registration statement.

Among matters which must be disclosed are the following:

Salaries (if over $30,000) paid to the three highest paid officers.

Receivables at any time during the period from officers, directors, or principal stockholders.

Material contracts (including patents) not made in the ordinary course of business which are to be executed in whole or in part subsequent to the filing of the application for registration or which were made within the two years prior thereto.

Reporting requirements to bring the information up to date will presumably be similar to current requirements, which call for the filing of certain information on an annual basis (usually on Form 10-K), as well as semiannual reports of income on Form 9-K (which need not be certified), and reports at a month end (where applicable) on Form 8-K of certain other information, including copies of material contracts not made in the ordinary course of business.

Insider-trading requirements are the same as for listed companies. Officers, directors, and "10 percent stockholders" must file statements of their holdings, direct and indirect, of securities of the company at the time it registers, and must report any changes in such holdings by the 10th of the month following the change. Such insiders may not sell such securities short, and any profits made on sale or purchase of securities held less than six months inure to the company. Individuals becoming "insiders" after registration must file their initial report within 10 days.

PROXY REQUIREMENTS

Proxy requirements are also the same as for listed companies. It is not practical to explain all the proxy requirements but I will mention a few of interest.

Three copies of the preliminary proxy statement must be submitted to the SEC at least 10 days prior to the date the proxy statement is sent to security holders. The SEC may suggest changes in the proxy statement and, after the proxy statement has been changed, may have further changes to suggest. Four copies of the final proxy statement must be sent to the Commission.

If a security holder submits a proposal he intends to present at the meeting to the company, 60 days before the proxy solicitation material is to be mailed, the company must, subject to various rules, include the proposal in its proxy solicitation material. However, relief is provided from annual solicitation of rejected proposals.

The requirements for the proxy statement may vary depending on the purpose of the meeting of stockholders.

If the proxy relates to authorization or issuance of securities otherwise than for exchange, or to modification or exchange of securities, certified financial statements of the issuer and its subsidiaries such as would currently be required in a registration statement must be included. If the proxy relates to mergers, consolidations, acquisitions, and similar matters, similar statements of the company and its subsidiaries, as well as for companies being merged or acquired, must all be included. Financial statements need not include schedules, except for the schedule of supplementary profit and loss information. Financial statements not material for the exercise of prudent judgment may be omitted.

In the case of the usual annual meeting relating to the election of directors, an annual report containing adequate financial statements must precede or accompany the proxy, or be in the hands of the stockholders at least 20 days prior to the meeting. The proxy statement for such a meeting must disclose the shares held by continuing directors and by individuals nominated to be directors. Remuneration of each director, and of each of the three highest paid officers whose aggregate remuneration exceeded $30,000 must be shown, as well as one figure for directors and officers as a group. Similar information must be included as to pension contributions and anticipated benefits, as to options, and as to certain other matters. Proxy statements must disclose shares held by anyone owning more than 10 percent of the outstanding voting securities.

The amendments authorize the SEC to change the proxy rules to include a new requirement that, even if proxies are not being solicited, the SEC and stockholders of record must be furnished (1) prior to any *annual* meeting, with annual reports and information about proposed directors up for election, and (2) prior to *any* meeting, with appropriate information as to any matters on which the stockholders are to vote. The SEC in 1934 Act Release 7512, has proposed that companies registered under the 1934 act which do not solicit proxies be required to distribute to equity security holders an "Information Statement" containing information similar to that required in a proxy statement.

ISSUING PUBLISHED REPORTS

In connection with the proxy requirements, it should be borne in mind that Rule 14(a)-3 of the proxy rules has been amended in such a way that companies subject to the proxy rules must now take special care in issuing published reports. This rule provided, among other things, that, where the management of an issuer solicits proxies for an annual meeting of security holders for the purpose of electing directors, its proxy statement shall be accompanied or preceded by an annual report to such security holders containing, under the original rule, such financial statements for the last fiscal year as will, in the opinion of management, adequately reflect the financial position and operations of the issuer.

As amended, the rule now requires the inclusion of *consolidated* financial statements of the issuer, and its subsidiaries, in such annual reports to security holders if said statements are necessary to reflect adequately the financial position and results of operations of the issuer and its subsidiaries. Compliance with the requirements of financial statements filed with the Commission is not required, but *any material differences* between the principles of consolidation or other accounting principles or practices, applicable to such statements and those reflected in the report to security holders must be noted. The effect thereof must also be reconciled or explained in the annual report to stockholders.

The amended rule also provides that the financial statements included in reports to security holders shall be the certified by independent public or certified public accountants, unless certification is not required in annual reports filed with the Commission, or if the Commission finds that certification would be impracticable or would involve undue effort or expense.

This amendment to the proxy rules was a logical outcome of cases such as the Atlantic Research case in which the company published corporate financial statements showing a profit, and filed consolidated financial statements with the SEC showing a loss.

The amended rule also requires, in many cases, that the annual report contain such information as to the business done by the company and its subsidiaries during the year as will indicate the general nature and scope of their business.

Considering together, first, the extension or reporting and proxy requirements to additional companies and, second, the change in Proxy Rule 14(a)-3, we see that many companies will not only have to disclose more information than in the past, but they are also going to have to review the form of their published reports to ensure such reports do not differ in material respects from financial reports submitted to the SEC.

IMPACT ON SPECIAL INDUSTRIES

Our second category is companies in special industries:

A. Regulated investment companies registered under the Investment Company Act of 1940 are not affected by the amendments.

B. Railroads are covered, but they may use statements prepared for the ICC in lieu of other financial statements. Their reports need not be certified by public accountants.

C. Banks — although the Exchange Act applies to all banks, the registration, periodic reporting, proxy solicitation, and insider reporting and trading provisions with respect to bank securities, whether listed or unlisted, will be administered and enforced by the federal bank regulatory agencies; the Comptroller of the Currency with respect to securities issued by national and District of Columbia banks; the Board of Governors of the Federal Reserve System with respect to state banks which are members of the Federal Reserve System; and the Federal Deposit Insurance Corporation with respect to all other insured banks. The relevant regulations have been issued by these bodies; they do not require that financial statements be audited by independent certified public accountants.

Banks which are not subject to regulation by a federal bank regulatory agency will be required to comply with the requirements as administered by the SEC. It is believed there are only four such banks.

D. Insurance companies are accorded special treatment. They are exempt from the new registration requirements contained in the new provisions of the Exchange Act provided the home state imposes reporting and proxy requirements meeting the standards of the National Association of Insurance Commissioners and, effective July 1, 1966, imposes insider-trading regulations substantially equivalent to those in the Act. The state requirements do not include certification of financial statements by independent public accountants. The periodic reporting requirements which formerly applied to insurance companies which have registered under the 1933 Act will continue to be applicable to them as well as to insurance companies which file 1933 Act registration statements in the future. Insurance companies registered on a national securities exchange, or which register under the amendments pursuant to Section 12(g), will be subject to the periodic reporting, proxy solicitation, and insider reporting and trading provisions of the 1934 Act.

E. Other companies filing financial statements with the Federal Power Commission (FPC), the Interstate Commerce Commission, or the Federal Communications Commission may file such reports, supplemented by descriptions of the securities being registered, in lieu of reports otherwise required. Where this procedure is followed, the financial statements in the published annual report are also submitted; such statements for companies subject to the FPC must be certified.

F. Exemptions are contained in Section 12(g) for (1) securities listed and registered on a national securities exchange; (2) securities issued by registered investment companies; (3) securities (other than stock generally representing nonwithdrawable capital) of savings and loan associations and similar institutions; (4) securities of certain nonprofit organizations operated exclusively for religious, educational, benevolent, fraternal, charitable, or reformatory purposes; (5) securities of certain agricultural marketing cooperatives; and (6) securities of certain nonprofit mutual or cooperative organizations which supply a commodity service primarily to members.

Companies not engaged in a business affecting interstate commerce and whose securities are *never* traded by use of mails nor by any means or instrumentality of interstate commerce are exempt.

UNLISTED COMPANIES ALREADY REPORTING

We now turn to special industries to consider the impact of the 1964 amendments on the third category of companies, those that are already reporting to the SEC but whose securities are unlisted.

There are many companies which have not listed their securities on any exchange but whose securities of one class or another have been registered with the SEC, *under the 1933 Act,* at the time such securities were sold. When such a company filed a registration statement under the 1933 Act prior to August 20, 1964, it was required to include what was called an "undertaking" to the effect that, if the issue being registered plus all other securities of the same class amounted to $2 million based on the offering price, the company would comply with certain reporting requirements prescribed in the 1934 Act. It would continue to report until that class of securities was reduced to less than $1 million. Thus, such companies have been filing reports, usually on Form 10-K, every year, to "update" financial and certain other information included in the original filings. These firms, however, were not required to comply with the 1934 Act proxy rules or provisions relating to insider trading which applied to listed companies.

As a result of the 1964 Act amendments, every such company which has 750 or more stockholders (500 or more July 1, 1966) and $1 million in assets, will have to register under Section 12(g) of the 1934 Act, and will become subject to the registration, proxy, and insider-trading provisions of the 1934 Act, already briefly described. This is a matter of considerable importance to such companies.

INSIDER-TRADING PROVISIONS

It is undoubtedly true that the managements of some companies have not yet realized the extent to which they will be affected. The management and principal holders of the company's securities probably should be particularly concerned with the insider-trading provisions and the corollary necessity for giving particularly careful consideration to them before selling any securities of the company which they own. These provisions sound quite innocent, but it is very easy to engage in a transaction in such a way that, quite inadvertently, the profit will be considered a short-swing profit under the rules as interpreted, and the profit on the transaction must be turned over to the company.

The management of some of these firms may be concerned, too, by the necessity for disclosure of executive compensation. Accountants are particularly concerned with the necessity for sending out certified reports to holders of equity securities, and the application of Proxy Rule 14(a)-3 as revised (as previously described). In some cases, this may require careful study to make certain that the published annual report is in acceptable form. It is especially important to determine if there are any differences reflected in financial statements in the report to security holders, from the principles of consolidation or other accounting principles or practices (or methods of applying accounting principles or practices), applicable to the financial statements filed, or proposed to be filed, with the SEC.

Companies in this latter category will find it easy to file a registration statement under Section 12(g) because most of the information about the company, including its financial statements, has already been submitted to the SEC. The SEC has revised its old Form 8 (A) to permit that form to be used for a Section 12(g) registration by unlisted companies already reporting to the SEC. The revised form is quite simple. It requires no additional financial statements.

"UNDERTAKING" TO FILE

As indicated, filings under the 1933 Act prior to August 20, 1964, required an "undertaking" to file subsequent periodic reports described in the 1934 Act. This undertaking is not included in filings after August 20, 1964, because the law has been changed to require, in practically every case, the filing of such information for the registrant's fiscal year during which its 1933 Act registration statement became effective. Except in respect to that year, the requirement to file later periodic reports regarding any fiscal year is suspended if, at the beginning of said year, the securities of each class to which the 1933 Act registration statement relates are held of record by less than 300 persons. Under the old undertaking, the reporting requirements stopped when the related security fell below $1 million. Dropping under $1 million is not a cause for suspension of reporting requirements under the new rule.

The amendments expand the reporting requirements to include the filing of copies of material contracts not made in the ordinary course of business not wholly executed prior to July 1, 1962, with the SEC.

IMPACT ON LISTED COMPANIES

The fourth and last category of companies to consider includes those that are listed on a national exchange (excluding companies with unlisted trading privileges, and companies listed on exempt stock exchanges). They are exempt from the requirement for registering under Section 12(g). This is because they are already subject to the full reporting and proxy in insider-trading rules of the 1934 Act. These requirements have been expanded to include a regulation that listed companies must file with the SEC, and with the exchanges on which they are listed, copies of material contracts (including patents) not made in the ordinary course of business unless wholly executed prior to July 1, 1962. Furthermore, these companies are affected by the revisions of Proxy Rule 14(a)-3 already described.

GENERAL TOPICS

In the area of general matters, there has been some confusion arising from the use of the word "registration" in connection with the various Securities Acts. This has been compounded by the fact that, while we have for many years had registration statement requirements under the 1934 Act for companies listing on a national securities exchange, we now have registration statement requirements for unlisted companies under Section 12(g) of the same Act, which is actually called the Securities *Exchange* Act of 1934. To clear one area of possible general confusion, let it be noted that the requirements for registering under the Securities Act of 1933 have not been reduced. For instance, a life insurance company offering $500,000 of its securities for sale, interstate, would still have to register under the 1933 Act and that 1933 Act registration would still have to include certified financial statements.

A word as to the auditor. If the auditor has not had experience with SEC filings, one of the first things he should do is study the rules on independence with special attention to the Accounting Series Releases which relate to independence. If he is not independent under the rules, his certification usually is not acceptable to the SEC; in the case of a filing under Section 12(g), an accountant who has been, in fact, independent but has not fully met the prescribed rules, should resolve his situation by discussion with the SEC. A company required to register with the SEC should expect its independent public accountants to have a good working knowledge of the pertinent statutes, of the rules and regulations issued by the SEC, and its organization.

Any accountant who practices before the SEC—and this includes every accountant whose opinion is included in a registration statement, application, or report filed with the SEC—is assumed by that organization to be informed concerning its accounting and auditing requirements. This knowledge is essential to the practicing accountant; he should advise the client as to the form and content of the financial statements to be filed, and should consult effectively with lawyers and other experts involved in preparing documents for filing.

In conclusion, the unusual opportunities for constructive service arising from the enactment of these amendments, and a particular paragraph from a speech by Manuel Cohen, the present Chairman of the SEC, should be noted:

> The 1964 Amendments to the Securities Acts will bring into contact with the Commission many heretofore "unregulated" companies. Undoubtedly, in many cases, the accountant will be a primary bridge between the issuer and the Commission. He will be called on to explain the "hows" of the Commission's rules. He should also explain the "whys." The accountant should advise on the establishment of systems and controls which will promote the most effective and comprehensible form of compliance. A little foresight can avoid many unnecessary, and possibly embarrassing, problems. For example, when it is contemplated that a company will have to register in the future—as when the shareholder limit under the 1964 Amendments drops to 500 after about two years—the appropriate internal controls should be established now to avoid potential problems which might preclude the issuance of an unqualified certificate. In short, good practices and procedures should be adopted and followed at the earliest possible time.

FOURTEEN

"Truth in Securities"
Three Decades Later

FRANCIS M. WHEAT

Former Commissioner, Securities and Exchange Commission

A little over thirty years after the enactment of the Securities Act of 1933, the Securities Acts Amendments of 1964 were adopted. Francis M. Wheat, at the time a Securities and Exchange Commission commissioner, discusses the changes brought about by these amendments and how they result in a more extensive disclosure system consistent with the vitality and flexibility required of such a process. Together with Mr. Youngdahl's article, Wheat's comments provide the basis for studying the important changes of the 1964 amendments.

The time is late March, 1933. The Pecora hearings on the causes of the great stock market crash have produced a shocking indictment of the financial community.[1] Demands have been mounting for legislation under which the federal government, like certain of the state blue-sky commissioners, would have life-or-death powers over the raising of capital by public offering of securities.

Such powers are not desired by the new President. In his message to Congress on March 29th he said:

> There is ... an obligation upon us to insist that every issue of new securities to be sold in interstate commerce shall be accompanied by full publicity and information and that no essentially important element attending the issue shall be concealed from the buying public ... this proposal ... puts the burden of telling the whole truth on the seller. It should give impetus to honest dealing in securities ...[2]

On the very date of the President's message, however, a bill was introduced in Congress providing, in substance, for a federal blue-sky law.[3] Securities to be sold must be registered. A federal commission (to quote the language of the bill) "may revoke the registration of any security ... if it shall appear ... that ... the business of the issuer ... or the security is not based upon sound principles, and that the revocation is in the interest of the public welfare."[4] The bill represented the antithesis of a law founded on an obligation of full disclosure.

These divergent approaches to the problem of securities regulation, delivered to Congress on the same day, furnish the backdrop for a dramatic interlude in the history of early

Reprinted from Francis M. Wheat, "'Truth in Securities' Three Decades Later," 13 *Howard Law Journal* 100 (1967) with permission of the Howard University School of Law.

New Deal legislation. The House Committee, led by Sam Rayburn, quickly concluded that it needed help to head off the drive for a federal blue-sky law. Rayburn turned to President Roosevelt, who called upon the late Justice Felix Frankfurter. The Justice, in turn, drafted a team consisting of Benjamin Cohen, Thomas Corcoran, and James Landis. Over one weekend, working into the night (or so the story goes) these men completed the first draft of what was to become the Securities Act of 1933. For obvious reasons, they gave to their work the title of "perfecting amendments" to the wholly dissimilar bill already introduced in Congress.

With his legendary political skill, Sam Rayburn thereafter guided the proceedings to a conclusion with the enactment of the first federal securities laws — aptly termed, at the time, the "truth-in-securities act."[5]

More than a generation after these events occurred, Professor William L. Cary was appointed to the Commission as its fourteenth chairman. In an article written for the *Harvard Business Review* a year or so later, he confessed: "When I first came to the Securities and Exchange Commission, I thought that the philosophy of disclosure had been fully depleted."[6] It was not long after his appointment that he revised his thinking. One of the consequences of the reevaluation which took place during his tenure as chairman of the Commission was the adoption of the Securities Acts Amendments of 1964,[7] which gave substantial new scope and importance to the philosophy of disclosure as a regulatory tool. Fundamentally, the amendments make the disclosure requirements of the Securities Exchange Act of 1934,[8] which had previously been applicable only to listed companies, equally applicable to larger over-the-counter companies.[9] These requirements include the filing with the Commission of an initial registration statement,[10] the filing of periodic reports,[11] and compliance with the Commission's proxy rules.[12] In addition, officers, directors, and ten percent stockholders must report their transactions in the stock of their companies, and are subject to liability to the company for short-swing profits derived from the purchase and sale, or sale and purchase, of corporate securities within six months.[13]

The Securities Act of 1933 used disclosure as a means of reforming practices which had characterized the public distribution of *new* securities offerings prior to the great crash. The legislation of 1964, in contrast, is concerned not so much with *new* securities offerings as with the protection of those who purchase *already outstanding* securities in the trading markets. Recent developments of the disclosure concept have tended to emphasize this latter aspect of securities regulation together with a third aspect — the search for a means by which to lessen the inherent advantages of the corporate insider over the ordinary investor.

These recent developments demonstrate that disclosure remains a concept full of vitality and versatility. Its effectiveness is by no means dependent upon action taken by the Commission pursuant to federal law. In private civil litigation, in the rule of the self-regulatory institutions of the securities industry, in the administration of state blue-sky laws, refined uses for this durable concept are constantly being discovered.

In the remainder of this article, I will try to touch upon a few aspects of this process.

A recent Commission proposal concerns the availability, as well as the character, of disclosure. The reports filed by companies with the Commission on the widely used Forms 10K and 8K provide a wealth of information concerning reporting companies. This information is of value not only to individual investors and people in the securities industry but, if consulted and properly utilized, it can be of great assistance to practicing attorneys. In connection with merger negotiations, for example, an attorney can often learn significant facts about the business and operations of a proposed merger partner by referring to the Commission's public files. I have heard of one or two instances where resort to this simple precaution uncovered material facts which led to drastic modification of the terms of agreement.

In the past, the 8K and 10K reports were available only in Washington, D.C., unless the reporting company's stock happened to be listed on a national stock exchange. If so, the forms were readily accessible at the offices of the exchange. In order to facilitate a wider use of these reports, the Commission's recent *Special Study of the Securities Markets* recommended a change in this traditional pattern.[14] In response to this recommendation, our rules are being revised so that copies of these reports, and of proxy statements as well, will henceforth be kept on file not only in Washington but also in the three principal regional offices of the Commission in San Francisco, Chicago, and New York.[15]

While in the past company annual reports on Form 10K have for the most part gathered dust in Washington, the practice of sending large and colorful annual reports to stockholders has been steadily growing. The Commission has avoided setting explicit standards for reports of this sort and even for the financial statements which accompany them.

Not long ago, the Commission became convinced of the need for at least one significant qualification to this pattern, in the interest of full and fair disclosure. That qualification, announced in 1964 as an amendment to Exchange Act Rule 14a-3,[16] requires a company to use the same accounting principles and practices in preparing the financial statements sent to its shareholders in its annual report as are used in preparing the financial statements filed as a part of required reports to the Commission, unless any material differences are plainly noted and their effects explained. A rather dramatic episode led to the change in this rule. Briefly, a corporation in which there was widespread public interest sent an annual report to its shareholders which included only an unconsolidated income statement. The statement augured well for the company, since it showed a net profit of almost $1.5 million. The financial statement filed with the Commission, however, was required to be on a consolidated basis, and this one disclosed a net loss of over $1 million for the same reporting period.

That sort of thing should not happen again.

Other recent instances of the Commission's historic reliance on full disclosure could be mentioned, but let us instead look briefly at the activities of other groups concerned with "truth in securities" and the implications which that phrase holds for them.

The annual report to stockholders is an excellent vehicle for the transition. Here, where Commission action has been severely restrained, others with an interest in providing information to investors have played a part.

The Financial Analysts Federation, composed of some thirty-six member organizations in the United States and Canada, has a significant program aimed at upgrading annual reports. A committee of the Federation prepares standards by which the reports of leading companies are judged for adequacy. The standards are detailed and apply both to the items of the financial statement and to the text of the report. For example, one of the items in the annual report rating chart for chemical companies, which provided the largest range of grading points, reads as follows:

> *Current Operations: [are they] fully reviewed by major products or divisions, including such items as price and cost trends, competitive factors, major new products and plants, significant start-up costs, [and any] special factors affecting earnings?*[17]

On the basis of these standards, the reports are judged and graded, to the end that the company in each selected industry preparing the best and most informative report to stockholders may be given a citation for excellence in corporate reporting.

A recent report of the Federation's Corporate Information Committee which came across my desk was no faint-hearted document. It rated the steel industry high for leadership in good corporate reporting.[18] By contrast, life insurance industry reports were labeled generally poor and, in the Committee's words, at least half of the reports analyzed could not, by even the most minimal standards, be called stockholders' reports as the term is generally understood.[19]

Another private organization, one without which the exercise of constructive regulatory jurisdiction by a number of government agencies would be considerably more difficult, is the American Institute of Certified Public Accountants (AICPA). A significant change of policy was announced last fall by this body,[20] culminating many months of study and debate.

By way of background, it is apparent to all of us, I think, that the application by different auditing firms of differing accounting principles to the same, or relatively similar, situations, will inevitably produce financial statements which even the sophisticated person finds difficult to compare, and which may result in confused decisions by ordinary investors. The program of the AICPA, and the objective of its Accounting Principles Board, have been to seek to reduce the number of alternative accounting principles which can be classified as "generally accepted."

This is both a notable objective and a difficult task. In the interim, the protection of investors has been advanced by application of the principle of disclosure. Members of the Institute have been advised that in preparing audited financial statements for years beginning after December 31, 1965, they must see to it that any departures from the Opinions of the Accounting Principles Board, or the former Committee on Accounting Procedure, are disclosed in the statement or the accompanying opinion. Failure to make such disclosures would be deemed to be substandard reporting.

Improvement in the comparability of financial statements is a matter of great importance to the Commission. However, the certified public accountant normally conducts his audit of the financial records but once a year. What about the equally important task of keeping the public investor, and his adviser, fully informed regarding the current developments in the affairs of a company?

It must be frankly acknowledged that the Commission's reporting requirements for such current developments do not furnish a complete answer. The number of significant events which must be reported on Form 8 K is limited. Moreover, the reports are not required to be made before the tenth day of the month following the occurrence of the event to be reported.

Where practical considerations restrained Commission action, however, the major stock exchanges have taken a hand. Their rules have long required that the exchange be promptly notified, and that immediate publicity be given to a number of specified events,[21] such as action declaring or passing a dividend, which would clearly affect investment decisions.

Certain of the exchanges, including both the New York and American, have also followed a policy of urging listed companies to make prompt public disclosure of any material developments in their affairs, whether favorable or unfavorable, which might significantly affect the market price of their securities or influence investors. Last December, the American Stock Exchange became the first exchange to adopt a specific requirement of such disclosure as a part of its listing agreement form.[22] As a commentary on the new requirement, the exchange stated that henceforth it will expect all listed companies, in making the necessary disclosures, to adhere to the facts, to avoid overoptimism, to eschew forecasts not warranted by the facts, and to omit premature description of new products.

No mention has yet been made of the National Association of Securities Dealers (NASD), the self-regulatory agency for over-the-counter brokers and dealers. As many of you are aware, the NASD made effective last February a major change in its quotation system for those over-the-counter securities which appear on its national list.[23] Under the system previously in effect, newspapers were furnished with actual interdealer-bid quotations. Interdealer-asked quotations, however, were increased, before being furnished, by an amount which ranged from 2 to 5 percent, depending on the price of the particular security. As a result, the prices published in the newspapers did not reflect either actual wholesale or retail quotations.

The *Special Study* criticized this procedure and the recent Securities Acts Amendments changed the Securities Exchange Act to require that the NASD's rules contain provisions designed to produce fair and informative quotations and to prevent misleading quotations.[24] Under the new system, newspapers are being furnished with actual interdealer quotations on both sides of the market. This change, which the Commission approved, is in keeping with developing tradition of full disclosure to investors.

* * *

I fear these remarks might lead to the conclusion that their author conceives full disclosure to be a simple panacea for all the ills in the securities markets. Such a one-sided approach, however, would deny validity to much that the Commission, the exchanges, and the NASD have sought to accomplish for the protection of the markets from abuse.

Disclosure, however, remains the essential mechanism which makes possible, in an increasingly complex society, the preservation of effective freedom of choice for the investor. If a buyer neglects the available information and there has been no concealment of material facts, a wrong choice is more likely to evoke sympathetic amusement than indignation. The story is told out in my country of an old prospector who walked triumphantly into an assay office and laid down a piece of glittering ore. "How much silver in this?" he demanded. "Mica," said the assayer turning it over in his hand. "Ain't it silver ore?" said the prospector. "Nope, not a trace of it." "What's it worth an ounce?" "Nothing." At this the prospector gripped the assayer by the arm and cried, "Look, man, you've got to do something. I just married a widow with nine children because she owned a ledge of this."

NOTES

1. Stock Exchange Practices, Report of Com. on Banking and Currency, S. Rep. No. 1455, 73d Cong., 2d Sess. (1934).

2. S. Rep. No. 47 at 6–7 and H.R. Rep. No. 85 at 1–2, 73d Cong., 1st Sess. (1933).

3. S. 875 and H.R. 4314, 73d Cong., 1st Sess. (1933).

4. *Id.*, Sec. 6(c), (e), (f).

5. Securities Act of 1933, 15 U.S.C. § 77a–77aa (1958).

6. Cary, "The Case for Higher Corporate Standards," *Harv. Bus. Rev.,* Sept.–Oct. 1962.

7. 78 Stat. 425, 565, 569, 520, 574, 579, 580, amending various sections of Title 15 U.S.C.

8. 15 U.S.C. § 78a–78jj (1958).

9. Exchange Act, Sec. 12(g), 78 Stat. 565–568 (1964) 15 U.S.C. 78 L (g) (1964).

10. *Id.,* Act, Sec. 12, 78 Stat. 565–568 (1964) 15 U.S.C. 78 L (1964).

11. *Id.,* Act, Sec. 13, 78 Stat. 569 (1964) 15 U.S.C. 78m (1964).

12. *Id.,* Act, Sec. 14, 78 Stat. 569–570 (1964) 15 U.S.C. 78n (1964).

13. *Id.,* Act, Sec. 16, 78 Stat. 579 (1964) 15 U.S.C. 78p (1964).

14. *Report of Special Study of Securities Markets of the Securities and Exchange Commission,* H.R. Doc. No. 95, 88th Cong., 1st Sess.

15. E.g., Securities Exchange Act Release No. 7544 (March 5, 1965) Adopting Amendments to Form 10.

16. 17 C.F.R. 240. 14a-3.

17. Sixteenth Annual Report of the Corporate Information Committee, Financial Analysts Federation, 1963–64, p. 16.

18. *Id.,* pp. 29–32.

19. *Id.,* pp. 21–24.

20. Accounting Principles Board, Special Bulletin, October 1964.

21. E.g., NYSE — Company Manual, A–19 — A–23.

22. American Stock Exchange Guide, 8959, Listing Form L. Listing Agreement No. 3. The New York Stock Exchange subsequently adopted a similar requirement. NYSE Company Manual A–20.

23. In November 1966 the NASD made this change effective in its quotation system for those securities which appear on its local lists.

24. Exchange Act, Sec. 15A(b) (12), 15 U.S.C. 780-3(b) (12) (1964).

FIFTEEN

Some Thoughts on Substantial Authoritative Support

MARSHALL S. ARMSTRONG

Chairman Emeritus, Financial Accounting Standards Board

Based on the evolution of accepted practice as perceived by the Securities and Exchange Commission's Accounting Series Release No. 4, the concept of substantial authoritative support is important for CPAs in defending their professional judgment on a particular matter. This article by Marshall S. Armstrong, who later became the first chairman of the Financial Accounting Standards Board, presents some ideas about what constitutes substantial authoritative support and how extensively it should be defined by the accounting profession.

A few weeks ago, I received a telephone call from a practicing certified public accountant who was trying to decide whether he should accept a change in an accounting principle proposed by one of his clients for use in preparing year-end financial statements. He explained that his client had just returned from a convention where a competitor had told how he intended to improve earnings merely by adopting the proposed accounting method. The acceptability of the new method was in doubt.

I asked whether any authoritative support had been found for the proposed principle and he replied, "Well, I looked for an example in *Accounting Trends & Techniques* but found none, so I thought I should give you a call."

Obviously he was thanked for the expression of confidence, and then I proceeded to comment on his failure to undertake a more thorough search for substantial authoritative support concerning the proposed accounting principle.

Certainly this experience was not unique. Many practicing CPAs have had similar phone calls or discussions during their professional lives. My friend should be complimented, since a CPA should always counsel with his partners or with other experienced colleagues whenever a serious question of professional judgment is involved. The exercise of professional judgment can be put to no stronger test than in a case which requires acceptance or rejection of an accounting principle, practice, or method of application. My comments in this case concerned the need for a more complete search for authoritative support, rather than placing reliance upon such a limited "one publication" type of search.

It is important, in my view, for the CPA to be able to produce evidence in support of all professional judgments which he makes in his capacity as the independent auditor of financial statements. Furthermore, since the corporate financial executive normally initiates accounting principles and practices for his company, he must find support for his accounting decisions by reference to authoritative sources. Where the acceptability of an accounting principle or practice is in doubt, the financial executive and the auditor may have difficulty in satisfying their respective responsibilities in this regard.

Present accounting and auditing literature does not provide adequate guidelines on how auditors or financial executives should proceed in developing evidence to support judgments in this area. While I believe it would be inappropriate for our profession to develop a list of specific rules to be followed, some general guidelines should be helpful to practicing CPAs and to business financial management.

The purpose of this article, therefore, is to present some thoughts on substantial authoritative support and, also, to consider the question of whether the profession should define that term specifically or merely develop guidelines to help the practitioner and financial executive find adequate support for accounting principles. By following the latter approach an acceptable definition may evolve.

STATEMENT OF THE PROBLEM

It is well known that the Council of the American Institute of Certified Public Accountants (AICPA) is an elected body of about 230 members, established for the principal purpose of serving as the governing board of the Institute. Decisions of Council influence the actions of all Institute members as well as many segments of the business and financial community.

Those elected to serve on Council are experienced, intelligent, and astute professional men. Their decisions are usually sensible and objective. However, on occasion a decision of Council makes one wonder to what extent implementation techniques were considered before the issue was resolved.

Take for example the action of Council in October of 1964, which included these three statements:

1. "Generally accepted accounting principles" are those principles which have substantial authoritative support.

2. Opinions of the Accounting Principles Board constitute "substantial authoritative support."

3. "Substantial authoritative support" can exist for accounting principles that differ from Opinions of the Accounting Principles Board.

As a result of this 1964 action, Institute members are required to see to it that departures from Opinions of the Accounting Principles Board (APB) are disclosed either in footnotes to financial statements or in the audit reports of members in their capacity as independent auditors.[1] When the auditor is faced with such a situation, he is required to determine that substantial authoritative support exists for the alternate principle before he is permitted to express an unqualified opinion on the financial statements.

---

[1]Special Bulletin, "Disclosure of Departures from Opinions of Accounting Principles Board," published October 1964, by the AICPA.

Obviously, if substantial authoritative support can exist for accounting principles that differ from APB opinions, the auditor must be able to find such support for the alternate principle being used. In fact, it is necessary for the auditor to determine whether substantial authoritative support exists for all principles used in financial statements, particularly in those areas on which the APB has not expressed opinions or which are not dealt with in Accounting Research Bulletins.

Council's 1964 edict seems ambiguous, particularly the first statement previously quoted — "'Generally accepted accounting principles' are those principles which have substantial authoritative support."

Recently a prominent certified public accountant stated his opinion in these words:

> *I doubt that any member of the Council... could have given an adequate explanation of what was meant by the adopted recommendation.... It sounded good and was not controversial even if it was not understood. It was a compromise between the two opposing viewpoints expressed in the Council. However, an undefined term was used to describe another undefined term, and the problem was merely deferred.*

Another recent comment by a leading accounting authority is apropos. He said:

> *It seems to me, we are putting the cart before the horse. How can we say that a particular principle has substantial authoritative support without first setting forth which principles are generally accepted accounting principles? We must start with something more basic — the purpose or purposes of financial statements.*

Even though this 1964 action of Council represents a step forward in the continuing effort to define generally accepted accounting principles, it certainly creates many questions of substance. For example, what is the source of substantial authoritative support on a brand-new development? Is the practice of any one industrial firm or the extensive practice of a group of firms sufficient to constitute substantial authoritative support for an accounting principle? Is one financial report or a small number of reports a source of substantial authoritative support where the nature of the item is such that it is not likely to arise frequently? If there are several authoritative sources of support, what weight should be given to each source? What source is sufficiently authoritative to be on a par with an opinion of the Accounting Principles Board? These are only a few of the questions that come to mind.

In any case, it did not take Council long to recognize some of the difficulties involved in the situation. In the spring of 1965, Council gave the Accounting Principles Board several recommendations. The first one is very important in any consideration of substantial authoritative support. It reads thus:

1. At the earliest possible time, the Board should:

   a. Set forth its views as to the purposes and limitations of published financial statements and of the independent auditor's attest function.

   b. Enumerate and describe the basic concepts to which accounting principles should be oriented.

   c. State the accounting principles to which practices and procedures should conform.

d. Define such phrases in the auditor's report as "present fairly" and "generally accepted accounting principles."

e. Consider, with the committee on auditing procedures, the possibility of improving the terminology of the auditor's report, and in particular the words "generally accepted" in the expression "generally accepted accounting principles."

f. Define the words of art employed by the profession, such as "substantial authoritative support," "concepts," "principles," "practices," "procedures," "assets," "liabilities," "income," and "materiality."

At this time, the board is hard at work on most of the points contained in that recommendation. For example, an exposure draft of a statement or an opinion entitled "Basic Concepts and Accounting Principles Underlying Financial Statements of Business Enterprises" is currently being developed. The present draft deals with many of the matters contained in Council's first recommendation. It considers purposes of financial accounting, basic concepts of accounting, generally accepted accounting principles, and purposes of financial statements—just to name a few of the subject items. These are not easy matters to delineate. They are complex, controversial, and very elusive. The board and the accounting research division of the Institute have been working about three years on this project. Completion prospects look good at the moment.

How can we define words of art such as substantial authoritative support? One way would be to construct a definition based on deductive reasoning. Such reasoning would probe the fundamental meanings of the terms *substantial, authoritative,* and *support.* These meanings would be analyzed and combined into a definition of the term that would serve as a guide to practitioners and financial executives. The definition would then be confirmed or altered via its repeated testing in practice. In this way, the definition would be rooted in logic, and made operational.

A second way, the one chosen here, would be to scrutinize practice to see how substantial authoritative support is now discovered in the light of present-day standards of accounting practice and financial reporting. In a way, we will inventory the state of the art with respect to substantial authoritative support. By describing "how substantial authoritative support is found" rather than pinpointing "what substantial authoritative support means" in an airtight, logical sense, we will better appreciate the complexity of the term and why the problems of implementation must play a major part in the evolution of an acceptable *operational* definition.

BRIEF HISTORICAL BACKGROUND OF THE TERM

One of the historical landmarks which outlines the problem inherent in defining or searching for substantial authoritative support is contained in 1932 correspondence between a committee of the American Institute of Accountants (now AICPA) and a companion committee of the New York Stock Exchange.

In one part of this correspondence, the American Institute committee made these points:

In considering ways of improving the existing situation (i.e., improving financial reporting for listed companies), two alternatives suggest themselves. The first is the selection, by competent authority out of the body of acceptable methods in vogue today, of detailed sets of accounting rules which would become binding on all corporations of a given class.... The arguments against any attempt to apply this alternative to industrial corporations generally are overwhelming.

The more practicable alternative would be to leave every corporation free to choose its own methods of accounting ... but require disclosure of the methods employed and consistency in their application from year to year.

Thus started the debate — should the profession write a rule book of accounting principles for all business enterprises or should business management be free to choose principles and practices from various alternatives? Obviously, the "rule book" approach would eliminate the need to search further for substantial authoritative support. In my judgment, most people today are seeking the middle ground between the two extremes. The goal should be to eliminate alternative accounting principles which are not justified by different circumstances.

In 1936, another historical landmark appeared. The American Institute revised and published a bulletin entitled "Examination of Financial Statements." The following extract is relevant:

It is an important part of the accountant's duty, in making his examination of financial statements, to satisfy himself that accounting practices are being followed which have substantial recognition *by the accounting profession. This does not necessarily mean that all companies will observe similar or equally conservative practices. Accounts must necessarily be largely expressions of judgment, and the primary responsibility for forming these judgments and preparing the financial statements in which they are reflected must rest on the management of the corporation. But unless the difference is of minor importance, the accountant must assume the duty of expressing his dissent through a qualification in his report or otherwise, if the conclusions reached by the management are, in his opinion,* manifestly unsound, *though he is not entitled to substitute his judgment for that of the management when the management's judgment has* reasonable support *and is made in good faith. (Emphasis added.)*

You will note the bulletin contained terms which implied a need to measure the acceptability of accounting practices; e.g., "substantial recognition," "manifestly unsound," and "reasonable support." Although management was free to choose the accounting principles which it considered applicable, and also the method of their application, the independent auditor was required to express his opinion on the financial statements. The same general pattern of responsibility of management and of the auditor has continued from 1936 to the present time. Accounting practices which do not have "substantial recognition" will not receive an unqualified opinion from the auditor.

The term "substantial authoritative support" appeared in accounting literature in 1938 in Accounting Series Release (ASR) No. 4, issued by the Securities and Exchange Commission. This release expresses a fundamental concept:

In cases where financial statements filed with this Commission pursuant to its rules and regulations, under the Securities Act of 1933 or the Securities Exchange Act of 1934, are prepared in accordance with accounting principles for which there is no substantial authoritative support, *such financial statements will be presumed to be misleading or inaccurate despite disclosures contained in the certificate of the accountant or in footnotes to the statements, provided the matters involved are material. In cases where there is a difference of opinion between the Commission and the registrant as to the proper principles of accounting to be followed, disclosure will be accepted in lieu of correction of the financial statements themselves only if the points involved are such that there is* substantial authoritative support *for the practices followed by the registrant and the position of the Commission has not previously been expressed in rules, regulations, or other official releases of the Commission, including the published opinions of its chief accountant. (Emphasis added.)*

In effect, ASR No. 4 takes the position that accounting principles *with* substantial authoritative support will be accepted by the Commission, and those *without it* will be presumed to be misleading or inaccurate. However, the release is silent with regard to the source of such support. The implication seems to be that support can originate outside of the Commission itself.

Clearly, the crux of the matter is where and how to find substantial authoritative support.

When we look for guidance in publications of our own profession, we find little comfort. For example, the first standard of reporting requires that the auditor's report "shall state whether the financial statements are presented in accordance with generally accepted principles of accounting."

A discussion of generally accepted accounting principles is found in Chapter 7 of Statements on Auditing Procedure No. 33. Maybe that discussion will give us guidance. This is what it says:

The determination of whether financial statements are presented in accordance with "generally accepted accounting principles" requires exercise of judgment as to whether the principles employed in the statements have found general acceptance. The determination further requires a familiarity with alternative principles, sometimes more than one, which may be applicable to the transaction or facts under consideration, and a realization that an accounting principle may have only limited usage but still have general acceptance. *(Emphasis added.)*

Frankly, little help comes from that statement. The only expressed guideline here is to exercise our own professional judgment. Does it really assist in solving the problem of finding substantial authoritative support? On the other hand, as professional men, do we *need* more than this?

Based on observations of current practice, which have shown some lack of knowledge as to how one should proceed in an attempt to find support, it is obvious that we *do* need something more.

A SUGGESTED APPROACH TO FINDING SUBSTANTIAL AUTHORITATIVE SUPPORT

In my judgment, we need guidelines to assist in organizing the search for evidence which will justify decisions of financial executives or practicing CPAs as to whether, in fact, substantial authoritative support does exist in those cases where the acceptability of an accounting principle is in doubt. Bear in mind, we should be searching for present-day standards of practice — we should not be attempting to write a new set of principles.

Possibly most of the problems in this area can be resolved by systematically proceeding through five basic steps: (1) define the problem, (2) survey relevant literature, (3) survey present practice, (4) evaluate the information so developed, and (5) reach a conclusion. Obviously, search for support should not be done in isolation. Group investigation and discussion are essential to the success of such a process. As to practicing CPAs, counseling with partners in their own firms or with other experienced and knowledgeable practitioners is implicit in the "five basic steps" approach.

The summary of this approach, which appears at the end of this article, is not all-inclusive as to details of each step in the proposed process since it is intended only to be suggestive. Obviously, the circumstances of each case will dictate both the sources and the depth of search that may be required in various phases of the process.

In my view this five-step decision-making process is not unlike that of the auditor as he searches for and evaluates evidential matter in other areas in his examination of financial statements. The suggested approach is neither new nor unique — I believe it is being followed frequently by financial executives and practicing CPAs today.

As previously stated, most of the cases encountered can be solved by proceeding through the five basic steps enumerated; the real test of finding substantial authoritative support, however, may come in the remaining few but difficult cases. How does one find substantial authoritative support for a brand-new development or, in other cases, where there is no recorded evidence in support of, or in opposition to, the proposed accounting treatment? On the other hand, it may be that the available material is out of date or obsolete and indicates a position the opposite of that which the CPA or financial executive feels is proper in the particular circumstances, possibly in the light of recent refinements in accounting thought.

Obviously, different CPA firms or individual practitioners may approach these special cases in different ways. The "special case" approach varies from the "basic five-step" process only in the source of substantial authoritative support as will be noted in the following brief summary:

As the first step, a thorough search is made into all aspects of the particular situation and a written statement of the problem and of the proposed solution is prepared.

Second, this material, which would mention all references, pro and con, is subjected to intensive scrutiny by a group of firm partners with wide experience whose opinions on the matter are usually documented in a memorandum for the files.

As the third step, considered reactions are obtained from experienced members of other prominent CPA firms, and, if the consensus of the parties supports the proposed accounting position, no further action is taken.

One exception might exist. If the principle in question were one on which the SEC had previously taken an informal position contrary to the present consensus, discussions would take place with the staff of the SEC, particularly if the company were subject to SEC regulations.

Finally, since existing literature is silent as to authoritative views on the particular practice in question, or fails to reflect recent refinements in accounting thought, these proceedings and memorandums become a part of the firm's record and thus constitute "substantial authoritative support."

In the instance of a new development, which requires origination of an accounting treatment, the importance of analogy should not be overlooked. Here, the search for substantial authoritative support should include an analysis of situations which are similar to the new development and for which sound accounting has been established.

THE WEIGHT OF AUTHORITY

Much could be written on the relative weight that should be given to various sources of authority. In the minds of some people, if the Accounting Principles Board has not spoken on an issue, widespread use by industry is the main source of authority. On the other hand, rare use of such an accounting principle creates something of a negative presumption that needs to be overcome. *Previous use* of a principle is insufficient evidence if there are indications that a large part of the accounting profession no longer accepts the principle. Others believe that industry practice should be viewed as the most authoritative support for an accounting principle in every instance. Obviously, pronouncements by the Securities and Exchange Commission carry great weight for those companies that are required to file their financial statements with the Commission.

In my own judgment, the most objective and unbiased source of authority, and therefore number one in authoritative weight, is found in publications of the American Institute of Certified Public Accountants. In an *amicus curiae* brief filed recently in a United States District Court case, the Institute clearly supported its "number one weight position" in these words:

> *The Institute is the oldest and foremost professional organization of public accountants in the United States. Founded in 1916, it now has a membership of more than 64,000 certified public accountants in the country. The Institute has throughout its existence assumed a principal responsibility for the development, promulgation and enforcement of the professional standards which guide and govern the practice of public accounting in the United States. The formal Opinions of the Institute's Accounting Principles Board and its predecessor constitute the most authoritative and comprehensive statements of generally accepted accounting principles; and the series of Statements on Auditing Procedure, issued by the Institute's committee on auditing procedure, sets out in definite form the generally accepted auditing standards and furnishes guidance in the application of those standards. Such generally accepted accounting principles and auditing standards are incorporated by reference in a code of ethics dealing with relations between the Institute's members and their clients, and public and fellow members of the profession, which is enforced by the Institute through disciplinary proceedings. Although governmental agencies, principally the Securities and Exchange Commission, and others also exercise authority to establish and enforce profes-*

sional standards for accountants as to matters within their respective jurisdictions, the Institute, as principal spokesman for the profession itself, has long borne and exercised the primary responsibility in this field. The Commission has itself recognized the primacy and the importance of the Institute's role in this regard.

While an attempt should not be made to substitute inflexible rules for good judgment or to reduce the determination of substantial authoritative support to a mechanical exercise, some guidance as to the relative importance of various types of support should be helpful to all practitioners and to the business community in general. It has been suggested that sources of authority could be divided into two classes.

Class 1 should include those sources of support for accounting principles which would be sufficient evidence in themselves to constitute substantial authoritative support—for example:

- Opinions of the Accounting Principles Board
- Accounting Research Bulletins of the committee on accounting procedure
- Industry audit guides of the AICPA
- Regulation S-X and accounting series releases of the SEC
- In the absence of the first four items, predominant practice within an industry if peculiar to that industry, or of business enterprises in general if not peculiar to a particular industry.

Class 2 would include sources of support which in themselves would not be sufficient evidence to constitute substantial authoritative support but which, in combination with other such sources, may contribute toward sufficient evidence. Further, all Class 2 sources might not be accorded the same relative importance. If this thought were to be accepted, Level A sources would be considered more significant than Level B sources; Level B sources would be considered more significant than Level C sources, etc. Without attempting to indicate levels of relative importance, Class 2 sources of support might include:

- Pronouncements of industry regulatory authorities
- Substantial practice within an industry
- Accounting research studies of the AICPA
- Published research studies of authoritative professional and industry societies
- Federal, state, and local laws
- Accounting textbooks and reference books of individuals whose views are generally respected
- Publications of recognized industry associations
- Published articles and speeches of distinguished individuals.

If our profession were to adopt such a classification of authoritative support, changing circumstances undoubtedly would warrant the addition of new sources of support for accounting principles or perhaps the deletion or reclassification of some of the sources of support currently suggested.

In any event, the question of proper weighting of authoritative sources needs careful consideration and final resolution if guidelines in the area of substantial authoritative support are to be meaningful and helpful to practitioners and to financial executives.

Throughout this article, an attempt has been made to justify the earlier premise that it would seem to serve no useful purpose to concern ourselves at this time with a deductively reasoned definition of substantial authoritative support. Hence, some thoughts have been offered on how a practicing CPA or a financial executive might proceed in determining whether substantial authoritative support exists for a particular accounting principle or practice. As usual in our profession and in the financial community, one must exercise his best judgment in the face of each circumstance.

It is my hope that our profession and others will eventually come to the conclusion that substantial authoritative support rests on the considered opinions of experienced practicing certified public accountants, experienced objective corporate officials, and learned academicians which, as you have seen, is the foundation for the suggested five-step approach to finding substantial authoritative support.

This concept was expressed well by a subcommittee of the Accounting Principles Board during its preliminary work on a board project entitled Basic Concepts and Broad Accounting Principles. They put it this way:

> Generally accepted accounting principles are primarily conventional in nature. They are the result of decisions; they represent the consnsus at any time as to how the financial accounting process should operate and how financial statements should be prepared from the information made available through the financial accounting process.
>
> Inasmuch as generally accepted accounting principles embody a consensus, they depend heavily on notions such as "general acceptance" and "substantial authoritative support," which have not been and probably cannot be precisely defined. There is concurrence, however, that the notions of "general acceptance" and "substantial authoritative support" relate to the propriety of the practices, as viewed by informed, intelligent, and experienced accountants in the light of the purposes and limitations of the financial accounting process.

Finally, by having described in this article "how substantial authoritative support is found" rather than pinpointing "what substantial authoritative support means" in a purely logical sense, I trust an acceptable *operational* definition of the term has been developed. If financial executives and practicing CPAs will be helped thereby in their search for support, indeed it will be gratifying.

FIVE BASIC STEPS IN SEARCHING FOR SUBSTANTIAL AUTHORITATIVE SUPPORT

I. Define the Problem

A. This step includes preparation of a complete description and documentation of the business event or transaction in question. The memorandum should describe the economic and other objectives sought by the various parties as well as all pertinent facts relating to the event or transaction.

B. In addition, there should be set forth a complete description of the proposed accounting practice or alternative practices that are to be considered. Describe the timing and amounts of entries to be recorded, the financial statement presentation of the various elements, and the facts which would be disclosed in notes to the financial statements.

II. Survey Relevant Literature

Having defined the problem in complete detail under Step I, a thorough survey of relevant literature should be undertaken. Hopefully, this second step will provide evidence of what may be standards of acceptable practice currently in use. Without attempting to produce an exhaustive list of reference points, the following are representative but will vary on a case-by-case basis:

A. Pronouncements of the American Institute of Certified Public Accountants—for example:
   1. Opinions of the Accounting Principles Board
   2. Accounting Research Bulletins, including Terminology Bulletins.

B. Other publications of the AICPA:
   1. Statements of the APB
   2. Accounting research studies
   3. Industry audit guides.

C. Pronouncements of other professional societies, including those of foreign countries in some circumstances.

D. Rules and regulations of the Securities and Exchange Commission.

E. Written views of individuals.

   Accounting textbooks, reference books, accounting articles, and speeches are a vital part of professional literature. Care must be taken to distinguish between those that describe accounting which is presently regarded as sound and acceptable in the financial community and those which strive to describe a logical theory of accounting for the future regardless of its present use or acceptance.

F. Federal, state, and local laws.

G. Pronouncements of industry regulatory authorities, which may provide some acceptable evidence. (See Addendum to APB Opinion No. 2 for guidance in this area.)

H. Publications of industry associations such as those for colleges and universities, hospitals, health and welfare organizations, retail merchants, and the petroleum industry. (These frequently contain descriptions of principles of accounting that are appropriate for such specialized endeavors.)

III. Survey Present Practice of Organizations with Similar Problems

In searching for substantial authoritative support, the importance of knowing "what is going on in practice today" cannot be overemphasized. In fact, many practitioners, and financial executives as well, believe that "generally accepted" when used in the phrase "generally accepted accounting principles" literally means that the majority of companies are using the particular principle or practice in preparing their financial statements. On the other hand, this "head count" interpretation of the phrase is rejected by many. They prefer to view the phrase "generally accepted accounting principle" to mean a "sound accounting principle," which may not be the principle in predominant use.

It is the author's view that "generally accepted" principles should always be "sound" principles in the sense that results of financial transactions must be presented in financial statements without defect as to truth, justice, or reason.

However, regardless of one's own preference, the search for substantial authoritative support must include a careful survey of present practice. The American Institute of Certified Public Accountants annually publishes *Accounting Trends & Techniques*. This study is based upon a review of 600 published financial reports of publicly held companies and is a good starting point for the survey of present practice. Also, several industry studies are published by industry groups or associations. They may provide good information relevant to the accounting question under consideration.

In addition, a practitioner can usually receive for his own files copies of published reports by any publicly held company, merely by asking to be placed on its mailing list.

IV. Evaluate the Information Developed

V. Reach a Conclusion

The responsibility for evaluating the information developed under the first three steps of this process, and that of determining the precise weight of evidence necessary to constitute substantial authoritative support in a given situation rests with the individual practitioner or financial executive. He must make these determinations in each instance by exercising his best judgment on the matter after examining all facts relevant to the particular case.

SIXTEEN

Required Disclosure and the Stock Market: An Evaluation of the Securities Exchange Act of 1934

GEORGE J. BENSTON

University of Rochester

Benston examines the disclosure benefits of the Securities Exchange Act of 1934 and the consequences for the securities market. He concludes that the disclosure requirements of the 1934 Act had little or no measurable effect on the securities traded on the New York Stock Exchange and argues that there is little need for more disclosure requirements.

The Securities Exchange Act of 1934 was one of the earliest and, some believe, one of the most successful laws enacted by the New Deal. The stock market crash of 1929 and the Great Depression provided the impetus for reform of the stock markets in the belief that weaknesses of the institutions and ineptitude and/or chicanery among brokers and bankers were partially responsible for the losses incurred by stockholders. Although many critics, reformers, and congressmen wanted Congress to enact "blue skies" legislation that would require all securities sold and traded to be approved by the federal government, President Franklin Roosevelt preferred the concept of "disclosure" (see Francis Wheat [1967]). Rather than having the government approve or disapprove securities, corporations whose securities are publicly sold or traded are required to disclose a large amount of predominantly financial information to the Securities and Exchange Commission (SEC) who make these data available to the public. Indeed, the Securities Exchange Act is described in its title and usually referred to as a "disclosure statute."

Although the financial community generally opposed this legislation and the preceding Securities Act of 1933,[1] most brokers, investors, and government officials probably would find it difficult to conceive of the successful operation of the stock markets without the Securities Acts. Yet the economic rationale for the regulation of the securities markets was not examined carefully before the legislation was passed (which is not surprising, given turbulent times) nor has it been since,[2] even though the Securities Act of 1934 was extended in 1964 to include most corporations whose stock is publicly owned. Such an examination of one important part of the law—the financial disclosure requirements—is presented here. This analysis is particularly timely because the SEC appears to be shifting its emphasis toward increasing the disclosure requirements of almost all corporations whose stock is traded in the markets.[3]

Reprinted from *The American Economic Review,* Vol. 63, No. 1, March 1973, pp. 132–155, with permission of the American Economic Association.

I. THE DISCLOSURE REQUIREMENTS OF THE SECURITIES EXCHANGE ACT OF 1934

The '34 Act requires that a corporation whose stock is traded on a registered stock exchange or who registered a stock issue:

a. file detailed balance sheets, income statements, and supporting substatements (Form 10K) within 120 days after the close of its fiscal year;

b. file a much less detailed semiannual report (Form 9K) within 45 days after the first half of the fiscal year;

c. file a "current report" (Form 8K) 10 days after the end of any month in which certain "significant" events occurred (such as a change of control of the corporation, material legal proceedings undertaken, material changes of securities outstanding, and revaluation of assets).

In 1964, the disclosure requirements were extended to almost all corporations with at least 500 stockholders or $1 million in assets. (Exceptions are regulated companies whose statements were prescribed, such as banks and insurance companies.) Thus, all but the smallest corporations now are covered by the Act.

Section 13(b) of the '34 Act (and Section 19(a) of the '33 Act) gives the SEC the power to prescribe the form and content of the financial statements filed under the Act. In general, the SEC has followed generally accepted accounting procedures, although it has influenced these procedures by insisting that assets not be revalued upward, goodwill be amortized rapidly, and other "conservative" biases be reinforced. In this regard, the SEC has not followed the "disclosure rather than approval" philosophy of the Securities Exchange Act. This policy was established by Accounting Series Release No. 4 in 1938, which states that

> ... where financial statements filed ... are prepared in accordance with accounting principles for which there is no substantial authoritative support, such financial statements will be presumed to be misleading or inaccurate despite disclosures contained in the certificate of the accountant or in footnotes to the statements provided the matters involved are material. (Emphasis added.)

Whether disclosure, as defined and required by the SEC, has been meaningful and beneficial, is the question asked here — not whether disclosure, as such, is good or bad.[4]

II. THE RATIONALE UNDERLYING THE LEGISLATION

It would seem that any argument against disclosure is equivalent to an argument for secrecy. But such is not the case. Prior to passage of the Securities Exchange Act, corporations could disclose what they wished to their current and potential stockholders and, if they were listed on the New York Stock Exchange (NYSE), American, Chicago (Midwest), or other regional exchanges, had to submit balance sheets and income statements to the Exchange. For the year ended December 31, 1933, all NYSE corporations were audited by CPA firms, all listed current assets and liabilities in their balance sheets, 62 percent gave their sales, 54 percent the cost of goods sold, and 93 percent disclosed the amount of depreciation expense. These percentages had been increasing fairly steadily prior to 1933, although there was little change after 1928. (See Benston [1969b], p. 519.) One could argue (as did the NYSE), that the legislation was not needed.

One could also argue that the disclosure policy followed by corporations in the absence of legislation is in the best interests of their stockholders. If management believed that the marginal revenue to the stockholders as a group from disclosure would exceed the marginal cost of preparing and supplying the information, they would disclose their financial and other data. The marginal revenue might include the savings to stockholders of not having to gather the data privately, the reduced cost of capital to the firm if prospective stockholders' uncertainty about the firm were reduced, improvement in the marketability of the firms' shares if investors desired financial information, etc. The marginal costs of disclosure might include the cost of preparing and distributing the statements, the costs incurred in informing competitors, suppliers, customers, and government officials, and the cost of misinforming stockholders when accounting statements report economic events incorrectly or inadequately (as when all research and development and advertising expenditures are charged to expense currently).

However, management might not issue financial statements (or might issue incomplete statements) if they underestimate the value of these statements to their current or potential investors, mismanage the corporation, intend to defraud investors, or if there are positive externalities in the efficient allocation of resources when all (or most) companies disclose financial data. Thus, one cannot immediately dismiss the argument that there is need for required disclosure solely by reference to the invisible hand of the market. Rather the question must be examined with respect to the rationale upon which the the Securities Exchange Act of 1934 is based.

Underlying the disclosure requirements of the '34 Act is the belief that required disclosure of financial data is necessary for the fair and efficient operation of capital markets. The SEC's 1969 Wheat Report (and most other writings on the subject) view disclosure as necessary to (1) prevent financial manipulation and (2) provide investors and speculators with enough information to enable them to arrive at their own rational decisions (Wheat Report, p. 10).[5] Perhaps even more important is the concept of "fairness," the belief that all investors, big and small, insiders and outsiders, should have equal access to relevant information. Whether these objectives can be achieved, a priori, by disclosure of financial data, and if they can, whether or not the evidence supports or rejects the hypothesis that they were, is considered in the balance of the article. To facilitate the presentation of the material, fraud and manipulation are discussed first in Section III, followed by an empirical analysis of information and investors' decisions in Section IV, and the effects of the '34 Act on traded securities in Section V, on losses by stockholders in Section VI, and on investors' confidence in the market in Section VII.

III. FRAUD AND MANIPULATION

Fraud and manipulation may be of two different types with respect to disclosure. Published statements may contain false or misleading data or desired data may not be published at all but may be released in the form of news stories, rumors, etc., to manipulate the public's expectations and so affect stock prices. These are discussed in turn.

It is very difficult to determine whether the '34 Act prevented the publication of fraudulent or misleading financial statements or even whether much fraud existed to any greater extent before or after the passage of the Act. In a situation of personal fraud by self-dealing or simple defalcation, required disclosure is of little value. Certified Public Accountants insist that they do not audit explicitly for fraud nor does the SEC ask them to do this, although I believe a good case could be made for this requirement. With respect to fraudulently prepared financial statements, I have reviewed such evidence as exists in another article (Benston [1969a], pp. 51–55). A search of the available literature, including the Senate and House hearings on the proposed securities legislation, fails to reveal much evidence of fraud in the preparation or dissemination of financial statements prior to 1934. For example, Wiley Rich, the author of a comprehensive survey of the legal responsibilities of accountants, states that, "An extensive search has revealed not a single American case in which a public accountant has been held liable in a crime for fraud" (p. 100). It appears that the feeling in the early 1930s that published accounting statements were fraudulent or misleading was based on "exposes" of William Ripley and others of the behavior of some large corporations at the turn of the century. Further, the recent BarChris, Yale Transport, Green Department Store, Continental Vending, and other cases show that fraud in financial statements, while relatively rare, has not been banished from the land.

The lack of evidence on fraudulent financial statements does not imply that published financial statements were or were not misleading. Prior to the passage of the Securities Act, it was very difficult for third parties, such as prospective stockholders, to sue accounting firms for negligently prepared financial statements. The courts held, under the rule of privity, that these reports were prepared for management only. (See *Landell* v. *Lybrand.*)

However, accountants were (and still are) liable for fraud "if their audit has been so negligent as to justify a finding that they had no genuine belief in its adequacy for this again is fraud." (See *Ultramares Corp.* v. *Touche, Niven and Co.* N.Y. p. 185, N.E. p. 488.) The Securities Act changed accountants' liability dramatically, and now an investor may sue an accountant if, having relied on false or misleading statements, he "shall have purchased or sold a security at a price which was affected by such statement" (Section 18). It is important to note that the accountant must prove that the investor's loss was not a consequence of the financial statements rather than that the investor prove that he actually was misled by or even saw the statements.

In contrast to the lawmakers' expectations, an important consequence of this change in the law and of the SEC's administration of the Acts appears to be that financial statements are more misleading than they were. The considerable liability of accountants under Section 18 has contributed to accountants following conservative, often worthless practice, since it is difficult to sue them successfully for preparing misleading statements if they follow traditional procedures. In addition, the SEC has insisted on historically based accounting, discouraging price level and other revaluation of assets and liabilities, refusing to permit publication of sales and income projections and other valuable economic data, etc. The published financial statements are more misleading than they otherwise might have been. Although accountants might not have made much progress in reporting the economic position and progress of corporations had there been no Securities Act, there is no empirical or a priori basis for an assertion that the '34 Act has had a net positive effect on the publication of fraudulent or misleading financial statements.

While there is little direct evidence that corporate managers issued fraudulent financial statements, they may have refused to disclose information to create a climate in which they could manipulate stock prices by means of "pools" and "bear raids." At least such is the opinion of the SEC. In their booklet, *A 25 Year Summary of the Activities of the Securities and Exchange Commission , 1934-1959,* they say these practices

> *... resulted in a situation in which no one could be sure that market prices for securities bore any reasonable relation to intrinsic values or reflected the impersonal forces of supply and demand. In fact, the investigation record demonstrated that during 1929 the prices of over 100 stocks on the New York Stock Exchange were subject to manipulation by massive pool operations. One of the principal contributing factors to the success of the manipulator was the inability of investors and their advisers to obtain reliable financial and other information upon which to evaluate securities (pp. xv–xvi).*

To test this assertion, the financial statements (as published in *Moody's Investors Services*) of those over-100 corporations whose securities were subject to pools, as revealed by the Senate Committee on Banking and Currency, were examined for years before, during, and after the pools. Table 1 gives the percentage that disclosed such important information as sales and cost of goods sold. (All except four corporations included in the 1929 pools and two included in the 1930 pools had otherwise complete balance sheets and income statements published in *Moody's.*) The percentages with respect to sales were almost the same as those found for all companies listed on the New York Stock Exchange and a little lower with respect to cost of goods sold. Thus, while "pools" and "bear raids" may or may not have been unfair to investors, it is clear that their operations (successful or not) owed little to the non-disclosure of accounting data.

IV. INFORMATION AND RATIONAL DECISIONS OF INVESTORS AND SPECULATORS

The second rationale for the disclosure requirements is to allow "investors [to] make a realistic appraisal of the merits of securities and thus exercise an informed judgment in determining whether to purchase them" (Securities and Exchange Commission, 1967, p. 1). This rationale is based on a belief that the data required by the SEC are "information." That is, the financial statements must provide data about a corporation that affect investors' expectations about its future prospects and relative riskiness and that were not previously known, such that information was completely discounted and impounded in the market price of the securities before the time of disclosure.

There is a serious question whether the financial data approved by the SEC can provide the investor with information. The SEC does not allow current market valuation of assets, estimates of future sales or projection of the effects of discoveries, favorable regulatory rulings, public acceptance of new products, and other economic events. Additionally, the present value of many important occurrences such as management changes, styling, advertising campaigns and other marketing strategies, changes in the competitive environment, and the like cannot be estimated very well even if the SEC allowed accountants or others to publish their efforts. While this information need not come to the public through the financial state-

Table 1   Disclosure of financial data by corporations whose securities were subject to pools

		Percentage Disclosing[1]	
Pool year	Statement year	Sales	Cost of goods sold
1929 pools	1927	58	47
(103 corporations)[2]	1928	58	48
	1929	61	50
	1930	60	52
1930 pools	1928	70	50
(30 companies)[3]	1929	70	53
	1930	70	60
	1931	63	70
1931 pools	1929	67	50
(6 companies)	1930	67	50
	1931	67	50
	1932	33	50
1932 pools	1930	100	100
(2 companies)	1931	100	100
	1932	50	100
	1933	50	100
1933 pools	1931	67	42
(12 companies)[4]	1932	67	42
	1933	67	42

Source: Pools: U.S. Senate Committee on Banking and Currency, part 17, pp, 7948–50, Financial Data: *Moody's Investors Service,* various years.

[1] Corporations whose statements were not in *Moody's* (4 of the 1929 pools and 2 of the 1930 pools) are included as "nondisclosure."

[2] Number of securities = 105; 2 securities of two corporations were listed

[3] Number of securities = 31; 2 securities of one corporation were listed

[4] Number of securities = 13; 2 securities of one corporation were listed

ments, the SEC's requirement that these statements be prepared in a specified form implies that they include some relevant quantitative financial information.

But even if financial statements do contain information that is of value to investors, the data may not be made available to the public before insiders (including bookkeepers, secretaries, accountants, typists, and printers) see and take advantage of them. In requiring the filing of financial statements, the SEC is caught in a choice between speed and accuracy (in the sense of reporting to the letter of the formal and informal regulations), a choice which is resolved in favor of accuracy. As is noted above, the annual reports (10K) need not be filed with the SEC until 120 days after the close of a corporation's fiscal year. Whether the statements that have been filed are meaningful to investors and sufficiently timely to be of value is, of course, an empirical question, to which I now turn.

A. The Information Content of Published Financial Data — Financial Statements and Stock Prices

If the SEC's disclosure requirements are meaningful, the statements they require should contain information, and thus investors' expectations about a corporation's earnings and prospects, riskiness, relationship to other firms, etc., should be affected by the information. Since numerous studies show that the market adjusts rapidly to new information,[6] the effect, if any, of previously unexpected data published in the financial reports of a corporation (j) should be reflected in changes in its stock prices (ΔP_{jt}) in the period t when these unexpected financial data (F_{jt}^{*}) become publicly available. Other factors also may occur during the same period and must be accounted for. Principal among these are changes in general market conditions (ΔM_t), changes in expected dividend payments (which often are announced at the same time that earnings data are announced) (ΔD_{jt}), and changes specific to the corporation's industry (ΔI_{kt}). In summary,

$$(1) \qquad\qquad \Delta P_{jt} = f(F_{jt}^{*}, \Delta M_t, \Delta D_{jt}, \Delta I_{kt}, U_{jt})$$

where U_{jt} are other unspecified factors. This model was specified and tested, and the results were reported in a paper I published in 1967. They are summarized very briefly here. The specified model whose description follows was used for these tests, used in another study reviewed below (Ray Ball and Phillip Brown), and in further tests described below in Section V.

A two-stage estimating procedure was used that is based on a "market model" originally suggested by Markowitz and first applied in a context similar to the present study by Eugene Fama et al.

$$(2) \qquad\qquad \tilde{r}_{jt} = \alpha_j + \beta_j r_{Mt} + \tilde{u}_{jt}$$

where $\tilde{r}_{jt}$ is the rate of return for security j for month t (defined as $ln((P_{jt}+D_{jt})/P_{jt-1})$ where P_{jt} is adjusted for stock dividends and splits and P_{jt} is dividend payments declared); r_{Mt} is a similarly measured rate of return on a market index M; α_j and β_j are parameters that can vary from security to security; and $\tilde{u}_{jt}$ is a random disturbance.[7] Tests applied by Fama et al., and Marshall Blume (1968, 1970) indicate that equation (2) "...is well specified as a linear regression model in that (i) the estimated parameters α_j and β_j remain fairly constant over long periods of time [e.g., the entire post–World War II period in the case of Blume], (ii) r_{Mt} and the estimated $\hat{u}_{jt}$ are close to serially independent, and (iii) the $\hat{u}_{jt}$ seem to be independent of r_{Mt}"(Fama, p. 403). The $E(\hat{u}_{jt}|F_{jt}^{*})$ may not = 0. This is what was tested.

Equation (2) was applied in my 1967 paper to a sample of 483 companies traded on the New York Stock Exchange in 1964 (the latest year data were available at the time of the study). These included almost all NYSE traded companies from whom annual and quarterly financial data were available on the Compustat tapes. The statistics $\hat{\alpha}_j$ and $\hat{\beta}_j$ were computed from data that excluded months when the financial statements were made public. These statistics were then "plugged" into equation (2a) to compute the residuals, $\hat{u}_{jt}$ for the months when the financial data were published:

(2a) $$\hat{r}_{jt} - \hat{\alpha}_j - \hat{\beta}_j r_{Mt} = \hat{u}_{jt}$$

The $\hat{u}_{jt}$ computed with equation (2a) were regressed on estimated unexpected financial data, unexpected dividends, and variables that accounted for industry effects.

An expectation model had to be specified in order to estimate the unexpected financial data (F_{jt}^*). Since the SEC's regulations require disclosure of accounting statements for prior periods as well as the present period,[8] expected financial data were taken to be a function of previously published data. Three averages of past data (a weighted average with geometrically declining weights determined by a variant of the Koyck transformation and simple averages of three and five years' data) and a naive model (previous year's data) were used. Unexpected financial data F_{jt}^*, then, is measured by the difference between the reported and the expected data. Although the SEC did not require companies to report their quarterly data until recently, such data were required by the NYSE. Since investors' expectations would be affected by these reports, their effect is estimated by including third-quarter financial data in the regressions in forms analogous to those used for the annual data.[9]

Since it is not clear which specific financial data investors use, the financial variables were defined alternatively as sales, cash flow net income, current operating income, and net income after extraordinary gains and losses. Thus sixteen regressions were computed for the month when the financial data were sent to the SEC and stockholders (four expectations models and four definitions of income).

The regressions reveal that, except for the sales definition of financial data, none of the financial data variables in any of the expectations forms has a greater than minimal economic relationship to changes in stock prices, although the coefficients estimated are statistically significant. On the average, a 100 percent unexpected increase (or decrease) in the rate of change of income is associated with a 2 percent increase (or decrease) in the rate of change of stock prices in the month of announcement. Similar regressions were computed for the month when earnings were announced (which usually is a month before the SEC receives them), and similar results were found. The findings are not very dependent on the form of the expectations model used, although the naive model, where last year's rate of change is expected this year (a sort of "no-expectations" model), performed the best. This finding is contrary to the SEC's requirement that companies provide comparative data for several past years. Thus, I conclude that this evidence is not consistent with the underlying assumption of the legislation, that the financial data made public are timely or relevant, on average.

Corroborative findings are reported by Ball and Brown, whose study used a variant of the model described above in equation (2). Their sample consists of 261 firms who reported on an annual basis. For most of these firms, data were available in the period 1946 through 1968 on the Compustat tapes. Ball and Brown considered each firm's year as an independent observation. They separated the data into two samples, one consisting of years in which income increased and the other of years in which income decreased unexpectedly, as determined from an expectation model in which a firm's expected income is a function of the income reported by the other firms. However, they did not account for dividend changes or for the information content of quarterly reports. Ball and Brown found that cumulatively, over a year, firms that show greater (or lesser) than expected income changes averaged greater (or lesser) than normal stock price returns. However, they calculate that "... of the value of information contained in reported income no more than 10 to 15 percent ... has not been anticipated by the month of the [preliminary] report ..." and compute that the marginal monthly rate of return of buying or selling short a portfolio of stock based on the information contained in the preliminary report is less than 1 percent (pp. 175–76). By the time of the final (SEC-required) report, there is almost no information that has not already been impounded in the price of the stock.

Another study of interest was made by William Beaver, who measured the volume of trading in the weeks before and after the announcement of preliminary earnings. He analyzed weekly price and volume for a sample of 143 firms (those included on the Compustat tape, traded on the NYSE, with other than December 31 fiscal years, with no dividends announced in the same week as the announcement, no stock splits in the quarters around that date, and with relatively few other "announcements"). A model similar to that given in equation (2) was used to abstract from market effects. Beaver found that the variance, average volume, and residual positive or negative return are much greater in the week that the preliminary reports are announced (without regard to the sign or magnitude of the earnings) than in the previous or following eight weeks. Further, the greater than normal activity appears to continue for about two to three weeks after the announcement date, but with a considerably smaller magnitude. Contrary to the other studies, Beaver's results seem to indicate that financial statements do contain information or are at least used in some way. One interpretation is that investors use the announcements of preliminary earnings to switch their portfolios. Another is that brokers use the earnings reports as an excuse for "churning." The third explanation, one consistent with the findings of Robert Hagerman on the effect of requiring commercial banks to report earnings to the public in forms specified by regulatory agencies, is that while financial statements, as such, provide information, required reporting adds nothing. (Recall that all NYSE companies published some sort of statement before passage of the '34 Act.[12])

One other study has been published that considers directly the usefulness of published annual financial statements in purchasing securities. Richard McEnally tested the value of using low price/earnings (P/E) ratios to choose portfolios of stocks. He used a randomly selected sample of 100 calendar-year stocks from which five portfolios of 20 stocks each were chosen for each of five years, 1961–65. High or low P/E ratios were the basis for forming portfolios. The stocks are assumed to be purchased on April 1 and held for a year. When the earnings used in the P/E ratio were those of the previous year (E_{t-1}), the portfolio with the lowest P/E_{t-1} outperformed the others slightly in terms of mean return, there being little difference among the other four portfolios.[10] McEnally then used the ratio of price to earnings of the year in which stocks were purchased, P/E_t (which assumes perfect forecast of the year's earnings in April), to choose portfolios. Except for the little difference between the third and fourth groups, the portfolios so chosen provided consistently higher holding period returns according to the P/E criterion. Since market participants do not have perfect knowledge of the year's earnings, McEnally used the earnings forecasts of the three most popular advisory services of the P/E ratios. The results were almost the same as those reported for published earnings. Thus the research is consistent with Ball and Brown's study in that financial data seem to reflect the economic situations of corporations but either are completely discounted by the market before they are published or do not predict the economic future. In either case, the data are not useful to investors at the time the SEC requires disclosure.

B. Returns to Sophisticated Users of Financial Data

It may be that the studies cited above approach a complicated problem in too simple a way. It often is claimed that the detailed reports required by the SEC are more useful to trained analysts than to the ordinary stockholder. The analyst then passes on his information to his clients, or, in any event. trades on the information, thereby bringing its effects to the market. No doubt information about firms does get to the market. But does it get there by means of the financial reports required by the SEC?

One way to answer these questions is to examine whether well-trained analysts outperform the market. I am aware of two studies that test directly the ability of security analysts to use published financial data. John G. Cragg and Burton Malkiel recorded predictions made by five investment firms of the earnings of 185 corporations whose stock is widely held. In particular, they compared the earnings' growth rate forecast by the analysts with the actual growth rates. They report that ". . . the remarkable conclusion of the present study is that the careful estimates of security analysts participating in our survey, the bases of which are not limited to public information, perform little better than the past growth rates"[the naive predictor, that the future will be like the past] (p. 83). The second study, by Lyn Pankoff and Robert Virgil, was a controlled, laboratory study. They allowed security analysts to "buy" financial statements of companies in whose stock they can invest. The data are actual data and the stock prices are those that actually prevailed for the stocks whose identity they disguised. While their study is not yet complete, Pankoff and Virgil found that analysts who use financial data (or any other data) do not do as well as they could have had they followed a "naive" buy and hold strategy.

Several indirect tests of the ability of trained analysts to use financial data publicly can be derived from studies of the performance of mutual funds and research departments of brokerage houses. F. E. Brown and Douglas Vickers, William Sharpe, and Michael Jensen studied the performance of mutual funds compared to that of random selections of securities with similar risk characteristics. They used different techniques and all came to the same conclusion. Mutual funds do not earn for their investors a higher rate of return than would have been earned had the investors held a similarly diversified market portfolio, gross of research costs. Nor is the record of the research departments of brokerage houses any better. A study by R. E. Diefenback of the market performance of stocks whose purchase or sale was recommended by twenty-four institutional research services found that their recommendations, if followed, would have yielded returns equivalent to those earned by investments in the Standard and Poor's (S and P) 425 Index. Thus, even mutual fund and brokerage house research department analysts do not benefit from detailed analysis of SEC reports, among other data.

Even though the evidence reviewed does indicate that the financial reports required by the SEC, when made available, have almost no information content, this does not prove that the required disclosure is not valuable to investors. One might argue that the statements provide a confirmation of data previously released. Because investors know that a corporation's sales, operating expenses, extraordinary gains and losses, assets and liabilities will be reported, they may have some assurance that the preliminary reports, press releases, etc., are not prevarications. Thus when the financial statements are made public the data they contain are fully anticipated. But had it not been for the SEC's disclosure requirements, such a state of affairs might not exist. It is to this consideration that I turn next.

V. AN EMPIRICAL ANALYSIS OF THE EFFECT OF THE '34 ACT ON NYSE SECURITIES

When the Securities Exchange Act was enacted in June 1934, the United States was in the midst of the Great Depression. Hence, it is difficult to separate the effect of the legislation of the stock market from other economic events, and the effect of the disclosure requirements of the act from its other provisions. In addition, it is necessary to determine when the legislation affected the stock market, since it might have been anticipated such that, when passed, its impact already had been discounted.

Fortunately the data and the particular legislative history of the '34 Act allow an unusual opportunity to test the effect of legislation. Hearings on the '34 Act did not begin until February 1934, nor was there much belief before this date by most observers that such legislation would be enacted (see Sobel). Prior to this time, it was not considered part of the President's legislative "package." Nevertheless, the bill was signed by President Roosevelt in June 1934 and took effect that year, although full compliance did not occur within the year. Therefore, I have considered the period of adjustment to include February 1934 through June 1935. Thus there is a relatively short and distinct period over which the effect of the legislation may be measured.

The effect of the disclosure provisions of the Act may be tested by examining its differential effect on the securities of corporations that were and were not affected by the legislation. At the time of the passage of the Securities Exchange Act of 1934, about 70 percent of stock exchange transactions were made on the NYSE, 13 percent on the American (Curb) Exchange, 1.6 percent on the Chicago (Midwest) Stock Exchange, and the balance on nineteen other regional exchanges. The three principal exchanges, at least (the others didn't reply to my inquiries), had similar rules that required listed companies to send certified income statements and balance sheets to stockholders in advance of the annual meeting. The principal reporting requirement imposed by the '34 Act, in addition to the filing of detailed forms, was the required disclosure of sales. Of the 508 corporations whose stock was traded on the NYSE in 1934, 193 (38 percent) did not disclose their sales.[11] Since sales are considered very important information by analysts, and the study reported above (Benston [1968]) found sales the only relatively important accounting number, these corporations are considered as those most likely to be affected by the disclosure requirements of the '34 Act.[12]

Thus two samples of NYSE corporations can be distinguished: the 314 (62 percent) "disclosure" corporations and the 193 (38 percent) "nondisclosure" corporations (with respect to sales). These data allow a fairly comprehensive test of the law, since the '34 Act applied (until 1965) only to corporations whose stock is traded on registered exchanges, and most of these corporations were listed on the NYSE in 1934. If disclosure of the sales data required by the '34 Act were meaningful to investors, these effects should be observed in the market returns of the securities affected in the period after the law was effective. As was discussed above in greater detail, if the data disclosed are information, investors would alter their previous estimates of the relative value and/or riskiness of the firms.

The model given by equation (2) above can be used to measure these effects. The $\hat{u}_{jt}$ measure the returns on a security after the effect of changes in the return for the market as a whole is accounted for. A change in the $\hat{u}_{jt}$ represents a revaluation of the present value of future returns from a security. As such, it provides a valuable measure of the information content of mandated disclosure.

The $\hat{\beta}_j$ provide a measure of the relative systematic portfolio risk of a security, its covariance with the market relative to the market's variance.[13] As such the $\hat{\beta}_j$ might be affected if the data disclosed in the financial statements provide information about the risk class of a company and the relation of its economic value to changes in the economy (as reflected by the market).

The variance of returns from a stock may be stated as:[14]

$$(3) \qquad \sigma^2(r_j) = \beta_j^2 \sigma^2(r_M) + \sigma^2(u_j)$$

where the variables are as defined for equation (2) above. The variance of returns on a security, j, can be reduced by reducing the variance of the market, $\sigma^2(r_M)$ the sensitivity of the security to the market, β_j, and/or the residual variance, $\sigma^2(u_j)$. Fisher and Lorie's study shows that the dispersion of the market index is higher for the immediate post–'34 Act period than it was in the years before 1932. It is not until 1945 that it is of a lower magnitude than the late 1920s. A reduction in the β_j, though, would reduce the variance in stocks' returns. While a reduction in the variance of the residuals of a stock, $\sigma^2(u_j)$, also reduces the variance, it should be noted that investors can reduce or eliminate this "risk" by holding a portfolio of securities. Let

$$r_p = \sum_{j=1}^{n} \frac{1}{n} r_j$$

be the returns on a portfolio of securities with an equal dollar investment in each security. The variance of the returns on such a portfolio is given by

$$(4) \qquad \sigma^2(r_p) = \left(\sum_{j=1}^{n} \frac{1}{n} \beta_j \right)^2 \sigma^2(r_M)$$
$$+ \sum_{j=1}^{n} \frac{1}{n^2} \sigma^2(u_j)$$
$$= \bar{\beta}^2 \sigma^2(r_M) + \frac{1}{n} \overline{\sigma^2(u)}$$

assuming that $\text{cov}(u_i, u_j) = 0$ for $i \neq j$. As n, the number of stocks in the portfolio increases, the residual variance of the portfolio goes to zero (as long as the $\sigma^2(u_j)$ are bounded from above). Nevertheless, the legislators and many economists believe it is desirable to reduce the riskiness of individual stocks, since "small investors" cannot purchase enough different securities for efficient diversification.[15]

Thus, three statistics derived from equation (2) are of interest: $\hat{u}_{jt}$; $\hat{\beta}_j$; and $\sigma^2(\hat{u}_{jt})$ Equation (2) was computed for each NYSE-traded security on monthly data for the period January 1926 through January 1934 (pre-SEC period) and July 1935 through November 1941 inclusive (post-SEC period). January 1926 was taken as the initial month because this is the first month for which data are available on the Center for Research on Security Prices (CRSP) tape of NYSE monthly security prices.[16] November 1941 was taken as the last month because it allowed for the longest post-SEC period that did not include the next major dislocation — World War II. There are 98 months in the pre-SEC period and 90 in the post-SEC period. To allow for a sufficient number of observations for the regressions, securities that were traded for less than 10 months in each time period were excluded.[17] This left 466 companies, of whom 290 are disclosure corporations (62 percent) and 176 nondisclosure corporations (38 percent).[18]

Five hypotheses about the effectiveness of required disclosure can be tested with observations of the $\hat{\beta}_j$ and $\sigma^2(\hat{u}_{jt})$ for the periods before and after disclosure and of the $\hat{u}_{jt}$ for the adjustment period following immediately after required disclosure.

1. Managers avoided disclosure to hide their poor performance:

If the managers did not publish financial data because they wanted to hide their poor performance from their stockholders, the $\hat{u}_{jt}$ of the nondisclosure companies compared to the disclosure companies would be negative, since investors would revalue downward the returns to the securities. Similarly, such managers might not disclose financial data to mislead investors about the relative riskiness of the firm, in the hope that stockholders might be willing to hold stock having a lower rate of return if they believed the firm to be less risky than it really was. In this event, disclosure would result in higher $\hat{\beta}_j$ if the market (portfolio) risk of the nondisclosure firms was underestimated and greater $s^2(\hat{u}_{jt})$ if the individual, diversifiable security risk was underestimated and not diversified away.

2. Managers did not disclose because they did not realize the value of the information to investors:

If required disclosure provided investors with valuable information, the $\hat{u}_{jt}$ would change, and the $\hat{\beta}_j$ and $\sigma^2(\hat{u}_{jt})$ might change. However, the direction of the changes cannot be predicted.

3. Required disclosure imposes a cost on corporations without compensating benefits to stockholders:

If managers were disclosing adequately before the legislation was passed (the marginal cost of disclosure equaled its marginal benefits), investors might view disclosure as a net cost imposed on the firm. (Included in this cost is the value of the information to competitors.) In this event, the $\hat{u}_{jt}$ would decrease (as in hypothesis (1)), but there is no reason to believe that the $\hat{\beta}_j$ and $\sigma^2(\hat{u}_{jt})$ would be affected.

4. Required disclosure results in benefits to the market as a whole because investors would prefer stocks on registered exchanges to alternative investments, such as over-the-counter stocks or real estate. However, some costs are imposed on those firms that would not otherwise have disclosed:

If this hypothesis holds, the $\hat{\beta}_j$ and $\sigma^2(\hat{u}_{jt})$ should not be affected, the $\hat{u}_{jt}$ of the firms that were required to disclose might decrease and the $\hat{u}_{jt}$ of firms that were not so affected might increase, as investment in equities traded on the stock exchanges became relatively more attractive to investors. Thus the difference in the $\hat{u}_{jt}$ between disclosure and nondisclosure firms should be positive.

5. Required disclosure did not impose sufficient costs or benefits to be measured:

Should the "null" hypothesis obtain, there would be little change in the $\hat{u}_{jt}$, $\hat{\beta}_{jt}$, or

Table 2   Estimate of portfolio risk $\hat{\beta}_j$: differences and correlations
Post-SEC period less pre-SEC period

	Disclosure corporations (290 observations)	Nondisclosure corporations (170 observations)
Algebraic differences		
mean	.0320	.0264
standard error of mean	.0218	.0227
Absolute differences		
mean	.2722	.2133
standard error of mean	.0149	.0159
Correlation of pre and post periods	.5725	.7326
Data underlying β_j statistics average number of observations (months)		
Pre-SEC period	79.0	80.6
Post-SEC period	75.3	76.9
standard deviation of observations (months)		
Pre-SEC period	20.9	22.3
Post-SEC period	10.1	6.9

[a] Pre-SEC period: Jan. 1926 through Feb. 1934; Post-SEC period: July 1935 through Nov. 1941.

$\sigma^2(\hat{u}_{jt})$. Of course there could be costs to firms not traded at the time (such as the cost of newly registering with the SEC) or costs or benefits too small to be measured by the model.

Tests on the $\hat{\beta}_j$ are discussed first because, if the $\hat{\beta}_j$ are stable between periods, the $\hat{u}_{jt}$ can be computed more efficiently by using data from the entire data set, excluding the adjustment periods.

Table 2 gives the mean differences of the $\hat{\beta}_j$ computed for the pre and post-SEC periods in both algebraic and absolute terms.[19] Distributions of the $\hat{\beta}_j$ show them to be approximately normally distributed, so the standard errors of the means given in Table 2 can serve as valid summary statistics.[20]   Since the stability of the $\hat{\beta}_j$ are dependent, in part, on the number of observations used to compute them, the average number and standard deviations of the underlying observations also are given in Table 2. These data do not indicate any bias between the groups from this source. The algebraic differences between periods for both groups are positive, but hardly greater than zero and almost of the same magnitude and dispersion for the disclosure and nondisclosure groups. The absolute differences are presented because several of the hypotheses do not specify a change in the $\hat{\beta}_j$ of any particular sign, and the algebraic means could mask significant changes. Of course, the absolute means are larger than their algebraic counterparts. Most important, the absolute mean change of the disclosure group is somewhat greater than that of the nondisclosure group, which indicates a smaller change in perceived portfolio riskiness for those corporations affected by the '34 Act. An additional test of this conclusion was made by correlating the $\hat{\beta}_j$ from the pre-SEC period with the $\hat{\beta}_j$ from the post-SEC period for each group. The correlation coefficient of the pre-and post-SEC $\hat{\beta}_j$ (reported in Table 2) is higher for the nondisclosure group, which again indicates a lesser change in the $\hat{\beta}_j$ between periods.

In summary, the tests indicate that the disclosure requirements of the 34 Act had a somewhat lesser effect on the securities of corporations that did not previously disclose sales as compared with those that did. This finding is inconsistent with hypothesis (1) and casts doubt on hypothesis (2).

The stability of the $\hat{\beta}_j$ between periods (or, at the least, a small differential change between the groups) provides support for estimating the $\hat{u}_{jt}$ with the following procedure.[21] Equation (2) was computed for each security that was traded on the NYSE for at least five months prior to February 1934 and five months after July 1935, allowing at least ten observations. A total of 487 securities was included under this rule, of which 306 (63 percent) had disclosed their sales and 180 (37 percent) had not prior to the '34 Act. While the number of observations is slightly higher than those used for the $\hat{\beta}_j$ tests, the percentages in the disclosure and nondisclosure groups were almost identical. The $\hat{u}_{jt}$ were computed by running the following "market model" regression for each security

$$(5) \qquad\qquad r_{jt} = \alpha_j + \beta_j r_{Mt}$$

where t excludes February 1934 through June 1935. The computed $\hat{u}_{jt}$ and $\beta_j r$ then are used to compute the α_j for each month during the "adjustment period," February 1934 through June 1935:

$$(5a) \qquad\qquad \hat{u}_{jt} = \hat{\alpha}_j + \hat{\beta}_j r_{mt} - r_{jt}$$

where t runs from February 1934 through June 1935. The expected value of the $\hat{u}_{jt}$ is zero in the absence of an unanticipated change in the economic environment, such as the disclosure of previously undisclosed information.

The average (algebraic mean) residuals for each month of the j securities ($[\sum_1^n \hat{u}_{jt}]/n$, n = number of securities in each month) were computed for the disclosure and nondisclosure groups. Since several of the hypotheses do not predict a sign of the $\hat{u}_{jt}$, the average absolute residuals for each month ($[\sum_1^n |\hat{u}_{jt}|]/n$) also were computed for each group. Plots of these data were made and summary statistics are given in Table 3 for several subperiods before and after the adjustment period to contrast the behavior of the residuals during that period.

Two basic conclusions can be derived from these data. First, there appears to be somewhat less variance of the residuals of both groups during the months of the adjustment period of February 1934 through June 1935 compared to the following and preceding months. These data indicate that by the time the initial hearings on the Securities Act were begun, the impact of the Great Depression on the revaluation of individual shares was largely spent. Second, there is little difference in the behavior of the average residuals of the nondisclosure compared with the disclosure groups. The plots (not presented) show that their residuals behaved almost the same over time, with differences between the two groups being far overshadowed by differences between time periods.

Table 3. Average monthly residuals in subperiods*

Subperiod	Algebraic Means ÷ .001			Absolute Means ÷ .001		
	Disclosure	Non-disclosure	Disclosure-Non-disclosure	Disclosure	Non-disclosure	Disclosure-Non-disclosure
2/26 thru 1/28	.074	.206	−.132	6.653	6.459	.194
	(.742)	(.986)	(1.429)	(.919)	(.919)	(.774)
2/28 thru 1/30	.020	.075	−.056	8.028	7.647	.381
	(.924)	(1.086)	(1.634)	(1.604)	(1.460)	(.748)
2/30 thru 1/32	.026	−.002	−.024	10.475	9.795	.680
	(1.181)	(1.525)	(1.742)	(2.214)	(1.913)	(1.007)
2/32 thru 1/34	−.349	−.325	−.024	14.452	12.884	1.568
	(1.638)	(1.892)	(2.328)	(3.707)	(2.875)	(1.375)
2/34 thru 6/35 (adjustment period)	.125	.728	−.603	8.435	7.802	.633
	(.865)	(.968)	(1.124)	(1.115)	(1.250)	(.812)
7/35 thru 6/37	.227	−.263	.491	8.221	7.332	.888
	(.941)	(1.624)	(1.676)	(1.813)	(1.592)	(.728)
7/37 thru 6/39	.017	.203	−.186	6.972	6.225	.747
	(.773)	(1.226)	(1.314)	(1.185)	(1.299)	(.609)
7/39 thru 6/41	.077	.085	−.008	7.151	6.196	.955
	(.910)	(1.093)	(1.175)	(2.961)	(2.378)	(.743)

*Standard deviation shown in parentheses.

Table 3 is not quite adequate to test the hypothesis that the '34 Act affected each group differently, since the algebraic or absolute mean monthly values and standard deviations over months may not describe the underlying distribution of the individual $\hat{u}_{jt}$. Therefore, Figures 1 and 2 were prepared in which the fractiles (.05 and .95, .10 and .90, .75 and .25, and the median) are plotted for each group over time. If the plot of residuals for one group could have been printed as a transparency and placed over the plot of the other, the reader could see that there is almost no difference in the distribution of residuals between the groups.

The data presented thus far are based on monthly averages of the $\hat{u}_{jt}$. However, it also is necessary to consider the effect of the disclosure statute on individual securities. The possible revaluation of the present value of returns on individual securities need not have taken place entirely in any given month. In addition, it is not clear exactly when corporations made their financial data available as required by the '34 Act. Therefore, the $\hat{u}_{jt}$ were cumulated algebraically for the adjustment period ($\sum_{t=1}^{17} \hat{u}_{jt}$ where t = 2/34 through 6/35). As a further check, the $\hat{u}_{jt}$ were cumulated for an additional year ($\sum_{t=1}^{29} \hat{u}_{jt}$ where t = 2/34 through 6/36).

Figure 3 presents the data in the form of histograms, in which the distribution of the cumulative residuals for the corporations in the disclosure and nondisclosure group are

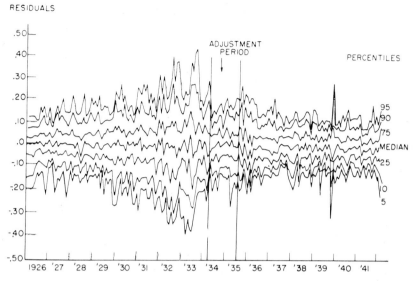

Figure 1 *Nondisclosure corporations distribution of residuals* $(\hat{u}_{jt})$

plotted together. It is clear from these histograms and from the summary statistics (not presented)[22] that there is little difference between the two groups and that neither group experienced a revaluation of its rates of return that is significantly different from the expected value of zero.

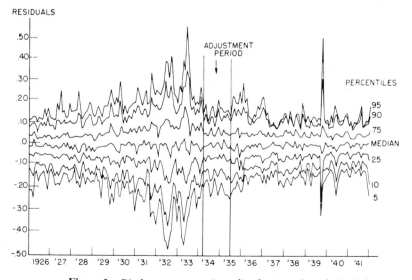

Figure 2 *Disclosure corporations distribution of residuals* $(\hat{u}_{jt})$

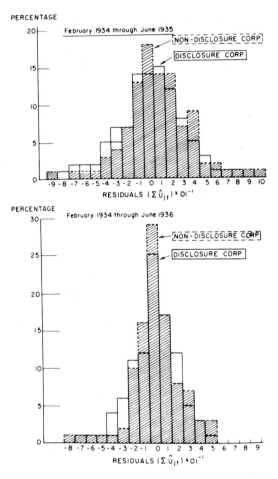

Figure 3 *Histograms of cumulative residuals disclosure and nondisclosure corporations*

The variance of the residuals of each company, $\sigma^2(\hat{u}_{jt})$, provides an estimate of the volatility of the individual security. A comparison of the mean and distribution of the standard deviations of the residuals of the disclosure and nondisclosure corporations are given in Part A of Table 4. The disclosure corporations show a slightly higher mean standard deviation of residuals in the pre-SEC period and, surprisingly, an even greater mean standard deviation in the post-SEC period. It is possible, however, that the means of the standard deviations of the $\hat{u}_{jt}$ of each group in the pre- and post-SEC periods obscure changes in the variance of individual securities. To test for this possibility, the differences between the standard devia-

Table 4   Variance of residuals ($\hat{u}_{jt}$) of individual companies pre- and post-SEC periods

	Disclosure	Nondisclosure
A. Means		
Pre-SEC period (1/26–2/34)		
Mean of standard deviations	.1496	.1351
Standard deviation of mean	.0623	.0507
Outlyers		
> mean $\pm$ 1σ	29.1[a]	30.9[a]
> mean $\pm$ 2σ	4.2[a]	3.1[a]
Number of observations	309	191
Post-SEC period (7/35–11/41)		
Mean of standard deviations	.1033	.0885
Standard deviation of mean	.0535	.0363
Outlyers		
> mean $\pm$ 1σ	14.9[a]	20.3[a]
> mean $\pm$ 2σ	5.1[a]	2.8[a]
Number of observations	296	177
B. Change in variances: Post-SEC less pre-SEC period		
Mean algebraic differences	−.0433	−.0435
Standard deviation of mean	.0534	.0385
Mean absolute differences	−.0540	−.0469
Standard deviation of mean	.0435	.0343
Number of observations	290	176

[a] Shown in percent.

tions of the residuals of each company in each period were computed. The mean and distribution of these changes is presented in Part B of Table 4. The mean change is negative for each group, consistent with Part A of the table. Most important, the change in variance of individual stock prices (after accounting for the variance of the stock market as a whole) once the Securities Act of 1934 was effective, is almost the same for those corporations that were and were not affected by the act.

From these data and the data reported above, I conclude that the '34 Act did not contribute to a reduction in the variance of returns from securities traded on the NYSE, as measured by the $\hat{\beta}_j$ (the covariance-variance ratio of security j to the market as a whole) and the standard deviations of the residual returns on securities, $\sigma^2(\hat{u}_{jt})$.[23]

Considering the evidence presented above, I must conclude that the data are consistent only with the hypothesis (5), that the disclosure provisions of the '34 Act were of no apparent value to investors.

VI. LOSSES BY STOCKHOLDERS

The data used in the tests presented above are of NYSE corporations that survived the depression, at least until December 1935 (five months of post-adjustment period data were required for the regressions). A question that should be raised is whether stockholders of corporations that disclosed their sales fared better than those who held stock in nondisclosing corporations. Should this be the case, the findings presented above could be biased because the worst offenders, with respect to disclosure would have been delisted from the NYSE.

To determine whether such was the case, the listing of NYSE corporations was traced. The base year chosen was 1929, because this is the last year before the depression and because I could use a study made by Standard Statistics Company, reported by Lawrence Sloan, pp. 66–74. This study of the income statements of 484 corporations listed on the NYSE revealed that 266 (55 percent) reported gross income in 1929 and 218 (45 percent) did not. Table 5 presents the listing history of these securities, showing whether the security was delisted because it went over the counter (OTC) or the corporation was merged. Either event is taken to mean a greater than normal loss for stockholders. If this assumption is correct, it is clear that stockholders of corporations that did not disclose gross income in 1929 fared better than those who held stock in the disclosure corporations.

This conclusion is interesting, because it implies that companies that did not disclose their sales were, in fact, better investments than those that did. Such investigations as I could make did not reveal the reasons that some companies disclosed their sales and others did not. A reason consistent with the data would be that those who disclosed had a greater real need to assure their stockholders of their worth than those who did not.

VII. INVESTORS' CONFIDENCE IN THE MARKET — RISK AND FAIRNESS

A major reason for enactment (and continuance) of the disclosure provisions of the '34 Act was the belief that disclosure was necessary to restore the confidence of investors in the stock market. It is obvious that depressions and the reduction of stock values (either with a "crash" or gradually over a relatively short period) reduce investor confidence and that such events have occurred before and since the passage of the '34 Act and were little affected by it. Therefore, a more meaningful (and charitable) definition of "investor confidence" might be related to the riskiness of returns from securities and to the concept of fairness, that all investors should have equal access to financial information about a company whose shares they own or contemplate buying. Each of these somewhat related concepts is considered in turn.

A reduction of the riskiness of returns, *ceteris paribus,* is considered a benefit because this would reduce the cost of capital to firms and increase investors' confidence in the market. Both assertions are based on the belief that investors are risk averse. (Speculators may prefer risk, but they are considered by legislators to be a nonpreferred group.) Of course, disclosure, as such, cannot reduce the inherent riskiness of corporations except where disclosure reduces or prevents the risk of fraud. However, disclosure might reduce the risk to the investor of not knowing about significant events (such as a large loss, lawsuit, discovery, etc.) and/or diversifiable risk by reducing the residual variance of security returns (as is discussed above in Section V).

Table 5. NYSE delisting of corporations that did and did not disclose gross income in 1929

Number	Disclosure corporations			Nondisclosure corporations		
	OTC	Merged	Total	OTC	Merged	Total
Delisted in:						
1929	1	1	2			
1930	1	4	5	1		1
1931	4	2	6	3		3
1932	6	5	11	6		6
1933	5		5	5		5
1934	3		3	1		1
Subtotal: Pre-SEC	20	12	32	16		16
1935	4		4	3	1	4
1936	2	1	3			
1937	2	1	3			
Subtotal: 1935–1937	8	2	10	3	1	4
1938	5	1	6	2		2
1939	4	1	5			
1940	2	1	3	1		1
Subtotal: 1938–1940	11	3	14	3		3
Total 1929–1940	39	17	56	22	1	23
On NYSE in 1941			210			195
Total			266			218
Percentages						
Delisted 1929–1934	7.5	4.5	12.0	7.3		7.3
Delisted 1934–1937	3.0	.8	3.8	1.4	.4	1.8
Delisted 1938–1940	4.1	1.2	5.3	1.4		1.4
Subtotal	14.6	6.5	21.1	10.1	.4	10.5
Not delisted as of 1941			78.9			89.5
Total			100.0			100.0

The evidence presented above indicates that disclosure as required by the '34 Act did not reduce fraud, nor did corporations who disclosed their sales fare better in the depression than those who didn't. The data on the variance of the securities of disclosure firms compared to that of nondisclosure firms (Tables 2 and 4), discussed above, indicates that the '34 Act did not have the desired effect on risk (as measured herein). The percentages of large residuals (outlyers) reported in Table 4 also provide evidence on the effectiveness of the '34 Act in reducing the risk of large, presumably unanticipated stock movements. The percentage of outlyers in the pre-SEC period was about the same for the disclosure and the nondisclosure firms. However, in the post-SEC period, there were relatively fewer mean$\pm 1\sigma$ outlyers for the disclosure group but more mean$\sigma \pm 2$ outlyers for the nondisclosure group.

Some additional evidence on the effect of the '34 Act on the stock market is provided by a study of corporate total capital information met by stock market issues and publicly sold debt issues compared to private placements in the pre- and post-SEC years (through 1954). As I reported in 1969 (see Benston 1969b), the percentage of new issues (net of redemptions) to expenditures on plant and equipment gross and net of price-level adjusted depreciation was the following:[24]

1900–24	30.9 (gross)	58.3 (net)
1919–29	36.8 (gross)	354.3 (net)
1932–38	— (gross)	— (net)
1938–46	6.5 (gross)	51.2 (net)
1946–49	23.1 (gross)	50.2 (net)
1949–54	20.6 (gross)	68.6 (net)

I also found that a ranking of industries by the percentage of private placements to total debt issues was almost exactly the same as a ranking of the extent of bias of the SEC's conservative accounting rules against a fuller reporting of economic events (such as the extent of mining claims, the value of airline routes, etc.). Thus it appears that, contrary to the expectations of its supporters, the '34 Act may have reduced the value of stock markets to corporations and, therefore, to investors.

The concept of fairness is difficult to define operationally. The belief that all investors should have equal access to financial information about a company whose shares they own or contemplate purchasing is perhaps the most important concept, politically, that supports the federal disclosure requirements. While some writers, such as Henry Manne, have argued that investors and the economy are served better when insiders are allowed to profit from information before it is disclosed, legislators argue that all current and potential owners of a corporation have an equal right to information without regard to cost. But since any information must be available to someone before it is known to all, this is a nonoperational concept in its extreme form. And, insofar as the SEC's disclosure requirements require the publication of useless or untimely data (as seems to be the case), the '34 Act has not served its purpose.

Nevertheless, the stock market could be considered "fair" if the prices of securities at any point in time are unbiased estimators of their intrinsic values, at least with respect to the financial data which corporations must disclose under the '34 Act, Then whenever an investor decides to buy or sell or hold a security, he can be assured that the market price has discounted completely the financial information. The average investor need not worry about discovering some important financial information about which he is unaware. He will just as often find himself buying or selling a security that is "overvalued" as "undervalued." In this event, the market would be "efficient" in what Fama calls the semistrong form of the martingale hypothesis.

Fama reviews the theory and evidence on efficient capital markets and concludes that "for the purposes of most investors the efficient markets model seems a good first (and second) approximation to reality. In short, the evidence in support of the efficient markets model is extensive and (somewhat uniquely in economics) contradictory evidence is sparse" (p. 416). But this evidence is based on data from years after enactment of the '34 Act. The act may have altered the way in which information gets to the market and the speed with which it is dispersed such that a previously inefficient market became efficient.

The data presented above, that the disclosure required by the '34 Act had no measurable effect on the residual market prices of companies that did and did not disclose their sales, are consistent with the hypothesis that the market was efficient before the legislation was enacted, at least with respect to the financial data.[25] In addition, runs tests on the signs of price changes before 1934 of the securities of the disclosure and nondisclosure corporations revealed that the price changes of both groups confirmed to a random walk.[26] The results of this weaker test of the efficient markets hypothesis is consistent with the belief that the '34 Act did not make the stock market a "fairer game" for investors.

VIII. SUMMARY AND CONCLUSIONS

The Securities Exchange Act of 1934 is called a "disclosure statute" because its purpose is to force corporations to provide the public with financial data as prescribed by the SEC. The Act was passed and extended because of the belief that such disclosure was required to correct the abuses of the pre–Great Depression period, provide information necessary for investors to allocate their resources wisely and efficiently, and make the stock market a "fair game" for the average investor.

A review of the evidence on fraudulently or misleadingly prepared financial statements prior to enactment of the '34 Act revealed very little evidence of abuses in reporting. The assertion by the SEC that "pools" and other presumably manipulative devices were made possible by inadequately disclosed financial information is not supported by the data. Proportionately, there was little difference between the reporting practices of corporations whose securities were subject to pools as those who were not.

The value of reported financial data for investors' decisions is based on the assumption that the data the SEC requires be made public is useful and timely. The SEC's adherence to historically based, "conservative" accounting procedures reduces the value of the numbers. Nevertheless, the question is an empirical one for which an empirical answer is sought. The extant statistical studies that relate published accounting statement data with stock prices all lead to the conclusion that the data either are not useful or have been fully impounded into stock prices before they are published.[27] Since these studies use relatively simple decision models, evidence on the ability of professional analysts to use financial data for stock choices was reviewed. The evidence supports the conclusion that the accounting statements either are not useful, timely, or both.

However, these findings are based on data from the post-SEC period. It may be that the SEC has created a climate of confidence in financial data such that the public can accept information as it becomes available during the year. In this event, the annual financial statements, when published, simply confirm that which was previously released, and therefore do not affect stock prices. Investors could believe the information because they know that a reputable government agency, the SEC, is concerned about the veracity of financial statements.

The hypothesis was tested by examining statistically the change in riskiness and returns in the stock prices on the NYSE before, after, and as a result of the Securities Exchange Act of 1934. Financial statements were available for almost all NYSE corporations, but only 62 percent reported their sales or other similarly important information. These corporations are a control sample against which effects of the '34 Act can be measured. The Sharpe-Markowitz "market model" was used to account for general stock market changes and to provide estimates of the market risk of stocks for each of the samples (disclosure and nondisclosure corporations) in the periods before and after the regulations became effective. Revaluations of securities as a result of the required disclosure of information also were measured with the model. All of the many measurements and analyses show that the '34 Act's financial disclosure requirements had no measurable effect on the securities of the corporation presumedly affected.

The effect of the '34 Act on investors' confidence and on the fairness of the market also was analyzed. Riskiness of securities, as measured by the variance of market prices net of covariance with the market, does not seem to have been reduced by the Act. Nor were the relative percentages of large price movements reduced. Also, the effect of the '34 Act on the capital market may have been perverse, since the percentage of corporate expenditures on plant and equipment financed with new public stock and debt issues was lower in the post-than in the pre-SEC decades. With respect to fairness, the evidence that the disclosure requirements did not result in a revaluation of the securities of the affected firms and the conformity of price changes before 1934 to a random walk indicates that the pre-SEC stock market was a fair game for investors.

The conclusion of this study, then, must be that the disclosure requirements of the Securities Exchange Act of 1934 had no measurable positive effect on the securities traded on the NYSE. There appears to have been little basis for the legislation and no evidence that it was needed or desirable. Certainly there is doubt that more required disclosure is warranted.

NOTES

1. A recent history by Ralph DeBedts reviews these events uncritically.

2. George Stigler (1964a, b) and Irwin Friend and Edward Herman provide the first quantitative analysis of the Securities Act of 1933 of which I am aware. The only other analyses are in two papers which I published in 1969.

3. A rather detailed "Report and Recommendations to the Securities and Exchange Commission" from the Disclosure Policy Study headed by Wheat recommends

> ... that for the future, greater attention be paid to those continuing disclosures which benefit the trading markets in securities. Prior to 1964 the continuing disclosure reached only those issues whose securities were listed on exchanges and those which had voluntarily registered securities under the '33 Act. Full exercise of that authority might have deterred listing. This is no longer the case, and a serious impediment to progress in disclosure policy has been removed (Wheat Report, 11).

4. The possible detrimental effect on the SEC's definition of disclosure on the development of improved and innovative accounting procedure has been argued elsewhere (Benston, 1969b). While the issue is important to the question of the efficient operation of securities market, it is not emphasized in this article.

5. Also mentioned is "the belief that appropriate publicity tends to deter questionable practices and to elevate standards of business conduct" (p. 10). These goals are inherently nonoperational, except as they refer to the prevention of fraud and manipulation, which is discussed below, or perhaps to insider stock dealings, which are not affected by the disclosure of financial data and hence are outside the scope of this article. However, see Henry Manne for one view contrary to the SEC's position.

6. See Eugene Fama for a summary and review.

7. Fama shows that this model is consistent with the Sharpe-Markowitz expected return model.

8. The SEC requires that companies who float a stock issue under the provisions of the Securities Act of 1933 publish at least five years of comparative data, three of which must be certified by an independent certified public accountant.

9. There is some possibility that these third-quarter data could be collinear with the annual data, which might reduce the significance of the measured coefficients. I am indebted to Ross Watts for pointing out this possible error.

10. The geometric mean return for the lowest P/E_{t-1} portfolio is 1.20 compared to the average of all portfolios of 1.15. No significance tests were made. However, McEnally reports that "Simple correlation coefficients between P_t/E_{t-1} and the next year's holding period return for these five holding periods...cast doubt on the validity of any relationship" (p. 30).

11. Fifty-four percent did not report "cost of goods sold," almost all of whom also did not report sales. (See Table 1 in Benston [1969b].)

12. The analysis was also carried out for the corporations that did and did not disclose cost of goods sold, with similar results to those reported.

13. See Fama, pp. 401–04, for a more complete exposition of this concept.

14. I am indebted to Michael Jensen for clarifying my thinking on this issue and for the equations presented.

15. While small investors can purchase mutual funds to obtain diversification, this alternative may not be considered sufficient or even desirable by legislators.

16. The center is at the University of Chicago. The tape presently is administered by the Standard Statistics Corporation.

17. A study of the disclosure practices of corporations who left the NYSE before February 1934, and hence were excluded from the analysis, is presented below.

18. Since the percentages of disclosure and nondisclosure corporations are the same, this procedure does not appear to have introduced any obvious bias.

19. The means (and standard errors of the means) of the $\hat{\beta}_j$ in the pre-SEC period is .9968 (.0202) for the disclosure corporations and .9854 (.0312) for the nondisclosure group. In the post-SEC period, these statistics are 1.0115 (.0248) for the disclosure corporations and 1.0006 (.0328) for the nondisclosure companies. The $\hat{\beta}_j$ are lower in both periods for the disclosure group, but insignificantly so.

20. The standard errors of the means (SEM) are relatively small, in part because the sample size (n) is large (SEM standard deviation/$\sqrt{n-1}$).

21. The correlation coefficients between the $\hat{\beta}_j$ in the pre- and post-SEC periods reported above may not be sufficiently high for some readers to accept this procedure. The alternative procedure would have been to use fewer observations to calculate the statistics, which, I believe, introduces more severe possible biases. In any event, the $\hat{u}_{jt}$ were calculated with $\hat{\beta}_j$'s from the pre-SEC period for the adjustment period and the results were little different from those reported below.

22. The algebraic means (and standard deviations) of the cumulative residuals in the February 1934 through June 1935 adjustment period are .0010 (.0307) for the disclosure corporations and .0072 (.0290) for the nondisclosure corporations. In the February 1934 through June 1936 adjustment period, the statistics are −.0004 (.0228) and .0022 (.0206).

23. The smaller mean values of the standard deviations of the residuals of securities in both groups in the post-SEC period compared to the pre-SEC period is due primarily to the period of May 1932 through June 1933.

24. Stock redemptions exceeded new issues in the 1932–1938 period.

25. These data also are consistent with the hypothesis that published financial data have no information content.

26. The mean percentage deviations between actual and expected (assuming a random distribution) total runs in the pre-SEC and post-SEC periods are –1.2 and 4.9 percent for the disclosure corporations and –1.5 and 7.5 percent for the nondisclosure corporations. On a probability basis, the percentage of individual stocks whose runs were significantly different at the 5 percent level from expected are 4.3 and 7.8 for the pre- and post-SEC disclosure corporations and 2.3 and 12.2 for the pre- and post-SEC nondisclosure corporations. It appears that the security prices of both groups more nearly conformed to a random walk in the pre-SEC period than in the post-SEC period. Most interesting for present purposes, prices of the securities of corporations that did disclose appear to reflect a less efficient market after the '34 Act became effective than did those of corporations that did not disclose their sales.

27. An exception may be Beaver's study of preliminary reports.

REFERENCES

R. Ball and P. Brown, "An Empirical Evaluation of Accounting Income Numbers," *J. Accounting Res.*, Autumn 1968, *6*, 159–78.

W. H. Beaver, "The Information Content of Annual Earnings Announcements," *J. Accounting Res., Empirical Research in Accounting: Selected Studies 1968*, 67–92.

G. J. Benston, "Published Corporate Accounting Data and Stock Prices," *J. Accounting Res., Empirical Research in Accounting: Selected Studies 1967*, 1–54.

————, (1969a) "The Effectiveness and Effects of the SEC's Accounting Disclosure Requirements," in H. G. Manne, ed., *Economic Policy and the Regulation of Corporate Securities*, Washington 1969.

————, (1969b) "The Value of the SEC's Accounting Disclosure Requirements," *Accounting Rev.*, July 1969, *44*, 515–32.

M. Blume, "The Assessment of Portfolio Performance," unpublished doctoral dissertation, Univ. Chicago 1968.

————, "Portfolio Theory: A Step Towards its Practical Application," *J. Bus. Univ. Chicago.*, Apr. 1970, *43*, 152–73.

F. E. Brown and D. Vickers, in I. Friend et al., *A Study of Mutual Funds*, Washington 1962, ch. 5, 289–358.

J. G. Cragg and B. G. Malkiel, "The Consensus and Accuracy of Some Predictions of the Growth of Corporate Earnings," *J. Finance*, Mar. 1968, *22*, 67–84.

R. F. DeBedts, *The New Deal's SEC*, New York 1964.

R. E. Diefenbach, "How Good is Institutional Research?" *Financial Analysts J.*, Jan/Feb. 1972, *28*, 54–60.

E. Fama, "Efficient Capital Markets; A Review of Theory and Empirical Work," *J. Finance*, May 1970, *25*, 383–417.

————, L, Fisher, M. Jensen, and R. Roll, "The Adjustment of Stock Prices to New Information," *Int. Econ. Rev.*, Feb. 1969, *10*, 1–21.

L. Fisher and J. H. Dorie, "Some Studies of Variability of Returns on Investments in Common Stocks," *J. Bus. Univ. Chicago*, Apr. 1970, *43*, 99–134.

I. Friend and E. Herman, "The SEC Through a Glass Darkly, *J. Bus. Univ. Chicago*, Oct. 1964, *37*, 382–405.

R. Hagerman, "An Investigation of Effects of Disclosure and Audits on the Efficiency of the Market for Bank Stock," unpublished doctoral dissertation, Univ. Rochester 1972.

M. C. Jensen, "The Performance of Mutual Funds in the Period 1954–64," *J. Finance*, May 1968, *23*, 389–416.

H. G. Manne, *Insider Trading and the Stock Market*, New York 1966.

H. M. Markowitz, *Portfolio Selection: Efficient Diversification of Investments*, New York 1959.

R. McEnally, "Information Effect and P/E Ratios," *Miss. Vall. J. Bus. Econ.*, spring 1970, *5*, 24–38.

L. D. Pankoff and R. Virgil, "Some Preliminary Findings from a Laboratory Experiment on the Usefulness of Financial Accounting Information to Security Analysts, *J. Accounting Res., Empirical Research in Accounting: Selected Studies 1970.*

W. D. Rich, *Legal Responsibility and Rights of Public Accountants*, New York, 1935.

W. Z. Ripley, *Trusts, Pools and Corporations*, rev. ed., New York 1916.

_____, *Main Street and Wall Street*, Boston 1927.

W. F. Sharpe, "Capital Asset Prices: A Theory of Market Equilibrium Under Conditions of Risk," *J. Finance*, Sept 1964, *19*, 425–42.

L. H. Sloan, *Everyman and His Common Stocks*, New York, 1931.

R. Sobel, *The Big Board: A History of the New York Stock Market*, New York 1965.

G. J. Stigler, (1964a) "Public Regulation of the Securities Markets," *J. Bus. Univ. Chicago*, Apr. 1964, *37*, 117–42.

_____, (1964b) "Comment," *J. Bus. Univ. Chicago*, Oct. 1964, *37*, 414–22.

F. M. Wheat, "'Truth in Securities' Three Decades Later," *Howard Law Review*, Winter 1967, *13*, 100–107.

_____, Wheat Report, *Disclosure to Investors, A Reappraisal of Administrative Policies Under the '33 and '34 Securities Acts*, Report and Recommendations to the Securities and Exchange Commission from the Disclosure Policy Committee, Mar. 1969.

Landell v. *Lybrand*, 264, Pa. 496, 107 Atl. 783, 1919.

Moody's Investors Services, *Manual of Investments, American and Foreign*, Industrial Securities, New York, various years.

Securities and Exchange Commission, *The Work of the Securities and Exchange Commission*, Washington, May 1967.

_____, *A 25 Year Summary of the Activities of the Securities and Exchange Commission*, Washington 1959.

Standard and Poor's, Industrial 425 Index, New York, various years.

Ultramares Corp. v. *Touche, Niven & Co.*, 229 App. Div. 581, 243 N.Y. Supp. (1st Dept. 1930), rev., 225 N.Y. 170, 174 N.E. 441, 1931.

U.S. Congress, Senate Committee on Banking & Currency, Stock Exchange Practices, *Hearings*, on S. Res. 84 and S. Res. 56, 73 Cong., Part 17, Washington 1934.

SEVENTEEN

Statement of Policy on the Establishment and Improvement of Accounting Principles and Standards

RELEASE NO. 150

December 20, 1973, 38 *F.R.* 1260

Statement of Policy on the Establishment and Improvement of Accounting Principles and Standards

Following the formation of the Financial Accounting Standards Board (FASB), the Securities and Exchange Commission announced that the FASB pronouncements are considered to have substantial authoritative support, and that any practices contrary to their pronouncements will be considered not to have such support.

Various Acts of Congress administered by the Securities and Exchange Commission clearly state the authority of the Commission to prescribe the methods to be followed in the preparation of accounts and the form and content of financial statements to be filed under the Acts and the responsibility to assure that investors are furnished with information necessary for informed investment decisions. In meeting this statutory responsibility effectively, in recognition of the expertise, energy, and resources of the accounting profession, and without abdicating its responsibilities, the Commission has historically looked to the standard-setting bodies designated by the profession to provide leadership in establishing and improving accounting principles. The determinations by these bodies have been regarded by the Commission, with minor exceptions, as being responsive to the needs of investors.

The body presently designated by the Council of the American Institute of Certified Public Accountants (AICPA) to establish accounting principles is the Financial Accounting Standards Board (FASB). This designation by the AICPA followed the issuance of a report in March 1972 recommending the formation of the FASB, after a study of the matter by a broadly based study group. The recommendations contained in that report were widely endorsed by industry, financial analysts, accounting educators, and practicing accountants. The Commission endorsed the establishment of the FASB in the belief that the Board would provide an institutional framework which will permit prompt and responsible actions flowing from research and consideration of varying viewpoints. The collective experience and expertise of the members of the FASB and the individuals and professional organizations supporting it are substantial. Equally important, the commitment of resources to the FASB is impressive evidence of the willingness and intention of the private sector to support the FASB in accomplishing its task. In view of these considerations, the Commission intends to continue its policy of looking to the private sector for leadership in establishing and improving accounting principles and standards through the FASB with the expectation that the body's conclusions will promote the interests of investors.

In Accounting Series Release No. 4 (1938) the Commission stated its policy that financial statements prepared in accordance with accounting practices for which there was no substantial authoritative support were presumed to be misleading and that footnote or other disclosure would not avoid this presumption. It also stated that, where there was a difference of opinion between the Commission and a registrant as to the proper accounting to be followed in a particular case, disclosure would be accepted in lieu of correction of the financial statements themselves only if substantial authoritative support existed for the accounting practices followed by the registrant and the position of the Commission had not been expressed in rules, regulations, or other official releases. For purposes of this policy, principles, standards, and practices promulgated by the FASB in its Statements and Interpretations[1] will be considered by the Commission as having substantial authoritative support, and those contrary to such FASB promulgations will be considered[2] to have no such support.

In the exercise of its statutory authority with respect to the form and content of filings under the Acts, the Commission has the responsibility to assure that investors are provided with adequate information. A significant portion of the necessary information is provided by a set of basic financial statements (including the notes thereto) which conform to generally accepted accounting principles. Information in addition to that included in financial statements conforming to generally accepted accounting principles is also necessary. Such additional disclosures are required to be made in various fashions, such as in financial statements and schedules reported on by independent public accountants or as textual statements required by items in the applicable forms and reports filed with the Commission. The Commission will continue to identify areas where investor information needs exist and will determine the appropriate methods of disclosure to meet these needs.

It must be recognized that in its administration of the Federal Securities Acts and in its review of filings under such Acts, the Commission staff will continue as it has in the past to take such action on a day-to-day basis as may be appropriate to resolve specific problems of accounting and reporting under the particular factual circumstances involved in filings and reports of individual registrants.

The Commission believes that the foregoing statement of policy provides a sound basis for the Commission and the FASB to make significant contributions to meeting the needs of the registrants and investors.

By the Commission.

NOTES

1. Accounting Research Bulletins of the Committee on Accounting Procedure of the American Institute of Certified Public Accountant and effective opinions of the Accounting Principles Board of the Institute should be considered as continuing in force with the same degree of au-

thority except to the extent altered, amended, supplemented, revoked, or superseded by one or more Statements of Financial Accounting Standards issued by the FASB.

2. It should be noted that Rule 203 of the Rules of Conduct of the Code of Ethics of the AICPA provides that it is necessary to depart from the accounting principles promulgated by the body designated by the Council of the AICPA if, due to unusual circumstances, failure to do so would result in misleading financial statements. In such a case, the use of other principles may be accepted or required by the Commission.

EIGHTEEN

Impact of the SEC on Accounting Principles and Auditing Standards

HALDON G. ROBINSON

Partner, Deloitte, Haskins & Sells

In this article Robinson examines the development of accounting principles and auditing standards and the effect of the Securities and Exchange Commission (SEC) on this process up to the early 1970s. The private sector, partially motivated by the SEC, has been reviewing the process through which accounting principles and auditing standards are developed. Robinson urges support of efforts by private sector agencies to avoid further SEC involvement in accounting and financial matters.

As a practicing CPA, I would like to be able to say that the Securities and Exchange Commission (SEC) has had no discernible impact on the development of accounting principles and auditing standards. I would also like to say that those principles and standards have been developed solely by the private sector without regulatory intervention. However, neither would be a true statement. The SEC has exerted significant influence on accounting and auditing matters, and realistically we must expect that it will continue to play a significant role in the future.

HISTORICAL REVIEW

Perhaps a brief review of the development of accounting principles and auditing standards, and of the history of the SEC, will help to focus on the SEC's role in the development of those principles and standards.

Accounting is an old art; however, it was only thirty-five years ago in 1939 that the accounting profession in this country initiated a formal procedure for issuing pronouncements on accounting principles and auditing standards. In that year the American Institute of Certified Public Accountants' (AICPA) Committee on Accounting Procedure issued its first Accounting Research Bulletin. The Committee was succeeded in 1959 by the Accounting Principles Board (APB) which in turn was succeeded in 1973 by the Financial Accounting Standards Board. The pronouncements issued by those three bodies constitute a substantial portion of what we ordinarily refer to as "generally accepted accounting principles."

Published in *Proceedings,* Sixth Annual Symposium, California State University. Reprinted in Haskin & Sells, *Selected Papers*—1974, copyright © 1975 by Haskins & Sells. Reprinted by permission.

Also in 1939, the AICPA's Committee on Auditing Procedure issued its first Statement on Auditing Procedure. In 1973 that Committee was succeeded by the Auditing Standards Executive Committee. The Statements of those Committees contain what we refer to as "generally accepted auditing standards." In addition, the profession has published various case studies in auditing procedure and internal control as well as numerous industry audit and accounting guides. Those publications and the evolution in practice of certain principles and standards have added to the bodies of generally accepted accounting principles and generally accepted auditing standards.

The SEC has been active over almost the same period. After investigating the 1929 stock-market crash, Congress concluded that federal legislation was necessary to protect the public against fraud, misrepresentation, excessive speculation, and other undesirable practices in the distribution or trading of securities. As a result, Congress enacted the Securities Act of 1933 and the Securities Exchange Act of 1934, creating the SEC itself in 1934 to administer both statutes. In later years the SEC was given administrative responsibility under other statutes, such as the Public Utility Holding Company Act of 1935, the Trust Indenture Act of 1939, the Investment Company Act of 1940, the Investment Advisers Act of 1940, and certain others.

Essentially, the SEC's tasks are:

1. To control the activities of persons dealing in securities, such as broker-dealers, investment companies, and investment advisers.

2. To assure full disclosure of information, both financial and nonfinancial, by registrants in connection with new security offerings.

3. To require reports from the companies whose securities are traded in the public securities markets.

The statutes give the SEC broad powers to prescribe rules and regulations for many facets of the securities markets. Among those powers is the authority to prescribe the form and content of financial statements and to establish accounting principles and, under certain acts, auditing standards.

SEC PHILOSOPHY

How has the SEC used that authority? What is its policy for establishing accounting and auditing rules and regulations?

The SEC has standardized the form and content of financial statements required to be filed with it and has issued a number of pronouncements on accounting and auditing matters. The basic SEC accounting and auditing documents are Regulation S-X and the Accounting Series Releases. Essentially, however, the SEC has refrained from a broad exercise of its powers. Generally, its policy has been to let the private sector establish accounting principles and auditing standards. This policy is in sharp contrast to that of some other governmental agencies, such as the Interstate Commerce Commission and Federal Power Commission, which have established uniform systems of accounts that dictate the detailed manner in which accounts must be kept. The SEC has prescribed uniform systems of accounts as well as a host of other regulations) only for public utility holding companies and their subsidiaries and affiliates. Thus, SEC prescription of accounting has been limited to a relatively small number of companies in the United States.

The SEC's policy of relying mainly on the private sector to develop accounting principles and auditing standards was set forth in Accounting Series Release (ASR) No. 4, issued in 1938, a year before the accounting profession implemented its formal machinery for issuing accounting and auditing pronouncements. In ASR No. 4, the SEC stated that it would accept accounting principles provided there was substantial authoritative support for the principles followed and the Commission had not previously expressed its opposition to the principles.

The SEC reiterated its philosophy in Accounting Series Release No. 150, issued in late 1973, in which the SEC supported the then newly established Financial Accounting Standards Board (FASB). The Commission stated that it intended to continue its policy of looking to the private sector for leadership in establishing and improving accounting principles and standards. Furthermore, that policy has been emphasized in recent speeches and articles by the SEC's commissioners and its chief accountant.

While I agree with the SEC's general policy, I object to two aspects of the current SEC philosophy.

Measurement versus Disclosure

The first aspect is the SEC's distinction between "measurement" and "disclosure." The SEC seems to equate the measurement or quantification of economic data with generally accepted accounting principles and to view that matter as the primary concern of the private sector — that is, the FASB. At the same time, it considers the disclosure aspect of accounting and financial matters as the primary concern of the SEC. Accounting Series Release No. 150 expressed that thinking. While supporting the FASB, the SEC also stated that there was a need for information in addition to that included in financial statements conforming to generally accepted accounting principles and that the Commission would determine the appropriate disclosure required to inform investors properly. That additional required disclosure often concerns information of an accounting nature. For example, the SEC considers its releases on leases (ASR No. 147), compensating balances (ASR No. 148), and income taxes (ASR No. 149) in late 1973 to be within the area of disclosure, not measurement.

I object to the distinction because disclosure is an integral part of generally accepted accounting principles. For example, the accounting principles on income taxes and leases, as set forth in APB opinions, not only deal with measurement of the debits and credits, but also stipulate certain disclosures that are essential to a fair presentation of financial information. Almost every professional pronouncement on accounting principles prescribes disclosure of certain matters as well as the manner of recording transactions and events. The reason is simple. In today's complex and changing world it is impossible to give the reader of financial statements all of the information he should have in the body of the statements. Therefore, notes to financial statements are necessary to provide the additional information. Accordingly, to attempt to establish generally accepted accounting principles without taking into account both disclosure and measurement is not realistic.

Professional Analyst versus Average Investor

The second disturbing aspect of the SEC's current philosophy is the Commission's distinction between the professional analyst and the average investor. In two recent Accounting

Series Releases — those on disclosure of compensating balances (ASR No. 148) and income tax expense (ASR No. 149) — the SEC stated that certain of its financial statement disclosure requirements were aimed at professional analysts rather than average investors. The SEC's classification of users of financial statements seems to be arbitrary. It offers no definition of either "professional analysts" or "average investors." Individuals within each category differ in the degree of their understanding of financial information. Since the dividing line is not clear-cut, I believe we should attempt to develop accounting principles that result in financial statements that meet the needs of reasonably well-informed users. If the SEC believes that supplemental information is necessary for special user groups, that information should be presented apart from the financial statements.

The FASB is presently studying the needs of financial-statement users as part of its project on the conceptual framework for financial accounting and reporting. It seems to me that it would be prudent for the SEC to await the FASB's conclusions before continuing its recent practice of suggesting different financial statements for different groups of users.

IMPACT ON ACCOUNTING PRINCIPLES AND AUDITING STANDARDS

As I see it, the SEC's impact on accounting principles and auditing standards is threefold: First, the mere existence of the SEC has influenced accounting principles and auditing standards. Second, the active cooperation of the SEC with the private sector has aided the development of accounting principles and of auditing standards. Third, SEC pronouncements have established some principles and standards.

Existence of SEC

First, there is the intangible impact of the SEC's existence. When the SEC was created in 1934 there was considerable support in Congress for federally legislated accounting rules and federally employed accountants to audit the financial statements of publicly held companies. Fortunately, the approach was not adopted, and the accounting profession was entrusted with the responsibility for accounting and auditing standards. However, the accounting profession was "under the gun." To some extent, the threat of federally legislated accounting and auditing rules exists today. I am sure that we would be squarely facing exactly that situation if the private sector had not made the progress that it has made in the last thirty-five years. There is, then, the feeling — you might even say the knowledge — that if the private sector does not fulfill its role in establishing accounting principles and auditing standards, someone else will step in. That someone presumably would be the SEC. It is, of course, impossible to measure how much that threat of outside intervention has helped in establishing accounting principles and auditing standards. But the experience in other countries has demonstrated that in the absence of governmental persuasion the development of adequate financial reporting does not progress rapidly.

Along the same line, but in a more positive vein, we must consider the SEC's support of the accounting profession as having an impact on the development of accounting principles and auditing standards. The SEC, as a general rule, will not accept financial statements if the accountants' opinion indicates a deviation from generally accepted accounting principles or generally accepted auditing standards. I am aware that accounting principles established by the profession have not always been wholeheartedly received by industry. At times, a company follows a principle only to avoid a qualification in the auditors' report, which would, among other things, make the financial statements unacceptable to the SEC. In that sense, the SEC does have an impact on the development of accounting principles and auditing standards by reinforcing the accounting profession's position concerning these principles and standards.

Cooperation with Accounting Profession

Now to the second point — the SEC's cooperation with the accounting profession. The SEC frequently brings specific topics to the attention of the profession and cooperates with it in developing specific pronouncements. Further, representatives of the SEC and the accounting profession meet periodically to discuss topics of current interest and to exchange views.

Among current topics that are of concern to both the profession and the SEC are:

1. The publication by companies of forecast information and the independent auditors' role in the forecasting process
2. Improved disclosure of interim financial information and involvement of accountants in the interim reporting process
3. Transactions among related parties
4. The reporting of inventory profits
5. Communications between successor and predecessor auditors
6. Liquidity considerations related to the current economic situation

I have omitted many items on the FASB agenda that are obviously of concern to all parties affected, including the SEC.

A good example of SEC-AICPA cooperation appears in *The Journal of Accountancy* for November 1974. I refer to the article that summarizes an informal discussion between SEC officials and AICPA representatives concerning the implementation of Accounting Release Series Nos. 146 and 146-A. These releases deal with the effect of treasury-stock transactions on the accounting for business combinations. I believe that cooperation between the SEC and the accounting profession, especially on that topic, is a healthy sign. Only about a year ago the matter was one of substantial disagreement.

Another matter that is presently being studied by the profession is reliance on other auditors. Specifically, the question is the portion of the reporting entity's financial statements that an auditor must examine to be considered the principal auditor. The SEC's concern is evidenced by the fact that the Commission's chief accountant wrote to the AICPA's Auditing Standards Executive Committee requesting that better guidelines be developed in that area.

There are many examples of professional pronouncements that have been areas of concern for both the profession and the SEC. Some professional pronouncements probably would not have been issued — at least not at the time they were — without the cooperation of the SEC. I believe that SEC cooperation has been an important factor, although it is not feasible to assess the extent to which the SEC has influenced accounting principles and auditing standards by cooperating with the accounting profession.

SEC Pronouncements on Accounting and Auditing

The third way in which the SEC influences accounting principles and auditing standards is the most obvious way — by issuing specific pronouncements. Notwithstanding the SEC's policy of looking to the private sector for the establishment of accounting principles and auditing standards, it has on a number of occasions prescribed accounting and auditing standards. This may seem to make its practice inconsistent with its policy. However, the SEC has always reserved the right to take an action that it deems appropriate to resolve specific accounting and auditing problems. If the Commission believes that certain standards set by the private sector are incompatible with the SEC's role of providing adequate protection to investors, it will not accept the private-sector standards but will set its own. Similarly, in the absence of pronouncements by the private sector in areas where the SEC believes a need exists, the SEC will issue its own regulations.

There are many examples of SEC regulations concerning accounting and auditing. I will touch on some of the more important ones to demonstrate their impact.

Auditing Standards

Two specific industries are greatly affected by SEC audit regulations — broker-dealers and investment companies. Broker-dealers report to the SEC under the Securities Exchange Act of 1934. Investment companies register with the SEC and report under the Investment Company Act of 1940. For broker-dealers, the SEC requires that certain detailed audit procedures must be performed. The report filed with the SEC (Form X-17A-5) must contain, among other things, the auditors' comments on material inadequacies found in the accounting system, internal accounting control, procedures for safeguarding securities, and certain other matters. For registered investment companies, the SEC has issued specific regulations relating to examination and valuation of investment securities. In addition, the report filed with the SEC (Form N-IR) must contain the accountants' opinion regarding their evaluation of internal control and certain supplemental data. To date, broker-dealers and investment companies are the only businesses for which the SEC has prescribed such specific requirements for auditing and for reporting by the auditors.

A recent example of a specific pronouncement influencing auditing standards, and one that also manifests a new approach by the SEC, is Accounting Release Series No. 144, issued in 1973. In that release the SEC censured an accounting firm for certain practices and established a procedure for professional review of the firm's practice. The procedures for professional review are by no means finalized, and AICPA and SEC representatives are working to establish policies and define procedures. Ultimately the mechanism will influence auditing standards, although it is not now possible to predict the nature and extent of the influence. In a related development the AICPA's Auditing Standards Executive Committee has issued an exposure draft on "Quality Control Considerations for a Firm of Independent Auditors." The document deals with the activities of an accounting firm that may affect the quality of its services on audit engagements.

Although the SEC has issued relatively few specific auditing regulations, it has expressed its views on auditing procedures in a number of cases involving specific problems. Some specific cases have been summarized and issued as Accounting Series Releases. Typically, the SEC discusses the problem areas and often is critical of the audit procedures performed in specific circumstances, even though the procedures may be generally accepted within the profession. Early in 1974, for instance, the SEC issued Accounting Series Release No. 153, a noteworthy release for a number of reasons. First, the release discussed at some length the problem of auditing transactions among related parties, was critical of the audit procedures performed in the particular case in question, and prescribed audit guidelines. Second, the release discussed another current problem, that of communication between predecessor and successor auditors. Third, the release reiterated the SEC's opinion that auditors should be expected to detect gross overstatements of assets or profits. Finally, the release was the second instance in which the SEC ordered an accounting firm to subject its practice to a professional review.

Accounting Principles

Accounting pronouncements by the SEC have been more frequent than pronouncements on auditing.

One of the first SEC opinions, expressed in Accounting Series Release No. 8, issued in 1938, dealt with accounting for property and appraisals and concluded that fixed assets should be stated at cost rather than at appraised or current value. The principle of stating fixed assets at cost is surely well established today, but it was not so clear thirty-five or forty years ago. Also, I believe that in certain areas — for instance, accounting for fixed assets in joint-venture situations — professional literature is not clear even now.

Other SEC pronouncements in its early years also dealt with specific accounting questions. It is not worthwhile today to elaborate on these pronouncements. They are important only in the sense that they served to demonstrate the SEC's willingness to issue pronouncements on accounting when it believed there was a need for them.

In the SEC's first three decades it generally followed its policy of avoiding rule making in the accounting area. Most of its accounting opinions were the result of specific matters coming to the SEC's attention or specific questions raised. The SEC's approach in those years might be characterized as a case-by-case approach, although a few of its pronouncements did have application wider than the isolated case in question.

Starting in the 1960s, however, the SEC seemed to change its approach and to commence taking a more active role in shaping accounting principles. Its pronouncements in more recent years have often been of a more general and far-reaching nature than were earlier ones. An example of the change was Accounting Series Release No. 85, issued in 1960. In that release the SEC set forth its administrative policy regarding the balance-sheet treatment of deferred income taxes. The SEC concluded that deferred taxes could not be included in stockholders' equity as restricted or appropriated surplus. Another example was Accounting Series Release No. 120, issued in 1965, dealing with the balance-sheet treatment of deferred income taxes arising from installment sales. The SEC concluded that the classification of those deferred taxes as current or noncurrent should be consistent with the classification of the related receivables.

The underlying reason for SEC pronouncements such as those just mentioned seems to have been a quest for uniformity. The essential facts surrounding those accounting questions were not likely to vary among companies. Thus the SEC believed that uniform treatment of these matters would be desirable.

Another example of the quest for more uniformity in accounting was Accounting Series Release No. 95, issued in 1962. The SEC was concerned that some profits on real-estate transactions were being recorded before their realization. The SEC responded by issuing ASR No. 95, which set criteria for recognizing profit on real-estate transactions and presented seven illustrative cases taken from SEC filings. Because of the absence of applicable AICPA pronouncements, the SEC release became the guide for accounting for real-estate transactions for over a decade. In the last year the AICPA has issued two Industry Accounting Guides on the subject, *Accounting for Retail Land Sales* and *Accounting for Profit Recognition on Sales of Real Estate.*

In reciting examples of SEC accounting pronouncements, I must mention the one that was perhaps the most publicized — Accounting Series Release No. 96, dealing with accounting for the investment credit. The APB issued its Opinion No. 2 on that matter in late 1962. The board concluded that the investment credit (which under the applicable tax laws at that time had to be deducted from the depreciable base of the asset) should be reflected in income over the productive life of acquired property and not in the year in which the property was placed in service. The SEC in January 1963 issued ASR No. 96, permitting the recording of the investment credit, net of tax effect, in the year in which the credit reduced taxes currently payable. But the SEC said that it would also accept the method prescribed by the APB. The matter was much publicized and criticized, and I will not dwell on it.

More recently, in early 1972, accounting for the investment credit resulted in a controversy. In the Revenue Act of 1971 Congress stipulated that both the flow-through and the deferral methods were acceptable methods of accounting for the credit. The APB at that time was still leaning to the deferral method only. But, of course, the Board had to yield to Congress. Officially, the SEC remained silent at the time, but unofficially it was prepared to support the board's view before Congress intervened.

Those two episodes are highly significant. For one thing, ASR No. 96 is one of the most important examples of the SEC's influence on the development of accounting principles. More than that, it is a reminder that the SEC will not necessarily agree with the private sector's pronouncements. The episode relating to the Revenue Act of 1971 is an ominous reminder to all of us that Congress also has the power to prescribe accounting rules. In that connection, we must also be mindful that the SEC is an organization created and financed by Congress and is therefore responsible to Congress and, through Congress, to the voters.

Recently we have seen a flurry of SEC activity in the accounting area. The increased activity seems to have started about three or four years ago and has accelerated since John C. Burton became the SEC's chief accountant. John Burton has been described as an activist, a description that I believe fits.*

A number of recent SEC pronouncements have dealt with controversial issues and current topics. Many recent pronouncements have required additional disclosure in notes to financial statements, reflecting the SEC's philosophy of attempting to identify the needs of

---

* *Editor's Note:* Mr. Burton resigned as Chief Accountant in 1976. Clarence Sampson is the current Chief Accountant.

investors for additional disclosure and taking appropriate action to provide that disclosure. Good examples of the so-called disclosure pronouncements are ASR Nos. 147, 148, and 149, dealing with leases, compensating balances, and income taxes. Of particular interest is ASR No. 147, pertaining to disclosure of financing leases and their impact on income. Shortly before that release was issued, the APB issued Opinion No. 31 dealing with the same topic. The SEC, however, believed that Opinion No. 31 did not go far enough. Specifically, it believed that disclosure of the present value of financing leases and of the impact on net income of capitalization of those leases, neither of which was required by APB Opinion No. 31, was essential to investors. Accordingly, the SEC decided to go ahead with its own release despite APB Opinion No. 31. In the release, the SEC stated that it had referred the basic problems of accounting measurement of leases to the FASB. Earlier, I expressed my views on the SEC's distinction between "disclosure" and "measurement." The entire subject of leases is, of course, being studied now by the FASB. No doubt the SEC, as well as many other interested parties, is anxiously awaiting the FASB's conclusion on this complicated subject.

The SEC's recent proposal to impose a moratorium on capitalization of interest cost pending the development of standards by the FASB is, in my opinion, a clear example of the SEC's attempt to establish the measurement feature of accounting principles. That action obviously runs counter to the SEC's stated policy. The AICPA, in a letter of comment to the SEC, opposed the proposed action and urged that the SEC adopt only certain disclosure requirements and await FASB action on the subject.

CONCLUSION

There is no doubt that we in this country have the highest financial reporting standards in the world. I believe a major portion of the credit for that status belongs to the private sector which, since the 1930s, has shown remarkable progress in establishing accounting principles and auditing standards. However, the examples I have cited make it clear that the SEC has also had a significant impact on the development of those principles and standards.

Partially as a result of the SEC's concern, the private sector has been reexamining its mechanisms for promulgating accounting principles and auditing standards. One result of the reexamination was the creation of the FASB. That body, composed of seven independent, full-time members representing the private sector is now responsible for developing financial accounting standards. For the first time, the primary responsibility for the development of financial accounting standards has been moved out of the AICPA's hands.

In the area of auditing, the private sector is reexamining the question of responsibilities of independent auditors. Just recently a seven-member commission was appointed to determine whether a gap exists between what the public expects of auditors and what auditors can reasonably be expected to accomplish. The commission is headed by Manuel Cohen, who was SEC chairman from 1964 to 1969, and has three other members from outside the AICPA. It is expected to complete its study by the end of 1975.

I am under no illusion that all pronouncements by the FASB and by professional bodies such as the Commission on Auditors' Responsibilities will be unanimously embraced. Many of the subjects being tackled are too controversial for unanimous agreement on the conclusions offered to be expected. However, we must recognize that the conclusions are the result of considerable research and deliberation, and I urge everyone — in particular the business community and professional accountants — to support the conclusions. If that support is not forthcoming, the organizations entrusted with the responsibility for promulgating accounting and auditing standards will be weakened, their progress will be inhibited, and the likelihood of greater involvement by the SEC in accounting and auditing matters will increase. Let us work together, then, to make the private sector responsive to our mutual needs with minimal governmental intervention being required.

NINETEEN

SEC Enforcement and Professional Accountants: Philosophy, Objectives and Approach

JOHN C. BURTON

Columbia University

Former Chief Accountant, Securities and Exchange Commission

The Securities and Exchange Commission (SEC) uses its enforcement powers to help ensure the quality and reliability of financial information available to the public. In this article, Burton, chief accountant of the SEC, reviews the Commission's enforcement program and concludes that over time the accounting profession has been strengthened by this effort.

I. THE PHILOSOPHY

The enforcement program of the Securities and Exchange Commission (SEC) is an important means by which the Commission moves toward the objectives of improved capital markets and the prevention of fraud. The regulatory authority under which the Commission is authorized to perform its enforcement activities prescribes that where "it appears that there may be a violation of the acts administered by the Commission or the rules and regulations thereunder, a preliminary investigation is generally made."[1] If, as a result of this investigation, it appears that a violation has been or is about to be committed, the Commission may then order a formal investigation.[2] If the investigation reveals that a violation has taken place the Commission can institute administrative proceedings looking to the imposition of remedial sanctions, initiate injunctive proceedings, or refer cases to the Department of Justice for criminal prosecution.[3] Thus, except for this last alternative, the SEC enforcement program is designed to maintain the integrity of the marketplace and deter fraud, rather than punish wrongdoers.

While the regulatory language is clear and its authorizations broad, the Commission has limited resources and finds it impossible to investigate and prosecute every violation. Consequently, the Commission has sought in recent years to focus its enforcement efforts at key points where maximum impact can be achieved. For this reason, enforcement efforts involving professionals, such as accountants and lawyers, have been important even though the number of cases in which professionals were so involved has not been great. The reasoning of the Commission is simple: these professionals are an essential element in providing access to the marketplace, since the sale of securities cannot take place without their involve-

---

Reprinted from *The Vanderbilt Law Review*, January 1975, pp. 19–29, with permission.

ment. Professional responsibility at these points of access can prevent many questionable activities before they occur.

The enforcement program as it relates to professional accountants, therefore, is part of the Commission's broad effort to encourage improved professional performance. By insisting upon high standards of performance by accountants, more reliable and meaningful financial information for the investing public will be assured. This information is the cornerstone of the analytical process whereby sound investment decisions can be made.

It must be understood that enforcement is only one part of the Commission's program to improve the quantity and quality of information available to the public. The regulatory authority granted the Commission is used extensively, and the potential of its further use has proved a valuable incentive to the development of corrective institutions within the private sector. Regulation and exhortation alone, however, are not enough. An enforcement program has proved to be an essential ingredient in the process and it must be understood as such.

It should be emphasized that the enforcement program is not used as a vehicle by which fundamentally new professional standards are established. The present generally accepted auditing standards of adequate technical training, independence of mental attitude, due professional care, adequate planning and supervision, and sufficient competent evidential matter are perfectly adequate to assure sound auditing if conscientiously applied to each case.[4] In addition, the fundamental accounting principle of fair presentation under the particular circumstances of each case remains the basis of good financial reporting.

II. THE OBJECTIVES

A. Giving Effect to Auditing Standards

Within the above broad standards the Commission's enforcement program deters shoddy performance by the increased risk of a Commission injunctive action and private actions for money damages.

As a result it becomes desirable for individuals and firms to devote greater resources and more care to the avoidance of such performance. While professionals in general have a desire to do a good job, excellence is costly, and in a world of competing claims and equities, a program which raises the cost of deficient work should have the impact of improving performance. On an individual firm basis, an injunctive action should restrain a repetition of the conduct in question and require improved compliance with professional standards while subjecting those responsible to prosecution if there is a repetition of the unacceptable behavior. On a professionwide basis, the threat of an enforcement action and the costs of an adverse determination by a court — unfavorable publicity, possible civil judgments, the financial burden of litigation, and, ultimately a loss of professional stature with a consequent decline in business — all combine to reduce the likelihood of defective professional performance.

B. Encouragement of Quality Control Procedures

It is also intended that the Commission enforcement actions encourage the implementation of professionwide quality controls within firms. Examples of these initial controls are: procedures involving recruitment, training, and promotion of a highly competent professional staff, specific review procedures governing engagements, and internal audit systems by which the management of a firm can be assured these controls are working adequately. In recent years, accounting firms have been devoting substantial resources to these procedures, and professional standards are giving recognition to their importance.[5]

General procedures assuring adequate professional staff probably are of the greatest importance, because competent, well-trained professionals with an alert and independent attitude are the key to effective auditing. If the staff in the field and the partner in charge of an engagement do not have these attributes, it is unlikely that specific review procedures will provide assurance of a good audit.

On the other hand, well-designed review procedures are useful in reducing the danger to the public and the firm of an error or faulty judgment by one or a few individuals. These procedures should be designed to disclose breakdowns within the audit and provide a mechanism for their correction before a report is issued. They may include formal steps by which various levels of work-paper review are undertaken by audit personnel on an engagement. Additional procedures include: provisions for consultation as problems arise, a means by which staff persons who disagree with judgments reached by an engagement partner may bring these matters to the attention of senior persons in the firm; independent reviews of financial statements and summary work papers by a partner or technical staff member not directly responsible for the engagement; and the use of industry specialists.

Finally, quality control systems within firms include an after-the-fact "internal audit" system designed to provide assurance to the management of the firm that adequate audits are being done and that timely review procedures are achieving their objectives. This system normally encompasses postaudit reviews on a sample basis utilizing personnel from other offices or a designated central quality assurance group for the firm as a whole.

In response to Commission actions, actions by private litigants, and some generally perceived public concern about the adequacy of audits, accounting firms have been increasing substantially their commitment of resources to all forms of improved quality controls. It is hoped that this investment will result in fewer auditing errors and a substantial reduction in the frequency of future enforcement actions. In those cases in which errors still occur, review procedures will lessen the likelihood that these errors will go undetected and result in the auditor's acceptance of misleading financial reporting.

C. Improving Auditing Standards

In addition to encouraging better quality controls, enforcement actions may have the benefit of directing attention to areas in which auditing standards may be more effectively articulated and applied. Although Commission actions are based on the facts of particular cases, in some situations the facts may be typical of general problem areas, and Commission opinions, orders, and complaints may emphasize audit deficiencies that require professionwide attention.

In one recent opinion,[6] for example, the Commission set forth in considerable detail its view of a deficient audit in which transactions with related parties played a major role. In the same opinion, comments were made by the Commission with respect to relationships between predecessor and successor auditors that the Commission believed were inadequate in the particular case. Both areas are now being considered by the Auditing Standards Executive Committee of the American Institute of Certified Public Accountants (AICPA), which is attempting to articulate specific guidelines to be applied in these areas. In addition, the Commission's emphasis, in a number of cases, on overall fairness in financial reporting has communicated to the profession the Commission's expectation that accountants' responsibilities go beyond the mechanical application of defined accounting principles.

D. Improving Public Confidence

The Commission is aware of the overall impact on public opinion of the enforcement program, and to this end a major objective is to increase the level of public confidence in financial reporting. If this is to be achieved, there must be greater confidence in the accounting profession and in the reporting environment. The investor must be assured that redress will be achieved in situations where deficiencies are found to exist. While some accountants suggest that confidence in the public accounting profession would be enhanced if all actions against accountants were kept private and many were not brought at all, this is a short-sighted view. As the level of professional performance rises, the public must be persuaded that an overwhelming majority of public accountants do a good job and that in those cases where they do not, vigorous action will be taken by public agencies to call them to task. A cover-up of deficient professional performance, no matter how justified, will ultimately tend to erode rather than enhance public confidence.

Confidence in the SEC is an important part of this total package that also must be considered. If investors are satisfied that the Commission, as the principal regulatory agency in the area, is alert and effective in discovering abuses and bringing effective sanctions against those involved in significant wrongdoing, there will be an increase in the level of investor confidence in financial reporting. While it is conceivable that an excessive number of such suits might erode public confidence, the temporary building of confidence through the process of deluding the public as to the reality of the situation would be far more destructive when the facts of the matter finally emerge.

At the same time, the need for public confidence in the SEC serves as a deterrent against the Commission bringing enforcement actions in marginal cases where the auditor involved was guilty of a simple error in judgment that was not particularly egregious. Although such errors might create some legal responsibility to private litigants, it does not seem desirable for the Commission to bring an enforcement action every time it may conclude that an auditor has made a mistake.

III. THE APPROACH

In deciding whether to institute an enforcement action, the Commission considers the case in light of several major factors, including the seriousness of the professional deficiency and the extent to which the auditor had knowledge of what was happening. The Commission also considers the degree to which the auditor appeared to be an active participant in a scheme to mislead the public through artful or incomplete disclosure or through the creative selection of accounting principles designed to present a picture inconsistent with reality. All factors relevant to the particular case must be considered.

In this connection, it should be emphasized that there are many enforcement actions brought by the Commission involving deficient financial reporting in which auditors are not named as defendants. In fact, auditors are named in only a minority of such cases. The Commission does not have a policy of pursuing all professional deficiencies that can be found simply for the joy of the hunt. Selectivity in the use of resources and attention to the more serious cases are the keys to an effective program.

Because of the selectivity in bringing cases, it must be recognized that the failure to name an auditor in a case does not necessarily represent an endorsement of the job done. The Commission sometimes concludes that while an auditor has done less than would have been hoped, the performance does not warrant a formal action. In such situations, the Commission sometimes instructs the staff to request that the management of the accounting firm involved come in for an informal conference. At such a conference, the management is advised that although no action is being instituted, the Commission does not feel that the level of performance in the case was up to the standards it believes that the profession should achieve. The management is then questioned with regard to remedial actions taken by the firm to improve future performance. In this way, appropriate corrective action can be encouraged in marginal cases without formal proceedings.

A. Sanctions

The sanctions imposed in Commission proceedings must serve a remedial purpose for firms in which improvements in the quality of work can reasonably be anticipated. In other cases, it is necessary to protect the public from continued practice before the Commission by unqualified persons and firms. Some circumstances arise in which it must be concluded that the performance of particular individuals or firms is so deficient that their continued practice before the Commission in the public marketplace carries too great a risk and hence is unacceptable. While small firms have more commonly been involved in such cases, a consistent pattern of deficient work by a large firm might lead to a conclusion that its continued practice would expose the public to greater risks than the Commission could reasonably deem to be acceptable.

1. *Rule 2(e) Action* — In cases involving unacceptable performance, the Commission has the authority under Rule 2(e) of its Rules of Practice to bar an individual or firm from practice before the Commission.[7] It may also suspend the professional from Commission practice until an appropriate showing of fitness to practice has been made. The ultimate sanction of a permanent bar is not frequently used, since the Commission usually believes that a professional firm can take actions to bring its performance up to an acceptable level and provide the Commission with assurance that such a level is being maintained. Even when an accountant has been barred from practice before the Commission, his right to practice may be reinstated after the passage of time, usually upon a showing that he no longer poses a danger to the public.

2. *Quality Control Review and Inspection* — Over the years the Commission has attempted to use sanctions which will meet the needs presented in each particular case. In the past two years, new sanctions have been developed in consent situations that the Commission believes hold some promise. Where cases raise questions concerning the adequacy of an accountant firm's quality control procedures, the Commission may require the firm to submit its procedures to the Commission's staff or to a group of outside professionals for re-

view. As a result of this review, the firm and the Commission agree on certain quality control and audit procedures to be followed. Such procedures may emphasize particular areas of practice that relate to the specific enforcement action, but they are generally not limited to such areas. After agreement on procedures, the firm undertakes to have its subsequent practice inspected for a period of time by a group of its peers in professional practice to determine whether the standards are adequate and whether they are being implemented. This inspection team reports its findings to the Commission, which retains jurisdiction of the matter until the final report is received and evaluated. If the report is not satisfactory, further action is required. Although this sanction has a number of variants tailored to particular situations, it certainly is not a panacea, and may not be appropriate in every case. The Commission believes, however, that it will have the effect of promoting improved professional performance, and has been working closely with the AICPA on this program.

In one case where this sanction was imposed, it appears that it had a beneficial effect in improving the firm's operating procedures and controls. In addition, the existence of an outside inspection team aided the senior management of the firm in upgrading the firm's professional practice. It is important, however, not to overemphasize the value of this program, because it is apparent that the attitudes of people and their training are of greater importance in assuring general audit excellence than are formal control procedures. Clearly, it is not productive to load a mountain of review on a pinhead of audit field work.

3. *Limiting New Firm Business* — In addition to the inspection sanction, in some cases the Commission has imposed a partial or complete limitation on new SEC business for a firm, either for a prescribed period or until such time as a peer review group is able to inspect a practice and report thereon to the Commission. In this way the Commission feels it has obtained outside evidence that the program has been effectively implemented before the firm is allowed to grow further, either in the aggregate or in the areas that are affected most. Since the establishment of improved control procedures and the need for extended training of personnel will necessarily require the commitment of substantial managerial and personnel resources, it may be appropriate to require that when evidence of control problems arises, growth should be substantially curtailed until there is independent evidence that such problems are effectively eliminated. This seems particularly appropriate in cases where the problems have not been of a limited nature but have encompassed several areas of practice.

The Commission will continue to monitor the results of these sanctions and to appraise their success in achieving better financial reporting and auditing. As new situations that require different solutions are confronted, the Commission will try to develop additional approaches to the problem of sanctions.

B. Review of the Reviewers

While it is appropriate to consider the Commission's enforcement program in terms of broad objectives, it is also important that the program be a fair one to specific firms and individuals affected in each separate case. I believe that adequate safeguards to insure fairness do exist in the procedures followed by the staff and the Commission, and although various parties may disagree with conclusions reached, the judgments made are based on a full consideration of the facts, including, if desired, written presentations from the proposed defendant.[8]

At each stage in the process of bringing a new case, review of staff actions takes place at the Commission level. When the staff initially concludes that a situation warrants investigation to determine whether an enforcement action is needed, it must present the basis for this judgment to the Commission and request a formal order of investigation under which documents and witnesses may be subpoenaed. Such an order is not issued unless the Commission is persuaded that a reasonable basis exists for the investigation.

When an order is issued, the investigation is undertaken with due regard for the rights of all. Any person being questioned has the right to counsel and is fully informed of his rights by the staff. Accountants from the Division of Enforcement staff are involved early in the procedure when financial statements are part of the investigation.

In many cases during the early stages of an investigation, the staff is not fully aware of the facts that ultimately are developed, and, accordingly, it is not always clear whether the professional accountant is a potential defendant. Nevertheless, where the professional accountant and his counsel seek information, the staff will attempt to advise them of the progress of the investigation to the extent it is feasible for them to do so. Moreover, during the course of the investigation the professional may make a submission setting forth his view of the case. Any submission made is furnished to the Chief Accountant and to the Commission. Representatives of the Office of the Chief Accountant are frequently consulted by the Division of Enforcement and regional office staffs as an investigation proceeds so that any questions concerning auditing and accounting can be answered in the course of the investigation.

Before a case involving an accountant is sent to the Commission, it is submitted to the chief accountant for review of the merits. At this time, the assistant chief accountant (Investigations) in the Office of the Chief Accountant generally reviews the testimony and other evidence and reports his conclusion to the Chief Accountant. In many cases the proposed defendant will request a meeting with the Chief Accountant to discuss the case, and, if thought desirable by the staff, this meeting will be held before any recommendation is forwarded to the Commission. After careful review of the evidence, the Chief Accountant then makes his recommendation, which is submitted to the Commission along with the recommendation of the Division of Enforcement. In my tenure with the Commission, no case against an accountant has been brought without my concurrence. If the case involves novel or particularly difficult questions, the Commission's Office of General Counsel will also review the recommendations.

After recommendations have been sent to the Commission, together with any submissions by proposed defendants, the Commissioners and their legal assistants review the case with great care. The staff will frequently receive questions about details in connection with this review. Then the case is discussed at the Commission table before any decision is reached, and these discussions are substantive in nature. The staff is subjected to vigorous questioning, and the principles and objectives underlying the proposed action are considered in depth.

All of these procedures occur prior to an action being brought by the Commission, since it is recognized that the bringing of an action against a professional has a substantial impact on his reputation even before any judicial determination is made. After the action is brought, the normal due process of the legal system is still available to provide protection against unjust actions.

While virtually all Commission cases are civil in character, on rare occasions it is concluded that a case is sufficiently serious that it should be referred to the Department of Justice for criminal prosecution. Referrals in regard to accountants have only been made when the Commission and the staff believed that the evidence indicated that a professional accountant certified financial statements that he knew to be false when he reported on them. The Commission does not make criminal references in cases that it believes are simply matters of professional judgment, even if the judgments appear to be bad ones.

CONCLUSION

The Commission's enforcement program in regard to professional accountants is one of the means by which it seeks to improve the quality and reliability of financial reporting in the United States. Effective utilization of this program can achieve an increasing quality of professional performance and the implementation on an industrywide basis of improved quality control procedures, thereby assuring the vitality of auditing standards and public confidence in the profession as a whole. These objectives are being achieved through a selective, albeit vigorous, application of enforcement program powers and the continued use of flexible and innovative approaches by the SEC. While the accounting profession may sometimes feel that it has been damaged by this effort, I am confident that in the long run the profession has in fact been strengthened in performing its essential function for the investing public and the free capital market system.

NOTES

1. 17. C.F.R. § 202.5 (1974).

2. *Id.*

3. *Id.*

4. *See* 1 CCH AICPA Prof. Stands., SAS No. 1, AU § 150.02 (1972).

5. *See, e.g.,* AICPA SAS No. 4, "Quality Control Considerations for a Firm of Independent Auditors," Dec. 1974.

6. SEC Accounting Series Release No. 153 (Feb. 25, 1974), 4 CCH Fed. Sec. L. Rep.   72,175, at 62,399.

7. SEC Rules of Practice 2(e), 17 C.F.R. § 201.2(e) (1974).

8. 17 C.F.R. § 202.5 (1974).

TWENTY

Disclosure Rules and Annual Reports: Present Impact

RAY GARRETT, JR.

Former Chairman, Securities and Exchange Commission

In this 1975 article then Chairman Ray Garrett, Jr., defends newly adopted disclosure rules of the Securities and Exchange Commission (SEC) which impact corporate annual reports and explains their purpose, including the insurance of full disclosure and the establishment of confidence in the country's business management.

Last fall, the Securities and Exchange Commission (SEC) amended its rules relating to the contents and distribution of annual reports to shareholders. Briefly, most publicly owned companies will now be required to include at least the following information in their annual reports:

- certified financial statements for the past two fiscal years;
- a summary of operations for the last five fiscal years and management's analysis of the summary with special attention to significant changes occurring during the most recent three years;
- a brief description of the company's business which, in the opinion of management, indicates the general nature and scope of the company's business;
- a line-of-business breakdown of total revenues and of income (or loss) before income taxes and extraordinary items for the last five fiscal years;
- the name and principal occupation or employment of each director and executive officer of the company;
- the market price ranges and dividends paid for each quarterly period during the last two fiscal years with respect to each class of equity securities entitled to vote at the company's annual meeting.

In addition, the annual report, or the proxy statement, must contain an undertaking that the company will provide, without charge, to any security holder as of the record date, upon written request, a copy of the company's Form 10-K or 12-K annual report, except for

Reprinted from *The Financial Executive*, April 1975, pp. 16–21, with permission of the Financial Executives Institute.

the exhibits thereto, as filed with the Commission. Companies must also undertake to make copies of the exhibits to their Form 10-K or 12-K available, but may impose a fee limited to their reasonable expenses for providing the copies.

Finally, these companies will be required to contact known record-holders, such as brokers, banks, and their nominees, who may be reasonably expected to hold securities on behalf of beneficial owners; to inquire of them as to the number of sets of material needed for distribution to beneficial owners for whom they hold securities; to furnish the material to them; and to pay the reasonable expenses of the record-holders for distributing the material to the beneficial owners.

This has long been standard practice for well-run companies, but there are enough which do not do this to justify a rule. A note to this requirement calls the attention of issuers to the fact that broker-dealers have an obligation pursuant to applicable self-regulatory requirements to obtain and forward proxy statements and annual reports in a timely manner to beneficial owners for whom they hold securities.

OUTLINING OBJECTIVES

The Commission had several objectives in adopting these relatively far-reaching amendments. Basically, the Commission has attempted to assure that all annual reports to shareholders contain at least a minimum quantum of meaningful business and financial information. Beyond this, the Commission has also attempted to improve the distribution of reports so that all security holders, including beneficial owners who hold their securities in nominee accounts or "street names," receive an annual report and, if interested, have ready access to the more detailed information contained in the company's Form 10-K or 12-K annual report filed with the Commission.

These rules reflect the thorough consideration and hard work of many individuals — both inside and outside the Commission — during the past decade. Based upon the work of the Wheat Report, our Industrial Issuers Advisory Committee, and the analyses and recommendations of the New York Stock Exchange, as well as our own experience, the Commission, in January 1974, published various proposals relating to the annual report for public comment. The proposed amendments drew more than 165 letters of comment from interested persons, including a large number of public companies and many private individuals, most of whom were presumably small shareholders. Based upon our consideration of all the letters of comment and our own experience, the Commission adopted the previously described amendments.

I was troubled, however, by certain of the comments expressed by various public companies, including, for example, that:

- the rules will mark the beginning of making the annual report another government report;
- annual reports will become too detailed, confusing, and complex;
- the rules represent a substantial infringement upon the free-writing aspect of the annual report.

In my judgment, these complaints reflect a serious misconception of the Commission's intent in adopting the recent amendments.

We are not attempting to bootstrap our almost plenary authority over proxy statements in order to gain direct jurisdiction over the contents and format of annual reports. And we certainly do not want to transform the annual report into a prospectus or "another government report" filled with legalistic and technical terminology.

To the contrary, we are aware that annual reports have substantially improved over the years without any SEC rules, except with respect to financial statements, because many companies have presented meaningful data in an understandable, and often innovative, form. I might note that the release announcing the amendments "continues to encourage issuers to improve voluntarily the content and format of their annual reports to security holders." The Commission recognizes that annual reports are probably the most effective means of communication between management and shareholders, and the Commission is sensitive to the free-writing aspects of the annual report and does not want to infringe unnecessarily upon management's discretion to choose the content and format of annual reports.

Parenthetically, last spring I saw several reports of informal surveys on annual report readership. They were, to me, surprisingly negative, suggesting that even the annual report does not get much attention from ordinary shareholders. Even so, it at least gets more attention than any other disclosure device.

INCONSISTENT INPUT

You may well ask, if all that I'm saying is true, why did the Commission adopt disclosure rules for annual reports? It is quite simple. The Commission has become aware of:

- companies whose annual reports are inconsistent in material respects with the annual reports filed on Form 10-K with the Commission;
- companies which issue flashy and detailed annual reports for good years, but which issue sparse annual reports containing limited information for bad years; and
- companies which consistently present little meaningful information regarding their operations other than the basic financial information previously required by the Commission.

Because of the recurring frequency of these situations, the Commission felt it appropriate to adopt rules embodying the good reporting practices so that all companies subject to the proxy rules would be required to disclose certain basic information regarding their business, management, operations, and financial position.

In adopting these requirements, we have attempted to permit management as much latitude as possible in communicating effectively with its shareholders. For example, the rules are quite clear that the annual report may be in any form deemed suitable by management and that the required disclosures may even be presented in an appendix or separate section of the annual report. A note has been included in the rules encouraging the use of tables, charts, and graphic illustrations to present financial information in an understandable manner so long as the presentation is consistent with the underlying financial data.

As an administrative policy, the Commission's staff, which is available for assistance in this area, will be interpreting the new requirements liberally during this first proxy season, which will serve as a shake-out period for the new rules.

Lest I lull you into thinking that "anything goes" for the 1974 annual reports, I should mention briefly the applicability of the antifraud provisions of the Securities Exchange Act. The recent amendments have not changed the legal status of annual reports. While these reports are not "filed" documents under the Exchange Act and are not ordinarily soliciting material under the proxy rules, so that annual reports to shareholders are not subject to Section 18 of the Exchange Act, they continue to be subject to the broader antifraud provisions of Rule 10b-5.

FUTURE CONCERNS

As to the future, I think there is a strong temptation to utilize the annual report for a multiplicity of purposes. For example, during Senator Metcalf's and Muskie's hearings on corporate disclosure in May 1974, it was suggested that the annual report would be a suitable vehicle for disclosing all corporate affiliations of officers and directors, the 30 largest shareholders, all control relationships, including any management contracts with other companies, all debt obligations and environmental responsibilities, and litigation. The Commission probably will focus its attention in these areas on the Form 10-K requirements rather than imposing additional rules on annual reports.

During this coming year, the Commission's staff will be issuing interpretative letters on, and making any necessary recommendation for technical changes to, the recent amendments, but I doubt the Commission will substantively amend the annual report rules, with the possible exception of requiring additional liquidity and working capital disclosures in annual reports, if objective standards can be developed in that area.

During the past three months the Commission's staff has conducted a public fact-finding investigation *In the Matter of Beneficial Ownership, Takeovers and Acquisitions by Foreign and Domestic Persons.* One of the specific inquiries of that proceeding was whether the Commission should adopt rules to facilitate communications between issuers and the beneficial owners of their securities. Based on the testimony during the hearing and the written comments on that inquiry, it appears necessary for the Commission to take some direct or indirect action to improve the distribution of annual reports to the beneficial owners who hold their securities in nominee accounts or street names.

And something more may be expected with regard to disclosure of stock, and perhaps long-term debt, ownership. We are, of course, well acquainted with the futility of simply requiring more disclosure of record ownership, and any meaningful solution may well require legislation, but the pressure for more information on corporate ownership and control is growing.

The desire of corporate management for direct communication with its security holders and the desire of others to smoke out informal affiliations and control are now joined by a widespread desire for at least the identification of foreign involvement. How this will work out I cannot say at this time.

As to the last of these, the Departments of Commerce and Treasury are presently engaged in a two-year study of all foreign ownership of American business. Perhaps some device usable for corporate disclosure purposes will come from this, although we can expect legislation to be proposed in this Congress for restrictions on foreign ownership without awaiting the results of the study. Similar bills in the last Congress did not receive much support, but it may be different this time.

ETHICALLY SPEAKING

When environmental and equal employment matters became of such widespread concern, the Commission's eventual response was to require disclosures in these areas largely to the extent that the company had problems that might materially affect its earnings. The ethical investor, it is urged, wants to know if the company is behaving badly in these respects, whether or not its earnings appear to be threatened.

Who are these ethical investors, and are they entitled to such consideration? I suppose anyone can be an ethical investor, but the outspoken and self-styled ones seem to be universities or other educational endowment funds, certain church funds, some pension funds, public interest groups (who may not, in fact, be investors except in a nominal sense), and several new investment companies set up to invest only in companies whose activities meet a set of prescribed ethical standards. Of course, there has always been some of this. All investors have never been pure "economic" men. Church funds have avoided investments in tobacco and liquor companies, and so on. But the degree of concern today may be sufficiently increased to make it a new problem.

But the Commission has not been solely concerned with the economic investor. At least we have required, and do require, some disclosures where the dollar amount is insignificant so that the requirement must be based on something else, whether or not that something else is clearly articulated by us. Indeed, this additional rationale for compulsory disclosure has been around from the beginning.

Everyone is no doubt familiar, perhaps too familiar, with Justice Brandeis's oft-quoted dictum about sunshine being the best disinfectant, and it is true that disclosure may deter certain questionable business transactions from occurring. I doubt that there is anyone left today who questions that basic utility of disclosure. After all, the practical alternative may well be substantive federal regulation of corporate business transactions that the authors of the federal securities laws thought ought primarily to reside with the states. And I am inclined to agree.

As a recent example of this basis for disclosure, the Commission has no direct substantive responsibility to police the federal campaign contribution laws. Nevertheless, we have brought suit against a number of companies, and are investigating a fair number of other companies, concerning their failure to disclose possible violations of these critical federal statutes. In all cases of which we are aware thus far, companies that have engaged in unlawful conduct have generally failed to disclose their conduct, which we think is material, for obvious reasons. The amounts of money involved are, as a general matter, insignificant from the company's point of view. And, in terms of practical benefit to shareholders, the money may have been well spent. Why, then, require disclosure?

It is possible to relate such disclosures to the concerns of the purely economic investors. It may affect earnings if the president is sent to jail. It may affect the quality of earnings if they are dependent to any significant extent on illegal expenditures. If a company can prosper at its present business only by successfully bribing the local fire inspector, or what have you, that information is material to even the most heartless and amoral investor. But, in bringing our cases, we have not attempted to base the need for disclosure on any such analysis. We simply think reasonable investors want to know if management is making illegal political contributions, and we think the need for disclosure will discourage these contributions.

WHERE DO WE GO FROM HERE?

But how far should we go down this road? Illegal political contributions seem obvious and of much current concern. Perhaps the same rationale should apply to any clearly illegal conduct. At least there we have a reasonably concrete standard, although so many things can be illegal in a technical sense that some notion of "material" illegality seems necessary. I shouldn't think, for instance, that we should require a trucking company to disclose that its drivers regularly exceed the 55-miles-per-hour speed limit. (Maybe that's a poor example inasmuch as such disclosure would be mere surplusage, but you get the point.)

But, even if material illegality is a workable concept, what about "material unethicalness"? Is this workable at all? Of course, the present controversy over environmental and equal opportunity matters also involves putative illegality, but its supporters argue for the ethical investor who, I presume, has higher standards than mere illegality. He might, for instance, be concerned with doing business in South Africa. The trouble is that he may be concerned as well with a lot of other things, many of which might be unexpected and idiosyncratic. Dollars and serious criminal conduct we can all understand. What is ethical for modern business is something else. I know people who seem to think it's unethical to make a profit or even to want to.

We have a further quandary whether exposure of material undesirable corporate conduct is sufficient. Let me give you an example.

The whole trend involved with companies desiring to "go private" raises a question about the fairness of the transaction to minority shareholders. If a company fully discloses to its shareholders how unfair a particular transaction may be, and that the transaction is being entered into solely for the benefit of the insiders of the company, should the Commission be content simply with full disclosure, particularly where the shareholders involved may not be in a position to prevent the transaction in question from occurring? At least one court has said that, if full disclosure is made, this is no concern of the federal government under our general antifraud powers, and there are many who agree with that proposition. But the court in question was a district court, and its opinion is presently on review by the Court of Appeals in New York.

To sum up, is it accomplishing all of the purposes of disclosure if we continue to employ a test of materiality limited solely to economic, and perhaps illegal matters? There are certainly numerous areas of corporate activity today that are not precisely unlawful, but are ethically or morally odoriferous. Yet this conduct may not adversely affect the economic well-being of the company. Worse, the conduct might actually enhance the corporation's status. Should the full disclosure concept be used to deter these kinds of activities? And, if so, can we adhere to the standard of materiality that we have employed so effectively for so long?

The difficulty is that, unless a careful balance is drawn, something the Commission tried to do when it last considered environmental disclosure proposals, our disclosure documents could really become unduly cumbersome and bloated. And, at some point, even if the Commission did want to assume responsibility for deterring unethical or immoral conduct, we would be forced to recognize that some corporate activities, however troublesome, are the substantive responsibility of either other federal agencies or of state governments and that, if appropriate and complete disclosure has been made, the Commission's role is, and should be, at an end.

I think we all share a deep concern for establishing confidence in American business management, not just to make money, important as that is, but to achieve socially desirable goals. And I don't need to remind you of the widespread disenchantment with, and even hostility toward, our present system of economic organization. The total process of rehabilitation involves much more than the federal securities laws, but it surely includes them. Corporate disclosure is an important part of the process, the importance of which is by no means limited to enabling individual investors to make simple buy or sell decisions. We are concerned with preserving our present economic structure as against the disastrous alternatives.

TWENTY-ONE

Regulation in America:
A Review Article

THOMAS K. McCRAW

Harvard University

McCraw examines the history of economic regulation in the United States. In his analysis, he considers several models of regulation — a public interest ideal, the capture thesis, and the role of self-preservation in policies developed by regulatory agencies.

With accelerating momentum over the last quarter century, the subject of economic regulation by state and federal commissions has undergone rigorous reinterpretation. Although the process of revision is far from mature, studies in each relevant discipline — history, political science, law, and especially economics — have begun to reshape the terms of discussion and to advance alternative models of regulatory behavior. In so doing, they have questioned not only some long-held views of business-government relations, but also associated themes such as the nature and results of Progressive and New Deal reforms, the wisdom and efficacy of planned interference with market forces, and the character of the American polity itself.

Certain difficulties still block the formation of a satisfactory new synthesis. For one thing, the scope of "regulation" defies precise definition, since every economic activity is regulated in some degree.[1] Commissions of various types exist in all fifty states and throughout the federal establishment, but some have little in common with others besides the presence of "board" or "commission" in their titles. Then, too, regulation properly conceived includes structurally different (commissionless) but functionally similar roles played by institutions like the Antitrust Division of the Department of Justice and the price support apparatus of the Department of Agriculture. It also includes intra-industry regulatory mechanisms such as trade associations, rate bureaus, and price leadership systems. This article will address only the commission aspects of regulation, beginning with two widely known but troublesome concepts or images: the "public interest" notion, and the recently dominant "capture" thesis. Some of the scholarship of regulation, and practically all of the journalism, converges on one or the other, or on some combination of the two.

PUBLIC INTEREST

The "public interest" seems an unusually vague construct, indefinable and analytically coun-

Reprinted from *Business History Review*, Vol. 69, No. 2 (Summer 1975), pp. 159–183, with permission. Copyright © 1975 by The President and Fellows of Harvard College.

terproductive. Part of the problem comes from its multiple meanings and evolving redefinitions over time. In the nineteenth century public interest enterprises had social overhead functions, such as banking, transportation, and several other industries later called "public utilities." Some of these enterprises combined great economic power with a propensity toward corruption, and they required regulation for the protection of potential victims. Others, notably railroads, tended toward "natural monopoly" and needed a surrogate for the lost discipline of the market. More recently, still other industries, such as broadcasting and air transport, appeared to need regulation as an escape from chaotic or destabilizing competition, which injured not only themselves, but the public as well.

American law reflected these economic premises. Beginning in the nineteenth century and culminating in the *Nebbia* decision of 1934, the law marked off certain types of enterprise as "affected with a public interest" and therefore subject to a strong application of the police power. But as society became more and more interdependent, and as consumer markets for standardized products became larger and larger, the number of industries logically "affected with a public interest" grew unmanageably large. As time passed, the public interest as an economic and legal notion had less and less utility, and became an unsatisfactory litmus test of why some industries in America are closely regulated and others are not.[2]

In the political sense, insofar as it can be distinct from the legal or economic one, public interest has been roughly analogous to such phrases as "public good," "common good," or "general welfare," expressing in the eighteenth and nineteenth centuries a conviction that the societal whole is greater than the sum of its parts, and by the mid-twentieth an intuition that consumer interests are more vital than they used to be. In political science, the notion is related to the theory of public goods, and also to pluralist thought, for which it serves as a point of departure.[3]

In a confusing amalgam of these usages, public interest is a thread of continuity at the heart of regulatory ideology, from its origins down to the present. The phrase "the public good," for example, appeared in the statute that created the first important regulatory tribunal, the Massachusetts Board of Railroad Commissioners, established in 1869 and dominated throughout its first decade by Charles Francis Adams, Jr. In commissions, Adams, like many others, detected "a new phase of representative government," made necessary by the unprecedented complexities of industrial technology. Commissions would take as their guide "the interest of the community," which informed regulators would harmonize with the interests of businesses. Unlike legislatures, the new agencies would sit continuously, investigating and deliberating within a universe of dispassionate expertise. Shunning turmoil, they would deal with industrial problems not as dramatic episodes, but as evolving processes calling for careful, meticulously considered responses. Statistics would replace emotions as the basis for action.[4]

For seven decades afterward, from the 1870s through the New Deal, state and federal commission regulation proliferated over railroads, gas and electric utilities, radio and television broadcasting, truck and air transport, and a few other enterprises. Although the reasons for regulation varied according to the industry involved, the notion of the public interest continued to dominate the rhetoric of reformers, the utterances of presidents, and the decisions of commissioners. It served as an ideological glue binding together the quasi-legislative, quasi-executive, quasi-judicial duties of regulators. In the 1930s, the doctrine reached its rhetorical zenith, a paradoxical result in view of the New Deal's frequent recognition of and assistance to private interest groups. Legislative draftsmen inserted the phrase repeatedly into the flood of regulatory law that created the Federal Communications Commission (FCC), the Securities and Exchange Commission (SEC), and the Civil Aeronautics Authority (now Board) (CAB). The public interest occurs a dozen times in the Communications Act, a dozen and a half in the Securities Exchange Act, and more than two dozen in the Civil Aeronautics Act, as a guide for regulators and as a justification for the immense discretionary powers those statutes bestowed.[5]

The New Deal also produced the outstanding theoretical elaboration of administrative regulation, written by James Macauley Landis, a draftsman of both the Securities Act and the Securities Exchange Act. Pupil and friend of Felix Frankfurter, commissioner of the Federal Trade Commission (FTC) and the SEC (and, later, dean of the Harvard Law School and member of the CAB), Landis was one of the brightest men of his time. In his Storrs Lectures at Yale, published in 1938 as *The Administrative Process,* he delivered the most eloquent celebration of commission regulation ever written. Recognizing the ambiguity of the public interest, Landis nonetheless affirmed the validity and efficacy of broad administrative discretion founded on that doctrine.[6]

THE "CAPTURE" IMAGE

Significantly, Landis devoted much of his analysis to a defense of regulation, for the idea had long since encountered critical attack. Deriving from many different sources and premises, this critique resolved into an alternative image of regulation at once more tough-minded, easily grasped, and above all more descriptive of what seemed to be going on within the regulatory agencies.

Early skeptics had questioned just how independent the regulatory machinery was likely to be, or should be. For one thing, the appointment of expert, nonpartisan regulators (or even bipartisan commissions) and their removal from the normal political process seemed a step toward elitism, away from the nation's democratic traditions. For another, genuine independence might be unsustainable against presidents or governors who wished to interfere with scientific deliberation, or thwart it through the appointment of cronies and hacks. Even more likely, considering what usually went on inside the lobbies of legislatures, regulated corporations could direct their potent economic influence as readily toward regulators as toward other public officials. These arguments, all related to experience as well as to deductive notions of "capture," persisted as a running debate throughout the Progressive Era. In 1925, President Calvin Coolidge symbolically crystallized the capture theme by appointing to the Federal Trade Commission a man (William E. Humphrey) who brought a 3–2 majority against what most old progressives conceived as the public interest. The ensuing despair brought loud protest, together with calls for the FTC's abolition from some of its erstwhile friends.[7]

The New Deal temporarily quieted criticism of this sort. Franklin D. Roosevelt appointed aggressive regulators like Landis and William O. Douglas, and attempted to undo history by firing Humphrey. Thus, during the thirties, intellectually respectable criticism of regulation came from other sources, many of them based on theoretical objections that it held to be "a headless fourth branch of government," unresponsive to executive leadership.

It was to this kind of attack, rooted more in political science than in evidence of sellout, that Landis replied when he wrote *The Administrative Process.*[8]

The capture idea persisted nevertheless. The New Deal's multiplication of regulatory agencies, together with its programs of assistance to specific interest groups, simply multiplied the fields available for capture. Over the next two decades, observers noted that the CAB and FCC in particular seemed to follow doctrines that equated the public interest with whatever the most powerful elements of the communications and airline industries wanted. By the 1950s, scholars such as Samuel P. Huntington and Louis L. Jaffe had begun to analyze the ties between regulator and regulated, and the inherent flaws in regulatory thought. In 1955, Marver H. Bernstein published a devastating book that synthesized into a coherent whole all the diverse objections that had gathered force since the New Deal. And in 1960, James M. Landis, in a stunning turnaround, catalogued the breakdown of the regulatory system he himself had celebrated twenty-two years before.[9]

By that time, the attack on regulation had become a staple of the broad re-evaluation of American institutions that began in the 1950s and reached maturity in the 1960s. Liberal reform as a whole underwent a searching critique and redefinition, its viability questioned by disillusioned analysts who looked beneath society's veneers and found the results of pluralist democracy ugly and repulsive. In a context of prolonged national crisis and self-examination, the regulatory agencies remained prime targets. By the late 1960s, a common assumption held that the commissions, like so many American institutions, had sold out, that they had suffered capture by regulated interests, that the public interest had become a tragic joke.

Detailed indictments quickly followed. Portraits of uniformly abysmal performance emerged from a series of immature, predictable, but incisive exposes published by the young associates of Ralph Nader. Less sensational but equally damning studies by other journalists and scholars suggested that however flawed the work of "Nader's Raiders" might be, their conclusions had merit. By the 1970s, the public interest as a credible standard for interpreting regulatory behavior had few defenders. In its place reigned the capture thesis, which was rapidly nearing the status of a truism, a cliche of both scholarship and popular perceptions. "If nearly a century of regulatory history tells us anything," observed economist Robert Heilbroner, "it is that the rules-making agencies of government are almost inevitably captured by the industries which they are established to control."[10]

HISTORIANS AND REGULATION

Over much of the literature of capture, one historian exerted a uniquely powerful influence. Gabriel Kolko anticipated the crest of the thesis in each of his two books on regulation, *The Triumph of Conservatism* (1963), and *Railroads and Regulation* (1965). In Kolko's models, argued a priori and buttressed by impressive new evidence of the sort conventionally esteemed by historians, capture inhered in the American polity, because of the centrality of capitalist power. Thus, wrote Kolko, railroad men themselves "were the most important single advocates of federal regulation from 1877 to 1916." From the beginning, "the Interstate Commerce Commission entered into a condition of dependency on the railroads, and the railroads quickly began relying on the Commission as a means of attaining their own ends." Even more startling, what was true of the railroads applied to American business in general: "Federal economic regulation was generally designed by the regulated interest to meet its own end, and not those of the public or the commonweal."[11]

Kolko's ideas failed to convince many of his colleagues. Some historians pointed out that he ignored contrary evidence and misunderstood basic economics; others argued that he fallaciously assumed a polarity between the public interest and private interests; still others asserted that even the selective evidence he did present, though useful, did not begin to sustain his thesis, in part because he often failed to distinguish what businessmen received from what they originally wanted.[12] Still, Kolko's books asked new, challenging questions, and neither the questions nor his evidence could be dismissed easily. Consequently, they became staples of graduate seminars and professional convention sessions. Activists enlisting in the causes of the 1960s found Kolko's the most usable of pasts. More important, his work influenced scholars in disciplines other than history. Here the attraction seemed to be neither the strength of evidence nor the conclusiveness of argument, but the distinctly theoretical approach. At bottom, Kolko's analysis was a straightforward deductive system, very like the deductive models of economists and sociologists. The Kolko model argued not only that capture inhered in the system from the outset, but also that the American political economy made the design and subsequent behavior of commissions inevitable, and therefore predictable. Such a theory had immense appeal, the more so because it seemed a uniquely clear explanation of contemporary experience. Nor was the appeal confined to Kolko's ideological allies on the Left. His insistence that competition in the American economy was increasing at the turn of the twentieth century, and his implicit ideal of a decentralized society attracted admiration from many quarters, notably the "Chicago school" of free market economists.[13]

As capture became first an alternative to public interest, then a cliche in its own right, questions arose about *its* validity. How could the Interstate Commerce Commission (ICC) be simultaneously the captive of railroad, truck, and barge transporters, when these industries had overlapping markets and were partial competitors? In what sense was the Federal Power Commission (FPC) the captive of the natural gas industry, whose field prices it regulated so stringently that production brought inadequate returns, leading to what critics called "regulation-induced shortages"?[14] How well did the capture thesis fit those few points of regulatory history where scholars had made detailed investigations?

Most of the existing histories pertain to railroad regulation alone, probably because it offers the richest source materials and the longest perspective for evaluation. In consequence, however, the aggregate portrait of regulation by historians is very narrow. Of eight book-length studies to appear since Lee Benson's pioneering *Merchants, Farmers, and Railroads,* all except three have concerned railroad regulation.

Benson's thesis, that "New York merchants constituted the single most important group behind the passage of the Interstate Commerce Act," seems in retrospect less convincing and less significant than the other points he established in arguing it. His vast body of evidence demonstrated that the movement for national railroad legislation was a many-faceted phenomenon that embraced agricultural, mercantile, and eventually railroad interests themselves. On this last point, a pivotal one for capture, Benson found the railroad men belated supporters who joined the movement because "it would have been fairly dangerous to attempt to cap it tight." As for the public interest, Benson portrayed the struggle as hardly "a victory by the 'people' over the 'corporations,'" but instead a fight over who would receive what proportion of the new wealth generated by the economic explosion of the period. Fundamentally, the origin of the ICC was a story of warring interest groups, no one of which represented the entire public or felt motivated by an ideology of the general welfare. Instead, economic men fought each other over the division of industrial spoils. Without regulation, the railroad magnates had the power to keep a disproportionate share for themselves, even during periods of instability within the industry. Benson's behavioral methodology, informed by pluralist theory from political science, cut through the rhetoric of the period, and in the process demonstrated the inadequacy of both public interest and capture as models of the origins of national railroad regulation.[15]

Studies by Gerald D. Nash, Edward A. Purcell, Jr., and K. Austin Kerr confirmed the pluralist implications of Benson's book, though Nash differed in his nomination of the leading interest group (Pennsylvania oil men in place of Benson's New York merchants), and Purcell argued that the very process of suggesting one leading proponent disguised the national consensus basic to the ICC's creation. Kerr carried the model of group interaction into the period of World War I, showing how external conditions favored first one interest, then the other, and especially how the growing potency of railroad brotherhoods injected a third major force into the old dualism of carriers versus shippers.[16]

These same point emerged in Albro Martin's *Enterprise Denied*. Yet Martin consistently viewed the struggle from the perspective of railroad executives and took rhetoric and ideology much more seriously. Evaluating congressional and ICC action between 1897 and 1917, Martin contended that railroad entrepreneurship was stunted by "archaic progressivism." He thus portrayed the era as a starving time for railroads, accompanied by a rise in the political fortunes of shippers, with whose cause midwestern legislators identified "reform." Though the book suffered from an untenable conclusion,[17] Martin exhibited an unusually sure sense of the ways in which businessmen made decisions. In effect, the book, together with a later article by Martin that clarified the controversy over pooling, totally inverted the thesis of Kolko's *Railroads and Regulation*. Whatever capture had occurred was the railroads by the ICC. Wherever Kolko had found "political capitalism" operating to the benefit of the industry, Martin discovered "archaic progressivism" undermining it. Where Kolko's implicit premise appeared to be the illegitimacy of the American polity, Martin's seemed to be the nonsense of regulatory meddling with a market system.[18]

Two state studies provided additional insight into early railroad politics, in its midwestern setting. These were George H. Miller's *Railroads and the Granger Laws* and Stanley P. Caine's *The Myth of a Progressive Reform*.[19] Miller's book, a model of careful scholarship, argued that although the so-called Granger legislation of the four upper-midwestern states in the 1870s may have had the support of farmers (some of whom were more or less "radical"), the laws derived more directly from the region's shippers. "When set against the background of previous rate law and policy," observed Miller, "the laws appear far less radical and in no sense agrarian."[20] In the Middle West, the railroad problem meant discriminatory rates, not general rate levels. It meant interstate and intercity rivalry as much as carriers versus shippers. The dilemma pressed hard: if regulation were too stringent, railroads might refuse to extend their services, or stop them altogether, cutting the umbilical lifelines of towns serving as trans-shipment points for agricultural commodities. Within such a context of total dependence, the public interest had a sharper, more self-evident substantive meaning than it had for other regions and other industries. As for capture, it was irrelevant to regulatory experience in the Granger states. The railroads fought commission regulation with every tool they possessed. When this effort failed, they often ignored the new laws, and when that policy proved unsatisfactory they turned to the courts for relief. Thus Miller's book again confirmed the group-struggle pattern of regulation. It also provided a valuable institutional approach to a question too little explored by historians — the transitions and continuities in nineteenth-century state economic policies from optimistic promotion to disillusioned regulation.[21]

In Stanley P. Caine's monograph on Wisconsin, the principal actor was Robert M. La Follette, who, as the state's governor from 1901 to 1906, attempted to add railroad regulation to his list of essential programs. As La Follette himself told the story in his autobiography, he managed to secure a genuinely progressive commission, which inaugurated an era of regulation in the public interest. Several historians accepted this version uncritically, but Caine did not. Instead, he argued that the alleged victory over corporate interests was an illusion; that the new law did not give the commission clear power to initiate rates, but made it a judicial institution of appeal from the decisions of railroad corporations. The new tribunal quickly assumed an accommodating posture, and the railroad men who had fought its creation grew to admire it. To Caine, this sequence indicated "a betrayal of reform ideals." The very title of his book, *The Myth of a Progressive Reform*, implied a normative judgment that the public interest had not been served.[22]

Although most regulatory histories pertained to railroads, three studies addressed other aspects of the subject. The best known of the three, Kolko's *The Triumph of Conservatism*, argues the same thesis as his *Railroads and Regulation*, substituting business in general for the railroads' role. The other two examine the early careers of the Federal Trade Commission and the Securities and Exchange Commission. The first to appear was G. Cullom Davis's article, "The Transformation of the Federal Trade Commission, 1914–1929." Davis found in the FTC the same sort of inconsistency within one agency that scholars of railroad regulation had collectively discovered among different railroad commissions. As the FTC struggled with its vague mandate during the Progressive Era, World War I, and the prosperity of the twenties, "unfair methods of competition in commerce" successively acquired different meanings for different groups. By the close of the commission's first decade, its early enemies had become champions, its early advocates new opponents. In Davis's scheme, the public interest alternated with capture depending on the identity of the commissioners, which in turn varied with the incumbent of the White House and ultimately with the mood of the nation. In effect, Davis found the commission, like Mr. Dooley's Supreme Court, following the election returns. The high court itself added to the FTC's woes by confining its discretionary powers to the narrowest of functions.[23]

Michael E Parrish's fine study, *Securities Regulation and the New Deal*, emphasized the intelligence and professionalism of the architects and early members of the Securities and Exchange Commission, but also noted the effects of concentrated industry pressure both on the shape of the legislation and on the policies of the SEC. Even during a national economic depression, when businessmen in general and securities dealers in particular were in extremely low repute, industry input could still have powerful impact. The SEC confronted entrenched economic arrangements that antedated the New Deal, and that were likely to be upset by an overturning of the exchange apparatus, with devastating effects not only on the guilty few but also on innocent multitudes of investors. The SEC negotiated a fine line between merely symbolic action on the one hand and overkill on the other, a policy that represented neither a rout of the villains nor a surrender to them, but "half a loaf." Considering the complex situation, this was a substantial achievement. It minimized the effects of private corruption on the national economy and "held the possibility of more orderly, enduring economic growth in the future."[24] Parrish detailed the financial community's utter hostility toward regulation, its near-willingness to hold national recovery hostage to its determination to avert reform. During the post-enactment period, the mutual reliance between industry and commission for information, the shifts back and forth of important personnel, were characteristics consistent with the possibility of capture, but not in themselves conclusive evidence.

Taken as a whole, historical writing offers few clear patterns of regulatory behavior, except that it demonstrates the inadequacy of either capture, the public interest, or the two in tandem as satisfactory models. Most historians have emphasized the political aspects of regulation, with the one common conclusion that regulatory politics involved in an intricate, complex struggle among intensely competitive interest groups, each using the machinery of the state whenever it could, to serve particularistic goals largely unrelated to public interest ideology except in the tactical sense.

ECONOMISTS AND REGULATION

A continuing problem for both scholars and reformers has been the elusiveness of hard evidence concerning regulation's actual effects. Unlike their corporate counterparts, commissions issue no profit-and-loss statements telling in an instant whether the quarter or year has been good or bad. No regulatory agency lists its common stock on traders'exchanges, where a rise or fall might indicate success or failure. Nor do most commissioners, like elective politicians, face voters at regular intervals for endorsement or rejection. Consequently, the new attention that economists gave to regulation in the 1960s and 1970s had prodigious significance. In these studies, a "bottom line" appeared, purporting to provide quantitative assessments of regulation's impact.

Economists had long been interested in the subject. Institutional economics supplied some of the intellectual foundations of the commission movement, and prominent scholars like John R. Commons, William Z. Ripley, Balthasar H. Meyer, and Rexford G. Tugwell sometimes wrote regulatory laws, served on commissions or commission staffs, and made regulation an academic subdiscipline. By the 1930s, however, institutionalism had begun to wane, and the subsequent triumph of Keynesianism and macroeconomics inevitably made regulation a less exciting topic, prosaic in comparison with the glamour of fiscal policy, growth economics, and "fine tuning."

The studies emerging in the 1960s and 1970s grew less out of the old institutional tradition than from the intellectual revival of price theory, whose methods in themselves raised questions about the pricing functions exercised by state utility commissions and by federal agencies such as the ICC, CAB, and Federal Power Commission. Adding a measure of ideology to the cold logic of price theory was the related work of scholars associated with the Chicago school, whose near-worship of the market as allocator of resources led to a distaste for that very interference with market forces that lay at the heart of the commission movement. Irrespective of premises Left or Right, the explicit test for most economists was the performance of an industry under regulation. The collective conclusion, much more decisive than those of the empirically oriented historians, held that regulation was an expensive failure. In a harsh summary verdict, one influential economist wrote in 1963: "What the regulatory commissions are trying to do is difficult to discover; what effect these commissions actually have is, to a large extent, unknown; when it can be discovered, it is often absurd."[25]

The ICC, the oldest federal commission, which had weathered innumerable storms and had by the 1930s attained a uniquely high reputation, was now found guilty of enormously costly errors. Its policies of minimum rate regulation, its reluctance to allow market forces to accept optimal modes for particular freights, its custodial preservation of obsolete services, were ill serving the industries concerned and making a mockery of the public interest. By the 1970s, "the immediate cost to the economy of such regulation-induced inefficiencies in surface freight transport is estimated at $4 billion to $10 billion a year."[26]

For airline regulation, the same dismal picture emerged. The Civil Aeronautics Board had prevented since its creation during the New Deal the entry of a single new trunk line carrier into the business. It had facilitated the rise of fares to unnecessarily high levels, preventing normal price competition and indirectly promoting useless and expensive types of competition, such as excessive flights, elaborate decors, massive media advertising, and extravagant inflight services. For the one important city-pair market not subject to CAB regulation, the intrastate Los Angeles–San Francisco route, normal business competition had cut the going rate nearly in half, suggesting what deregulation might accomplish elsewhere. In focusing its policies on other priorities, such as the promotion of new, technologically advanced aircraft, the subsidized extension of air service to small towns, and an apparent determination to maximize the size of the industry, the CAB had lost sight of the overall consumer interest.[27]

Price regulation of the natural gas industry by the Federal Power Commission brought similar inefficiencies, according to the leading student of this question.[28] In the first place, gas field production bore little resemblance to "natural monopoly," being instead diversified among numbers of relatively small producers. Regulation therefore lacked the logical foundation that supported early railroad commissions. Then too, the policies of the FPC tended to freeze prices during periods of sustained inflation, discouraging a proper market level of production, retarding the development of the industry, and diverting users to less economical sources of energy. By the 1970s, the policy had injured the entire economy, as the energy problem became acute and one important fuel source lay poorly developed because of regulatory constraint.

Within the states, public utility commissions seemed to pursue unwise policies toward the electric power industry. One influential hypothesis held that regulation had no serious effect at all.[29] In an equally challenging argument, two scholars theorized that utilities tend to overcapitalize, and consequently to operate at outputs other than the optimal. This excessive-capitalization theory encouraged a host of spinoff studies, and gave its originators a type of immortality by incorporating their names into the phenomenon they described: "the Averch-Johnson effect." Still other scholars discovered additional errors common to state utility commissions.[30]

Economists tended to be less critical of those commissions with few or no pricing powers, but they hardly ignored them altogether. Scattered throughout the literature were indictments of the Federal Communications Commission, the Securities and Exchange Commission, state insurance commissions, and others. Sometimes regulation itself was held to inhibit technological innovation, a grievous charge to lay at the door of a uniquely American institution.[31]

The distinctive contributions of the economists were their theoretically based methodology, their quantification of regulatory inefficiencies, and their ability to predict probable effects of hypothetical changes in commission policy. Partly because their inquiries were typically less holistic than those of the historians, they were better able to keep a rigorous focus, and to specify precisely what it was they were trying to show. On the other hand, they paid less attention to historical sequence and factual detail. Seldom did they attempt the kind of combined cultural and economic analysis so fruitful in the work of historians such as Ellis W. Hawley and Richard Hofstadter.[32]

A few economists did theorize about the entire regulatory process. One ambitious statement came from George J. Stigler, a leading member of the Chicago school, who propounded a rudimentary model of regulation from its origins, through enactment, and into operation. Unhappy with assumptions that the public interest emerged automatically from regulation, Stigler showed equal impatience with the capture thesis: "This criticism seems to me exactly as appropriate as a criticism of the Great Atlantic and Pacific Tea Company for selling groceries, or as a criticism of a politician for currying popular support." In some respects, Stigler's was the Kolko model updated. Whatever capture had occurred was not so much of the commissions as it was of prior political power, which expressed itself through the creation of a regulatory mechanism. The new apparatus did not necessarily take the form of a commission, but could be an import quota system or tariff schedule. The virtue of Stigler's argument was its recognition that the regulatory process goes beyond purely economic phenomena, that "the problem of regulation is the problem of discovering when and why an industry (or other group of like-minded people) is able to use the state for its purposes, or is singled out by the state to be used for alien purposes."[33]

REGULATION IN THE LITERATURE OF POLITICAL SCIENCE AND LAW

An appropriate source of answers to Stigler's question would appear to be political science and law. As was the case in economics, the contributions from scholars in each of these two disciplines outnumbered those of historians, a logical circumstance considering that regulation is barely a century old, that it remains controversial, and that the commissions' embrace of legislative, executive, and judicial roles within a single institution raised theoretical and practical issues of keen interest to lawyers and students of government.

Although the characteristic approaches of the two disciplines were not identical, each one emphasized matters of procedure, responsibility, and equity. Where the distinctive method of historians was empirical, and of economists a theory-oriented testing of market efficiency, that of political scientists and lawyers centered on due process, legitimacy, and reform. The resulting scholarship fell into two broad categories. The first included a number of quasi-histories, written within a generation of the establishment of particular commissions and directed toward prescriptions for improvement as well as toward analysis. A second category focused on elaborations or critiques of interest group politics in America and included books addressing the questions of public interest and capture. This second category fitted into the pluralist versus antipluralist debate within both political science and law.

Three books on the Federal Trade Commission typified the first group, the prescriptive quasi-histories. In *The Federal Trade Commission: A Study in Administrative Law and Procedure,*[34] Gerard C. Henderson, a practicing lawyer, found the early FTC insufficiently judicial in its proceedings, sometimes guilty of unfairness, and ready to dissipate its energies in cases involving no broad public concern. Some of the same suggestions appeared in another study of the FTC, published in 1932 by Thomas C. Blaisdell.[35] Anticipating much New Deal scholarship, Blaisdell found the commission's performance during the 1920s clearly unsatisfactory. The vague FTC Act implicitly identified competition *as* the public interest, on the apparent assumption that competition in all cases promoted socially desirable results. Such a premise Blaisdell found controverted by American economic history. "Means were confused with ends," he wrote, in a comment significant not only for the FTC but for other aspects of regulatory experience. Blaisdell contrasted the Federal Trade Commission's woes with the more successful record of the ICC, whose problems with the courts were resolved only through repeated action by Congress.[36] In still a third book on the FTC, former commissioner Nelson B. Gaskill identified some of the same problems, suggested a few new remedies, and, like both Henderson and Blaisdell, advanced the hope that intelligent trade regulation could be achieved, despite the FTC's manifest failures. The overriding need, wrote Gaskill, was a clear enunciation of policy, by both Congress and the commission.[37]

In 1962, Henry J. Friendly updated these views, in a brief but important book entitled *The Federal Administrative Agencies: The Need for Better Definition of Standards.* Ending with a prescriptive chapter typical of regulatory scholarship, Friendly sought salvation through the creation of "a body of substantive law." Delineating the ways in which procedural delay denied justice, Friendly showed how due process carried to extremes could actually thwart the public interest. Even so, he rejected the remedy of heavy reliance on presidential control over commissions recommended in the Landis report of 1960, and also in the extensive work of Emmette S. Redford, a leading figure among scholars of regulation within political science.[38] Displaying a faith in regulation consistent with the book's dedication to Felix Frankfurter, a pioneer of legal scholarship and teaching in the field, Friendly concluded with an affirmation: "The administrative agencies have become a vital part of the structure of American government. Nothing is accomplished by merely negative criticism or by petulant proposals to abolish them."[39]

Such feelings echoed the tradition of reform-oriented scholarship emblematic of the 1930s. In that decade I. Leo Sharfman completed his huge study, *The Interstate Commerce Commission,*[40] which comprises five thick books and remains the most exhaustive analysis of a commission yet written. Its conclusions tended to confirm the ICC's high reputation of the time. Also in the thirties, E. Pendleton Herring published a thoughtful analysis of several agencies, and a short prosopographical study of the careers of federal commissioners.[41] At the close of this productive decade of scholarship, Robert E. Cushman completed the broadest of the prescriptive quasi-histories, *The Independent Regulatory Commissions,* a massive study that grew out of Cushman's work on Franklin D. Roosevelt's Committee on Administrative Management.[42] Packed with suggestions for improvement, Cushman's book also contained a cross-national analysis of the American and British experiences in regulating business—a useful methodology mostly neglected since.

A landmark of regulation in the scholarship of political science was Marver H. Bernstein's book of 1955, *Regulating Business by Independent Commission*.[43] In a survey of the entire field, Bernstein weighed arguments for and against regulation and came down heavily on the negative side. Generalizing freely, the author propounded a "life cycle" theory, which held that commissions typically pass through successive phases, beginning with exuberant prosecution of mandate but ending with ossification and debility. In the area of documentation, the book left something to be desired, but Bernstein's arguments seemed so thoughtful, reasonable, and self-assured that they practically set the terms for the critical attack that followed in the 1960s.

This attack, as noted above, came largely from economists and from reformers like Nader's Raiders, who made heavy use of the economic literature and of the theories and arguments summarized by Bernstein. In political science, the analysis tended to become much broader, and to address issues of which regulation formed only a part. Especially noteworthy was the work of the critics of pluralism. Dismayed by the results of "broker-state" government in the New Deal pattern, unpersuaded by celebratory assurances from 1950s writers that countervailing pressures from diverse interest groups yielded a genuine public interest, these scholars detailed the distance between the aims of Progressive and New Deal reformers on the one hand, and the contemporary reality of American life on the other.

Three books both exemplified and influenced the antipluralist persuasion: Henry S. Kariel's *The Decline of American Pluralism*, Grant McConnell's *Private Power and American Democracy*, and Theodore J. Lowi's *The End of Liberalism*.[44] The three differed in many particulars but held unanimously that pluralist theory disguised the exploitation of public authority by private groups for private purposes. The public interest, far from emerging automatically from the intergroup struggle, was simply lost in the shuffle. Regulated industries were the clients of their commissions. The American Farm Bureau Federation, in alliance with other powerful groups, dictated policy to the Department of Agriculture. Big Labor won big gains for itself, but often ignored the rest of society. Meanwhile, the public interest led nobody's list of priorities.

Capture, in other words, applied not just to commissions but to the entire American polity. The system had degenerated from an original dream of constitutional democracy and the general welfare to a hopelessly fragmented melange of small, autonomous constituencies sensitive only to self-interest. The tragedy was that the government had lent its authority to these constituencies, piece by sovereign piece, and that the pluralist postulate of universal access to power had encountered the incontrovertible fact that such access depended on systematic, articulate, well-funded organization. Some groups could not meet these tests. Unorganized or, as in the case of the poor, unorganizable, they stayed out in the cold, away from the American banquet.[45]

The antipluralist indictment inspired a variety of responses, some of them holding that the legal order in the United States had always provided mechanisms to protect the weak and unorganized. As one scholar put it in 1972, "probably never before in our history has legal policy been so supportive of the rights of individuals and groups affected by administrative action to be heard and to influence the action taken." To some writers, the advent of public interest law—an institutional adaptation to some of the problems identified by the antipluralists—represented a hopeful sign that the existing system might yet work, given adequate funding for public interest lawyers.[46] Some of the most promising studies by legal scholars, such as those of Richard A. Posner, attempted to combine economic theory with jurisprudence, in order to establish first principles of regulation, whether of the commission variety or of the older market-common-law type.[47]

AN ASSESSMENT

The collective findings in history, economics, political science, and law have been sufficient to establish a few broad conclusions:

1. Neither public interest nor capture, nor the two in combination adequately characterize the American experience with regulation over the last century. Sometimes regulation materialized with the support or even initiative of the industry involved (as with broadcasting), sometimes with the reluctant assent (as with the ICC), and sometimes against the rigid opposition (as with the Granger commissions and the SEC). Commissions often came into existence with broad popular support, sometimes amid obvious public apathy, but never in the face of mass-based, articulate opposition.

2. Once established, commissions did respond readily to pressures from organized interest groups. Such groups included not only the regulated industry, but also the industry's market elements (shippers, for example, in the case of the ICC), and occasionally the industry's labor force. Whenever actual capture by one of these elements did occur, it followed patterns not peculiar to commissions but common to a whole range of bureaucratic interdependency between government agencies and organized interest groups, whether in labor, agriculture, defense, or other private interests able to use the power of the state for their own benefit.

3. Regulation in America has been a multifunctional pursuit, a circumstance that has offered scholars a choice, when they generalize about the regulatory process as a whole, between extreme caution on the one hand, and extreme likelihood of error on the other. Regulation is best understood as an institution capable of serving diverse, even contradictory ends, some economic, some political, some cultural. Regulatory experience over the last century suggests several major ends or functions:

a. the function of disclosure and publicity

b. the function of cartelization

c. the function of containing monopoly or oligopoly

d. the function of economic harmony among industries

e. the function of promotion or advocacy

f. the function of legitimizing parts of the capitalist order

g. the function of consumer protection

Obviously, such a list could be longer, or differently stated. The functions could overlap, as in early railroad regulation, when efforts to control rates through disclosure and publicity aimed at stabilization and economic harmony. More often than not, regulatory functions among different commissions, and sometimes even with the same agency, could conflict. The Civil Aeronautics Board, to take one example, has not succeeded in its efforts to promote orderly airline development and technologically advanced aircraft, while simultaneously trying to stabilize rates at levels attractive to travelers with modest incomes. In the broader sense, items (b) and (c) above proceed from conflicting premises concerning the efficacy of competition, reflecting not only different market imperatives of different industries, but also ideological splits within American society. The perennial conflict over competition underlies a large proportion of the controversy over regulation, including both the public interest and capture images of it.

Despite the danger of internal inconsistency, regulators have identified whichever function they wished to emphasize at the moment with the public interest. They could hardly have done otherwise. Almost nobody ever declares his hostility to the public interest. Yet such rhetoric could go beyond either symbol or cant. It could often signify an intelligent conviction that a particular policy would yield broad societal benefits. For scholars, the notion has little use as a static entity, but it may offer a helpful signal at those points where it visibly changes. Industries or societies in different stages of development need different things. The same industry or society, moving from one phase to another, fulfills or forgets old needs and acquires new ones. The public interest, therefore, however defined, cannot remain static, even within the mind of an individual. Time makes it dynamic; and historians specialize in change over time.

They have less experience, however, in other aspects of regulation equally essential to understanding: the structures, markets, and competitive characteristics of the industries involved. As the histories of railroad regulation suggest, a firm grasp of the "railroad problem" and the distinctive features of the industry — its high ratio of fixed to variable costs, its powerful tendency toward huge integrated systems — are indispensable to the study of attempts at its public control. If, as seems likely, the inherent nature of an industry is the most important single context in which regulators must operate, then the range of policies open to them has been narrower than many observers have hitherto believed.[48]

These problems indicate once more that regulation is so broad a topic that its proper study compels the use of methods from many disciplines. Besides those discussed — history, economics, political science, and law — another promising perspective might come from organizational theory.[49] Despite the vast literature on regulation, scholars still have only a vague idea of what went on inside the commissions, in the interplay of contending subgroups, the relationships among commissioners and career staff members, and especially the connections between regulatory policy and perceived bureaucratic imperatives. Like other organizations, commissions seldom followed paths that would diminish their own importance, but instead promoted policies that would insure their institutional survival and growth. The inconsistent patterns of regulatory behavior over the last hundred years may mean not only that regulation is a multifunctional undertaking, and that different industry structures governed regulators' options, but also that commissions' highest loyalties sometimes went neither to the public interest nor to the regulated industry, but to regulation itself. Regulation was their business, and they did not intend to close up shop.[50] In promoting regulation as a value in itself, they generated an independent social force whose cumulative influence over time may have been substantial, but which remains mostly unexplored by scholars.

Multiple approaches are therefore essential for the realization of the major dividend available from the study of regulation: the illumination of that shadowy zone where public and private endeavors met and merged, where regulator and regulated experienced a confusion of identity and assumed each other's roles. Seldom in American history did the goals of private groups form a perfect identity with those of the rest of society, but seldom a perfect antithesis, either. Instead, sets of goals overlapped, now finely, now amply. Within the zones of overlap, private groups plausibly claimed service to society, and capture coexisted in fleeting calm with public interest. Fleeting, because each zone suffered a double indeterminacy: who made the decisions, the public official or the businessman? And what were the precise boundaries of the zone? Constantly shifting from internal and external pressures, the zones formed arenas whose only permanent qualities were confusion, controversy, and uncertainty. Did a given action by a businessman or regulator denote the presence of public interest, or of capture? Did it deserve congratulation, or condemnation? Prize, or prosecution?

The theme is ancient, of course, a continuous thread of American history back at least to the time of Hamilton. Writing twenty years ago, Robert A. Lively described "the incorrigible willingness of American public officials to seek the public good through private negotiations," and offered as a leading exhibit the early corporate enterprises promoted by the states.[51] In this sense, capture and public interest derived from a single source, and have been intertwined ever since. The gradual obsolescence of the public purpose corporation, and the concurrent rise of modern industrial capitalism, set a context hospitable to the evolution of a regulatory system with as many private purposes as public, as many promotional functions as restrictive, and as much continuity with a recent past as divergence in a new age.

NOTES

1. Even public utility regulation raises definitional issues. See James W. McKie, "Regulation and the Free Market: The Problem of Boundaries," *Bell Journal of Economics and Management Science,* 1 (Spring 1970), 6–26.

2. On the "public interest" in American utility law, see Harry N. Scheiber, "The Road to *Munn:* Eminent Domain and the Concept of Public Purpose in the State Courts," *Perspectives in American History,* V (1971), 327–402. *Nebbia* v. *New York,* 291 U.S. 502 (1934). Most textbooks of public utility economics provide a summary of the evolution of "public interest" law; an example is Part I of Paul J. Garfield and Wallace F. Lovejoy, *Public Utility Economics* (Englewood Cliffs, N.J., 1964).

3. The concept is examined at length in Glendon Schubert, *The Public Interest* (Glencoe, Ill., 1960); Richard E. Flathman, *The Public Interest: An Essay Concerning the Normative Discourse of Politics* (New York, 1966); Carl J. Friedrich, ed., *The Public Interest* (Nomos V, New York, 1962); and Virginia Held, *The Public Interest and Individual Interests* (New York, 1970).

4. Massachusetts *Acts and Resolves,* 1869, Chapter 408, Section 4, p. 701; Charles Francis Adams, Jr., "Boston, I," *North American Review,* CVI (January 1868), 18, 25; Adams, "Railroad Inflation," *North American Review,* CVIII (January 1869), 158, 163–164.

5. A typical declaration of the principle came from Commissioner Joseph B. Eastman of the ICC, who wrote to his colleagues in 1931: "For a long time I have quarreled with the idea that in a complaint case involving freight rates this Commission is merely a jury to decide between the parties upon the basis of the particular facts which they happen to bring to our attention in that case. The Commission is much more than that; it is an expert tribunal with a definite responsibility for the railroad rate structure of the country and its proper adjustment in the general public interest." ICC Docket No. 22876, May 4, 1931, Eastman Papers, Robert Frost Library, Amherst College, Amherst, Massachusetts.

6. Landis, *The Administrative Process* (New Haven, Conn., 1938). On the public interest, see especially 51–52.

7. G. Cullom Davis, "The Transformation of the Federal Trade Commission, 1914–1929," *Mis-*

sissippi Valley Historical Review, XLIX (December 1962), 452 ff.

8. The Humphrey episode is examined in William E. Leuchtenburg, "The Case of the Contentious Commissioner: Humphrey's Executor v. U.S.," in Harold M. Hyman and Leonard W. Levy, eds., *Freedom and Reform: Essays in Honor of Henry Steele Commager* (New York, 1967), 276-312. The focus of Landis's attention is evident in *The Administrative Process,* 4.

9. Huntington, "The Marasmus of the ICC: The Commission, the Railroads, and the Public Interest," *Yale Law Journal,* LXI (April 1952), 467-509; Jaffe, "The Effective Limits of the Administrative Process: A Reevaluation," *Harvard Law Review,* LXVII (May 1954), 1105-1135; Bernstein, *Regulating Business by Independent Commission* (Princeton, N.J., 1955); Landis, *Report on Regulatory Agencies to the President-Elect* (U.S. Senate, Committee on the Judiciary, 86th Cong., 2d Sess., 1960).

10. Edward F. Cox, et al., *"The Nader Report" on the Federal Trade Commission* (New York, 1969); Robert Fellmeth, *The Interstate Commerce Omission* (New York, 1970); Mark J. Green, *The Closed Enterprise System* (New York, 1972); Green, ed., *The Monopoly Makers* (New York, 1973). Examples of additional critical literature include Louis M. Kohlmeier, Jr., *The Regulators: Watchdog Agencies and the Public Interest* (New York, 1969); and Paul W. Mac-Avoy, ed., *The Crisis of the Regulatory Commissions* (New York, 1970). The quotation is from Heilbroner, et al., *In the Name of Profit* (Garden City, N.Y., 1972), 239.

11. Kolko, *Railroads and Regulation 1877-1916* (Princeton, N.J., 1965), 3, 233; Kolko, *The Triumph of Conservatism: A Reinterpretation of American History, 1900-1916* (New York, 1963), 59.

12. A collection of Kolko criticism appears in Otis L. Graham, Jr., ed., *From Roosevelt to Roosevelt: American Politics and Diplomacy, 1901-1941* (New York, 1971), 70-109; see also Robert U. Harbeson, *"Railroads and Regulation, 1877-1916,* Conspiracy or Public Interest?" *Journal of Economic History,* XXVII (June 1967), 230-242.

13. Membership in the "Chicago school" is not a hard-and-fast category, but one important member is George J. Stigler (see note 33 below). Other Chicago-associated scholars apparently influenced by Kolko include Thomas G. Moore, *Freight Transportation Regulation: Surface Freight and the Interstate Commerce Commission* (Washington, D.C., 1972); and George W. Hilton, "The Consistency of the Interstate Commerce Act," *Journal of Law and Economics,* IX (October 1966), 87 ff.

14. This point is discussed briefly in James Q. Wilson, "The Dead Hand of Regulation," *The Public Interest,* XXV (Fall 1971), 46-49; on the FPC, see Paul W. MacAvoy, "The Regulation-Induced Shortage of Natural Gas," *Journal of Law and Economics,* XIV (April 1971), 167-199.

15. Benson, *Merchants, Farmers, and Railroads: Railroad Regulation and New York Politics, 1850-1887* (Cambridge, Mass., 1955), 212, 245. An earlier work that included substantial analysis of the nineteenth-century state commissions in one area was Edward Chase Kirkland, *Men, Cities and Transportation: A Study in New England History, 1820-1900* (2 vols., Cambridge, Mass., 1948). Benson's conclusion that railroad men supported regulation somewhat reluctantly was consistent with an earlier report by Thomas C. Cochran, in *Railroad Leaders 1845-1890: The Business Mind in Action* (Cambridge, Mass., 1953), 189-199.

16. Nash, "Origins of the Interstate Commerce Act of 1887," *Pennsylvania History,* XXIV (July 1957), 181-190; Purcell, "Ideas and Interests: Businessmen and the Interstate Commerce Act," *Journal of American History,* LIV (December 1967), 561-578; Kerr, *American Railroad Politics, 1914-1920* (Pittsburgh, 1968).

17. Martin, *Enterprise Denied: Origins of the Decline of American Railroads, 1897-1917* (New York, 1971). Martin concluded that the ICC's regulatory action in the decade following passage of the Hepburn Act (1906) induced a capital starvation that precipitated the secular decline of American railroads. The fallacy here was Martin's insufficient emphasis on a much stronger factor in the railroads' eclipse—the onset of severe intermodal competition, both for freight, from trucks, and for passengers, from interurban electrics, automobiles, and airlines.

18. Martin, *Enterprise Denied, passim*; Martin, "The Troubled Subject of Railroad Regulation in the Gilded Age — A Reappraisal," *Journal of American History*, LXI (September 1974), 339–371.

19. Miller, *Railroads and the Granger Laws* (Madison, Wis., 1971); Caine, *The Myth of a Progressive Reform: Railroad Regulation in Wisconsin 1903–1910* (Madison, Wis., 1970).

20. Miller, *Railroads and the Granger Laws*, ix.

21. The litigation over the Granger laws produced one of the landmark cases in public utility law, *Munn* v. *Illinois* [94 U.S. 113 (1877)], in which the opinion of Chief Justice Morrison R. Waite explicitly relied on the public interest doctrine in affirming the power of states to regulate enterprises that "stand in the very 'gateway of commerce' and take toll from all who pass." Miller's book provided an insightful new perspective on this decision, tying it to earlier state policies, as did Harry N. Scheiber in the article cited in note 2 above.

22. Caine, *The Myth of a Progressive Reform*, especially Chapter 10. Caine's analysis was strongest in clarifying the motives of La Follette and other principals, the legislative trade-offs that usually characterize regulatory statute making, and the policies of the new commission itself. Nowhere, however, did he show that rates in Wisconsin were too high, or that a substantial general decrease would have benefited the shippers or the public without unduly injuring the corporations. Instead he seemed to take this difficult question for granted.

23. Davis, "The Transformation of the Federal Trade Commission, 1914–1929," *Mississippi Valley Historical Review*, XLIX (December 1962), 437–455.

24. Parrish, *Securities Regulation and the New Deal* (New Haven, Conn., 1970), 219, 232. This book covered much of the same ground as Ralph F. De Bedts, *The New Deal's SEC: The Formative Years* (New York, 1964), but was better researched and more analytical.

25. Ronald H. Coase, "Comment," *American Economic Review*, LIV (May 1964), 194. The rapid rise of interest in regulation among economists may be traced through two relatively new journals, both devoted largely to regulatory topics: the *Journal of Law and Economics*, and the *Bell Journal of Economics and Management Science*. A third indication is the large project begun in the late 1960s by the Brookings Institution, which resulted in a number of books on regulation, many of which are cited below.

26. The quotation is from John R. Meyer and Alexander L. Morton, "A Better Way to Run the Railroads," *Harvard Business Review*, LII (July–August 1974), 143, citing an unpublished paper by Thomas G. Moore. Moore's views are elaborated also in a book that conveniently surveys the literature of its subject: *Freight Transportation Regulation: Surface Freight and the Interstate Commerce Commission* (Washington, D.C., 1972). Important studies include John R. Meyer, Merton J. Peck, John Stenason, and Charles Zwick, *The Economics of Competition in the Transportation Industries* (Cambridge, Mass., 1959); Ann F. Friedlaender, *The Dilemma of Freight Transport Regulation* (Washington, D.C., 1969); George Wilson, *Essays on Some Unsettled Questions in the Economics of Transportation* (Bloomington, Ind., 1962); Wilson, "The Effect of Rate Regulation on Resource Allocation in Transportation," *American Economic Review*, LIV (May 1964), 160–171; and Richard N. Farmer, "The Case for Unregulated Truck Transportation," *Journal of Farm Economics*, XLVI (May 1964), 398–409. An interesting attempt to apply theory to early railroad experience is Paul W. MacAvoy, *The Economic Effects of Regulation: The Trunk-Line Railroad Cartels and the Interstate Commerce Commission Before 1900* (Cambridge, Mass., 1965).

27. Richard E. Caves, *A Sir Transport and Its Regulators — An Industry Study* (Cambridge, Mass., 1962); William A. Jordan, *Airline Regulation in America: Effects and Imperfections* (Baltimore, 1970); George C. Eads, *The Local Service Air Line Experiment* (Washington, D.C., 1972); Theodore Keeler, "Airline Regulation and Market Performance," *Bell Journal of Economics and Management Science*, III (Autumn 1972), 399–424; George W. Douglas and James C. Miller III, *Economic Regulation of Domestic Air Transport: Theory and Policy* (Washington, D.C., 1974).

28. Paul W. MacAvoy, *Price Formation in Natural Gas Fields* (New Haven, Conn., 1962); Mac-Avoy, "The Effectiveness of the Federal Power Commission," *Bell Journal of Economics and Management Science,* I (Autumn 1970), 271–303; MacAvoy, "The Regulation-Induced Shortage of Natural Gas," *Journal of Law and Economics,* XIV (April 1971), 167–199.

29. George J. Stigler and Claire Friedland, "What Can Regulators Regulate? The Case of Electricity," *Journal of Law and Economics,* V (October 1962), 1–16; see also Harold Demsetz, "Why Regulate Utilities?" *Journal of Law and Economics,* XI (April 1968), 55–65. An enlightening discussion of the evolution of utility pricing theories is R. H. Coase, "The Theory of Public Utility Pricing and Its Application," *Bell Journal of Economics and Management Science,* I (Spring 1970), 113–128. Elaborations of this theme may be found in any of several standard textbooks on public utility economics, one of the best of which is Alfred E. Kahn, *The Economics of Regulation* (2 vols., New York, 1970, 1971).

30. Harvey Averch and L. L. Johnson, "Behavior of the Firm Under Regulatory Constraint," *American Economic Review,* LII (December 1962), 1053–1069; discussions of the "A–J effect" are summarized in William J. Baumol and Alvin K. Klevorick, "Input Choices and Rate-of-Return Regulation: An Overview of the Discussion," *Bell Journal of Economics and Management Science,* I (Autumn 1970), 162–190.

31. The following are examples of recent scholarship on these topics: on the FCC, Roger G. Noll, Merton J. Peck, and John J. McGowan, *Economic Aspects of Television Regulation* (Washington, D.C., 1973); R. H. Coase, "The Federal Communications Commission," *Journal of Law and Economics,* II (October 1959), 1–40; on technological aspects, William M. Capron, ed., *Technological Change in Regulated Industries* (Washington, D.C., 1971); on one aspect of SEC regulation, Jeffrey F. Jaffe, "The Effect of Regulation Changes on Insider Trading," *Bell Journal of Economics and Management Science,* V (Spring 1974), 93–121; on state insurance commissions, Paul L. Joskow, "Cartels, Competition and Regulation in the Property-Liability Insurance Industry," *Bell Journal of Economics and Management Science,* IV (Autumn 1973), 375–424.

32. Many of the institutions did approach problems in this way, as have a few more recent economists, such as J. K. Galbraith. For the historians, see, in particular, Hawley, *The New Deal and the Problem of Monopoly: A Study in Economic Ambivalence* (Princeton, N.J., 1966); and Hofstadter, "What Happened to the Antitrust Movement? Notes on the Evolution of an American Creed," in Earl F. Cheit, ed., *The Business Establishment* (New York, 1964), 113–151.

33. Stigler, "The Theory of Economic Regulation," *Bell Journal of Economics and Management Science,* II (Spring 1971), 3–21. See also Stigler, "The Process of Economic Regulation," *The Antitrust Bulletin,* XVII (Spring 1972), 207–235. A few other economists have attempted interdisciplinary approaches. See, for example, Roger G. Noll, "The Behavior of Regulatory Agencies," *Review of Social Economy,* XXIX (March 1971), 15–19; and Paul L. Joskow, "Pricing Decisions of Regulated Firms: A Behavioral Approach," *Bell Journal of Economics and Management Science,* IV (Spring 1973), 118–140.

34. New Haven, Conn., 1924.

35. Blaisdell, *The Federal Trade Commission: An Experiment in the Control of Business* (New York, 1932).

36. *Ibid.,* 293, 307. The comparison was made central in Carl McFarland, *Judicial Control of the Federal Trade Commission and the Interstate Commerce Commission 1920–1930* (Cambridge, Mass., 1933). Also on the important subject of judicial review of regulation, see Louis L. Jaffe, *Judicial Control of Administrative Action* (Boston, 1965); and Martin M. Shapiro, *The Supreme Court and Administrative Agencies* (New York, 1968).

37. Gaskill, *The Regulation of Competition* (New York, 1936). This book examined not only the FTC, but also the recently expired National Recovery Administration. It was a broadside more than a scholarly work.

38. Friendly, *The Federal Administrative Agencies: The Need for Better Definition of Standards*

(Cambridge, Mass., 1962). Friendly was a federal judge at the time. His book, heavily footnoted, provided a convenient guide to the legal literature on administrative procedure, a topic I have only touched on in this discussion. Representative of the voluminous publications of Emmette S. Redford are *Administration of National Economic Control* (New York, 1952); *American Government and the Economy* (New York, 1965); and *The Regulatory Process: With Illustrations from Commercial Aviation* (Austin, Texas, 1969).

39. Friendly, *The Federal Administrative Agencies*, 175; one example of the influence of Friendly's views may be found in William L. Cary (a former chairman of the SEC), *Politics and the Regulatory Agencies* (New York, 1967).

40. Sharfman, *The Interstate Commerce Commission: A Study in Administrative Law and Procedure* (4 vols. in 5, New York, 1931–1937). Sharfman was an economist, not a lawyer or political scientist. I have included his work in this section because it more closely resembles the work of the 1930s political scientists than that of recent economists.

41. Herring, *Public Administration and the Public Interest* (New York, 1936); Herring, *Federal Commissioners: A Study of Their Careers and Qualifications* (Cambridge, Mass., 1936).

42. Cushman, *The Independent Regulatory Commissions* (New York, 1941). The Committee, known popularly as the "Brownlow Committee," after its chairman, Louis Brownlow, was one of a long series of ad hoc groups studying regulation and organization in the federal establishment. Subsequent studies produced the Hoover Commission Report (numbers 1 and 2), the Landis Report, and the Ash Council Report.

43. Princeton, N.J., 1955. In the mid-1950s, there was nothing like a consensus on regulation within political science. Bernstein's views may be contrasted with those of Redford, *Administration of National Economic Control* (note 38 above), and of Robert E. Lane, *The Regulation of Businessmen* (New Haven, Conn., 1954). See also the uncritical quasi-history by James E. Anderson, *The Emergence of the Modern Regulatory State* (Washington, D.C., 1962).

44. In the order listed: Stanford, Cal., 1961; New York, 1966; and New York, 1969.

45. The solutions offered by the antipluralists varied, and in each book, the diagnosis seemed superior to the prescription. Lowi proposed a return to basic constitutional principles and the promotion of "juridicial democracy." McConnell suggested the strengthening of mechanisms that permitted the entire people to act as one. Invigoration of broad constituencies would limit the scope of capture, promote citizen participation, and give substantive content to the public interest.

46. Carl A. Auerbach, "Pluralism and the Administrative Process," *The Annals*, CD (March 1972), 1. On public interest lawyers, see Simon Lazarus, *The Genteel Populists* (New York, 1974), Chapter 10; Joseph C. Goulden, *The Superlawyers* (New York, 1972), Chapter 10; and Richard C. Leone, "Public Interest Advocacy and the Regulatory Process," *The Annals*, CD (March 1972), 46–58.

47. Posner, "Natural Monopoly and Its Regulation," *Stanford Law Review*, XXI (February 1969), 548–643; Posner, "Taxation by Regulation," *Bell Journal of Economics and Management Science*, II (Spring 1971), 22–50; Posner, *Economic Analysis of Law* (New York, 1973); Posner, "Theories of Economic Regulation," *Bell Journal of Economics and Management Science*, V (Autumn 1974), 335–358.

48. The logical starting place here is the work of Alfred D. Chandler, Jr., though it customarily deals less with regulated enterprises than with manufacturing. See, in particular, *Strategy and Structure: Chapters in the History of the Industrial Enterprise* (Cambridge, Mass., 1962); "The Structure of American Industry in the Twentieth Century: A Historical Overview," *Business History Review*, XLIII (Autumn 1969), 255–298; and Chandler, ed. and comp., *The Railroads: The Nation's First Big Business* (New York, 1965). See also Alfred S. Eichner, *The Emergence of Oligopoly: Sugar Refining as a Case Study* (Baltimore, 1969). A superior analysis of both the evolution of big business and of its historiography is Glenn Porter, *The Rise of Big Business 1860–1910* (New York, 1973), which emphasizes the capital-intensive nature of modern enterprise. A strong statement of the relationship between production process and industry structure appears

in Robert T. Averitt, *The Dual Economy: The Dynamics of American Industry Structure* (New York, 1968), Chapter 3.

49. Discussions of historians' application of organizational theory include Louis Galambos, "The Emerging Organizational Synthesis in Modern American History," *Business History Review,* XLIV (Autumn 1970), 279–290; James H. Soltow, "American Institutional Studies: Present Knowledge and Past Trends," *Journal of Economic History,* XXXI (March 1971), 87–105; and Robert D. Cuff, "American Historians and the 'Organizational Factor'" *Canadian Review of American Studies,* IV (Spring 1973), 19–31. Cuff's own *The War Industries Board* (Baltimore, 1973), is in many respects a model organizational study.

50. An early suggestion of "regulation-mindedness" appears in Louis L. Jaffe, "The Effective Limits of the Administrative Process: A Reevaluation," *Harvard Law Review,* LXVII (May 1954), 1113.

51. Lively, "The American System: A Review Article," *Business History Review,* XXIX (March 1955), 93.

TWENTY-TWO

Public (U.S.) Compared to Private (U.K.) Regulation of Corporate Financial Disclosure

GEORGE J. BENSTON

University of Rochester

The securities markets in the United States and United Kingdom have many similarities, but the U.S. market is publicly regulated and the U.K. market is privately regulated. In this article George J. Benston examines the differences between the two systems, concluding that the private system is preferable, primarily owing to excessive costs of disclosure in the public system.

Though the United States and the United Kingdom are dissimilar in many important respects, their security markets are rather alike. In both countries, almost instantaneous purchases can be made of securities representing claims on thousands of companies. The securities are owned and traded by a large number of individuals and institutions at prices that are made public. The companies whose securities are traded are required to publish financial statements that conform to legally required minimum standards of disclosure, and the accounting on which these statements are based is surprisingly similar. However, the United States relies on public regulation of financial disclosure (SEC); whereas, the United Kingdom relies on private regulation (the Stock Exchange). This article explores the differences, costs, and benefits of the two systems and concludes that, in many important respects, private regulation is preferable.

Though the U.S. Federal Securities Acts were modeled after the U.K Companies Acts (which predated them by almost a century), they are administered quite differently. In 1934, the United States established the Securities and Exchange Commission (SEC), giving it the authority to prepare and administer regulations governing the financial disclosure mandated by the Securities Act of 1933 and the Securities Exchange Act of 1934. In contrast, the U.K. Companies Acts (1948 and 1967) stand on their own in the sense that the specific disclosure required is given in the Acts rather than in regulations promulgated by the Department of Trade (DT). Although the DT has the power to investigate failures of directors to conform to the requirements of the Acts, particularly when such an investigation is requested by security holders, it serves primarily as a repository for the statements filed pur-

Reprinted from *The Accounting Review*, July 1976, pp. 483–498, with permission of the American Accounting Association.

suant to the Acts. However, in the United States, the SEC actively investigates situations that its staff believes may mislead investors and obtains stop-orders preventing trading in or issuance of the securities. It also reviews the financial statements files in accordance with the Securities Acts and rejects those which, in its opinion, do not conform to its regulations. This "screening" is particularly extensive with respect to prospectuses. In the United Kingdom, a somewhat similar function is performed by private regulatory agencies, i.e., by the Quotations Department of the (London) Stock Exchange[1] and the issuing houses (investment bankers and underwriters).[2] Before considering the costs and benefits of the regulatory systems, the scope of legally required corporate disclosure in each country is sketched.

THE SCOPE OF REGULATION OF CORPORATE FINANCIAL DISCLOSURE IN THE UNITED STATES AND THE UNITED KINGDOM

Unlike the U.K. Companies acts, the U.S. Securities Acts do not apply to all incorporated (limited liability) companies. Since 1966, the Securities Exchange Act of 1934 requires periodic reporting by all corporations that have more than $1 million in assets and a single class of equity securities that has more than 500 holders. In 1975, some 10,500 companies filed financial statements with the SEC (a number that has grown steadily over time). Of these, about 3500 were listed on registered stock exchanges. Additionally, the SEC registers prospectuses of all corporations who wish to offer securities to the public (except when the offering is entirely intrastate). In 1974, 2890 registration statements were declared effective (down from the high of 3712 in 1972).

The U.K. Companies Acts apply to all limited liability companies, whether widely held or not. In 1974, 598,000 companies not in liquidation were registered.[3] Of these, 15,500 were public companies, about 27 percent of which were listed on the (London) Stock Exchange. The prospectus requirements of the Companies Act 1948 apply to all new securities offered to the public. However, unlike the United States, which has a large over-the-counter market, such an offering usually is made in conjunction with obtaining a stock exchange listing. Also unlike the situation in the United States, prospectuses are not required for rights offerings or other issues that are in all respects similar to securities already listed. Furthermore, many instruments, such as interests in petroleum wells, limited partnership interests, and investment plans, are considered securities in the United States but not in the United Kingdom. Consequently, only about 120 prospectuses per year are issued in the United Kingdom (though the number varies widely).

The extensiveness of the regulations, and hence the cost of complying with them, reflects the regulatory structures adopted by the countries. The SEC, having been given the authority and responsibility of drawing up and enforcing disclosure regulations by Section 19(a) of the '33 Act and Section 13(b) of the '34 Act, at first delegated much of this task to the public accounting profession. In part because of this delegation, the accounting profession, primarily through the American Institute of Certified Public Accountants (AICPA) and the Financial Accounting Standards Board (FASB) and its predecessor committees, has adopted a large number of rules and suggestions for recording specific situations. On the other hand, the stock exchanges have adopted few additional rules governing financial statements, though before enactment of the Securities Acts they had established some reporting standards.

However, the SEC has become increasingly more active in assuming its regulatory responsibilities. Regulation S-X, supplemented by Accounting Series Releases (ASRs), which codifies the specific disclosure required of corporations subject to the Securities acts, increasingly is more detailed. Additional requirements are added and few, if any, are removed. As instances of poor or apparently fraudulent reporting by individual companies come to public attention, the SEC has assumed more control over public reporting by all subject corporations. For example, in 1967, the SEC extended its authority over annual reports to shareholders (Rule 14a–3), in part because of the revelation in 1962 that the Atlantic Research Corporation of America did not report a large loss in its annual report to shareholders, though it disclosed this information in its 10K report, which is available to the public. The SEC now requires that financial statements in annual reports must conform to those filed with the SEC or must contain a reconciliation or explanation of all such differences. Another example is the near failure of Penn-Central and the subsequent belief that more information about its short-term borrowings might have been useful. This led to the requirement that all corporations must report their compensating balance arrangements. Most recently, the Watergate revelations apparently have led the SEC into requiring disclosure of illegal campaign contributions and into "suggesting" disclosure of legal, though perhaps immoral, payments to foreign government officials.

In contrast, the U.K. Companies acts simply list the specific items that must be disclosed. Additionally, the statutes provide that financial statements shall "give a true and fair view" of the company's state of affairs and profit and loss (Companies Act 1948, Sec. 149[1]). This important phrase is not further defined nor is there recent case law that provides a definition. However, U.K. accountants generally understand it to require accounts that present a layman's definition of "a true and fair view" of specific circumstances, within the constraint that financial statements are not expected to report completely current realizable or other definitions of economic value.[4]

The DT is given the power to adapt the disclosure provisions of the Companies acts to the circumstances of individual companies (Companies Act 1948, Sec. 149). Though the DT also has the power to alter the Acts' financial disclosure requirements, it cannot render them more onerous (Companies Act 1948, Sec. 454[1]). Hence, the U.K. counterpart to the SEC has not extended, or rarely has even interpreted, the specific disclosure mandated by the Companies Acts.

The U.K. professional accountancy bodies have not been as active as their U.S. confreres in promulgating disclosure rules.[5] Regulation differences, in part, explain this relative lack of activity.[6] The U.K. statutes do not give anyone the authority to promulgate financial disclosure rules and procedures. Hence, unlike the SEC, the DT could not delegate this authority to the official accounting profession.

However, the (London) Stock Exchange has authority over companies whose securities are listed thereon. It has exercised this authority to promulgate disclosure rules, primarily for prospectuses. Since virtually all U.K. companies whose shares are traded publicly must be listed on the Exchange, its rules dominate. Its Quotations Bureau operates rather like the SEC in accepting or rejecting prospectuses before they can be issued to the public. In addition, the issuing houses (investment bankers and underwriters) exercise control over the contents of prospectuses, since public acceptance of a security depends importantly on the reputation of its sponsor. Consequently, most prospectuses include a statement by a generally well-known firm of chartered accountants (called reporting accountants) in addition to the statement of the company's auditor. The role of U.S. investment bankers and underwriters (with respect to financial disclosure) is negligible relative to that of their U.K. counterparts, since the SEC's regulations and prospectus registration procedures are so extensive and the Securities Act of 1933's provisions so encompassing that they dominate all others. Consequently, strict conformance with the law and regulations is required, leaving little room for deviations or extensions.

THE COSTS OF REGULATION IN THE UNITED STATES AND THE UNITED KINGDOM

The cost of financial disclosure regulation reflects, in large measure, the structures adopted by each country. The United States' disclosure regulations, codified in Regulation S-X and supplemented by ASRs, are much more detailed and explicit than those which face a U.K. company and accountant. An indication of this difference may be gathered from a comparison of the number of specific items required to be disclosed in each country. With respect to the balance sheet, Regulation S-X (as extended and amended) calls for more than sixty-five items compared to the thirty-nine required in the United Kingdom by the Companies Acts and the Stock Exchange.[7] In the income statement, the United States requires about fifty-three items compared to thirty-seven required in the United Kingdom. Regulation S-X and the instructions to the forms also specify rules for consolidating statements of a company and its subsidiaries, for disclosing contingent liabilities, etc. In addition, quarterly statements and monthly reports are required in the United States but not in the United Kingdom.[8] The recent adoption of ASR 177, which requires inclusion of quarterly data in annual reports certified by public accountants, probably will increase costs to clients considerably.

One important aspect of cost is the necessity of learning and following the disclosure regulations. Though comparative figures are not available, it is obvious that these direct costs are greater for the U.S. than for U.K. companies. This is particularly true for periodic reporting, which is much simpler in the United Kingdom.

Prospectuses are also more detailed and extensive in the United States; e.g., a prospectus in the United States (which must be printed at considerable cost because even a small error can be the basis of an expensive lawsuit) usually runs to 50 or more 7½ by 9" pages. In the United Kingdom, a legally required prospectus is, and must be, printed on one to two pages of two daily London newspapers. The prospectus provided to the public, though, may be longer at the option of the issuer.

A corollary is the indirect cost of delay and inconvenience in fulfilling the more complex, more highly structured U.S. administrative rules, particularly with respect to prospectuses. In the United Kingdom, an auditor can call the manager of the Quotations Department of the Stock Exchange; discuss a question about whether a requirement is met by a particular procedure or can be modified to meet a special circumstance; and get an answer often within the day or with a delay of no more than about three days if a decision is required of a panel of members. Generally, no more than a few days will elapse between the day a prospectus proof goes to the Quotations Department and the time of its acceptance for further proofing. Completion of the work necessary to comply with the comments of the department usually is achieved within one week.

The more complex and formal U.S. rules and procedures do not permit as much flexibility or speed. The SEC staff attempts to answer telephoned questions. However, conferences involving top officers of the company, senior auditors, and legal counsel with SEC officials are often needed. The time for clearance is longer—a median of 36 days in 1974 (down from 45 in 1973, possibly because of the greatly decreased number of filings).

In part, the greater U.S. costs of preparing acceptable prospectuses are due to the greater number of prospectuses that the SEC must process—some 3000 compared to about 120 processed by the Stock Exchange's Quotations Department. The greater number in the United States is not only a function of its considerably greater size, but it is also a function of the SEC's regulations. In the United States *all* issues of securities by companies, except private placements and intrastate offerings, must be registered. Unlike the prevailing rule in the United Kingdom, it matters not whether the security issued is in all respects similar to securities currently being traded and quoted on a stock exchange. In addition, U.K. law applies only to security issues by a company and by underwriters who are acting in a professional capacity. However, in the United States, secondary offerings are subject to the SEC's regulations. As a consequence of these differences, it is estimated that from one-half to two-thirds of all registration statements filed in the United States would not be required in the United Kingdom (Krauss, 1971, p. 64).

The larger number of activities regulated by the SEC, the greater complexity of its disclosure regulations, and the greater formality of its administrative procedures necessarily require a more extensive and expensive bureaucracy. For fiscal year 1975, the SEC expects to employ 2219 people and expend $43 million. It is difficult to compare these figures with those of the U.K. authorities, since both they and the SEC do more than process financial statements. Nevertheless, it does appear that the Quotation Department's (1972) complement of fifteen professionals and twenty-five assistants, typists, etc., is proportionately smaller than the number employed by the SEC. Thus, both the costs to companies and to society appear relatively lower under the U.K. system than under the U.S. system.

Proponents of the U.S. system, though, claim that its benefits more than offset its greater costs. These benefits are listed, described, and evaluated next.

DELINEATION AND EVALUATION OF THE PRESUMED BENEFITS FROM ADMINISTRATION BY AN ACTIVE PUBLIC REGULATORY AGENCY

Several benefits may be achieved by having an administrative agency, such as the SEC, actively regulate financial disclosure. The seven benefits outlined are not mutually exclusive nor are they exhaustive. However, they do give something of the "flavor" of the arguments for an agency such as the SEC. While they are not "authoritative," they appear to be more complete than the rationale generally found in the SEC's publications and in most textbooks and articles.

The following advantages are thought to flow from a continuing professional administrative agency such as the SEC: (1) adaptability, (2) professional implementation of the securities statutes and regulations, (3) less discriminatory application of the securities statutes, (4) an expert and public interest source of information for legislative changes, (5) uniformity with respect to the type and format of data disclosed, (6) improvement of the quality of information disclosed, and (7) protection of the small investor and prevention of fraud. Each "benefit" is described and analyzed in turn. In the analysis that follows, all of the evidence of which this author is aware is applied to the evaluation of the SEC's administration of the Securities Acts.[9] Unfortunately, except for studies of the reaction of security prices to published financial data and of the behavior of share prices, few "hard" empirical studies have been published. Consequently, this study is based more on reasoning and "hearsay" evidence than desired. Nevertheless, this evidence is, in general, sufficient for most of the questions considered.

First, an agency like the SEC is claimed to be *adaptive* in determining the specific disclosure presumably needed to meet the public's "legitimate" demand for information. The agency can propose new rules, receive the opinions of interested parties, interpret these opinions in the light of its experience and draft new disclosure rules and revise old rules to meet the present needs of investors. In contrast, disclosure required of U.K. companies is specified in the Companies Acts by Parliament. If a given requirement appears unneeded, ineffective, or inadequate, it generally is not changed except by the passage of a new or amended act.[10] Since passage of new legislation rarely occurs more often than each decade (in the past in the United Kingdom, at about twenty-year intervals), it appears that the Companies Acts lack the currency that can be achieved by the SEC.

However, the SEC's power to promulgate disclosure requirements also serves to reduce the adaptability of the Securities Acts. Because the SEC is given broad power to implement the disclosure provisions of the Securities Acts, it has been forced to specify detailed rules and regulations that necessarily apply to a wide variety of circumstances. At first, the addition of a rule or regulation or publication of an opinion may serve to adapt the law to specific circumstances. But later, circumstances change and the regulations remain. Even though the regulations no longer may be meaningful to a changed environment or to the circumstances of specific corporations, the Commission appears reluctant to eliminate or even to change them: at least, that is an inference one can draw from the fact that the SEC's regulations are almost never withdrawn or even changed except to increase their specificity or coverage. Once a regulation is adopted or a rule formally interpreted, the Commission's staff understandably is reluctant to waive a requirement to meet particular circumstances. If they do, they risk being accused later of favoritism or even bribery, should it occur that the petitioner misled them or proved, or appeared, guilty of fraudulent acts. Thus as time passes, the SEC's administration of the Securities Acts' disclosure requirements tends to become less adaptive to changed environments and individual situations.

A private regulatory agency, such as the (London) Stock Exchange, can in practice be more adaptive than the SEC since it need not, and in general does not, promulgate a detailed set of rules and regulations. It has the power to adapt reporting standards to the circumstances of individual corporations, since it is not prevented by law or established precedent from waiving or adding requirements. The Quotations Department also can answer questions and resolve problems more quickly than can the SEC's staff because it need not be as concerned with uninformed ex post criticism.

It should be noted, though, that the considerably greater number of prospectuses processed by the SEC compared to the Quotations Department necessitates more formal, and hence less flexible, procedures. It may be that were the U.K. financial market as great as is the U.S. market, the United Kingdom would tend to adopt similarly formal written rules and regulations.

Second, an active administrative agency can provide *professional implementation of the securities statutes and regulations.* The SEC is staffed with accountants, lawyers, and financial experts who specialize in administering the Securities Acts. Consequently, they are presumed to be much more competent to determine investors' needs and the costs of compliance by companies than are legislators. Few legislators are expert or even very knowledgeable about the securities markets, accounting principles and procedures, financial institutions, and the like. Nor do they come into regular contact with market participants and the day-to-day problems of investors, brokers, accountants, comptrollers, and others who are concerned with financial statements. In contrast, the staff and administrators of an agency such as the SEC are in daily contact with the parties who are affected by the securities legislation. Further, since the agency is charged with enforcing the law, it is assumed to be the best judge of how the regulations should be most effectively written. In particular, an SEC type of agency can "plug" a loophole in the regulations which allows an unscrupulous issuer of financial statements to mislead the public.

It does seem correct to conclude that the SEC provides professional implementation of the law. The agency is well staffed with lawyers and accountants. However, while many (if not most) of these professionals administer the law, they also serve an apprenticeship for private practice in which they will earn fees from clients for steering them through and around the law. For lawyers, in particular, a profession that deals entirely with the regulation of the securities industry has developed in the United States. The securities bar, as it is called, is perhaps unaware of the inherent self-interest of its position as drafters and interpreters of the securities laws whose complexity is the primary source of the bar's marketable expertise. This conflict and confusion of interest is intensified by the apprenticeship served in and constant dealings with a regulatory agency. As Manne (1974, pp. 94–95) describes it:

> *To be a leader of the securities bar, one must be on extremely friendly terms with important SEC staff members and even commissioners. Such a "social" position is not reached automatically by studying law-books. Rather, typically, it requires an apprenticeship at the Commission and then practice in one of the important corporate law firms. Then begins the gradual ascendancy through the committee structure of the American Bar Association or related organizations to the exalted position of "leading securities lawyer."*
>
> *If at any point along the way an individual begins to wonder out loud whether the whole system of regulation is actually in the public's interest, he will not appear to other leaders to have the stuff from which leadership is made. He may also find that he is less able to serve his clients well, since a continuing friendly relationship with the SEC staff is essential to that function. The circle will then be complete, for certainly one cannot be a leading securities lawyer without numerous or important clients.*

I believe that the extant empirical evidence (reviewed in Benston, 1976, Chapter 4) is consistent with the hypothesis that the multitude of rules and regulations, court cases, releases, journal articles, and conferences generated by the SEC and the securities bar have benefited investors only slightly, if at all. The bar, though, does appear to have benefited.

Third, an agency such as the SEC is thought to be less *discriminatory in its application of the securities statutes,* because it makes its rules, regulations, and rulings public and minimizes its informal dealings with registrants. An extensively detailed set of regulations and publications of opinions and rulings permits all companies and accountants to file the required documents without benefit of an "inside connection." In contrast, critics of the U.K. system (Stamp and Marky, 1970) charge that the more informal regulation by the Stock Exchange gives rise to an "old boy network" in which established public accounting firms and issuing houses have a decided advantage over others who are not acquainted personally with Stock Exchange officials. In addition, they claim that less information is available to the ordinary investor and poor performance by "members of the club" is covered up. While few, if any, such instances are cited by the critics, they claim that the limited disclosure required by the Exchange does not permit revelations that otherwise would occur.

A related advantage claimed for the U.S. system is that, because it is funded by Congress, it serves the general public rather than private persons or groups. A private agency, such as the (London) Stock Exchange, critics claim, rather will serve the Exchange members and related parties. Aside from possibly covering up these insiders' wrongdoings, a private agency may prevent outsiders from competing with its constituency.

Though there is little evidence of cover-ups or similar scandals in the United Kingdom, it does seem that Stock Exchange rules restrict the establishment of new companies. The Stock Exchange rarely permits a company to apply for listing unless it can show at least five years of successful operations. The Stock Exchange is also the only market in which shares can be traded publicly. In contrast, a new company in the United States is not restricted by the SEC from offering its shares to the public, regardless of its "track record." Indeed, the shorter its financial history, the less onerous are the SEC's prospectus requirements. This difference between the United States and the United Kingdom may be a consequence of the fact that the SEC's constituency is more diverse than is the Stock Exchange's, since several stock exchanges and over-the-counter stockbrokers and dealers vie for the public's business in the United States compared to the monopoly situation in the United Kingdom.

The Stock Exchange's limitation of new companies also may reflect the desire of all regulators, indeed, most persons, to reduce risks as well as costs to themselves and their constituency, *ceteris paribus*. Should a newly listed company fail, the Stock Exchange, established issuing houses, and accountants and listed companies will be damaged if the public loses investments in ventures that, in retrospect, appear to be fraudulent or to have been more risky than was expected. While the public and economy might benefit from investments in risky enterprises, established firms generally only lose. If the new ventures are successful, the newcomers provide unwanted competition to established firms and few gains to the Stock Exchange. If they are unsuccessful, investors may blame their losses on poor administration by Exchange officials.

However, the situation in the United States, while better for new companies, presents considerable difficulties to them as well. First, though the SEC's regulations and rulings are available to anyone who subscribes to a good reporting service, considerable professional expertise is required to interpret them and file properly the required statements.[11] This professional help necessarily is expensive, so much so that many smaller companies cannot afford to sell shares to the public unless they can qualify for the private placement or intrastate exemptions. Second, the SEC tends to reduce the risk of registrants' failing, as does the Stock Exchange, since it is criticized should companies fail but is not rewarded should they succeed. Consequently, it has interpreted the permitted exemptions of securities from registration to limit them severely; has extended its authority to require registration of ventures such as franchises and condominium apartments; has accepted only conservative and easily administered accounting procedures (such as requiring write-offs of goodwill and not permitting upward revaluations of assets); has tended to restrict diversity of permissible accounting procedures; has refused to accept for registration statements of corporations which appear to have inadequate working capital to operate successfully,[12] etc. Though many of these actions may benefit the public, they also tend to complicate the disclosure requirements, which makes access to securities markets more costly, particularly for small companies, and limits accounting for registrants to auditors (generally the large firms) who are expert in SEC practice. Thus the public regulatory agency may, in fact, be as discriminatory as private monopoly.

Fourth, the *expertise and public interest orientation of an SEC may be an invaluable source of information to legislators* in evaluating proposals to change the law. The agency can carry out studies requested by the legislature. Examples in the United States are the 1963 *Special Study of Securities Markets* and the 1972 *Study of Institutional Investors* requested by the Congress, and the 1969 SEC-initiated study of *Disclosure to Stockholders* (Wheat Report) prepared by the Commission. Since the agency is not supported directly by accountants (as are the American Institute of Certified Public Accountants and the Institute of Chartered Accountants in England and Wales), lawyers (as are the bar associations), brokers (as are the stock exchanges), or others, it presumably acts in the public interest. In effect, then, the agency may be thought of as a continuous Royal Commission.

This benefit, though, is of limited value because of the inherent self-interest of the securities bar and of the SEC as a regulatory agency. The more complex a law, the more work for lawyers and regulators. Though simplification and/or elimination of many disclosure requirements may result in a net benefit to investors, the SEC rarely conducts rigorous benefit-cost analyses. The Commission employs few professional economists and sponsors almost no economic research, despite the fact that the Securities Acts are based on presumed economic problems. Consequently, the economic effect of its regulations is measured rarely and economic analyses are not undertaken to determine whether the present regulations are beneficial, in some sense, or even effective.

Nor is the SEC necessarily concerned with the interests of the general public when their interests conflict with those of the analysts, public accountants, investment bankers, brokers, stock exchange officials, and others who constitute perhaps its most influential constituency. The general public might not want (in the sense of being willing to pay for) additional detailed disclosure, as evidenced by the relatively few requests by shareholders for 10-K Reports.[13] Since the public has no means of telling the SEC that less information is wanted (there being no market mechanism), the SEC tends to interpret the vocal demand by security analysts for "more" as the voice of the public. As a consequence, perhaps, the Commission tends to add disclosure requirements and rarely removes them, though it has this power.

In addition, the Commission tends to suggest legislative changes that only increase regulation on the assumption that additional regulation almost always is in the public interest. Thus, despite good intentions, the SEC cannot serve the legislature as an unbiased expert source of information as to what changes in the Securities Acts will best serve the public interest.

Fifth, the SEC can impose a *uniformity with respect to the type of data disclosed* by companies. Ambiguities in the interpretation of law and regulations can be reduced by means of decisions and opinions on accounting practices. This uniformity may reduce the cost of gathering and analyzing financial data.

It is questionable, though, that the benefits from detailed regulations exceed the costs thereof.[14] Nonadministered legislation, such as the Companies Acts, can provide analysts and other company data users with specialized data which can be processed as readily by a nonregulatory agency, such as the DT, as by an SEC.

Sixth, proponents of the U.S. system (such as Kripke, 1970) believe that the SEC also can *improve the quality of the financial data available to investors* by enforcing the maintenance of minimum standards with the threat of sanctions should the data be misleading. In addition to the extreme threat of criminal charges, these sanctions include court orders stopping the sale or trading of a security, injunctions against corporate officers and directors, and temporary suspension of, or barring from practice, public accountants who prepare misleading statements, are not independent, or conduct grossly inadequate audits.

Assuming that the "quality of information" is an operationally meaningful term, there is little evidence to support the belief that the SEC has improved the quality of information disclosed. Regulatory agencies, in general, tend to remove ambiguity and judgment to reduce their risk. As a consequence, the data reported are necessarily less useful to investors. As SEC Commissioner Sommers put it (before he became a commissioner) after reciting specific examples: "You could often predict with precision what a prospectus would say about various problems. There was always a consensus that conservatism was the safest course" (1973, p. 507). Schneider agrees, saying, "Historically, certain types of highly relevant information — which I will call 'soft' information — have been largely excluded from filings by the SEC" (1973, p. 506). He goes on to say, "Generally, filings are treated as insurance policies against liability, and all of the juicy soft information is disseminated through oral selling" (1973, p. 507). As Schneider says, the potential legal liability of accountants and others results in rigid conservatism and following the letter (though not the spirit) of the regulations and law. Accountants and managers appear concerned primarily with following the rules and regulations in a manner that will avoid lawsuits and problems with the SEC. Unfortunately, this approach also limits presentation of judgments that could be valuable to investors.

Last, because a public regulatory agency receives its support from the government, many believe it will be particularly concerned with *protecting the small investor and preventing fraud.* In addition, an agency that specializes in securities laws, such as the SEC, should be able to prosecute criminals and other wrongdoers more efficiently than ordinary police and legal officers. Security law specialists also should be better equipped to promulgate and enforce regulations and propose disclosure and other laws to counter new methods devised by swindlers to cheat the public.

This "service" of the SEC is considered by many to be the most important benefit derived from a public regulatory agency. Many, perhaps most, small investors see the SEC as their "ombudsman." Should they have a dispute with their brokers, not be able to get information from a company, think they were misinformed by a security salesman, etc., the SEC is there to help. The SEC assures them that their brokers execute their order at the best price, that insiders do not profit at their expense, etc. While many of these expectations no doubt are met, recent and past history indicates a considerable failure by the SEC to meet this obligation to the public.[15] However, these considerations are beyond the scope of this study which is limited to financial disclosure of corporations.

Considering fraud related to financial statements, it is difficult to determine whether the SEC has been a more effective "policeman" than a police fraud squad would have been. It is not useful to compare the record of the U.S. Justice Department (which works with the SEC, since the SEC can only recommend criminal prosecution) with that of the U.K. police fraud squad, since the commission of frauds is not known, only arrests for fraud. Nor can one even know the extent to which fraud was prevented because wrongdoers fear the SEC or the police fraud squad.

Nevertheless, it is clear that securities fraud is still a problem in the United States and does not appear to be nearly as much a problem in the United Kingdom. The SEC's Annual Report gives a very brief summary of the actions taken. Each year, several hundred companies and persons are investigated; stop-orders are issued preventing securities from being sold or traded when the financial statements of the companies involved appear materially misleading; and some thirty to fifty cases are referred to the Justice Department for criminal prosecution. While very few of these cases involve certified public accountants and financial statements, the impact of an SEC action of any kind upon an accountant, even a temporary suspension from practice, is great. Even the threat of such an action is powerful. Therefore, one cannot measure the SEC's effectiveness in preventing fraudulently prepared financial statements simply by counting the number of cases filed.

However, there were very few cases of fraudulently prepared financial statements before the Securities Acts were enacted.[16] Most security specialists believe that SEC prosecution has little effect on anyone who really is dishonest. In particular, a lawyer who worked for the SEC and the Justice Department said (in personal conversation, after recounting the cases he had worked on and the need for an agency like the SEC):

> *I must admit, the principal difference between now and the 1920s is that you need the help of a lawyer to commit a successful fraud. But it's still a good business. These people are almost never caught. If caught, they're almost never indicted. If indicted, they rarely are found guilty. If found guilty, they almost never are fined much or sent to jail. If sent to jail, they get out on parole in a few months or years at most and then are welcomed back to their country club in Westchester.*

While the SEC may reduce the amount of fraud, it may be that an individual investor's best defense is still caveat emptor. It is possible that the SEC has made the small investor too complacent about purchasing securities by giving him the impression that the "bad old days" no longer are with us. For as former SEC Chairman Garrett stated: "We have had cases of fraud and mismanagement and disregard of investor interests that rival anything known to the men of 1933 who set about to construct a system that would make the world safe for small investors" (1974, p. 9).

One other dysfunctional aspect of the SEC's role in preventing fraud should be mentioned. Law enforcement officers, in general, often tend to see prevention of crime and punishment of wrongdoers as more important than the presumption of innocence and protection of civil liberties. The courts and even the prosecuting attorneys act as a balance against the understandable bias of the police who, coming into direct contact with the consequences of crime, may become rather zealous concerning the need to punish criminals. Unfortunately, a public regulatory agency, such as the SEC, has the power of a policeman, prosecutor, and judge over an accountant, lawyer, or other professional who represents clients before it. When the client (company) wishes to offer a security to the public, the SEC also has almost total power over it, by delaying registration.

One prominent accountant, H. Kapnick, Chairman and Chief Executive of Arthur Andersen and Co., commented after members of his firm were found innocent of criminal fraud charges brought by the SEC:

> *Too often today, it appears that the SEC staff is wielding power to attempt to discipline and control accountants with utter disregard for the effect on the public interest at large. The SEC, more so perhaps than other government agencies, should understand that allegations made by it, even though unsubstantiated, are accepted as fact by a large portion of the public. The mere allegation carries more impact than the ultimate resolution of the allegation. In fact, even though certain accountants recently were found innocent of charges alleged by the SEC [Four Seasons trial], a senior officer of the SEC recently stated publicly that such accountants were not vindicated by the jury but that the jury found that there was reasonable doubt as to their "criminal conduct." If this attitude is right, how does a professional ever eliminate the unproven charges? No longer, it seems, is one deemed innocent until proven guilty! (Kapnick, 1974).*

Lawyers apparently have been more subject to possible abuses of power by the SEC. In a well-documented paper, M. H. Freedman, Dean of Hofstra University Law School, concluded:

> *In sum ... securities regulation is characterized by denial of the right to counsel, corruption of the independence of the Bar and of the traditional professional standards of lawyers' obligations to their clients, a police state system of investigations, and denial of a variety of other basic due process rights (Friedman, 1974, p. 288).[17]*

CONCLUSION

I believe that the U.S. regulatory system, with all its benefits and costs, evolved and will continue to evolve as a consequence of the establishment in 1934 of an active regulatory agency, the SEC. It is no criticism of the SEC (which most observers acknowledge to be as honest and efficient an agency as exists in Washington) to say that it strives to extend its authority beyond the statutes under which it was created; that it avoids risks, even though it imposes costs on others; and that it tends to serve those who support or who are likely to support it rather than the general public. Similar behavior is expected of any agency, public or private.

However, a public agency, unlike a private company or agency, cannot benefit from risks assumed — it can only lose. For example, consider a company that undertakes a risky research project. It may lose its investment, but if the project proves successful, it gains the benefits. However, if the SEC allows the company to publish subjective estimates of the value of the research, it risks public criticism if the estimates prove overoptimistic, but gains nothing should the estimates prove correct. Similarly, if a new company turns out to be a failure, in retrospect its prospectus may appear misleading, even fraudulent. Even though the prospectus states (in block letters), "these securities have not been approved or disapproved by the Securities and Exchange Commission nor has the Commission passed on the accuracy or adequacy of the prospectus," purchasers of the company's securities may blame the SEC for "passing" the registration. Therefore, it is not surprising that the SEC prohibits appraisals of assets, since these later may prove vastly incorrect; forbids estimates, since these cannot be "objectively" determined; and requires reporting of very detailed data and analyses by all companies, despite the relevance of these numbers to relatively few companies and situations. If even one fraud or scandal is prevented thereby, or if it occurs and the SEC is not blamed, to the agency the benefits exceed the costs since it does not assume the costs imposed on the general public, including the cost of not getting possibly useful information (such as valid appraisals and estimates).

It is also not surprising that the SEC attempts to expand its activities. Thus when specific items are added to the list of requirements by the SEC in response to specific situations, they rarely are removed, since they may serve some purpose or group. In a particular case, analysis of depreciation accounts might be helpful to an analyst. In another case, knowledge of the amount of specific intangible assets not yet written off may be valuable. An analyst might want to know the amount of the provision for doubtful accounts or royalties or advertising expenses or maintenance and repairs, etc. Addition of each requirement seems to place but a small burden on corporations and may yield some benefits. But, even after it is clear that the amount of the benefit is nonexistent or very small, the requirement for disclosure remains and is imposed on all registrants. Aside from the natural aversion of public regulatory agencies toward contracting their activities, the SEC must be concerned that it will drop a reporting requirement that someone later claims would have been useful in a specific case.

In seeking to expand its activities, the SEC must be cognizant of the fact that its budget is approved by the President and voted by Congress. Hence it must be concerned to serve those who approve the budget and to obtain a "good press." Therefore, it is not surprising that it has extended its authority over annual reports (most recently by requiring in 1974 that the reports contain five-year summaries of earnings, information about the business, disclosure of its principal occupation, and employer of each director and executive officer, etc.), has ruled that a complete 10-K report must be provided to shareholders free of charge upon request; and has been concerned publicly about corporate contributions to politicians and payments to overseas officials and persons. These actions apparently are popular with analysts and the general public, whose support the SEC needs, even though they might harm shareholders, whom the SEC is charged with protecting.

A private regulatory body, such as the (London) Stock Exchange, also acts to maximize its welfare. Thus it serves *its* constituency—the companies listed on the Exchange, issuing houses, brokers, bankers, and the major public accounting firms. Consequently, it is unlikely to require disclosure of superfluous or embarrassing information. And, as is discussed above, it tends to reduce its risk by excluding new, untried companies from listing. With respect to growth, since the Stock Exchange derives its budget from its members rather than from the government, its incentive to expand is restricted by the unwillingness of its constituents to pay for this expansion.

The issuing houses also serve as private regulatory agencies, as do the reporting accountants. In conjunction with the Stock Exchange's Quotations Department, they determine the content of prospectuses and the investigations of company data that underlie them. The issuing houses and reporting accountants have a very great incentive for ascertaining that the prospectuses they issue and sign are not fraudulent or misleading — protection of their reputations. The issuing house's reputation is a direct function of the after-issue performance of the companies it sponsors. Should subsequent events show that the prospectuses issued misstated the companies' economic position and prospects, the issuing houses will "pay" by losing public confidence. Similarly, the signatures of reporting accountants are valued in prospectuses because they are known to be independent, careful auditors. Should the public's faith turn out to have been misplaced, the auditors' perhaps most valuable asset, their reputations, may be lost or damaged seriously. Thus, though these private regulators may wish to protect their client from bad publicity, they may do so at the peril of their own fortunes.

In conclusion, the evidence reviewed provides very little reason to believe that the U.S. system gives the public greater benefits, on the whole, than does the U.K. system. The cost of the U.S. system, though, appears considerably greater. On balance then, there is little (if any) evidence that the disclosure regulations promulgated by the SEC provide a benefit, net of costs, to the public. Rather, the U.S. experience shows that once powers are granted to an active, regulatory agency, they almost never contract and almost always expand, regardless of their demonstrated lack of efficacy for solving problems or propensity to create new problems. Perhaps, though, the more formal, more explicitly codified, more regulated U.S. system is politically necessary for a large diverse country where there are relatively few restrictions (though considerable costs) on a company that wishes to sell its share to the public.

Consequently, were I asked, I would recommend that the United States move toward the U.K. system by reducing the authority and power of the SEC. The c⚫.cept of "disclosure" should be restated to make it clear that the SEC is primarily an agency to which corporations report what they have disclosed to shareholders and how they determined the numbers rather than an agency that determines what and how corporations must report to the public.

NOTES

1. There is only one stock exchange in the United Kingdom.

2. See Benston, 1976, Section 2.2.2, for a more detailed description.

3. See Benston, 1976, Chapter 2, for a more extensive discussion.

4. Based on interviews and a review of the literature.

5. As of December 1975, there are fifty-one Accounting Research Bulletins, thirty-one Accounting Principal Board Opinions and four statements, and twelve statements and six interpretations of the Financial Accounting Standards Board in the United States. In contrast, the U.K. Institute of Chartered Accountants in England and Wales issued fifteen Recommendations on Accounting Principles and the Accounting Standards Steering Committee has issued eleven Statements of Standard Accounting Practice, one of which is an amendment to another statement.

6. Professional, economic, and legal environmental differences between the United States and the United Kingdom also explain this phenomenon. These are analyzed in Benston, 1975.

7. The count of items is taken from Benston, 1976, Chapter 3, which lists the specific items re-

quired in each country. The counts reported are likely to be inexact because this listing was made for purposes of reference rather than for the present purpose.

8. See Kellogg and Poloway, 1971, and Rappaport, 1972, for annotated manuals of the SEC's disclosure requirements.

9. Evidence on the extent to which many of these benefits are achieved by administration of the U.S. Securities Acts is reviewed in Benston, 1976, Chapter 4. This evidence does not support the contention that the Securities Acts have increased significantly the reliability or usefulness of published financial statements. There is little evidence that financial statements published before passage of the Acts were more fraudulent or misleading than they are today or that, as a consequence of required disclosure, they are more useful to investors. But since one cannot ever be certain that some unmeasurable (or unmeasured) benefit does not flow from the SEC's administration of the Acts, it is necessary to analyze the arguments for an SEC type of agency.

10. Statutory Instruments are issued occasionally by the DT which clarify or extend (to a small degree) the Companies Acts.

11. The standard SEC accounting practice manuals contain 1217 (Rappaport, 1972) and 929 (Kellogg and Poloway, 1971) pages of outlined requirements and commentary. In addition, most large CPA firms maintain their own manuals to keep up with the changes (proposed and adopted) by the SEC in increasing numbers and complexity. Similar manuals do not exist in the United Kingdom, apparently because they are not necessary.

12. See Shefsky and Schwartz (1973) for an analysis of ASR 115.

13. A survey of fifty companies that included a notice in their 1973 annual reports advising shareholders that they could obtain a copy of Form 10-K on request revealed the following: (1) .16 of the companies' total number of investors requested the material; (2) in most cases, inclusion of the notice of availability of Form 10-K did not appear to have elicited favorable comment from shareholders or others; (3) there was no correlation between the percentage of shareholder requests and the size of the company or number of shareholders of a particular company ("Shareholders exhibit lack of interest in 10-K data," 1974).

14. See Benston, 1976, Chapter 4, for a review of evidence that supports this assertion.

15. Among the important instances that could be described are the failure of the SEC to prevent brokers from mishandling transfers and from maintaining inadequate capital and the SEC's past support of the stock exchanges' minimum commission schedules.

16. The evidence is reviewed in Benston, 1969.

17. Also see Guzzardi, 1974, for additional material.

REFERENCES

Benston, G. J., "The Effectiveness and Effects of the SEC's Accounting Disclosure Requirements," in Henry G. Manne, ed., *Economic Policy and the Regulation of Corporate Securities.* American Enterprise Institute for Public Policy Research, 1969, pp. 23–79.

_____, "Accounting Standards in the U.S. and the U.K.: Their Nature, Causes and Consequences," *Vanderbilt Law Review,* Vol. 28 (January 1975), pp. 235–268.

_____, *Corporate Financial Disclosure in the U.K. and the U.S.: A Comparison and Analysis.* Institute of Chartered Accountants in England and Wales; D. C. Heath, 1976, forthcoming.

Freedman, M. H., "A Civil Libertarian Looks at Securities Regulation," *Ohio State Law Journal,* Vol. 35 (November 1974), pp. 280–289.

Garrett, R., Jr., "New Directions in Professional Responsibility," *The Business Lawyer,* Vol. 29 (March 1974), pp. 7–13.

Guzzardi, W., Jr., "Those Zealous Cops on the Securities Beat," *Fortune* Vol. XC (December 1974), pp. 144–147, 192 ff.

Kapnick, H., "Concern or Crisis? The Deteriorating Relationship Between the SEC and the Accounting Profession Is Not in the Public Interest," *Executive New Briefs,* Vol. 2. Arthur Andersen and Co., April 1974.

Kellogg, H. L., and Poloway, *Accountants SEC Practice Manual.* Commerce Clearing House, 1971.

Krauss, R. L., "Securities Regulation in the United Kingdom: A Comparison with the United States," *Vanderbilt Journal of Transnational Law,* Vol. 5 (Winter 1971), pp. 49–132.

Kripke, H., "The SEC, the Accountants, Some Myths and Some Realities," *New York University Law Review,* Vol. 45 (December 1970), pp. 1151–1205.

Manne, H. G., "Economic Aspects of Required Disclosure Under Federal Securities Laws," in *Wall Street in Transmission: The Emerging System and Its Impact on the Economy.* University Press, 1974, Charles C. Moskowitz lectures, pp. 21–110.

Rappaport, L. H., *SEC Accounting Practice and Procedures,* Third Edition. Ronald Press, 1972.

Schneider, C. W., "Nits, Grits, and Soft Information in SEC Filings," *University of Pennsylvania Law Review,* Vol. 121 (1972), pp. 254–305.

"Shareholders Exhibit Lack of Interest in 10-K Data," *Journal of Accountancy,* Vol. 138 (November 1974), pp. 20, 22, 24.

Shefsky, L. E., and E. J. Schwartz, "Disclosure and Reporting Under SEC's ASR No. 115," *Journal of Accountancy,* Vol. 136 (September 1973), pp. 53–61.

Sommers, A. A., Jr., "New Approaches to Disclosure in Registered Security Offerings: A Panel Discussion," *The Business Lawyer,* Vol. 28 (January 1973), pp. 505–535.

Stamp, E., and C. Marley, *Accounting Principles and the City Code: The Case for Reform.* Butterworth, 1970.

TWENTY-THREE

The Significance
of the *Hochfelder* Decision

ALLEN KRAMER, LL.B.

General Counsel, Deloitte, Haskins & Sells

In this article the author examines the Supreme Court's ruling in the case of Ernst & Ernst v. Hochfelder *and the question of auditor liability under the 1934 Act. He discusses the significance of the decision and concludes that this case leaves uncertain the future of litigation in this area.*

The Supreme Court of the United States on March 30, 1976, handed down its decision on the case of *Ernst & Ernst* v. *Hochfelder.*[1] The decision is of considerable significance to everyone whose business or profession involves questions of federal securities law because it places an important limitation on the scope of civil liability for damages under Rule 10b-5 under the Securities Exchange Act of 1934.

The plaintiffs in the *Hochfelder* case had invested in a securities scheme perpetrated by the president of a brokerage firm. They had been brokerage clients of the firm and had received investment advice from the president. He advised each of them that he was able to offer an opportunity to invest in a so-called escrow which would yield a high rate of interest. He told them that the escrow fund would be used as the principal from which a small loan company would make loans at very high interest rates, but he was vague and secretive about the details. The plaintiffs sold securities through the firm to obtain cash to invest in the escrow. The cash was paid to the plaintiffs, who then drew their personal checks payable to the president for what they were told by him was investment in the escrow. He paid some interest from time to time on the purported escrow funds which for a number of years he made to appear to be legitimate investments although they were never in fact handled through the firm. In 1968 the president murdered his wife and committed suicide, leaving a suicide note which described the firm as being bankrupt because of his thefts and described the escrow as "spurious."

The Securities and Exchange Commission brought a receivership action against the firm in which it was held that there had been a violation by the president and by the firm of Rule 10b-5.[2] Ernst & Ernst had served as auditors for the firm throughout almost all the period during which the fraudulent transactions had occurred. The plaintiffs sued Ernst & Ernst on a theory of "negligent nonfeasance," claiming that they had been negligent in auditing the firm, thereby aiding and abetting the violations by the firm and its president of Rule 10b-5.

Reprinted from *The CPA Journal,* August 1976, pp. 11–14, with permission.

The alleged negligence consisted of the failure by Ernst & Ernst to detect and report an alleged lack of adequate internal accounting controls of the firm which resulted from its "mail rule." The mail rule was an office rule that all mail addressed to the president or to the firm was to be opened by no one other than him and, according to plaintiffs, was the key to the fraudulent scheme. They contended that adequate inquiry on the part of Ernst & Ernst would have led to discovery of the fraud and subsequent disclosure would have led to its prevention. The plaintiffs specifically disclaimed the existence of fraud or intentional misconduct by Ernst & Ernst.

The United States District Court for the Northern District of Illinois granted a motion by Ernst & Ernst for summary judgment and dismissed the action. The Court of Appeals for the Seventh District reversed, holding that one who breaches a duty of inquiry and disclosure owed another is liable in damages for aiding and abetting a third party's violation of Rule 10b-5 if the fraud would have been discovered but for the breach. There were genuine issues of fact as to whether Ernst & Ernst's failure to discover and comment upon the mail rule constituted a breach of its duties of inquiry and disclosure and whether inquiry and disclosure would have led to the discovery or prevention of the fraud.

Thereupon, in the words of the Supreme Court:

> *We granted certiorari to resolve the question whether a private cause of action for damages will lie under §10(b) and Rule 10b-5 in the absence of any allegation of "scienter"—intent to deceive, manipulate or defraud.... We conclude that it will not and therefore we reverse.*

THE SUPREME COURT'S REASONING

The Court's conclusion is based primarily on the language of Section 10(b) of the Securities Exchange Act of 1934, which provides as follows:

> *It shall be unlawful for any person, directly or indirectly by the use of any means or instrumentality of interstate commerce or of the mails, or of any facility of any national securities exchange....*
>
> *(b) To use or employ, in connection with the purchase or sale of any security registered on a national securities exchange or any security not so registered, any manipulative or deceptive device or contrivance in contravention of such rules and regulations as the Commission may prescribe as necessary or appropriate in the public interest or for the protection of investors.*

The opinion states that the words "manipulative," "device," and "contrivance" in the statute clearly show that it was the congressional intent to proscribe a type of conduct quite different from negligence, and the use of the word "manipulative" particularly connotes intentional or willful conduct designed to deceive or defraud investors by controlling or artificially affecting the price of securities.

It also points out that there are provisions of the Securities Act of 1933 in which a civil cause of action premised on negligent behavior is clearly recognized, such as Sections 11, 12(2), and 15. Furthermore, the structure of the 1934 Act and the 1933 Act does not support a contention that civil liability can be based on negligent action or inaction under Section

10(b) because it is not by its term expressly limited to willful, knowing, or purposeful conduct, unlike certain other sections, such as Section 9 of the 1934 Act. In fact, according to the Court, where Congress intended a cause of action based on negligent behavior, as in the sections of the 1933 Act mentioned above, it is expressly recognized.

Another argument made in the opinion is that each of the express civil remedies in the 1933 Act allowing recovery for negligent conduct — i.e., Sections 11, 12(2), and 15 — is subject to significant procedural restrictions not applicable under Section 10(b), and to allow actions premised on negligent wrongdoing to be brought under that section would nullify the effectiveness of the carefully drawn procedural restrictions on the express actions.

Arguably, portions of Rule 10b-5 itself could encompass both intentional and negligent behavior. However, since the rule was adopted by the Securities and Exchange Commission pursuant to the power granted to the Commission in Section 10(b), the scope of the rule cannot exceed the power so granted. An analysis of the legislative history of the statute was also advanced by the Court in support of its conclusion.

EVALUATION OF DECISION

In evaluating the *Hochfelder* decision, it is necessary to consider both what it does do and what it does not. The most important reason why it is significant is the obvious one — the Supreme Court held that Ernst & Ernst was not liable to the defrauded investors under Rule 10b-5 because, whether or not they had been negligent in their audit and whether or not they had any duty to the plaintiffs, they had no intent to deceive, manipulate, or defraud.

If the Court had come to the opposite conclusion and affirmed the decision of the Court of Appeals, the consequences for potential defendants in civil securities litigation, particularly under Rule 10b-5, would have been extremely unfortunate because the decision almost certainly would have inspired a large volume of securities litigation. Anyone who works in the securities field is aware of the proliferation in recent years of lawsuits in the federal courts by disappointed purchasers of securities. The suits have been not only against issuers and sellers but increasingly against other persons who have been brought in as defendants even though they had no direct connection with the securities transactions in question. Where allegedly false or misleading financial statements have been involved, accountants in particular have found themselves in this situation. The *Hochfelder* case is unusual in this respect only in that the plaintiffs did not base their claim on a contention that the financial statements were inadequate or incomplete but rather on the contention that Ernst & Ernst had not conducted a proper audit and, if they had, the fraud would have been discovered or prevented.

Before the *Hochfelder* decision a number of federal courts had held that negligence alone could be a basis for civil liability under Rule 10b-5, and while there was no absolute uniformity, in general the trend of decisions was to keep extending the boundaries of liability. The *Hochfelder* decision in the Court of Appeals is a good example. Viewing the situation with reasonable objectivity, it seems fair to say that it would be holding the defendants to an unusually high standard of conduct and subjecting them to an unusually harsh penalty to find for the plaintiffs, but the Court of Appeals did hold that there were genuine issues of fact that could have been resolved against the defendants after full evidentiary development at a trial, and two Justices of the Supreme Court were sufficiently persuaded by the arguments advanced by the plaintiffs to dissent from the majority opinion.

The *Hochfelder* decision will certainly make it less attractive to potential plaintiffs to institute actions under Rule 10b-5 which are based on negligence alone, but it certainly will not cause securities litigation to disappear. Among the actions that will not be directly affected by the decision are actions under the various sections of the Securities Act of 1933 and the Securities Exchange Act of 1934 that provide for civil liability, actions under Rule 10b-5 that are not based on negligence, and actions in the state courts.

One effect of the extension by lower federal courts in recent years of liability under Rule 10b-5 has been to make it more attractive in many cases for plaintiffs in securities cases to sue in the federal courts under the rule than to sue under applicable state laws. Under the Securities Exchange Act of 1934, the federal courts have exclusive jurisdiction of violations of any provision of the Act or any rule under the Act. For this reason, all 10b-5 cases must be brought in the federal courts. In this connection, it is interesting to note that a number of state securities laws contain a section which is almost identical in its language to Rule 10b-5. The source is the Uniform Securities Act, which has been adopted, with variations, in more than 30 states. The Uniform Securities Act itself contains another provision which is designed to assure that a violation of the section will not be made the basis for civil liability. In some states, however, this provision has not been adopted and in some there have been various other departures from the Uniform Securities Act, so in certain states civil liability could be based on a violation of the section. The *Hochfelder* decision is an interpretation of the federal law only and will not of itself be binding on any court as an interpretation of the law of any state. Therefore, where these state statutes are applicable and could lead to civil liability, there is nothing to prevent a court from concluding that they can be the basis for damages based on negligence of the defendants, even though they may not have had any intent to deceive, manipulate, or defraud. Similarly, the *Hochfelder* decision will not of itself control the result to be reached under state common law or other state statutes. It is too early to tell whether the *Hochfelder* decision will lead to an increase in the number of negligence-oriented civil securities suits brought under state law, but it is at least possible that it may.

The *Hochfelder* decision is significant also for another reason, namely, the indication it gives of the attitude of the Supreme Court toward securities fraud cases. In *Blue Chip Stamps* v. *Manor Drug Stores*,[3] decided in June 1975, the Supreme Court held that only a purchaser or seller of securities could maintain a private cause of action for damages for a violation of Rule 10b-5. One of the bases for the decision was the view expressed by the Court that it is desirable for a variety of reasons to limit vexatious litigation under Rule 10b-5 which is brought primarily for its nuisance value in the hope of inducing a settlement by the defendant. A similar rationale would appear to underlie the *Hochfelder* decision even though it is not stated in the opinion, and in any event the *Blue Chip* and *Hochfelder* decisions do indicate an approach by the Supreme Court to limit the bounds of civil liability under the federal securities law. This is decidedly contrary to the trend of the cases decided over the last 20 years, in which the concepts of civil liability were expanded to what in retrospect seems to be almost an incredible degree. From the point of view of potential defendants, it is to be hoped that the attitude of the Supreme Court will not be unnoticed by the federal courts and the securities bar.

SUBSTANTIAL QUESTIONS REMAIN

There are several questions left open by the *Hochfelder* decision that should be kept in mind. One that may be significant is that it does not consider and in fact expressly leaves open the question whether scienter is a necessary element in an action brought by the Securities and Exchange Commission for an injunction against violations of Section 10(b) and Rule 10b-5. There are several opinions of lower federal courts to the effect that negligence alone can be the basis for an injunction in a suit brought by the Commission even though it might not be the basis for damages for a private plaintiff in the same circumstances. Until the actual case is presented to a court, there is no way to know whether the *Hochfelder* decision would lead to the opposite conclusion, but the reasoning of the Supreme Court does seem equally applicable to injunctive proceedings.

The decision of the Court on the question of liability under Rule 10b-5 for negligence alone is not quite as all-encompassing as might have been hoped, because in a footnote to the opinion the Court expressly leaves open the question whether, in some circumstances, reckless behavior may be sufficient for civil liability under Rule 10b-5. The dictionary definition of the words "manipulative," "device," and "contrivance" in Section 10(b) is one of the bases for the decision. Unfortunately, the definition of "reckless" in Webster's *Third International Dictionary* may suggest to attorneys for potential plaintiffs a way to dampen if not avoid the effect of the *Hochfelder* decision. The definition is "lacking in caution...foolhardy, rash; careless, neglectful, thoughtless...irresponsible." In a proper case, at least until the matter is resolved by further decisions, it may be that an allegation in a complaint under Rule 10b-5 of recklessness on the part of the defendant will, to some extent, serve as a substitute for an allegation of intent to deceive, manipulate, or defraud. It is worth observing that there was no noticeable decline in civil securities litigation in courts in the Second Circuit after the Court of Appeals for that circuit in a 1973 opinion[4] reached substantially the same conclusion with respect to the scope of Rule 10b-5 as the Supreme Court did in the *Hochfelder* decision.

It may also be that it will be possible to avoid the effect of *Hochfelder* in some cases based on what is essentially negligent conduct on the part of the defendant by alleging routinely that there was intent to deceive, manipulate, or defraud on the part of the defendant. There are, however, provisions of the Federal Rules of Civil Procedure that should at least limit this alternative. Finally, as the Court points out in the *Hochfelder* decision, actions under certain sections of the 1933 Act and 1934 Act may be premised on negligence or even an entirely innocent mistake. None of these sections is as broad in its potential application as Rule 10b-5, but many actions that could be brought under Rule 10b-5 can be brought under one or more of these sections, without running into the limitations imposed by the *Hochfelder* decision.

NOTES

1. CCH Fed. Sec. L. Rep. § 95,479 (U.S. Sup. Ct. March 30, 1976).
2. Rule 10b-5. Employment of Manipulative and Deceptive Devices.

> *It shall be unlawful for any person, directly or indirectly, by the use of any means or instrumentality of interstate commerce, or of the mails, or of any facility of any national securities exchange,*

(a) to employ any device, scheme or artifice to defraud,

(b) to make any untrue statement of a material fact or to omit to state a material fact necessary in order to make the statements made, in the light of the circumstances under which they were made, not misleading, or

(c) to engage in any act, practice or course of business which operates or would operate as a fraud or deceit upon any person in connection with the purchase or sale of any security.

3. 421 U.S. 723 (1975).

4. *Lanza* v. *Drexel & Co.*, 479 F.2d 1277 (2d Cir. 1973).

TWENTY-FOUR

Economic Foundations of Stock Market Regulation

IRWIN FRIEND

University of Pennsylvania

Professor Friend discusses the effects of stock market regulation on the market and the economy as a whole. After considering the evidence he concludes on both economic and equity grounds that the market and the economy have benefited from regulation.

Before considering the economic impact of stock regulation in the United States, which has pioneered in this area, it is desirable to review briefly the general purposes of such regulation. The two basic aims of the original legislation—the Securities Act of 1933 and the Securities and Exchange Act of 1934—were: (1) protection of investors and (2) promotion of broader public interest as this interest is affected by trading in securities. The first aim has an equity orientation, and the second has an economic orientation because the public interest in the area of securities regulation relates largely to the impact of regulation on the economic performance of securities markets.

These two aims were to be achieved largely by policies designed: (1) to require full disclosure of material facts on securities sold in the primary and secondary markets; (2) to prevent manipulation of securities prices; (3) to curb unfair trading practices; (4) to maintain orderly and liquid markets; and (5) to control "excessive" use of credit. This listing is not intended to indicate mutually exclusive groups, since there can be broad overlapping. Similarly, while some of the specific policies followed are directed primarily to either an equity or an economic objective, others are directed to both. Some policies apply to the market for new issues, a number apply to the market for outstanding issues, and still others apply to both.

The period subsequent to the original legislation which set up the U.S. Securities and Exchange Commission (SEC) to implement these objectives and policies has seen that agency, both through new legislation and new regulations, greatly expand its powers and assume a much more active and direct role in the regulation of securities issuance and trading. This trend has culminated in the recently enacted Securities Act Amendments of 1975, which give the SEC substantial new powers to structure the central market system and, at the same time, represent another major move away from industry self-regulation.

Reprinted from *Journal of Contemporary Business,* Summer 1976, pp. 1–27, with permission.

The comments in this article will be directed first to the economic rationale of stock market regulation and second to the available evidence relating to the economic impact of such regulation. The attention here is confined largely to economic effects, though equity considerations are obviously also relevant. We shall not consider here several peripheral areas of securities regulation, e.g., mutual funds, holding companies, and the recent extension of corporate disclosure requirements to social policy issues.

Before considering the technical materials to follow, it is important to note that it is this author's belief that securities legislation in the United States has had, as a whole, a beneficial impact on the economy, totally apart from its effect in reducing inequities among different participants in the securities markets. This does not mean that the economic case for every major facet of securities legislation has been proved beyond doubt, but simply indicates that the economic case for some major facets is rather strong and that for other facets the case "for" seems to be stronger than the case "against."

It seems amusing that the most vociferous economic critics of securities legislation have taken the tack that the case for such legislation must rest on irrefutable evidence that it has benefited the economy, not that the evidence for should be stronger than the evidence against. We would argue further that even if this legislation, with due consideration given to the costs involved, were neutral in its effects on the economy, much of it would be desirable on equity grounds.

To summarize my own views as to the effectiveness of different facets of securities regulation, the evidence that fuller disclosure has benefited the market for new securities issues seems rather strong. The position that fuller disclosure has improved the market for outstanding issues seems more defensible on the basis of the available evidence than the position that it has not, though the case is not as strong as for new issues. The evaluation of the success of the policies designed to maintain orderly and liquid markets and to control "excessive" use of credit in the stock market is that they probably have done more economic good than harm, but, again, the case is not very strong. The economic rationale for some specific measures taken by the SEC to prevent manipulation of securities prices and to curb unfair trading practices might be questioned, without much empirical support either way, but such policies frequently can be justified on equity grounds. In the subsequent discussion of the available evidence relating to the economic impact of securities regulation, we shall present only selected highlights and refer to the literature for further support of the position taken here.

The second section of this article presents a discussion, in turn, of the ways in which the stock market might be expected, at least in theory, to impinge on the economy; the third section presents a discussion of the economic rationale for believing that stock market regulation would affect the market favorably; and the fourth section presents empirical evidence relating to the performance of such regulation in furthering its economic goals. Parts of these sections rely heavily on earlier studies, but we also introduce new material, including a brief discussion of some recent, relevant literature. While a wide variety of regulatory policies is covered, special attention is paid to securities disclosure. The reasons for this emphasis are that disclosure is probably the most basic mechanism of securities regulation and that disclosure is currently under attack not only by antiregulation elements in the academic and business communities, but also apparently by the new chairman of the U.S. Securities and Exchange Commission.

THEORY OF MARKET IMPACT ON ECONOMY

The stock market affects the functioning of the economy in two principal ways.[1] First, market developments may affect the national income through their influence on the aggregate propensities to consume, to save, and to invest. Second, even with a given level of saving and investment, market arrangements can affect the efficiency of the allocation of investment funds.

This article is concerned primarily with the second of these two potential influences, namely, the impact of the market on economic efficiency — the type of impact to which economists have directed most of their attention.

However, it might be noted here that economists have given inadequate consideration to the fact that a highly volatile stock market may decrease aggregate investment by increasing the cost of capital to business enterprises. It may also result in substantial swings in the level of consumption and, hence, income through an asset effect. Thus a less volatile stock market might stimulate a higher secular level of investment and less pronounced cyclical swings in the level of consumption and income. Presumably, since all available evidence suggests that people are risk-averse, their expected utility would be increased by smaller cyclical fluctuations, perhaps even if the average level of the national income were lowered somewhat in the process.

Concepts of Market Efficiency

Economic theorists have shown, by making assumptions they consider reasonable — including management acting in the stockholders' interests and the costless and immediate availability of all information to all investors — that a firm's output decisions under capital market equilibrium will be optimal for all its stockholders. It will also be optimal in the sense that in long-run equilibrium each firm will be operating at minimum average costs.[2] In such a world, the need for securities regulation would be nonexistent, but this, of course, is not the world in which we live. Even if it is assumed that management can be counted on through moral pressures, competition, or fear of legal consequences to act in the stockholders' interest, it makes little sense to assume that in the absence of appropriate regulation all relevant information will be made immediately available at no cost to stockholders or to the marketplace. As a result, it can be shown from theoretical considerations, that the public enactment of disclosure rules may well help to create a more efficient market.[3]

Perhaps the most common conception of an efficient market in recent studies of stock market phenomena is one in which every price fully reflects all the available information, so that any new relevant information is reflected in prices extremely rapidly and cannot be used to make abnormal returns.

However, there are a number of difficulties with this definition. First, the market, in some fashion, must reflect all available information. The important question is the relevance of the information to the subsequent earnings or riskiness of the stock. How is information to be distinguished from misinformation? Second, is a market in which prices fully reflect the scanty information available as efficient as a market in which much more information is available and reflected in stock prices? In other words, what is the justification for considering the information set fixed? Third, is the efficiency of the market independent of the costs incurred? It seems desirable to have two measures of efficiency, one measuring the quality of the service rendered (sometimes referred to as "allocational efficiency") and the other measuring its cost (or "operational efficiency"). Finally, even if the markets are efficient according to any reasonable definition, this would not ensure a flow of economic resources into the most productive real investment. However, efficient markets should ensure that the markets are providing the appropriate guidelines for the flow of capital.

For some purposes, it is desirable to break down allocational efficiency, to which economists have devoted most of their attention, between informational and production efficiency. The former refers to the correctness of information supplied by the marketplace and the latter refers to the correctness of decisions, made by management, based on the market information. Market efficiency also may be defined more narrowly to refer to exchange efficiency which relates to the adequacy of exchange arrangements in the market — i.e., the extent to which the exchange instruments which could be created to fulfill investor needs do, in fact, exist.

Another approach to appraising market efficiency has been to set up two standards: (1) the extent to which short-run fluctuations in price — i.e., those not matched by changes in equilibrium price, are eliminated or, alternatively, the extent to which transaction costs to the public are minimized; and (2) the success with which changes in equilibrium prices are anticipated.[4] The first standard may be considered to lead to an appropriate measure of the market's operational efficiency. For a given volume and quality of services, and for given factor costs, operational efficiency is an inverse function of underwriting and other flotation costs of new issues and transaction costs in public transfer of outstanding issues (including any relevant regulatory costs). The transaction costs in the transfer of outstanding issues from a public buyer to a public seller include not only two commissions but also either all or part of the bid-ask spread.

The second of these standards, which is addressed to the market's allocational efficiency, introduces all of the difficulties in defining and in attempting to measure equilibrium price.[5] Equilibrium price is apparently taken to represent the intersection of the investors' demand schedule for a security with the amount outstanding, no matter how temporary or ill-advised retrospectively the price turns out to be. Again, no consideration is given either to the market role of misinformation or to the adequacy of the information set.

Probably the most satisfactory way of evaluating the allocational efficiency of decisions made in the securities markets is to inquire about whether the outcomes are the best obtainable with the available information. It is also relevant to ask whether the information is the best that *could* have been made available at that time, with the costs involved reflected in the measurement of operational efficiency. The best outcomes would be obtained if the markets maintained equivalent rates of return and hence, equivalent costs of financing on comparable investments. This quality of the markets would help to ensure that funds are channeled from savers to those users who will apply them most profitably and that portfolio shifts can be made to the mutual advantage of different investors. The efficiency of this allocation process can be asserted in retrospect by the extent to which there are variations in market return and by the extent to which these variations can be explained by differentials in risk.

While it is not too difficult to obtain a retrospective view of allocational efficiency by analyzing returns and risks associated with different investments, it is virtually impossible to tell how the actual outcomes compare with the best possible obtainable outcomes at the time the decisions were made. Retrospective data permit an absolute appraisal of the optimality of outcomes only with the benefit of hindsight. Yet they do provide an indication of the departure of outcomes from ex post optimality. If ex ante measures of return and risk at the beginning of a period bear little relationship to ex post measures at the end of the period, the value of the ex ante magnitudes would be quite limited.

In spite of the deficiencies in reliance on retrospective data to supply an adequate measure of absolute market efficiency, they probably do provide a reasonably satisfactory index of relative market efficiency. This index can be used to analyze the impact of different financial developments and practices, including the impact of securities regulation.

ECONOMIC RATIONALE OF MARKET REGULATION

The economic justification for disclosure, which is perhaps the most basic mechanism of securities regulation, is the belief that the provision of information to prospective investors is a necessary condition for efficient markets.

> *With full disclosure we would expect less drastic shifts in estimates of expected profitability of a given issue as a result of the greater initial level of economic information (and, presumably, the reduction in the possibility of surprises from this source), a greater scope for scientific investment analysis, a diminished reliance on and use of rumors, and a reduction in the scale of manipulative practices.*[6]

Information is a basic ingredient for rational economic behavior. Therefore, we would expect improved disclosure to increase allocational efficiency. Though less important, it also might increase operational efficiency as a result of greater public knowledge concerning underwriting and other transaction costs and reduce private expenses of investigation. However, the provision of new information entails additional costs which may offset some or all of these operational savings. Most people also would regard disclosure as enhancing equity among different groups in the market.

The economic as well as noneconomic justifications of regulations designed to prevent the more flagrant types of manipulation of securities prices require little explanation. Theoretically, such regulations might be expected to improve both efficiency and equity in the capital markets. It also, perhaps, might improve general economic stability, even though empirical evidence is required to assess whether the benefits achieved are worth the costs. Restrictions on certain types of speculation to maintain orderly and liquid markets and limitations on the use of securities credit frequently are rationalized on similar grounds. However, the existence of economic benefits from such policies is not clear from theory alone and must depend on evidence. For example, it is easy enough to use theoretical considerations to "demonstrate" that under plausible conditions speculators, on the average, must stabilize stock prices as long as it is assumed that their activities do not affect the demand schedules of investors. This, however, is an heroic assumption and requires direct or indirect empirical verification.

ECONOMIC PERFORMANCE OF MARKET REGULATION[7]

Some of the most convincing evidence on the SEC's accomplishments in the markets for new and outstanding issues is provided in the Pecora hearings,[8] two other U.S. Government pre–World War II studies,[9] and the postwar SEC *Special Study*,[10] These sources document the massive securities abuses of the earlier period and the much healthier post-SEC experience and provide substantial reason for believing that the effects of disclosure and related aspects of securities legislation have been beneficial. Vast amounts of money demonstrably were lost in the pre-SEC period as a result of activities which have been reduced greatly by securities legislation. These amounts would appear to dwarf any reasonable estimate of the costs of such legislation.

Stock market pools, bucket shop operations, misuse of insider information, and other types of manipulation and fraud, which frequently relied on the deliberate use of misinformation and the absence of full disclosure, were widespread in the pre-SEC period and involved vast sums of money. Today, these abuses seem less prevalent. At the time, enormous losses were absorbed by the public in excessively leveraged, highly speculative, and frequently manipulated new issues of public utility holding companies, investment companies, and foreign bonds, each of which was sold under disclosure conditions bordering on fraud. It is undoubtedly true that a substantial share of the blame for such losses lies elsewhere, but an important share is attributable to inadequate and deliberately misleading information and widespread violations of fiduciary responsibilities by market and corporate insiders.

The Pecora investigation catalogued 107 issues on the New York Stock Exchange (NYSE) and 71 issues on the New York Curb in which members of these exchanges participated in pools in 1929. It also documented an impressive number of cases of new issue sales in the mid-to-late 1920s with inadequate disclosure and disastrous results. Both the nature of the facts and statements by the investment bankers involved make it quite clear that these issues could not have been sold with a modicum of disclosure of known facts.

Impact on New Issues

There is additional evidence in the postwar *Special Report* suggesting a beneficial effect on new issues of the full disclosure requirement under the SEC. For example, during 1960–61 a law firm representing seventeen issuers filed thirteen Regulation A statements which do not require full disclosure and four registration statements which do require full disclosure. Eleven of the thirteen Regulation A statements, but none of the four registration statements, became effective. Of the eleven Regulation A issues subsequently marketed, all went to a premium immediately after the offering; however, by November 1962, eight were no longer mentioned in the quotation sheets and three were quoted below their offering price. Through a variety of arrangements, the public monies raised through these offerings substantially were siphoned off to persons affiliated with the law firm representing the seventeen issuers. The *Special Study* also shows that while Regulation A issues in 1959–61 fared better than registered issues in the immediate postoffering period (up to one month after offering), they fared worse by 30 September 1962. This can be construed by suggesting that in the short run full disclosure may prevent unwarranted price rises and that in the longer run it can ensure a closer coincidence between initial price and intrinsic value.

One of several tests of the effect of full disclosure compares the market experience from 1958 to 1963 of unregistered new industrial common stock below $300,000 in 1958 with the smaller registered issues of more than $300,000, where both groups of stocks are adjusted by movements in the market averages.[11] Only nonrights, publicly offered, primary issues were included to maintain comparability. While this test was of rather limited scope, it pointed to a superior after-issue price performance of the registered issues. The price relatives for the registered small issues were not very different from those typically found for the larger issues, but they were appreciably better than the price relatives for the very small issues not subject to registration.

Another test of the effect of full disclosure carried out in connection with the criticism of a similar earlier test by George Stigler[12] was to compare the price performance relatives of comparable large new stock issues in the pre-SEC (1923–28) and post-SEC (1949–55) periods over a five-year period subsequent to their offering.[13] These price performance relatives were obtained by adjusting the price trends of new issues for the price trends of outstanding issues as measured by the Standard and Poor's Industrial Index in an attempt to eliminate the effects of general market conditions. Such a test assumes that any differences in the relation of the markets for new and outstanding issues in the two periods were mainly a reflection of the SEC, with the disclosure provisions for new issues likely to be particularly important.[14] The deficiencies in this assumption are obvious, but the results of this test are still of interest.

In this comparison of the 1923–28 and 1949–55 periods, we found that the price performance of new issues was inferior to that of outstanding issues, but that it was closer to outstanding issues in the post-SEC than in the pre-SEC period, suggesting an increase in allocational efficiency. The price performance of new issues relative to outstanding issues was, as a result, superior in the post-SEC period. The superiority was least marked in the first year or so after the issue date. This finding can be explained by two facts: (1) the extensive price pegging and numerous manipulative pools in the 1920s, which might be expected to be particularly active in the first year after the public sale of a new issue, and (2) the extreme difficulty of securities valuation in the absence of full disclosure until there is some record of operating experience. In connection with the first point, it might be noted that a sample of new issues which, according to the Pecora hearings, were subject to pool operations in the 1920s had an above-average price performance in the first year after the issue date.[15]

We extended the pre-SEC and post-SEC comparisons in which we had covered the same time period and size categories of issues used by Stigler to include 1958 and the first half of 1959 and also to include small issues for 1923, the first half of 1928, and the first half of 1958. Again we obtained the same qualitative results when comparing the pre-SEC and post-SEC periods.

Another significant result of this comparison of pre- and post-SEC price performance of new common stock issues relative to outstanding issues is that the variances of the price ratios for each of of the five years after issue date were much larger in the pre-SEC period. In other words, there was much less dispersion in relative price performance of new issues in the post-SEC period. The result is consistent with theoretical expectations of the effects of improved information and a reduction of manipulative activity and, again, could be construed as evidence that securities legislation has improved the structure of stock prices.

In a subsequent analysis, we pointed out that another measure of performance advanced by Stigler suggested a statistically significant improvement in the structure of new issue prices from the pre- to post-SEC periods.[16] Thus, the correlation in the pre-SEC period between new issue prices and prices one year later, with all new issue prices deflated by the price index for outstanding issues, seems to have been significantly lower than the average correlation for adjacent pairs of years after issue. However, these correlations are identical (and higher) in the post-SEC period.

The only comprehensive data updating the comparative performance of new and outstanding issues[17] covers the price performance of SEC-registered, underwritten, unseasoned common stock issues during each month of the 1960–69 period over a postissuance five-year period through 1971. This study finds that after a short-lived initial premium, these new issues are indistinguishable from other outstanding stock. If these results are taken at face value, they would seem to suggest the virtual disappearance in the post-SEC period of the inferior performance of new issues. Thus, to the extent that such data are relevant, they support an improvement in the efficiency of the new-issue market in the post-SEC period.

In the light of all these findings, it is not surprising that in an article in the *American Economic Review,* this statement appears: "We interpret the evidence on the 1933 Act as clearly favorable to disclosure."[18] Therefore it may be useful to consider a different evaluation by George Benston which appeared in that same issue,[19] both to examine its validity and perhaps its conformance with elementary standards of full disclosure. Benston, in referring to the papers by Stigler, Herman, and myself, which cover all the results summarized above except those obtained by Ibbotson, states that:

> The data presented in these papers indicate an insignificant difference in the mean rate of return (relative to the market) on stocks floated in the years 1923–27 compared to flotations in the period 1949–55. However, the standard deviations of the returns are higher in the pre–Securities and Exchange Commission (SEC) period, which F-W* assume is favorable.

Then Benston proceeds to attack the relevance of the standard deviations and concludes that from such evidence "one should not interpret the evidence as clearly favorable to disclosure."

Benston clearly states (1) that the 1923–27 and 1949–55 comparisons provide insignificant differences in mean rates of return and strongly implies (2) that these are the only relevant results available and (3) that our conclusion is exclusively or primarily based on respective standard deviations, which do not constitute terribly relevant evidence. The first point is grossly misleading, and the second and third points are false. I can begin to understand Benston's distaste for full disclosure.

Turning to the first point, both Stigler and Friend and Herman make two different comparisons of the pre- and post-SEC performance of new issues. The first comparison covered 1923–28 for the pre-SEC period and included Class A stock as common, following Stigler's original procedures. The second comparison covered 1923–27 and excluded Class A stock for common, following Stigler's revision of his original procedures when we pointed out that the original results, appropriately corrected, suggested a favorable SEC effect in the new-issue market.

What Benston does not point out — and this would seem to be a glaring omission — is that for the first set of comparisons, the post-SEC period was superior in the performance of new issues for each of the five years tested subsequent to their offering and was significantly

---

* Friend and Westerfield; see note 18.

superior (at the 5 percent level) for four of the five years. When the pre-SEC period is terminated at 1927, which had the best relative price experience of the pre-SEC years included, instead of 1928, which had the worst, *and* when Class A stock is excluded, the differences between the pre- and post-SEC results for the five years subsequent to the offering are not statistically significant in any year. However, Benston neglects to point out that the post-SEC performance is superior in four of the five years. While the differences in two of the five years are quite small, they range from 6 to 17 percent in the other three years, with the post-SEC results superior in these years. If 1928 is retained in the earlier period but Class A stock still is omitted, the post-SEC performance of new issues in all the five years rose by from 9 to 37 percent a year. Moreover, even for the pre-SEC comparison, which is least unfavorable to Benston's position, a serial correlation measure of performance commented on earlier in this article seems to show a statistically significant superiority of the post-SEC period.[20]

The second point implied by Benston — that the 1923–27 and 1949–55 comparisons to which he refers are the only evidence in the paper cited on mean relative rates of return on new issues — is without any foundation. Totally apart from the several other 1923–27 and 1923–28 comparisons referred to and the comparison of standard deviations of returns to which Benston refers, it may be recalled that there previously was discussion of five other reasonably independent statistical tests and a substantial amount of qualitative information. All of this was favorable to the efficacy of the 1933 Act disclosure requirements and was cited in the literature referred to by Benston.

The last point implied by Benston — that our favorable conclusion on 1933 Act disclosure depended basically on the comparison of standard deviations of returns in the pre- and post-SEC periods — is thus completely incorrect. As for the relevance of such a comparison, the reduction in variance of new-issue price ratios from the pre- to the post-SEC periods, since it clearly was not associated with a reduction in relative return, can be regarded from the investor's viewpoint as a positive achievement of the SEC, making the usual assumption that investors are risk-averse. Benston advances the strange argument that such evidence has no relevance to the effectiveness of the SEC, relative to private individuals, in screening out fraudulent issues and, apparently in view of the covariance problems, in measuring potential risk. The evidence would seem to be directly relevant to the effectiveness of the securities regulation in screening out fraudulent issues. Moreover, in the theoretical world to which covariances apply, any desired level of risk could be obtained by a suitable combination of the market portfolio and the "risk-free" asset. If Benston is implying that the variance of the market portfolio has increased over this period as a result of covariance developments in the new-issues markets, this seems far-fetched, and in any case, the available data do not support this hypothesis.[21]

A question might be raised as to the effect of securities regulation on the costs of new issues. In other words, has the apparent increase in allocational efficiency been offset by a reduction in operational efficiency or an increase in new-issue costs, including the costs of the SEC as well as private costs? Of course, to the extent that registration costs are already reflected in price performance, our performance relatives already have adjusted for any difference in registration costs in the pre- and post-SEC periods. However, in any case, the evidence suggests a decline in underwriting compensation from the pre-SEC and the early SEC to the subsequent period,[22] and other information points to an inconsequential upward movement — in the aggregate, a fraction of 1 percent — in other expenses associated with new issues.[23] The cost of SEC registration activities is estimated at well under one-tenth of 1 percent of the proceeds of registered issues. There are some other social costs as well as savings associated with required disclosure, but these are not quantified readily, are not clear in direction, and, in my opinion, are not very large. The costs of disclosure would seem to be a small fraction of the savings suggested by the various tests referred to earlier.

Impact on Market for Outstanding Issues[24]

Several direct tests of the market's relative allocational efficiency in different periods have been derived from market equilibrium theory. This demonstrates that under plausible assumptions, the return on an individual stock over time should bear a simple linear relation to the return on the stock market as a whole (or on all risky assets). The return of an individual stock in a cross section should be related linearly to its risk as measured by the covariance of its return with that on the market. The residual variation in these relationships provides a basis for assessing the efficiency implications of changes in the market structure. Thus a study which regresses the monthly individual returns for 251 NYSE stocks against the average market return for all of them finds that the variance of the residuals for 247 issues was smaller in the post–World War II period than in the period from 1926 through the 1930s.[25] The total variance of return on these 247 issues, which measures variance in the market return as well as residual variance, was also smaller in the postwar period.

A supplementary analysis carried out several years ago[26] regresses on time the standard deviation of residuals from a series of cross-section relationships of portfolio monthly return and risk for twenty-one periods of twenty-four months, from July 1926 through June 1968. Each of the twenty-one cross-section relationships regressed the average monthly return on the estimated beta[27] of approximately ten portfolios, each consisting of approximately eighty NYSE stocks stratified by beta in a preceding period. The twenty-one standard deviations of residuals obtained from these relationships then were regressed on time, and a significant downward time trend was found.

Both of these last two tests derived from market equilibrium theory suggest an improvement in market structure from the 1920s to the period after World War II. Since they abstract from factors affecting return on the market as a whole, they supply some support to the thesis that changes in securities regulation may have improved efficiency in the market for outstanding stock. However, the evidence here is not very strong.

Moreover, there are two more recent studies which purport to provide evidence that securities regulation in the market for outstanding stock has had no significant impact on market efficiency. The first study by R. R. Officer[28] concludes that the decline from the pre- to the post-SEC periods in the one-year standard deviation of monthly returns on the New York Stock Exchange stock as a whole was "not attributable to the SEC." The second study by Benston[29] concludes that empirical evidence provides no support for the belief that the disclosure and related provisions of the Securities Exchange Act of 1934 had any effect on the market for outstanding issues.

The conclusion by Officer differs from that reached in earlier analyses of the variability of returns of NYSE stocks as a whole. Officer's results are, to a substantial extent, dependent on an extension back to February 1897 of the series on NYSE average returns from the reasonably satisfactory data covering all NYSE stocks starting with January 1926. The first part of the extension goes back to January 1915 on the basis of a 20-stock Dow Jones index, and the second part, prior to 1915, is on the basis of a 12-stock Dow Jones index. In view of the major incomparabilities between the data before and after January 1926, and presumably the much higher quality of the Dow Jones stocks as compared to the market as a whole, the new evidence by Officer does not appear at all cogent, though he asserts that the biases introduced by these incomparabilities are relatively unimportant. Moreover, it should be noted that Officer addresses himself only to variance in the market return and not at all to variance in residual returns.

The analysis by Benston is of somewhat greater interest since it is directed specifically at measuring the impact of SEC-mandated disclosure on the market for outstanding stocks on the basis of two tests of the impact of the 1934 Act disclosure. The first test estimates the impact of changes in accounting data on common stock prices by deriving cross-sectional regressions in 1964 between changes in prices of individual stocks on the New York Stock Exchange (adjusted for movements in the market) and "unexpected" changes in each of a number of different financial variables (net sales, cash flow, net operating income, and adjusted net income). Expected changes in these financial variables were obtained from several simple autoregressive models based on past data. Then they were compared with subsequent published data to obtain estimates of unexpected changes. A similar but more limited analysis was carried out for 1963.

As pointed out in a comment on this analysis, Benston, for obscure reasons, *uses more than one* of these unexpected changes in financial variables in the same regression, *but only one at a time*.[30] Even so, his findings point to statistically significant relations between price changes and the unexpected changes in each of these financial variables. Nevertheless, in view of what he considers the small size of the regression coefficients, he concludes that "this evidence is not consistent with the underlying assumption, that the financial data made public are timely or relevant, on average." There does not seem to be any justification for his willingness to dismiss out of hand the economic importance of these statistically significant results. Thus, he in effect does not consider as relevant for stock prices knowledge about changes in financial variables, in spite of the fact that he finds that an increase of 100 percent in the annual rate of net sales is associated with an increase in price of 10.4 percent in the month of the announcement, and that changes in other variables also are associated with significant, though proportionately smaller, changes in price.

Moreover, it seems clear that Benston's regressions considerably understate the usefulness of published financial statements. They do not allow for the joint effects of unexpected changes in the different financial variables. Also, they make no adjustment for the substantial understatement of the relevant regression coefficients arising from the very large random measurement errors associated with any empirical measures of unexpected change.

Finally, we pointed out that on the basis of independent analyses, "many writers have concluded that published accounting profile variables can be useful in making investment decisions and contribute to market efficiency,"[31] Benston alleged that almost all previous empirical work relating published accounting data to stock price changes also leads to the conclusion that the data are not useful or are redundant.

In attempting to refute our comments on the first of his two tests discussed previously, Benston's rejoinder[32] advances six arguments (2–7) of which three (2, 3, and 5) might be regarded as substantive and shall be considered here. In reply to our above quotation on earlier analyses of the utility of published accounting profiles, Benston states categorically that, "No such conclusions are drawn in the articles they cite." Let me quote directly from the Martin article cited. Martin concludes (pp. 20–21):

> *We have presented empirical evidence in support of the decision-relevance of accounting annual report data for investment decisions. In our view, this evidence is complementary to evidence provided by existing studies examining various aspects of accounting information utility. This study uniquely provides an explicit test of the usefulness of a series of accounting variables taken together.... Finally, we consider legislation to increase the scope and amount of reported data as potentially beneficial to investors, based on the ability of current information to explain investor expectations...*

Clearly Benston's categorical assertion is unwarranted. May's summarization of the two implications of his results (p. 151) again seems consistent with the above quotation to which Benston takes exception.

Interestingly enough, even Nicholas J. Gonedes, whom Benston cites in his continued refutation of the above quotation and indeed at several different points in his rebuttal, concludes in a recent paper,

> *The results of our tests — which involved tests on means, variances, and covariances — are consistent with the statement that special accounting items convey information pertinent to establishing firms' equilibrium values. Also, our results are not consistent with the statement that no effect is asscciated with the disaggregation represented by the separate disclosure treatment accorded to special accounting items...* [33]

In reply to our criticism that "Benston does not use more than one of these expected changes in financial variables in the same regression ...," he agrees this criticism is correct but says that Gonedes obtained similar results when he used a number of accounting data ratios simultaneously. [34] Surely it is disingenuous of Benston to make such a statement without pointing out the main conclusion which Gonedes reached:

> *Our major purpose was to determine whether the accounting numbers jointly reflect new information. The results of our multivariate tests assign a high probability to the statement that the numbers do jointly provide information pertinent to assessing equilibrium expected returns.*

From the viewpoint of statistical theory and elementary logic, perhaps the strangest point made by Benston is in response to our reference to the "substantial understatement of the relevant regression coefficients arising from the very large random measurement errors associated with any empirical measures of unexpected change." The clear import of this reference is that under plausible and well-known statistical assumptions, substantial random errors in an independent variable in a regression will bias substantially downward the absolute value of the coefficient of that variable. As a result, the impact of disclosure which Benston found statistically significant in spite of this problem clearly is understated in his analysis — probably substantially. Benston's reply, apart from referring again to the unpublished study by Gonedes which uses a grouping technique to reduce this measurement error, is that we "should question why the SEC has done so little to reduce these errors, or even to provide investors with some indication of their magnitude and effect." Nothing in Benston's analysis casts any light on the SEC's accomplishments in these areas, since this would require comparable results for the pre-SEC period.

Benston's second set of tests of the impact of SEC-mandated disclosure on the market for outstanding stocks is similarly flawed. This set attempts to determine whether a large sample of individual NYSE stocks which were affected by sales disclosure provisions of the 1934 Act subsequently behaved "better" relative to the market as a whole than stocks for which such sales data were already available prior to the act. The deficiencies in these tests were spelled out in some detail in the comment by Westerfield and Friend[36] and were responded to in the rejoinder by Benston.[37]

First, Benston objects to our statement that, "We have indicated that Benston's analysis suggests that the 1934 Act did improve estimates of expected return." He goes on to state, "I have been unable to detect where in their analysis F-W so indicate." Here, Benston is forgetting his first set of tests where, as indicated earlier, he does find a statistically significant effect of accounting disclosure of financial items such as sales and net income on stock prices. If we assume, as Benston does that the effect of disclosure on risk is marginal, then the effect on stock prices must reflect change in expected return.

Second, Benston states that "F-W then somewhat overstate the reported usefulness of accounting data [in several external studies] for forecasting betas." This point is significant, since his finding that the market evaluation of risk as measured by beta did not change more in the post-SEC period for pre-SEC "nondisclosure" firms than for pre-SEC "disclosure" firms is essentially the only evidence Benston has to support his position that disclosure had no effect. We pointed out that "there are several external studies showing that current accounting data can be used to make at least as good and possibly superior forecasts of future asset risk (as measured by beta) than forecasts dependent only on historically estimated asset risks . . ." and "The accounting data which turn out to be useful for this purpose are balance sheet and income account items other than sales." Sales, it will be recalled, is the only variable Benston used in estimating the value of disclosure in this second set of tests. Benston's rejoinder is that the analysis in the external studies we referred to is flawed and again refers to the unpublished study by Gonedes, which asserts that some of the results we relied on may reflect "spurious correlation."

Nothing Benston says or that we have seen in the literature is inconsistent with our assertion that the available external studies[38] can be used to make "as good and *possibly* superior forecasts of future asset risk" than can be obtained from past market-derived betas. Our view was and is that there is some weak evidence to support the position that disclosure can and does help in the assessment of risk of outstanding stock measured by beta. There is stronger evidence that disclosure affects stock price in the theoretically expected and desired direction. Such a price effect, even in the absence of a beta effect, would be sufficient to justify 1934 Act disclosure unless associated costs were excessive.

The last consequential point in Benston's rejoinder takes issue with our statement (quoted here more fully):

> *Contrary to Benston's assertions, none of the assumptions that the portfolio approach depends upon appears strictly correct and empirical evidence on the valid-*

ity of the beta coefficient is not conclusive. Therefore, it might have been illumi-nating to have included total variability estimates to supplement the analysis.

Benston objects both to our criticism of the assumptions and to our evaluation of the empir-ical evidence. Both the simple capital asset pricing theory which he relies on and the portfolio approach he uses to justify almost exclusive reliance on beta assume that investors will at-tempt to minimize risk of their portfolio for given expected rates of return. The relevant measure of risk is total variability of return on the portfolio they hold. If investors hold a perfectly diversified portfolio of risky assets, as is implied by the capital asset theory, each will hold a microcosm of all stock and other risky assets in the same proportion to the total of their risky assets. Under these circumstances, the total variability in the portfolio would be determined mainly by the betas of the individual assets held, but this is no longer true for portfolios which are not well diversified. For investors with such portfolios, the average standard deviation or some other measure of total variability of returns on individual assets is also important.

Therefore, it is highly relevant to point out that convincing statistical evidence is avail-able which indicates that a high proportion of portfolios is dominated by a small number of assets; thus, the portfolios are not well diversified.[39] Nearly 33 percent of all stock owned by U.S. individuals in 1971 was held in portfolios with fewer than five stocks, and more than 55 percent was held in portfolios with fewer than ten stocks. One or two stocks dominated not only such portfolios but also a surprisingly high percentage of portfolios with a larger num-ber of stocks. To assume that investors with such portfolios would use beta to the exclusion of total variability as the measure of risk is to assume they are irrational and to vitiate both capital asset pricing and portfolio theory.

Turning to Benston's objections to our evaluation of the empirical evidence on the de-sirability of a total variability measure "to *supplement* the analysis," he quotes or paraphrases Merton Miller and Myron Scholes (whom we also cited),[40] Michael Jensen,[41] and Eugene Fama and James MacBeth[42] to the contrary. He clearly misinterprets Miller and Scholes and Fama and MacBeth and presumably Jensen. Miller and Scholes and Fama and Mac-Beth state in reasonably clear language that it is *possible,* though not proved, that the empir-ical data they investigate are consistent with capital asset pricing theory, which implies that beta of an individual stock, if we could measure it properly, is the only relevant measure of its risk. Jensen, whom Benston quotes out of context (see rest of footnote 35, p. 367, to which Benston refers), is making the statement quoted about portfolios rather than individual se-curities and depends on Fama and MacBeth for its extension to individual assets. It seems to me, at the present state of the art in capital asset pricing theory, that if we are concerned with realistic explanation of real world phenomena — not the most elegant theory which may or may not be applicable — it is unfortunate that Benston did not examine total variability estimates.

Impact of Margin Regulation

Of the various regulatory policies which have been directed toward the maintenance of or-derly markets, the one of perhaps greatest interest to the general economist is the regulation of margin trading. This regulation originally reflected congressional concerns about the possibly excessive use of securities credit on the economy as a whole as well as on the stock market itself. Neoclassical economists in the United States seem to consider this type of securities regulation as especially distasteful, presumably because it interferes with the freedom of behavior of the beneficent speculators, substitutes selective credit controls for the free market, and has no obvious strong equity rationale.

In an earlier paper,[43] casual empiricism led to the conclusion that margin requirements probably have tended to reduce stock price volatility and increase market efficiency, though such evidence is obviously not at all convincing. In that study, it was pointed out that a rather comprehensive analysis of margin trading completed a little earlier,[44] which concluded that "margin requirements have failed to achieve any of their objectives," was subject to deficiencies which, when corrected, appear to present a more favorable case for margin regulation.

Since that time, two other studies — one by George Douglas[45] and the other by James Largay[46] — have presented favorable evidence on the effectiveness of margin regulation, and one study, by Officer,[47] argues for the ineffectiveness of such regulation. The Officer argument is based on two annual time-series regressions, apparently over the 1934–68 period, between each of two forms of the standard deviation of stock market return and both margin requirements and the standard deviation of industrial production. The two forms of the market return variable lead the margin requirements in one regression and follow them in the other, with the lead and lag both one year in duration. The lead form turns out to have a much higher correlation, and the margin requirement variable is statistically insignificant in both, with the same negative coefficient and a t-value of somewhat more than one.

The Douglas analysis regresses the standard deviation of the rate of change in price, both on the standard deviation of the rate of change in dividends and on margin requirements for the period 1926–60, where each observation is a subperiod of five-year length (with the exception of four-year for the last) for each of 100 stocks. The coefficient of margin requirements is again negative but now is highly significant which, according to the author, "suggests that margin requirements tend to reduce price volatility."

The Largay paper analyzes the price and volume characteristics of seventy-one NYSE and thirty-eight American Stock Exchange (AMEX) stocks placed under special margin requirements during 1968–69. The price and volume characteristics of these stocks are explained both around the times when 100 percent margins were imposed and, subsequently, when they were removed. The author concludes that "The empirical results support the a priori hypothesis that banning the use of credit for transactions in individual issues is associated with a moderation or cooling off of speculative activity in these stocks." This conclusion is based on several key findings: Imposition of 100 percent margin was associated with the termination of the marked upward price movement and a reduction of the heavy volume of trading, both of which typically had preceded the new margin restriction. As the author notes, the NYSE stocks actually declined in price after they were placed under this restriction. Prices of the restricted stocks generally declined preceding removal of the special margin requirement. After removal, only prices of the AMEX stocks tended to rise again though the volume of trading began to accelerate for both the NYSE and AMEX stocks.

My own appraisal of this material is that the evidence of a favorable effect of margin regulation on at least stock market volatility is stronger than the evidence on the other side. However, this assessment may reflect personal biases; the evidence is far from conclusive.

Impact of Other Restrictions on Trading Activity

The other major restrictions on trading activity affected by securities regulation will be touched on only briefly. These restrictions include those on short sales, on ordinary floor trading by members of an exchange, on stock specialists' activities, and on trading by corporate insiders (officers, directors, and principal stockholders) in stocks of the corporations with which they are affiliated. Since specialists are considered as having a responsibility for helping to maintain fair and orderly markets, their trading activity has not been subjected to regulatory restrictions that are as severe as those imposed on the other types of speculative activity.

In the paper referred to earlier,[48] the interpretation of the available evidence was that the trading activity of NYSE floor traders appeared, as a whole, more likely to be destabilizing than stabilizing; that the reverse was true of NYSE specialists, and perhaps also of corporate insiders, at least in the post-SEC period; that the evidence on short selling was mixed;[49] and that none of this evidence was terribly strong. I also noted that even if restrictions on insider trading did not have a favorable impact on stock market volatility and market efficiency, they might be justified on equity grounds.

Since that earlier paper, an interesting new analysis of insider trading has been published by J. F. Jaffe.[50] The analysis indicates that three legal actions which might have been expected to lead corporate insiders to expect stricter enforcement of the SEC insider-trading rules (specifically SEC Rule 10[B]-5) did not, in fact, have a statistically significant effect on the profitability and volume of insider trading. Actually, the two legal actions which might have been expected to have the largest impact (the Cady, Roberts and Texas Gulf Sulphur decisions) *were* associated with drops in insider profitability, while the third (the Texas Gulf Sulphur indictment) was associated with an increase in profitability. However, the changes were not statistically significant, and the volume of insider trading increased slightly after all three actions (again without statistical significance). As a result, at least these specific changes in the prospects for implementation of regulatory constraints on insider training seemed to have very little effect on the profitability and volume of such activity.

While this new evidence is certainly relevant to the effectiveness of these three legal actions involving the SEC, the relevance it has for the broader effectiveness of Section 16B of the 1934 Act (relating to corporate recovery of short-term profits by insiders) is not clear, and it would seem to have very little relevance for the effectiveness of Section 16A (relating to full disclosure provisions for insiders).[51] Thus, if these provisions of the 1934 Act had been extremely effective well in advance of the first of the three legal actions, i.e., the November 1961 Cady, Roberts decision, Jaffe would have obtained the results he did, but the interpretation of his results would be radically different. Given the extreme variability of stock price changes and rates of return, it would not have been surprising to find apparently little effect of stricter enforcement of the SEC insider-trading rules. Even prior to Cady, Roberts, there were both the prospect and, I suspect, actuality of private litigation for recovery of insider profits.

Clearly what is required for a more convincing answer to the overall effect of insider regulation is a careful comparison of pre-SEC and post-SEC insider behavior from the scattered pieces of evidence available. After reading the major U.S. Government investigations of the stock market and related abuses of the 1920s cited earlier in this article, it seems that insider abuses have declined substantially subsequent to that period. This is attributable, at least in part, to the disclosure provisions and restrictions imposed on insiders by the 1934 Act. A careful documentation of all such evidence would provide more relevant evidence than we now have available for assessing the effectiveness of the insider provisions of the 1934 Act.

Finally, there is no comment here on the ultimate type of interference with free market processes in the securities markets when trading in individual stocks or, on rare occasions, in the market as a whole is temporarily stopped in the face of major disruptions in the market. It is indicated elsewhere that under certain extreme circumstances (e.g., the assassination of President Kennedy) such action is desirable.[52]

To conclude, it is my view that securities legislation in the United States has, as a whole, benefited the stock market and the economy. However, as I stated in the past, it is not yet clear whether a number of specific policies have been beneficial. Further exploration of the impact of such policies would be highly desirable.

NOTES

1. Part of this discussion is based on Irwin Friend, "The Economic Consequences of the Stock Market," *American Economic Review* (May 1972).

2. For example, see Hayne E. Leland, "Production Theory and the Stock Market." *Bell Journal of Economics and Management Science* (Spring 1974). See also Robert C. Merton and Marti G. Subrahmanyam, "The Optimality of a Competitive Stock Market," in the same issue of *Bell Journal.*

3. For example, see Jeffrey F. Jaffe and Mark Rubenstein, *The Value of Information in Impersonal and Personal Markets,* Working Paper No. 16–75, Rodney L. White Center for Financial Research. See Mark Rubenstein, "Securities Market Efficiency in an Arrow-Debreu Economy," *American Economic Review* (December 1975), for a very brief discussion of securities market efficiency, in general, and a more detailed discussion of informational efficiency.

4. George Stigler, "Public Regulation of the Securities Markets," *Journal of Business* (April 1964), p. 117.

5. See Irwin Friend and Edward S. Herman, "The SEC Through a Glass Darkly," *Journal of Business* (October 1964), p. 399, and (January 1965), p. 109.

6. Friend and Herman, "Through a Glass Darkly."

7. Part of this discussion is based on Irwin Friend, "The S.E.C. and the Economic Performance of Securities Markets," in Henry G. Manne, ed., *Economic Policy and the Regulation of Corporate Securities* (American Enterprise Institute for Public Policy Research, 1969).

8. *Stock Exchange Practices: Hearings before the Senate Committee on Banking and Currency* (72d and 73d Cong., Parts 1–17) (Washington, D.C.: 1933–34).

9. *Report of the Federal Trade Commission on Utility Corporations* (70th Cong., 1st Sess., Sen. Doc. 92) (Washington, D.C.: 1935, esp. Parts 22, 71A, 72A, and 73A); and *Report of the Securities and Exchange Commission on Investment Trusts and Investment Companies* (Washington, D.C.: 1939–42).

10. *Report of Special Study of the Securities Markets of the Securities and Exchange Commission* (Washington, D.C.: U.S. Government Printing Office, 1963).

11. Friend and Herman, "Through a Glass Darkly."

12. Stigler, "Public Regulation of the Securities Markets."

13. Friend and Herman, "Through a Glass Darkly."

14. While the SEC has effected significant increases in disclosure for both new and outstanding issues, the disclosure requirements for new issues are more extensive and started in the pre-SEC period at a much lower base.

15. Friend and Herman, "Through a Glass Darkly."

16. Irwin Friend and Edward S. Herman, "Professor Stigler on Securities Regulation: A Further Comment," *Journal of Business* (January 1965), and George J. Stigler, "Comment," *Journal of Business* (October 1964).

17. Roger G. Ibbotson, *Price Performance of Common Stock New Issues* (University of Chicago, 1973).

18. Irwin Friend and Randolph Westerfield, "Required Disclosure and the Stock Market: Comment," *American Economic Review* (June 1975).

19. George J. Benston, "Required Disclosure and the Stock Market: Rejoinder," *American Economic Review* (June 1965).

20. I will not comment here on the appropriateness of a longer versus a shorter period for assessing the performance of new issues since Benston does not raise it and because it is covered fully in Friend and Herman, "Professor Stigler on Securities Regulation."

21. See Irwin Friend and Marshall E. Blume, "The Demand for Risky Assets," *American Economic Review* (December 1975). The data there indicate that the standard deviation of return on New York Stock Exchange stocks as a whole was smaller in each of the decades 1942–51, 1952–61, and 1962–71 than for the decades 1922–31 and 1932–41 or than for the entire period 1872–81 or for the period 1926–71 for which the data are much more reliable.

22. Irwin Friend et al., *Investment Banking and the New Issues Market* (World Publishing, 1967).

23. Friend and Herman, "Through a Glass Darkly."

24. Part of this discussion is based on Friend, "Economic Consequences."

25. Marshall E. Blume, "The Assessment of Portfolio Performance: An Application to Portfolio Theory" (Ph.D. diss., University of Chicago, 1967).

26. Friend "Economic Consequences."

27. Beta is a measure of an asset's risk based on the covariance of its rate of return with that on the market (normalized by dividing this covariance by the variance of the market's rate of return).

28. R. R. Officer, "The Variability of the Market Factor of the New York Stock Exchange," *Journal of Business* (July 1973).

29. Benston, "Required Disclosure."

30. Friend and Westerfield, "Required Disclosure: Comment."

31. For example, see A. Martin, "An Empirical Test of the Relevance of Accounting Information for Investment Decisions," *Journal of Accounting Research, Empirical Research in Accounting: Selected Studies, 1971,* and R. G. May, "The Influence of Quarterly Earnings Announcements on Investor Decisions as Reflected in Common Stock Price Changes," *Journal of Accounting Research, Empirical Research in Accounting: Selected Studies, 1971.*

32. Benston, "Required Disclosure: Rejoinder."

33. Nicholas J. Gonedes, *Risk, Information, and the Effects of Special Accounting Items in Capital Market Equilibrium,* Report 7429 (University of Chicago: Center for Mathematical Studies in Business and Economics, June 1974).

34. Ibid. A number of other studies could be cited to support the usefulness of accounting disclosure, including most recently Daniel W. Collins, "SEC Product-Line Reporting and Market Efficiency," *Journal of Financial Economics* (June 1975).

35. "Capital Market Equilibrium and Annual Accounting Numbers: Empirical Evidence," *Jour-

nal of Accounting Research (Spring 1974).

36. Friend and Westerfield, "Required Disclosure: Comment."

37. Benston, "Required Disclosure: Rejoinder."

38. The most comprehensive listing (and summary) I have seen of such studies appears in Stewart C. Myers, "The Relation between Real and Financial Measures of Risk and Return," in I. Friend and J. Bicksler, eds., *Risk and Return in Finance* (Cambridge: Ballinger Publishing, 1976).

39. Marshall E. Blume, Irwin Friend, and Jean Crockett, "Stockownership in the United States: Characteristics and Trends," *Survey of Current Business* (November 1974); and Marshall E. Blume and Irwin Friend,, "The Asset Structure of Individual Portfolios and Some Implications for Utility Functions," *Journal of Finance* (May 1975).

40. Merton H. Miller and Myron Scholes, "Rates of Return in Relation to Risk: A Re-examination of Some Recent Findings," in M. C. Jensen, ed., *Studies in the Theory of Capital Markets* (New York: Praeger, 1971).

41. Michael Jensen, "Capital Markets: Theory and Evidence," *Bell Journal of Economics* (Autumn 1972).

42. E. F. Fama and J. MacBeth, "Risk, Return and Equilibrium: Empirical Tests," *Journal of Political Economy* (May 1973).

43. Friend, "S.E.C. and Economic Performance."

44. Thomas Gale Moore, "Stock Market Margin Requirements," *Journal of Political Economy* (April 1966).

45. George W. Douglas, "Risk in the Equity Markets: An Empirical Appraisal of Market Efficiency," *Yale Economic Essays* (Spring 1969).

46. James A. Largay III, "100% Margins: Combating Speculation in Individual Security Issues," *Journal of Finance* (September 1973).

47. Officer, "Variability of the Market Factor."

48. Friend, "S.E.C. and Economic Performance."

49. A similar conclusion on short selling is reached in Thomas H. Mayor, "Short Selling Activities and the Price of Equities: Some Simulations and Regression Results," *Journal of Financial and Quantitative Analysis* (September 1968).

50. J. F. Jaffe, "The Effect of Regulation Changes on Insider Trading," *Bell Journal of Economics and Management Science* (Spring 1974).

51. Actually Cady, Roberts involved activities which did not require corporate insider disclosure.

52. Friend, "S.E.C. and Economic Performance."

TWENTY-FIVE

SEC Commentary: Recommendations of the SEC Advisory Committee on Corporate Disclosure

ROBERT P. LIENESCH

Cincinnati Milacron Inc.

The results of the deliberations of the Securities and Exchange Commission's Advisory Committee on Corporate Disclosure, ACCORD, and the preliminary recommendations are discussed herein. This article suggests the types of improvements that are needed in the corporate disclosure system.

INTRODUCTION

The SEC's Advisory Committee on Corporate Disclosure has been meeting periodically for over a year to formulate recommendations for improvements in the corporate disclosure system. The prestigious 17-member committee has considered a wide array of disclosure issues, and has reached some tentative conclusions that could have a long-range impact on corporate reports filed with the SEC and sent to stockholders. Although the committee's final report is not expected until later this summer, the SEC has already proposed adoption of some of its recommendations.

The purpose of this article is to highlight the more important of the committee's tentative recommendations,[1] some of which may eventually be adopted by the SEC.

BACKGROUND

In January 1976, Roderick Hills, then Chairman of the SEC, announced the formation of the SEC Advisory Committee on Corporate Disclosure. The committee's charge was to define the purposes and objectives of the corporate disclosure system, including an overall assessment of its effectiveness, and to compare its costs to the resulting benefits.

The committee is chaired by former Commissioner A. A. Sommer, Jr. Other members include prominent accountants, attorneys, corporate executives, professors, financial analysts, an investment banker, and a representative of a public interest group. Harold Williams served on the committee until his recent appointment as Chairman of the SEC.

Reprinted from *The CPA Journal,* July 1977, pp. 54–56, with permission.

METHODOLOGY

In addition to considering a vast amount of research already publicly available, several original research projects were initiated by the committee. In the most significant of these, it solicited views from those associated with the corporate disclosure system, including registrants, financial analysts, individual and institutional stockholders, financial news disseminators, and the general public. This process included interviews with over 60 financial analysts, and corporate executives of approximately 25 registrants. In addition, over 60 comment letters were received from registrants, accounting firms, attorneys, and professional organizations in response to the SEC's request for comments on 12 specific issues (SEC Release No. 33-5707). Questionnaires were also sent to over 11,000 individual investors. While the final results of the research project have not been tabulated, the preliminary results enabled the committee to reach many of its tentative conclusions.

CONCLUSIONS AND RECOMMENDATIONS

Disclosure guides. One of the first substantive issues considered by the committee was a perceived lack of uniformity of financial disclosures within specific industries. Most of the concern centered around the requirement in most SEC filings and the annual shareholders report for a "description of business." The committee concluded that the SEC should establish, on an experimental basis, "disclosure guides" for specific industries to encourage uniformity of disclosure by companies in the same industy. These guides were viewed as analogous to the recent Guide 61, "Statistical Disclosure Requirements for Bank-Holding Companies."

Further, the committee concluded that the SEC should receive input from users and preparers of this financial information within the industry affected before the guides are published as proposals. This provision was aimed at ensuring that the proposed guides would be both adequate and practical.

The committee understands that, as a result of these recommendations, the SEC is proceeding with an experimental program to develop guides for the railroad, gas and electric utility, airline, and casualty insurance industries. In fact, the guides for the railroad industry have already been drafted and projected for issuance (SEC Release No. 33-5824).

Forecasting. The committee considered the SEC's current policy, which neither encourages nor discourages the inclusion of forecasts of future economic results in SEC filings (Release No. 33-5699). Because of the acknowledged importance of forecasts in the marketplace, it was agreed that the SEC should take a more active role in encouraging registrants to issue them. The committee felt that registrants should have wide latitude in deciding what to disclose — whether it be estimated sales, earnings, earnings per share, or some other appropriate measure. The latitude should also extend to whether or not to:

- Disclose the underlying assumptions.
- Compare the forecast with actual results.
- Update previously issued forecasts.
- Discontinue or resume issuing forecasts.

- Have an independent review.

However, the committee warned that forecasts should include cautionary language about the inherent uncertainties of forecasted data.

Committee members recognized that registrants are often fearful of legal liability when forecast results are not achieved. Therefore, a "safe harbor" rule was drafted and approved. This rule is designed to protect from legal liability registrants which prepared forecasts on a reasonable basis and issued them in good faith. The provisions of the rule are very similar to those included in ASR No. 203 to protect registrants from liability resulting from disclosure of replacement cost information.

Segment reporting. Upon the issuance of FASB Statement No. 14, "Financial Reporting for Segments of a Business Enterprise," the committee considered the implications of the statement on reports filed with the SEC and sent to shareholders. It was agreed that the textual portion of the SEC forms (e.g., description of business) should be amended to require segmented disclosures where this would be consistent with the spirit of FASB Statement No. 14. The Commission already has proposed to adopt this recommendation.

But more important, the committee voted to require segmented financial information on a quarterly basis in Form 10-Q. This recommendation, if adopted by the SEC, would be most helpful to financial analysts. However, it could also prove to be most burdensome to registrants. The SEC considered this recommendation in April and, while not specifically proposing the requirements, requested comments from interested parties of the advisability of requiring segment data in Form 10-Q.

Rule-making procedures. Concern was expressed by some committee members that, on occasion, disclosure standards have been established through enforcement or administrative procedures (for example, disclosures of improper or illegal payments). It was felt that disclosure standards are best established, in most cases, through formal procedures which allow interested parties to comment before new rules are adopted. The committee concluded that the SEC should initiate the formal rule-making process promptly after identifying a disclosure issue for which standards should be established or modified.

One finding of the research project was that many who would be affected by proposed new disclosure standards do not respond to the SEC's requests for comments because they feel a sense of futility, i.e., a feeling that the new rule will be adopted substantially as proposed regardless of the input received from affected parties. To alleviate this problem, the committee agreed to recommend that the SEC issue a "concept release" prior to issuance of a formal proposal. The purpose of such a release would be to explain the issue and alternative disclosure approaches along with the SEC's preliminary preference. The release would request comments from interested parties. After considering the comments, the Commission would then proceed with a formal proposal. It is hoped that this approach will encourage a greater participation by registrants, analysts, and others in the disclosure standard-setting process. The same approach was recently used in announcing consideration of segment reporting requirements for Form 10-Q (as discussed above) and simplified disclosure requirements in Form S-14 for certain business combinations (SEC Release No. 33–5806).

Management discussion. In 1974 the "Management's Discussion and Analysis of the Summary of Operations" (Guides 1 and 22) was first required in SEC filings (ASR NO. 159) and annual shareholders reports (SEC Release No. 34–11079). In light of the first few years of experience, the SEC is generally disappointed with the quality of these analyses. After considering several ways to improve them, the committee concluded that the SEC should amend the guides to emphasize the latitude given to registrants in explaining the results of their operations. At the same time, the SEC should discourage the mechanistic exercise which many registrants seem to use to explain changes in line items of the summary of operations. (The current rules require changes in every item in the summary of operations to be described if they meet certain percentage tests.) Similarly, the committee wants more discussion of historical facts and, more importantly, their potential effect on future operations. Therefore, the committee recommended requiring a letter to accompany the filing, signed by the chief financial or accounting officer, acknowledging that the registrant has fully considered the provisions of the guides, including the requirement to discuss any facts known to management which would cause the historical financial statements to not be indicative of the future.

"Form CD." Perhaps one of the most significant recommendations made by the committee is to rescind most of the frequently used registration and reporting forms, including Forms S-1, S-7, S-8, 10, 8-K, 10-K, and 10-Q. These forms would be replaced by a new Form CD, "Continuous Disclosure." The intent of this form is to integrate the disclosure requirements of the 1933 and 1934 Acts and to eliminate duplication and inconsistency. The form would contain 77 disclosure items, taken principally from Forms S-1, S-8, 8-K, 10-Q, and 10-K. Its adoption would have the effect of taking all disclosure items now contained in these and other forms and including them in one form. Where duplications now exist (e.g., "Summary of Operations" in Forms S-1, S-7, 10, 10-K), one set of instructions would be selected (e.g., from Form S-1) for inclusion in Form CD. It would not create new disclosure items but simply codify existing ones.

To determine the disclosure requirements of a registration statement, a registrant would be classified into one of three categories:

Level 1. These would be the larger, more actively traded companies — generally those registrants currently permitted to use Form S-7.

Level 2. This category would include any other registrant having been registered for over three years which met all the periodic reporting requirements for the last three years.

Level 3. All others.

The effect of this categorization is that a registration statement for a Level 1 registrant need not contain as much data as a statement for a Level 2 or 3 registrant. Similarly, a statement for a Level 2 registrant would be shorter than one for Level 3.

For example, a registration statement for a Level 1 registrant would rely heavily on incorporation by reference for many of the disclosures now included in a registration statement, and the prospectus itself would contain only the following disclosures, if applicable: (1) Selling security holders; (2) Distribution spread; (3) Plan of distribution; (4) Treatment of proceeds; (5) Identity of issuer; (6) Securities to be offered and manner of offering; (7) Securities to be offered on conversion of other securities; (8) Securities to be offered upon the exercise of warrants; (9) Information regarding any adverse changes since the end of the previous fiscal year and any changes in control of the registrant; (10) Incorporation by reference of certain documents (including financial statements).

However, a prospectus for a Level 3 registrant, for example, would contain all of the typical S-1 disclosures and would not permit incorporation by reference.

For the most part, adoption of Form CD would not affect disclosure content or the due date of quarterly or annual reports or reports on significant corporate events. For example, quarterly and annual financial statements would still be due within 45 to 90 days, respectively, of the end of the reporting period.

Social and environmental issues. The committee also considered recommending changes to the current SEC standards for disclosure of social and environmental matters. In essence, the committee endorsed existing SEC policy that such matters need be disclosed only when deemed "material" to informed investment or corporate suffrage decision making. In this context the committee viewed materiality in the economic sense or as being related to the integrity of management.

CONCLUSION

It is obvious that the committee, in analyzing these and other disclosure issues, left few stones unturned. Although the SEC has already proposed some of its recommendations for adoption, there is no telling how many of them, or which ones, will eventually be adopted. But one thing seems reasonably certain: the findings of the SEC Advisory Committee on Corporate Disclosure will strongly influence the evolution of the corporate disclosure system for a long time to come.

NOTE

1. Although the committee has reached agreement on various issues, the members have reserved the right to change or modify these recommendations before the final report is issued.

TWENTY-SIX

The SEC and Its Chief Accountants: Historical Impressions

GARY JOHN PREVITS

Case Western Reserve University

In this revised version, the author discusses the history of the Securities and Exchange Commission (SEC) regulation of accounting by closely examining the actions of five chief accountants and, in turn, each officeholder's effect on the role played by the SEC and the accounting profession.

A PERSPECTIVE

The stability and progress of business and government in a socety as complex as ours are unlikely to persist without strong capital markets, and it seems equally unlikely that confidence in capital markets can persist without confidence in the people who operate them and in the Securities and Exchange Commission (SEC) and other governmental agencies that supervise them. The role of adequate information in the process of trading securities and valuing securities is interlaced and imbedded in this overall social order. Revelations in the past decade of excesses, frauds, and abuses in the institutions of government, business, and the professions have brought the existing capital market structure and its ability to command the public trust into question. The ability of the public accounting profession to command the respect and confidence of the individuals and institutions of the capital markets would appear to be central to the issue of reexamining the balance and worthiness of our economic, political, and social order.

The market crash of 1929 and the trauma of the early 1930s, capped by the collapse of the Kreuger and Toll empire, heightened the legislative ardor to investigate the operations of the securities markets. Also, Ferdinand Pecora had begun a series of investigations under the U.S. Senate Committee on Banking and Currency relative to investment bankers and the banking system. A Senate committee subsequently engaged in extensive inquiries about the Kreuger and Toll collapse even though the principal accounts of Kreuger and Toll had been audited by Swedish accountants (a U.S. subsidiary had been audited by Price Waterhouse & Co. and another American accounting firm was also indirectly involved). The financial press highlighted this episode and generated substantial pressures on the accounting profession, referring to inadequate auditing and accounting safeguards. In the capital markets, confidence had reached an all-time low. The newly elected President Franklin D. Roosevelt, as a part of his New Deal platform, proposed reform of the capital markets. Among his confidential advisers was a young Columbia University law professor, Adolph A. Berle. Berle had been influenced by the writings of Professor William Z. Ripley, the author of a series of articles that first appeared in the *Atlantic Monthly* in the 1920s and were later published in the book *Main Street and Wall Street.*

In 1932, Berle and Gardiner Means, an economist also on Columbia's faculty, published *The Modern Corporation and Private Property.* This work identified and analyzed the phenomena of the modern corporation and the separation of ownership and management relative to securities and property control. John L. Carey and other writers assert that Berle's influence in the Roosevelt Administration (as Berle was a member of the young intellectual "brain trust") led to the structure of securities legislation to address the basic bifurcation of management control and ownership.

The key words in this new legislation were "full and fair disclosure." James M. Landis, who served as a commissioner during the early years of the SEC, commented with regard to the legislative history of the 1933 Securities Act that among the multiple considerations in the minds of those who drafted the legislation, it was clear that the government did not seek to pass upon the investment quality of any security. Landis further stated that the theory of the English Companies acts was fundamental in guiding the deliberations of that small group who were charged with constructing the provisions and exemptions under this initial "registration" act.

Edward N. Gadsby, then chairman of the SEC, wrote in the *George Washington Law Review* in 1959, "It is doubtful that history affords an example of more timely and necessary legislation than the federal securities acts." In his view, the Federal Securities Acts responded to the need to restore confidence in order to maintain an important source of investment identified as "people's capitalism" (a view that, during the 1920s, public subscription of corporate securities had followed upon the favorable experience of individual investors in the liberty bonds of World War I). After the casinolike atmosphere of the 1920 stock market with speculation and market manipulation, the basis for public confidence in the investment process had been eroded, if not all but destroyed.

The 1933 Securities law first required registration of new offerings of securities upon the public exchanges. The registration of such securities required the certification by an *independent* public or certified accountant. This requirement had not initially been in the drafts of legislation, but had come about through the testimony of Arthur H. Carter, then managing partner of Haskins & Sells and, at that time, president of the New York State Society of CPAs. Carter's testimony before the Senate Banking Committee is acknowledged to have influenced Congress to include this requirement for certification of financial statements. The 1934 legislation, which established the SEC and other requirements for periodic reporting to that Commission, contained no certification requirement. However, the broad powers granted to the Commission under the law were later specified by the Commission to require such certification of the 1934 Act periodic reports filed. With the passage of the 1934 law, all the filings for public disclosures of registrant companies under the 1933 Act were transferred from the Federal Trade Commission to the SEC. These laws had given the Commission power to prescribe the accounting disclosure policies (Sec. 19 — 1933 Act; Sec. 13 —

1934 Act) to be followed in filings and had also placed responsibility and liability on accountants who undertook to practice and present statements to the Commission.

THE CHIEF ACCOUNTANTS

Carman G. Blough (December 1935–May 1938). Blough had come to the SEC after several years of professional experience and teaching accounting at several universities. While working at the Commission, he accepted the newly created position of chief accountant in December 1935. The task before Blough was to establish a basis of policy to provide formal interpretation of the law the Commission was to enforce with regard to the practice of accountants. While Blough was not encumbered by precedent, he was not afforded any of the guidance that is normally provided by such precedent. The literature of the profession of this period, as characterized by the editorial by Eric Kohler in *Accounting Review,* refers to the fact that the profession was "nervous" as to the outcome of its role in its new relationship with the SEC. The stipulation of independence, while not new, had never before been clearly defined as a legal or operational term. Furthermore, the authority of the Commission extended not only to filings with it but, under the proxy rules, the potential for the Commission's authority to extend to periodic and annual reports, normally provided by management to shareholders, also existed (but it was not exercised in these early years). The profession was to find that the decision of the Commission (in Accounting Series Release [ASR] No. 4, April 25, 1938) to permit financial statements to be filed with the Commission in accordance with accounting principles which had "substantial authoritative support"— was the start of a new generation of accounting thought and practice. The term "substantial authoritative support" was the key concept in this generation. Earlier, Blough had remarked:

> There is, of course, a dividing line between acceptable and unacceptable accounting practices; that line is a hairline, the location of which is a matter for the individual judgment of the accountant.

Only ASR Nos. 1 through 8 are attributed directly to Blough, as he resigned from office in 1938; but the role of the chief accountant for several years had been set in the precedent of his path-breaking judgments, precedents such as in ASR No. 4[1] and the notion of substantial authoritative support. As John Carey has observed,[2] Blough was "not only a competent accountant, but was temperamentally ideally qualified for the job. A minister's son, he was attracted by public service. He was vigorous, industrious, and self-confident, but open-minded and judicious — not doctrinaire. When convinced he was right, he stood his ground, but he could disagree without being disagreeable. His candor, complete honesty, and good nature inspired confidence. He was not without a gift of diplomacy. He got along well with people. He had a sense of humor. He could relax convivially. He had no pretensions."

William W. Werntz (May 1938–April 1947). Historically, we must acknowledge the significant influence of Blough in guiding the Commission's ruling on ASR No. 4 with regard to accounting principles. Similarly, we find under the chief accountantship of Werntz an important precedent as to the establishment of auditing standards under the direction of the profession in the wake of the *McKesson-Robbins* case.

In December 1938, McKesson-Robbins, a large, widely known company principally engaged in drugs and chemicals, was suspended from trading in the New York Stock Exchange in light of a suit and other revelations with regard to the financial representations of the corporation. Assets approximating $19 million (total consolidated assets, $87 million) were subsequently found to have been fictitious. For the prior year ended December 31, 1937, the financial statements had been certified by Price Waterhouse & Co. Other investigations revealed that the president of the corporation was in reality an individual who had previously been convicted of several commercial frauds and that other principal officials in McKesson had been acting under assumed names. All this added up to a juicy bit of scandal.

The SEC commenced hearings on the McKesson-Robbins frauds in 1939, shortly after the revelations had been made. In the meanwhile, the CPA profession began to act independently, establishing a special committee to deal with auditing procedures. At issue was whether the generally accepted auditing procedures for the examination of assets and the presentation of financial statements were adequate to discover such frauds and to protect the investing public. The outcome, in part because of the expeditious action of the profession, was the issuance of the first auditing standard, Statement on Auditing Procedure (SAP) No. 1, *Extensions of Auditing Procedure.* The gist of this pronouncement was to require that the observation of inventories and confirmation of receivables be required where reasonable and practicable to do so. When the SEC concluded its hearings in April 1939, it began to deliberate the appropriate course of action with regard to the professional competence of independent accountants as a result of the deficiencies determined. By this time, however, the procedures that had now been set forth under SAP No. 1 had been approved by the Council of the American Institute. ASR No. 19, issued in December 1940, revealed the findings and conclusions of the SEC with regard to McKesson-Robbins. While noting that the auditors had failed to employ the degree of vigilance and inquisitiveness necessary in a professional undertaking, the Commission also acknowledged that the profession had acted promptly to address the overall procedural deficiencies through the issuance of SAP No. 1. In this way, the Commission recognized auditors' efforts to establish their authority over their own rules of work. While some may contend that such authority was not in question, since the language of the law does not clearly authorize the Commission or its principals to mandate auditing procedures, others have held that had the profession not acted promptly and appropriately, action or legislation to empower the SEC to do so might have been forthcoming.

Also in 1939, a significant precedent emerged in the *Interstate Hosiery Mills* case. While this case did not primarily involve an issue of the responsibility for financial information, the judgment indicated that the management of a company subject to SEC jurisdiction had the responsibility for the financial information filed with the Commission. The findings in this case tended to establish and reinforce a prevalent belief that management had primary responsibility for the selection and application of accounting principles and that the auditors' duties extended to the satisfaction of their own judgment as to the propriety of such principles under the norm of substantial authoritative support.

In February 1940, the Commission established a revision of previous filing rules relative to the acts that it had now taken the responsibility for enforcing. This revision had been directed by Werntz since he had come to the Commission as a member of the Forms Division under Harold Neff. Werntz had compiled the rules for what had originally been identified as Regulation Z, later retitled Regulation S-X, issued in 1940. Regulation S-X specified the form and content of financial information and statements to be filed with the Commission.

It was also during Werntz's term as chief accountant, in 1941, that Regulation S-X was revised to require that the certificate of the independent accountant refer to conformity with generally accepted auditing standards.

During his term as chief accountant, Werntz also tackled the difficult issue of independence, which had been rather unclearly dealt with on a preliminary basis in ASR No. 2, wherein a net worth measure of conflict of interest had been established. In ASR No. 25, using the issue of independence as the basis of decision, Werntz ruled that the agreements between registrants and accountants to hold the accountant harmless from all losses and liabilities arising out of his certification (i.e., to idemnify the accountant) would seriously impair the independence of the accountant, such that the chief accountant would not recognize the independence of the public accountant in certifying financial statements to be registered with the Commission. Werntz sought to further operationalize the concept of independence by citing specific cases relative to the matter of independence in ASR No. 47, issued in January 1944. The principles of compiling and considering these cases had been set forth a few months earlier in ASR No. 44, wherein the Commission had stated that an accountant would not be considered independent with respect to a registrant in whom he had a substantial interest, direct or indirect, or with whom he was, during the period of the report, connected as a promoter or underwriter, voting trustee, director, officer, or employee.

The notion of independence had by now become one of considerable importance to the public accounting profession, the registrant, and the SEC. It continues today to be a critical matter in the nature of the professional service offered by the accountant who certifies the statements of the publicly held corporation filing with the Commission.

As if addressing the issues of authority over auditing rules, the matter of management responsibility for the selection of accounting principles and the issuance of Regulation S-X were not enough, it was Werntz who instituted proceedings under Rule II(e) of the rules of practice of the Commission (wherein the disciplined practitioners were found to be deficient in independence and competence with regard to their practice before the Commission). All of this activity, of course, was taking place during the very difficult and demanding years of World War II.

After resigning from the Commission in May 1947, Werntz turned to public practice as a member of the firm Touche, Niven, Bailey & Smart. Among his early responsibilities at that firm were duties relative to the Seaboard Commercial Corporation. The annual report of that corporation for the fiscal year ended December 31, 1947, became the basis for an Accounting Series Release issued nearly a decade later (ASR No. 78, March 25, 1957). In instituting proceedings under Rule II(e), the Commission asserted that the financial statements of Seaboard at December 31, 1947, were materially misleading, in that inadequate reserves had been reflected for accounts known to be doubtful of collection and that current assets were overstated as a result. Because of the newly formed status of the firm, and because of the involvement of Werntz on that assignment, the determination of the Commission as to the degree of responsibility held by Werntz was unclear. Nevertheless, the firm and Werntz were sanctioned and denied the privilege of practicing before the SEC for 15 days.

In studying the history of the Commission, the irony of this situation is that someone who formally was in charge of the accounting policy of a regulatory agency could subsequently be considered to have practiced improperly before it immediately after departing from the Commission.

In his writings, Werntz not only evidences his scholarship, but his understanding of the relationship between law and accounting. Among his cogent notions is the following, made with regard to accounting as a control device:

> *It was impossible that this development of accounting as a control device origi-*
> *nating in the business world would go unnoticed by legislative bodies and judicial*
> *and administrative officials. It was inevitable, in the search for an effective means*
> *of obtaining data as a social and economic phenomena, [that] early resorts should*
> *be had to accounting data. Thenceforth, it was but a short and logical step to*
> *reliance on the accounting process, first, as a means of regularly observing the*
> *activities of economic units, and then as a means of prescribing and proscribing*
> *courses of action. It is most interesting to note, in passing, that the effective use*
> *of accounting as a control over government itself has lagged far behind the use*
> *of accounting by government as a means of policing and controlling those whom*
> *it governs. Only recently have some of the most obvious improvements of busi-*
> *ness accounting been enlisted in an effort to control governmental activities.*[3]

Werntz observed that administrative agencies had been a significant influence on the development of accounting in the last half century predating 1950, and that overall they enforced and enlarged a greater amount of detail data collecting and probably contributed by the improvement of accounting methods that might not otherwise have been developed. On balance, he concluded, it seems probable that accounting thought and practice progressed further and faster under the stimulus of such agencies than it would otherwise have done.

Werntz's writings suggest not only the awareness as to the potency of accounting as a control device, but also of the potential for legislative and governmental agencies to use accounting information primarily for social control and economic planning.

Earle C. King (April 1947–November 1956). King had come to the Commission's Registration Division in 1934 and was assigned to Blough when the chief accountant's office was created. In April 1947, he succeeded William Werntz and continued in that position until November 1956, when he resigned. King is perhaps the least well known of the chief accountants of the SEC. This lack of recognition deserves to be addressed. An editorial in the June 1947 *Journal of Accountancy,* pertaining to the years preceding King's chief accountantship, suggests that "a happy state of affairs" had existed relative to the tenure of Werntz and Blough. And it seemed, since fewer than two dozen Accounting Series Releases were issued under King, that this condition continued. (One might saucily observe that such a modest number of ASRs would not even have been a fair night's work for "Sandy" Burton in his heyday during the mid-1970s.)

The lack of productivity, however, does not necessarily indicate a lack of activity on the part of the Commission in matters relating to financial reporting and disclosure. King's philosophy was not to use the Commission filings as a proving ground for innovations in reporting techniques. One might observe that the existing rules for reporting and measurement were deemed to be suitable and in the eyes of the chief accountant innovation or "proving" of new disclosure techniques should take place in the periodic reports (management's reports to shareholders), rather than in the statutory disclosures in the Commission. King, much like his predecessors, was attuned to the "disclosure qua remedy" theme that had been sounded by Professor Ripley 25 years earlier. An important accomplishment of the King term as chief accountant includes the major revision of Regulation S-X set forth in ASR No. 70. This comprehensive amendment of Regulation S-X included eliminating old, awkward, and unsuitable terminology, such as reserves and surpluses, as had been recommended and encouraged during the preceding decade. The release was finally issued in December 1950, undertaken amidst an environment of the rapidly changing expectations and multiple economic uncertainties of the post–World War II period.

Confrontation on Income Disclosure

Battle lines became drawn on the issuance of Accounting Research Bulletin (ARB) No. 32, under the authority of the Committee on Accounting Procedure (CAP) of the Institute. The committee had issued the bulletin, which endorsed the current operating concept of net income. The Commission had previously expressed a preference for an all-inclusive concept of income and, in keeping with this, King requested that in conjunction with the published announcement of ARB. No. 32, his letter to the committee be published in the *Journal of Accountancy*. It was so published in the January 1948 issue. The letter, dated December 11, 1947, contained the following statement: "The Commission has authorized the staff to take exception to financial statements which appear to be misleading, even though they reflect the application of Accounting Research Bulletin No. 32."

The CAP attempted compromise by issuing ARB No. 35 but the clash continued and subsequently was to be accented by other conflicts, although as we have observed, King had otherwise limited the number of ASRs as to technical matters.

The accounting academic community also exercised its view with regard to the controversy between the SEC and the CAP on the matter of accounting for net income. In one of its moments of academic decisiveness (during the term of Professor Perry Mason's presidency), the American Accounting Association passed a resolution at its annual meeting "condemning" the SEC for deciding accounting principles. It is not known what the effect of this resolution was on the Commission, but it is important to note that academics mustered the resolve to take a position.

The interchange between the Institute and the SEC did lead to the resolution of some differences. The Commission withdrew the term "principles" in its revised text of Regulation S-X and left it as a "disclosure" requirements document. This was undertaken with the understanding that the Institute would get to work to create the proper accounting principles.

It is probably important to note from the point of view of hindsight that income statement disclosure as it now is established takes the form of a "modified, all-inclusive" arrangement. While the term "modified" suggests compromise, the form indicates that an all-inclusive versus a current operating approach has been followed, and would seem to indicate that the Commission influenced the profession as to the approach.

Lest the reference to the "happy state of affairs" above and the lack of a deluge of Accounting Series Releases be taken to indicate that King had become "soft on the accounting profession," it should be noted that during his term as chief accountant, the first Rule II(e) proceedings against one of the eight largest international CPA firms was instituted (ASR No. 73) in the matter of Haskin & Sells and Andrew Stewart and their client Thomascolor.

The results of the hearings resulted in the suspension of practice for both Haskins & Sells and Andrew Stewart for 10 days. While the suspension seems to be a minor penalty, it should be remembered that when a firm itself is denied practice before the Commission for a period of time, other clients of the firm are inconvenienced and punished. Therefore, the Commission does not take lightly the imposition of such a suspension. And since suspensions of this nature tended to inconvenience clients, they served as an economic sanction for firms, in that clients who were prohibited from entering the public capital markets during this period, because they lacked CPA representation, might choose to be represented by other independent accountants.

Andrew Barr (November 1956–January 1972). Barr had been recruited to the SEC by Carman Blough in 1938. When Earle King resigned his position, Barr, who had been assistant chief accountant, was selected as King's successor. His tenure was to last until January 1972, and the number of ASRs issued during his term as chief accountant would number nearly 60. Because of his extensive experience at the Commission, Andy Barr quickly stepped in and accepted the responsibility for continuation of the policies that had been established by his predecessors. He was equally familiar with the personalities and predilections of each, having served with them over a period of almost 20 years.

Barr's views on independence provided the basis for the actions that led to the current Institute rule of professional conduct with regard to that subject. Furthermore, his innovative techniques for disclosing nonconsolidated significant subsidiaries (as in the *Atlantic Research Corporation* case of 1964) provided a precedent for adequate disclosure within the maze of conflicting alternatives for consolidated reports during the merger period of the 1960s. Barr also dealt with the issue of the Commission position on the investment credit in the early 1960s. He was also involved in the deliberations relative to the 1964 amendments to the Exchange Act, which extended the authority of the Commission and its accounting rules to the wide body of "over-the-counter securities" for companies with $1 million of assets and (now) 500 shareholders. The significant extension of the 1964 amendments to include such companies was in part a response to concern that many insurance companies and bank corporations whose securities had not been traded on public exchanges were employing woefully inadequate accounting and disclosure practices. The annual report to the Congress by the SEC for 1964 describes the intent in the 1964 legislation. Transportation companies such as railroads were now included as a result of the 1964 amendments; that is to say, they were subject to file with the SEC for the first time but were permitted to use statements prepared for the Interstate Commerce Commission (ICC), and because the ICC had prescribed the disclosure requirements, the reports were not required to be certified by public accountants. However, following the Penn-Central disaster in the late 1960s, the Commission now requires that information follow the rules established for other commercial companies. As a result of the 1964 amendments, banks that were under the control of federal bank regulatory agencies would not be required to file under regulations of the Commission, but any banks not subject to federal bank regulatory agencies would be so required under the 1964 amendments. Reporting by insurance companies, while extremely complicated by the fact of state regulations, was expanded to include insurance companies that were involved in interstate commerce and that met the size test of $1 million of assets and 500 security holders.

Barr's term might be characterized as one of dedication to the processes that were initiated by his predecessors. ASR No. 4 remained at the heart of the administration of the Securities Acts relative to accounting principles. But the difficulty of abiding by the partnership as established on those terms (substantial authoritative support) was becoming all too apparent as evidenced in the matter of ASR No. 96 on investment credit, issued January 10, 1963. Prior to this ASR, the Accounting Principles Board (APB), the newly formed senior technical committee of the Institute, which was vested with the authority to establish accounting principles for practitioners, had directed to treat the investment credit on the deferred basis. The Commission had to decide to accept this treatment in filings or to accept either the deferred or the flow-through treatment. As the day of final deliberation was reached, it was noted that in the area of public utilities, where the treatment of investment credit was a most critical factor, major firms and utilities were about equally split with regard to the treatment between deferral and flow-through. The Commission had no basis in practice for preferring one treatment over the other. Further, the APB was not sufficiently constituted by all major firms to insure that its promulgations would be followed. Necessary professional sanctions did not exist as a means to discipline those who might choose to disagree with an APB pronouncement. Thus, perhaps with some reluctance, the Commission directed that either approach would be acceptable.

In the history of the accounting profession's attempts at self-regulation and development of accounting principles, this episode is often regarded as a critical one, in that the SEC, by the effect of this release, is considered to have "broken the back" of this attempt by the APB.

When viewed from the position of the chief accountant, the lack of clear support in law or theory for one approach over the other, it is understandable that the Commission chose to permit either technique. This episode was also a bellwether of the fact that industry had come of age in recognizing the importance of alternative treatments of accounting principles with regard to potential economic consequences. Without precedent and without research to determine the potential outcomes of investment credit legislation, the Commission had little choice but to allow either treatment.

Despite the profession's setback on the issue of authority related to the matters of investment credit, the SEC worked cooperatively with the APB affording the profession the opportunity to deal with such issues as leases, pensions, and earnings-per-share disclosures.

Critics of the Commission have claimed that this period of SEC policy was clearly one of abandoning the duties and responsibilities of the Commission by permitting the APB to establish, or attempt to establish, accounting principles. But from the Commission's point of view, it would appear that the willingness to accept the profession's leadership was consistent with the policy set in ASR No. 4, as well as with a belief that management had a right to express its point of view in the periodic reports. Without Barr's patience and the cooperation of the Commission, it seems likely that the trial-and-error procedures which the APB underwent in the process of perfecting a private sector-standard setting approach might never have taken place, particularly if the Commission has acted vigorously during this period.

But we can reserve speculation on such a matter and point to the fact that as the chief accountantship of Andrew Barr came to a close, new studies, to be identified as the Wheat and Trueblood reports, would alter the partnership between the Commission to reflect the changing technological and investment forces which were impacting the capital market structure of the country.

John C. "Sandy" Burton (June 1972–September 1976). Burton came from the Graduate School of Business at Columbia University to the office of chief accountant at the age of 39. His prior experience as an academic, including host coordinator of the Seaview Symposia (which dealt with important disclosure and ethical considerations in the capital markets of the 1960s and 1970s), familiarized him with the concerns of the many parties who had a vested interest in the disclosure system as it existed under the securities laws. One might appropriately term these the years of "the sound and the fury," but that might be unfair and a poor attempt to add humor to a very important period in the history of our profession.

With the economy of the early 1970s struggling to maintain the confidence of the American people, and the political environment not being necessarily conducive to extensive capital market adventure, Burton's record, one of clear activism, displays an impressive innovation. To begin with, in the areas of lease disclosure and of treasury shares, we find attempts to halt questionable accounting practices, and in later pronouncements we find disclosure rules and disciplinary actions that suggest some degree of intestinal fortitude.

From the end of 1945, when the Institute numbered a mere 9000 members, to the mid-1970s when its membership numbered over 130,000, it became clear that the rapidly growing public accounting profession had lost the ability to give itself clear direction.

Resource managers in the capital markets, who had grown to depend on the representations of the independent accountant, were getting misty information signals. Double-digit inflation was also eroding the meaningfulness of financial disclosures. Periodic management reports to shareholders submitted in support of proxy solicitations were still prepared under generally accepted accounting principles as determined by "substantial authoritative support" which afforded no clear basis of authority. Watergate, Equity Funding, Lockheed and other political and economic affairs had laid low the confidence of the general investing public. Burton dealt courageously and creatively with the many issues he encountered. First, he indicated support for the attempt of the accounting profession to establish its own independent rule-making agency (ASR No. 150). Indeed ASR No. 150 was the cornerstone of a new era of disclosure policy, just as ASR No. 4 had been the cornerstone of the previous one. ASR 150 recognized the Financial Accounting Standards Board (FASB) as the agency whose pronouncements were considered to have substantial authoritative support.[4]

When considered along with ASR No. 159 and the related amendments to the proxy rules (which accomplished what had long been recognized as feasible under the acts, namely that the Commission had the authority to dictate not only the contents of the reports filed with it but also the contents of any reports submitted in solicitation of proxies), ASR No. 150 stands as the policy hallmark for this new generation of chief accountants. ASR No. 159 was the start of the end of the "dual stream" of financial reporting (the 10-K and the corporate annual report). Notwithstanding Burton's commitment to "differential disclosure," what has now evolved is the policy tool to afford the Commission the control over both 10-K and periodic report contents. Even more, when viewed as the constructs of a new disclosure policy, ASR Nos. 150 and 159 amalgamate the authority of the private sector and the public sector over both the filings with the Commission and management disclosures in the annual report to shareholders.

Burton's exhortations via ASRs and his innovative Staff Accounting Bulletins (SABs) were not limited to the matter of the authority of the Commission in relation to the accounting principles. Indeed, in the area of auditing policy an important issue with regard to interim reports involving "the auditor of record" became a matter of confrontation. In an attempt to add credibility to the limited review of interim financial statements as required under ASR No. 177, Burton sought the assistance of the Auditing Standards Executive Committee (AudSEC) to develop guidelines for such reviews. The controversy surrounding Statement on Auditing Standards (SAS) No. 10 included some important last-minute changes in posture by AudSEC such that an "acceptable" audit "disclosure" was finally achieved.

Burton initiated several important precedent-setting sanctions against national public accounting firms, one of the most important of which was the sanction of Peat, Marwick, Mitchell & Co., as detailed in ASR No. 173. Such creative sanctioning introduced the concept of a firm peer review. It is important to recognize that the process of disciplining a firm, at that time, was unavailable to the Institute through its rules of professional conduct, which were capable of individual sanction only. The notion of peer review established a basis for evaluating the competence of a firm as well as the policies of that firm to include its internal quality controls.

If the sanctions imposed and the pressures relative to SAS No. 10 were not sufficient to draw the fire of the accounting profession on the new chief accountant, his actions with regard to the independent accountant's responsibility for newly adopted principles, set forth in the interpretation of ASR No. 177, clearly afforded a choice target. Whether such a preferability judgment need be made by the independent accountant may one day need to be decided by the courts.

Burton's innovations did not stop with ASR No. 177. In fact, they did not reach a zenith until ASR No. 190, requiring the unaudited disclosure of replacement costs by certain large registrants. ASR No. 190, and its accompanying safe-harbor provision, ASR NO. 203, were attempts by Burton to address the issue of inflation accounting. Taken in perspective, ASR Nos. 190 and 203 represent a logical extension of the hallmark of the term of this "first" chief accountant in this "new" generation. ASR No. 190 is consistent with a structure of unaudited interim information data, other socially relevant data, and the proposal for forecast information within a new trend of soft data. "Soft data" accountability distinguishes this generation of chief accountants from the preceding one, which was identified with historical cost and financial data disclosure.

If all these changes are taken in light of the "scienter" limitations established by the Supreme Court ruling on the 1934 Act liability provisions (the *Hochfelder* decision), perhaps the accounting profession can find some solace when considering the Burton years. One might note that this is what would be expected from the son of a former managing partner in a national public accounting firm. My view is that Burton was gutsy and he had gusto.

ACCORD AND COMING ATTRACTIONS

When Sandy Burton resigned his position and took on the task of Deputy Mayor of Finance for the City of New York, the job of chief accountant fell vacant and has remained so.*

---

* A Clarence Sampson, serving as Associate Chief Accountant under Burton, was appointed Acting Chief Accountant. In August 1978 Sampson was named Chief Accountant.

Some have suggested that the new chairman of the Commission, Harold M. Williams, is in effect serving in the chief accountant capacity, as well as fulfilling the duties of the chairmanship. In one respect, with the able talent of A. Clarence Sampson, acting chief accountant, there may be little concern for the ability of the Commission to continue to implement the innovative policies that were introduced by Burton.

New issues have also evolved and new pronouncements (some of which were to some extent initiated under Burton's tenure as chief accountant) have come to fruition, including segment reporting, another proposal for forecast disclosure and the potential for involvement by public accountants in the process of disclosing questionable or illegal payments by registrants. All this has occurred under the close political scrutiny of Congressional committees (and others charged with a public-spirited curiosity and wrath) relative to the problems of disclosure and the capital markets.

The deliberations of the Advisory Committee on Corporate Disclosure (ACCORD), as contained in its report of November 1977, provides added insight to the role which the SEC may play in this new era. While the Commission's position toward the recommendations of the advisory committee falls short of a blanket endorsement of the recommendations, its response (as contained in Release 34–14471) endorses the recommendations made by the committee and, in many respects, action that has already been taken by the SEC tends to strengthen the prospects for accomplishing a major number of important recommendations in ACCORD, including additional soft information disclosures, such as earnings projections and other future-oriented information, and the study of differences in the cost-benefit relation of various disclosure rules of the Commission with regard to large and small registrant companies.

The Commission also has embarked recently on investigations relative to corporations' policies for payments of perquisites to management. The chairman of the Commission has gone on record as encouraging limited participation by active members of management on the board of directors of registrants.

Further, an amendment to the 1934 Securities Act created by the passage of the Foreign Corrupt Practices Act of 1977 will likely increase the involvement of the Commission and the office of the chief accountant in matters of internal control policies and as to disclosure of the adequacy of such systems.

A final observation with regard to recent developments includes noticing comments by the newest SEC commissioner, Roberta Karmel, as to the interest of the Commission in matters of "competition." In a speech before the U.S. Air Force Academy on alternatives to government regulations, she said

> *Government regulations are necessarily a reactive force which seems to have lim-*
> *ited ability for creating initiatives in the economics sphere. One of my concerns*
> *about overregulation is that it is a drag on private sector development and inno-*
> *vation. There are at least two alternatives to greater government regulation which*
> *play an important role in the SEC's administration of the federal securities law,*
> *namely disclosure and competition (emphasis added). Disclosure enables investors*
> *to exercise their judgment through their voting rights as to whether or not direc-*
> *tors and officers have acted in a company's best interest. Disclosure may lead to*
> *public debate on the morality of public conduct.* [Later she said,] *I believe that a*

*competitive environment is generally more conducive to responsible business be-
havior than an environment characterized by regulatory controls.*

Does this statement suggest that the SEC will become active in judging disclosure in
light of competition? Is such a role consistent with its legislative authority and conducive to
the free enterprise notion of market derived competition? Only time will tell the significance
of these statements.

As to the period that began with the term of Carman Blough and ended with the term of
Andrew Barr, we can note (1) the establishment of the notion of professional independence
as contained in the rules of professional conduct and (2) the development of the concept of
substantial authoritative support which is linked to the second generation through ASR No.
150. We also find established a customary view of the role of recognizing management's responsibility for the determination of appropriate accounting principles and policies and we
see the evolution of the "strong, silent type of cooperation" between the chief accountant
and the accounting profession. Overall, this initial generation is characterized by concern
with disclosure of historical cost-based financial data.

It is probably appropriate to characterize this initial era as one of mixed "public interest"
and "capture." The critical Accounting Series Releases number at least a half dozen, including ASR Nos. 4, 19, 62, 78, 90, and 96.

By the end of the first generation of chief accountants, the capital markets in the American economy, not to mention the American public accounting profession, had matured and
evolved into a different interdependent state, one that was characterized by the high technology of computers and mass communication facilities. The new and yet to be fully characterized second generation of chief accountants, as established by the policies of John C. Burton,
is one of "soft data" and social "accountability." Much remains to be decided about where
this disclosure philosophy will lead. Does the prospect for social and political control as
noted in Werntz's writings in the 1950s exist, and is there a chance that it will be enhanced
under this approach? Only time will tell. What is clear about the new generation is that it has
afforded the accounting profession both the opportunity, through creative new disclosure
programs (including quarterly and replacement cost disclosures) and through programs
which provide for firm discipline (namely, peer review), to reestablish a positive and respected public image among consumers of accounting information within the capital markets.

In conclusion, two observations are required. First, the office of the chief accountant
has become an institution, not only in the United States but in the Western World. Second, accountancy as an economic institution is in a phase of evolution such that it must now
be examined from the point of view of political science, as well as from that of an art of recording and reporting financial-based transactional data.

NOTES

1. Accounting Series Release No. 4, April 25, 1938, 11 F.R. 10913.
    The Securities and Exchange Commission today issued the following statement of its ad-
ministrative policy with respect to financial statements:

> *In cases where financial statements filed with this Commission pursuant to its rules and regulations
> under the Securities Act of 1933 or the Securities Exchange Act of 1934 are prepared in accordance
> with accounting principles for which there is no substantial authoritative support, such financial state-*

> *ments will be presumed to be misleading or inaccurate despite disclosures contained in the certificate of the accountant or in footnotes to the statements provided the matters involved are material. In cases where there is a difference of opinion between the Commission and the registrant as to the proper principles of accounting to be followed, disclosure will be accepted in lieu of correction of the financial statements themselves only if the points involved are such that there is substantial authoritative support for the practices followed by the registrant and the position of the Commission has not previously been expressed in rules, regulations, or other official releases of the Commission, including the published opinions of its chief accountant.*

2. Carey, J. L. "The CPA's Professional Heritage — Part IV," The Academy of Accounting Historians — Working Paper Series, December 1977.

3. Werntz, W. W., "The Influence of Administrative Agencies on Accounting," *Handbook of Modern Accounting Theory,* 1955, pp. 99–118 (Morton Backer, ed.).

4. Accounting Series Release No. 150, issued December 20, 1973, says, in part:

> *The [SEC] intends to continue its policy of looking to the private sector for leadership in establishing and improving accounting principles and standards through the FASB with the expectation that the body's conclusions will promote the interests of investors.*
>
> *In Accounting Series Release No. 4 (1938) the Commission stated its policy that financial statements prepared in accordance with accounting practices for which there was no substantial authoritative support were presumed to be misleading and that footnote or other disclosure would not avoid this presumption. It also stated that, where there was a difference of opinion between the Commission and a registrant as to the proper accounting to be followed in a particular case, disclosure would be accepted in lieu of correction of the financial statements themselves only if substantial authoritative support existed for the accounting practices followed by the registrant and the position of the Commission had not been expressed in rules, regulations, or other official releases. For purposes of this policy, principles, standards, and practices promulgated by the FASB in Statements and Interpretations will be considered by the Commission as having substantial authoritative support, and those contrary to such FASB promulgations will be considered to have no such support.*
>
> *Accounting Research Bulletins of the Committee on Accounting Procedure of the American Institute of Certified Public Accountants and effective opinions of the Accounting Principles Board of the Institute should be considered as continuing in force with the same degree of authority except to the extent altered, amended, supplemented, revoked or superseded by one or more Statements of Financial Accounting Standards issued by the FASB.*
>
> *It should be noted that Rule 203 of the Rules of Conduct of the Code of Ethics of the AICPA provides that it is necessary to depart from accounting principles promulgated by the body designated by the Council of the AICPA if, due to unusual circumstances, failure to do so would result in misleading financial statements. In such a case, the use of other principles may be accepted or required by the Commission.*

TWENTY-SEVEN

Line of Business Reporting and Security Prices: An Analysis of an SEC Disclosure Rule: Comment

RICHARD R. SIMONDS

Michigan State University

and

DANIEL W. COLLINS

State University of Iowa

In an earlier article in The Bell Journal of Economics, *Horowitz and Kolodny reported that imposition of the SEC's line of business reporting requirements did not affect investors' assessments of the riskiness of multisegment firms. We suggest that shortcomings in their sample-selection and hypothesis-testing procedures may have led to this result. Our empirical analyses indicate that LOBUR disclosure did convey useful information to investors and that the average effect was a downward shift in their assessment of a multisegment firm's market riskiness.*

1. INTRODUCTION

In a recent article appearing in this *Journal,* Horowitz and Kolodny (1977) attempted to assess the impact of Securities and Exchange Commission (SEC) line of business reporting (LOBUR) requirements on the securities markets. Specifically, one major aspect of their study dealt with the investigation of whether or not changes in perceived market risks of multisegment were significantly greater than those of single-segment firms around the time previously nondisclosed line of business information became public in 1970 10-K reports.[1] As the authors note, significantly greater changes in market riskiness at the time of initial disclosure of LOBUR data would suggest that such reporting does convey information to

---

investors which is useful in assessing the risk and, therefore, return prospects of multiseg-ment firms.

On the basis of their analyses, however, Horowitz and Kolodny (H-K) draw the follow-ing conclusion:

> *The null hypothesis that the required disclosure had no effect on the risk and return of securities close to the time of its reporting could not be rejected at the 0.05 level in any of the tests. Thus the authors' results provide no evidence in support of the universally accepted contention that the SEC required disclosure furnished investors with valuable information (Horowitz and Kolodny, 1977, p. 247).*

H-K's results and conclusions would seem to have direct relevance to the deliberations of the Special Advisory Committee on Corporate Disclosure which was recently formed to conduct a comprehensive investigation and evaluation of SEC reporting rules and practices.[2] Indeed, one of the charges given this committee was the determination of the effect various SEC disclosure practices have had on security prices. Presumably, this effort was under-taken with the intent of eliminating or revising those reporting requirements which have had little or no demonstrated effect on the pricing of securities.

With the obvious policy implications of H-K's research results in mind, it seems to us most important to investigate thoroughly the basis for their conclusions concerning the ef-fects of LOBUR disclosure on market risk changes. For as Sunder has recently warned:

> *Before we can convincingly argue that the role of accounting in security markets is minor or nonexistent, we must demonstrate that the procedures used for its detection are sufficiently powerful to have detected a role if it exists.... How large an effect will there have to be in order to have a good chance of appearing significant in statistical testing in various types of research approaches? In the absence of the knowledge of the power of resolution, it is difficult to conclude that the accounting system does not play a certain type of role simply because our chosen instrument of market price data has failed to render any trace (Sun-der, 1976, p. 7).*

We believe H-K's analyses and associated conclusions concerning the effect of LOBUR on market risk are vulnerable to the challenge offered by Sunder. Accordingly, the first ob-jective of this article is to identify certain deficiencies in H-K's sample-selection and hypothe-sis-testing procedures which appear to have biased their results in favor of finding "no effect." Second, we propose alternative procedures designed to overcome some of these deficiencies. Finally, using these procedures, we present summary results of our own empirical research which suggest, contrary to H-K's findings, that the initiation of SEC LOBUR did have an effect on the perceived riskiness of multisegment firms.

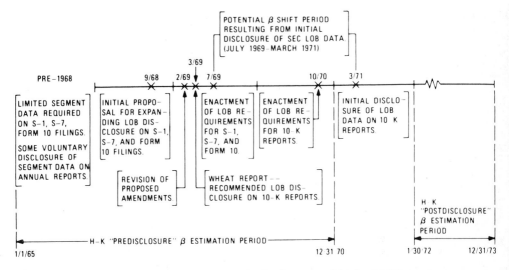

Figure 1. *Time continuum of critical events in the development of SEC LOBUR requirements*

2. H-K'S SAMPLE SELECTION

Two critical aspects of H-K's analysis of the market effects of LOBUR regulation were: (1) the identification of a set of "treatment" firms whose public reporting was most affected by the new SEC reporting requirements; and (2) the identification of a critical time during which to test for the market effects of LOBUR disclosure. In Figure 1 we present a time continuum which depicts the critical events in the evolution of SEC LOBUR. Also indicated are the periods over which H-K estimated the "predisclosure" and "postdisclosure" market risks (beta) of each sample firm. Analysis of this diagram reveals potential biases in their selection of a critical cut-off date for pre-LOBUR disclosure versus post-LOBUR disclosure conditions and in their selection of LOBUR "treatment" firms.

H-K center their analysis on the initial disclosure of LOBUR data in 1970 10-K reports issued within the first three calendar months of 1971. We note, however, as they do, that the SEC LOBUR program was initiated in July 1969, for registration statements S-1, S-7, and Form 10 filings. Accordingly, firms floating new security issues subsequent to this time were required to disclose in these nonperiodic reports *both revenue and profit data by line of business.* Moreover, subsequent to July 1969, such data were frequently disclosed in proxy statements issued in connection with merger proposals.

In view of these facts, it was somewhat surprising that H-K selected their primary treatment sample of LOBUR firms based only on segmental revenue disclosures in annual shareholder reports.[2] Registration and proxy statements which may have been filed by these companies were apparently not examined by H-K. Thus, to the extent that any of H-K's 50 treatment firms were involved in merger activities or floated new securities during the 18-month period from July 1969 to December 1970, LOBUR *revenue and profit data* are likely to have been disclosed and, in an efficient market,[4] impounded in security prices prior to the release of such data in 1970 10-K reports. Failure to consider these alternative sources of LOBUR data represents an obvious bias if one is interested in selecting "treatment" firms which are expected to be most affected by LOBUR disclosure on 1970 10-K reports.

As noted earlier, failure to consider LOBUR disclosure on registration and proxy statements from July 1969 to December 1970 also suggests a bias in H-K's definition of predisclosure versus postdisclosure conditions. Since H-K's "predisclosure" period (January 1965–December 1970) includes this critical 18-month period, any market adjustments to LOBUR data disclosed durring this time would obviously affect their "predisclosure" market risk estimates (beta) and make it less likely that they would find a significant difference between the beta changes estimated for the LOBUR firms and those estimated for the non-LOBUR (control) firms.

In our own research (discussed below) registration and proxy materials, in addition to annual shareholder reports, were studied to determine the extent of segmental disclosure during the 1967–1970 period. In a substantial number of cases both segment revenue and profit data were publicly disclosed in registration or proxy statements (although not in annual shareholder reports) prior to the release of these data in 1970 10-K reports. This suggests that the risk-information impact of LOBUR disclosure for some of H-K treatment firms may well have occurred prior to the end of the "predisclosure" period employed in their analyses.

3. H-K'S STATISTICAL TEST

Another factor which is likely to have contributed to H-K's finding of "no effect" relates to the statistical procedure they used to test the hypothesis that the beta changes were more extreme, on the average, for LOBUR firms than for non-LOBUR firms. In their analysis two separate estimates of beta were computed for each security in the LOBUR and non-LOBUR samples — one for the "predisclosure" period and a second for the "postdisclosure" period. Each estimate was obtained using OLS and the familiar "market model" of the following form:

$$\tilde{R}_{it} = \alpha_i + \beta_i \tilde{R}_{mt} + \tilde{\epsilon}_{it},$$

where α_i is a constant intercept; $\tilde{R}_{it}$ and $\tilde{R}_{mt}$ are the returns on security i and the market portfolio, respectively; β_i is the systematic or market risk of security i defined as $\text{cov}(\tilde{R}_{it}\tilde{R}_{mt})/\text{var}(\tilde{R}_{mt})$; and $\tilde{\epsilon}_{it}$ is an error term independently and identically distributed across t. The absolute value of the change in the estimated beta for each firm was computed and the average of these values determined for each sample group. The averages were then computed using a standard t-test for the difference in means.

Two aspects of this procedure warrant examination. First, how does the large estimation error that exists when beta is estimated at the individual-firm level affect the power of the test? It has been well established empirically (Fama and McBeth, 1973) that at the individual-firm level beta is estimated with considerable error. However, by combining individual securities into portfolios the standard error on beta can be reduced substantially.[5] Since the ability of a testing procedure to detect a change in the level of beta is directly related to the precision of the underlying beta estimates, an investigator may be better off constructing portfolios when trying to detect risk changes. However, doing so comes at some cost. There is no strong *a priori* basis for expecting a beta shift in the same direction for all firms in the LOBUR sample. Therefore, the possibility exists that most of the LOBUR effect present at the individual-firm level might be obfuscated when securities are combined into portfolios.[6] Consequently, beta estimates at the firm level should not be avoided entirely. The challenge is to develop a test at the firm level that has a good prospect of detecting a LOBUR effect, if indeed such an effect exists. We propose one such test in a later section of this article.

Our second aspect of concern is H-K's decision to work with the absolute values of beta changes. Recall that they were interested in detecting whether or not LOBUR led to more extreme changes in beta. It would appear that a more powerful test for the difference in the dispersion of $\Delta\beta$'s for LOBUR and non-LOBUR firms would be a standard F-test assuming underlying normality or a nonparametric test such as that proposed by Moses.[7] The unconventional use of a test for central tendency applied to absolute values to detect dispersion differences is not likely to perform well. Furthermore, if a difference in central tendency does exist between the distributions of raw β changes, it is unclear whether a t-test on the absolute values would detect such a difference.

To investigate these two concerns further, the statistical power of H-K's testing procedure was evaluated using simulated $\Delta\beta$ data with known distributional properties.[8] Three results of this evaluation are noteworthy. First, even if the dispersion of the actual beta changes for the LOBUR firms is four times greater than for non-LOBUR firms, the chance of detecting that difference using the H-K test (α level = 0.05) is only about 0.16. The standard F-test for a difference in variances is superior to H-K's test, but the power is still very low. This arises because of the very large estimation error involved in $\hat{\beta}_i$, particularly in the second estimation interval. Second, if in fact there exists a difference in the means of the distributions generating actual raw beta changes (but equal variances), the t-test conducted using the absolute values is very weak compared to a t-test using raw data. Third, when the mean and variance both differed, one was better off not to use H-K's test. On the basis of our simulations, we feel the H-K "no effect" result is not unexpected and not particularly meaningful.

4. AN ALTERNATIVE APPROACH TO ASSESSING THE RISK-INFORMATION EFFECTS OF LOBUR

In the remainder of this article we briefly describe an alternative approach to assessing the risk-information effects of LOBUR. In addition, we summarize our own experience using this approach in a recently completed inquiry into the market risk effects of LOBUR disclosure. The interested reader can find more complete details of the sample selection process, testing procedures, and empirical findings in Collins and Simonds (C-S) (1977).

The ANCOVA or "Chow" Test

In the market model of equation (1), β_i is the slope of the linear time series relationship between $\tilde{R}_{it}$ and $\tilde{R}_{mt}$ and, as was noted earlier, is a measure of the systematic or market risk of an asset. A common technique of testing for a change in the slope of a linear time series is the analysis-of-covariance (ANCOVA) procedure (sometimes referred to as the "Chow" test) as described by Fisher (1970) and Johnston (1972). This technique, based on an F-statistic,

Table 1.   Summary description of (C-S) sample groups

I. Multisegment treatment group (MST) (78 firms)	Firms that had no or limited segmental disclosure (segment revenue disclosure only) in annual reports, prospectuses, or proxy statements in the period 1967–1970 prior to initiation of SEC LOBUR in the 1970 10-K.
II. Multisegment control group (MSC) (70 firms)	Firms that disclosed both segment revenue *and* segment profit data in annual reports, prospectuses, or proxy statements prior to initiation of SEC LOBUR in the 1970 10-K.
III. Single-segment control group (SSC) (67 firms)	Firms that had no segmental disclosure either before or after initiation of SEC LOBUR in the 1970 10-K.

provides an exact test of the equality of the beta coefficients for two time subperiods. Furthermore, the F-statistic has a noncentral F-distribution given a known value of $\Delta\beta_i$ which may be used to calculate the power of the ANCOVA test procedure.

Empirical Test Results: Portfolio-level Analysis

To test the market risk effects of LOBUR disclosure it was first necessary to segregate sample firms according to the level of their segmental disclosure in annual reports and registration statements or proxy statements issued prior to the filing dates of their 1970 10-K reports. Data sheets were obtained from *Accounting Trends & Techniques* which identified the level and type of segmental disclosure by individual firms in their 1967–1970 annual reports. This list was supplemented with firms whose level of pre-1970 segmental disclosure was identified in the Kinney (1971) and Collins (1976) studies. Next the registration and proxy materials of these firms were examined along with their 1970 10-K reports. Finally, if monthly return data on the CRISP tapes for the time period of October 1965 through July 1974 were not available, the firm was eliminated. This procedure yielded a list of 215 firms that were classified into three distinct groups as described in Table 1.

The firms within each group were further identified by 3-digit SIC industry codes. Each company was classified on the basis of its major line of business as reflected by gross revenues. The results of this classification are presented in the Appendix and suggest that the three sample groups are reasonably comparable in terms of industry representation with the possible exception that the single-segment control firms tend to be more heavily concentrated in service and/or regulated industries. One might expect this group of firms, therefore, to exhibit a lower average beta, since returns of firms operating in such industries tend to be less volatile than the market as a whole. However, this fact should have little bearing on our

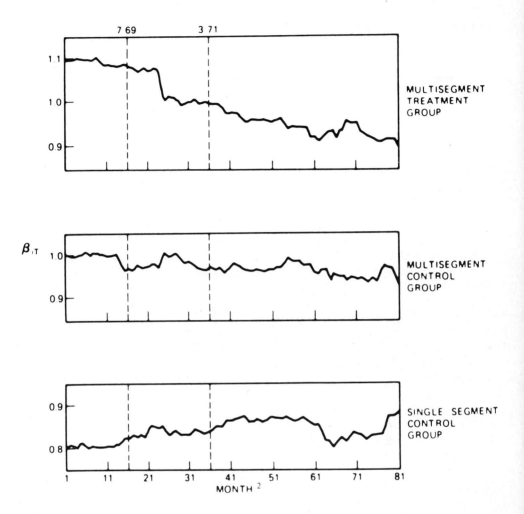

Figure 2. *Estimated moving beta coefficients[1] for April 1968 to December 1964 computed for the multisegment treatment, multisegment control, and single-segment control groups.*

[1] The moving beta coefficient for each month was estimated using the OLS procedure and the market model on return data for a 40-month period ending with that month. For example, in estimating the moving beta for month 1 (April 1968), monthly returns from January 1965 through April 1968 were regressed against the market index for that period.

[2] The designated critical SEC LOB disclosure period is 7/69 to 3/71.

Table 2   Portfolio-level ANCOVA test statistics [a]

	Multisegment treatment group portfolio	Multisegment control group portfolio	Single-segment control group portfolio
F_i Score[b]	12.2	0.188	0.006

[a] Calculated at March 1970.
[b] Critical value for $\alpha = 0.05$ is 3.96.

subsequent tests since our focus is *not* on comparing levels of beta between groups but, rather, on comparing *relative changes* in beta (from pre-LOBUR to post-LOBUR) for treatment versus control groups.

Moving-beta estimates ($\hat{\beta}_{iT}$) were calculated via equation (1) using OLS for each of the three groups or portfolios employing monthly return data for $t = T - 39, \ldots, T$ and Fisher's equally weighted market index as a surrogate for R_{mt}. The results are plotted in Figure 2. Inspection of these graphical results reveals a noticeable downward drift in the beta level of the multisegment treatment group with the most dramatic shift occurring within the *designated critical period* near March 1970 (month 24 in figure 2), which is eight months after the initiation of SEC LOBUR reporting for registration statements and twelve months before the initial disclosure of LOBUR data in 1970 10-K reports. In contrast, the average betas of the multisegment and single-segment control groups reveal considerable stability overall with little change apparent within the designated critical period.

To evaluate the observed beta changes for each of the three groups of firms in a more formal way, the ANCOVA procedure referenced earlier was applied at March 1970, which falls near the middle of the 21-month designated critical SEC LOBUR disclosure period.[9] The test statistics were computed by using contiguous time periods of 40 months and are presented in Table 2.

The results of the ANCOVA tests strongly suggest that the multisegment treatment group portfolio (MST) experienced a significant shift in beta while the multisegment control group portfolio (MSC) and single-segment control group portfolio (SSC) revealed no significant beta change during the designated critical period. The fact that the beta change for the MST portfolio appears to have occurred before March 1971 suggests that SEC LOBUR data were being developed and disseminated to the market well in advance of the time that such data were published as part of the registrant's 1970 10-K report.

Individual Firm-level Analysis

Summary measures of the F_i-statistics computed at March 1970 for the individual firms in each of the C-S test groups are presented in Table 3. The distribution of the sample mean $\tilde{F}_i$ score ($\bar{F}_i$) computed for n firms is well approximated by $\chi^2(n)/n$ under the null hypothesis

Table 3   Individual-firm ANCOVA test statistics for the treatment and control groups [a]

	Mean F_i $(\bar{F}_i)$ [b]	Proportion of significant F_i values [c]
Multisegment treatment group	1.63	11/78
Multisegment control group	1.11	4/70
Single-segment control group	1.19	6/67

[a] Calculated at March 1970.
[b] The value of $\bar{F}_{i(0.05)}$ equals 1.27, 1.29, and 1.30 for the treatment, multisegment control, and single-segment control groups, respectively.
[c] The value of $F_{i(0.05)}$ equals 3.96.

Table 4.   Results of H-K test applied to the C-S samples [a]

	H-K t-test (t-test using absolute value of beta changes)	F-test (for equality of variances)	t-test (using raw beta changes)
MST vs. MSC	1.33 (0.185)	1.14 (0.587)	−2.42 (0.017)
MST vs. SSC	0.48 (0.631)	1.02 (0.915)	−2.63 (0.010)

[a] Significance level shown parenthetically.

$H_0: \Delta\beta_i = 0$, for all i.[10] As can be seen from Table 3, the constant-beta hypothesis is not rejected at the 0.05 level for the two control groups since the $\bar{F}_i$ values of 1.11 and 1.19 are below the critical values of 1.29 and 1.30. The hypothesis is rejected, however, for the treatment group, since the $\bar{F}_i$ statistic of 1.63 exceeds the 0.05 critical value of 1.27. Also, the proportion of $\bar{F}_i$ scores exceeding the critical value of 3.96 is approximately twice as great for the treatment group versus either control group. Therefore, on an individual-firm basis, as well as on a portfolio basis, the treatment group appears different.

As a further comparison of the test employed by H-K and the ANCOVA test used by C-S, the H-K test was applied to the MST, MSC, and SSC samples. The results are shown in Figure 3 and Table 4. The betas were estimated using two contiguous subperiods of 40

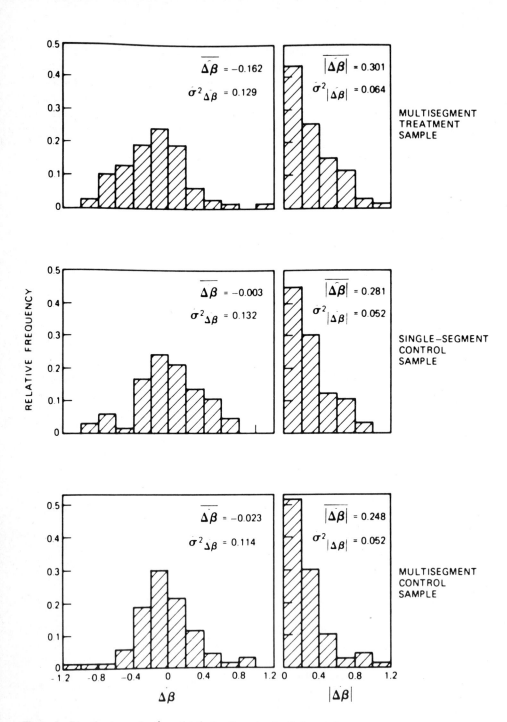

Figure 3 *Distributions of* Δ^b *and* $|\Delta\beta|$ *for firms in the C-S samples*

months centered on March 1970. As was anticipated, the distributions of $|\delta\hat{\beta}|$ for all three samples are highly skewed. When using the H-K procedure, the null hypothesis of no difference between the treatment and control group was not rejected in comparing MST and MSC or MST and SSC. Neither was it rejected using the standard F-test for equality of variances. If the t-tests were conducted using the raw beta changes, however, significant test statistics would have been obtained. This result occurs because the average beta changed by −0.162 for the treatment group, while the average changes were only −0.023 and −0.003 for the MSC and SSC control groups, respectively.

5. SUMMARY

We presented shortcomings in H-K's sample-selection and hypothesis-testing procedures which may have been responsible for their finding that LOBUR did not affect investors' assessment of the riskiness of multisegment firms. The results of our empirical analyses suggest, contrary to H-K's findings, that the initiation of SEC LOBUR disclosure did convey useful information to investors for assessing the market riskiness of multisegment firms. Furthermore, the average effect was a downward shift in beta.

One possible explanation for the observed decline in market risk is suggested by Kochanek (1974):

> ... *if segmental disclosure does provide a more objective basis of evaluating the future earnings performance of a diversified firm and thereby currently valuing the firm's stock in line with these expectations, then stock price fluctuations due to investor ignorance should be lessened and therefore price dispersion should be narrowed over time (p. 247).*

The results of Konachek's empirical tests suggest that predictions of future earnings were facilitated by the availability of segment data and that those firms voluntarily disclosing subentity data exhibited lower weekly stock price variability over time than firms not providing such information.

Additional evidence of the improvements in earnings forecasts from the use of LOBUR data is provided in the Kinney (1971) and Collins (1976) studies. Moreover, Barefield and Comiskey (1973) have demonstrated a positive relationship between beta and the level of forecasting error in firm earnings as reflected in analysts' forecasts. Together, these results suggest that the observed decline in market beta, on average, may be a consequence of improvements in earnings forecastability, which results from LOBUR data.

APPENDIX

Industry Membership of Sample Firms*

3-digit SIC Industry code	Industry Name	Multi-segment treatment group (78 firms)	Multi-segment control group (70 firms)	Single product control group (67 firms)
10–14	Mining			
100/104	Metals, Copper Ores, Gold	2		4
121	Coal		1	
131	Oil — Crude Producers	1	1	
20–39	Manufacturing Industries			
200	Food — Packaged	1	2	1
201/203	Meat, Dairy, Canned Foods		3	
205/206	Foods — Bread and Cakes/Sugar	1	1	4
208	Beverages	1	1	2
211/212	Cigarettes, Cigars	3	2	
220/230	Textiles/Textile Apparel	1		2
240	Forest Products	1	2	
251	Home Furnishings	1		
260	Paper/Paper Containers	2		1
272/275	Peridicals/Books/Printing		2	2
280	Chemicals	5	7	
283	Drugs	3	4	
284	Soap and Cosmetics			1
289	Chemicals and Chemical Preparations	2		
291	Oil — Integrated	4	2	
295	Building Materials — Roof and Wallboard	2		
300	Tire and Rubber Goods	2	1	1
313	Boots and Shoes — Cut Stock		1	
321	Glass Products		1	
322	Containers — Metal and Glass	3		1
324	Building Materials — Cement	1		1
327	Concrete Gypsum and Plaster	3		
329	Abrasives & Refractory Products	3		
331	Steel — Major	3		2
333	Primary Smelting & Refining	1		1
335	Rolling and Draw Nonferrous Metals		2	1
343	Building Materials — Heat, Air Conditioning, Plumbing		1	
344	Metal Work		1	
352/353	Machinery — Agricultural/Oil and Construction	2	1	
355	Machinery — Specialty/Industrial	3	3	2
357	Office and Business Equipment	1	3	

Industry Membership of Sample Firms* *(continued)*

3-digit SIC Industry code	Industry Name	Multi-segment treatment group (78 firms)	Multi-segment control group (70 firms)	Single product control group (67 firms)
358	Machinery — Pollution Control	1		
360/362	Electrical Equipment and Controls	1	2	1
363/365	Electric — Household Appliance/ T.V., Radio	1	2	2
366/367	Transmitting Equipment/Electronics	4		
371	Motor Vehicles	6	5	1
372	Aerospace and Aircraft	2	2	
374	Railroad Equipment	2		1
381	Engineering, Laboratory, and Research Equipment	1		
382	Mechanical — Measuring — Control Instruments	1		1
386	Photographic	1	1	
394	Games — Toys — Leisure Time Products	1		
399	Manufacturing Industries	2	2	
40–49	Transportation, Communication, Other Public Utilities			
451	Air Transport	1		4
481	Telephone Companies		1	1
491	Electric Utilities			8
492	Natural Gas	1		4
50–59	Wholesale/Retail Trade			
519	Wholesale — Nondurables			1
531/591	Retail — Department, Variety, Food Shoe, Furniture, Drug		1	9
60–67	Finance, Insurance, Real Estate			
612	Savings & Loan Institutions			4
614/633	Finance, Insurance/Securities Industry		3	3
70–79	Services			
701	Hotels — Motels			1
781/794	Motion Pictures, Amusement		2	
999	Conglomerates	1	7	0
	Total	78	70	67

*The sources of classifications are the *COMPUSTAT Industrial Manual* and the *Directory of Companies Filing Annual Reports with the Securities and Exchange Commission* (1970). Each company was classified on the basis of its major line of activity as reflected by gross revenues.

NOTES

1. By greater changes, H-K were referring to more extreme changes either upward or downward, since a direction of change was not posited.

2. Securities Act of 1933, Release No. 5673, Securities Exchange Act of 1934, Release No. 12064 (February 2, 1976), Appendix 1. For details concerning the objectives of this Advisory Committee see Securities and Exchange Commission, "First Progress Report to the Securities and Exchange Commission from the Advisory Committee on Corporate Disclosure," August 23, 1976.

3. While H-K state that only two of their 50 LOBUR treatment firms disclosed segment profits in 1969, one cannot automatically conclude that segment profit contributions had not been reported in prior years. In our review of firms surveyed by *Accounting Trends & Techniques* from 1967 to 1970, we found a number of instances where firms actually decreased the level of segmental disclosure from previous years.

4. An "efficient market" as used in the present context is one in which all publicly available information pertinent to evaluating the risk and/or return prospects of a firm is immediately impounded in security prices in an unbiased fashion. For a review of the theory and empirical evidence in support of the efficient market hypothesis in its various forms, see Fama (1970).

5. See Evans and Archer (1968) and Fama and MacBeth (1973) for a demonstration of how forming securities into portfolios can reduce the residual or unsystematic risk $[\sigma^2(\epsilon)]$ and, therefore, enhance the precision of beta estimates.

6. We acknowledge this possibility in our own analysis to be presented below and, therefore, conducted tests at both the individual-firm and portfolio levels.

7. See Siegel (1956) for a discussion of the Moses test of extreme reactions.

8. The simulation procedure and complete test results are available from the authors upon request.

9. Recall from Figure 1 that SEC LOBUR requirements for S-1, S-7, and Form 10 were enacted in July 1969, and at that time the Wheat Report had recommended that these disclosure requirements be extended to the SEC's periodic 10-K reports. Given this fact, and given the pressures from the financial community for expanded segmental disclosure, it does not seem unreasonable to expect that SEC LOBUR data were being developed and disseminated to the market prior to the time that such data were published as part of a registrant's 1970 10-K report. Only in those instances where such "leakages" did not take place would we expect the potential shift point to coincide with the publication of the 10-K report

10. See Merrington and Thompson (1943) for a discussion related to this approximation.

REFERENCES

American Institute of Certified Public Accountants. *Accounting Trends and Techniques.* New York: AICPA.

Barefield, R., and Comiskey, E. "Earnings Variability as a Risk Surrogate." Working Paper No. 423, Krannert School of Industrial Administration, Purdue University, 1973.

Collins, D. W. "Predicting Earnings with Subentity Data: Some Further Evidence." *Journal of Accounting Research* (Spring 1976), pp. 163–177.

———, and Simonds, R. R. "SEC Line of Business Disclosure and Market Risk Adjustments." Working Paper, Graduate School of Business, Michigan State University, 1977.

Evans J., and Archer, S. H. "Diversification and the Reduction of Dispersion: An Empirical Analysis." *Journal of Finance* (December 1968), pp. 761–767.

Fama, E. F., and MacBeth, J. D. "Risk, Return, and Equilibrium: Empirical Tests." *Journal of Political Economy* (May/June 1973), pp. 607–636.

Fisher, F. M. "Tests of Equality Between Sets of Coefficients in Two Linear Regressions: An Expository Note." *Econometrica* (March 1970), pp. 361–366.

Horwitz, B., and Kolodny, R. "Line of Business Reporting and Security Prices: An Analysis of an SEC Disclosure Rule." *Bell Journal of Economics,* Vol. 8, No. 1 (Spring 1977), pp. 234–249.

Johnston, J. *Econometric Methods,* 2nd ed. New York: McGraw-Hill, 1972.

Kinney, W. R., Jr. "Predicting Earnings: Entity versus Subentity Data." *Journal of Accounting Research* (Spring 1971), pp. 127–136.

Kochanek, R. "Segmental Financial Disclosure and Security Prices." *Accounting Review* (April 1974), pp. 245–258.

Merrington, M., and Thompson, C. M., "Tables of Percentage Points of the Inverted Beta (F) Distribution." *Biometrika* (1943), pp. 73–88.

Securities and Exchange Commission. Securities Act of 1933. Release No. 5673. Securities Exchange Act of 1934, Release No. 9000, 12064.

_____. "First Progress Report to the Securities and Exchange Commission from the Advisory Committee on Corporate Disclosure." August 23, 1976.

Siegel, S. *Nonparametric Statistics for the Behavioral Sciences.* New York: McGraw-Hill, 1956.

Singhvi, S., and Desai, H. "An Empirical Analysis of the Quality of Corporate Financial Disclosure." *Accounting Review* (January 1971), pp 129–138.

Stigler, G. J. "The Economics of Information." *Journal of Political Economy* (June 1961), pp. 212–224.

Sunder, S. "Empirical Research in Accounting and Security Markets." Unpublished manuscript, University of Chicago, 1976.

TWENTY-EIGHT

Line of Business Reporting: A Rejoinder

BERTRAND HORWITZ

State University of New York, Binghamton

and

RICHARD KOLODNY

University of Maryland

In this response to Simonds and Collins the authors defend their 1977 article on the line of business reporting (LOBUR) disclosure, restating the conclusions of their previous article: that the LOBUR disclosure has had little or no significant impact on the securities market.

The lengthy comment of Simonds and Collins (1978) to our study on the market effects of the Securities and Exchange Commission (SEC) requirement for segmented profit data by diversified companies is a welcome and important addition to a field that is now under close scrutiny. The implications of both studies are not only of "direct relevance to the deliberations of the [SEC's] Special Advisory Committee on Corporate Disclosure" (Simonds and Collins, p. 647), but also relevant to the studies of the Federal Trade Commission and the Commission on Federal Paperwork. Indeed, both studies are concerned with the general problem of the economic effects of required disclosure. Simonds and Collins (S-C) criticize our study in two respects, both of which are claimed to bias the results: (1) deficiencies in sample selection and (2) deficiencies in the techniques of testing the hypothesis. In this brief rejoinder, we intend to show that we remain convinced that our conclusions are warranted.

S-C are correct in asserting that "[r]egistration and proxy statements which may have been filed by these [sample] companies were apparently not examined by H-K" (p. 648) between July 1969 and December 31, 1970. Further, they imply that the "treatment" group is inadequate since "in a substantial number of cases both segment revenue and profit data were publicly disclosed in registration or proxy statements ... prior to [their] release in 1970 10-K reports" (p. 649). In a subsequent examination of the companies in the treatment group, we discovered that only three companies from the sample of fifty had released segmented profit data prior to December 31, 1970, hardly enough to affect the results significantly.

In their comment, S-C report the results of their own empirical work. They conclude that there was a significant downward shift in beta (market risk) for firms which disclosed line of business reporting (LOBUR) information for the first time. A firm's market risk is the responsiveness of the return on its security to the return on the securities market in general. Consequently, if LOBUR contained information previously unavailable to investors which changed this responsiveness (either made the company return more sensitive or less sensitive to the market), a shift in beta would follow" (Horwitz and Kolodny, 1977, p. 238). This might occur if the line of business data revealed that the earning power of the company was more or less sensitive to economy-wide swings than was earlier believed. In this context, the decrease in beta observed by S-C implies that LOBUR disclosure caused the returns to security holders to become less responsive to market returns.

This conclusion is surprising, and the explanation provided by S-C is, we believe, unsatisfactory. The results are surprising, because there is no theory to explain why, if there is a shift in beta, it should be in a systematic downward direction across the treatment group. The additional disclosure by an individual firm may reveal that the firm's earnings and return are either more or less correlated with analogous market variables. There is no reason to expect average lower correlations, or equivalently, lower betas. In fact, the opposite result might be hypothesized. For, if the market were efficient and a firm recognized that reporting LOBUR profit data would have *reduced* its market risk, it would be inclined to make that information public *prior* to the regulatory requirement in order to lower its cost of capital. Firms most likely to have withheld the information would be those for which disclosure would increase market risk and cause a greater cost of capital. Therefore, with the imposition of the requirement, one may have hypothesized an increase in the risk level for the treatment group (those firms which had not previously released the information).

S-C offer but one explanation for the market risk decrease observed for the treatment group. They suggest that the market risk is reduced because segmented profit data permit analysts to forecast earnings more accurately. Two assumptions are implicit in their explanation: (1) Segmented profit data improve earnings forecasts and thereby reduce uncertainty; and (2) A reduction of the uncertainty associated with earnings forecasts reduces market risk. Let us examine each of these assumptions by referring to previous studies cited by S-C.

Assume a security market participant formulates a distribution for the firm's future earnings which can be summarized by two parameters, its expected value and variance. LOBUR profit information may change either or both of the distribution parameters. The expected value of the distribution may shift, i.e., the participant may now expect higher or lower earnings than previously, and/or the variance may change. It is important to stress that the variance of the distribution may increase or decrease. For instance, it might increase if LOBUR information revealed that the profitability of segments is more highly correlated than was earlier estimated or that the total operating risk of the firm was greater than earlier believed. In either case, after disclosure, the participant would estimate that there was more uncertainty associated with the earnings of the firm than before disclosure.

The analyses of H-K and S-C are at the market level, rather than the individual participant level. When we move from the individual to the market level, it is important to recognize that the market assessment of return and risk is some weighted composite of individual assessments, and that, to some extent, individuals interpret information differently. Therefore, when information is released, it is possible that the changes in the predicted earnings distribution of one investor may partially offset changes of another, thereby having little effect on the market assessment (consensus). With this in mind, let us examine S-C's position.

In the concluding section of their comment, S-C suggest that the prediction of future earnings improves when segmented profit data are available. Kinney (1971), cited by S-C, does demonstrate that segmented revenue data permit better mean forecasts than the use of aggregated data. However, with respect to profit data (the issue of concern in both the S-C and H-K studies), Kinney does not find improved forecasts by using segmented profit data. Even Collins (1976a, p. 126), himself, using seven forecasting models, finds virtually no improvement by using disaggregated profit data once sales data are known:

> Moreover the main advantage of segment data appears to accrue from segment revenue disclosure, since predictive ability was enhanced only nominally when segment profit margin data were utilized in addition to segment revenue data. This suggests that arbitrary allocations of joint costs may limit the reliability and predictive usefulness of segment profitability data.... Investors should avoid placing undue reliance on segment profit figures as presently reported under SEC guidelines.

Should we expect a decline in beta when Collins himself has shown that segmented profit data do not reduce forecast error after segmented sales data are known?

A comprehensive study which analyzed the effect of segmented profit data on the accuracy of analysts' forecasts (rather than examining the performance of mechanical trading rules, such as in Collins [1975]), was conducted by Barefield and Comiskey (1975). Their results indicate that there is no evidence whatsoever to support the claim that the average error of analysts (bias) was reduced when disaggregated data were available:

> [D]ata were examined to see if forecasting performance [of analysts] improved as a result of the implementation of the disclosure requirement. Again, no significant impact was noted on bias [average error] scores (p. 19.)

Because it is reasonable to assume that the market assessment of earnings is an average of analysts, it follows that mean market predictions were no better with segmented information. Barefield and Comiskey did find that the mean forecast of each analyst was closer to the market (average) forecast when LOBUR information was available. However, this is not to say that the level of uncertainty associated with each analyst's earnings forecast, or the uncertainty associated with the market's earnings forecast, was lessened. Thus, the assumption that segmented profit data improve earnings forecasts and reduce uncertainty is, at the least, highly questionable.

It may be noted that the quotation by S-C of Kochanek's study (1974) is not quite appropriate for supporting their statistical conclusions. Kochanek also concludes that segmented disclosure is useful, but *not* that segmented profit data, given segmented sales, are useful.

The second implicit assumption by S-C also deserves consideration. Disregarding the above discussion for the moment and assuming that the variances of individual analysts and the market's earnings distributions decreased when LOBUR profit data became available, it still does not follow that the total variability of security returns or the betas decreased as S-C hypothesize.

The total variability of a security's return and that portion explained by the market, as summarized by the security's beta, are measured ex post. One cause of return variability and possibly a larger beta is uncertainty which presents itself ex post in the form of surprise. Thus, if price and earnings are related as assumed, then the more the market is surprised by a firm's earnings, the greater the volatility of security prices and returns. As noted above, Barefield and Comiskey (1975) show that the forecasting error of the market (average analyst error) is neither increased nor reduced. Therefore, we would not expect the disclosure of LOBUR profit to reduce the level of market surprise or decrease return variability. However, even if there were a reduction in surprise and return variability, there is no reason that such a reduction would present itself in terms of a lower beta. It would be more likely that the reduction would be in unsystematic variability, since there is no reason in particular for it to be market-related.

In sum, the explanation which S-C offer for their results rests on assumptions that are weak and partially incorrect. Also, if the tests performed by H-K were not strong enough to detect a true average reduction in beta as S-C purport, this should have been evident in H-K's residual analysis. In particular, the average betas (based on pooling predisclosure and post-disclosure period return observations) which H-K use to calculate residual returns would be less than the (higher) predisclosure betas and would be greater than the (lower) postdisclosure betas. If these biases existed, there would be a tendency for the H-K LOBUR firms to exhibit positive residuals prior to disclosure and negative residuals after disclosure. An examination of Tables 1 and 2 and Figures 1 and 2 (Horwitz and Kolodny, 1977, pp. 242–244) indicates that neither tendency existed.

On pages 649–650 of their comment, S-C are critical of two aspects of the statistical procedures we used to test for significant changes in betas: (1) the use of tests at the firm level, rather than the portfolio level, and (2) the decision to evaluate absolute values of beta changes. The reason for both decisions relates to the fact that there was no a priori reason to believe that the additional LOBUR information would either increase or decrease market risk. Accordingly, if individual firms were combined into portfolios before measuring beta changes, we would expect a tendency for individual beta changes to offset one another. Similarly, when testing for average group changes, if absolute values were not used, positive and negative changes would be offset.

The ANCOVA or "Chow" test which S-C suggest for testing for beta changes is an appropriate and well-conceived method to test for shifts at a certain point in time. However, a few aspects of its application and the interpretation of results by S-C raise questions. First, the "Chow" test assumes that betas are stable before and after the month at which a change is being hypothesized. This is inconsistent with the hypothesis that betas are changing throughout the disclosure period and with the general instability of betas reported in other studies. Nevertheless, this technique is most appealing.

Other questions are raised if one carefully examines the moving beta estimates calculated by S-C and presented in Figure 2 (p. 652) for each of their three test groups. S-C point out that the graphical results "reveal . . . a noticeable downward drift in the beta level of the multisegment treatment group with the most dramatic shift occurring within the *designated critical period* near March 1970" (p. 652). Examination of Figure 2, however, also reveals a downward shift in average beta which appears to continue for the treatment group, and to a lesser extent, the multisegment control group a full three years after the required disclosure date. This suggests that there may have been a gradual reduction in beta for multiproduct firms unrelated to LOBUR disclosure, perhaps due to changes in operating or financial risk characteristics or attitudes toward diversified firms.

Both the portfolio and the firm ANCOVA test statistics presented by S-C focus on March 1970, the month as noted above wherein there appeared to be the most dramatic shift in beta for the treatment group. With respect to the portfolio tests, S-C do not report on the outcome of the tests at other points during the designated critical period. With respect to the individual firm level tests, statistics are presented again only for March 1970. There is no a priori reason why March 1970 should be the critical month. Furthermore, it is likely that S-C's findings are biased, since they apparently first observed that in this month the most dramatic shift in beta occurred and then tested for a shift in that period. An examination of Figure 2 suggests that if the same tests were conducted for January 1971, it would not be surprising if the multisegment control group exhibited a significant beta reduction, whereas the treatment group did not.

Lastly, implicit in the conclusions of the S-C study is the notion that disaggregated data provide a better forecast than aggregated data. This is not always the case, however. It has been demonstrated (Barnea and Lakonishok, 1976; Grunfeld and Griliches, 1960) that there are circumstances in which aggregate forecasts are superior to forecasts which utilize disaggregated data. This may be particularly true for disaggregated profit data because of the difficulty in classifying segments and the arbitrariness of joint cost allocation.

In conclusion, for the reasons outlined in the foregoing comments, we find it difficult to accept either S-C's evaluation of our study or the explanation they provide for their findings. We believe that the techniques introduced by S-C are useful additions to the analyses of the economic effects of required disclosure. However, with respect to line of business reporting of profit data, we remain unconvinced that the SEC requirement had any significant impact on the securities markets.

REFERENCES

Barefield, R., and Comiskey, E. "The Impact of the SEC's Line of Business Disclosure Requirement on the Accuracy of Analysts' Forecasts of Earnings Per Share." Purdue University Working Paper, March 1975.

Barnea, A., and Lakonishok, J. "An Analysis of the Usefulness of Disaggregated Accounting Data for Forecasts of Corporate Performance." Cornell University Working Paper, June 1976.

Collins, D. "SEC Line-of-Business Reporting and Earnings Forecasts." *Journal of Business Research* (May 1976a), pp. 117–130.

———. "SEC Product-Line Reporting and Market Efficiency." *Journal of Financial Economics* (June 1976b), pp. 125–164.

Grunfeld, Y., and Griliches, Z. "Is Aggregation Necessarily Bad?" *Review of Economics and Statistics* (February 1960), pp. 1–13.

Horwitz, B., and Kolodny, R. "Line of Business Reporting and Security Prices: An Analysis of an SEC Disclosure Rule." *Bell Journal of Economics,* Vol. 8, No. 1 (Spring 1977), pp. 234–249.

Kinney, W. R., Jr. "Predicting Earnings: Entity versus Subentity Data." Journal of Accounting Research (Spring 1971), pp. 127–136.

Kochanek, R. "Segmental Financial Disclosure and Security Prices." *Accounting Review* (April 1974), pp. 245–258.

Simonds, R. R., and Collins, D. W. "Line of Business Reporting and Security Prices: An Analysis of an SEC Disclosure Rule: Comment." *Bell Journal of Economics,* Vol. 9, No. 2 (Autumn 1978), pp. 646–658.

TWENTY-NINE

SEC Roundup: Developments Affecting the Director in 1978

IRWIN L. GUBMAN

Secretary and Assistant General Counsel, Bank of America, San Francisco

Irwin L. Gubman summarizes the 1978 Securities and Exchange Commission (SEC) actions relative to disclosures about managers, directors, and insider activity. A long-term trend he notes is the increasing importance of the proxy in providing both "hard" and "soft" information about corporate governance.

Securities and Exchange Commission (SEC) rule-making related to corporate governance and accountability was unusually active during 1978. Corporate lawyers, executives, and directors have had an increasingly difficult time in maintaining an awareness and understanding of SEC developments. As a result, there has been a high level of frustration in the corporate community with both the substance and the process of SEC rule-making.

For example, there were instances of important rule changes being adopted in final form on the very day that amendments to those rules were being proposed for comment!

This failure by the full Commission to coordinate SEC staff projects is most unfortunate and renders even more difficult efforts by the corporate community to play a constructive and thoughtful role in commenting on proposed rule-making and adapting to change in corporate governance.

This article seeks to shed light on the substantive outcome of this apparently confused rule-making effort by relating the origins of SEC activity in key corporate governance areas to the current status of the more important rules and SEC forms. This article makes an occasional effort to suggest directions the SEC and others may take in the future in the corporate governance area. The focus of concern is requirements for increased corporate disclosure affecting boards of directors.

One long-term trend that affects many of the changes described in the article is the increasing importance being given to proxy statements and annual reports as principal disclosure documents, rather than registration statements and prospectuses. This change reflects an emerging disclosure system based on company registration through an integration of reporting requirements under the principal Securities Act which have the effect of expanding periodic reporting under the 1934 Act in preference to infrequent reporting in conjunction with the registration of securities offerings.

This article is neither all-inclusive of important SEC rule-making activity during 1978 nor definitive as to the legal responsibilities of directors and companies in complying with the new rules and interpretations. It is, rather, intended only as a guide, and advice of counsel should be sought regarding the applicability of any particular change in rules.

INDEPENDENT AUDITORS

Since 1971, the SEC has required disclosure in an 8-K report of any change of principal independent accountants by a reporting corporation, including disclosure of any disagreements on matters of accounting principles or practices, financial statement disclosure, or auditing scope or procedure which led to such change of accountants. Beginning in 1974, similar disclosures were required to be made in proxy statements.

Recognizing the increasing importance of independent accountants in the assurance of accurate financial reporting, the SEC moved in 1977 to expand the disclosure of changes of accounting firms. Rules[1] were proposed which would have required the disclosure of the reasons behind any change of accountants and whether the change had been approved by the corporation's board of directors or its audit committee. In May 1978, the SEC issued these rules in final form.[2] The section dealing with expanded disclosure of reasons for changing accountants was dropped. Although the SEC in its final release encouraged such disclosure on a voluntary basis, the weight of negative opinion from the business community was apparently convincing. Comments to the SEC suggested that any required disclosure would consist of useless "boilerplate." Even those who commented favorably were generally unable to articulate any specific benefits which would accrue to investors as a result of this disclosure. The final rules do require disclosure of any board or audit committee approval of a change in accountants. Such a disclosure is now required to be made in both an 8-K and the next proxy statement the corporation issues following such change.

Another set of rules dealing with independent accountants was proposed in 1977[3] and adopted in July 1978.[4] The proposal stemmed from the SEC's concern that the size and profitability of the total relationship between a corporation and a CPA firm might undermine the independence of the outside auditors. Since the early 1960s, CPA firms have been providing management consulting assistance to many of their audit clients. In those situations where both functions were performed by a firm's same employees, the SEC maintained there might be some loss of objectivity in the audit. Similarly, it was suggested that an accounting firm might be more willing to compromise on a certification of a client's financial statements if that client were a rich source of nonaudit revenues.

The SEC attacked these issues with several proposed changes in the proxy statement. First, the Commission proposed that corporations be required to disclose the nature of any nonaudit services performed by the principal independent accountant and the amount of the fees charged for both audit and nonaudit services. In the version finally adopted, however, the SEC decided not to require disclosure of the dollar amounts involved. Critics had exposed several disadvantages: investors might mistakenly compare the charges of two accountants without regard to the relative difficulty or extensiveness of audits involved; pressures to reduce accounting fees might develop, causing a decline in audit quality. But the new disclosure requirements do include:

1. the identification of all services provided by the independent accountants to the company and its affiliates;

2. the percentage relationship which the fees for all nonaudit services provided by the independent accountants bear to the fees paid for the audit of the company's books and records;

3. the percentage relationship which the fees for each nonaudit service (which exceeds 3 percent of the fees paid for the audit) bear to total audit fees;

4. the nature of any services furnished at rates that were not "customary"; and,

5. the existence of any limits on fees regardless of problems encountered during the audit.

Second, a rule was proposed and later adopted that requires disclosure of whether nonaudit services, and their possible effect on accountant independence, received prior approval by the board of directors or its audit committee.

Issues regarding independent accountants remain high on the SEC's agenda. For example, it has solicited comment and information on the scope of services provided by accountants and is currently considering whether certain nonaudit services should be prohibited entirely.

DISCLOSURE OF BENEFICIAL OWNERSHIP

Disclosure of the beneficial ownership of securities received frequent attention from the SEC during 1978. For the most part, these actions can be characterized as either technical adjustments or regulatory implementation of past congressional mandates.

The SEC made numerous changes in the rules and forms under the Williams Act. This law, designed to remove the element of surprise from takeover attempts, generally requires the filing of information whenever anyone acquires 5 percent or more of the equity securities of a company. Among the recent changes are:

1. a limitation that provides that 5 percent of the *voting* equity securities must be acquired to invoke the law;

2. a clarification of the treatment of options and convertible securities, for example, an acquisition of 5 percent of a class of securities convertible into at least 5 percent of the common stock of a company would create the obligation to report upon both issues simultaneously;

3. an expansion of the applicability of short form filing by institutional investors who disavow any intention of acquiring control of a company; and,

4. an exemption from reporting by some purchasers in private placements, under certain conditions.[5]

In December 1977, Congress moved to close a loophole in the Williams Act. Previously, investors who had acquired their 5 percent interest before December 22, 1970, or who acquired their 5 percent interest in a registered stock-for-stock exchange, or who acquired their 5 percent interest at a rate of less than 2 percent in any one year were exempt from filing.

New Section 13(g) of the Exchange Act authorized the SEC to require disclosure of all 5 percent interests, no matter how obtained. In 1978, therefore, the SEC proposed a new form, Form D-G, to be filed by all such investors.[6] While the SEC has admitted to the obvious duplication between old and new forms and has attempted to combine and simplify them, at the moment the area has to be described as unclear.

In 1975, Congress added new Section 13(f) to the Exchange Act. This section authorized the SEC to require the filing of reports by any institutional investment manager who exercised investment discretion with respect to equity accounts aggregating at least $100 million. This section had originated in the SEC's Institutional Investor Study Report in 1971, which cited important "gaps in information" and recommended legislation of new disclosure requirements.

In 1978, the SEC adopted Rule 13f-1 and Form F to implement this authority.[7] While Form F is relatively straightforward, the interlocks between this form and other reporting forms are not. Due to the confusion between the "investment discretion" test of 13(f) and the beneficial ownership test of 13(d) and 13(g), an investment manager required to file under Section 13(f) who also controls more than 5 percent of any one security must then decide whether to file Form 13D (or 13G or perhaps 13D-G) as well.

Portions of the beneficial ownership rules were also incorporated in new item 6 of Regulation S-K. For this reason, their concepts now apply to SEC forms and types of stock ownership never before affected. See, for example, the discussion of item 6 of Regulation S-K below.

REGULATION S-K

As part of its commitment to consolidating forms and reducing the overall burden of financial reporting, the SEC has begun the development of an integrated disclosure rule, Regulation S-K. It is designed to unify forms such as S-1, the main 1933 Act registration form, and the 10-K as well as Schedule 14A, applicable to proxy statements.

The first two items of Regulation S-K were adopted in December 1977.[8] The main innovation was the requirement that data be broken down into "industry segments." The justification claimed by the SEC was that it wished to integrate its requirements with those of Financial Accounting Standards Board (FASB) Statement No. 14, "Financial Reporting for Segments of a Business Enterprise," issued in 1976. It did decide, however, not to require a segment breakdown in quarterly reports at this time. In a later release, the SEC emphasized methods of defining such segments. Segments can be based on: (1) the nature of the product — similar products or services, similar risks or rates of profitability, similar rates of growth; (2) the nature of the production process — similar labor forces, similar degree of capital intensity; or (3) the nature of the markets and marketing methods. A segment is reportable if it accounts for at least 10 percent of profit or loss, 10 percent of revenue, or 10 percent of identifiable assets.

Item 1 is entitled "Description of Business." It requires: a discussion of the "general development of business" during the preceding five years; specified financial information by segment for five years; a "narrative description of business" broken down by segment but only to the extent that such detailed information is material to the business as a whole; and a financial breakdown between foreign and domestic activities.

Item 2 is entitled "Description of Property." It makes a different use of the segment concept. While a registrant must list only properties materially important to itself and its subsidiaries, it must then identify the industry segments which use these properties.

In July 1978, four additional items were incorporated into Regulation S-K.[9] New item 3 is entitled "Directors and Executive Officers." For the first time, the ages of directors will be a required disclosure in the proxy statement. Additional directorships held by directors or director-nominees must also be included. The time period covered by disclosure of background information on directors and officers was uniformly made five years instead of ten. Detailed rules covering the disclosure of the involvement of directors and executive officers in legal proceedings was adopted. Disclosures include:

1. involvements of such persons in a bankruptcy, or in a criminal proceeding; and,

2. injunctions prohibiting such persons from engaging in specified securities-related activities.

The rule provides that a discussion of any mitigating circumstances may also be included.

Item 4 is entitled "Management Remuneration and Transactions." The current contents of this requirement will be discussed later in this article; however, its adoption provides a useful insight into the problems business has had in following recent developments. The so-called management remuneration rules, which are amendments to Regulation S-K, were proposed the same day the above four items of S-K were adopted. These four items were themselves partly a product of changes first proposed in November 1976 and partly of the move toward integration announced in December 1977.

Item 5 is entitled "Legal Proceedings." It not only requires disclosure of material legal proceedings involving the registrant, but also requires disclosure of any proceedings materially involving a director, officer, or 5 percent stockholder where such person holds an interest adverse to the registrant.

Item 6 specifies the requirements for disclosing the stockholdings in the registrant officers, directors, and 5 percent stockholders. These requirements incorporate part of Exchange Act Rule 13d-3. Thus, while 5 percent owners have already had to contend with the beneficial ownership concepts of shared voting powers and shared investment powers, directors and officers of the reporting company now must face the same problems with respect to the securities of the reporting company. For example, if an officer or director of a reporting company also sits on the board of another entity which happens to invest in securities of the reporting company, such board membership may be deemed a shared investment power under these rules. At this time it is unclear how remote and inconsequential such powers must be before they need not be reported. There is no limit to materiality in the rules. Consultation with counsel seems essential to officers and directors who have a variety of board affiliations.

PROJECTIONS OF FUTURE ECONOMIC PERFORMANCE AND THE 10-K

One principal recommendation made by the SEC's Advisory Committee on Corporate Disclosure which has been accepted by the SEC concerns projections and forecasts of "soft" data. In the past the SEC took the position that such statements concerning the future are not facts, are inherently misleading, and therefore must be kept out of disclosure statements.

In August 1978, the SEC proposed a completely revised format for Form 10-K,[10] the principal annual reporting form under the 1934 Act. The main distinguishing characteristic was that the disclosure of forward-looking information was encouraged, although not required.

Businessmen are justifiably wary of including projections in their SEC filings. If forecasts·turn out later to have been highly inaccurate, charges of misrepresentation and deceit seem likely to follow. Many businesses have indicated that, despite the most sophisticated computerized planning tools, they have no great confidence that they can accurately predict even the next quarter's results.

To alleviate these concerns, the SEC issued in November 1978 a proposed safe-harbor rule for projections and a related guide for preparation and filing of reports under both the 1933 and 1934 acts.[11] The proposed safe-harbor rule can be summarized as follows: A statement containing a projection of revenues, income, earnings per share, or other financial items shall not be the basis of civil liability if such statement was (1) prepared with a reasonable basis and (2) disclosed in good faith. Note particularly that this proposed wording would, in any litigation, put the burden on the defendant corporation to prove its reasonableness and good faith.

The guide is not law but rather represents practices which will be followed by the SEC's Division of Corporate Finance in administering the disclosure rules. The guide contains, among other things, the following comments:

1. a company need not have a history of operations to formulate projections with a reasonable basis;

2. although independent, outside review of projections is not officially encouraged, it is discussed in the guide as a possible form of additional protection to the corporation;

3. management may prefer to state a range of forecast values rather than one number, but such range may not be so wide as to be meaningless. Varying assumptions might be stated to determine where in the range a value will fall; and

4. investors should be cautioned as to the absence of certainty in the projection. They should be warned of the inaccuracy of past projections. They should be apprised of any assumptions on which the accuracy of the forecasts depend.

Future developments in this area may well depend on how many companies respond voluntarily, and on how significant such disclosures seem to the investment community. It is possible that forecasts may some day be required. The SEC indicated in this release it has under advisement proposals for disclosure of planned capital expenditures and financing, management plans and objectives, statements of dividend policies, and statements of capital structure policies.

MANAGEMENT REMUNERATION

The SEC listed in several recent releases its justifications for additional rule-making in the area of management remuneration. It noted that noncash forms of remuneration were increasingly likely to be presented either in narrative text or in footnotes rather than in numerical tables. This often made it difficult for a shareholder to determine from the proxy statement the total compensation of any single officer. The SEC also urged that shareholders generally should be better informed about the management of their corporation, and that accurate knowledge of officers' remuneration, compared to the corporation's performance, would be a valuable tool. With this in mind, new remuneration rules were proposed in July 1978.[12] After extensive comment and revision, they were adopted in December 1978[13] and are effective for proxy statements and other filings that contain information with respect to years ending on or after December 25, 1978, when such filings are initially made on or after January 15, 1979.

There is a major change in the requirement concerning individuals whose remuneration must be reported. Formerly, the rule required disclosure of remuneration for all directors and for the three top officers, so long as the direct remuneration to each exceeded $40,000. Now the rule specifies that the five most highly compensated executive officers or directors must have their remuneration disclosed if each earns over $50,000. The added word "executive" has special meaning: If a company has less than five directors or officers who have policy-making responsibility, disclosure can be limited to only these persons. Such disclosure, however, could include an officer of a subsidiary who, in fact, exercises policy-making functions in the parent corporation. The SEC had originally proposed disclosure for an additional five persons: the five most highly compensated officers or directors of the reporting company or any wholly owned subsidiaries whose remuneration exceeded $150,000. This proposal was met with protests during the comment period, including claims of invasion of privacy, immateriality, and danger to overseas executives.

A new format was adopted for the new remuneration disclosures. Column A names the individuals; column B describes the capacities in which these individuals serve; column C1 contains all vested cash remuneration; column C2 contains all vested remuneration in the form of cash equivalents such as property, insurance benefits, personal benefits, or similar perquisites. Certain personal benefits can be excluded if they:

1. cannot be determined without unreasonable effort or expense;
2. amount to less that $10,000; and,
3. would not render the table materially misleading if omitted.

These benefits are to be valued at their incremental cost to the company, unless the recipient had to pay significantly more to obtain the same benefits, in which case appropriate disclosure, including the value to the recipient, should be made in a footnote. Now personal or insurance benefits need be included if they are available to a large group of employees and not only to officers and directors. If the amount of personal benefits disclosed in column C2 exceeds 10 percent of the total of columns C1 and C2, or $25,000, whichever is less, a footnote describing the benefits and stating the dollar amount of percentage of column C2 must also be included.

A final column D contains remuneration whose vesting, payment, or measurement is subject to future events. Prime examples are pension benefits, stock option plans, and stock purchase plans. The number shown for these items should generally be the amount expensed by the reporting company for financial reporting purposes. An exclusion is permitted if contributions to a plan on behalf of any individual cannot readily be calculated by plan actuaries.

The Commission considered the idea of a final Column E, which would have totaled Columns C1, C2, and D, but rejected it. The reader can readily make such a calculation if he believes it to be helpful.

The new rules also provide for the disclosure of remuneration for services rendered to the reporting company paid by third parties in transactions where the primary purpose is to benefit the officer or director. Transactions where such benefits are incidental are addressed by other disclosure requirements. The rules also provide for adjustments based on prior year remuneration calculations. For example, if in year 1 an amount of remuneration based on the prices of a company's stock is disclosed, a decrease in the price in year 2 may result in a loss of some of these benefits. Such a loss, if it is proper to recognize it under financial accounting standards, may be deducted from the remuneration shown for such officer or director in year 2.

The remuneration rules also have a separate section entitled "Proposed Remuneration." As to any retirement plan not already disclosed in the table described above, a separate table showing the estimated annual benefits payable on retirement must be included. Other plans for nonvested payments to be made in the future must be disclosed. An exception is included for certain insurance plans that do not discriminate in favor of officers or directors.

The last section of the new rules deals with the remuneration of directors. It requires disclosure first of the reporting company's standard practice regarding director compensation. It then asks whether any directors received remuneration different from or in addition to this norm. If so, the names of the directors and the amounts involved must also be disclosed.

CORPORATE GOVERNANCE

The most noteworthy developments of the year were in the field of corporate governance. A series of releases and hearings on the subject, beginning in April 1977, culminated in a set of rules which were proposed in July 1978.[14] The proposals evoked an enormous public response—almost 600 persons and organizations submitted comments to the SEC. A pervasive theme was that the SEC was attempting to move beyond merely requiring additional disclosure toward federal regulation of the corporate structure. Because of the controversies they engendered, the proposals will be explored separately. Final rules appeared in December 1978[15] and are effective for all filings made on or after January 15, 1979, with respect to years ending on or after December 25, 1978.

1. Disclosure of Board Composition

During public hearings held by the SEC, there was general support for the proposition that a strong board of directors, able to exercise independent judgment, is a crucial element of corporate accountability. Suggestions on how to increase this accountability varied greatly. What resulted was a proposal to label each director or director-nominee in the proxy statement as either "independent," "affiliated nonmanagement," or "management."

This was the most controversial proposal of all. Critics claimed the SEC, through pejorative labeling, was seeking to force corporations into increasing the number of "independent" directors on the board—a power not granted to the SEC under existing statutes. Basically, "independence," as used in the proposal, only depended upon the mechanically determined absence of business affiliations, disregarding an individual's qualities of sound judgment and creative thought. There was the unstated implication that "independent" directors, so determined, are automatically the most qualified directors.

The SEC abandoned the proposal to label directors in its final rules and instead decided to require increased disclosure of relationships which could affect a director's relations with a corporation. The proxy now must disclose, as applicable, that:

1. the director or nominee has had a principal employment with the reporting company or its affiliates during the past five years;

2. the director or nominee is related to an executive officer of the company by blood, marriage, or adoption no more remote than first cousin;

3. the director or nominee owns at least 1 percent of a business which transacts a specified level of business with the reporting company. There is a similar requirement regarding a specified amount of indebtedness between a 1 percent–owned company and a reporting company;

4. the director or nominee is associated with a law firm which the reporting company has retained in the last two years or proposes to retain in the current year;

5. the director or nominee is associated with an investment banking firm which has performed services for the reporting firm during the past two years or is proposed to perform services during the current year;

6. the nominee or director is a control person of the reporting company (other than solely as a director); and,

7. the existence of other similar relationship between the reporting company and the director or nominee which the company is aware of.

The SEC noted some companies are already labeling directors in their proxy statements. Because of the lack of consensus on what a given label should represent, however, the SEC has advised against this practice. Until labels are generally accepted and understood, their use, arguably, could render the proxy statement materially misleading.

2. Committee Disclosure

The SEC believes that active board audit, nominating, and compensation committees are important components of corporate governance. Thus, their existence and structure received a good deal of attention in the proposed rules. The first proposal was that the reporting company disclose the existence or nonexistence of the three above-named committees. Critics objected that requiring a statement of nonexistence served no disclosure purpose but in fact coerced companies to establish such committees. This accusation was denied by the SEC, which found the disclosure did have a "valid informational purpose" and was adopted accordingly.

Second, the SEC proposed disclosure concerning the structure and function of each such committee: The company was required to identify each member, indicate whether the member was "independent," "affiliated nonmanagement," or "management," disclose whether any of these committees did not perform functions which such committees customarily perform, and state the number of meetings held by such committees during the last year. In the final rule, the label test fell in the committee context as well. There was a strong protest over the question of "customary" committee functions. The SEC was charged with going beyond mere disclosure to, in effect, prescribe uniform standards for these three committees in all reporting companies. The final rule requires the company to affirmatively "describe briefly the functions performed by such committees." Such descriptions, those concerned with 1979 proxy statements could take "boilerplate" shape.

The most recent proposal was that, if a nominating committee exists, a disclosure should be made as to whether it is receptive to shareholder nominations of director candidates. If so, then the procedures to be followed by shareholders in submitting such nominations should be described. This proposal was adopted in the form originally proposed.

3. Attendance and Number of Meetings

Under this heading the SEC first proposed disclosure of the number of meetings held by the board during the year. While some commentators stated that this was not a reliable measure of a board's effectiveness, the SEC concluded that the information "may be helpful" and adopted the proposal.

A more controversial proposal involved the reporting of each director's meeting attendance. The proposal required the naming of each director who failed to attend either 75 percent of all board meetings or 75 percent of all board committee meetings since the last annual meeting. In the face of protests that this was a misleading statistic in representing a director's value to the company, that 75 percent was too high, and that explanatory excuses would proliferate in the footnotes, the final rule was changed. The SEC agreed to aggregate an individual's board and committee attendance in part because some committees met too infrequently to provide reliable statistics. Aside from technical modifications, the proposal was otherwise adopted as presented, so that an individual need be identified only if his or her aggregate board and committee attendance falls below 75 percent.

4. Resignation of Directors

As proposed, this rule would have (1) required that any disagreement resulting in a director resigning or not standing for reelection be disclosed in an 8-K report and (2) given the affected director the right to present his own reasons for departing to the shareholders in the proxy statement.

It was objected that not all disagreements are appropriate for disclosure, some relating to personal quarrels or being otherwise immaterial. As adopted, nothing need be reported by the company unless the affected director furnishes the company with a letter describing the disagreement and requests that the matter be disclosed. If he does so, the company shall summarize his views and disclose them in the 8-K and the proxy statement. The company can, if it wishes, also publish its views on the subject. The SEC recognized in its release that probably few directors will choose this course of action and this rule may therefore be of little importance.

5. Shareholder Proposals

The SEC maintained that a shareholder-proponent of a proxy proposal is in the best position to recognize whether management's statement opposing the proposal in the proxy materials is false or misleading. Accordingly, the SEC has adopted a rule requiring that all such management statements in opposition to shareholder proposals be transmitted to the proponent for review not later than ten days prior to the date preliminary copies of the proxy statement are filed with the SEC. In the event the proponent believes there are materially false or misleading statements contained therein, the proponent should promptly notify the SEC.

In its release, the SEC emphasized its view of the equities inherent in the new rule: the prefiling period is a better time to informally resolve any such disputes than by means of litigation after the annual meeting. It pointed out that a recent federal court decision has questioned the availability of any remedy to a "victimized" proponent of a precatory proposal. Most criticisms received during this proposal's comment period dealt with the increased time pressures the new rule would create. While the SEC made limited efforts to alleviate these fears, it emphasized that the rule was "experimental" and would be reexamined if serious timing problems were encountered.

6. Settlement of Election Contests

One proposed rule change received little criticism. Disclosure will now be required in the proxy statement and the corporation's quarterly 10-Q of the terms of the settlement of any election contest, together with the extra costs incurred by the company in connection with the contest.

In addition, another proposal which would have required disclosure of voting policies and procedures of institutions with respect to equity securities held for their own accounts or for the accounts of others was withdrawn, with an indication it will reappear in other vehicles in the near future.[16]

POSSIBLE LEGISLATIVE DEVELOPMENTS IN CORPORATE GOVERNANCE IN 1979

Senator Metzenbaum of Ohio has indicated his intention to submit draft legislation affecting corporate governance in 1979. This legislation would apply to corporations with more than $1 million in assets and more than 500 shareholders. A review of the provisions of his proposed legislation may provide a valuable preview of the next round of debate over corporate governance in America, a debate which promises to become more intense over the next few years. Briefly, the bill is expected to include the following:

1. An important section defines a director's fiduciary duty to the shareholders, clearly supplanting a large body of state corporation law. A director must exercise the care of an ordinarily prudent person and act in good faith. He is entitled to rely, in the absence of suspicious circumstances, on the data supplied by company officers, counsel, public accountants, and committees of the board itself.

2. A majority of the board will be required to consist of "independent" directors, pre-

sumably those free of transactional relationships contained in the new corporate goverance proxy disclosure rules.

3. All corporations must have an audit committee. All members thereof must be considered "independent." They shall be required to perform a list of six functions specified in the legislation.

4. All corporations must have a nominating committee. A majority of the members thereof must be "independent." The power to nominate shall be vested solely in this committee.

CONCLUSION

The credibility of the corporation and its very legitimacy have come under sharp attack in the past decade. An unsettled economy has called into question the adequacy of corporate economic performance, while at the same time corporate critics and other claimants have attempted to place new demands on the corporation to help redress shortcomings with regard to the fulfillment of social goals. In the midst of such questioning and changing expectations, revelations of bribery and illegal payments at home and abroad by large public companies have given further impetus to those who would change the balance between corporations and society.

In the past two years, the SEC has become a leading participant in the reexamination of the role of corporations in this country. The nearly unmanageable series of releases over the past year bears unfortunate testimony to the scope of the SEC's interests in corporate governance and accountability. It has been suggested that the corporate community should welcome the SEC's active stance on the grounds that SEC actions are preferable to those that could emanate from the legislative process. While it is true that individual SEC commissioners are attempting to proceed calmly and deliberately in the face of calls for federal chartering and other panaceas, the same can hardly be said for many of the SEC's staff who, given a free hand, seem desirous of taking action at least as onerous as any legislative prescription.

Corporate critics, having so far been unable to generate support for outright federal chartering of corporations, strongly support efforts to achieve other modes of corporate change, efforts to strengthen the proxy mechanism (to enable shareholders to more readily gain membership on corporate boards and otherwise influence the choice of corporate managers), and efforts to increase corporate disclosure. Most of the SEC's efforts in the past year, in fact, have been oriented toward mandating increased disclosure. It should be recognized that a reasonably constructed and orderly process of rule-making in the disclosure area can be helpful in encouraging change in many aspects of corporate governance. Indeed, many corporations have already demonstrated an awareness of the desirability of change in corporate governance in order to meet reasonable expectations of shareholders and other claimants. It would be preferable that such change continue to evolve voluntarily and in ways that meet the needs of individual corporations. Disclosure can be a catalyst in furthering such change.

On the other hand, change in corporate governance mandated by government regulation, with its inherent bureaucratic confusion, should be avoided. To do so, however, will require private efforts which minimize the need for government action. Many in the business community profess to see in the SEC's recent actions merely a first and relatively painless step down the road toward mandated change in the corporate governance process. It is known, for example, that SEC staff are developing positions on a number of governance issues for full Commission consideration in the next year. One of the most troublesome issues under consideration concerns the corporate electoral process. It seems likely that the staff will propose changes in the proxy mechanism to provide shareholders with access to management's proxy for the purpose of electing their candidates to boards of directors. Should such changes be implemented, the movement to place "constituency directors" on major boards will become a serious possibility, with attendant divisiveness within the board and potential economic inefficiencies generally. The issue before the corporate community is whether self-initiated changes in corporate practices, voluntary industry attempts at self-regulation, and independent oversight by boards of directors will be undertaken in sufficient measure to mitigate demands for restrictive regulation.

NOTES

1. Securities Act Release No. 5868, Exchange Act Release No. 13989 (September 26, 1977).

2. Securities Act Release No. 5934, Exchange Act Release No. 14808 (May 26, 1978).

3. Securities Act Release No. 5869, Exchange Act Release No. 13990 (September 26, 1977).

4. Securities Act Release No. 5940, Exchange Act Release No. 14904 (June 29, 1978).

5. Securities Act Release No. 5925, Exchange Act Release No. 14692 (April 21, 1978).

6. Securities Act Release No. 5926, Exchange Act Release No. 14693 (April 21, 1978).

7. Exchange Act Release No. 14852 (June 15, 1978).

8. Securities Act Release No. 5893, Exchange Act Release No. 14306 (December 23, 1977).

9. Securities Act Release No. 5949, Exchange Act Release No. 15006 (July 28, 1978).

10. Exchange Act Release No. 15068 (August 16, 1978).

11. Securities Act Release Nos. 5992, 5993, Exchange Act Release Nos. 15305, 15306 (November 7, 1978).

12. Securities Act Release No. 5950, Exchange Act Release No. 15007 (July 28, 1978).

13. Securities Act Release No. 6003, Exchange Act Release No. 15380 (December 4, 1978).

14. Exchange Act Release No. 14970 (July 18, 1978).

15. Exchange Act Release No. 15384 (December 6, 1978).

16. Exchange Act Release No. 15385 (December 6, 1978).

THIRTY

An Analysis of the SEC Monitoring of Prospectuses

TEDDY L. COE

New York University

This article studies the Securities and Exchange Commission's (SEC's) review of compliance in registration statements filed for new securities offerings. Its focus is on the comment letters sent to registrants.

The role of regulatory agencies in monitoring and influencing the American economic system has been subjected to a closer scrutiny in recent years than in former years. The Securities and Exchange Commission (SEC) was the subject of an intense investigation by the SEC Advisory Committee on Corporate Disclosure, and that committee has now made its report.[1] One of the committee's recommendations was that the SEC's monitoring of compliance with the regulations be critically reviewed. This article focuses on a single aspect of the monitoring system—the SEC's process of insuring that the registration statement for new securities fully complies with the applicable forms and regulations.

This study is designed to (1) provide information on the registration process, (2) determine the type of information that is most carefully scrutinized by the SEC, (3) determine the type of information that is most often inadequate in the registration statement, and (4) provide information on the adequacy of the monitoring process. The study should also provide information for making some initial judgments about how the SEC is fulfilling its legislated role in the American economy.

MONITORING PROCESS FOR NEW SECURITIES

Normally, the first contact between the registrant and the SEC comes when the registration statement is filed, although some large firms request and receive a prefiling conference where certain questions are raised and, often, resolved to the satisfaction of both parties. After receipt of the registration statement, it is assigned to a branch chief who has available for the examination an assistant branch chief, two accountants, two lawyers, two or three analysts, and, occasionally, an expert in a particular field such as engineering. There are fifteen branch chiefs who handle not only the examination of new security offerings, but also the annual filings with the SEC. Typically, a company's registration statement is examined by the same

Reprinted by permission from the *Journal of Accounting, Auditing and Finance,* Vol. 2, No. 3, Spring 1979, pp. 244–253. Copyright © 1979, Warren, Gorham and Lamont Inc., 210 South Street, Boston, Mass. All Rights Reserved.

group of examiners responsible for the registrant's annual filings with the SEC.

Registration statements must conform with the rules and regulations promulgated by the SEC under the authority granted by the Securities Act of 1933 and the Securities Exchange Act of 1934. The regulations take the form of Securities Act Releases, some of which are issued as Accounting Series Releases. . . . In addition to the requirements of these regulations, the SEC also uses various registration forms to stipulate other rules. The basic registration statement is Form S-1, although other registration forms are required or permitted in special circumstances, such as Form S-8, which is used by those firms registering securities offered to employees.

The SEC's review of the registration statement takes the form of a deferred, cursory, limited, or full review. The deferred review is given to those registration statements that are so inadequate that the SEC will not even comment on the statement. A cursory review limits the scope of the review process and results in no comments either by phone or letter. A limited review is also an abbreviated review of the registration statement, but a letter of comment is issued to the company. Since significant problems may go undetected by this process, the SEC requires the chief executive office to acknowledge in writing that it is fully aware that the responsibilities for a complete and true filing rests with the registrant and not with the SEC. A full review results in oral and/or written comments covering the full scope of the registration process.[2]

A letter of comment to the registrant provides detailed information and instructions on what actions must be taken to conform the registration statement to SEC requirements. The letters of comment are normally written letters; however, in recent years, the SEC has adopted a policy of providing some registrants with these letters by phone. This is done to speed the registration process. Normally, the examiner will have made notes about the phone call, and these notes are included in the registrant's files.

The review process that results in a letter of comment is not a highly structured process; the examiners are expected to determine what should be carefully investigated and to develop their own "audit" plan of the statement. It is expected that the examiners have sufficient familiarity with SEC regulations, accounting standards, and general business "sense" information to develop such an "audit" plan. While the SEC does not use a "checklist," it does have a few items with which it is particularly concerned for a particular year; for example, in recent years it has been particularly concerned with real estate accounting problems, prior period adjustments, and accruing for liabilities.

The examiners' comments can be categorized according to the type of action that the registrant is expected to take. The examiners may instruct the registrant that an error exists that must be remedied. This type of comment most often occurs in regard to an inappropriate or wrong application of an SEC regulation, to the failure to include information required by an SEC regulation, and to language or format of the statement believed to be misleading or confusing.

A second type of comment results in the registrant providing additional information to the SEC on items that require amplification. This type of inquiry may lead to changes in the registration statement; however, the additional information may satisfy the examiners, and a change in the registration statement is not required. This type of comment occurs in relation to transactions involving affiliated parties, to use of proceeds from the proposed sale of stock, and to information about the risks of uncertainty associated with the business.

THE STUDY METHOD

The registration statements and the SEC's letter of comment in this study include those for all publicly negotiated U.S. stock offerings (except for utilities) during 1976 of $5 million or more, and, in the case of initial public offerings, of $2.5 million or more. There were 130 such public offerings during 1976.[3]

The letters of comment were obtained from the SEC through a request based upon the Freedom of Information Act (FOIA). A total of ninety-three letters of comment, both formal letters and notes on phone letters, were received from the SEC. Thirty-seven letters were not provided for the following reasons: The FOIA did not extend to the content of those letters; the files could not be located; and the files did not contain a letter of comment. The files may not have contained a letter because the comments were given by phone without any written record made (and, apparently, this does happen).

A copy of the firm's "red herring" prospectus was obtained to relate the SEC's comments to the registrants' filings. If the "red herring" was unavailable, the final prospectus was used.

The letters of comment were analyzed by categorizing the various comments into the categories shown below:

□ *Foreign payments.* Categorizes comments relating to illegal or questionable payments to foreign nationals.

□ *Financial statements.* Categorizes comments concerning the financial statements and is broken into the following subcategories:

- *Accounting standards.* Categorizes references to specific provisions of the authoritative accounting literature.
- *Disclosure.* Categorizes comments on the adequacy of disclosures in the financial statements.
- *Accounting policy.* Categorizes comments relating to the accounting policy statement and comments relating to the accounting methods used.
- *Auditor's opinion.* Categorizes comments concerning the appropriateness of the auditor's opinion.

□ *SEC regulations.* Categorizes the comments which require the registrant to comply with or reference specific SEC regulations.

□ *Use of proceeds.* Categorizes comments concerning the expected use of the funds and is broken into the following subcategories:

- *Purpose of funds.* Categorizes the comments regarding disclosure of the purposes for the expected funds.
- *Earnings per share.* Categorizes the comments on the effect that the issuance of the securities will have on earnings per share.

□ *Affiliation — certain transactions.* Categorizes the comments concerning related party and other "non-arm's-length" transactions.

□ *Stock options.* Categorizes the comments concerning the adequacy of disclosure on stock option plans.

□ *Format—language.* Categorizes the comments regarding the ordering, classification, and presentation of information.

□ *Business.* Categorizes comments on the description of the registrant's business activities and is broken into the following subcategories:

* *Risk and uncertainty.* Categorizes comments on the adequacy of disclosure regarding the risks and uncertainties faced by the registrant.

* *Lines of business.* Categorizes comments on the registrant's product lines, geographic markets, and types of business activities,

* *Other business.*Categorizes comments about business activities not included above.

□ *Other regulatory agencies and laws.* Categorizes comments on the applicability of regulations and laws administered by agencies other than the SEC.

□ *Capitalization.* Categorizes comments on what the registrant's capital structure will be if the sale of securities is successful.

□ *Financing agreements.* Categorizes comments on the underwriting agreement.

□ *Other comments.* Categorizes comments not covered by other categories.

ANALYSIS OF THE SEC COMMENTS

Of the ninety-three letters of comment, there were three letters which contained no comments requiring any action on the part of the registrant. Comments in the remaining ninety letters are categorized in Table 1. In column one, the total number of times a comment type was made about the registration statements for all firms is tabulated. In column two, the number of firms receiving comments in each category is counted. Columns three through seven show the number of firms receiving the noted frequency of comments.

The SEC's monitoring of corporate filings for the registration of new securities is designed to insure a reasonable degree of compliance with SEC regulations. The letters of comment analyzed in this study reveal those areas of greatest general concern to the SEC and/or those areas where noncompliance with SEC regulations regarding the registration of new securities is the greatest. The subcategories of business ("risk and uncertainty"and "lines of business") seem to be of greatest concern followed closely by the categories "financial statements," "affiliation—certain transactions," and "use of proceeds."

In general, the SEC seems to be more concerned with descriptive information than with quantitative information and with "soft" information rather than with hard information. This can be discerned from reviewing the types of comments given in the "accounting standards" versus "disclosure" subcategories and in reviewing the types of comments in the "business" category.

The SEC examiners did not comment on accounting measurements for the valuation of property, plant, and equipment, and the allowance for depreciation, intangibles, or long-term investments or long-term debt. The SEC examiners made a few inquiries into the capitalization of leases, the early application of Financial Accounting Standards Board (FASB) Statement No. 8, and the adequacy of the provision for doubtful accounts and the provision

Table 1. Letters of comment tabulation

Categories	Total number of times referred to	Number of firms receiving comment on item	Number of firms receiving the following frequency of comments				
			0	1–2	3–4	5–8	9+
Foreign payments	3	3	89	3	0	0	0
Financial statements							
Accounting standards	34	23	67	20	2	1	0
Disclosure	251	68	22	33	18	11	6
Accounting policy	19	13	77	12	1	0	0
Auditor's opinion	19	12	78	10	2	0	0
SEC regulations	161	57	33	32	19	7	1
Use of proceeds							
Purpose of funds	52	36	54	33	3	0	0
Effect on EPS	12	12	78	12	0	0	0
Affiliation—certain transactions	95	38	52	24	7	7	0
Stock options	28	18	72	16	1	1	0
Format—language	82	37	53	25	7	3	2
Business							
Risk and uncertainty	203	67	23	36	18	10	3
Lines of business	151	56	34	31	15	10	0
Other business	89	41	59	27	12	2	0
Other regulatory agencies and laws	27	19	71	18	0	1	0
Capitalization	33	16	74	11	4	1	0
Underwriting	49	26	64	21	3	2	0
Other comments	75	36	54	28	5	3	0

of warranty and defect allowances. The examiners showed greater concern with the calculation of the earnings per share figure than with any other number on the financial statements. The relative sparsity of comments on accounting standards, especially those related to measurement, can be attributed to (1) the SEC's primary concern with disclosure and (2) the fact that registrants had already adapted and adequately implemented the appropriate accounting standards; therefore, few comments on the standards were necessary.

The examiners, however, showed far greater concern with the adequacy of disclosures of financial accounting information than with the accounting measurement. Comments in this area seem to be directed to providing information of a more explanatory type, information concerned with adequately assessing or interpreting the accounting measurements, including descriptions of accounting policy and information about unusual risks and uncertainties. The SEC examiners' more frequent comments on disclosure can be attributed in part to the fact that without precise standards of disclosure, different individuals will make different judgments about the information necessary for a full and fair disclosure.

The SEC's concern with soft data is reflected in the large number and types of comments made about the lines of business and risk and uncertainty. The examiners seem to place considerable emphasis on the description of the firm's areas of activities and competitive pressures faced in those markets. The descriptive information requested by examiners includes not only descriptions of current activities, but also information about significant pending matters such as the possibility of dropping product lines. In some cases, the examiners asked the registrant to state how the firm would react if a major supply of raw materials were not available or a significant customer dropped the company's products. The comments under the "business" category often dealt with enlarging the information set to fully reflect management's judgments about the risks facing the firm and how management was prepared to deal with those risks.

Further evidence of the SEC's concern with the soft data can be detected under the categories "use of proceeds" and "affiliation — certain transactions." Under "use of proceeds," the SEC not only wanted the registrant to disclose the general purpose of raising the funds, but also the specific purposes, even to the extent of asking the registrant to describe contingency plans for using the funds if the stated uses failed to materialize. Under the "affiliation — certain transactions" category, the SEC comments seemed to be directed toward insuring that individuals or groups accorded special terms would be disclosed.

ANALYSIS OF THE OVERALL RESULTS

Reviewing the letters of comment and the large number of comments in some of the categories leads to an understanding of those areas of concern to the SEC; however it is useful to review the number of comments received by firms in all categories in order to even make initial judgments about the registrants' compliance with SEC regulations. In Table 2, the number of firms receiving the noted number of comments is tabulated for all categories.

Table 2.   Number of firms receiving noted
number of comments

Number of comments	Number of firms
0	3
1–5	19
6–10	20
11–15	24
16–20	5
21–25	8
26–30	1
31–35	5
36–40	4
41–45	1
46–50	0
51 + *	3

*These firms received 53, 62, and 76 comments.

Relatively few firms received a large number of comments on their registration statements; in fact only twenty-seven out of ninety-three firms received more than fifteen comments, and sixty-six firms received less than sixteen comments on their registration statement. Three firms received no comments, and nineteen firms received from one to five comments. These statistics point to a relatively high degree of compliance with SEC regulations by the vast majority of firms included in this study. It should be remembered, however, that some of the registrations were given a limited or cursory review rather than a full review. A limited review should reveal any significant areas of noncompliance, but would not necessarily result in finding all areas of noncompliance.

The letters of comment directed to the firms with the largest number of comments, fifty-three, sixty-two, and seventy-six, reflect a pattern similar to that shown in the analysis of comments section. The categories of greatest concern include disclosures in the "financial statements," comments on "risk and uncertainty" and on "lines of business." Firms in general seem to file registration statements which meet the registration standards.

CONCLUSIONS

The categories that received the largest number of comments, as shown in Table 1, include "disclosure," "SEC regulations," "risk and uncertainty," and "lines of business." With the exception of the category "SEC regulations," the comments in the other categories were directed toward "hot" issues. The "line of business" comments were directed toward gaining a disclosure of business segments — a topic that was the subject of exposure drafts of both the FASB and the SEC. The comments under the "disclosure" category also dealt with issues of concern at the moment, such as leasing and unrealized appreciation on securities. In general, the areas that received the largest number of comments are those that would have been expected, given the financial reporting environment of 1976.

The categories "disclosure" and "risk and uncertainty" contained a large number of comments requiring additional disclosures or asking the registrant to provide additional information about the item under question. The number of comments in these categories were far more numerous than in the categories "accounting standards," "accounting policy," and "auditor's opinion." The few number of comments about these areas can perhaps be attributed to the fact that requirements in these areas are better understood and less ambiguous. Disclosure requirements and requirements for the discussion of risk and uncertainty are less precise, and when individual examiners attempt to determine compliance with these requirements, it is more difficult than in an area such as accounting standards. If the standards for disclosures of financial information and for risk and uncertainty were more carefully constructed, registrants might file registration statements that would more fully comply with SEC requirements.

While ninety-three of 130 letters of comment were received from the SEC, the remaining thirty-seven were not available for review. Some letters of comment were not available because the FOIA did not extend to them. However, some letters were not available because the registrant's file could not be located and others were not available because the registrant's file did not contain such a letter. In some cases (perhaps most), the letters were not available because only oral comments were given. The practice of giving oral comments without any written records makes it difficult for anyone, including the SEC, to review the work of individual examiners and of the SEC monitoring process itself. This is an unfortunate situation and should be corrected if the public and the SEC are to gain an understanding of the role and impact of the SEC on providing financial information to investors and on the general economy.

NOTES

1. SEC, "Report of the Advisory Committee on Corporate Disclosure" (Washington: U.S. Government Printing Office, 1977).

2. SEC, Securities Act Release No. 4394, Nov. 1968; Securities Act Release No. 5231, Jan. 1972.

3. These firms are reported in "Who Financed in the U.S.," *Institutional Investor* (1977).

THIRTY-ONE

Analyzing Effective Corporate Tax Rates

CLYDE P. STICKNEY

Dartmouth College

ASR No. 149 requires reporting companies to publish a reconciliation between their report-ed income tax expense and an amount equal to the statutory federal tax rate of 48 percent multiplied by income before taxes. It defines the effective tax rate for this purpose as income tax expense divided by book income before taxes.

The author questions whether income tax expense is the best measure of a firm's tax burden, based as it is on book income, which is affected by the choice of generally accepted accounting principles. Taxes currently payable, on the other hand, are based on taxable in-come and relatively unaffected by alternative accounting principles.

Using income taxes currently payable divided by estimated taxable income as the defi-nition of the effective tax rate, the author develops a framework for reconciling effective and statutory rates. He also discusses the problems that certain items—taxes on nonrecurring income, taxes on earnings of unconsolidated subsidiaries, deferred tax provisions that may not reverse, and investment tax credits—may create for the interpretation of effective rates.

Since a firm's cash flow and earnings depend critically on its effective tax rate, analysis of a firm's past effective rate can lead to a better understanding of the firm's future cash flow and earnings. The kind of analysis described by the author can also be useful in determining whether apparent differences in firms' effective tax rates reflect genuine competitive differ-ences or mere differences in accounting.

In its annual report for the year ended January 31, 1978, Sears reported an effective tax rate of 49.5 percent. For the same period, J. C. Penney reported an effective tax rate of 47.6 per-cent. Are the tax burdens of these two firms essentially the same, or do different methods of accounting and reporting submerge the very real differences? If so, are these differences tem-porary or long-term factors?

Since the issuance of Accounting Series Release No. 149 (ASR No. 149) in 1973, corpo-rations have been required to provide a note to their financial statements containing detailed information concerning income tax expense.[1] Given this information, it is possible to ana-lyze effective tax rates in considerable depth. The analysis, however, must be done with care. Reported effective tax rates are usually not comparable across companies because of vary-ing treatments of the investment credit, income taxes of unconsolidated subsidiaries, minor-

Reprinted from *Financial Analysts Journal*, July–August 1979, pp. 45–54, with permission.

ity interest in the income taxes of consolidated subsidiaries, and other items. In addition, the various reporting formats used often prove more confusing than enlightening. This article discusses several of the more important factors affecting the measurement and disclosure of income taxes and suggests a standardized framework for analyzing effective tax rates.

REQUIRED DISCLOSURES UNDER ASR NO. 149

Exhibit I presents the income tax note from the 1977 annual report of E.I. du Pont de Nemours & Company to illustrate the disclosures required by ASR No. 149. Companies are required to disclose all components of income tax expense (including taxes currently payable, taxes deferred because of timing differences between book and taxable income, taxes reduced because of net operating loss carryforwards, and the net effect of investments credits) and the amounts of income taxes payable to the federal government, foreign governments, and state and local governments.

The income tax note must reconcile any difference between reported income tax expense and an amount equal to the statutory federal income tax rate of 48 percent multiplied by income before taxes. In addition, if a company expects that the cash outflow for income taxes in any of the succeeding three years will substantially exceed the income tax for the year, it must disclose the amount of the expected excess, the year of its occurrence, and the reasons for it.

ASR No. 149 states:

> *The objectives of these disclosure requirements are to enable users of financial statements to understand better the basis for the registrant's tax accounting and the degree to which and the reasons why it is able to operate at a different level of tax expense than that which would be incurred at the statutory tax rate. By developing such an understanding, users will be able to distinguish more easily between one time and continuing tax advantages enjoyed by a company and to appraise the significance of changing effective tax rates. In addition, users will be able to gain additional insights into the current and prospective cash drain associated with payment of income taxes.*

DEFINITION OF THE EFFECTIVE TAX RATE

The required reconciliation between income tax expense and an amount equal to the statutory federal rate of 48 percent times income before taxes is usually expressed in percentage form rather than in dollar amounts. (See, for example, du Pont's reconciliation of its effective 43.6 percent tax rate in Exhibit I.) ASR No. 149 defines the effective tax rate for this purpose as:

$$\text{Effective income tax rate} = \frac{\text{Income tax expense}}{\text{Book income before income taxes}}$$

Is this in fact the appropriate definition of the effective tax rate? One might ask, for one thing, whether income tax *expense,* rather than income taxes *currently payable,* is the best

Exhibit I.   E.I. du Pont de Nemours & Company income tax footnote in 1977 annual report

Provision for income taxes	1977	1976
Federal		
Current	$346.0	$296.6
Deferred	50.8	34.8
Investment tax credit		
amortization	(41.4)	(31.7)
Foreign		
Current	27.7	21.1
Deferred	6.7	7.5
State and local	37.4	29.5
	$472.2	$357.8

The current portions of the federal and foreign tax provisions are based on taxable income. Current federal taxes are before deduction of investment tax credit. Investment tax credit generated in 1977 was $70.6 and in 1976, $95.8. For financial accounting purposes, investment tax credit is deferred and the cumulative amount amortized over the expected lives of the related assets. Deferred federal and foreign taxes represent the adjustment to provision for income taxes to recognize timing differences between financial accounting income and taxable income. The sources of these differences in 1977 and 1976 and the tax effect of each are as follows:

Tax deduction over (under) book provision for:

Incentive compensation	$(6.4)	$(19.1)
Depreciation	26.1	19.6
Other — net	37.8	41.8
	$57.5	$42.3

The current portion of cumulative deferred taxes, $178.5 at December 31, 1977, and $152.5 at December 31, 1976, is included in the Consolidated Balance Sheet caption "Income Taxes," and the noncurrent portion is classified as "Deferred Income Taxes."

The company's provision for income taxes is 43.6 percent of earnings before income taxes and minority interests in 1977 and 43.5 percent in 1976. A reconciliation of these rates to the statutory federal income tax rate of 48 percent follows:

Statutory federal income tax rate	48.0%	48.0%
State and local income taxes, net of		
federal income tax benefit	2.0	1.9
Amortization of investment tax credit	(4.2)	(3.8)
Lower effective tax rate on export sales	(1.4)	(1.4)
Other	(0.8)	(1.2)
Effective income tax rate	43.6%	43.5%

measure of a firm's tax burden. The income tax expense is based on book income and is affected by the use of alternative "generally accepted accounting principles." The amount of taxes currently payable is based on taxable income and is relatively unaffected by the use of alternative accounting principles. The latter measure has the additional advantage of focusing on cash flows — an important variable in most investment valuation models.

One might also ask whether book income before taxes is superior to taxable income as a base for scaling. Book income amounts are not comparable across firms because of the use of different accounting methods. There is much less diversity in the accounting methods used to calculate taxable income. This second issue is of particular concern when comparing different firms' effective tax rates.

We now have two alternative definitions of the effective tax rate:

Alternative 1

$$\text{Effective income tax rate} = \frac{\text{Income taxes currently payable}}{\text{Book income before income taxes}}$$

Alternative 2

$$\text{Effective income tax rate} = \frac{\text{Income taxes currently payable}}{\text{Book income before income taxes} - \dfrac{\text{Deferred income tax expense}}{0.48}}$$

The first alternative shifts the focus from income tax expense to income taxes currently payable. But alternative accounting methods will still affect the tax base in the denominator. In the second alternative, deferred income tax expense is divided by the statutory federal rate of 48 percent to obtain an estimate of the dollar difference between book income before taxes and taxable income. This amount is then subtracted from pretax book income to arrive at an estimate of taxable income. The second alternative definition therefore relates taxes currently payable to estimated taxable income.

Exhibit II presents the effective tax rates of the Dow Jones 30 industrial companies for 1977, using the three definitions of effective tax rates. The amounts shown in column 1, based on the definition prescribed by ASR No. 149, conform (with a few exceptions) to the amounts reported in published financial statements for the year. Column 2 uses the first alternative definition and column 3 the second alternative definition. Some firms — like Eastman Kodak and United Technologies — show only minor differences in the effective rates depending on the definition used. The effective tax rates of most of the firms, however, vary significantly depending on the definition (e.g., Allied Chemical, Esmark, and Union Carbide).

As a basis for assessing the impact of income taxes on cash flows and analyzing the reasons for differences in tax burdens between firms, the definition in column 3 (taxes currently payable divided by estimated taxable income) seems preferable. This definition, which corresponds to our second alternative, focuses on cash flows and adjusts for the effects of alter-

Exhibit II.   Dow Jones 30 industrial companies 1977 effective tax rates

Firm	Income tax expense/Income before taxes (1)	Income taxes currently payable/Income before taxes (2)	currently payable/Estimated taxable income (3)
Allied Chemical[1]	42.9%	29.3%	52.6%
Alcoa	33.3	32.3	32.9
American Brands	53.6	44.4	54.4
American Can[1]	47.6	48.2	47.6
American Telephone & Telegraph	41.1	9.4	17.0
Bethlehem Steel[2]	(50.8)	—	—
Chrysler	42.8	44.1	31.7
du Pont	43.6	34.8	39.6
Eastman Kodak	46.4	45.4	46.4
Esmark	34.1	12.7	22.9
Exxon	70.1	64.9	72.8
General Electric	40.9	43.6	40.3
General Foods[6]	48.7	50.9	48.7
General Motors	46.8	50.9	45.7
Goodyear	46.7	41.6	46.5
Inco	43.1	31.9	41.6
International Harvester	45.0	31.7	43.9
International Paper	31.1	18.7	25.3
Johns-Manville	46.4	36.0	46.0
Minnesota Mining	46.3	43.3	46.2
Owens-Illinois	29.9	24.1	27.4
Procter & Gamble[4]	46.1	42.2	45.9
Sears[5]	29.8	20.6	25.5
Standard Oil of California	42.7	35.8	41.8
Texaco	54.0	43.8	55.6
Union Carbide	30.0	13.7	16.7
U.S. Steel[3]	(35.3)	(89.8)	—
United Technologies	49.5	49.9	48.7
Westinghouse[1]	35.4	24.2	31.5
Woolworth[5]	48.1	48.7	48.1

[1] Amounts exclude taxes and income from discontinued operations and extraordinary items.
[2] Pretax book loss and no income taxes paid for the year.
[3] Pretax book profit, negative estimated taxable income, and a net refund of taxes for the year.
[4] For the year ending June 30, 1977.
[5] For the year ending January 31, 1978.
[6] For the year ending April 1, 1978.

native accounting principles. The adjustment rests, however, on one important assumption —i.e., that firms use the statutory 48 percent rate in calculating deferred taxes.

While this is the appropriate rate for most deferred federal taxes (e.g., deferred taxes on depreciation, pension, warranty, and other differences), it may not be appropriate for deferred foreign taxes. If the foreign marginal tax rate differs significantly from 48 percent, and if a company has a significant deferred foreign tax expense for the period, use of column 3's definition will bias the estimate of taxable income. In such cases, it may be desirable to use a different rate for foreign timing differences. We develop below a framework for analyzing effective tax rates, using as the definition of the effective tax rate income taxes currently payable divided by the estimated taxable income.

SUGGESTED ANALYTICAL FRAMEWORK

Exhibit III presents a standardized framework that can be used to analyze and compare effective tax rates. The amounts shown are based on information taken from Exhibit I.

Lines (1) through (6) of Exhibit III represent the components of taxable income — the base for measuring the effective tax rate. Lines (1) through (4) calculate book income before taxes (i.e., net income plus income tax expense plus minority interest in earnings). Pretax book income is then reduced (or sometimes increased) for differences between book and taxable income. Du Pont reported a deferred tax expense for depreciation of $26,100,000, a negative deferred tax expense for compensation of $6,400,000, and other deferred tax expenses of $37,800,000. Dividing the net sum of these amounts by 48 percent results in a dollar difference between book and taxable income of $119,792,000 (= $54,375,000 — $13,333,000 + 78,750,000), with estimated taxable income amounting to $859,908,000.

Income taxes payable for the year — line (13) — amount to $340,500,000. This total comprises $275,400,000 in federal taxes ($346,000,000 reported as "current" less the *realized* investment credit of $70,600,000), $27,700,000 in foreign taxes, and $37,400,000 in state and local taxes. The company's effective tax rate for the year thus works out to 39.6 percent (= $340,500,000 / $859,908,000).

The remaining steps in the analysis reconcile the difference between the effective tax rate and the statutory federal rate of 48 percent — shown on line (7). The number and types of items that account for the difference vary among firms. The more common items include foreign, state, and local taxes, the investment tax credit, and the operating loss carryforward. Line (8) in Exhibit III shows the net effect of foreign taxes at rates greater or less than 48 percent. Line (7) assumes that all income (domestic and foreign) is subject to a 48 percent rate. The incremental or decremental taxes resulting from a different foreign rate are entered on line (8).

Line (9) shows the net effect of state and local taxes. State and local taxes paid raise the effective tax rate above 48 percent. The amount added is, however, net of any federal tax benefit. For du Pont, the $19,448,000 in line (9) represents 52 percent of the state and local income tax expense of $37,400,000.

Line (10) adjusts for other permanent differences. These might include tax savings from lower capital gain or loss rates, lower tax rates on the income of domestic international sales corporations (DISCs), percentage depletion allowances in excess of the cost of depletable property, the 85 percent dividends received reduction on intercorporate dividends, and other items. Du Pont shows a reduction of $13,716,000 for lower tax rates on export income and aggregates other permanent differences of $7,388,000.

The investment tax credit shown on line (11) represents the investment credit actually realized as a reduction in taxes payable for the year, rather than the amount amortized. Du

Exhibit III.   Framework for analyzing effective tax rates illustrated with data for du Pont for 1977 (Dollar amounts in thousands)

	Amounts	Percentages
(1) Net income	$545,000	
(2) Plus income tax expense	427,000	
(3) Plus minority interest in earnings	7,400	
(4) Equals income before taxes	$979,700	
(5) Less timing differences between book and taxable income (deferred income tax expense/48%)		
Depreciation	(54,375)	
Compensation	13,333	
Other	(78,750)	
(6) Equals estimated taxable income	$858,908	100%
(7) Federal taxes at 48%	$412,756	48.0%
(8) Net effect of foreign taxes at rates greater (or less) than 48%	—	
(9) Net effect of state and local taxes	19,448	2.3
(10) Plus or minus the effects of permanent differences		
Capital gains and losses	—	
Percentage depletion	—	
Export company rate differences	(13,176)	(1.6)
Equity in earnings of affiliates	—	
Other	(7,388)	(0.9)
(11) Less investment tax credit	(70,600)	(8.2)
(12) Less net operating carryforward	—	
(13) Equals income taxes payable	$340,500	39.6%

Pont realized a credit of $70,600,000 during 1977. For book purposes, du Pont recognizes the investment credit using the deferral method. The credit recognized as a reduction in income tax expense during 1977 was $41,400,000; see Exhibit I. As discussed later, "deferral" amounts must be converted to "flow-through" amounts in the reconciliation.

Tax savings realized from carrying forward net operating losses of prior years are entered on line (12). In the case of large, publicly held companies, loss carryforwards are relatively rare. When they do appear, however, they can have a significant impact on the cash outflow for taxes and should be set out for separate analysis.

SOME COMPLEXITIES

The preparation of effective tax rate reconciliations is generally a straightforward exercise, once the analytical framework becomes familiar. Certain items may nevertheless present difficulties. Four such items—(1) income taxes on nonrecurring income, (2) income taxes

Exhibit IV.   Effective tax rates on continuing operations, discontinued operations, and extraordinary items

	Continuing Operations	Discontinued Operations	Extraordinary Items	Combined
Allied Chemical	24.4%	—	(32.9%)	23.6%
Armstrong Cork	49.0	—	34.0	46.7
Motorola	44.9	(76.2%)	—	42.7
Owens-Illinois	34.9	—	3.7	22.1
White Motor	30.0	48.0	(12.6)	28.9

on earnings of unconsolidated subsidiaries and affiliates, (3) deferred tax provisions on book-tax differences that may not reverse, and (4) investment credits measured under the deferral and flow-through methods—are discussed below.

Income Taxes on Nonrecurring Income

Some firms report income gains or losses from discontinued operations or extraordinary gains or losses in addition to income from continuing operations. These nonrecurring sources of income are generally shown net of their tax effects, which are usually disclosed parenthetically. The taxes on these sources of income should be analyzed separately from taxes on continuing operations. In this way, it will be easier to distinguish between tax advantages that are expected to recur and those due to temporary conditions.

Exhibit IV shows five corporations' effective tax rates on various types of income. Note that the effective rates on income from discontinued operations and extraordinary items differ significantly from the tax rate on income from continuing operations. The combined effective rate can be misleading, particularly since taxes on nonrecurring sources of income are often tax savings (i.e., a negative effective tax rate), rather than tax payments.

The analytical framework illustrated in Exhibit III can be expanded to include nonrecurring items by adding to the reconciliation columns labeled "Continuing operations," "Discontinued operations," and "Extraordinary gains and losses."

Income Taxes on Earnings of Unconsolidated Subsidiaries and Affiliates

A second and more important concern is the treatment of taxes on the earnings of unconsolidated subsidiaries and affiliates. Two types of income tax are at issue here—(1) taxes payable by the subsidiary or affiliate on its income during the period and (2) taxes that may be payable in the future when the parent company receives a dividend from the subsidiary or affiliate. The question of concern in the first case is whether the taxes and income of the subsidiary or affiliate should be combined with those of the parent in computing effective tax rates. The question of concern in the second case is whether the parent should allow for deferred taxes to cover the future payments that will arise if dividends are received from the subsidiary or affiliate. The first question is addressed in this section. The second question is addressed in the next section.

Exhibit V.   Effective tax rate calculation when unconsolidated subsidiaries exist

Illustration data	Parent company	Subsidiary
Income before taxes from separate company activities	$100	$40
Income tax expense (all current)	(40)	(10)
Net income	$ 60	$30

Calculation of effective tax rate

Numerator	Denominator	Calculation
1. Taxes currently payable by parent company	Pretax income of parent company plus aftertax income of subsidiary	$\dfrac{\$\,40}{\$130} = 30.8\%$
2. Taxes currently payable by parent company	Pretax income of parent company (excluding equity in earnings of subsidiary)	$\dfrac{\$\,40}{\$100} = 40.0\%$
3. Taxes currently payable by parent company plus parent's interest in taxes currently payable by subsidiary	Pretax income of parent company plus equity in pretax income of subsidiary	$\dfrac{\$\,50}{\$140} = 35.7\%$

The tax reconciliations of parent companies presented in published annual reports show three different measurement and disclosure formats used in the treatment of taxes of subsidiaries and affiliates. These are illustrated in Exhibit V. The top half of this exhibit presents the pretax incomes, income taxes, and aftertax incomes of both parent and wholly owned subsidiary. To simplify matters, all taxes shown are assumed to be currently payable (i.e., there is no deferred income tax expense). The lower portion of Exhibit V illustrates the various treatments of taxes.

When calculating effective tax rates, some firms include only the taxes payable on their parent company income in the numerator, but include their share of the *aftertax* earnings of unconsolidated subsidiaries and affiliates in the denominator. In the first calculation in Exhibit V, the parent's taxes of $40 are divided by the parent's pretax income of $100 plus the subsidiary's aftertax income of $30 to obtain an effective tax rate of 30.8 percent. Standard Oil Company of California used a similar method in its 1977 report. It recognized an equity in net income of associated companies of $357,464,000 for the year, and included this amount in the tax base in reporting an effective tax rate (according to ASR No. 149's definition) of 42.7 percent. One of the items in its tax reconciliation schedule was a 13.3 percent reduction — $235,736,000 — resulting from "equity in net income of affiliated companies recorded on an aftertax basis thus excluding income taxes paid by the affiliate."

A second reporting format includes only the parent company's taxes and income in the effective rate calculation. In the second calculation in Exhibit V, the parent company's taxes payable of $40 are divided by its pretax income of $100 to obtain the effective tax rate of 40 percent. Sears uses this format in reporting its income from Allstate Insurance Company. Defining its tax base as net income before taxes and before equity in earnings of unconsolidated subsidiaries and affiliates, Sears reported an effective tax rate for the year ending January 31, 1978 of 49.5 percent. If its equity in the aftertax earnings of Allstate had been included in the tax base, Sears would have reported an effective tax rate (ASR No. 149 definition) of 29.8 percent — a dramatic difference.

A third reporting format includes both the parent company's income and taxes and the parent company's equity in the pretax income and taxes of the subsidiary in the calculation. In the third calculation of Exhibit V, the sum of the parent's and subsidiary's taxes, $50, is divided by their combined pretax incomes of $140 to obtain an effective tax rate of 35.7 percent. International Harvester uses this reporting format. For 1977, it reported a combined income tax expense of $166,717,000, amounting to an effective tax rate (ASR No. 149 definition) of 45 percent. It disclosed the components of this expense as follows:

Consolidated group	$116,559,000
Nonconsolidated companies	58,890,000
Wisconsin Steel division	(8,732,000)
Total	$166,717,000

If Sears had included both the income and taxes of Allstate in its calculation, it would have reported an effective tax rate (ASR No. 149 definition) of 35.4 percent (versus 29.8 percent under the first treatment and 49.5 percent under the second treatment).

There are obviously significant differences in the treatment of income and taxes of unconsolidated subsidiaries and affiliates in corporate annual reports. Furthermore, these reporting differences can create significant differences in reported effective tax rates. Before doing any interim comparisons, some adjustment for these differences must be made.

In the case of wholly owned, unconsolidated subsidiaries, which operate under the control of the parent as a single economic entity, the tax policies of the subsidiaries are usually dictated by the parent, and the income and taxes of the subsidiaries are likely to be affected by production, pricing, financing, and other decisions of the parent. Given these interrelationships, it is desirable to calculate a "fully" consolidated effective tax rate, using the information available in the separate-company financial statements of each subsidiary. First, include the taxes payable by the subsidiaries in the numerator of total taxes payable for the period (as done by International Harvester). Then estimate the taxable incomes of the subsidiaries and the taxable income of the parent (as illustrated in the first four lines of Exhibit III) and combine them to form a fully consolidated tax base. Exhibit VI gives an example of this procedure.

In addition to its appealing logic, the fully consolidated approach offers an added advantage. The effective tax rates of firms with wholly owned, *unconsolidated* subsidiaries will be more comparable to those of firms that consolidate their wholly owned subsidiaries (e.g., J.C. Penney, which does not consolidate its finance subsidiary, with Sears, which does).

Exhibit VI.   Calculation of consolidated effective tax rate for Sears and Allstate for the year ending January 31, 1978

(Dollar amounts in thousands)

Line in Exhibit III	Sears	Allstate	Elimination Debit	Elimination Credit	Combined
(1) Net income	$ 837,982	$395,104		$395,104[1]	$ 837,982
(2) Income tax expense	356,019	103,900			459,919
(4) Pretax book income	$1,194,001	$499,004			$1,297,901
(5) Timing difference/48%	(229,167)	(18,006)			(247,173)
(6) Estimated taxable income	$ 964,834	$480,998			$1,050,728
(7) Federal taxes at 48%	$ 463,120	$230,879			$ 504,349
(9) Net effect of state and local taxes	23,039	—			23,039
(10) Other permanent differences					
Equity in earnings of unconsolidated subsidiaries	(227,536)	(20,519)	189,650[2]		(58,405)
Other	3,377	(115,103)			(111,726)
(11) Investment tax credit	(16,000)	—			(16,000)
(12) Tax loss carryforward	—	(88,047)			(88,047)
(13) Income taxes payable	$ 246,000	$ 7,210			$ 253,210
Income tax expense/pretax book income (ASR No. 149 definition)	29.8%	20.8%			35.4%
Income taxes payable/ estimated taxable income	25.5%	1.5%			24.1%

[1] Amount is already included in Sears net income of $837,982
[2] Amount is equal to equity in net income of Allstate times 48 percent.

A similar case can be made for consolidating the pretax incomes and taxes of less than wholly owned subsidiaries and affiliates. As long as the parent can control or exert significant influence over the subsidiary or affiliate, the logic of the consolidation approach remains sound. A major difficulty in this case, however, is obtaining the information. Since separate financial statements of less than wholly owned subsidiaries are seldom included in the parent's annual report, the interested analyst must often incur additional search costs. It might therefore be more practical to consolidate only significant unconsolidated subsidiaries and affiliates and to treat remaining companies by consistently following either of the first two procedures illustrated in Exhibit V.

Deferred Tax Provisions on Questionable Timing Differences

Deferred taxes must be provided on revenues and expenses that are recognized in different periods for book and tax purposes. The reversals of taxes for most items (e.g., a particular item of depreciable property) occur at a reasonably predictable time with a high degree of certainty. Generally accepted accounting principles require that deferred taxes be provided in these cases. There are several other cases where it is highly uncertain if and when differences will reverse. Three common examples are discussed below.

Income from an unconsolidated subsidiary is typically recognized for book purposes as it is earned by the subsidiary (using the equity method) but recognized for tax purposes only when a dividend is received. Accounting Principles Board Opinion No. 23 indicates that this "may result in a timing difference, in a difference that may not reverse until indefinite future periods, or in a combination of both types of differences, depending on the intent and actions of the parent companies."[2] In fact, if certain relatively subjective criteria for "indefinite reversal" are met, a firm may not have to provide deferred taxes on these earnings.

Indefinite reversal criteria most commonly apply to earnings of foreign subsidiaries. According to Texaco's 1977 annual report: "The undistributed earnings of subsidiary companies and nonsubsidiary 'corporate joint venture' companies accounted for on the equity method, for which deferred income taxes have not been provided at December 31, 1977, because of reinvestment of earnings by the companies involved and the availability of foreign tax credits, amounted to $908,540,000 and $1,190,845,000, respectively."

For book purposes, the income of domestic international sales corporations (DISCs) is typically recognized by the parent as earned. Fifty percent of this income is taxed as it is earned; the remaining 50 percent is taxed only if and when dividends are paid to the parent. As in the previous case, firms have discretion as to whether to provide deferred taxes on this second half of DISC income.

A third item giving rise to a questionable timing difference has appeared with increasing frequency in the last few years. This is the difference between the foreign exchange gain or loss recognized for book and for tax purposes. For book purposes, the Financial Accounting Standards Board's Statement No. 8 requires that firms recognize both realized and unrealized exchange gains and losses.[3] For the most part, only realized exchange gains and losses are recognized for tax purposes.

There are differences of opinion as to whether unrealized exchange gains and losses will ever reverse themselves, particularly when they apply to monetary assets and liabilities denominated in the home currency of a foreign unit. As a consequence, corporate annual reports evidence wide differences in treatment. For 1977, United Technologies reported an unrealized foreign exchange loss for book purposes, but provided no deferred taxes to cover the possible future income tax savings from deducting the loss. Because the loss was not deductible for tax purposes, the tax reconciliation showed an additional $2,899,000 of taxes, thereby increasing the effective tax rate.

American Brands also reported an unrealized exchange loss for 1977. It provided deferred taxes for the unrealized loss on long-term debt, but did not provide deferred taxes on the remaining items giving rise to the loss. Other firms provide deferred taxes for all unrealized gains and losses.

For each of these three items, management has considerable latitude in deciding whether or not to provide deferred taxes. Since ASR No. 149 defines the effective tax rate as income tax expense divided by pretax book income, a firm's reported effective rate will be affected by management's decision. Because the second alternative effective tax rate calculation suggested in this article uses income taxes payable, rather than income tax expense, the amount in the numerator will not be influenced by the presence or absence of deferred tax provisions.

Unfortunately, the denominator amount is affected in that estimated taxable income starts with pretax book income — line (4) in Exhibit III — and then adds or subtracts amounts for timing differences. The estimated taxable income of various firms will not be comparable if some firms provide deferred taxes for these "questionable reversal" items and others do not. When comparing the effective rates of firms that have significant amounts of income from unconsolidated subsidiaries and affiliates, DISC income, and unrealized foreign exchange gains and losses, the analyst should make an effort to put the firms on a comparable basis. This can be done by adjusting the tax bases of the firms that do not provide deferred taxes for these items by dividing the reported *permanent* different amounts by 48 percent and subtracting the result from the estimated taxable income.

Investment Tax Credits

The tax savings realized from investment credits are one of the most important reasons why effective tax rates differ from statutory rates, particularly for capital intensive firms. The tax savings currently realized, however, may differ from the amount reported for the investment credit in corporate annual reports. Proper analysis of the effects of the credit sometimes requires adjusting the reported data.

Investment credits are accounted for by using either the flow-through method or the deferral method. Under the flow-through method, investment credits realized in computing taxes payable for the year are immediately recognized as a reduction in income tax expense (i.e., the benefits flow through to the current year's income statement). Under the deferral method, the benefits realized in computing taxes payable for the year are deferred for book purposes and the deferred credit amortized over the life of the asset giving rise to the credit.

Under the flow-through method, the amount of the reported investment credit corresponds to the amount currently realized. Under the deferral method, however, the amount reported represents a portion of the credit realized in the current and prior years.

Exhibit VII illustrates the significance of this difference in reported amounts. It shows for each of the three firms that use the deferral method the amount of the investment credit currently realized and the amount amortized for 1977. These amounts are also expressed as percentages of the tax base (estimated taxable income) to provide an indication of their impact on the effective tax rate. For American Telephone & Telegraph Company and Union Carbide Corporation, the credit currently realized substantially exceeds the credit amortized. For Allied Chemical Corporation, the amount amortized exceeds the amount currently realized.

In preparing effective tax rate reconciliations, all firms should be placed on a flow-through basis. That is, line (11) in Exhibit III should show the credit actually realized as a reduction in taxes currently payable for the year. This simply requires replacing the amount reported as amortized with the amount realized during the year. For example, the income tax note for du Pont in Exhibit I reports $41,400,000 in investment credits amortized during 1977. Du Pont reported as realized a credit of $70,600,000, and line (11) in Exhibit III shows this amount.

Exhibit VII.   Realized and amortized investment credits of selected firms for the year ended December 31, 1977

	(1) Amount realized	(2) Amount amortized	(3) Income taxes payable	(4) Realized/ payable	(5) Amortized/ payable
Allied Chemical	$ 1,682,000	$ 11,014,000	$ 70,993,000	2.4%	15.5%
American Telephone & Telegraph	1,044,992,000	224,756,000	754,423,000	140.2	30.2
Union Carbide	60,300,000	15,400,000	81,300,000	74.2	18.9

When a firm uses the deferral method, the denominator of the effective tax rate calculation requires no adjustment, since the tax base calculation starts with *pretax* book income. The effects of using flow-through versus deferral methods are already filtered out of the tax base at this point.

USING EFFECTIVE TAX RATES FOR TIME SERIES AND CROSS-SECTIONAL ANALYSES

The ability to predict a firm's future effective tax rates can significantly improve predictions of its cash flows and earnings. A time series analysis of prior years' effective tax rates can determine the level and trend of effective tax rate in the past, those reconciling items that remain a relatively stable percentage of estimated taxable income, those that should not be expected to continue, and those that account for most of the change in the effective tax rate from year to year.

Exhibit VIII illustrates the approach, using the partial tax reconciliations for du Pont for the years 1975, 1976, and 1977. The effective tax rate has increased steadily over this three-year period, from 27 to 39.6 percent. The effect of state and local taxes has been relatively stable, increasing the effective tax rate by 2.0 to 2.5 percent each year. Between 1975 and 1976, there was a significant reduction in tax savings from export company rate differences, probably indicating that income generated through export companies had become a smaller percentage of the total income generated by du Pont. The tax saving leveled out at 1.6 percent in 1977, suggesting that the preceding year's reduction was not a temporary condition.

Most of the change in du Pont's effective tax rate over the three-year period can be attributed to a proportionally smaller and smaller investment credit. Accurate information about du Pont's capital investment plans should permit estimation of its likely investment credit for current and future years. During 1976 and 1977, the credit approximated 10 percent of capital expenditures—very close to the statutory investment credit rate. Since the statutory rate changed during 1975, it is difficult to generalize about the relation between the credit realized and the statutory rate for that year.

Exhibit VIII.   Reconciliation of effective and statutory tax rates for du Pont for 1975, 1976, and 1977

Line in Exhibit III	1975		1976		1977	
(6) Estimated taxable income	$ 359,875	100.0%	$733,975	100.0%	$859,908	100.0%
(7) Federal taxes at 48%	$ 172,740	48.0	$352,308	48.0	$412.756	48.0
(9) Net effect of state and local taxes	9,568	2.7	15,340	2.1	19,448	2.3
(10) Plus or minus the effects of permanent differences						
Export company rate differences	(14,043)	(3.9)	(11,509)	(1.6)	(13,716)	(1.6)
Other	(9,665)	(2.7)	(8,939)	(1.2)	(7,388)	(0.9)
(11) Less investment tax credit	(61,600)	(17.1)	(95,800)	(13.1)	(70,600)	(8.2)
(13) Equals income taxes payable	$ 97,000	27.0%	$251,400	34.2%	$340,500	39.6%
Capital expenditures	$1,066,000		$904,000		$780,000	
Investment credit/capital expenditures	5.8%		10.6%		9.1%	
Statutory investment credit rate	7.0/11%[1]		11.0%[1]		11.0%[1]	

[1] Based on the statutory rate of 10 percent plus the one percent allowed for contributions to employee stock ownership plans.

Effective tax rate analysis can also be used to determine whether particular firms or industries have competitive tax advantages. Tax advantage should affect cash flows, rates of return, and other important variables. Exhibit IX presents an analysis of four segments of the petroleum industry — large integrated international firms (6 companies), large integrated domestic firms (15 companies), small integrated domestic companies (8 companies), and exploration and extraction companies (21 companies). The amounts shown represent the averages for the companies in each group.

It is evident from Exhibit IX that large, international firms tend to have higher effective tax rates than smaller, domestic firms, and that the difference is primarily the result of higher effective rates on foreign-source income. Exploration and development firms have the lowest effective rates, enjoying as they do relatively large deductions for percentage depletion and capital gains (included in "other" permanent differences). A recent study has shown that these effective tax rate patterns tend to persist over time and apply to most firms within each industry subgroup.[4]

CONCLUSION

The first paragraph of this article asked whether Sears's reported effective tax rate of 49.5 percent and J.C. Penney's reported effective tax rate of 47.6 percent indicated essentially similar tax burdens. In fact, adjusting for nonrecurring income, foreign exchange gains and losses, and investment credits, and calculating the effective tax rate as income taxes currently

Exhibit IX.   Average effective tax rates for firms within various segments of the petroleum industry

	Large integrated international companies	Large integrated domestic companies	Small integrated domestic companies	Exploration and extraction companies
Statutory income tax rate				
Federal taxes	48.0%	48.0%	48.0%	48.0%
Foreign taxes	19.7	13.7	—	1.2
State and local taxes	1.1	1.3	2.1	1.2
Total	68.8%	63.0%	50.1%	50.4%
Investment tax credit	(5.3)	(7.2)	(5.3)	(5.5)
Total	63.5%	55.8%	44.8%	44.9%
Permanent differences				
Percentage depletion	(0.8)	(1.6)	(1.1)	(9.4)
Other	(4.1)	(1.0)	(4.9)	(8.6)
Taxes payable	58.6%	53.2%	38.8%	26.9%

payable divided by estimated taxable income for the year, yields a 24.1 percent effective rate for Sears and a 45.5 percent rate for J.C. Penney. Minor differences in reported effective tax rates can mask major differences in actual tax burdens.

NOTES

1. Securities and Exchange Commission, "Amendment to Regulation S-X to Provide for Improved Disclosure of Income Tax Expense" (November 28, 1973).

2. Accounting Principles Board Opinion No. 23 (1972), para. 9.

3. Financial Accounting Standards Board Statement No. 8 (1976), para. .019.

4. Clyde P. Stickney and Ralph B. Tower, Jr., "Effective Tax Rates of Petroleum Companies," *Oil and Gas Tax Quarterly*, June 1978, pp. 445–456.

THIRTY-TWO

Accounting Series Release No. 264: Scope of Services by Independent Accountants

This Accounting Series Release attempts to address the issue of how management consulting services affect an auditor's independence. The Securities and Exchange Commission (SEC) does not prohibit management consulting services, nor does it deny that there are benefits in such services. However, the release points out that the Commission will take action to ensure auditor independence, consistent with its responsibilities under the law.

SECURITIES ACT OF 1933
Release No. 6078/June 14, 1979

SECURITIES EXCHANGE ACT OF 1934
Release No. 15920/June 14, 1979

PUBLIC UTILITY HOLDING COMPANY ACT OF 1935
Release No. 21100/June 14, 1979

INVESTMENT COMPANY ACT OF 1940
Release No. 10737/June 14, 1979

ACCOUNTING SERIES
Release No. 274/June 14, 1979

PART 211—INTERPRETATIVE RELEASE TO ACCOUNTING MATTERS

AGENCY: Securities and Exchange Commission.

ACTION: Interpretation.

SUMMARY: The federal securities laws impose upon the Commission responsibilities regarding the independence of those accountants who issue reports on financial statements which are required to be filed with the Commission. Accordingly, in this interpretative release the Commission states its views concerning certain factors which accountants should consider in assessing the possible effects upon their independence of the performance of nonaudit services for publicly held audit clients. In addition, because of the impact which any impairment of the auditor's independence, either in fact or in appearance, could have on the credibility and usefulness of the audit report, the Commission also sets forth certain factors which audit committees, boards of directors, and managements should consider in determining whether to engage their independent accountants to perform nonaudit services.

DATE: June 14, 1979.

ADDRESSES: The Commission invites written submissions concerning the interpretation set forth in this release and the practical experience of accountants and registrants with its application. All comments should be filed, in triplicate, with George A. Fitzsimmons, Secretary, Securities and Exchange Commission, 500 North Capitol Street, Washington, DC 20549. Submissions should refer to File No. S7–785 and, unless confidential treatment is authorized, will be available for public inspection and copying at the Commission's Public Reference Room, 1100 L Street, N.W., Washington, D.C. FOR FURTHER INFORMATION CONTACT: Clarence M. Staubs (202-755-0222) or Edmund Coulson (202-472-3782), Office of the Chief Accountant, Securities and Exchange Commission, 500 North Capitol Street, Washington, DC 20549.

SUPPLEMENTARY INFORMATION: Scope of Services by Independent Accountants

I. BACKGROUND

Since its inception, the Commission has considered the independence of the auditors who examine financial statements filed with the Commission as central to the effective implementation of the Federal Securities Laws.[1] More recently, in response to the rise, primarily in the last decade, of the performance of nonaudit or "management advisory services" (MAS) by accounting firms, the Commission has been concerned particularly with the effect of the performance of MAS on the independence of public auditors and on the resulting reliability of documents filed with the Commission.

These issues have been the subject of much discussion. The problem has been addressed in various fora by the accounting profession,[2] scholars,[3] the Commission,[4] the Congress,[5] and most recently the Public Oversight Board (POB) of the SEC Practice Section of the Division for CPA Firms of the American Institute of Certified Public Accountants.[6]

While there has been no firm consensus resulting from this dialogue, the growing array of nonaudit services offered by some independent public accountants—and the growing importance of management advisory services to the revenues, profits, and competitive position of accounting firms—are a cause for legitimate concern as to the impact of these activities on auditor independence, objectivity, and professionalism. The issue is both one of appearance and fact; if public confidence in the integrity of financial reporting is to be maintained, it is of the utmost importance that public confidence in the objectivity of independent auditors be similarly maintained. That goal demands continuing awareness and sensitivity to concerns about the independence of accountants. Auditors of publicly held companies have a duty to investors and other users of financial information—and to the accounting profession—to assure that their audit engagements have been conducted, in fact and in appearance, with the highest degree of integrity and objectivity.

In light of these concerns, in September 1977, the Commission issued for comment proposed amendments to Schedule 14A of the Securities Exchange Act of 1934.[7] The proposed amendments would have required disclosure of all nonaudit services performed by an independent auditor for audit clients, as well as of the specific fees charged for each nonaudit service. As indicated in Release No. 5869, the Commission sought this disclosure to "provide objective evidence of the types and amounts of services being provided by auditors," and to permit shareholders to compare fees paid by similar companies for similar services. At the same time, the Commission solicited comments and information on the scope of services accountants actually provide to their audit clients.

In June 1978, after considering the public comments regarding this proposal, the Commission, in Accounting Series Release No. 250,[8] adopted a rule requiring disclosure in proxy statements of services provided by the registrant's principal independent accountant and disclosure of whether the board of directors or its audit or similar committee had approved each service and considered its possible effect on independence. In ASR No. 250, the Commission also indicated that it had not yet determined whether it should propose rules to prohibit public accountants from rendering certain types of services to their publicly held audit clients. The Commission noted that the SEC Practice Section had asked the Public Oversight Board to consider the matter and stated that the board should be given the opportunity to present its conclusions before the Commission acted. This view was reaffirmed in the July 1978 Commission "Report to Congress on the Accounting Profession and the Commission's Oversight Role."[9]

On March 9, 1979, the board submitted its report to the Executive Committee of the SEC Practice Section.[10] The board indicates that it generally rejects any limitations on MAS practice on the theory that available "empirical evidence" does not reveal any actual instances where the furnishing of MAS has impaired independence. However, as the board concedes, the absence of evidence does not necessarily mean that such abuses do not exist or have not occurred,[11] nor does it allay the concerns which arise because certain relationships between the auditor and his client may reasonably appear to compromise the objectivity of the independent auditor. The board, nonetheless, concluded that proscriptive solutions to the scope of services issue are not necessary at this time.[12]

II. COMMISSION'S POSITION

The Commission has reviewed the report of the POB and believes that it does not adequately sensitize the profession and its clients to the potential effects on the independence of accountants of performance of nonaudit services for audit clients. While the Commission is not proposing proscriptive rules at this time, it believes that continued surveillance of the potential effects of such services on independence is essential. Therefore, the Commission is urging those responsible for decisions with respect to nonaudit services—including accounting firms, audit committees, boards of directors, and managements—to give careful attention to the performance of nonaudit services for audit clients. While each of these participants has somewhat different perspectives, all should be concerned about the effect that a possible impairment of the objectivity and professional image of independent accountants may have on the credibility and integrity of auditors' reports and on corporate financial reporting in general.

For these reasons, the Commission has determined to set forth its views concerning certain factors which accountants should consider in assessing the possible effects upon their independence of the performance of nonaudit services for publicly held audit clients. In addition, because of the impact which any impairment of the auditor's independence, either in fact or in appearance, could have on the credibility and usefulness of the audit report and thus the client's financial reporting, the Commission is setting forth certain factors which audit committees, boards of directors, and managements should consider in determining whether to engage their independent accountants to perform nonaudit services.

A. Independent Accountants

Accounting firms and individual accountants who act as independent auditors for public corporations have a statutory responsibility to safeguard their independence, both in fact and in appearance. As the POB Report indicated:

> While it is, of course, essential that an auditor preserve his objectivity and integrity from his own viewpoint, commonly called "independence in fact," it is also important that the auditor appear independent to all users of the financial information he provides. This latter concept is a key ingredient to the value of the audit function, since users of audit reports must be able to rely on the independent auditor. If they perceive that there is a lack of independence, whether or not such a deficiency exists, much of that value is lost.[13]

In a fundamental sense, independence is not an attitude which can be mandated by rule,[14] but rather is a goal which must be addressed by individual accountants in their day-to-day activities. However, public confidence is influenced not only by fact, but also by appearances, impressions, and perceptions. The Commission believes that public confidence is significantly lessened if auditors engage in activities and services that the public perceives as foreign to the expected role of the auditor.[15] Accountants — as individuals, firms, and as a profession — must consider the appropriateness of the nonaudit services provided to audit clients.[16] Public trust and confidence in the integrity of the financial reporting system and the auditor's report should be of prime importance to every accountant.

Accountants who audit publicly held companies should exercise self-restraint and judgment in determining which nonaudit services are appropriate in specific cases. In discharging this obligation, there are several key factors which the Commission believes that accountants should bear in mind.

1. Dependence on MAS Accountants should consider the aggregate revenues derived from MAS and the relationship of those revenues to total firm revenues.[17] Similarly, in considering a particular MAS engagement for a publicly held audit client, the accountant should examine the relationship between the audit fee and the proposed MAS fee. While hard-and-fast lines cannot be drawn, any firm which finds that a substantial portion of its aggregate revenue arises from nonaudit engagements should seriously evaluate the resulting impact on its image as a professional accounting firm and from the standpoint of the potential for impairment of its independence. Similarly, where the firm's revenues from a given audit client are heavily weighted toward MAS revenue, the impact on both the fact and appearance of independence merits thoughtful review. Although the Commission does not advocate that accountants forego MAS engagements solely on the basis of the magnitude of the related fee, the Commission does believe that this is an issue which requires the profession's scrutiny.

2. Avoidance of supplanting management's role Accountants must exercise care to ensure that they serve only in an advisory capacity. They cannot make management decisions and they must avoid situations which will give that appearance. In Accounting Series Release No. 126, the Commission described this relationship as follows:

> *A part of the rationale which underlies any rule on independence is that managerial and decision-making functions are the responsibility of the client and not of the independent accountant. It is felt that if the independent accountant were to perform functions of this nature, he would develop, or appear to develop, a mutuality of interest with his client which would differ only in degree, but not in kind, from that of an employee. And where this relationship appears to exist, it may be logically inferred that the accountant's professional judgment toward the particular client might be prejudiced in that he would, in effect, be auditing the results of his own work, thereby destroying the objectivity sought by shareholders. Consequently, the performance of such functions is fundamentally inconsistent with an impartial examination. However, it is the role of the accountant to advise management and to offer professional advice on their problems. Therefore, the problem posed by this dilemma is to ascertain the point where advice ends and managerial responsibility begins.[18]*

Where a registrant's managerial expertise in a particular area is weak, there is an increased possibility that outside individuals providing MAS will find themselves called upon to assume a de facto managerial role, rather than merely to provide advice. Accordingly, accountants engaged to perform nonaudit services for their audit clients must be particularly careful not to accept engagements where management does not have the expertise[19] or the inclination to utilize their advice as a basis, rather than a substitute, for management decision making.

3. Avoidance of self-review A related problem which MAS engagements may raise is that, as the auditor — through an MAS practice — becomes enmeshed, for example, in structuring the client's internal accounting controls or designing its accounting system, the client loses the benefits which normally result from the outside auditor's dispassionate review of these systems.[20] Stated simply, the auditor, as the architect of the system, can no longer provide management with the "second look" normally expected from an independent, professional accountant. Accountants must recognize that, particularly in areas where management is weak, there is a great potential for the inadvertent creation of auditor self-review. In such situations, auditors take on special obligations if they elect to proceed with the MAS work. For example, when an accounting firm has assisted in the design of an internal accounting control system for an audit client, the auditor must recognize the need to exercise extreme care and a heightened sensitivity to assure an objective evaluation of the implementation of that system at a later date.[21].

4. Impact on audit quality Consideration should also be given to the possibility of enhanced audit quality which might result from the performance of certain nonaudit services. An in-depth understanding of a client's business is essential to an effective audit. The broader base of knowledge about, and greater understanding of, the business which often results from the performance of nonaudit services may improve the efficiency and thoroughness of the audit. This broader perspective on the audit is healthy and desirable, and the Commission recognizes it as a potential positive benefit of MAS.[22] Of course, if MAS is performed by a separate department or official of the accounting firm, with little or no interaction, this transference value would not appear to exist.[23] And, in this connection, auditors must recognize that the acceptance of an MAS engagement may well carry with it the corresponding obligation to bring the knowledge gained in the course of the MAS work to bear on the audit. Auditors who failed to act upon information known to their MAS colleagues would, in the Commission's judgment, run a substantial risk.

5. Relation of engagement to audit skills In 1977, the Senate Subcommittee on Reports, Accounting, and Management — while rejecting the more sweeping position of its staff[24] — stated that the best policy with regard to management advisory services:

> is to require that the independent auditor of a publicly owned corporation per-
> form only services directly related to accounting. Non-accounting management
> services such as executive recruitment, marketing analysis, plant-layout, product
> analysis and actuarial services... should be discontinued.[25]

Subsequently, the Executive Committee of the SEC Practice Section proposed, on May 8, 1978, to amend the section's organizational document to prohibit members from furnishing services to publicly held audit clients when those services would require skills "not related to accounting or auditing."[26] The POB, in its report, recommended against adoption of this limitation.[27]

The Commission recognizes that this is an area in which bright lines cannot easily be drawn and that the difficulties in identifying those advisory services which are rationally related to auditing are formidable.[28] For that reason, the Commission is not of the view that this factor be explicitly included among the considerations to be addressed in deciding whether to enter into a particular MAS engagement. However, the Commission does wish to emphasize the fact that it appears difficult to isolate any substantial benefits to either the public's trust and confidence in the integrity of the accounting profession or in the quality and thoroughness of the auditor's work which accrue when auditors engage in what becomes principally a management consulting business. There may, however, be negative consequences. To the extent, for example, that a substantial part of the staff of an accounting firm views itself as consultants, and its relation with the firm's clients as that of an advisor, the firm's commitment to independence and integrity may be eroded. Moreover, as a practical matter, accounting firms offer their audit services to potential clients on the basis — not solely of the audit services they can render — but on the basis of the entire range of client services available from the firm. For this reason, there may be an unfortunate tendency for firms to compete with one another as to the scope of nonaudit services available, and some firms may feel compelled to match the services offered by their competitors. This phenomenon tends to result in a constant expansion in the range of MAS which accounting firms offer; whether or not this is healthy for the professionalism and reputation of accountants is open to serious question.

The Commission believes that, in considering any nonaudit engagement with a public audit client, the accountant should test the services in question against each of these factors and proceed when satisfied that the total balance of considerations favors proceeding with the engagement and that none of the factors tilts strongly against performance of the nonaudit work involved. In each instance, an exercise of judgment is necessary, and auditors should bear in mind their responsibility — not only to the financial welfare of the accounting firm — but also to the integrity and reputation of the profession as a whole.[29]

B. Audit Committees, Boards of Directors, and Managements

Audit committees, boards of directors, and managements have a responsibility to act in the best interest of their shareholders and must therefore be concerned about the credibility of their financial reporting. To the extent that the independence, in fact or in appearance, of the entity's auditor may be called into question, the credibility of the financial statements will be similarly questioned. Accordingly, the impact on auditor independence of potential MAS engagements should be of direct concern to the issuer and especially its independent audit committee.[30] Set forth below are certain factors which the Commission believes should be weighed in discharging this responsibility.[31]

1. Economic benefit Often there are economic and other benefits associated with having the independent auditor provide nonaudit services, and, since corporate management and directors owe primary allegiance to their shareholders, this is certainly a legitimate consideration in their decision making. However, while there may be demonstrable benefits associated with such services as corporate tax return preparation and internal accounting control review, the benefits, in many other instances, such as the rendering of actuarial services, plant layout, and market studies, may be more imaginary than real. Therefore, care must be exercised to assure that the benefits, weighed against the potential adverse effects, of engaging an auditor to perform nonaudit services represent a real advantage to the client. Potential benefits may include the savings in time and money which the auditor's specific knowledge of the accounting records and financial transactions of a company will yield in connection with the MAS engagement. For example, tax advisory services frequently involve working with many of the same accounting records and financial transactions as were utilized in performing the audit. Thus, where someone other than the auditor performs this service very substantional additional costs — in terms of professional fees consumed while obtaining knowledge of the company, internal costs to the company, and the quality of the resultant advice — could result. Audit committees, boards of directors, and managements should recognize the need to gather sufficient information in order to make this comparison in reaching judgments.

Conversely, certain services, such as executive recruiting and employee compensation and benefit counseling, can be rendered by persons without audit experience at a cost comparable to that charged by the auditor. In these situations, the possible adverse impact upon public confidence in auditor independence should weigh more heavily in the analysis.

2. Avoidance of supplanting management's role As discussed above, in performing nonaudit services, independent accountants should serve in an advisory capacity only and must not make management decisions or participate in the conduct of a registrant's operations. Management should share the problems and concerns of its independent accountants in this regard, and it should ensure that it has sufficient competence in the area involved in the proposed nonaudit service to make appropriate management decisions.

3. Avoidance of self-review Similarly, management, like the auditor, must be sensitive to the fact that registrants, in engaging their auditors to perform services such as design of accounting systems, lose the opportunity for the "outside look" normally obtained when the audit is performed. To some extent, this may be mitigated by the benefit to the registrant of using its independent accountants to perform those services heavily dependent on the auditor's knowledge of the company, and the registrant's audit committee or board of directors should weigh carefully the projected benefits against any potential adverse effect. Considerations of relative cost and alternate availability of services may take on a greater significance in the deliberations of smaller businesses than would be expected in other instances.

4. Auditor's dependence on MAS Finally, the audit committee, board, and management should consider the relation of the aggregate amount of nonaudit service fees to audit fees. The Commission recognizes that this relation may vary from year to year depending on a registrant's need for particular services and does not believe it desirable to establish a particular percentage relation as a maximum in any given year. The relation should be evaluated regularly, however, in terms of both relative magnitude and trend.[32]

III. CONCLUSION

The possible effect upon auditor independence of performing nonaudit services for audit clients is a complex issue. The Commission, in identifying the factors set forth above, is neither proposing to proscribe particular nonaudit services regardless of the surrounding circumstances nor is it seeking to deprecate the very real benefits which may accrue from certain auditor MAS engagements. Rather, the Commission's objective is to reinforce the sensitivity of interested parties of the considerations involved in judging whether particular nonaudit services should be rendered by a particular registrant's auditor. In each case, the ultimate issue is one of informed professional judgment; no set of factors or criteria can substitute for the careful, case-by-case evaluation which the exercise of that judgment entails.

This release is not the end of the examination of the scope of services issue. The Commission has the responsibility and authority under the securities laws to assure that accountants who practice before it are independent and will continue its oversight of this area, principally through staff monitoring of the disclosures required under ASR No. 250 and of the profession's response to both the views expressd in this release and to the Public Oversight Board's recommendations. The Commission's staff will also continue to examine particular cases in which questions arise concerning the independence of accountants who practice before the Commission, and compilations of such inquiries will be published from time to time.[33]

The Commission recognizes that the question of independent auditor MAS activity is both difficult and controversial. If future events indicate that further action is necessary, the Commission stands ready to reconsider this issue in order to assure the confidence of investors in the financial reporting of publicly held companies. In order to facilitate that process, the Commission invites public comment on the factors set forth in this interpretation and on the experience of the profession and the corporate community in applying them to concrete fact patterns. All comments should be filed, in triplicate, with George A. Fitzsimmons, Secretary, Securities and Exchange Commission, 500 North Capitol Street, Washington, DC 20549. Submissions should refer to file S7–785 and, unless confidential treatment is authorized,[34] will be available for inspection and copying at the Commission's Public Reference Room, 1100 L Street, N.W., Washington, D.C.

By the Commission.

George A. Fitzsimmons
Secretary

June 14, 1979.

NOTES

1. Rule 2-01 of Regulation S-X, 17 CFR 210.2-01, provides in part:

> *(b) The Commission will not recognize any certified public accountant or public accountant as independent who is not in fact independent.*

> *(c) in determining whether an accountant may in fact be not independent with respect to a particular person, the Commission will give appropriate consideration to all relevant circumstances, including evidence bearing on all relationships between the accountant and that person or any affiliate thereof, and will not confine itself to the relationships existing in connection with the filing of reports with the Commission.*

In various Accounting Series Releases, beginning with ASR No. 47 (January 25, 1944), the Commission has provided guidance concerning the circumstances which it would consider indicative of a lack of independence on the part of a public auditor.

2. E.g., "Reports, Conclusions and Recommendations," The Commission on Auditors' Responsibilities (1978) at Section 9.

3. E.g., R. K. Mautz and Hussein A. Sharaf, "The Philosophy of Auditing," American Accounting Association (1961): 228; Abraham J. Briloff, "Old Myths and New Realities in Accounting," *Accounting Review* 41 (July 1966): 484–95; Ronald V. Hartley and Timothy L. Ross, "MAS and Audit Independence: An Image Problem," *Journal of Accountancy* (November 1972): 42–51; David Lavin, "Perceptions of the Independence of the Auditor," *Accounting Review* 51 (January 1976): 45–51; Arthur A. Schulte, Jr., "Compatibility of Management Consulting and Auditing," *Accounting Review* 40 (July 1965):587–93; Pierre L. Titard, "Independence and MAS: Opinions of Financial Statement Users," *Journal of Accountancy* (July 1971): 47–52.

4. E.g., Securities Act Release Nos. 5869 [42 FR 53635] (September 26, 1977), and 5940 [43 FR 29110] (June 29, 1978).

5. E.g., "Improving the Accountability of Publicly Owned Corporations and Their Auditors," Report of the Subcommittee on Reports, Accounting and Management of the Committee on Governmental Affairs, 95th Cong., 1st Sess., (Committee Print 1977) at 16–17.

6. Public Oversight Board Report, "Scope of Services by CPA Firms," published for the Public Oversight Board of the SEC Practice Section of the Division for CPA Firms of the American Institute of Certified Public Accountants (AICPA 1979). [Hereinafter referred to as the "POB Report"] Copies are available from the AICPA, 1620 Eye Street, N.W., Washington, DC 20006.

7. Securities Act Release No. 5869 [42 FR 53635] (September 26, 1977).

8. Securities Act Release No. 5940 [43 FR 29110] (June 29, 1978).

9. Securities and Exchange Commission, 95th Cong., 2nd Sess. (Committee Print 1978), p. 16.

10. The board's conclusions and recommendations are set forth on pp. 4–6 of the POB Report.

11. POB Report, p. 35. The Commission encourages additional empirical study of this issue.

12. The board has recommended that the SEC Practice Section's peer review program should be expanded to review MAS engagements to determine whether such engagements impaired the auditor's independence in rendering an opinion of the fairness of the client's financial statements [POB Report, p. 45]. The Commission also believes this expansion of the peer review program is necessary, recognizing that the peer reviewers should consider all the pertinent facts of particular cases in evaluating any MAS impact on independence.

13. POB Report, p. 27.

14. Certain situations exist where the potential for an appearance of a conflict of interest is so great that the Commission or the profession has prohibited them — e.g., financial interest in an audit client. [Rule 2-01 of Regulation S-X (17 CFR 210.2-01)].

15. See text which accompanies note 25 *infra*. As the Commission on Auditors' Responsibilities stated: "Firms should not expand their offerings of other services without careful consideration of the trade-offs involved." The Commission on Auditors' Responsibilities: "Report, Conclusions and Recommendations" (1978), p. 103. As to the risk that dependence on MAS fees will jeopardize auditor independence, see text following note 17, *infra*.

16. As indicated by the board: "There is enough concern about the scope of services in responsible quarters so that the question cannot be dismissed as a nonproblem. The board believes that there is potential danger to the public interest and to the profession in the unlimited expansion of MAS to audit clients, and some moderating principles and procedures are needed." POB Report, p. 56.

17. In this respect, the board indicates that the reporting requirements for membership in the SEC Practice Section include a statement of gross fees for accounting and auditing, tax, and MAS expressed as a percentage of total gross fees. The board further indicates: "With these figures, shareholders and the general investing public can review the relative amount of nonaudit work individual auditing firms perform and assess whether their primary service of auditing financial statements is being diluted. If the public or boards of directors are concerned with any such trend, they can respond by engaging audit firms that have not chosen that course." In addition, the board recommends adding a requirement that the members' annual disclosure statement reveal the relative importance of MAS to accounting and auditing as furnished only to audit clients. The board believes that such data could be helpful to observers concerned with this question and to the board in any further examination of this question" [POB Report, pp. 43–44].

18. Securities Act Release No. 5270 [37 FR 14294] (July 5, 1972).

19. Such expertise could, however, be provided by consultants or experts (other than the auditor) outside the company.

20. For example, the board, in discussing actuarial services, concludes that an independent auditor who serves as enrolled actuary of an employee benefit plan and who also audits that plan is simply performing an independent professional service outside of management's traditional area

of operation and expertise. The auditor is not making management decisions and should not be viewed as being part of management's team. However, when furnishing actuarial services to insurance company audit clients (where actuarial considerations are integrally related to the role and responsibility of management), care must be taken to limit those services to advice and technical assistance. To avoid the appearance of exceeding such an advisory role, accounting firms should not furnish such services unless they are supplemental to primary actuarial advice furnished by another actuary not associated with the accounting firm. POB Report, pp. 52–53.

The Commission agrees that accounting firms should restrict their actuarial services for insurance company clients to supplementing the work of unaffiliated actuaries. In other situations, such as the provision of actuarial services to employee benefit plans of audit clients, the Commission believes that the factors identified in this release must be considered.

21. See Securities Exchange Act of 1934 Release No. 15772 [44 FR 26702] (April 30, 1979).

22. The auditor's review of internal accounting control systems, for example, would appear to have high potential benefits of this nature.

23. To foster continued improvements in audit quality, the board has suggested that accounting firms should apply their MAS expertise to the audit function to the fullest extent possible [POB Report, pp. 18–19].

24. "The Accounting Establishment," A Staff Study, prepared by the Subcommittee on Reports, Accounting , and Management of the Committee on Government Operations of the United States Senate, 95th Cong., 1st Sess., March 31, 1977, at 22.

25. Report of the Subcommittee on Reports, Accounting, and Management of the Committee on Governmental Affairs of the United States Senate, "Improving the Accountability of Publicly Owned Corporations and Their Auditors," 95th Cong., 1st Sess., Novemver 1977, at 16.

26. Proposed Amendment to Section IV, 3(i) of the Organizational Structure and Functions of the SEC Practice Section of the AICPA Division for CPA Firms, included as Addendum B to the POB Report. The effective performance of an audit requires some familiarity with virtually every phase of the client's business. Accordingly, the executive committee's constraint that MAS be limited to services "not related to . . . auditing" may be considerably narrower than that contemplated by the Senate subcommittee. Because of the breadth and vagueness of the executive committee's proposal, the Commission staff did not support it.

27. Specifically, the board recommended that:

> . *At this time no rules should be imposed to prohibit specific services on the grounds that they are or may be incompatible with the profession of public accounting, might impair the image of the profession, or do not involve accounting or auditing related skills* [*POB Report, p. 5*].

In the March 9, 1979, letter transmitting its Report to the Executive Committee of the SEC Practice Section, the board stated that it: "has not viewed favorably the effort of the executive committee to engage in a series of determinations on hypothetical situations with respect to which management advisory service (MAS) engagements do, and which do not, involve skills related to accounting or auditing. The board believes that this approach would involve the executive committee in an array of ad hoc judgments which would become, or appear to be, increasingly arbitrary, and that it lends itself to logical extensions beyond the policy purpose sought to be achieved. We believe that it is wiser for the executive committee to adhere to the concept of independence and the appearance thereof as sole the governing principle." [Transmittal letter, p. 1].

28. See n. 26, *supra.*

29. Some MAS services for audit clients which have become increasingly common in recent years may, in many cases, prove difficult to justify on the basis of the tests set forth above. For example, actuarial services; psychological testing; consumer surveys and opinion polls; plant layout services; and employee compensation and benefit consulting are some of the more obvious services which seem to carry a potential for impairment of independence, jeopardization of the profession's reputation, creation of self-review situations, or other undesirable consequences; at

the same time, such services may have little potential benefit to the profession's stature and effectiveness. In special cases, of course, justification may exist for the rendering of some of these services to audit clients.

Some services have been banned by the SEC Practice Section and thus the application factors set forth in this release to those services is irrelevant for section members. For example, the Organization Document, as amended by the executive committee on May 26, 1978, of the SEC Practice Section of the AICPA Division for CPA Firms proscribes both acting, for a fee, as a finder for mergers and acquisitions and executive recruiting services. Similarly, the Commission believes that the application of the factors set forth in this release would normally preclude non-members from performing these services for their clients.

30. As the Commission on Auditors' Responsibilities stated: "An audit committee of the board of directors is ideally suited to evaluate the trade-offs involved in having audit and other services performed by the same public accounting firm. Knowledge of active participation by the board or audit committee may lessen the concern of some users about potential conflicts." "Reports, Conclusions and Recommendations," The Commission on Auditors' Responsibilities (1973) at p. 103.

31. Several of these factors correspond to those treated earlier in this release. In applying the criteria addressed to the client's audit committee, board, and management, careful attention should be devoted to the discussion of the accountant's obligations in each of the areas of common consideration.

32. Information concerning the percentage relation between fees for nonaudit services and audit fees is presently required to be included in a registrant's proxy statement in accordance with ASR No. 250.

33. E.g., Accounting Series Release No. 234 [42 FR 64304] (December 13, 1977).

34. The Commission recognizes that comments reflecting specific experience with this interpretation may, in some cases, reflect confidential business information not appropriate for public dissemination. Those wishing to make application for confidential treatment of any part of their submission should state that fact promptly on the first page or cover sheet thereof. See generally Section 23(a)(3) of the Securities Exchange Act of 1934, 15 U.S.C. 78w(a)(3).

THIRTY-THREE

The Internal Auditing Profession: Challenges and Opportunities

A. CLARENCE SAMPSON .

Chief Accountant, Securities and Exchange Commission

This article focuses on the future of an internal auditing profession. Sampson discusses the effects of recent federal legislation upon the internal auditor and the challenges facing internal auditors, particularly because of the Foreign Corrupt Practices Act.

Probably no other group like internal auditing has been, and will be, more fundamentally affected as a result of the increasing focus on corporate accountability. That focus is apparent in various public and private sector initiatives — the increasing formation and effective functioning of independent audit committees, the Foreign Corrupt Practices Act, the American Institute of Certified Public Accountants' Special Advisory Committee on Internal Accounting Control, the Commission's recent rule proposals for reporting on the effectiveness of systems of internal accounting control, the broad reexamination of the nature and structure of the accounting profession, and the Institute's own *Standards for the Professional Practice of Internal Auditing* — to name a few. Virtually all of these initiatives have resulted in increased attention to, responsibilities for, and visibility of internal auditors and the internal auditing profession.

The greatest impact on internal auditors, however, has probably come from the Foreign Corrupt Practices Act.

That act, which was effective upon enactment in December of 1977, includes not only antibribery provisions, from which it takes its name, but also certain accounting provisions which require reporting companies to:

- maintain accurate books and records
- devise and maintain a system of internal accounting control which provides reasonable assurances that the broad objectives of internal accounting control are achieved

Those broad objectives, which were taken directly from authoritative auditing literature, can be summarized as follows:

1. Transactions are recorded as necessary to permit preparation of reliable financial statements and other reported financial information.
2. Transactions are appropriately authorized by management.
3. Assets are appropriately safeguarded.

That seems fairly simple and not very novel — indeed, few would argue that these statutory objectives are not necessary to sound business practices. However, the codification of those objectives into law has had significant practical implications, particularly in today's environment where corporate accountability is receiving increased attention. The result is, corporate managements are asking such questions as:

- How do we evaluate whether our system of internal accounting control provides reasonable assurances that the broad objectives are achieved?
- What must we do differently to make sure we comply with the law?
- What level of documentation of our system, and of our evaluation of it, is necessary?
- Should we be changing the emphasis of our internal audit control?
- Or, should we have an internal audit department?

In addition, boards of directors, and particularly audit committees and outside directors, are becoming more actively concerned with these same kinds of questions.

It is not surprising that many companies are relying heavily on internal auditors to help answer these questions — and probably even more heavily to implement the solutions. The emphasis certainly will not be short term. Indeed, I expect that it will continue to increase, particularly if the Commission adopts final rules that require public reporting on the effectiveness of registrants' systems of internal accounting control. The Commission recently proposed such rules for public comment.[1]

The proposed rules, if adopted, would require inclusion of a statement of management on internal accounting control in Form 10K and in annual reports to shareholders furnished pursuant to the proxy rules. The rules are proposed to be adopted in two stages. For years ending after December 15, 1979, and prior to December 16, 1980, the statement of management on internal accounting control would be required to include the following:

1. management's opinion as to whether, as of the date of the audited balance sheet, the systems of internal accounting control of the registrant and its subsidiaries provided reasonable assurances that the broad objectives of internal accounting control specified in the Foreign Corrupt Practices Act were achieved;
2. a description of any material weakness in internal accounting control communicated by the independent accountants of the registrant or its subsidiaries which have not been corrected, and a statement of the reasons why they have not been corrected.

For years ending after December 15, 1980, the statement of management on internal accounting control would be required to include a similar management opinion regarding reasonable assurances of achievement of the specified broad objectives of internal accounting control; however, the opinion would extend to conditions which existed throughout the period, not just as of the end of the year.

In addition, the statement of management on internal accounting control would be required to be examined and reported on by an independent public accountant for periods ending after December 15, 1980. The specific disclosure requirement relating to uncorrected "material weaknesses" would, therefore, drop out.*

Challenges to, and pressures on, internal auditors, both individually and as a profession, are abundant as a result of the Foreign Corrupt Practices Act. Those challenges and pressures will only increase—in some instances very significantly—if, or when, reporting on the effectiveness of internal accounting controls is required. I say that with particular confidence in light of the Commission's articulated views about the considerations attendant to representations about the effectiveness of systems of internal accounting control. Simply stated, the Commission recognizes that management judgment is inextricably involved in virtually all such considerations. Consequently, the Commission has not proposed detailed, prescriptive rules for control procedures and techniques which will ensure effective internal accounting control. Quite to the contrary, the Commission has recognized that systems of internal accounting control must be designed to fit individual circumstances, and, accordingly, the control procedures which are necessary to achieve the objectives of internal accounting control must be determined by each company.

The Commission also recognizes that the cost-benefit criterion underlying the concept of "reasonable assurance" is one that is rarely likely to involve precise quantification. Rather, considerations of costs and benefits of controls—particularly qualitative elements such as the reputation of the company and its management—will often depend in part on estimates and judgments by management.

Similarly, while setting forth certain conceptual elements which it believes should be encompassed in evaluations by managements of systems of internal accounting control, the Commission recognizes that *specific methods* of approaching and implementing such evaluations will vary from company to company and that the extent and timing of review and monitoring procedures in connection with such evaluations are among the cost-benefit judgments involved in the concept of reasonable assurance.

To put it another way, each company must maintain a system of internal accounting control, and a method of reviewing and monitoring that system, that makes sense in the circumstances. Reviewing, monitoring, and evaluating the system require a great deal of familiarity with the company and understanding of its potential exposures and related controls. If these requirements sound like they were taken from a description of prerequisites for an internal audit position then I think I have made my point.

I alluded to certain conceptual elements which the Commission believes should be encompassed in evaluation of systems of internal accounting control.

- first, evaluation of the overall control environment

---

* *Editor's Note:* In June 1980, the SEC decided not to adopt the rules for public reporting on internal controls. See Accounting Series Release 278, June 1980. This decision reflects a view that private sector action should be permitted an opportunity to develop the processes herein described.

- second, translation of the broad objectives of internal accounting control into specific control objectives applicable to the particular business, organizational, and other characteristics of the individual company
- third, consideration of the specific control procedures and individual environmental factors which should contribute to achievement of the specific control objectives
- fourth, monitoring of control procedures to determine whether they are functioning as intended; and
- finally, consideration of the benefits (consisting of reductions in the risk of failing to achieve the objectives) and costs of additional or alternative controls

Some of these conceptual elements will be more familiar than others. Monitoring compliance with control procedures, of course, fits very comfortably within the traditional (although sometimes narrow) view of the internal audit function. This is not to say that it is not important. Indeed, it is an essential element of an evaluation of controls. However, it is only one of the essential elements. If the role of internal auditors is restricted to compliance testing, the high expectations which so many have for the profession will not be fulfilled. The reason for that should be fairly obvious: there is little benefit in monitoring compliance with controls if the controls are not appropriate to begin with.

If the internal auditing profession is to make opportunities of the challenges I have mentioned, internal auditors must make positive contributions in more judgmental areas. Internal auditors must play an active, and successful, role in determining what controls *should be* in effect. To do that requires specific identification of the control exposures which companies face—that is, translation of the broad objectives of internal accounting control into specific objectives applicable in a company's particular circumstances.

It will also require a determination of the specific control elements which, when functioning as intended, contribute to achieving the specific control objectives.

In addition, internal auditors must contribute to the cost-benefit decisions which underlie the concept of reasonable assurance. I am not suggesting that internal auditors should have ultimate responsibility for making those decisions. Generally that will be the province of management. However, I believe it is essential that internal auditors contribute to the decision-making process by participating in identification and estimation of both benefits and costs of additional or alternative controls, and by maintaining and communicating an objective view regarding the cost-benefit decisions to be made by management.

One other point before returning to the conceptual elements. I think it is worth emphasizing that appropriate documentation is important to *each* aspect of an evaluation of internal accounting control. I am sure internal auditors are familiar with the importance of documenting tests of compliance with controls, and, in varying degrees, that is a discipline they have traditionally incorporated in their work. However, is that equally true of documentation of specific control objectives or of the control procedures which are in place which should contribute to achieving those objectives? Whether or not it is equally true, because of the dynamic nature of internal accounting control, it is certainly equally important. I will very confidently speculate that not more than a few companies have, at least until recently, documented the bases for cost-benefit decisions. However, the judgmental aspects of cost-benefit analyses make such documentation particularly important.

There are likely to be very practical benefits to thorough documentation of evaluations of internal accounting control as well. To the extent that independent accountants are involved in a "second look" capacity in reporting on internal accounting control, I suspect that the magnitude of their fees will be heavily dependent on the quality of the evaluation, and documentation thereof, performed by internal auditors. In addition, to the extent that internal auditors are successful in increasing the effectiveness of a company's internal accounting controls, the independent accountant will be able to rely increasingly on those controls, rather than on extensive substantive testing, in examining the financial statements.

Let's revisit the first conceptual element of an evaluation of internal accounting controls — the overall control environment.

In discussing internal accounting control, and evaluations thereof, it is important to keep in mind that systems of internal accounting control are not limited to *specific* control procedures.

Since enactment of the Foreign Corrupt Practices Act there has been considerable discussion about which controls are *accounting* controls and which controls are *administrative* controls. In my view, those discussions are generally misguided — misguided because they focus on *types* of control procedures. The scope of internal accounting control cannot be defined in terms of types of control procedures or in terms of organizational or functional departments. The focus must be on objectives of internal accounting control — preparation of financial statements, authorization of transactions, and safeguarding of assets. Anything which affects the achievement of those objectives must be considered in evaluating whether reasonable assurances of their achievement are provided.

Certain factors are critical to the effective functioning of any system of internal accounting control, including:

- effectiveness of the organizational structure as a framework for authorization and control of transactions
- role of the board of directors in overseeing the establishment and maintenance of strong systems of internal accounting control
- communication of corporate procedures, policies, and related codes of conduct
- communication of authority and responsibility
- competence and integrity of personnel
- accountability for performance and for compliance with policies and procedures
- objectivity and effectiveness of the internal audit function

The AICPA's Special Advisory Committee on Internal Accounting Control quite descriptively termed these factors the "internal accounting control environment" — the simple point being that it is only possible to realistically assess the effectiveness of specific internal accounting control procedures and techniques in the context of the environment in which they operate.

For many internal auditors, consideration of the control environment may require an excursion into largely untested waters. If internal auditors are to succeed in meeting the challenges which face them — in making them opportunities, not vulnerabilities — it is essential that they navigate — and chart — some untested waters.

I think it is quite clear that the challenges to the internal auditing profession — and to individual internal auditors — are great. Converting those challenges to opportunities will require increasing competence, objectivity, and professionalism.

The internal auditing profession has taken a significant step in promulgating the *Standards for the Practice of Internal Auditing*. It is, nevertheless, only a first step. It is essential that auditors incorporate those standards in their practice and continue to improve their capabilities to effectively meet the increasing responsibilities and fulfill internal auditing's changing role.

Internal auditors must accomplish this not only as individuals, but also as a profession through the Institute of Internal Auditors, Inc. The IIA, institutionally and through its members, has a responsibility to ensure that the auditing profession continues to grow and respond to changing circumstances. To do that, the Institute must assume a leadership role and speak out on issues — not only issues which impact internal auditors, but perhaps more importantly, issues on which internal auditors can, and should, have an impact. This is an important distinction. It is the distinction between a trade association and a professional organization. If the IIA is to fulfill the latter role, it must provide a substantive voice on issues like internal accounting control, not merely a call for increased recognition of internal auditors.

As individuals, to be in a position to be *able* to meet increased responsibilities requires that auditors function as objectively as possible within their organizations. SEC Chairman Harold Williams has stressed the importance of an organizational structure that promotes the ability of internal auditors to function objectively. Williams's remarks that, in most instances, the director of internal auditing should not report to the chief financial officer or chief accounting officer have prompted considerable controversy. However, I do not think his point was to be proscriptive about internal auditors' reporting responsibilities. Rather, it was to stress the importance of an organizational structure which allows internal auditors to function objectively and to be responsible to someone high enough in the organization to ensure appropriate consideration of their recommendations. For the same reasons. I think it is also important that internal auditors are able to communicate directly with the board of directors. These concepts are, of course, recognized in your *Standards*. I think they are critical to success in meeting the challenges internal auditors are facing — and the related opportunities available to them.

I sincerely hope internal auditing succeeds in meeting these challenges. Such a success is important to the entire business community.

NOTE

1. Securities and Exchange Commission's Release No. 34-15772, April 30, 1979. The comment period extended through July 31, 1979.

THIRTY-FOUR

Using Replacement Cost Data in the Bank Loan Pricing Decision

MICHAEL A. DIAMOND

California State University, Los Angeles

and

JERRY L. ARNOLD

University of Southern California

In this recent study the authors have examined the utility of replacement cost information for bank loan officers in making decisions, particularly about loan pricing. They conclude that replacement cost has no effect on the loan pricing decision. Along these lines they state that Accounting Series Release No. 190 disclosures are often questioned by loan officers and are likely to be supplanted by professional judgment.

Commercial lending decisions are based largely upon financial statements and related disclosures. These data are keys in assessing a prospective borrower's worth and profit potential. Until very recently, disclosure of only historical cost data has been required in published financial statements. However, in this period of continuous inflation, many questions have been raised about the adequacy of historical cost data in credit and investment decisions. It has been argued that some form of current value information should be available, at least on a supplemental basis.

The accounting policy setters have responded to this viewpoint. First, the Securities and Exchange Commission (SEC) in March 1976 issued Accounting Series Release (ASR) No. 190, which required certain registrants to disclose limited replacement cost information. In particular, ASR No. 190 pertains to all firms whose total inventories and gross property, plant, and equipment exceed $100 million and 10 percent of total assets. It requires them to disclose the replacement cost of their inventories, productive capacity, and the related cost of goods sold and depreciation expense.

In 1978, the Financial Accounting Standards Board (FASB) issued an exposure draft of a statement which would require all companies to disclose supplemental inflation-adjusted information on either a specific replacement cost or general price level.[1]

The stated purpose of these SEC and FASB requirements was to provide an improved basis for assessing a company's worth and profit potential. An unanswered question, however, has been whether this information would actually be used by loan officers and if it would affect their decisions. Several studies have looked at loan officers' perceptions of the reliability and thus usefulness of current cost data. For instance, in his study, Ralph Estes found that 90 percent of the bankers that responded to his survey felt that current cost data would be useful.[2] However, a recent study by Keith Stanga reported upon in this *Journal* found "bankers do not have much faith in the (current cost) figures."[3] There has been no evidence, however, about how bankers would actually react to this information once presented with it.

The purpose of this article is to report upon a study which looked at the effects, if any, of supplemental replacement cost data on bank loan decisions. The replacement cost measure was selected since it is already part of the required disclosures of large public companies (per ASR No. 190). Specifically, two related questions were investigated:

1. What is the effect, if any, of replacement cost data on the loan officers' term loan pricing decision?

2. To what extent do loan officers actually use these data in making their individual pricing decisions?

The methods used to address these questions and the results obtained are described in the following text.

THE EXPERIMENT

Overview

Over 100 loan officers from six major California banks participated in this study. In addition, a high level executive from each bank served as consultant to the study. The design of the experiment, which is briefly described below, resulted from numerous discussions with these consultants. The main purpose of these discussions was to ensure that the design of the experiment was as realistic as possible.

Each of the participating loan officers was requested to evaluate a set of financial statement ratios for 40 independent firms and to recommend an interest rate at which each loan would be granted. Half of the loan officers made decisions based upon historical cost ratios while the other half made decisions based upon both historical and replacement cost ratios. The decisions of the loan officers were then analyzed to determine if, and in what manner, the supplemental replacement cost data were used.

Data Set

The loan officers were presented with data on 40 different actual firms selected from four industries. These industries were chosen on the basis of capital intensity to allow an examination of the relation between level of capital intensity and impact of replacement cost data on the loan decision. The industries and firms used in the study are presented in Table 1.

Table 1. Firms selected for study

Highly capital intensive	Medium capital intensive
Steel industry	Tire and rubber industry
1. Armco	1. Armstrong
2. Bethlehem	2. Uniroyal
3. Inland	3. Carlisle
4. Lykes	4. Goodyear
5. National	5. Firestone
6. Republic	6. General Tire
7. U.S. Steel	7. Mansfield
8. Allegheny Ludlum	8. Mohawk
9. Interlake	9. Goodrich
10. Carpenter	10. Cooper Tire and Rubber
Capital intensive	**Low capital intensity**
Machinery industrials	Textile
1. Aeroflow	1. HSM
2. DORR	2. Bobbie Brooks
3. Chicago Pneumatic Tool	3. Cluet Peabody
4. Cooper Ind.	4. Jonathan Logan
5. Gardner-Denver	5. Levi-Strauss
6. Mesta	6. Manhattan Ind.
7. Hobart	7. Munsingwear
8. Ingersoll-Rand	8. VF Corp.
9. Milton Roy	9. Phillips Van Heusen
10. Parker-Hannifin	10. McGregor

The loan officers were asked to make pricing decisions using only ratio data, a subset of the information normally used. Discussions with the project consultants and a survey of the relevant banking literature indicated that this should not have a limiting effect on the ability of the loan officers to make reasonable decisions. A number of studies have shown that bankers use ratio data in evaluating the credit worthiness of a firm and perceive this analysis to be worthwhile. For instance, on the basis of his study of loan officers, Robert Libby observed that "the traditional confidence in ratio analysis for credit rating seems justified, and speaks highly of the accountant as an information provider and the banker as professional decision maker."[4]

The decision as to what specific ratios to use was also based on discussions with the study's consultants, a survey of the relevant literature, and a pilot study. From the information obtained from these sources came the ratios exhibited in Table 2, which were used in the study.

Replacement cost ratios are calculated in the same manner only with replacement cost adjusted data. The historical cost data were adjusted by the researchers to replacement cost in a manner consistent with the suggestions of ASR No. 190.

Table 2.   Ratios used in study

1. Current ratio	Current assets
	Current liabilities
2. Debt to net worth	Total liabilities
	Total stockholders' equity
3. Times (×)—Interest earned	Income from operations before interest and taxes
	Interest expense
4. Income to total assets	Income before taxes and extraordinary items
	Total assets
5. % change in profits	Percentage change in profits. This trend is based on the change over the last five years in the firm's income before taxes and extraordinary items.

The Loan Decision

As noted previously, each participant was requested to evaluate a set of financial statement ratios and to recommend an interest rate at which each loan would be granted.

All loan requests were for five-year unsecured term loans. This time period was selected to increase decision relevance, since the replacement cost of inventory, plant, and equipment is more likely to be an issue in longer-term loans than in shorter-term loans. In addition, the loan officers were told that although this was a new client, the bank expected a long-term continuing relationship. The dollar amount of the loan request was varied according to the size of each firm. Specifically, each loan request was 5 percent of common stockholders' equity except that no loan exceeded $50 million or was less than $1 million. This procedure assured that the requested loan was related to the size and the financial characteristics of the individual firm and that the amount was reasonable for a term loan of this nature. The use of 5 percent of common stockholders' equity was the result of discussions with the study's banking consultants.

There are, of course, other variables relevant to the loan decision. And we tried to get the loan officers to disregard them so to speak or at least to assume that they were constant in all the subject companies. Furthermore, implementing the loan decision once it is made is itself a multidimensional process in that the officer must simultaneously determine several loan terms, such as interest rate, compensating balance, and dividend and working capital restrictions. However, according to bank executives, the interest rate is a most important—and realistic—variable.

The Participants

As already indicated, over 100 loan officers participated in the study. An analysis of their backgrounds indicated that they were experienced loan officers with high levels of education. Their main function within the bank was evaluating loans for large corporate customers.

Although their backgrounds and attitudes were diverse, there were no significant differences between the loan officers who received the historical cost data and those who received the replacement cost data.

RESULTS

The results from the experiment were analyzed at two levels. First, the actual decisions of the two groups were statistically compared to determine the effects, if any, of the replacement cost data. Further, each loan officer's decision process was modeled to determine the relative impacts of the individual historical and replacement cost ratios. The results are considered in turn as follows.

Decision Analysis

The purpose of this analysis was to determine if replacement cost disclosures affected the loan pricing decision. The decisions of the loan officers receiving the historical cost data were statistically compared to those of the loan officers receiving both the historical and replacement cost ratios. The results of this analysis indicated that the decisions were not statistically different. Thus, given the sample of firms used in this study, the disclosure of supplemental replacement cost data did not have a different effect across industries. Thus, there was no relationship between capital intensity and replacement cost data.

A further test was conducted to determine if the replacement cost data affected the degree of consensus among the loan officers. If replacement cost has information value to the loan officers, it was felt that there might be more consensus in the pricing decisions of the replacement cost group than in the historical cost group. However, statistical tests indicated that there was no difference in consensus between the groups.

The results from this part of the experiment indicate that supplemental replacement cost data had no statistically significant effects on the bank loan pricing decisions. It neither changed the loan officer's pricing decision nor increased the consensus of those decisions. Possible explanations for these results are explored in the following section dealing with the loan officers' decision-making process.

Process Analysis

It was noted previously that the final pricing decisions of the loan officers receiving the replacement cost data were not different from those of their "historical cost" counterparts. This does not necessarily imply, however, that the replacement cost data were ignored. It was possible that the loan officers used the data in their decision process without its changing their assessments of the sample companies. To test for this, the decision process of each loan officer in both groups was modeled to determine the relative impact of the specific historical and replacement cost ratios.[5] This analysis indicated that replacement cost ratios were, in fact, substantially ignored by the loan officers. When asked to evaluate the usefulness of replacement cost ratios subjectively, the loan officers consistently indicated that the ratios had little effect. Thus, in terms of both the actual decisions and the underlying processes, the replacement cost data had no significant impact.

INTERPRETATIONS

There are a number of possible reasons why the replacement cost data did not affect the loan officers' decisions. In the absence of replacement cost disclosures, the loan officers receiving the historical cost data may have adjusted for the effects of inflation in their analysis. And they may feel that these adjustments are as reliable as those provided by ASR No. 190. There is some evidence that this may be the case. In response to specific questions, the participants indicated they normally estimate the effect of inflation on a firm's financial statements and feel that their own estimates are reliable.

Another possible explanation for the results obtained in this study is that replacement cost is just "too new" to be used effectively by loan officers. This implies that there is a learning process involved, and at this time, loan officers have not had enough exposure to replacement cost information to process it effectively. However, this is doubtful. ASR No. 190 was adopted over two years ago, and the loan officers in this study indicated that they were reasonably familiar with the release. Therefore, the fact that the disclosures were relatively new was probably not influential to the results. It is possible, however, that the overall size of the data set presented to the replacement cost group did have an effect. This phenomenon is called information overload and is discussed below.

There are limits to the amount of information that can be processed effectively by a loan officer. And at a certain point, information overload occurs and some information is necessarily ignored. This situation could have occurred in this study. The loan officers could have used a selection process to filter out what was considered irrelevant information, in this case the replacement cost information. However, for whatever reason, it is clear the replacement cost data had no significant impact on the loan decisions in this study.

CONCLUSION

As noted earlier, it has been argued that to aid in analysis some form of current value information should be formally disclosed to loan officers. The results of this study challenge this argument. Supplemental replacement cost data had no significant effect on bank officers' loan pricing decisions. Further, it seems likely that the loan officers are already adjusting for the effect of inflation. This and other studies indicate that loan officers question the reliability of ASR No. 190 disclosures and are likely to continue to rely on their professional judgments.

NOTES

1. As of this printing—early November—the FASB has issued an accounting standard (Statement No. 33, "Financial Reporting and Changing Prices") requiring major companies to disclose the effects of changing prices as supplementary information in their published annual reports. The standard requires certain companies to disclose financial information using the "constant dollar" accounting method. It also requires disclosure of certain supplementary information using the "current cost" accounting method.

2. Ralph Estes, "An Assessment of the Usefulness of Current Cost and Price-Level Information by Financial Statement Users," *Journal of Accounting Research,* Autumn 1968, pp. 200–207.

3. Keith G. Stanga, "SEC Replacement Cost Information: How Reliable?" *Journal of Commercial Bank Lending,* May 1979, pp. 49–54.

4. Robert Libby, *Prediction Achievement and the Use of Simulated Decision Makers in Information Evaluation,* unpublished doctoral dissertation, University of Illinois, 1974.

5. Multiple regression analysis was used to model each loan officer's decision process. From this analysis the relative impact of each ratio on the decision process was determined. For more information on this analysis, please contact the authors directly.

THIRTY-FIVE

The 1980s:
The Future of the
Accounting Profession

HAROLD M. WILLIAMS

Chairman, Securities and Exchange Commission

Harold M. Williams, chairman of the Securities and Exchange Commission (SEC), discusses the problems the accounting profession will face in the decade of the 1980s. Among these problems are questions of self-regulation, independence, and the setting of accounting standards. Chairman Williams concludes that the profession's ability to face these and other problems on a timely basis will determine whether government regulation of the profession will be necessary. Williams cites his concern about problems with peer review, international accounting, the makeup of the SEC Practice Section of the American Institute of Certified Public Accountants, and the effectiveness of the section in disciplining members.

The decade of the 1980s has opened with the promise of a full plate of volatile and explosive issues which will test the relevancy and adequacy of many of our institutions and conceptions. For the accounting profession as well, this promises to be a period of challenge, innovation, and change. Events of the past few years have spawned significant progress toward the objective of creating the capability to assure that appropriate ethical and professional standards are developed and maintained timely and with a minimum of government legislation or regulation. The successful attainment of this goal will permit the accounting profession to emerge from the 1980s stronger and more vital than it entered them.

Much remains to be accomplished if the the profession is to realize this goal. During the past two years it has faced challenges embracing the full spectrum of the profession's activities. Criticisms directed at the accounting profession from without, as well as the profession's own efforts at self-assessment — such as the Cohen Commission — have served as the basis for change. While the profession can justifiably derive a sense of confidence and satisfaction from its ability to conceive and implement significant changes,it must guard against the tendency to become complacent, or to develop an attitude that enough, or too much, has been done, and that much of what is being done is not substantively necessary or cost justifiable, but rather a mandatory tithe to keep powerful, but misguided, external forces at bay. This must not happen. As I indicated at this conference last year, a major part of the stress that

---

An address to the AICPA Seventh National Conference on Current SEC Developments, January 3, 1980.

the profession is under stems from its own failure in the past to recognize in a timely manner challenges to its discharge of the only responsibility which justifies its existence today — insuring the credibility and reliability of financial reporting.

The Commission's view of the accounting profession's progress in response to the issues facing it has been described in our two reports to Congress on "The Accounting Profession and the Commission's Oversight Role." We will again report to the Congress during 1980. In the last analysis, the maintenance of an independent, private profession depends on the profession's progress, and I sincerely hope that the Commission will be in a position to be positive with respect to the profession's self-regulatory efforts. In this connection, I want to look at some specific areas which are, in my judgment, significant tests of the profession's efforts and direction.

SELF-REGULATION

The most visible change made by the accounting profession in response to criticisms directed toward it was the creation, just over two years ago, of the AICPA's Division for CPA Firms. The SEC Practice Section is the key to successful voluntary self-regulation and the problems in implementing its programs pose the greatest obstacles to success. Therefore, rather than focusing on the progress made by the profession — and significant progress has been made — I want to concentrate on three of the uncertainties which could hinder the section's ability to meet its objectives.

The first unresolved issue relates to membership in the section. On the positive side, it appears that 230 member firms audit almost 9000 public companies — including virtually all companies listed on the national stock exchanges and a significant portion of NASDAQ-traded companies. Unfortunately, however, approximately 600 accounting firms that have at least one SEC audit client have not yet joined the SEC Practice Section. The AICPA has undertaken to identify these firms and to ascertain why they are not yet section members. In response to concerns raised about cost, particularly for smaller firms, the section has recently taken action to reduce its insurance and dues requirements. The effects of these changes remain to be seen.

In addition, some smaller firms appear concerned about their ability to exercise influence over activities of the section, and, in fact, some have asserted that the AICPA and its self-regulatory effort are dominated by the larger accounting firms. In that vein, the Commission has urged greater participation by smaller firms in the self-regulatory effort. Nonetheless, because an overwhelming majority of public companies are audited by larger firms, it does not seem inappropriate that these firms have taken the lead in the self-regulatory effort. These firms have, of course, a heavy burden not to abuse their leadership to the detriment of the smaller members. The section's executive committee must also remain sensitive to the concerns of this segment of the profession and ensure that its interests are fairly represented.

I recognize that many smaller firms which audit only one or a few small registered companies may honestly be concerned that the increased costs of participating in the self-regulatory effort — either to themselves or to their clients in the form of higher fees — may exceed the benefits to the public interest. Perhaps they have other concerns as well. In this connection, the Commission and, I am confident, the section and the Public Oversight Board (POB), would be pleased to hear directly from these smaller firms as to the reasons for their positions and any suggestions as to how any unjustifiable burdens could be alleviated.

In my view, however, if the section functions as it is intended to, there will be increasing pressure on all firms with public clients, regardless of size, to join the SEC Practice Section. Membership in the section — with its attendant peer review requirements — provides a basic level of assurance of quality audits. Accordingly, the onus is shifting to the firms with SEC clients which have elected not to participate in the self-regulatory program. Inevitably, as time passes, either their clients or others will raise questions as to why they have not yet joined. Moreover, it may be important for investors to be informed as to whether a registrant's auditors are members of the section and whether the auditor has been subject to a peer review. The Commission's staff is presently considering this issue and may recommend that the Commission propose rules which would require disclosure on this point from issuers. I encourage companies to make this disclosure voluntarily since it may be useful to shareholders and other users of financial information in evaluating the overall quality of a registrant's financial reporting.

The second important but unresolved element in the profession's voluntary self-regulatory program is the peer review concept. Commitment to meaningful, in-depth peer reviews by independent and objective reviewers is a prerequisite to the success of the profession's voluntary self-regulatory program. Accordingly, delays in the effective implementation of the peer review program are a serious threat to the whole structure of self-regulation.

In July 1979, we reported to Congress that, although we remained optimistic that the peer review process would ultimately prove effective, only a few peer reviews had been conducted, and that the evidence was therefore too fragmentary to sustain any firm conclusions. At that time, we expected that a significant number of peer reviews would be scheduled during the coming year. In fact, however, only some forty peer reviews were conducted during 1979. This small number causes justifiable concern about the profession's commitment to self-regulation.

Another factor continues to impede the Commission's ability to evaluate the peer review program. That problem — Commission access to peer review work papers — must be resolved now. While the Commission can rely on the POB's supervision of the peer review process to a great degree, it is necessary for our staff to have sufficient access to permit an evaluation of the adequacy of the peer review process. If we were forced to rely exclusively on the POB's assurances that the process is working effectively, we would simply not be in a position to satisfy ourselves and apprise Congress as to whether the SEC Practice Section is an effective mechanism for professional quality control.

The profession's leaders look upon Commission access to peer review materials with some trepidation. I believe, however, that they understand the importance of reaching an appropriate solution. Representatives of the section and the POB have met with the Commission's staff in an effort to design a mechanism to achieve this goal. The problem is a difficult one, and we appreciate the profession's concern for client confidentiality. Further, I think it is important to emphasize that our need for access is not geared toward enforcement of the securities laws — an area in which we have ample existing authority — but rather to fulfill our oversight responsibilities. The Commission will maintain a position of flexibility in resolving this issue. Based upon my discussions with the Commission's staff, I am optimistic about the outcome of the ongoing efforts to resolve this issue in an acceptable manner.

I look forward to being able to report to Congress later this year that a breakthrough has been achieved in this very difficult area.

I want to comment on one final peer review related issue — the extent to which audit work performed outside the United States should be encompassed in the scope of peer reviews. This is a complex issue, and continuing efforts must be made to seek an effective resolution. While a worldwide peer review process concentrating on each firm's quality control system — regardless of the physical location of that firm — may be the ideal way to provide investors with assurance of audit quality, I recognize that differing legal and professional environments make progress toward this goal difficult. As we have discussed with the AICPA's and POB's staffs, one way to address the issue of worldwide peer review would be an engagement oriented focus. That is, a U.S. firm, as part of its quality control or audit standards, could be required to perform certain procedures where a significant portion of the audit work was performed outside the United States. These procedures — which would be documented — should be designed to provide assurance, at least to the extent of that particular engagement, that (1) the quality of financial reporting is consistent, (2) audit quality with respect to all phases of the audit is uniformly high, and (3) all aspects of the audit were conducted by independent accountants based on professional and regulatory standards applicable to U.S. firms. Using this approach, the peer review process would concentrate on the U.S. firm's overall policies and procedures for reviewing audit work done outside the United States. In my view, this would be a satisfactory interim resolution to a difficult issue.

The third area of uncertainty surrounding the self-regulatory initiative relates to the disciplinary measures the section will invoke against members who deviate from the profession's standards. As the Commission noted in both of its first two reports to Congress, the section's sanctioning process and procedures are not yet in place and are untested. Thus their timeliness, fairness, evenhandedness, and efficacy remain to be demonstrated.

INDEPENDENCE

I want to turn now to the issue of safeguarding auditors' independence. Like self-regulation, this subject occupied the profession's attention during the 1970s and will continue to be a focal point of debate during the 1980s. Two issues — independent audit committees and the scope of services which the auditor provides his client — are particularly important.

The audit committee issue is, of course, one I have addressed repeatedly in my prior appearances at this podium. Last year, I referred to the AICPA's then-recent response to our suggestion that it approach the issue from the perspective of adopting an ethical or auditing standard. As you will recall, the AICPA, on the recommendation of the special committee which it chartered to analyze this question, declined to establish an audit committee requirement. In my view, even if the AICPA were justified in rejecting such a standard, the accounting profession can and should contribute more leadership than the special committee's report recognizes. The profession should be in the forefront of the movement for institutional changes, such as independent audit committees, which can serve to reinforce auditor independence.

It is my firm belief that the 1980s will see audit committees functioning as an integral part of all public companies. The forces of public and peer pressure are presently working toward this goal. For example, the American Stock Exchange (AMEX) recently recommended that all AMEX-listed companies have audit committees consisting entirely of directors independent of management. While the AMEX initiative is only a recommendation, it will add to the existing pressures for the formation of independent audit committees. Whether direct Commission action is necessary to further this process remains to be determined.

The ultimate value of audit committees, however, depends on how well they actually function, rather than whether they simply exist in theory. And, in turn, whether or not they function effectively will depend on the combined efforts of the accounting profession, the corporate community, and individual audit committee members. This is the ultimate goal toward which we must all be working. Auditors are obviously the focal point of audit committee operations, and I urge the accounting profession, in its own self-interest, to continue its efforts to help create more effective audit committees.

The ultimate value of audit committees, however, depends on how well they actually function, rather than whether they simply exist in theory. And, in turn, whether or not they function effectively will depend on the combined efforts of the accounting profession, the corporate community, and individual audit committee members. This is the ultimate goal toward which we must all be working. Auditors are obviously the focal point of audit committee operations, and I urge the accounting profession, in its own self-interest, to continue its efforts to help create more effective audit committees.

A second issue bearing directly upon auditor independence is the scope of services performed by independent accountants. The Commission has addressed this area principally in two releases. First, in 1978, the Commission promulgated Accounting Series Release (ASR) No. 250, which requires disclosure of nonaudit services performed by independent auditors in terms of their percentage relationship to audit fees. We believe that ASR 250 will serve to provide data upon which users of financial information can evaluate the relationship between companies and their auditors — in effect, these disclosures should eliminate some of the mystique which has historically surrounded the scope-of-services issue. Similarly, these disclosure requirements will enable the Commission to monitor the nature and extent of services performed by independent accountants and will assist us in developing an empirical base from which to determine any need for further action in this area.

The second facet of the Commission's consideration of the scope-of-services issue is reflected in ASR 264. The impetus for this release was the Commission's judgment that the awareness of registrants and their auditors to the concerns surrounding the performance of management advisory services needed to be heightened. The profession, through the Public Oversight Board, had studied the question of scope of services by CPA firms and issued a report in March 1979. Dissatisfied with the lack of more specific guidance in that report, the Commission presented its own views in ASR 264 to detail the factors which the Commission believes management, the audit committee, and the accountant should consider in determining whether a proposed engagement should be offered or accepted and invited public comments.

ASRs 250 and 264 together provide an appropriate framework within which the parties who are primarily concerned with the independence which characterizes the audit relationship may determine the scope of services appropriate in the circumstances. In developing ASR 264, the Commission consciously determined not to prohibit particular management advisory services (MAS) engagements. Accountants, and not the Commission, must serve as the front-line guardians of their professional independence, as their own ethics literature recognizes. Similarly, corporate boards, and not the Commission, should have primary responsibility for the credibility of issuer financial reporting. ASR 264 seeks to guide the auditor and the issuer's board in discharging these responsibilities.

The reaction by the accounting profession to the issuance of ASR 264 has been, to put it mildly, negative. Indeed, the AICPA letter of comment to the Commission, voicing strong opposition to the release, stated that "unwarranted curtailment of nonaudit services is likely to be substantially realized simply by its issuance." While the accounting profession has not "called the SEC's bluff," as implied in a recent magazine article — if for no other reason than that the Commission is not bluffing — some concerns have been raised which deserve response and clarification. I would like to respond today to several recurrent comments on ASR 264.

First, the Commission in ASR 264 did not seek to deprecate the benefits which may accrue from certain MAS activities. Clearly, the benefits in many cases can be significant. For instance, in view of the accounting provisions of the Foreign Corrupt Practices Act, services performed by independent auditors in assisting their clients in the review of internal accounting control systems should be very helpful to registrants. The Commission, in ASR 264, also recognized that the knowledge gained from such services often is beneficial to the performance of the audit. With that in mind, we encouraged a careful assessment of both the benefits to the registrant and the potential impairment of independence which may accrue from the engagement of a company's own certifying accountants for internal accounting control reviews. I would expect that, in most cases, after considering these factors, auditors would continue to be engaged to perform reviews of internal accounting controls.

A second issue which has arisen respecting ASR 264 concerns its relation to ASR 250. Although we will monitor the disclosures as to the nature and extent of the particular services rendered, it never was the intention of the Commission to suggest in ASR 264 that it would question the independence of a company's auditor after the fact based solely on the percentage relation disclosed pursuant to ASR 250. Rather, the purpose of this monitoring activity is to assist us in developing an empirical base from which to determine the need for further action in this area. Any further action would, however, be prospective.

Third, commentators have raised questions with respect to the so-called global test relating to aggregate revenues generated from MAS and the relation of those revenues to total firm revenues. Some firms — particularly smaller firms — appear to be concerned that the Commission may have stigmatized firms that derive a significant portion of their revenue from, for example, tax work and "accounting and review services." This was not the Commission's intention. While ASR 264 uses "nonaudit" and MAS somewhat interchangeably, the Commission recognizes that the terms are different and that MAS encompasses a narrower range of services. In the context of services performed on a firmwide basis, the Commission's principal concerns relate to the magnitude of MAS activities and the potential impact on the quality of audits.

Another point raised by commentators relates to the fact that the global test focuses on the firm as a whole and transcends factors affecting individual engagements. Many in the profession, on the other hand, believe that independence should be evaluated in terms of individual engagements only, and that independence judgments should not be colored by the magnitude of the auditor's overall MAS work. While I agree that independence is primarily dependent on the nature of the accountant's relationship with individual audit clients,

I disagree with the notion that the profession may disregard the magnitude of MAS activities on a firmwide basis. I believe that an undue emphasis on MAS could ultimately translate into an effect on the quality of audit work performed. Similarly, I am concerned about the apparent tendency of some accounting firms — particularly larger firms — to compete on the basis of total revenues generated and the array of MAS services offered. Like a conglomerate facing the prospect of only modest, and perhaps even nominal, growth in its primary lines of business — audit, accounting, and review services, and tax work — some firms have expanded their MAS activities into areas with greater growth potential. Under this policy, a dollar of revenue is equally valued, regardless of its source. The ultimate result of such a philosophy could be a subtle shift in emphasis — perhaps real, perhaps apparent — away from the auditor's primary function. It is this eventuality, and the possible consequent effect on audit quality or on user confidence in the reliability of the auditor's report and the credibility of financial reporting — the profession's reason for being — that the Commission was attempting to warn against in ASR 264.

Before I leave the issue of management advisory services, I want to mention that I am somewhat disappointed by the tone and focus of the profession's response to ASR 264. While I appreciate the profession's concern, there is significant public interest and concern surrounding this issue. This interest was evidenced at the public hearings on the accounting profession conducted by Senator Eagleton in early August of 1979 as well as by the continuing controversy within the profession. Instead of attempting to explain away the concerns expressed with respect to the scope-of-services issue, the accounting profession should assume the initiative by focusing their efforts on meaningful action to reduce the underlying reasons for these concerns.

The Commission has not ended its examination of the scope-of-services issue. Rather, we view the issuance of ASRs 250 and 264 as part of a continuing examination of the relationships between registrants and their independent accountants. The Commission's staff will continue to review and evaluate ASR 250 disclosures. Over time, these disclosures will generate the data necessary to identify trends in the scope of services provided by independent auditors. ASR 264 is, of course, not a Commission rule — rather, it is a statement of views. After reviewing future proxy disclosures, the Commission may revisit this area, and I encourage comments, particularly from the corporate community, on the factors set forth in ASR 264 and, particularly, on their application to specific decisions.

STANDARD SETTING

The final broad area I want to examine is the setting of accounting standards. The need for timely and meaningful standards established within an effective and adaptive framework has never been clearer. In this regard, a shift toward increased reporting of soft data, while retaining historical cost data in the primary financial statements, has already begun. It may eventually necessitate substantial changes in the total reporting model with which we are all quite familiar — an idea that many accountants and businessmen seem to abhor.

The Financial Accounting Standards Board (FASB) appears willing to meet the challenge of setting meaningful accounting standards in a changing economic environment. Indeed, as we have reported to Congress, the FASB has made important strides in addressing some of the most fundamental issues inherent in the standard-setting process. Nonetheless, if the FASB is to be successful, it must continue to exercise positive leadership. Moreover, the board must be able to rely on the support and encouragement of the accounting profession and the corporate community — regardless of the effect of particular board decisions on particular reporting companies and regardless of whether those companies and their auditors fully agree with the board.

The FASB has made progress on its long-awaited and critically important development of a conceptual framework. It would, however, be difficult to overstate the importance of the FASB aggressively pursuing this project. While I do not envision the completion of the project as providing answers to all difficult accounting and financial reporting problems, it will provide direction for solving such problems in a timely, effective, and consistent manner.

The board's first concept statement — Statement of Financial Accounting Concepts No. 1, "Objectives of Financial Reporting by Business Enterprises" — establishes the objectives of general purpose external financial reporting by business enterprises. In my view, a major element of the conceptual framework should be to rethink the objectives of the primary financial statements — and, therefore, to rethink what type of information should be included and what information should be presented outside the financial statements. Ideally, the most relevant information would be a projection of cash flows for future periods. However, I recognize that such information may be highly uncertain and that surrogates may have to be used. The decision as to what that relevant information is and whether it should be included in the primary financial statements will be influenced by its measurability. The current exposure draft of the FASB on qualitative characteristics addresses this issue. In my view, the factors involved in the trade-off between reliability and relevance are the key to developing guidelines for the type of information that should be included in financial statements. It seems to me that a further clarification of this issue is necessary before display issues, such as the reporting of earnings, can finally be resolved. The development of the recognition criteria phase of the project will be critical to the board in its search for a definition of "earnings." I hope and expect that the board will give appropriate attention and priority to these important issues.

It might be useful to look at a practical example of a problem currently facing the profession which a comprehensive conceptual framework should help to resolve. One clear application is apparent in the board's current reconsideration of its Statement No. 8 on accounting for foreign currency translation — an issue which the FASB chairman has characterized as the most complex and difficult problem the FASB has faced. It appears that many of the issues the FASB is dealing with relate to basic conceptual questions. For example, the question of the appropriate disposition of translation adjustments has proved particularly troublesome. This question directly relates to the objectives of financial statements — that is, once one determines the objectives of an income statement, one can more appropriately determine whether certain items, such as translation adjustments, should be included.

Another area where the benefits of a completed conceptual framework project can be clearly seen is in the determination of the appropriate accounting and disclosure standards for oil- and gas-producing activities. While reserve recognition accounting (RRA) has been the subject of much criticism, it has the potential to provide significantly more useful information to present and potential investors, creditors, and other users in making rational investment, credit, and similar decisions — an important objective of financial reporting. Major standard-setting initiatives like RRA should be handled by the private sector, and the existence of a conceptual framework would help to assure that this is the case. Certainly, the Commission would benefit from the existence of a conceptual framework as it evaluates RRA. As a matter of fact, if the FASB has not made sufficient progress in this area, the Commission may have to deal with related issues on its own, as they impact RRA.

I would now like to turn briefly to the FASB's new standard on accounting for the effects of changing prices — Statement No. 33, "Financial Reporting and Changing Prices." This statement represents a significant breakthrough in the private sector standard-setting process. However, I think we would all agree that it will not be the final resolution to the difficult question of providing useful information on the effects of changing prices on business entities.

In my view, ultimate success in achieving this goal — measured in part by changes in public perception of the adequacy of corporate profits and in tax policy — will depend, in large part, on the efforts of the accounting profession and the business community in applying the standard, and evaluating and providing additional disclosures which may help users assess the impact of changing prices on particular entities and industries. With respect thereto, the new standard should be viewed as a requirement for the minimum information to be presented to investors — an area where the corporate community must make a positive contribution to the standard-setting process by volunteering additional information necessary to make the reporting most useful and meaningful in the particular corporate circumstances.

For example, a meaningful "management's discussion and analysis" approach is the appropriate vehicle for explaining the required information on changing prices. The additional explanation should focus on translating what some believe to be potentially confusing information into a meaningful discussion of the effects of changing prices on a particular business or segments of a business. In some cases a company may determine that a display of data in addition to what is required by the FASB may make the overall presentation more meaningful to users. In these circumstances, companies should not focus their discussion on explanations as to why the information required by the FASB may not be entirely appropriate for them. Rather, they should take advantage of this opportunity to present the additional quantitative and qualitative information that they believe will be useful to investors in evaluating their companies. This will not only add to the usefulness of financial reports but should contribute to the evolution of standards for presenting this data.

The FASB recognized that the measurement and use of information on changing prices will require a substantial learning process on the part of all concerned. In view of the importance of clear explanations to users of financial reports of the significance of the information called for by Statement No. 33, the board organized an advisory group to develop illustrative disclosures that might be appropriate as a guide to preparers in particular industries. While the illustrative disclosures recently published by that group are useful, they will not obviate the need for each company to determine the most appropriate disclosures in its own particular circumstances, including those additional disclosures that a meaningful presentation will entail.

Criticism has, of course, been directed at Statement No. 33 — criticism with which I am not unfamiliar in view of our replacement cost requirements in Accounting Series Release No. 190. As you know, the Commission believes that information on the effects of changing prices should not be limited to historic cost data adjusted for general inflation — that any meaningful approach must encompass specific price changes. While the application of macroeconomic data — such as general price level — is of some value, it does not serve adequately the microeconomic objective of assessing the impact of inflation and changing prices on the individual firm. The Commission has held this position despite the sometimes vocal criticism directed toward ASR 190. I believe the refinement of the replacement cost approach, as set forth in Statement No. 33, will further increase the utility and the use of this data and that the eventual results of the FASB's initiative in this area will be worthwhile.

In this connection, I read with interest the recent survey of financial analysts' attitudes toward ASR 190 conducted by SRI International as part of a research project on inflation accounting financed by the National Science Foundation. The results of this survey, while not overwhelming, do indicate that ASR 190 information is not "useless" as argued by some. The researchers conclude that ASR 190 data have been used more widely than generally acknowledged, and that continued reporting of such data and increasing familiarity would be expected to add to its importance.

I am confident that the 1980s will see the development of a conceptual framework for addressing emerging accounting problems. However, it is important to note that, in view of our changing economic environment, such a conceptual framework will require continuing review. I believe that this period will see the continuing development of a mechanism for providing public shareholders with useful information on the effects of changing prices on business entities. Finally, I believe that the 1980s will see increasing pressure from investors and other users of financial reports for more useful information — including more value-oriented data — to assist them in making investment, credit, and similar decisions.

CONCLUSION

I am pleased to note that most of the initiatives I have mentioned today are from the profession, rather than the Commission. Nonetheless, the Commission's statutory responsibility for the integrity of the financial information disseminated by public companies requires our continuing concern with the accounting principles by which that information is reported, the auditing standards by which it is reviewed, and the independence and competency of the profession that performs that review. My own preference is, however, to emphasize the role of nongovernmental bodies in resolving accounting and auditing issues. It is, therefore, incumbent upon the profession to face squarely and timely the difficult issues confronting it.

We are in a period of dramatic evolution within the accounting profession, and the profession deserves congratulations for the strides it has made. At the same time, however, accountants must recognize the importance of insuring that the momentum continues. The structures designed in the 1970s must stand the test of the 1980s.

I am hopeful your efforts will be successful.

THIRTY-SIX

SEC Reporting Rules Get Sweeping Revisions

DENNIS R. BERESFORD and GARY A. ZELL

Partners, Ernst & Whinney

In 1980, starting with a broadly based series of accounting disclosure and report changes, the SEC has begun to implement the so-called "integration project." This step represents an attempt to reduce duplicative and/or cost ineffective disclosures between the 10-K report to the SEC and the annual report to shareholders. The integration of the 10-K and annual report results in the annual report containing disclosures beyond those required by GAAP. The precedent for such a "takeover" of the annual report and the cost/benefit trade-off to the disclosure system will be studied carefully by preparers and users in the future.

The SEC has used the term "integration project" to describe its efforts to reduce the duplication in filings made under the 1934 and 1933 Securities Acts and between filings with the Commission and annual and quarterly reports sent to investors. Although integration has been discussed for some time, the current SEC initiatives come from the 1977 recommendations of the Advisory Committee on Corporate Disclosure. Among other things, that Committee recommended the Commission "adopt a single integrated disclosure form to be used for compliance with the registration, reporting, and proxy solicitation requirements of the Securities Act and the Exchange Act." The Commission's goal is to integrate the two disclosure systems under these Acts into a single system and to reduce the impediments to integrating or combining filings with the Commission with reports provided to security holders.

The SEC has issued a number of releases called by Chairman Williams "the single most important advance toward achieving the Commission's long-standing goals of an integrated and simplified disclosure system." The rules are effective for fiscal years ending after December 15, 1980, although they may be followed earlier.

ANNUAL REPORT TO SHAREHOLDERS

The consolidated financial statements in the annual shareholders report must comply with Regulation S-X. However, a proposal to require portions of the annual report to be incorporated by reference into Form 10-K was dropped.

Adapted, with permission, from Ernst & Whinney's *Financial Reporting Briefs,* September 1980.

The shareholders report must include a table of "Selected Financial Data" for five years, replacing the current summary of operations. The table lists such income statement and balance sheet amounts as revenues, income from continuing operations, and total assets. Only a requirement to state working capital was dropped from the proposal.

Management's discussion and analysis is now required to focus on financial condition as well as the income statement, and include discussion of liquidity, sources of capital, and results of operations. To encourage more meaningful discussion, the percentage tests have been replaced with general guidelines. All companies also must discuss the impact of inflation. Those not subject to FASB Statement No. 33 must provide a narrative discussion of the impact of inflation on revenues and income from continuing operations.

The often-criticized proposal to require that the principal executive, financial, and accounting officers, as well as a majority of the board of directors, sign Form 10-K has been adopted. Chairman Williams stated that "directors will be encouraged to devote the needed attention to reviewing the 10-K, and to seek the involvement of other professionals to the degree necessary to give themselves sufficient comfort."

UNIFORM FINANCIAL STATEMENT REQUIREMENTS

In annual shareholders reports and most SEC filings, income statements and statements of changes in financial position are required for three years and balance sheets for two years. Industry segment information has been reduced from five to three years, but differences between the FASB and SEC requirements remain. However, we understand that segment data may now be presented either in the financial statements or description of business and cross-referenced.

In most cases, interim financial information included in registration statements should be in the same detail as that required in Form 10-Q reports.

REGULATION S-X

"Compliance notes"—footnote disclosures formerly required in Form 10-K but not in annual shareholders reports—have undergone considerable change. Some have been eliminated altogether. Some will now be included in shareholders reports and thus become *de facto* GAAP. And a few are moved to the Form 10-K schedules (e.g., short-term debt borrowing information and weighted average interest rates). Supplementary profit and loss information was not moved to a footnote as proposed—it stays in a schedule.

Among the disclosures required by Regulation S-X that now will be included in annual reports:

> Reconciliations of tax expense to statutory rates, details of the deferred portions of tax provisions, and foreign and domestic pretax income. (However, the SEC did not adopt most of the proposed expansion of these disclosures.)

> Compensating balance information.

> Debt maturities for the next five years.

For the time being, banks, insurance companies, and investment companies are exempted from the requirement that the financial statements in annual shareholders reports comply with Regulation S-X. The SEC will review the special articles in the Regulation dealing with these industries to see what changes, if any, are necessary.

The proposed changes to the property, plant, and equipment schedules to show assets by depreciation method, major classification, and weighted average lives were deferred. The presently required information on lives and depreciation methods has been moved from a compliance footnote to the schedule, and the SEC expects to issue a revised proposal in the near future. A number of schedules have been deleted: Bonds, Mortgages, and Similar Debt; Capital Shares; and Warrants or Rights.

FORM S-15

This new Form for registering securities issued in connection with certain business combinations was adopted substantially as proposed. It may be used if the issuer qualifies to use Form S-7 and the transaction will have less than a 10 percent effect on the issuer's sales, net income, assets, and equity. The advantage of Form S-15 is that most of the business and financial information about the issuer can be provided by attaching the annual shareholders report to the prospectus.

RELATED SEC PROPOSALS

The Commission also approved rule proposals to revise Form 10-Q for quarterly reports and to propose three new registration statement forms. Form 10-Q would be revised to cover financial condition as well as results of operations in management's discussion and analysis, and the SEC is proposing uniform requirements for the interim financial information in both Form 10-Q and registration statements.

The three new registration forms would take the place of most existing forms and would establish different levels of disclosure in securities offerings depending on a company's size, financial stability, and public reporting history.

CONCLUSION

These adopted and proposed rule changes will certainly move forward the SEC's integration project. Because many of the disclosures required in SEC filings will now be identical to those required in reports to shareholders, many companies will "incorporate by reference" from one to the other, thus reducing the total amount of information prepared as well as the number of pages handled by security analysts and other users. The Commission's actions have resulted in disclosures beyond those required by generally accepted accounting principles being required in the financial statements in annual shareholders reports.

Some are concerned that these changes will result in more legalese and boilerplate being included in shareholder communications, thus detracting from the communicative style of reports to shareholders. The SEC recognizes that concern and intends to monitor closely the effect of the rule changes on shareholder communications. However, eliminating differences between the disclosure requirements will lessen confusion and facilitate incorporation by reference. This will eliminate some of the cost of the prior disclosure systems — both the cost to preparers and time spent by users.